The Origins of Cool in Postwar America

The Origins
of Cool
in Postwar
America

Joel Dinerstein

The University of Chicago Press
Chicago and London

The University of Chicago Press, Chicago 60637
The University of Chicago Press, Ltd., London
© 2017 by The University of Chicago
Published 2017
Printed in the United States of America

26 25 24 23 22 21 20 19 18 17   1 2 3 4 5

ISBN-13: 978-0-226-15265-3 (cloth)
ISBN-13: 978-0-226-45343-9 (e-book)
DOI: 10.7208/chicago/9780226453439.001.0001

Library of Congress Cataloging-in-Publication Data

Names: Dinerstein, Joel, 1958– author.
Title: The origins of cool in postwar America / Joel Dinerstein.
Description: Chicago ; London : The University of Chicago Press, 2017. | Includes
    bibliographical references and index.
Identifiers: LCCN 2016049319 | ISBN 9780226152653 (cloth : alk. paper) |
    ISBN 9780226453439 (e-book)
Subjects: LCSH: Popular culture—United States—History—20th century. | United
    States—Social life and customs—1945–1970. | Cool (The English word)
Classification: LCC E169.12 .D566 2017 | DDC 306.0973/0904—dc23 LC record
    available at https://lccn.loc.gov/2016049319

♾ This paper meets the requirements of ANSI/ NISO Z39.48-1992 (Permanence of
Paper).

To Dave and Kenny, the cool men I grew up with

Contents

Figure 1. Miles Davis in Paris with Juliette Gréco, "the muse of the existentialists," in 1949 (© Jean-Phillipe Charbonnier, Getty Images).

Prelude

Paris, 1949

At a table in the Club Saint-Germain, Jean-Paul Sartre sat with his regular inner circle: Simone de Beauvoir, his partner and fellow philosopher; Boris Vian—jazz trumpeter, cultural critic, agent provocateur, and author of *Guidebook to the Left Bank*; Juliette Gréco, the young French actress and already an existentialist icon, as elusive and cryptic as Vian was voluble. It was the second night of the Paris International Festival of Jazz at Le Salle Pleyel.[1]

Boris Vian had been trying to orient the ears of Sartre and Beauvoir to bebop—the new jazz idiom—for three years. A year earlier, Dizzy Gillespie and His Orchestra thrilled the group with their precision, humor, and drive, all played without charts that had been misplaced. The night before, the circle had gone to the festival to hear Charlie "Bird" Parker, Vian's favorite, "one of the gods come to visit us on earth," he wrote in *Jazz Hot*, "a God and a half!" Charlie Parker's single, "Cool Blues," had won France's Grand Prix du Disque (best record) of 1948.[2]

Earlier that evening the group had seen a quintet led by the young Miles Davis, featuring the pioneering bebop drummer Kenny Clarke. During the set, Miles espied Juliette Gréco in the audience, dressed in

1

her usual black, glowing without a spotlight. On a set break, he beck-oned her onstage with an index finger. They did not have a common language, yet mimed their way through a set of flirtations about music and voice using the trumpet as a prop and fell into love at first sight.

They spent a week together. Gréco thought Miles had an expressive manner like a Giacometti sculpture, "a face of great beauty."[3] Miles loved Gréco's style, autonomy, and charisma, her minimalist sense of expres-sion, the plasticity of her face, and lithe body. Later that year, Miles Davis would record the *Birth of the Cool* sessions. Gréco was on the verge of a successful singing career that would eclipse her film roles.

"Why don't you two get married?" Sartre asked Miles later that same week. He could stay in France, Sartre appealed, perhaps thinking of the author Richard Wright and his wife Ellen, close friends of existential-ism's first couple. Wright became a French citizen in 1947; James Bald-win had just moved there and joined the African-American expatriate group of artists in postwar Paris.

I can't do that to her, Davis thought but said aloud: "I love her too much to make her unhappy." Davis did not have to state the obvious. Both Sartre and Beauvoir had written eloquently about racial oppres-sion in the United States. "And it's much worse for white women mar-ried to black men," Davis added. Gréco recalled Davis telling her, "You'd be seen as a 'negro's whore' in the US . . . and this would destroy your career." And yet, and yet . . . to live in France and marry this woman, to feel the freedom, equality, and sense of belonging he'd never felt even as a middle-class black kid in St. Louis? It was tempting. "I had never felt that way in my life . . . the freedom of being in France and being treated as a human being, like someone important." *Like an artist.* Yet Davis also intuited—rightly, it turned out—that if he lived in France, he would lose touch with the currents of his art, with his fellow artists, with his coun-try, and with jazz's social and ethnic content.

So he left on schedule, heartbroken. Davis and Gréco saw each other in Europe now and then, especially in Paris, when he was touring. Five years later, Gréco toured the United States and invited Davis to dinner at the Waldorf Astoria in New York, where African-Americans were unwel-come. Gréco recalled: "After two hours [of waiting], the food was more or less thrown in our faces. The meal was long and painful, and then he left." Later that night, Miles Davis called in tears and told Gréco never,

ever to ask to see him again on American soil. The experience proved him prescient.

When he toured Europe in 1957, Miles Davis played the Club Saint-Germain, where drummer Kenny Clarke was now the musical director, having joined the considerable African-American expat community in Paris. That night at the club, Davis met director Louis Malle, who hired him on the spot to provide a score for his first movie, a film noir called *Elevator to the Gallows* (*L'ascenseur pour l'échafaud*, 1958). Davis was only going to be in Paris for a few days but took the job anyway.[4]

Davis hit on a simple, brilliant method to score the film: the musicians watched the rushes and improvised the music to the action. Miles called out when and where to stop—composing, arranging and playing only to those images best enhanced by music. Other scenes were left to run without music. To watch the film now, the soundtrack still deftly evokes nighttime in postwar Paris, the vibrating tension of a man in the midst of a criminal act, an agitated woman walking through the crowds of a busy boulevard. The musicians finished recording the soundtrack in one overnight session.[5]

The effectiveness of this soundtrack as ambient music for interior psychic moods points up an artistic tragedy: that in Jim Crow America, black jazz musicians were excluded from Hollywood, as composers, musicians, and even in studio orchestras. Jazz musicians would have been the natural composers for the genre of film noir. But there is one minor consolation: Davis's experience of improvising music to visual images helped trigger his next musical phase to the modal jazz of *Kind of Blue* (1959). Every Miles solo on the record—by far the best-selling jazz album of all time—can be heard as a scene in an unmade film noir. By 1959, Miles was an icon of cool and his quintet with John Coltrane was a gathering place for artists and celebrities: Marlon Brando and Ava Gardner often came together, and the audience often included Tony Bennett, Elizabeth Taylor, James Dean, Lena Horne, Frank Sinatra, and boxer Sugar Ray Robinson.

Like every artist, Miles Davis built his music from disparate artistic influences. In the 1950s, Davis's sonic signature was his spare, precise melodic phrasing on the muted trumpet. By his own admission, it owed a debt to Frank Sinatra's cadences and something as well to Orson Welles's radio voice. In the same year as Davis's visit to Paris—1949—Welles was an expatriate living in Europe and also involved in a romantic relationship across racial lines. Of his affair with singer and actress Eartha Kitt, Welles remarked: "She is the most exciting woman on earth."[6] In fact, he cast her as Helen of Troy in *Doctor Faustus*. It is unimaginable for Miles Davis to have uttered the same words about Juliette Gréco without incurring the wrath and revenge of white American men protective of "their" women.

In 2006, Gréco reflected back on the long arc of her relationship with Davis: "Between Miles and me there was a great love affair, the kind you'd want everybody to experience. Throughout our lives we were never lost to each other. . . . He would leave messages for me in the places I traveled in Europe: 'I was here, you weren't.'" In his autobiography, Davis claimed he had never loved a woman more. "Juliette was probably the first woman that I [ever] loved as an equal human being," he reflected in 1989.[7]

Davis remains the jazz avatar of cool today since he modeled an equipoise of both sound and person. Then throw in some mystery, intimidation, toughness, and a certain potential for violence. Just to read this list of adjectives is to understand why the postwar cool aesthetic was a masculine one. Yet Gréco influenced a cool female aesthetic: as a precedent for Audrey Hepburn, the lithe, resilient, urbane bohemian cool woman who charms everyone with feminine guile yet retains her self-possession. Sartre wrote songs for her and she acted alongside Orson Welles in two films.[8] In addition, Miles Davis is now often considered an "existentialist artist," as jazz scholar Eric Nisenson notes, since "music had no value [for him] unless the musician was willing to put his life on the line."[9]

Sixty years later, Gréco recalled that first week with Miles: "There was such an unusual harmony between the man, the instrument and the sound—it was pretty shattering." To call a *person* cool in the postwar era meant there was some internal harmony about his or her artistic voice, style, and physical being. As a journalist described the jazz singer Anita O'Day in 1946, "Anita is completely frank. She says what she thinks, wears what she pleases, and behaves as she prefers to behave." O'Day defined herself as a "hip chick," a female version of a "cool cat."[10]

"Cool" was then synonymous with authenticity, independence, integrity, and nonconformity; to be cool meant you carried personal authority through a stylish mask of stoicism. As everyone then knew: you can't buy it; you have to make it.

In the postwar era, to be cool meant negotiating a resistant mode of being in the world. And the *origins* of cool—as of nearly all art and aesthetics—can be found in the transmutation of pain and loss into something dynamic and uplifting.

Introduction

The Origins of Cool

Organic Existentialists

This is a theory of the origins and functions of the concept of cool in American culture as it manifested in the post–World War II arts of jazz, film, literature, and popular music.

In this era between 1943 and 1963, a new embodied concept and romantic ideal—*being cool*—emanated out of African-American jazz culture to become an umbrella term for the alienated attitude of American rebels. For the next two generations, being cool was an alternative success system combining wildness and composure; it was directly opposed to the social norms of a materialist and rapidly suburbanizing society. Within a decade of its emergence in the mid-1940s, this elusive concept was adopted and interrogated by artists, writers, intellectuals, bohemians, and youth culture. Authors such as Norman Mailer and Jack Kerouac struggled to create philosophies out of *cool* and its brother concept, *hip*. The sociologist Erving Goffman found that prisoners used the phrase "playing it cool" to refer to strategies for maintaining dignity against oppressive authority. When *West Side Story* was a hit on Broadway in

1957, it featured a production number called "Cool," sung by a character named Ice, who advised his fellow gang members to control their anger by cooling their jets.[1]

"Cool" represents a convergence of African-American and Anglo-American archetypal modes of masculine behavior. From England came the mythic reserve of the upper class, the Victorian ideal of the gentleman, the social value of keeping a stiff upper lip; the English themselves mock this emotional mode as the passionlessness of "God's *frozen* people." Duke Ellington, a world traveler for four generations, thought of Londoners as "the most civilized" people in the world and admired their "sense of *balance*" as a national trait and social value. Ellington hinted at his own adaptation of this sense of balance in his autobiography: "Self-discipline, as a virtue or an acquired asset, can be invaluable to anyone." Yet this social *class* ideal of stoicism had already begun to lose its allure among Americans after the various artistic and cultural rebellions in the wake of World War I: modernism in the arts and Communism in politics, working-class union socialism and anticolonialism, a populist rebellion in the arts through jazz, social dance, and the cinematic slapstick of Chaplin, Keaton, and Lloyd.[2]

Spurred by the disillusion resulting from the Great Depression, rogue figures arose as the shadow selves of Anglo-American positivism: the ethnic gangster, the jazz musician, the devil-may-care song-and-dance man, the hard-boiled detective, and later on, the spy. This symbolic shift from a British class ideal to a tough loner can be located in both popular music and literature, beginning with jazz and pulp fiction in the 1920s. In crime fiction, by the early 1930s, the puzzle solving of Sherlock Holmes and Watson in the drawing room became supplanted by the streetwise analysis of solo gumshoes Sam Spade and Philip Marlowe. These new detectives counted more on their street smarts than on brilliant rational analysis, and they were afoot in American cityscapes, as much prone to violence as any average working stiff. The shift to vernacular cool in music can be found in the abandonment of European classical music and ballet for the popular revolution of African-American music, arguably the most influential global artistic culture of the half century between 1920 and 1970. It was not just the global impact of musical practices and tastes through jazz, blues, gospel, swing, soul, rhythm and blues, and rock and roll, but also the style and slang, the physical gestures and kinesthetics that informed each genre shift as it hit American city streets and global dance floors.[3]

In 1955, Norman Mailer observed that the idea of cool underwent a sea change from the English gentleman to the American working-class male. The Englishman's reserve was a matter of upholding class dignity: "They had to be cool because to be cool is for the English the *social* imperative." In America, by contrast, cool was admired as an intrinsic projection of an individual. For Mailer, "cool" was a password synonymous with "grace under pressure," Hemingway's famous definition of courage. Mailer idolized Hemingway and he understood American cool as something achieved only in-the-moment: "Americans are more primal; for us to be *cool in action* is the basic thing." The value of being cool had shifted from a sign of social class to one of admirable and enviable self-mastery. *American* cool became synonymous with a certain stylish stoicism: emotional self-control carried off with a signature style.[4]

An illuminating connection between African-American jazz cool and Anglo-American outlaw cool can be found in the coming-of-age of actor Clint Eastwood, a postwar teenager who idolized jazz musicians. Born in 1930, Eastwood's model for *cool-in-action* was the soloing jazz musician of the late 1940s, and like Jack Kerouac, he hung out in jazz clubs in postwar Oakland during jazz's shift from swing to bebop. When soloing, the individual jazz artist creates spontaneous art on a blank aural canvas: this artistic practice imprinted Eastwood with a heroic ideal. As film critic David Denby perceived, Eastwood's "notion of cool—slightly aloof, giving only the central satisfaction and withholding everything else—is derived from those [jazz] musicians." It may be counterintuitive to link the respective tough-guy cools of Eastwood and Miles Davis but they are closely related as middle-class Americans born only four years apart.[5]

In 1946, Eastwood went to a Jazz at the Philharmonic concert expressly to see and hear his idol, saxophonist Lester Young. "I thought he was the cat's rear end," Eastwood humbly recalled.[6] Young is the primogenitor of cool: he disseminated the modern usage of the term and concept of cool; he modeled it as an embodied philosophy; his solos are the foundation for the genre of "cool jazz." Yet Eastwood was equally stirred that night by Charlie Parker's revolutionary bebop solos—his harmonic, supersonic virtuosity imposed on a blues foundation. Bird's angular musical feats were then foreign to Eastwood's tastes but he bought a few of

Parker's records. Three years later he saw Dizzy Gillespie's big band in San Francisco and realized he was "drawn to the whole improvisational element" of jazz, and in the 1950s, he became enamored of "cool jazz" through Stan Getz, Chet Baker, and Gerry Mulligan. Thirty years later Eastwood fulfilled a lifelong dream by directing *Bird* (1988), a biopic of Charlie Parker.[7]

Like jazz, acting is a spontaneous art from, even when scripted. Eastwood redirected the calm center required of the improvising jazz musician into the edgy composure at the center of his acting. Imagine *jazz cool* transported to the frontier: Eastwood took the impassive, aloof face of the postwar jazz musician and made of it the mysterious, intimidating, kinetic cool-in-action of a Western hero living by a private code. Denby calls it "Eastwood's mask," a grim, impassive gravity that managed to project a personal set of values severed from institutional loyalty and the law. In the *Fistful of Dollars* trilogy and *High Plains Drifter*, he plays an American *rōnin*: "He kept his head still, at a slight angle; he narrowed his eyes; he scowled and curled his upper lip . . . he looked mean, amused, coolly amoral." The obvious Hollywood precedent for this mask came from film noir—from Humphrey Bogart, Robert Mitchum, and Sterling Hayden—with a nod to John Wayne to the West and Paul Muni to the East. Denby suggested that this mask was "an arrogant teen-ager's idea of acting," but this is an anachronistic analysis. Arrogant, sneering teen-agers did not exist on-screen until the 1950s: that's the legacy of Marlon Brando, James Dean, biker films, Elvis, and rock and roll. This *now-archetypal* masculine mode was new to Hollywood in 1941. "Eastwood's mask" extended the stylistic and conceptual revolution of postwar cool into the 1960s and 1970s, as his alienated, elusive, and ethical scowl "establish[ed] an image of implacable male force."[8]

For all that Eastwood rose to stardom in *Rawhide* (1958–65) and spaghetti Westerns, for his directorial debut he chose to play a *cool cat* in *Play Misty for Me* (1971), a jazz DJ. The film features a score by pianist Erroll Garner and several scenes at the Monterey Jazz Festival, including two numbers by saxophonist Cannonball Adderley. Eastwood's second film was an existential western, *High Plains Drifter* (1973), and he plays a nameless protagonist known only as "The Stranger" (perhaps a nod to Camus). The Stranger exacts revenge on a town that once exiled him for his attempt to bring the local mining interests to justice. In a flashback, he recalls the night he was whipped like a slave by the company's hired thugs. The camera focuses on Eastwood's lined, emotionless face before and after the dream, signaling that his tight, stony gaze resulted from the need to repress the searing pain of that near-fatal whipping.

Given Eastwood's investment in jazz and its history, The Stranger's whipping should be seen as a complex combination of solidarity with cool-as-black-rebellion—the mask of stylish stoicism—and the substitution of a white rebel. In 1957, Elvis was whipped on film in *Jailhouse Rock* for his participation in leading a jailbreak over prison conditions. The camera frames him dead-on, his hands tied to an iron bar, in a pose that is half crucifixion and half indebted to slavery, the historical root of both the oppression and musical tradition Elvis inhabited. These are paradigmatic examples of the "love and theft" of African-American culture as it has always informed the concept of cool on the color line.

For Eastwood as for Miles Davis, the sign of rebellion was *the mask of cool*: the projection of toughness and self-mastery through a blank facial expression and a corresponding economy of motion. In 1949, Miles Davis did not yet carry himself with the fierceness now associated with his image. Photos of the time reveal a young man with an open face, intense and attractive yet trusting. (See fig. 1.) This is probably how Juliette Gréco saw him. But Davis was soon hardened by five years of a heroin addiction (1949–54), a period in which he was humiliated by drug dealers and Charlie Parker's arrogance, by his mistreatment by club owners and the New York Police Department. Yet there is a salient difference: even if Miles Davis's mask of cool was as archetypally defiant as Eastwood's, his *sound* was then romantic and melodic.

Miles's romantic postwar trumpet projected "a monk's sound," Boris Vian wrote, the sound of "somebody who is part of the century but who can look at it with serenity." That is the secret of a cool aesthetic: artistic relaxation that creates excitement in the listener or audience. In art or in life, it is the ability to be in the center of dynamic action and maintain a state of equipoise: cool head and relaxed, kinetic body. Miles Davis's trumpet floated apart, aloof, riding on the elegance of the rhythm section. What a nice idea if your mind and thoughts could *sound* like that, buoyant yet grounded. "[It] takes a healthy sense of balance," Vian wrote of Miles Davis's solos, to create "such complex constructions" and yet "land on your feet."[9] In other words, to use then-current jazz slang, Miles was a *very* cool cat.

Clint Eastwood's grizzled, sculpted face later offered something similar: the Western gunslinger *as a monk*—but a tough monk, a samurai monk. What a nice idea if your own presence carried such authority, a wordless integrity. In the early 1960s, Eastwood supplanted John Wayne—a.k.a. "the Duke"—as the rogue Western gunslinger, since the latter's rebel roles were mostly behind him, from *The Searchers* (1954) dating back to *Stagecoach* (1939). The Duke was now as iconic as Uncle Sam, his face like something carved in granite on Mount Rushmore, his persona set in stone. In contrast, Eastwood's cowboy brought *existential cool* to the Western figure: it signaled the hope that there was and would always be a free, autonomous American out there on the frontier, what I will call here an *ethical rebel loner*.

In postwar cities, the jazz musician was the emblematic cool existential figure. Through his public, improvisatory negotiation of a denied individuality, and as the creators of an Afro-Western musical culture, the jazz musician was global culture's first non-white rebel. Having been dehumanized at every level, African-Americans practiced cool through rituals of self-affirmation that Albert Murray once called "survival technology." Using the portable cultural resources of music, style, slang (as coded language), humor, and physical gesture, these rituals communicated crucial lessons for anyone in the process of social and self-reinvention, whether oppressed, Othered, or culturally lost. In the nightly public assertion of the self-in-resistance, the jazz musician performed the kind of existential freedom called for by French existentialists Albert Camus, Jean-Paul Sartre, and Simone de Beauvoir.[10]

◆ ◆ ◆

This work is concerned with three intertwined questions. First, what do we mean when we say a person is cool? Second, how and why did this word and concept emerge into postwar American life?

The word and concept of "cool" first surfaced in the postwar African-American jazz vernacular as an emblematic word synonymous with "relaxed intensity." A cool person projected a charismatic self-possession that was both "low-key and high-wattage," as one film critic described jazz singer Abbey Lincoln.[11]

In an artistic sense, cool came to refer to someone with a signature artistic style so integral as to exude an authentic mode-of-being in the world: Miles, Bogart, Brando, Eastwood, Gréco, Elvis, Lady Day, Sinatra. Such a person created something from nothing and gave the world some new artistic or psychological "equipment for living," to use a phrase of Kenneth Burke's. A signature style is *yours* and can only be carried *by you*: it cannot be abstracted except through dilution and commodification since it reflects an individual's complex personal experience. In this sense, cool was "making a dollar out of fifteen cents," to pull another phrase from the African-American vernacular. Lester Young was once at a bar when a tenor saxophone solo floated out of the jukebox. "That's me," he said happily. As he listened his mood collapsed—he realized it was one of his many imitators. "No, that's not me," he said sadly. To steal someone else's sound or style and capitalize on it has always been *uncool*, the pretense of posers.[12]

The new canvas for identity was a person's body and bearing, style and attitude, the outer signs of a new, modern *portable* self. Whether marked by fedoras or leather jackets or tattoos, our bodies were now the mobile canvas of identity. Consider the contrasting public personae and personal styles within the same artistic fields of Bogart and Brando, of Dizzy Gillespie and Sonny Rollins, of Lauren Bacall and Audrey Hepburn. Cool was originally associated with being distinctive, singular, and synthetic: an individual created his or her cool out of highly personal resources.

The third question refers to a historical conundrum of postwar cool. How is it that we can consider Bogart, Bacall, Sinatra, and Mitchum cool along with their seeming opposites, Kerouac, Brando, Dean, and Elvis? The answer concerns a necessary remapping of post-1945 cultural history into two distinct phases I will call here *Postwar I* (1945–52) and *Postwar II* (1953–63), as split by the end of the Korean War (1950–53).

In the first phase (1945–52), cool represented dignity within limits, a calm defiance against authority with little expectation of social change. By the late 1950s, in Postwar II, cool inflected toward a certain wild abandon, a bursting of emotional seams reflecting a hopeful surge against obsolete social conventions. The late 1940s (Postwar I) was a makeshift period of recovery from war, social instability, and trauma, while Postwar II was a period of expansive middle-class prosperity and American triumphalism masking the underlying tensions of the Cold War. In short, there was at first an anxious phase of instability and readjustment focused on American soldiers, followed by a slow-breaking prosperity in the mid-'50s as it registered on a new consumer cohort of teenagers. I treat each phase as a different cultural era. The first five chapters focus on Postwar I as a lived mindset (or *mentalité*) then there is an interlude explaining the shift in cool to set up six chapters analyzing the icons of the late '50s (Postwar II).

In short, the boomer generation had quite different cultural needs than the earlier Depression-and-wartime cohort that settled down in the late 1940s, and this shift can be read through patterns of popular culture. We are more familiar with the cool icons of Postwar II (Brando, Kerouac, Miles Davis), because the term itself surfaced along with them. It is important to keep in mind that cool is not a transhistorical concept: it is neither reducible to the clichés of timeless or classic style nor to its contemporary sense of commodified rebellion.

Here's an initial definition broad enough to cover both postwar phases: *cool* was a public mode of covert resistance.

Noir Cool

Humphrey Bogart's grizzled face was the mask of cool incarnate, with its flat affect, half grimace, and deadpan cynical gestures. It was the expression of your face at rest when life has made you "beat," a word Jack Kerouac co-opted from the African-American vernacular in his visits to jazz clubs in the 1940s. Theirs was a "beat generation," Kerouac moaned to his friend John Clellon Holmes in 1949. At the time he meant "beat" as in worn out, exhausted, almost without hope. Only in the late '50s did he revise his past by transmuting the connotation of "beat" from "exhausted" to "beatific" (or angelic). In effect, Kerouac's eliding of this one word symbolizes the shift in the concept of cool between Postwar I and Postwar II.[13]

The iconic power of the Bogart persona in Postwar I was to embody the attitude, stance and feeling of being *beat-but-not-beaten*. Bogart's face was the mask of survival—after the Great Depression and the unmasking of capitalist paternalism, after the regressions of fascism and the unmasking of Stalinist tyranny with the Nazi-Soviet pact, after a world war that involved the total mobilization of American life and left an arms race for a legacy. When French film critic André Bazin eulogized Bogart in 1957, he focused on this aspect of his appeal for European audiences: "The *raison d'être* of his existence was in some sense [simply] to survive. . . . Distrust and weariness, wisdom and skepticism: Bogey is a Stoic." And to be a Stoic is the ancient Greek philosophical precedent for being cool.[14]

The representative cinematic character of *noir cool* is Rick Blaine (Bogart), the owner of the Café Américain in *Casablanca* (1942). Living in exile during World War II, Blaine has committed an unnamed crime and has a track record of working for Leftist causes. He has no religion and proclaims neither virtue nor heroism, only that he looks out for number one. That's a lie, as we learn, but it is a front he keeps up so no one takes him for a sap. *Casablanca* manages to catch a little bit of the terror Europeans felt living under the Nazis, an experience not unlike the colonized under the colonizer, and one that has important implications for existentialism.

Cool represents inchoate social and psychological forces taking embodied form. In other words, a new figure of cool embodies the unspoken, unconscious emotional needs that have not yet reached consciousness in young people. Something new has arrived, its powerful energy amorphous and untheorized, but there he or she stands. It is this triangulation of social need, manufactured product, and artistic stylization that sustains the central importance of popular culture to American society. Cool is clarified through its icons: Astaire and Rogers in the '30s, Brando and Elvis in the '50s, Dylan and Hendrix in the '60s, Madonna and Prince in the '80s. In effect, popular culture represents society—or a generation—thinking out loud.

Why was it Bogart rather than James Cagney or Paul Muni who became the embodiment of American mythic cool? Bogart is still number one on the American Film Institute's esteemed list of male Hollywood icons. What were the social, cultural, economic, and political forces in play that made Rick Blaine the American anti-hero of 1941 and a man for all seasons? And why did cool itself emerge in Hollywood in 1940–41? Why *this* attitude *then*? And why wasn't it the tall, blond, suave, courageous Nazi hunter Victor Lazlo who became the icon of cool in *Casablanca*? "He's too good," a student of mine once quipped with a bit of class hostility, and his response gets to the heart of cool.

To be cool is not the same as being good or nice or heroic. To be cool is to disconnect from the religious framework of virtue and vice, of good and bad, of saints and demons. A cool person has engaged his or her dark side and strives to be ethical on his or her own terms. Victor Lazlo is a saint in *Casablanca*: honest and transparent, good and noble, he is guided by larger causes that map onto the messianic. The less saintly among us—that is to say, all of us—struggle simply to control our desires and instincts. And that's why Rick Blaine is the American anti-hero par excellence as the industrial world recovered from the Depression. Bogart's public mask revealed the costs of controlling his desires, the effort of suppressing his jealousy, rage, and hopes. The audience knows that Blaine will kill or betray someone if necessary to advance his cause or save a friend. He is not too good for any action in the service of survival.

Cool is a post-Christian concept, a devaluation of the virtuous (or good) man as an unrealistic ideal. Instead, cool assumes every human being has a dark side, and that to ignore its inappropriate temptations—or never chase one's desires—was to live as a "sap," a key Depression-era term. Rick Blaine keeps his dark side under control: he drinks in a darkened room, by himself, and lets out his desires only at extreme moments. Blaine both is representative of the influence of Freudian psychology on Hollywood and he also represents the revelations of the Depression in economics and geopolitics. The Depression left in its wake a set of busted ideals of capitalism and democracy while neither pacifism nor virtue was likely to defeat fascism, state Communism, or the Third Reich. Americans needed a new tough public face for the fight just as big band swing gave GIs a powerful, new machine-age soundtrack. *Casablanca* was marketed by the Warner Brothers studio in conjunction with the French government and film industry, a transatlantic pact emblematic of the cultural conversation in literature, film, and music throughout this work. Colloquially, the unconscious is the dark side, and audiences understood you needed to be *noir cool* to maintain spiritual balance. In fact, "transcendent balance" is one of the core definitions of cool as inherited from its West African origins. (See chapter 1.)

The masculine icons of film noir carried themselves as if each embodied the simplest colloquial translation of being cool: a guy who doesn't give a shit what anyone thinks of his actions. Take the case of Robert Mitchum, the protagonist of *Out of the Past* (1947), an iconic film noir second only to *Double Indemnity* (1944). Mitchum was raised in a working-class family of little means and often ran away to ride the rails during the Depression, bonding with vagabonds and fending for himself before he was thirteen. Tall, broad, and almost supernaturally impassive, Mitchum impressed every director with his work ethic, theatrical fellowship, and range of knowledge. He was a lawless soul and a total professional: hardworking, hard drinking, and hard smoking. Mitchum was arrested in a famous marijuana bust in 1948 and shook it off. Forced by the studio to go into rehab for alcoholism, he stopped in for a drink on the ride home. He looked like a veteran boxer who had learned something from every shot he'd ever taken: beat but not beaten. On-screen, Mitchum moved with reptilian aplomb. His cool aesthetic was effected by projecting a smoldering relaxation that created excitement.[15]

Actor Harry Carey Jr. grew up as a studio kid and his experience working under Mitchum's wing on the set of *Pursued* (1947) still left him awed a half century later. The only word that came to Carey's mind to describe Mitchum was "cool"—the supreme compliment of American culture— and he recalled correctly that the word was not yet in circulation.

> It's over fifty years later . . . and I still haven't met another guy like that in my life. He was just an overwhelming personality. Big. Powerful looking. I mean, I knew Duke Wayne, and Mitchum . . . was a much more overpowering figure than Duke Wayne was, no question. And Mitchum—I don't know if they even had the word then—[but] Mitchum was *cool*. If they didn't have that expression he must have invented it, because he was just the coolest guy that ever lived. He had his own outlook on life and he didn't let anyone interfere with it. Totally opposite from me.[16]

Mitchum was "totally opposite" from the young actor and schooled him on commanding respect on the set by being cool: (*a*) *carry yourself in a relaxed, nonchalant manner,* as if you can take the job or leave it; (*b*) *avoid eagerness*—people will take advantage of you; (*c*) *ignore the director if he gives you a command*—wait for a request; and (*d*) *treat all co-workers with respect,* regardless of status or salary. Carey was amazed that Mitchum hitchhiked home every night, taking rides in any kind of car, with anyone, to his home up in the hills. Mitchum was a radical egalitarian in a Hollywood that ran on nuances of hierarchical prestige. Carey's testimony carries considerable authority since he was the son of Harry Carey Sr., one of the original Hollywood cowboys, and grew up admiring his father's cohort on the studio back lots.

In essence, film noir was the Western's Other—an urban rather than a rural genre dealing in new masculine archetypes of cool. In the Hollywood studio typology of the 1940s, Bogart and Mitchum inhabited two distinctive cool personae in direct opposition to the epic heroism of John Wayne or the eccentric decency of Jimmy Stewart. There were existential and even noirish Westerns, of course. Yet in contrast to Mitchum, John Wayne was a muscular Christian saint regressed back to the frontier where Americans could imagine themselves innocent even as the apocalypse hung overhead like a cartoon anvil of doom.

In effect, cool represented an inquiry into the reassessment of conventional morality outside of Christian frameworks and Western philosophical grandstanding. Modernity had triumphed but without covering its losses. That's why the cool figure with his private code was—and remains—so appealing. Rick Blaine's cool signaled a populist desire for a new ethics, which, if not found, would result in a reversion to, say, fundamentalist religion. Many human beings seem unable to live without a transcendent belief system or purpose, or certainly this remains true of Americans.

Cool was a sign of change: it signified a populist upsurge searching for new symbols to critique society. Cool is a mask on Bogart's or Mitchum's face, one that is post-traumatic after the Great Depression and World War II. For audiences, this cool mask valorized rational despair as achieved through reflection on transgression, violence, impulsive desire, or criminality. Cool was the public face of postwar survival: it signified the rejection of innocence, optimism, and hypocritical morality. In chapter 2, I analyze film noir as a genre representing a deferred engagement with the social trauma of the Great Depression. Until now, film scholars and historians have mostly ignored the aesthetic continuity of noir with Depression-era urban life along with its class hostility.

In a capitalist society where social prestige is based on wealth and possessions, the mythos of cool is simple: *You don't own me.* You'll *never* own me.

Cool signaled an underground search for an ethics to guide individuals into an era of post-Christian imperfectibility.

Cool is a hidden transcript of the postwar era.

In the Beginning Was the Word

> *Howl* is all "Lester Leaps In."
>
> Allen Ginsberg[17]

Legendary jazz saxophonist Lester "Pres" Young first used the colloquial phrase "I'm cool" to mean being relaxed and under control, and in his own style. His intention was both psychological and situational: to invoke the phrase meant a speaker felt he or she was in a safe environment. Given the racism of the Jim Crow era, Young meant something like "I'm keeping it together—in my psyche and spirit—against oppressive social forces." To be cool was to keep the various factors of everyday existence in balance.

Jazz was the dominant postwar subculture of American life, especially in New York, so its innovative practices, slang, and styles spread quickly. The word "cool" was quickly adopted by writers and artists with an ear to both jazz and the street, such as Kerouac, Norman Mailer, and Leonard Bernstein. Young was an underground jazz culture-hero of the era, and Kerouac introduced Beat writers to the "spontaneous method of composition" he appropriated from jazz improvisation. Ginsberg scatted Young's composition "Lester Leaps In" to find the right rhythmic phrasing for "Howl." By 1954, even the *New Yorker* referred to Lester Young as the "pres of cool" at the Newport Jazz Festival, picking up on the nickname Billie Holiday gave him as "the president of all the saxophonists."[18]

"Cool" was more of a symbolic matrix than a single word. It was complex, elusive, multilayered, and protean in its associations. If "cool" first surfaced in the African-American vernacular in the 1930s, Young redirected it to mean an ideal emotional mode of balance—a calm, cerebral space of relaxation.[19] As Big Bill Broonzy sang to a woman in "Let Me Dig It" (1938), "Let me cool you, baby / before the ice man come." In the 1940s, to "be cool" meant the same thing as "being chill" does now. After "cool" was appropriated by the dominant white society, young black men found it necessary to recast cool as "chill" and "chillin'" in the early 1980s, a term with obvious linguistic similarities. As for Young's role in disseminating the concept, Kerouac revered him as "the cultural master of his generation" of modern jazz, the key to its "mysteries as well as masteries," the cultural leader of its "styles [and] sorrows."[20]

"Cool" also referred to a new musical aesthetic developed by Young, a melodic sensibility he rhythmically reconfigured from the styles of two of his influences, white saxophonists Frankie Trumbauer and Jimmy Dorsey. To have a cool approach to a jazz solo meant to favor the following aesthetic elements: flow and understatement, minimalism and relaxed phrasing, deep tone and nonverbal narration. Young's influence reached across genres and artistic forms such that B. B. King crafted his solo guitar phrasing from the style of "the man they called the President, [who] played that . . . tenor sax with a laid-back attitude that revolutionized the music. Prez invented cool. Rather than state a melody, he suggested it. . . . Prez was an abstract jazz man and he taught me the beauty of modern art." For B. B. King, only Miles Davis took Young's subtle cool revolution further by "us[ing] silence better than anyone. . . . I call him [the] King of Cool." In his autobiography, B. B. King invoked this cool aesthetic of sound and art only for Young and Davis.[21]

Here's an example of how cool was used among postwar musicians in a recording like Big Joe Turner's "Cherry Red" (1952). Turner first sings two verses of this raucous ode to sexual pleasure ("I want you to boogie my woogie / until my face turns / cherry red"), and then trombonist Lawrence Brown takes a slow, controlled solo that is the essence of how jazz musicians "talk" on their instruments. At the end of one soulful phrase, Turner shouts to Brown in the studio, "You're a cool one, you're a *cool* one!"[22] This was a double compliment referring to both Brown's solo (as musical communication) and his impressive emotional control (as technical skill). When cool seeped out of the jazz subculture of the

1940s, it was the opposite of pretentious style, superficial rebellion, or faddish consumerism, as it is often used today.

Lester Young and Billie Holiday together invented cool as an aesthetic mode of music. By carefully accenting only certain words or notes through rhythmic nuance and a sophisticated manipulation of musical space, they created a low-key, late-night emotional sphere of adult experience. In the process, they transformed the blues into an urbane American romanticism. Young created the style and phrasing while Holiday's vocal swinging built on the subtle power of cool understatement. Holiday's early recordings reveal a talented young blues singer, but while a journeywoman on the road with the Count Basie Orchestra in the late 1930s, she played Young's records "over and over to get the phrasing," Basie vocalist Jimmy Rushing recalled. In fact, Holiday thought of herself as more of an improvising horn player than a singer and she swung *with* the band, not above it. Between 1935 and 1943, backed by the cream of the Basie and Ellington orchestras, Billie Holiday recorded nearly fifty chamber jazz classics, "a milestone in Western music," jazz critic Will Friedwald declaims, on a continuum "from Bach to Mozart to Ornette Coleman." There is a distinctive ease to the two dozen tracks featuring Holiday and Young—including such classics as "All of Me" and "He's Funny That Way"—such that her voice and his saxophone curl around each other, shape the air into sound, rise into smoky swirls of late-night yearning, then settle into your clothes with the bittersweet taste of romance come and gone.[23]

In the '50s, Frank Sinatra retooled this cool aesthetic from the late '30s and made swing over into one of the most globally resonant styles. Sinatra and Billie Holiday were born the same year (1915), and his vocal storytelling was permanently altered after seeing Lady Day at a Chicago club in the late '30s. He understood her artistic genius was in narrating songs as if they were short stories. In addition, Sinatra and Young were musical favorites of one another. "I knew Lester well," Sinatra recalled. "We were close friends, and we had a mutual admiration society. . . . I took from what he did, and he took from what I did." Young admired how Sinatra told a story and how he swung. "If I could put together exactly the kind of band I wanted . . . Frank Sinatra would be the singer," Young told Nat Hentoff in 1956. "Really, my main man is Frank Sinatra."[24]

"Jazz turned the Cold War into a *cool* war," according to German cultural historian Reinhold Wagnleitner. The Nazis and the Soviets both banned jazz due to its popularity since neither ideological system had a "sonic weapon" to counter its ensemble individuality and rhythmic power, as Wagnleitner argued in "Jazz: The Classical Music of Globalization."[25] In other words, the popular music of Germany and Soviet Russia were retrograde and unable to engage modernity. Jazz was (and is) the antithesis of all collective ideologies due to the artistic freedom built into the musical form, both individually and within an ensemble. This was untenable for totalitarian societies as a reflection of the state's top-down values.

Through jazz culture, cool became a set of postwar codes: nonchalant attitudes instead of eager obedience, subversive slang instead of polished eloquence, sly symbolic gestures (suggesting unstated beliefs) instead of blind patriotism, emotional detachment instead of phony affability. During the wartime era, cool started off with a few iconic figures: the jazz musician, the private detective, the existentialist author, the bohemian hipster, the swinging vocalist, the politicized worker.

By the mid-'50s, cool came to represent cultural resistance to all authority rather than political resistance to a known oppressor. Dharma bum and poet Gary Snyder, the most dedicated Zen practitioner of the Beats, defined cool among San Francisco bohemians as "our ongoing in-house sense of [being] detached, ironic, fellaheen hip, with an outlaw/ anarchist edge." By 1964, novelist Ken Kesey called the Merry Pranksters' cross-country road trip "the search for a kool place."[26] "Cool" carried into the early 1960s certain kinds of unheralded music, an alternative canon of underground literature, and a set of films—it functioned as a loose, underground cultural semiotics.

"Cool" was an emblematic term representing a convergence of Anglo- and African-American masculine ideals from different traditions: this intersection is crucial to its popularity and accessibility. For example, the key '50s phrase "playing it cool" is a combination of valorizing the rational mind—"keep a cool head," an Anglo-American phrase—with the African-American phrase "keep cool," which added connotations of strategic silence and public detachment. For African-American men, "playing it cool" represented an embodied philosophy of survival, as Langston Hughes sketched it in near-haiku form in "Motto" (1951):

I play it cool
And dig all jive
That's the reason
I stay alive

The narrator announces he is streetwise and survives through constant vigilance and awareness. To "dig" means to understand at a deep level and "jive" refers both to the latest slang and to the hypocrisy of the dominant white society during Jim Crow. "Playing it cool" concerns surviving with style but ideally it is only a transitional mode. Hughes then imagines a better society based on reciprocal dignity and social equality.

My motto,
As I live and learn,
Is:
Dig And Be Dug
In Return.

Three years before *Brown v. Board of Education*, Langston Hughes suggested that African-American men should *be cool* until things change. Ralph Ellison claimed this was characteristic of black survival and protest: such "resistance to provocation" and "coolness under pressure" were "indispensable values in the struggle [for freedom]."[27]

By the early 1950s, the phrase "playing it cool" had worked its way into the American vernacular as an emotional mode, a strategy of masking emotion. To play it cool combined performed nonchalance with repressed vulnerability. In "Satin Doll" (1953), a hit for the Ellington orchestra and then a bigger hit for Sinatra, the singer explains his strategy of seduction: "She's nobody's fool / so I'm playing it cool as can be." Elvis riffed the phrase a few years later in "Fools Fall in Love" (1957)— "They've got their love torches burning / When they should be playing it cool"—and was in turn answered by his ex-girlfriend, rockabilly queen Wanda Jackson, in "Cool Love" (1957): "You been playing it cool / I been playing a fool / Now don't you give me that cool love." In 1952, Ralph Ellison wrote to a friend about shopping his novel *Invisible Man* around, "Good things are being said and the publisher's hopes are high, but I'm playing it cool."[28]

"Playing it cool" was a vernacular phrase picked up from jazz slang that came to represent a new emotional mode and style: *the aestheticizing of detachment*. These popular songs set up a resonant tension between felt emotion and performed nonchalance. *To be a fool* was to be vulnerable and open to love and warmth, while *playing it cool* signified emotional self-control through repression, wariness, circumspection, and calm deliberation. The opposite of *playing it cool* is *playing a fool*: being sincere or emotionally open, wearing your heart on your sleeve, being an eager beaver.

These songs support one of the original coded meanings of "cool" as inherited from both Anglo- and African-American cultural traditions: the strategic silence of the outlaw or the oppressed, of the Zen warrior or the method actor. Postwar cool was a low-key emotional register expressive of a desire for social change that as yet had no form. To be cool in the postwar era was an outward manifestation of hard-fought inner worth. In the aftermath of World War II, there was an awareness of a *cultural* Cold War: monolithic consumer capitalism versus monolithic centralized Communism. Social change seemed unlikely in this polarized geopolitical Cold War moment of two sumo-wrestling superpowers. Of what importance was a single, critical, independent human being? And if change was unlikely, one could not afford to be eager or enthusiastic. For precedent, postwar cool contained elements of stoicism, quietism, revolutionary consciousness, and moral resignation. So the cool person relaxes into a moment but with an edge.

To be cool was to project a calm defiance.

To be cool signified as the opposite of blind patriotism in the United States and marked a person out as an enemy of propagandists of all political stripes.

To be cool was to be a walking indictment of society.

Cool as an American Mythos

And yet if this was only a historical set of meanings, the word "cool" would have evaporated into thin air like so many other jazz slang terms: "heavy," "groovy, "drag," "mellow," "uptight," "outasight." Why doesn't "cool" lie on the historical junk-pile of once-common generational slang such as "swell" or "solid," "making the scene" or "cruisin' for a bruisin'"?

Here's my theory: cool is a myth or, more precisely, it is the password to an American mythos. Like any myth, it contains truths *we don't know* we know—unconscious beliefs, idealistic hopes, submerged fears, historical evasions. "Cool" carries as yet unrealized truths of the twentieth century. "Cool" is a bejeweled word with many aspects. In the postwar generation, it stood for inchoate rebellion against religious morality and corrupt politics, against repressive social norms and runaway technological worship.

Here's the crucial subtext of the concept of cool: the valorization of the individual against larger dynamic forces. The postwar arts discussed in this work are characterized by an attempt to recuperate the individual—meaning, quite simply, to hold out the potential significance of a single person's actions in the face of global economic, social, and technological forces. In retrospect, it is significant that this was precisely the crux of the argument that broke apart Sartre and Camus in the early 1950s over the latter's study of individual rebellion, *The Rebel*. (See chapter 3.)

To be cool meant to walk the line "between good and evil," to appropriate Nietzsche's phrase. To be cool meant an engagement of *both* good and evil within oneself, to have experimented with your dark side and to have come out in control (or so your convincing act suggests). Cool worked in opposition to traditional middle-class dualisms of right and wrong, moral and immoral. To be cool meant a quest for spiritual balance or authenticity through secular means; it was unrelated to contemporary meanings of celebrity or trendiness.

Even now, with the idea of cool long since commodified and diffused into the vernacular, to say *"he's* cool" or *"she's* cool" still carries a social charge of charisma, style, and integrity, of having developed an edge to walk that is all one's own. It remains an honorific redolent with populist admiration.

In the offices of the dot-com boom of Silicon Valley in the '90s, for example, "cool" retained its power as an iconic term for "the ethos of the unknown," as Alan Liu learned while researching his study, *The Laws of Cool*. In the technological workplace, "cool" remains the unique signifier of what is as yet "unencoded and unstructured" in our culture of information, and such unconscious, inchoate desire becomes filtered by an "imagination [that] begins with cool." That "cool" still carries such emblematic power makes of it a symbol we can follow back in time to a mythic struggle.[29]

Cool is an inchoate value awaiting explanation.

Cool is a myth invested in the recuperation of individual agency.

Cool and the End of Western Civilization: 1947

European nations suffered a profound spiritual crisis in 1945, as Tony Judt pointed out in his magisterial study of the continent, *Postwar*. How could it have been otherwise? Western civilization was a failure: the Germans became savage primitives slaughtering other races they found inferior and unclean; the French were humiliated as an occupied nation; the British lost an empire. Most Europeans lived on subsistence rations until the late 1950s while contending with the political agenda of the USSR, both within and without. Without the Marshall Plan, the recovery of postwar Europe might have taken another generation. By 1945, after two world wars and the worldwide depression, "the cumulative effect of these blows was to destroy a civilization," Judt reflects, and yet since 1989, this history has been rewritten in "a self-congratulatory, even lyrical key" obscuring this lost faith in civilization, Europe, and the West.[30]

In *Year Zero: A History of 1945* (2013), Ian Buruma writes of that year's palpable understanding among Europeans that "the Old World had collapsed in . . . disgrace, not just physically, but culturally, intellectually, [and] spiritually," and this was especially true in countries liberated by the Allies (France and Holland) or conquered by them (Germany, Austria, Italy), and then embodied by American soldiers. From 1945 to 1957, Europeans experienced a foreign army of occupation from an exotic American culture first symbolized by "swing music and . . . easygoing GI manners, and they greeted the soldiers as liberators." Many European theorists consider that being consumers in this era offered Europeans an outlet for redefinition, "a new freedom to define themselves and shape their own identity." This was certainly an improvement over the Nazi occupation or totalitarian rule yet carved out neither new national nor European identities. This collapse is the subject of Thomas Pynchon's epic novel *Gravity's Rainbow* (1972), set in 1944 amid images of chaotic migrations and the loss of coherent ideology in favor of technological progress and escapism. As Buruma asks rhetorically in his memoir, "How are societies, or 'civilization' (a popular word at the time), put together again?"[31]

The European Age was over for two reasons. First, Nazi Germany treated even non-Aryan white Europeans as Other. As Simone Weil first set out in *The Need for Roots* (1943), Nazi Germany treated Europeans the same as they treated *non*-white colonized peoples, slaughtering and stealing their lands at will. World War II revealed there was indeed but a thin veneer of civilization over the savagery usually kept off-shore in the colonies, just as Freud suggested in *Civilization and Its Discontents* (1931). Second, once white Europeans were treated as Others, it led to a slow-breaking recognition of colonial oppression and imperialism among European intellectuals and, more importantly, to a rise in revolutionary sentiment in these same colonies. As Pankaj Mishra reflected recently, Americans and Europeans seemed unaware until the 1960s that "liberal democracies were experienced as ruthlessly imperialist by their colonial subjects." Historian Mark Mazower was stunned at the lack of intellectual protest or sympathy he found among European leftists for the colonized before 1945: "One examines the resistance record in vain for indications of an interest in the predicament of colonial peoples." Nearly alone among European intellectuals, Weil saw a straight line of white, Western imperialism from the Roman Empire to European colonialism to Nazi Germany. Under the Nazi occupation in Paris, the French felt eviscerated as individuals, much like the colonized, a process rendered palpable on every page of Jean Guéhenno's *Diary of the Dark Years*. (See chapter 5.)[32]

Even more self-consciously, the eminent British historian Geoffrey Barraclough declared "the end of European history" in 1955. Barraclough spent thirty years recasting his field away from its default mode of universalizing the Eurocentric perspective and "the human" through Enlightenment models. Everywhere in his travels, Barraclough heard from laymen and intellectuals alike of the need for "a new view of European history." In 1947, he opened a talk this way: "As we sit here under the louring shadow of the atom-bomb—replete, well-fed, with a . . . courageous smile on our faces, but with inward foreboding, like convicts on the morning of the day of execution—it is a good opportunity to take stock of human history, and see what it is all about."[33] This sentence might have come from one of Camus's journals. Barraclough continued: "The European age—the age which extended from 1498 to 1947—is over," he wrote and future problems would have to be solved by "humanity as a whole." Three years earlier, Arthur Koestler forecasted the end of two convergent models that had sustained European intellectuals for half a century: (1) the Enlightenment model and (2) the Soviet Union as the model progressive society that would emerge from the revolution of the proletariat. In "The End of an Illusion," Koestler wrote of Communism as a romantic cult then in its death throes all across Europe. The revelation of the Soviet Union's totalitarian oppression in the late 1940s was like "the end of a chapter in history," a now-stunted revolutionary arc of "the whole development of the socialist idea since the French Revolution."[34]

Cool was a transitional mask of composure necessary for those rebels who realized that Western civilization had come to an end, at least in its European phase. A decade earlier, American critic Joseph Wood Krutch had pondered this question during the Depression in *Was Europe a Success?* (1934) by invoking Oswald Spengler's *Decline of the West* as a jumping-off point for the continent's implosion. Philosopher Emmanuel Levinas began developing his "post-rational ethics" in a series of papers in 1946–47—certainly "rational ethics" translates as "Western ethics."

As individuals and nations must, Europeans rewrote their wartime narratives—first in the late 1940s and then later in the 1980s. The French turned a complex wartime experience of passivity, collaboration, and silence into a myth of heroic Resistance. The Germans channeled lost imperial dreams into a massive economic engine fueled by the core-dumping of guilt. The British gave up their empire for democratic socialism. Italy eliminated Mussolini and fascism from public memory, emphasizing instead the partisans' battle for the North. Israel was born, an act of historical reparations for a millennium of European anti-Semitism. Yet European self-doubt remained an "obsession with a largely intra-Western dispute" over governmental form (liberal democracy vs. Communism or fascism) while a larger shadow loomed: the blowback from centuries of colonial oppression began to rise in Africa and Asia. If in the 1980s, Reagan, Thatcher, and the end of the Cold War reanimated pride in Western civilization, this work attempts to recapture the lived tensions and doubts of the postwar era.[35]

Cool was an intellectual's mask of composure in the face of nuclear anxiety, post-Holocaust meditations, and the concurrent rise of oppressed peoples. "In the face of the atomic bomb, everybody felt powerless," poet Lewis MacAdams reflected in *Birth of the Cool*, his oral history and study of postwar New York artistic culture. "After 1945, the idea that history was a steady progression toward perfection began to seem naïve." Working against runaway technological visions of centralized power, new reflections on Western imperialism, and visions of the apocalypse, artists were drawn to a new modality: "Cool—a way, a stance, a knowledge—was born."[36]

Here's an evocative intellectual matrix of 1947. In that year, Simone de Beauvoir toured the United States with Richard Wright as her guide: to jazz and Jim Crow, to the lived experience of the Other, and to the idea of race as a social construction. Beauvoir's excellent travel memoir, *America Day by Day* (1948) is dedicated to Wright and his family; its strongest sections are meditations on American race relations. A year later, Beauvoir's *The Second Sex* (1949) launched second-wave feminism using the analogy of race as the model for gender oppression through the concept of the Other. To illuminate the caste position of women, Beauvoir synthesized Wright's "phenomenology of oppression" with Gunnar Myrdal's sociology of race, *An American Dilemma* (1944). While writing *The Second Sex*, Beauvoir wrote of her ambition to her paramour, author Nelson Algren: "I should like to write a book as important as this big one about Negroes; Myrdal points [to] . . . analogies between Negroes' and women's status; I felt it already."[37]

In 1947, the French intellectual journal *Le Temps Moderne*, as edited by the circle around Sartre and Beauvoir, serialized three works alongside one another: Wright's *Black Boy* (1944), Beauvoir's *The Ethics of Ambiguity* (1947), and Sartre's *What Is Literature?* (1948). All three authors were friends in Paris, all three theorized the subjective landscapes of lived experience, all three influenced each other's work on colonialism, subjectivity, and existentialism, all three organized together for a political third way during the Cold War. To understand this intellectual moment, Paul Gilroy raised a key question a generation ago: "What would it mean to read Wright intertextually with Genet, Beauvoir, Sartre?"[38] It would mean we might start writing a *post-Western*, postwar cultural history since 1945. In fact, it turned out there was no third political way—at least, not until the so-called Nordic model of social democracy.[39]

Instead, individual rebellion as theorized through existentialism represented a third *cultural* way: ethical self-consciousness at a *cool* remove. Albert Camus theorized the figure of the rebel as a slave who suddenly says no without saying why: this "no" was in essence a verbal line in the sand, an inchoate rebellion. In other words, individual alienation precedes social and political protest. Such an attitude can also be applied to "the problem with no name" that Betty Friedan identified among white middle-class suburban woman in *The Feminine Mystique*. For the first wave of baby boomers, born in the 1940s, authors and theorists such as Camus, Friedan, and Wright built the ground on which '60s rebels stood. The African-American cultural critic Margo Jefferson recalled her own coming into consciousness as "admiring and trying to emulate the creeds and tastes of '40s and '50s hipsters." Jefferson followed these social rebels as they "modulated and diversified through the Civil Rights and youth movements, the counterculture, the New Left, and Black Power, feminism, and gay rights." These interrelated movements emerged under the sign of cool. To take only the most salient example from three of this work's iconic figures, Marlon Brando, Frank Sinatra, and Orson Welles were all staunch civil rights advocates in the '50s and '60s.[40]

Almost alone among American intellectuals, playwright and civil rights activist Lorraine Hansberry perceived the rise of non-white peoples as the primary cause of the postwar intellectual malaise. She railed against its manifestation in existentialism in a fictional dialogue between "He" (a Jewish intellectual) and "She" (Hansberry): "What other than the rise of subject peoples has brought Western Europe and its intellectuals to their present state? . . . What has induced the melancholy other than the collapse of empire[?] . . . In the modern world, 'the West' has mistaken its own self-glorified image for the world." *He* is confused so *She* explains: "I am talking about the death of colonialism." For Hansberry, the existential malaise was a form of intellectual cowardice, an inability to face up to the rise of oppressed peoples. Western writers and intellectuals floundered around with absurdity while anticolonial revolutions grew in strength every day. "To want to be free and equal is *not* to want to be white," *She* insists, then frames white people globally as a "misguided world-wide minority," one she hoped was "rapidly losing ground." *She* maintains that "the gloom and doom of so much of Western art and thought" was simply a white intellectual response to the revolutions of people of color in Africa and Asia, as well as to the civil rights movement. To Hansberry, Camus's melancholic vision and existential literature more generally were part and parcel of the same malaise, the "Death of the West."[41]

Hansberry's best friend, James Baldwin, sounded this note even more clearly in 1963: "All of the western nations have been caught in a lie, the lie of their pretended humanism; this means that their history has no moral justification, and that the West has no moral humanity." Even this was a more refined and political elaboration of the clarion note he hit in the final line of *Notes of a Native Son* (1955): "This world is white no longer, and it will never be white again."[42]

Cool at the End of World War II

Cool rises from the ashes of Western civilization: it is the endgame of the West provided by its internal dissidents. *Cool* was the sign of an attempt to recuperate the value of individuality after the failure of collective ideologies and it had three separate manifestations. I will first explore the wartime emergence of cool in jazz, film noir, and existentialism, and then analyze their intersections.

Euro-American cool was a working-class male response to both the trauma and capitalist hypocrisy of the Great Depression and found its artistic form in film noir. (See chapters 2, 5, and 7.)

African-American cool was a psychological and stylistic repudiation of the racial performance of Uncle Tomming as modeled by jazz musicians' art, style, and slang. In their role as creators and emblems of a post-Western, Afro-European musical culture, jazz musicians were the emblematic existential figures of cool. The inward turn of this revolution among African-American men required new language: jazz musicians followed Lester Young's lead in disseminating the terminology of cool itself (e.g., "be cool," "cool it!" "Cool!"). In fact, swing-era jazz culture was already influential and potent enough during World War II that certain phrases—such as "in the groove" or "lay it down"—were used as code by French Resistance fighters to transmit secret messages.[43] (See chapters 1, 4, 5, and 9.)

Existential cool in France was a response to both the trauma of Nazi occupation and the fallen promise of Marxism as carried out by the Communist Party. In the postwar era, the capital of Western culture moved from Paris to New York, from an exhausted and depleted Europe to a nation mostly untouched by the ravages of World War II. Existential cool found its narrative form in the detached voice of first-person narratives that remain the philosophy's most accessible expressions. These novels were indebted to the hard-boiled American literature of Hemingway, James M. Cain, Dashiell Hammett, Raymond Chandler, and others. (See chapters 3, 5, and 10.)

The triad of jazz, noir, and existential literature has not yet been explored. These were the popular arts of a distinctively American existentialism, itself a philosophy based on imagining each individual as a blank slate, purged of progress, fate, and innate morality. What happens to someone without a framework? In these art forms, he or she survives to prove that there is no life without dignity and then either proceeds to die trying (in film noir or existentialist fiction) or to turn one's self inside out (in jazz solos or method acting). Sartre distilled existentialism into three little words, "existence precedes essence." What will you do with your existence if your essence comes without a blueprint?

Jazz musicians sounded out the invisible structures of the postwar cage, both personal and social. The iconic actors of film noir walked such a walk. The existentialist writers came up with a new way to talk such a talk. All were only convincing inasmuch as a gait, a narrative tone, or an instrumental voice can communicate an honest rendition of personal experience. As Charlie Parker quipped, "If you don't live it, it won't come out of your horn." And it won't register in your bearing: this is the earned credit for trying to walk the daily tightrope and tell your story when you get to the other side.[44]

For jazz musicians, cool was a stage persona, a philosophy of relaxation, and a survival strategy. The mask walled off the invasive white gaze and allowed the deep excavation of experience transmuted into emotional communication and spontaneous art. In film noir, cool manifested as the world-weary stoicism of the private detective, a man whose integrity is a threat to both the cops and his clients. In existentialist fiction, it is the dispassionate narrative voice of a man who suppresses violence and sexual desire to project the illusion of emotional self-control.

Film noir has sometimes been considered something of a pulp existentialism, but it has rarely been analyzed as such. Some scholars pay lip service to the notion of the jazz musician as an existential figure, but there is little rigorous analysis of the musicians or the literature they inspired. In jazz, the mask of cool allowed your music its beauty or its protest—to burn or to churn—while the suited-up postwar musician remained cool at the core, his face blank, his body controlled. In existentialist fiction, the detachment of the narrative voice and the male protagonist serve to flatten underlying traumatic loss: it signifies emotion*less*ness rendered in style.[45]

Antonio Gramsci theorized "common sense" as a set of agreed-upon values in a society that manifest in distinctive artistic ways for separate social classes or ethnic groups. In this way, existentialist concepts might manifest in jazz for college students and African-Americans, in film noir for white working-class Americans, and in French literature and philosophy for intellectuals and self-conscious social rebels. In a variety of ways, cool was on the street and on the screen, on the tongue and on the page, on the air and in the music.

My theory of the origins of cool unifies the affinities of these three concurrent cultural forms around the search for new masculine modes of subjectivity and identity in the face of modernity, trauma, mass society, technological encroachment, and geopolitical crisis. In Postwar I, the mask of cool affirmed the sheer act of survival for audiences whose belief systems—religious, cultural, ideological, and teleological—had been shattered.

The cool mode was post-traumatic yet a form of affirmation.

Camus declared his philosophical intent in 1954: "I imagine a first man who starts at zero." The events of 1945 blew up the Western world: its social ideal of rational men (not women), its false Cartesian opposition of mind and body, its white racial arrogance. As early as 1939, Beauvoir suggested to Sartre that he abandon the ideas of "Cartesian thought" and revolutionary salvation: "The only thing left was to begin everything over again."[46] Or as Walker Percy distilled Camus's challenge to American writers: "How can one be a decent and moral man in an absurd world?" Camus sketched a fragmentary answer in a late journal entry: "*The First Man* . . . . He did not want to have, he did not want to possess, he wanted [only] to be. For that only obstinacy [is needed]."[47]

How do you look if you have the intellectual or spiritual guts to stare at zero? Maybe beat like Bogart. Maybe blank and impassive like Bird

(Charlie Parker). Maybe beautifully diffident like Barbara Stanwyck. In any case, you'd try to look cool.

Being cool was the performance of calm in the face of ideological breakdown.

Cool is what you need when the master narratives collapse (God and Christianity, civilization and nationalism, racial superiority and patriarchy) and the counternarratives fail (Marxist revolution, isolationism, primitivism). Cool is a transitional mode of a self-in-motion, surviving. For these reasons, the setting for Samuel Beckett's *Waiting for Godot* (1952)—the first truly postmodern work—had to be abstract and post-apocalyptic, set in a nameless post-Western nowhere without buildings or markers, a wide spot in the road where two wisecracking tramps wait for a message from God . . . who (it turns out) isn't coming. In an unconscious borrowing from both the philosophical past and the African-American present, European and American men turned to a renewed stylish stoicism—cool—to emotionally weather the postwar spiritual crisis.

Cool was an emergent structure of feeling in postwar America.

Figure 2. Lester Young brought the concept of cool into American culture (Institute of Jazz Studies, Rutgers University).

1

Lester Young and the Birth of Cool

Lester Young first invoked "cool" to refer to a state of mind and contemporary usage of this word and concept disseminated from jazz culture starting in the late 1930s.[1] When Young said, "I'm cool" or "that's cool," he meant "I'm calm," "I'm OK with that," or just "I'm keeping it together." Jazz musician and scholar Ben Sidran noted that this cool ethic reflected "actionality turned inward" and was "effected at substantial cost and suffering."[2] If Miles Davis's 1957 collection *The Birth of the Cool* often serves as a lightning rod for discussions of cool in jazz culture, a spate of jazz recordings testify to the importance of being cool starting in World War II as a strategy for dealing with the dashed hopes of social equality.[3] The messages of Erskine Hawkins's hit, "Keep Cool, Fool" (1941), Count Basie's "Stay Cool" (1946), and Charlie Parker's "Cool Blues" (1946) all testify to a new valuation of public composure and the disparaging of the outward emotional display long associated with stereotypes of blacks, from Uncle Tomming to the happy-go-lucky "Southern darky."

One of the two or three most influential jazz artists between the eras of Louis Armstrong and Charlie Parker, Lester Young created the so-called cool saxophone style and carved the melodic path to the "cool school" of jazz co-created by Miles Davis and Gil Evans. Young is little known outside the jazz world because his groundbreaking recordings were primarily made with either the Count Basie Orchestra or Billie Holiday. Young was the "genius soloist" of the classic 1930s Basie band and the saxophone complement to Billie Holiday's best vocal performances before 1945.[4] Young was Holiday's favorite musician, and they bestowed the nicknames on one another that stuck for life: she called him "Pres" as short for "the president of all the saxophone players," and Young dubbed her "Lady Day."

Young burst into recorded history in 1936 with two songs — "Shoe Shine Boy" and "Oh! Lady Be Good" — that featured his revolutionary, vibrato-less tenor saxophone sound: fast, floating, airy, clean, light.[5] His sound was so completely opposed to the then-dominant model of the tenor saxophone — Coleman Hawkins's rhapsodic, powerful, macho tone — that it confused many jazz musicians.[6] Young's combination of lightning speed, blues feeling, rhythmic balance, precise articulation, and inexhaustible melodic ideas made him, in retrospect, something like the Michael Jordan of jazz. Dizzy Gillespie called it a "cool, flowing style" to emphasize the long, fluid phrases, strategic use of silence and space, and rhythmic mastery. Young's sound and style represented a musical synthesis of early jazz history: from his childhood on the New Orleans streets and adolescence on the black vaudeville circuit to his responsiveness to white Chicagoan influences like Jimmy Dorsey and Bix Beiderbecke; from his mastery of the blues and his classical virtuosity to his involvement in "the big music workshop" of Kansas City in the 1930s. Young influenced hundreds of musicians between 1937 and 1944. After suffering a series of traumatic experiences at a Georgia army base in World War II (see below), he remained a perennial performer but withdrew into a quiet, gin-soaked nonconformity.[7]

Young's strategies of self-insulation in the postwar era — his shades, slang, and style — were as influential as his music on younger jazz musicians. Young's renowned use of hip slang influenced jazz culture, black cultural pride, Beat writers, and (through them) the counterculture of the 1960s. His prodigious consumption of marijuana and alcohol, renowned sense of humor, trademark porkpie hat, and silent, expressive sadness generated so much jazz lore he remains the exemplar of this golden age of jazz — as Dale Turner in the movie 'Round Midnight (1986) and Edgar Pool in John Clellon Holmes's novel, *The Horn* (1958). Young earned more than $50,000 a year during this period yet self-consciously drank himself to death in a small room in the Alvin Hotel on 52nd Street, neither proud nor ashamed of either his substance abuse or his sadness.[8] Between his dedication to expressing his inner pain artistically and the blank facial expression he wore to resist the white gaze, Young embodied two seemingly contradictory aspects of cool: artistic expressiveness and emotional self-control.

There were four core African-American cool concepts alive at the birth of cool, all of which still influence contemporary usage. Cool the first: to control your emotions and wear a mask of cool in the face of hostile, provocative outside forces. Cool the second: to maintain a relaxed attitude in performance of any kind. Cool the third: to develop a unique, individual style (and sound) that communicates your personality or inner spirit. Cool the fourth: to be emotionally expressive within an artistic frame of restraint, as in jazz, acting, or basketball. *Cool* is also the term used to express aesthetic approval of such a performance ("Cool!").[9]

Cool was an ideal state of balance, a calm-but-engaged state of mind between the emotional poles of "hot" (excited, aggressive, intense, hostile) and "cold" (unfeeling, efficient, mechanistic). "Cool" translated to "relaxed intensity," a common objective of jazz musicians in performance. Nelson George reflects that, for young urban black men in the late 1940s, "cool came to define a certain sartorial elegance, smooth charm, and self-possession that . . . suggested a dude that controlled not only himself but his environment." When jazz producer and scholar Ross Russell called Lester Young "the greatest bohemian and hipster in the jazz community," he meant Young was an anti-authoritarian, peace-loving, jive-talking nonconformist long before those qualities were acceptable in the average American man (of any ethnicity).[10]

Lester Young was a musical genius with a legendary sense of humor who influenced hundreds of musicians during the most dynamic years of the Great Migration, a time when American race relations were undergoing a radical shift. Young's whole life was self-consciously dedicated to being original—in his music, mannerisms, and detached style—on the Romantic model, as if being original was the vital force of life itself. He was often described as "'cool'—calm, imperturbable, unhurried, and balanced in his playing and personal demeanor."[11] Young died in 1959, and yet two generations later, bandleader Johnny Otis still declared Young to be "the one figure who stands above the entire field of music as the guiding spirit of African-American artistry." Here I will explore the West African, Anglo-American, African-American, and pop-cultural roots of the concept of cool, then show how Young's synthesis of these materials gave birth to American cool.[12]

From Blackface Minstrels to Jazz Artists

Even among jazz musicians, Lester Young was thought of as a visitor from another planet. A shy, reserved, and gentle man, Young was a fierce musical competitor but otherwise recoiled from interpersonal conflict. When insulted, he pulled out a small whisk broom and brushed off his shoulder; when a bigot was present, he said softly, "I feel a draft"; when a fellow musician made a musical mistake on the bandstand, he rang a little bell. Young's bandmate, the guitarist Freddie Green, reflected: "Most of the things he came up with were . . . things you'd never heard before. . . . He was a very original man." His stylistic trademarks were a slow, relaxed step no one could hurry and the flat, black porkpie hat he had custom-made from a Victorian woman's magazine. He seems to be the primary source for the essential jazz idea that it is more important to "tell a story" in your solo than to be virtuosic; his sage advice was "Ya gotta be original, man."[13]

After 1940, Young spoke a nearly impenetrable hip slang, and more than one fellow musician claimed it took several months to understand him.[14] To express desire for something, he had "big eyes" for it (or "no eyes" if he disapproved), an expression still used among jazz musicians; he called policemen "Bing and Bob," an old girlfriend "a wayback," and white jazz musicians "gray boys"; he addressed fellow musicians as "Lady" plus their last name (e.g., Lady Basie, Lady Tate, Lady Day) and stuck many of them with permanent nicknames.[15] His vocal inflections were so expressive, a New York clergyman called it "his personal poetry" and claimed that only "Prez could say 'mother-fucker' like music, bending the tones until it was a blues." He was that rare jazz musician whose use of slang "correspond[ed] with the popular magazine and radio concept of a jazz musician's jargon," critic Leonard Feather recalled, "'dig,' 'cool' and 'hip' are key words with him."[16]

Two strains of the African-American historical experience converged in the 1930s that helped create the conditions for the emergence of cool: first, a new impatience among blacks with the need to mask their feelings and smile in front of whites; second, the fight for recognition of individuality and artistic self-expression. As blacks moved north and west and became part of the national social fabric, a new sense of possibility arose along with economic success and this freedom of movement. The two most important cultural forms of what Cornel West calls "New World African modernity" were black vernacular English and jazz, "a dynamic language and mobile music." Blues, gospel, and big band swing, along with the urban slang then called "jive," became the influential portable expressions of American society's "perennial outsiders."[17] Black jazz musicians helped stimulate cultural pride and became national cultural heroes. In validating Southern black vernacular culture, they helped "nurture the undercurrent of protest in the black community between the 1930s and 1970s." In the mid-1930s, these changes were only bubbling beneath the surface.[18]

Ironically, the confluence of masked behavior with African-American artistic expression first occurred when blacks replaced whites as entertainers in the business of blackface minstrelsy in the 1870s. African-Americans created a professional class of singers, dancers, musicians, and comedians "under the cork," since minstrelsy was one of the only open paths to success at the time. Blues composer and bandleader W. C. Handy wrote that "the minstrel show was one of the greatest outlets for talented musicians and artists."[19] Minstrel performers forever shaped American comedy through character sketches, slapstick, syncopated music, and rhythmic-based dance (cakewalk, tap, flash).[20] Kansas City bandleader and arranger Jesse Stone grew up in his family's minstrel band, and he perceived a musical continuity between rhythm and blues and minstrel music, "the flavor of things I had heard when I was a kid."[21] But there was a serious social cost: white Americans believed real-life African-Americans were similar to the stereotyped characters portrayed on the idyllic Southern plantation of the minstrel show: the smiling "Sambo," the slow-witted, shuffling Southern darky (Jim Crow), the Northern urban dandy (Zip Coon), the black buck, Mammy, Uncle Tom, old Uncle and old Auntie.[22] These were the only "frames of acceptance," to use Kenneth Burke's term, through which whites saw blacks.

The social contradictions created by this overlap of performative skill, rhythmic genius, and smiling pretense still confound race relations today. Minstrelsy's most enduring legacy was "the grinning black mask . . . embedded in American consciousness," yet, ironically, it was one of the great stars of this theatrical tradition that inspired the earliest definition of black cool by a white observer, poet William Carlos Williams.[23]

In an essay entitled, "Advent of the Slaves" (1925), Williams perceived a certain "quality" among his working-class African-American neighbors in Paterson, New Jersey: "There is a solidity, a racial irreducible minimum, which gives them *poise in a world where they have no authority*" (my italics). It's hard to imagine a better first definition of cool. This poise was manifested locally in the homespun existential philosophy of the poet's neighbors and publicly in the comedian Bert Williams's performance of his signature song "Nobody." Bert Williams was the most famous black entertainer of the early twentieth century and the first to draw large white audiences. As half of the famous vaudeville duo Williams and Walker, he helped tone down the wilder minstrel antics into a "cooler [style that] more realistically mirrored actual black behavior," according to Mel Watkins. "Nobody" was an ode sung by a downtrodden man in tattered clothes who claimed "nobody did nothin' for him," and Bert Williams made of it a meditation on the basic rights of food, shelter, companionship, and love, managing to "express the existential desire to be treated as a person." "Nobody" was a huge hit at the turn of the century. William Carlos Williams expressed wonder at the performer's ability to bring dignity to "saying *nothing*, dancing *nothing* . . . [to] 'NOBODY,'" and how he amplified the message in dance: "waggin', wavin', weavin', shakin' . . . bein' nothin'—with gravity, with tenderness." The poet saw beneath the mask to a core affirmation at the heart of African-American ritual, the goal of imparting a sense of "somebodiness."[24]

Ralph Ellison maintained that blackface minstrelsy was a popular masking ritual that allowed for a "play upon possibility" for white men. The vicarious masking allowed white performers to act silly and irrational—and to express joy through movement—without sacrificing their public face and role responsibilities. Underneath the burnt cork, they found an escape from the work ethic, from Christian ideals of saintly behavior, and from Republican virtue; on stage, white minstrels displayed a more tolerant humanness for their working-class and immigrant audiences.

Minstrelsy provided therapeutic relief from a society whose then-heroic model required a combination of rational thinking, virtuous public behavior, and repressed emotion—an emotional "iron cage."[25] Although minstrel shows depicted African-Americans as happy-go-lucky slaves fit only for the hard work and dependence of plantation life, certainly whites were bestowing a twisted compliment on the African-American cultural elements they mocked, if only in the sense that imitation is the sincerest form of flattery. Eric Lott calls this conflicted admiration of black music, dance, humor, and kinesthetics the "love-and-theft" of African-American culture. In even more generous terms, Ellison suggested simply that "[in] America humanity masked its face with blackness."[26]

Why is this phenomenon related to cool? First, because the demise of minstrelsy and the beginnings of jazz overlap in the first three decades of the century; second, because white audiences brought minstrel-derived frames to their experience of the new urban music and its musicians. Louis Armstrong did not have to "black up" (as it was called) yet he wore the smiling mask of the happy-go-lucky darky on stage throughout his life. His mainstream success was probably dependent on allowing audiences to hold onto their ideas of white supremacy while enjoying his music as entertainment rather than as art. Gerald Early identified these historical tensions: "Did the whites love Armstrong for his undeniably powerful musicality or because he was a one-man revival of minstrelsy without blackface? . . . Could his genius be contained only by having it entrapped in a halo of intolerable nostalgia, of degrading sentiment about darkies on the southern campground?"[27]

Jazz musicians helped destroy these plantation images, but it was a slow process since the business of American popular entertainment was for so long *Southern* business. The very names of 1920s jazz bands and venues tell the story of how these stereotypes migrated: every city had a Cotton Club or a Plantation Club, a Kentucky Club or a Club Alabam; black bands drew on minstrel archetypes for their names, such as McKinney's Cotton Pickers, the Dixie Syncopators, or the Chocolate Dandies. Plantation themes often served as the content for much of the entertainment at Harlem's world-famous Cotton Club. "The whole set was like a sleepy-time down South during slavery," Cab Calloway recalled, "[and] the idea was to make whites who came feel like they were being catered to and entertained by black slaves."[28] The two highest-earning black orchestras, Cab Calloway's and Duke Ellington's, set national standards of jazz *and* jive, of new African-American economic success within predictable plantation-derived tableaux. Most Americans believed in the reality of these racial types as co-invented by Northern minstrels and Southern slave owners to emphasize black inferiority, and perpetuated both by pseudo-scientific theories of racial hierarchy and Hollywood imagery.[29]

Hiding one's feelings under "the grinning black mask" was a survival skill of great importance to all black males up through World War II. A black man could easily get lynched for pretending to be on equal terms with a white man under almost any circumstances. Cab Calloway's drummer Panama Francis remembered a man who used to come see his band every week in his Florida hometown and put a hole in his bass drum. The man always gave him five dollars to fix it, but the drummer hated the ritual humiliation. "I used to get so mad, but I had to smile because back in those days, you had better smile, so I smiled; but I didn't like it too well." In 1941, black sociologist Charles S. Johnson designated this emotional masking with the formal term "accommodation" to a white social order. Colloquially, it was known as "Tomming."[30]

Even the most successful African-American bandleaders needed to create a public front readable as a given racial stereotype. Cab Calloway played the joyful, energetic, out-of-control wild man: "I was . . . energy personified."[31] Duke Ellington played the debonair, gentlemanly dandy on stage. In a *Downbeat* profile otherwise extolling Ellington's musical leadership, the editor astutely noted: "He will not even talk to a white woman without his manager . . . know[ing] too well the inflammatory moods of a dominant race."[32] The classically trained violinist and bandleader George Morrison played the old "darky lament" of "Shine" for white audiences when he sensed any hostility—an act he deemed "black diplomacy."[33] Jimmie Lunceford's crack band of former college students flipped their instruments in the air and tap-danced in sections as part of their act.[34] These bandleaders all took pride in what was then called "showmanship"—and they had fun on stage—but these non-musical aspects enabled white audiences to de-emphasize the skill and intelligence of jazz as an art. Swing bandleaders such as Ellington, Calloway, Lunceford, and Count Basie were both bosses and artists, "heads of a business organization and public figures concerned with the artistic, emotional, and symbolic function[s] of a band and its music." These men were grossing as much as $10,000 a week in the 1940s yet they had to appeal to white expectations and provide the old symbolic associations of racial hierarchy.[35]

"Tomming" was the racial order of the era. African-American band-leaders who totally eschewed showmanship for musical artistry in the early 1940s—for example, Teddy Wilson and Benny Carter—did not succeed with the broader white public. They provided neither the wild energy of intoxication nor the therapeutic escape from guilt and the work ethic that white audiences desired from their black entertainers, the legacy of blackface minstrelsy. "Benny [Carter]'s band never caught on too well," saxophonist Howard Johnson recalled. "At that time they wanted Black musicians to 'get hot,' and nearly all bands had gimmicks of one kind or another. They were entertainers more than musicians, and we were not entertainers." Teddy Wilson's bassist Al Hall similarly claimed, "Everybody kept saying we sounded too white." George Simon, the (white) editor of the jazz trade magazine *Metronome* noted, "'Polite' black bands were hard to sell in those days." Many successful white bandleaders also had an identifiable gimmick or theme song, but audiences did not demand they ingratiate themselves as inferiors.[36]

Lester Leaps In

It was left to a swing band's star soloist—a performer who did not have to engage with the audience—to start a quiet, nonviolent revolt against Tomming. Lester Young was born and raised in Mississippi and New Orleans at a time when to speak out against racial injustice would have meant economic death, at the very least. At fourteen, for example, Young was called on to smuggle a gun to a member of the band who was being chased by a lynch mob. Between the ages of ten and nineteen, he was a member of his father's family band, the Billy Young Band, a staple attraction on the black vaudeville circuit (TOBA, or the Theatre Owners Booking Association). Young was proud to have grown up in "travelin' carnivals [and] minstrel shows," but he hated the South and spoke with pride about avoiding it as an adult: "Only time I went through the South was with Basie."[37]

Young made his only public statement about racism at the age of fifty, two months before his death—in France, significantly—and focused on the mask as the symbol of black male limitation. "They want everybody who is a Negro to be an Uncle Tom or Uncle Remus or Uncle Sam, and I can't make it." Young here clearly identified the masks through which he was most often seen: as the smiling, servile Southern servant who always agreed with white men (Uncle Tom); as the desexualized old man who distributed folk wisdom (Uncle Remus); as the regular-guy patriot or soldier who disowned his ethnic cultural heritage (Uncle Sam).[38]

Lester's father, Willis Young, was a school principal and trumpeter. He formed a carnival band and left the New Orleans area in the violent summer of 1919, when race riots broke out all over the country and lynchings increased for the first time in several years. The senior Young believed the music business held the greatest opportunities for blacks at the time; Lee Young (Lester's brother) recalls his father saying, "My son will never be a porter; my daughter will never be a maid. You're going to learn to play music." The Billy Young Family Band toured throughout the Midwest, South, and Southwest, playing carnivals, state fairs, minstrel shows, and theaters. The band was popular enough (and good enough) to have carried three future jazz giants for short periods—Ben Webster, Cootie Williams, and John Lewis—all of whom attested to Billy Young's ability as a musician and teacher.[39]

With his father as the front man during his formative years, young Lester focused on music and became the band's star. His siblings and cousins smiled, danced and did acrobatic flips while playing, but Young despised the "'Uncle Tomming that went on," and his idea of jiving was to play the saxophone upside down. Young was a disciplined musical apprentice: he ran scales and practiced seven hours a day along with the records of classical saxophone virtuoso Rudy Wiedoeft; he synthesized Louis Armstrong's powerful expressiveness with the so-called cleaner white jazz styles of Jimmy Dorsey, and his idol, Frankie Trumbauer. The senior Young knew Lester was gifted musically and rode him pretty hard—for example, when he forced him to learn to read music. When his father beat him, Lester ran away for short periods—he never could endure emotional discord—but he always returned, and never expressed any resentment toward his father later in life.[40]

In a telling example of generational change among young African-American men, Lester Young's declaration of independence from his father dovetailed with his rejection of Southern accommodation. In January 1928, the family band got ready for a series of Texas dates and Lester refused to go: "I told him [his father] how it would be down there, and that we could have some fine jobs back through Nebraska, Kansas and Iowa, but he didn't have eyes for that."[41] He said later, "I was just ready to be grown is all." Young stayed behind with two other bandmates in Salina, Kansas, and joined up for a year with a regional Midwestern band, Art Bronson's Bostonians. He barnstormed for the next four years, first touring with New Orleans legend King Oliver for a season, then settling in Minneapolis where the grapevine spread his reputation. In 1930, bassist and bandleader Walter Page offered him a spot in the Oklahoma City Blue Devils, a legendary Southwest territory band whose nucleus later formed the foundation of the Count Basie Orchestra in Kansas City in 1935.[42] Young freelanced with the Blue Devils, the Bostonians, and several Kansas City bands before joining Basie in 1934. He was then well-known enough among black musicians that when he temporarily replaced Coleman Hawkins in the Fletcher Henderson band in New York, two leading African-American newspapers referred to him as "one of the most celebrated tenor sax players in the music world."[43]

Young's refusal to accommodate to whites was representative of a new breed of jazz musicians, just as his cool style and nonchalant demeanor were responses to the "hot jazz" of the 1920s. Until bebop, jazz was widely known as "hot music," a reference to the music's faster, syncopated rhythms, its improvised component, and its ability to stir up an emotional and physical response. During the Jazz Age of the 1920s, the featured soloist was often called the "hot man." There weren't yet many musicians who could improvise well; the hot man's drive and originality propelled the jazz band to moments of peak excitement and emotional release. Clarinetist Mezz Mezzrow claimed that jazz musicians first introduced the word "swing" because the "unhip public" had taken over the word "hot" and would stand by the bandstand and yell at musicians, "Come on man, get hot! Get hot!"[44] Young helped change the idea of the *hot* man to the *cool* man.[45]

During the swing era, the structure of Tomming began to shift. The increased visibility of African-American cultural heroes (Joe Louis, Jesse Owens, Ethel Waters), the success of big band swing, the relative freedom of northern and western cities, the new economic and political power blacks felt after leaving the South—all contributed to the "swing hopes" that social equality was just around the corner. Historian Lewis Erenberg calls big band swing "the music of the black migration," since the musicians were walking advertisements of urban (and urbane) promise.[46] Calloway's bassist, Milt Hinton, said the bandleader often reminded them their job was to "uplift" people in the South and "elevate the black customer."[47] Musicians also validated African-American vernacular culture by naming its attitudes, heroes, dances, phrases, foods and sounds in song and on stage: Ellington's "Harlem Air Shaft," Calloway's "Pickin' Cabbage" and "Chili Con Conga," Basie's "Stompin' at the Savoy," Lunceford's "What's Your Story, Morning Glory?" Looking back from the 1970s, both Cab Calloway and Earl Hines referred to their big bands as the first "Freedom Riders" who went behind enemy lines to help change racist assumptions and inscribe a new set of urban, sophisticated images on African-Americans.[48]

Perhaps the most indirect, persuasive evidence of the cultural leadership of big band swing musicians can be found in *The Autobiography of Malcolm X*. Nearly a quarter of the book revolves around Malcolm Little's transformation from small-town country hick to hip city slicker between 1937 and 1943. The arenas of change were the great ballrooms where jazz heroes and dynamic dancers, speaking hip slang and sporting flamboyant clothes and hairstyles, took that nightly ride to a better future on the brash, chugging, confident, big band night train. Ralph Ellison recalled the effect of the sights and sounds of the Duke Ellington Orchestra in 1930s Oklahoma: "Where in the white community . . . could there have been found . . . examples such as these? Who were so worldly, who so elegant, who so mockingly creative? Who so skilled at their given trade and who treated the social limitations placed in their paths with greater disdain?" Nat Hentoff, the Jewish-American jazz critic, said much the same about the black jazz musicians (such as Jo Jones) who mentored him in 1930s Boston. African-American jazz musicians were the epitome of 1930s urban sophistication.[49]

Lester Young's contribution to these swing hopes was to help develop new strategies of self-presentation for the individual musician—without either drawing on the minstrel legacy of "the darky entertainer" or fading into the collective sheen of the big bands. At the time, most big band musicians wore tuxedos or uniforms on stage and exercised their sartorial tastes offstage; Young wanted to stand out *onstage*. His first stylistic trademark was a completely original way of holding a saxophone, up and out to the side at a forty-five-degree angle.[50] At the start of a solo, he looked about to "paddle a canoe"; once he really got going, it became "almost horizontal." He held it high in the air like a flute and blew musical worlds into the sky: fast, rhythmic flights of musical consciousness. It drove audiences wild.[51]

Ellison caught the saxophonist's dramatic synthesis of sight and sound in his hometown of Oklahoma City in 1929 when Young was just an unknown twenty-year-old kid with the Blue Devils:

> [An] intense young musician . . . who, with his heavy white sweater, blue stocking cap and up-and-out-thrust silver saxophone left absolutely no reed player and few young players of any instrument unstirred by the wild, excitingly original flights of his imagination . . . Lester Young . . . with his battered horn upset the entire Negro section of town. . . . [We tried] to absorb and transform the Youngian style."[52]

At twenty, Young stood out with a stocking cap and a sweater, probably adapted from the popular collegiate look of the 1920s (all big bands regularly played colleges). Fourteen years later, Young was a world-famous hipster, and one white soldier experienced the same excitement seeing him perform with the Al Sears band at a Texas air force base: "Lester was working with a fine group of Negro musicians . . . [but] when he stepped out in front with his pork-pie hat and dark glasses (no USO monkey suit for him), he blew the crackers, the hayseeds, and even we studiedly casual easterners right out of our seat."[53]

Young made the saxophone into a new weapon, an instrument of speed and flight; standing still, he sounded like he was taking off. Americans were obsessed with aviation in the 1930s: Charles Lindbergh flew solo across the Atlantic right before the decade started and Superman first appeared in the skies over Metropolis toward the end. Young belongs in their company: he flew across the middle ground, a man riding atop a big band train. The jazzman's horn also had an iconic sexual value as a phallic symbol at a time when any assertion of black male sexuality was a matter of life-or-death. Holding up your horn—first known as an "ax"—mediated a celebration of individual black male creative energy: physical, sensual, sexual, intellectual.[54] That Young brought the horn

down in front of him in the late 1940s underscores the sexual symbolism. Jack Kerouac, ever on the lookout for models of masculinity, judged
Young's mood over time from the position of the saxophone, from his
glory days "holding his horn high" to "when he let his horn half fall
down" through "when all our horns came down."[55]

Young's soaring saxophone style was "cool" because he generated
excitement without getting excited; he stayed cool. He dazzled listeners' minds with rhythmic surprise and melodic ideas, not technique or
flash. His fellow Basie bandmate Harry Edison described his solos: "He
didn't put a whole lot of notes in a solo. He put the right note in the right
place at the right time. . . . His timing was perfect."[56] The cool message
came through Young's rhythmic control—sure-footed solos in which he
cut lightly across the shouting brass and crisp rhythms, maintaining his
own personal beat even while being challenged by three trombones and
a drummer. The cool message came through Young's fast, fluid, floating tone, a counterforce to the rhapsodic style of Coleman Hawkins.[57]
Young's bandmate, Earle Warren, wondered even in 1980: "A thing I've
never been able to figure out . . . is why so many black players followed
Lester *and* so many white ones did." In short, Young had synthesized what
were then seen as African-American musical strengths (speed, rhythmic
depth, emotional feeling) with what were then seen as Euro-American
musical strengths (purity of tone, precise attack, clean phrasing).[58]

Young's second contribution to self-expression on the bandstand
was the strategic use of sunglasses. Young was the first jazz musician to
wear shades on stage, indoors and outdoors. Long before Charlie Parker
and Miles Davis became famous for turning their backs on the audience,
Young recognized the use of shades as a mask to deflect the gaze of others without causing conflict and to create an air of mystery. In July 1938,
he wore an early pair of wrap-around plastic shades on the stage of the
Swing Jamboree at Randall's Island in New York City, a concert featuring
twenty-six bands that drew twenty-five thousand young people.[59] Young
looked calm and aloof amid a noisy, joyous, outdoor throng; the Basie
band caught rhythmic fire but Young remained detached and dispassionate. Sunglasses became a key element of the stylistic rebellion of black
jazz musicians in the postwar era; in effect, wearing sunglasses at night
was the primary symbol of the cool mask.[60]

Third, Young introduced the aesthetic idea of relaxation into jazz soloing by incorporating a melodic combination of silence, space, phrasing, and accent into the structure of a solo. For example, on Count Basie's "Doggin' Around" (1939), Young starts his solo by holding one note for the whole bar, then slides into a long, fluid line for six bars then lays out for four beats.[61] Basie's rhythm section enabled Young's ability to soar. Universally considered "the greatest percussion combination in the history of jazz," the depth of its groove freed the soloists from having to accentuate the beat. The big band could be a fast, loud, chugging, shouting machine, but Basie's band created an easy, relaxed swing beat—call it a *cool groove*—that revolutionized big band swing.[62] Young sometimes soared over the melody, but more often set up exciting cross-rhythms and musical tension with his phrasing; according to musicologist Wilfrid Mellers, Basie's band brought creative conflict into swing music. Drummer Jo Jones insisted that just keeping the reins on the band required all his physical energy: "I didn't need to worry about [competing with drummers] Gene Krupa or Buddy Rich, I was catching hell sitting up there, trying to play in Basie's band."[63] The implicit challenge of playing in Basie's band was to maintain one's individuality in the face of a powerful collective rhythmic drive. Here, then, is the major contribution of big band swing to American cool: an art form that publicly displayed the fight for self-expression within a larger unit.[64]

Young spent his happiest and most productive years (1934–40) with the Count Basie band, first in Kansas City and later in New York. Before living in Kansas City, Young did not curse or drink or smoke pot or speak that "funny language."[65] He was an inwardly focused dreamer, a romantic musical artist whose rejection of the grinning black mask was now complete. But Kansas City was the Las Vegas of the Midwest during the Great Depression, a wide-open town where the clubs never closed and Prohibition was neither enforced nor recognized as law. Mayor Tom Pendergast's corrupt political machine was run in service to the big farmers, cattle ranchers, and oilmen of the region. "If you want to see some sin, forget about Paris and go to Kansas City," an Omaha journalist wrote at the time.[66] It was a lively city with steady work, a strong African-American community, and so much music pouring out of clubs that, as Jo Jones told Nat Hentoff, "people would go from one club to another, walking in time[,] *jazz time*." The Basie band worked seven nights a week, from 9 P.M.—5 A.M., and Young loved every minute of it: "I'd sit up all night and wait to go to work."[67] Then he would make the round of local jam sessions, and jam until noon or one o'clock. Impresario John Hammond wrote of Young in 1936: "He is the kind of guy who just likes to make music, with the result that he is always to be found jamming in some unlikely joint." Legendary trumpeter Roy Eldridge reflected that Young "was *always* a cat who loved to play."[68]

Kansas City jam sessions resonated with both Western frontier aesthetics and African-American humor. Musicians in territory bands thought of their artistry "in terms of self-reliant individualism," David Stowe has written, and their cutting contests were more like "performances associated with violent contests and gunfights."[69] Trumpeter Buck Clayton recalled his musical reception on his arrival in Kansas City from California once word got out he would be at the Sunset Club: "[When] two more trumpet players came in and started jamming . . . I figured we'd all have a ball. Then about half an hour later in came about three more trumpet players. . . . Then, as the evening went on, more and more trumpet players came in to blow. To me, it seemed as if they were coming from all directions."[70] When Coleman Hawkins, the reigning king of the tenor saxophone, came through with the Fletcher Henderson band in 1934, he got "hung up" at the Cherry Blossom battling tenor saxophonists Ben Webster, Lester Young, and Herschel Evans in the most famous jam session in jazz history. At four in the morning, Ben Webster begged pianist Mary Lou Williams to get out of bed: "Get up, pussycat, we're jammin' and all the pianists are tired out now. Hawkins has got his shirt off and is still blowing." Hawkins ruined his car engine by speeding to his next gig in St. Louis.[71]

Jazz drummer Lee Young saw this gun-slinging attitude as his brother Lester's motivation for jam session prowling: "Anyone who picked up a saxophone, you know, Lester wanted some of it . . . he really wanted to see who was the better man. It would be just like a prize fighter or a wrestler."[72] Young was a jam-session legend, renowned for his competitive zeal and his fertile imagination. Billie Holiday bragged that Young could blow fifteen choruses in a row, "each one prettier than the last," off the top of his head. "It took him several choruses to get started," the less-partisan pianist Mary Lou Williams said, "then, brother, what a horn." Perhaps Young spent so much time at jam sessions because it was the only public forum in U.S. life where black and white adult men exchanged ideas in a relaxed atmosphere.[73] At jam sessions, African-American men could display excellence unmasked—in their own faces—and receive respect from peers in a competitive African-American ritual. When John Hammond brought the Count Basie Orchestra to New York City in 1936, they brought this gun-slinging attitude to Harlem and permanently influenced the city's jazz culture.[74]

From the moment the Basie band came to New York until Young was drafted in 1944, he enjoyed the admiration of jazz musicians. He was erratically employed after quitting the Basie band in late 1940 but remained a brand-name player. Record reviewers referred to other saxophonists as "Lester Youngish"; his archrival Coleman Hawkins named him number one among tenor saxophonists for originality and flow of musical ideas; Benny Goodman had Young sit in with his band for a recording session, a direct insult to his own tenor saxophonist.[75] Up-and-coming tenors like Dexter Gordon and the young John Coltrane favored Young's sound over that of Hawkins.[76] Trumpeter Joe Newman saw Young at Alabama State College and was awed by his "flamboyant style . . . I mean it was smooth, it was easy, and it flowed so freely that it excited me."[77]

In 1944, Young starred in the best jazz film of the period, *Jammin' the Blues. Life* magazine photographer Gjon Mili directed the Academy Award–nominated ten-minute short and made jazz icons of Young's porkpie hat, his romantic tone, and his blank, pained facial expression. When Harlem jam-session enthusiast Jack Kerouac wrote that Young had "put it all together for this generation just as [Louis] Armstrong had for his," he meant Young combined a new sound and personal style to produce one of the culture's greatest artistic voices of the wartime era.[78]

White (Anglo) Cool and Black (West African) Cool

In Anglo-American culture, the adjective "cool" reflects the ability to repress one's emotions to think clearly and effect a more rational analysis. The archetypal cool characters of American popular culture—film noir's private detective, the Western gunslinger, the existential motorcycle wanderer—are untamable, self-sufficient male loners who live by their own code. They exist as free violent radicals on the fringes of society who cultivate a calm impudence regarding social norms. In the nineteenth-century vernacular they were called "cool characters": nonconformist, unpredictable, mysterious, adept at violence. There is an unbroken line from the Enlightenment philosophical ideal of living in "the middle state" between heaven and earth to the classic composure of the English gentleman to the romanticized British reserve of fictional models from Sherlock Holmes to James Bond. Anglo-American cool characters are loners valued for the ability to repress emotion and resist temptation (women, money) in exchange for an unimpeachable reputation for straight talk and the self-satisfaction of seeking the "truth," however personally or situationally defined.[79]

Among many West African peoples—especially the Yoruba— "coolness" has associations with smoothness, balance, silence, and order.[80] Robert Farris Thompson first noticed the high value on projecting coolness in music and dance across the African diaspora—in West Africa, the Caribbean, and the United States. Thompson found thirty-five West African languages with concepts similar to the Yoruban *itutu*— "mystic coolness"—a philosophical concept with non-Western "cool" associations such as "discretion, healing, rebirth, newness, purity." This West African mask of coolness is admired in the midst of pleasure as well as stress and has connotations of healing. In West Africa, an action of this kind can "cool the heart" or "make a country safe." Coolness is also associated with silence: to "cool one's mouth" (keep a "cool tongue") is to keep strategically silent; the familiar African-American analogue is the advice, "Cool it!" A common meaning of cool is to "restore order." There are many commonalities between coolness in West African and English modes: emotional control, the calm face, a demeanor "composed, collected, unruffled, nonchalant, imperturbable, detached," and especially under duress. Yet there is no West African equivalent of the European idea of coldness, as in "icy determination" or "cold efficiency."[81]

In West African public rituals of music and dance, coolness is a force of community—that is, of maintaining the social order. A cool West African performer stimulates the participation of others and generates community. For example, a master drummer directs the production of continuous, building rhythms to create a sound foundation for dancers. He shows coolness by contrasting the propulsive rhythms he creates with steady, calm execution in motion. A dancer might do the opposite, using fast, accelerated steps to work against slow, steady drumming. Both provide a public model of coping with dynamic forces with grace and composure. In West Africa, then, to be cool is to participate actively in an event while maintaining a detached attitude. The symbol of one's coolness is the relaxed, calm, smiling face.

American anthropologist John Miller Chernoff apprenticed for years with a Dagomba master drummer, Ibrahim Abdulai, who described cool as a kind of spiritual calm displayed in performance. "[The word] 'baalim' is not 'cool' in the way that water or the weather is cool, but rather it means 'slow' or 'gentle.'" The Dagomba term *baalim* applies to a drummer who controls the emotional dynamics of a ritual or situation by cooling or relaxing a given audience. "The one who has learned well, he plays with understanding, and *he has added his sense* and cooled his heart" (my italics). The pun of sense / cents is useful here. To add "your two cents" is a capitalist metaphor of participation and it means to give your opinion. In Dagomba musical ritual, a person adds his or her *musical sense* to the rhythmic discussion. Abdulai declared that only older men played drums coolly; they understand the essence of being generous with rhythms, whereas the young men are too busy "taking big steps and shaking their bodies when they dance"—in other words, *hot*-dogging. Abdulai contrasted the steady diffusion of sound by the older drummers to the coarse, thudding, heavy "beating" of the younger ones. When a drummer is uncool with his rhythms, he is relieved from his job: "Sometimes when we are playing hard and then come to make everything cool, and the one who knows only force is beating, we just hold his hand and collect his stick so that he won't play again."[82]

Coolness concerns balancing opposites publicly with style and within a community ritual: coolness is thus an aesthetic attitude of participation effected through an individual's ability to contribute his or her own rhythms to a larger communal experience. At a West African musical event, everyone is expected to participate and lend energy—and their individual styles—to the larger beat. West African cool is less about striving for the middle state than about partaking of both extremes—the "sweet" and the "pain"—without losing control. Cool balances the duality of hot and cold, of propulsive rhythms and smooth execution, of call and response. Just as colors opposite each other on the color wheel (say, blue and orange) bring out the most intense dynamics in each other, to "cool one's head" means first to heat it up—as when eating hot, spicy foods in the summer—so as to detoxify the built-up stress.

For a West African dancer, the analogy for cool, gentle drumming is the ability to maintain "facial serenity." A dancer often keeps time to three or more rhythms, using different parts of the body to dialogue with different rhythms. When a dancer smiles through this hard work, she celebrates the rhythms and her own vitality by implying that these graceful motions, this dialogue with the drums is effortless, easy, no sweat, a piece of cake. The dancer's mask of coolness projects both serenity of mind *and* mastery of the body: the cool performer thus shares with the community the joy of living in one's body, the pleasure one gets in contributing beauty and grace to an event, the skill of producing a distinctive rhythm that links up with other rhythms.[83] The objective is to turn difficult physical acts into smooth, fluid, easy kinesthetic motion—symbolically, to display a relaxed sense of control. Toni Morrison claims that any distinctively black art "must look effortless. It must look cool and easy. If it makes you sweat, you haven't done the work. You shouldn't be able to see the seams and stitches."[84]

There are two salient differences between West African and Anglo-European ideas of cool. The first is the modeling of a relaxed style within a stressful situation or a dynamic expressive cultural event. The second difference rests in the relationship of the individual action to the community. Anglo-American cool figures may save the community from external threats (criminals, official corruption) but they do not participate in the community. West African cool performers generate community by drawing the crowd into the performance and challenging others to make equal contributions to the event. The ultimate goal of a drummer's or dancer's balancing of several rhythms is to add depth and texture to the event—an event maintained collectively through the rhythms (or "the beat") itself. The display of self-mastery—of being what I call "cool in motion"—then provokes competitors to share the honor and glory of recognized excellence.

We should consider jazz jam sessions as the kind of public ritual in which West African coolness was admired and called forth. No one was paid to play and yet everyone was expected to contribute, often until wearing themselves out. In other words, this African-American musical event provided an opportunity to express excellence of personal character in relation to other participants. As Mary Lou Williams explained about jam sessions, "My whole thing is to needle the man to play their best for anybody who is soloing because if he plays a good solo then I have inspiration to play." This kind of competition was also common among African-American tap dancers, suggesting a broad, influential legacy across various genres of expressive culture.[85]

The legacy of West African coolness to African-American cool centers on the transition from community ritual performance to American popular culture and reflects three non-European strategies. First, the idea of playing *hot* or *cool* is derived from West African concepts and nomenclature, as applied to rhythms and performative modes. As Thompson analyzed these opposing modes: "It is *cool* to sweeten hurt with song and motion; it is *hot* to concentrate on the pain." Second, in the dialogue between the drummers and dancers, the boundary between performer and audience dissolves. Third, "relaxed, effortless grace" in a musical or dance performance is a valued achievement.

Jazz musicians had no direct access to the nomenclature of hot and cool modes from West African performance beyond an untraceable continuity of African retentions in the musical cultures of the Mississippi Delta and New Orleans. (For example, there is no proof that Young thought of his style as "cool" playing in an African mode.) Yet this quality still exists today within the jazz tradition. In his book *What Jazz Is*, jazz pianist Jonny King emphasizes the importance of striving for "relaxed intensity," explaining that when he would coast, his teacher would drive him harder, yet when he became too hot and his solos too busy, he was told he was "too intense."[86] In addition, two cardinal qualities of West African music are "propulsive rhythms" and the "clash of rhythms," lending more evidence to the continuity of musical practices and aesthetic objectives.[87]

The contrast between propulsive rhythms and calm execution is the essence of Lester Young's cool musical revolution in the swing era. Pianist Oscar Peterson claimed Young could cool any song and any rhythm section: "Lester . . . had this remarkable quality to transmit beauty from within himself to the rhythm section. . . . [He would] play some lines that were so relaxed that, even at a swift tempo, the rhythm section would relax."[88] Unlike swing tempo, which was called the "push beat," or playing "on top of the beat"—or the "kicking-your-ass" beat, as one dancer called it—the Basie band played slightly "behind the beat," a more relaxed modality that enabled Young to become the most creative solo exemplar of a cooler style.[89] Using long, flowing phrases punctuated by held notes and short honks, Young almost seemed to wait to see where the band's groove was headed, setting off the band's collective rhythmic drive by understatement and placement. But while adding his sense to the big band's collective power, Young always kept in mind a romantic artistic concept of self-expression: "Musicians wishing to say something really vital must learn to express their feelings with a minimum of outside influence."[90] Jazz trumpeter Johnny Carisi described how a typical Young solo provoked artistic participation from other musicians: "Just when you think he had done it [was finished], he would, like, back off a little bit, he would goof and then descend on you again, only more so than before, [and] get everybody crazy, man."[91]

At jam sessions, Young may have acted as a western gunslinger, but as a swing musician, he saw his role as something akin to a master drummer. Young always claimed he "missed the dancers," and specifically the dialogue of dancers and musicians. "I wish jazz were played more often for dancing," he reflected in 1956. "I have a lot of fun playing for dances because I like to dance, too. The rhythm of the dancers comes back to you when you're playing. When you're playing for dancing, it all adds up to playing the right tempo. After three or four tempos, you find the tempo they like. What they like changes from dance date to dance date."[92] Big bands found their musical cues by judging the tempo of each evening and each audience. At a time when many white musicians and critics were trying to make jazz into a concert form—they saw dancing as *the* symbol of commercialism—Young was proud of the social function of musicians: that is, to increase the level of participation of the dancers.

Young was central to a larger transfer of West African cool aesthetics into American popular culture between the wars.[93] First, there was an enormous reciprocal development between jazz and African-American vernacular dance. In the 1920s, black jazz musicians and chorus-line dancers in floor shows caught one another's rhythms, leading to a more sophisticated and elastic groove. As early as 1925, "jazz drummers were getting ideas from tap dancers," and many swing-era drummers *were* originally tap dancers.[94] The lindy hoppers at the Savoy Ballroom would stand in front of the band and beat out the rhythm they wanted from the band, an action common in the U.S. South and West Africa, but otherwise unknown in American society.[95] Many early black jazz musicians were good dancers and proud of it. Pianist and composer James P. Johnson reflected, "All of us used to be proud of our dancing—Louis Armstrong . . . was considered the finest dancer among the musicians. It made for attitude and stance when you walked into a place and it made you strong with the gals."[96]

A third factor in the dissemination of West African cool aesthetics into American society during the swing era was the emergence of the trap-set drummer. Black and white drummer-bandleaders like Gene Krupa, Chick Webb, Jo Jones, and Buddy Rich came to have responsibilities more akin to the master drummers of West Africa than the classical percussionist or other ethnic musical traditions. In the dance bands of the 1920s, the drummer was thought of mostly as a "timekeeper" on stage; in classical music, only the conductor controls the performance.[97] In a big band, jazz musicians needed a more solid rhythmic foundation—a clearer set of cues—to ground the more complex sound and to support their solos. In a sense, the role of the dancers in an African-American ritual was replaced by the interaction between the rhythm section and the melody instruments. As the pioneering folklorist Willis Lawrence James wrote in 1945, "The rhythmic feeling of the players, which would otherwise find expression in the dance, is expressed through the instruments."[98]

Classical composer Igor Stravinsky perceived the non-Western function of the jazz rhythm section through the same metaphor of cool: "The percussion and bass . . . function as a central-heating system. They must keep the temperature 'cool,' [or] not cool." Since the drummer commands the most powerful sonic forces, it became his job to manage the band's dynamics. Duke Ellington's drummer, Sonny Greer, explained how this worked in live performance: "A guy, naturally, playing a solo, he gets over energetic and he has a tendency to turn loose. You've got to hold it. Right away he wants to take it up to the sky. But no, we have to hold him down." Drummer Chick Webb called swing tempo "the push beat," because he pushed each individual soloist according to his needs: held him down (cooled him off) or kicked him into gear (heated him up). Count Basie said plainly: "The drummer is the boss of the band, not the bandleader. If the drummer's not right, nothing's happening."[99]

The modern swing-era drummer arrived at the head of a drum battery that combined the functions of four African drummers into one percussion point man. In fact, the now-standard trap set only came together in the late 1930s: the bass-drum pedal, the hi-hat, and brushes were first invented in the 1920s; Chinese cymbals and the African-derived tom-toms were added for nuance, texture, accent, and resonance. Jazz drumming has roots in military drumming, brass bands, minstrel bands, circus bands, and the pit drumming of silent movies, but the *role* of the jazz drummer came of age in the swing era due to the primary influence on the music from African percussive techniques.[100]

That the term "cool" arose in this period seems like an amazing historical accident, a semantic mystery, or an indication that African-American oral tradition carries more retentions than has been suspected. Young's adaptation of West African cool into American music, sound, and social function was a major inflection of American cultural style, but his adaptation of the Anglo-American pose of repressing emotion was an equally important symbol of postwar black cool.

The Cool Remove from Cold War America

Being "cool" (that is, toward white people) reflected the disappointment of African-Americans in the progress toward social equality during World War II. Cool was "an attitude that really existed," Amiri Baraka recalled of its origins in Harlem and defined it this way: "To be cool was . . . to be calm, even unimpressed, by what horror the world might daily propose," and the most important daily struggle concerned "the deadeningly predictable mind of white America."[101] In the early 1940s, examples abounded. Labor leader A. Philip Randolph had to threaten a march on Washington before President Franklin Roosevelt opened up federal defense jobs to African-Americans by executive order in 1941. Race riots broke out in several major cities in the summer of 1943 as whites rejected the presence of African-Americans in their neighborhoods and at the workplace. The internment of Japanese-Americans was a scary, foreboding precedent of racial judgment and disfranchisement. Harlem's Savoy Ballroom—a national symbol of social equality—was temporarily padlocked for the summer of 1943 on the false charge that black hostesses were selling sex to white servicemen. Black soldiers endured virulent racism from their own (white American) officers, served in separate units, and were generally assigned as mess attendants.[102]

African-Americans recognized the irony of fighting in Jim Crowed regiments against an enemy that believed in white supremacy (Nazi Germany) while they faced their own version of race war at home. As a young black college graduate put it in Chester Himes's first novel, "As long as the Army is Jim Crowed, a Negro who fights in it is fighting against himself." The editors of the influential African-American weekly, the *Pittsburgh Courier*, called for a two-front patriotism known as the "Double-V campaign": victory against fascism abroad and racism at home.[103] It was necessary to hide one's feelings behind "a bullet-proof vest known as cool," Ralph Ellison reflected, which was less a matter of Hemingway's heroic "grace under pressure . . . than of good common sense."[104]

Lester Young suffered a personal microcosm of America's domestic race war. Drafted in September of 1944 by an undercover agent who followed the Basie band in a zoot suit, he was denied a musical assignment at an army base by a middle-class black bandleader who thought he lacked proper musical education.[105] His inability to submit to discipline then drew the attention and hostility of his white commanding officer, who found marijuana and barbiturates in his trunk. Young was court-martialed in a Kafkaesque trial in which he calmly admitted his long-term drug use and proudly claimed he had never harmed a man; he was sentenced to nearly a year in solitary at Georgia's Fort Gordon, where he was often beaten. His only break from the solitude came when he played with the base's all-white big band since they wanted Young to practice with them. Every day, a white trumpeter would pick him up from the black side of the segregated camp and both would playact their Southern caste roles. The trumpeter would say, "Come on, nigger," and Young would answer "Yessir, Boss." Young rarely discussed his army experience. He wrote one song to commemorate it—"D.B. Blues" or "Detention Barracks Blues"—and in a 1948 interview said simply: "[It was a] nightmare, man, one mad nightmare. They sent me down South, Georgia. That was enough to make me blow my top. It was a drag."[106]

When Lester Young returned to playing in 1945, many writers and musicians commented on his blank face, his weary stride and the lack of joy in his playing. In general, white critics wrote about Young as a man who "numbed his feelings . . . with much alcohol and some marijuana and hid behind a disguise—his long . . . face, expressionless as a mummy's," and one critic wrote of his mask "that he seldom removed [it] even among the few people he trusted."[107] Many white writers of the time believed Young's creative years ended with his army and discussed his postwar life as a version of the tragic artist myth.[108] This myth of Young's dissipation has been overstated, as many recordings of 1946–47 show, but he was a less consistent player after the war, and his playing lacked its earlier joie de vivre.[109]

Still, young jazz musicians—both black and white—consistently called Young "a beautiful man" and commented on his good humor, gentle humanity, and "balanced mind."[110] Young's silence helped keep his sanity; several young musicians declared him to be the sanest, most human man in their experience. Many white writers observed that Young avoided the company of whites and wondered aloud why he didn't play like he used to.[111] Young always told them, in effect, "that was then, this is now." In short, it was not his job to be who he was in 1939 but, rather (he felt), "what are you going to play today?" Young treated white jazz musicians warmly but kept most other whites at arm's length and at a masked remove. By making his face blank and rejecting deference and geniality, Young refused to play up to white expectations in public encounters. His solitary resistance symbolized a movement among African-American musicians and writers to reject the racial order of Uncle Tomming.

Between 1938 and 1952, four major African-American male writers used their art to rebel against "racial accommodation" by symbolically executing the figure of Uncle Tom.[112] In Richard Wright's first collection of short stories, *Uncle Tom's Children* (1938), every male protagonist (literally, every son of Uncle Tom) either shoots a white man or refuses the orders of a white man. In 1941, Duke Ellington and a team of Hollywood writers produced a theatrical revue called *Jump for Joy* whose objective was to "take Uncle Tom out of the theatre [and] eliminate the stereotyped image that had been exploited by Hollywood and Broadway."[113] In Chester Himes's short story, "Heaven Has Changed" (1943), a soldier fighting overseas in World War II dreams he is back in a Southern cotton field, where he stumbles on a funeral procession of old sharecroppers who tell him simply, "Ol' Uncle Tom is dead." The first spoken lines in Ralph Ellison's *Invisible Man* (1952) comprise a deathbed confession by the protagonist's grandfather who explains that Tomming was actually a sophisticated form of rebellion: "Our [black] life is a war," he exclaims. He then implores his grandson to keep up the grinning and shuffling:

"Overcome 'em with yeses, undermine 'em with grins, agree 'em to death and destruction, let 'em swoller you till they vomit or bust wide open." Ellison later reflected on this scene as his own conscious "rejection of *a current code* . . . a denial become metaphysical" (my italics).[114]

The nameless "Invisible Man" symbolizes the larger black migration of the time—the South come north—and Ellison evoked the tense temporary balance between swing hopes of equality and the survival skill of masking. Invisible Man migrates north with the hope that social equality is within reach and so he rejects all the limited conceptions of African-American possibility. To his consternation, he finds that all black men wear masks in front of whites with authority; he watches with shock and disgust as even the president of his black college "compose[s] his face into a bland mask" before meeting with one of the school's white trustees.

Like Lester Young, Invisible Man was the symbol of a generation that refused to live by accommodation. Yet the novel ends with the protagonist living underground; without the old plantation stereotypes, there is no new face for him to wear in the postwar era. Invisible Man does find one clue for creating a new mask of self-preservation. Just before he goes underground, he observes a quietly intense new style among young black men on the street that reflects Young's serious, introspective mask of cool silence:

> It was as though I'd never seen their like before: Walking slowly, their shoulders swaying, their legs swinging from their hips in trousers that ballooned upward from cuffs fitting snug about their ankles; their coats long and hip-tight. . . . These fellows whose bodies seemed—what had one of my teachers said to me?—'You're like one of these African sculptures.' . . .
>
> They seemed to move like dancers in some kind of funeral ceremony, swaying, going forward, *their black faces secret* . . . the heavy heel-plated shoes making a rhythmical tapping as they moved. . . .
>
> They were men outside of historical time . . . *men of transition whose faces were immobile.* (my emphasis)[115]

They were new to Harlem, these cool boys, in their zoot suits, long coats, quiet, blank faces, rhythmic strides, and black vernacular slang,

men "speak[ing] a jived-up transitional language full of country glam-
our." Nelson George traces the new style to the new environments of
the black migration as "many Southern boys now wise to the concrete
jungle started to move with a fluid, no-sweat attitude everybody called
'cool.' . . . Cool was clearly an African-urban thing."[116] The new response
to the white gaze of superiority was to drop the grinning black mask—
the symbol of accommodation—and cool the face. In a novel based on
the rejection of masks, the cool mask provides the only new strategy of
self-presentation.

   Just as black male writers killed off Uncle Tom figures, jazz musicians
such as Dizzy Gillespie targeted Louis Armstrong's "plantation image"
for execution. Gillespie honored Armstrong's trumpet playing but never
his stage persona: "Handkerchief over his head, grinning in the face of
white racism, I never hesitated to say I didn't like it." Gillespie admitted
the need for Tomming at the time and he affected a new pose of nonchalance. His hip, ironic style became the prototype of Beatnik chic: a
beret, black-rimmed glasses, a goatee, hip slang.[117] Both Miles Davis and
Charlie Parker took another tack and became legends for literally turning their backs on audiences, while other bebop musicians kept a cool
silence on stage as befit classical musicians, even as they played the "willfully harsh, anti-assimilationist sound of bebop."[118] By refusing the role of
entertainers, bebop musicians displayed a cool remove from mainstream
American assumptions, rebelling simultaneously against masked modes
of behavior and the society's disrespect of jazz itself. According to the
prolific jazz producer Orrin Keepnews, the bebop rebellion "reflected
a protest against the position of the Negro [and] against the position of
the Negro entertainer."[119]

   Young was an elder statesman at the famous jam sessions at Minton's
and Monroe's Uptown House in Harlem where bebop was created and
a familiar musical presence to all the bebop pioneers (Dizzy Gillespie,
Charlie Parker, Kenny Clarke, Thelonious Monk). When Dizzy Gillespie
called the roll of musicians he had outlived to pay tribute to them in *To
Be, or Not . . . to Bop*, the only non-bebop musician he named was Lester
Young.[120]

   Young was the musical and stylistic bridge between Louis Armstrong's sambo act and Charlie Parker's audience-defying artistic blowing. Parker's musical mentor was alto saxophonist Buster Smith, but

he grew up watching and worshipping Young from the wings of Kansas City's Reno Club and often said he "attended Lester Young University." Parker took Young's records with him on a six-month gig in the Ozark Mountains and memorized each solo, note for note. Young once told Parker the whole challenge of music was "to shape the air," to use your whole body to create a personal sound. "I was crazy about Lester," Parker said. "He played so clean and beautiful . . . [but] our ideas ran on differently."[121]

A 1943 photograph of the Earl Hines big band provides iconographic evidence of Parker's co-optation of Young's defiant stage stance: he sits at the end of the front row, shades on, legs splayed, seemingly detached, leaning away from the saxophone section.[122] It is Parker—more than any other bebop musician—who used Young's hip slang to avoid conversation with those white fans and writers who idolized him, turning core hipster terms like "cool," "heavy," "dig," "solid," and "crazy" into one-word ideograms.[123] Amiri Baraka celebrated Lester Young's wordplay in "Pres Spoke in a Language":

> in the teeming whole of us he lived
> tooting on his sideways horn
> translating frankie trumbauer into
> Bird's feathers
> Trane's sinewy tracks
> the slickster walking through the crowd
> surviving on a terrifying wit
> its the jungle the jungle the jungle
> we living in

Bebop musicians were responsible for disseminating the word and concept of "cool," but they came to it through Lester Young.[124]

In terms of music and style, Young's most influential heir was Miles Davis. "Man, playing with Prez was something," Miles Davis wrote in his autobiography. "I learned a lot from the way he played the saxophone . . . [and] I tried to transpose some of his saxophone licks over to my trumpet." Davis was influenced by Young's "real, fast, hip, slick, Oklahoma style" and his combination of rhythmic flexibility with a "cool sonority." Davis liked the way Young "flood[ed] the tone," and the way he approached each and every note, rather than running up and down scales. Pianist Sadik Hakim often toured with Young in the early 1940s and recalled that Davis always came to see the band when it came through his hometown of St. Louis. "He'd sit in and he really dug Prez at the time . . . and much of his style, if you listen to him closely, was from Prez. He took many of the things Prez did and transformed them to his style, which we know as the cool style."[125] Davis's first session as leader of the Charlie Parker Quintet in May of 1947 rebelled against bebop's virtuosity with relaxed, melodic solos that were minimalist in comparison and "the liquid spirit of Lester Young hangs over the music."[126]

Davis's self-presentation featured a fierce reserve that said, "You don't wanna know—or ask." His music, like Young's, was accessible and admired by white fans, musicians, and writers; yet Davis symbolized the aloof, often hostile black jazz musician of the late 1950s. He turned his back on audiences and often walked off stage to smoke a cigarette while the band continued. Davis's Italian suits, his disregard for both artistic and social convention, his mix of personal mystery and artistic mastery, his tough, don't-fuck-with-me stance kept white jazz fans at a safe distance and suggested a churning inner complexity. Nightclub owner Max Gordon once asked why Davis didn't announce his songs or talk with the audience. "I'm a musician, I ain't no comedian," Miles answered. "The white man always wants you to smile, always wants the black man to bow. I don't smile and I don't bow. OK? I'm here to play music. I'm a musician." Young's strategic withdrawal set the stage for musicians like Miles Davis and Charles Mingus to give voice to their anger. Only a few perceptive white writers saw the hurt underneath the swagger, but more importantly, Uncle Toms were no longer welcome on the jazz scene.[127]

Cool is, in one sense, composed violence. At its most functional, "to keep your cool" has always meant not to "blow your top," phrases that suggest the potential for violence. For Young to have spoken out against racism as directly as Miles Davis (the son of a middle-class dentist in St. Louis) would have been suicide in the Deep South of the 1920s. In fact, jazz has always been chock-full of language that sublimated violence into musical combat: the horn was an ax (long before guitars were); musicians "cut" and "carved" each other at "cutting contests" and "carving sessions"; white people were called "ofays" (pig latin for "foes"). Young transmuted his hostility into long, flowing, well-structured solos "transform[ing] his life every night into what it ought to be." He imagined a better world through sound yet his dreamy romanticism always had enough rhythmic power and blues feeling to generate a "special intensity . . . with cool understatement."[128]

Like many jazz musicians, Young believed his *sound*, not the notes or songs he played, communicated his identity and personality to the world. Your sound *was* you, it was your literal voice—and the maintenance of that sound was effected at considerable artistic and emotional effort. Young had something of an identity crisis when many musicians adapted his melodic ideas and romantic tone—for example, the entire "Four Brothers" saxophone section of the Woody Herman band in the late 1940s took their cue from his innovations. Young often wondered aloud, "What am I to play? Should I copy them?" Tenor saxophonist Stan Getz—one of the most successful jazz musicians of the 1950s—often came up to Young's hotel room and asked him how he created certain sounds on his old records. Young enjoyed the attention but these exchanges left him sad and depleted. "The trouble with most musicians today is that they are copycats," he said in 1948.[129]

The love and theft of Young's sound was one factor in his physical deterioration through alcoholism; others included a perceived lack of recognition and simply the nomadic musician's life. Friends claim that Young drank two quarts of gin a day from the late 1940s until his death in 1959, and he often forgot to eat. He was seen by white writers as "slow and unsteady of movement, detached from reality [and] sealed off in a private world," and framed as a victim of a racist society. Although he married a second time in 1946 and enjoyed short periods of domestic stability in the early 1950s with his wife Mary, he was not a successful or attentive family man. After long stretches on the road, Young stayed in small hotels in midtown Manhattan, where he was often found by friends looking out the window, listening to his favorite "pretty music": Frank Sinatra, Doris Day, Jo Stafford. Nat Hentoff said he had "never seen anyone who was more alone wherever he was."[130]

But the younger musicians (black and white) who played with Young in the 1950s saw a different Pres, one they revered as a mentor, a poet, a spiritual figure, and something of a philosopher, especially on African-American culture. "[The] principles he taught me are the philosophy of the spirituals, the musician as a philosopher and a scientist, that we

[African-Americans] have made a major contribution to this country and [that] we are Americans," drummer Willie Jones III reported of Young's mentorship. "Prez opened up my eyes." Such statements, in sharp contrast to the view taken of white writers at the time, suggest the effort and success with which Young insulated himself from white people after his army experience. Basie drummer Jo Jones declared in 1973 that, for all his contacts with black civil rights leaders, "there has been nobody from Marcus Garvey up, that ever loved the black man like Lester Young, nobody!"[131]

If Lester Young was not one model for the ending of *Invisible Man*, he was certainly a real-life counterpart of Ellison's protagonist. Young was an original kind of American rebel who, despite his gentleness, remained an untamed free radical, a walking indictment of the society that denied the recognition of his accomplishments. A famous 1947 study of American hostility toward jazz concluded that the reaction to a new cultural form depends on "prestige of the donors," and that anti-jazz sentiments were based on the low status of African-Americans. "The jazz musician is an 'invisible man,'" sociologist Charles Nanry wrote, "contributing mightily to American cultural life yet usually rewarded with facelessness and anonymity."[132] The jazz world alone recognized Young's accomplishments. A year before his death, Young moved into the Alvin Hotel on 52nd Street "to look down on Broadway and look at Birdland [the jazz club]," according to Willie Jones III. Sick with alcoholism and malnutrition, Young was assisted in the move by Miles Davis, Max Roach, Sonny Rollins, and Jo Jones. A major musical innovator of the cultural form by which Americans signified "freedom" during World War II, this slow-walking, pot-smoking, monkishly dressed, gentle alcoholic wore a silent face and asked for no attention. Lester Young simply played his sadness every night, just as Billie Holiday sang in her cracked voice until the very end, and who knows, but at the lower frequencies, he spoke for the dashed swing hopes of social equality?

The Legacy of Black Cool

The cool mask was a blank facial wall, suggesting both a resistance to white social norms and an inner complexity few Americans ever suspected of their black entertainers. Cool can be seen as a three-front cultural civil war against social norms across racial lines: (1) a person wore a cool front or mask as invisible armor to hold off the prejudice, irrationality, and hostility of the society—"you didn't leave home without it," a television writer recalled in 1996; (2) "cool" stands as an umbrella term for a set of non-European aesthetic values traceable to West African sociocultural functions of music and dance that provided a base for the display of black aesthetic excellence; (3) cool heralded the necessary creation of a personal sound and style in a society that rarely saw African-Americans as individuals.[133]

The philosophical objective of African-American cool was (*is*) to combine expressive style with public composure. Jazz cool reflected a medium between West African cool and Anglo-American cool: the intelligent expression of one's human experience in the world at a given moment. Trumpeter and composer Thad Jones roomed with Young on a 1957 tour and recalled: "You could feel the pain in the man, I could, but he was still one of the most humorous [men]. . . . In the midst of all of the pain of it, he was able to laugh at it." Johnny Otis always heard both sadness and affirmation in Young's music, "a melancholy power and a lament . . . but [also] a joyous celebration of life, the human spirit, and sexuality." To be cool is to maintain a distinctive individual sound and style regardless of the potency of hostile outside forces. In 1964, Marshall McLuhan theorized that wearing sunglasses made any person into a "cool medium" since it created a sense of visual mystery in the observer. "Dark glasses . . . create the inscrutable and inaccessible image that invites a great deal of participation and completion." In shades, Young took his face out of the act and compelled white Americans to look deeper at an oppressed group long taken for granted and now newly visible, ironically, due to the mask of cool.[134]

Duke Ellington called jazz "freedom of expression music," and its universal symbol is probably a black man playing a tenor saxophone. John Szwed has called this image "the first truly non-mechanical metaphor for the twentieth century." It is certainly one of the first global icons of what Kenneth Burke once termed "man-as-communicant": how an individual communicates his or her emotional experience *in the moment* without losing control. It is an image that owes as much to Lester Young's life and art as to anyone.[135]

Cool—or the birth of cool—was a synthesis of West African aesthetic practices and Anglo-American ideas of self-mastery, braided and historically embedded in the African-American struggle for social equality in the United States. In valuing musical communication over technical virtuosity, Lester Young expressed his "somebodiness" without blowing his public cool. In the process Young dignified a stance and a pose—the cooled face—that his jazz heirs used to signify self-mastery and to resist American self-congratulation. The cool mask was a public face that displaced the smiling accommodation of Tomming and displayed instead *poise in a world where one had no authority.*

Figure 3. Bogart was the postwar global brand of noir cool (photo by Philippe Halsman ©
Halsman Archive).

2

Humphrey Bogart and the Birth of
Noir Cool from the Great Depression

In 1942, Paramount Studios attempted to float a new heroic category for rising star Alan Ladd: "the romantic heavy."[1] In studio parlance, the "heavy" meant *the villain* whereas previously the romantic lead was traditionally always the hero, so "the romantic heavy" is an oxymoron reflecting the need for a new category of leading man. "Romantic heavy" might be translated as the *heroic badass* (or rogue hero) but, in any case, it didn't take. Yet the studios were clearly confused by a new set of films and audience desires represented by actors such as Bogart and Ladd. For one thing, "good" men were not *badasses* in Hollywood films of the 1930s: justifiable violence could only be attributed to lawmen such as sheriffs or policemen; unjustified violence belonged to gangsters or outlaws and had to be punished on-screen. By the dictates of the Hays Code, any illegal or immoral act in a film had to lead to arrest or death. In American popular literature, the heroic badass was ubiquitous going back to James Fenimore Cooper's Natty Bumppo, Westerns, or dime novels. But in the popular imagination of the Depression, there was a class divide in American ideals of manhood—a cultural gap of class, prestige, and experience. In films, there were the conventional upper-class romantic leads of the Hollywood studios such as John Barrymore or William Powell, but in popular literature, there was a new working-class fantasy figure, the hard-boiled tough guy of detective novels and pulp magazines. As hopes for social mobility dimmed in the Depression, a new mode of popular masculinity surfaced in the genre of hard-boiled fiction or what I will call *literary noir*.[2]

Starting with *The Maltese Falcon* and then for the rest of Postwar I, Humphrey Bogart embodied this new American type, *the ethical rebel loner*. Yet Warner Brothers executives were surprised to find that Bogart received 75 percent of his fan mail from women after *High Sierra* and *The Maltese Falcon* (both from 1941), with most asking to see him in more romantic roles. Only within the context of the Depression can we explain the sudden stardom and sexual appeal of the short, older, grizzled Bogart, all five foot seven, forty-two years of him. One female film critic once wondered whether Bogart was, "objectively speaking, sexy?" Is an icon ever *objectively* sexy? Of course not: an era's icons are always historically bundled. Mae West could no sooner have been a sex symbol in the 1990s than Denzel Washington could have been in the 1930s. We can, however, register the cultural forces in play at a given historical moment and analyze the changes. In 1940, Bogart was on the Warner Brothers payroll, typecast as the studio's go-to gangster, yet suddenly the gritty, skinny, middle-aged tough was primed to be the studio's number one leading man, a rival to the likes of Clark Gable.[3]

Sometimes an audience chooses a veteran actor rather than a new face to represent a shift or a new desire in the cultural imagination. "An actor may work for years without becoming a star," David Denby reflects, "then, suddenly, looks, temperament, and role all come together—as they did for . . . Bogart in *The Maltese Falcon*." Suddenly the audience "sees what it desires" and in Bogart's case, it happened in two films that kickstarted an entire genre, first *High Sierra* and then *Falcon*. At such a moment, the iconic figure's redemption or resurrection represents "something that was true for the people who needed it to be true," Denby suggests cryptically, and the actor "becomes not only a star but a myth." At such a moment, a B movie like *Falcon* can unexpectedly triple its expected take at the box office and launch a new cinematic style. Less than a year after Bogart's iconic breakthrough as PI Sam Spade came *Casablanca*, a noir transposed in a patriotic key that forever remains near the top of the American Film Institute's prestigious top one hundred films.[4]

With *Casablanca* (1942), Bogart became a brand name for cool on a global scale, admired across race, nation, and class by writers and artists during wartime and then throughout Postwar I. Bogart is the only actor named by a twenty-year-old Malcolm X as he looked for models of style: "I loved the tough guys, the action, Humphrey Bogart in *Casablanca*." On the opening page of V. S. Naipaul's novel *Miguel Street* (1959), set in Port of Spain, Trinidad, we are introduced to the admirable protagonist Bogart. Single, stoical, a loner—this Trinidadian Bogart gained his nickname "the year *Casablanca* was made," Naipaul reflected, "[when] Bogart's fame spread like fire through Port of Spain and hundreds of young men began adopting the hardboiled Bogartian attitude." Naipaul recalled a Trinidad movie audience greeting Bogart's responses to Lauren Bacall in *To Have and Have Not* with shouts, applause, and cries of "*That* is man!"[5] In Jean-Luc Godard's *Breathless* (1960), Jean-Paul Belmondo meditates on a glossy eight-by-ten studio photograph of Bogart at a local theater: he is asking Bogart nonverbally how to *be* cool in his generation—in other words, how to survive with style. (Woody Allen asks the same question in a comic vein in *Play It Again, Sam* [1972].)

Noir cool marked everyday survival with style and dignity for working-class men caught in social and economic forces beyond their control and understanding. "He is an ordinary guy," the Caribbean theorist C. L. R. James wrote of Bogart in 1950, "that is his chief attraction." James analyzed Bogart as a reformed gangster type, tough and resilient at the core, "a symbol of a frustrated population."[6] *Noir cool* was akin to Lester Young's *jazz cool* in projecting alienation through silent protest and calm defiance. Just as aspiring white actors, musicians, or writers such as Kerouac or Eastwood or Stan Getz or Boris Vian took black jazz musicians as their models of cool artists, so white ethical rebel loners of these B movies were embraced as defiant rebels by Malcolm X or V. S. Naipaul.

By historical consensus, the first noir classic was John Huston's *The Maltese Falcon* (1941), starring Bogart as detective Sam Spade, and in the same year, *Citizen Kane* modeled the genre's signature visual style. The postwar French film critic André Bazin recognized the concurrent release of these two films as the start date of noir, "some secret harmony" that existed at "the end of the *prewar period*"—in other words, at the end of the Great Depression. For Bazin, *Kane* and *Falcon* brought two major cinematic innovations to Hollywood film: first, a literary type of narrative visual style (Bazin's "cinematographic *écriture*") and second, a turn toward subjective complexity "through Bogart" in particular as a herald of "the triumph of interiorization and ambiguity" in characterization. The full cycle of noir thrillers begins with *Double Indemnity* (1944), but a slow, steady release of noirs occurred during World War II. Nearly all film scholars maintain that noir responded to *post*–World War II social anxieties: Robert Porfirio refers to 1941–44 as an initial "experimentation" phase, while Frank Krutnik writes off *The Maltese Falcon* as a "false start." Yet how can an artistic breakthrough be a false start if its first auteurs have already fully mapped out the genre's visual, thematic, and narrative style?[7] These misreadings ignore the genre's Depression-era themes and street slang, its visual palate and cityscapes. Film noir reflects the deferred trauma of the Depression—not World War II—and it appears at the precise moment when audiences demanded a new register of masculinity for the transition into wartime.[8]

The crucible of this new white figure was his masking of emotion—literally, his *cool*. To be cool suggested self-control to the point of detachment and signified an insolent defiance as registered in facial expression and body language. Such masking of emotion communicated an inner intensity critical to the self-presentation and embodiment of Bogart, Mitchum, and Ladd. This was not the *sangfroid* of aristocratic nonchalance or the dullness of brute indifference: it was a near-kinetic detachment projected with a subdued intensity suggesting conscious (and conscientious) suffering. The assertive silence of such men created a resonance between actors and audiences that both validated private suffering and expressed the costs of survival. The philosopher of film Stanley Cavell called it the "banking [of] destructive feeling" through body language and physical gesture. For Cavell, encoding such restraint on the body becomes appealing precisely at historical moments when "society requires greater uniformity," since audiences seek a "[new] strategy of individuality and distinctness."[9]

Like jazz cool, noir cool is also a mask of composed violence. The mask of cool of the private detective or sympathetic criminal was noir's floating signifier for a society groping for a revitalized masculinity. The pain simmering through the mask validated the audience's experiences of the Depression precisely by putting a haggard face on it. Cavell refers to this hard-boiled masculinity as the "silent strength" and "hidden fire" of the romantic heavy. This blank, smoldering facial expression coupled with a relaxed body language together project this "banked [inner] fire." Cavell's analysis appeared in *The World Viewed* (1971), a memoir in which he reflected on the social function of Hollywood film for American audiences during the studio era. In contrast, Christopher Breu focuses on the violence and misogyny of noir cool, "the hard-boiled male's shell-like exterior" and his "*unemotive* violent masculinity." In any case, this persona—as embodied by Bogart, Mitchum, and Ladd—was immediately seized on by critics and audiences as a new stylistic mode of American manhood. Over the course of Postwar I, those gangsters in "The Rogue's Gallery" of Paramount Studios slowly transformed into a new, masculine type in the American dream factory: the cool man.[10]

Why did this working-class figure, so recently thought coarse and vulgar, suddenly become attractive to middle- and upper-class audiences— male *and* female—as the nation emerged from the Great Depression? This brand of gritty pragmatism resonated with the difficult economic choices of the era just as the tough guy of pulp magazines appealed to working-class readers. The mask of cool symbolized the repression of hostility toward authority figures and self-control during hard economic times. In gangster films, often the hard-boiled tough starts out as an uncouth gangster and then crosses over, polished up by money and style. Besides Bogart, the best example was the charismatic Irish gangster embodied by James Cagney—in particular, as Rocky Sullivan in *Angels with Dirty Faces* (1938). In this short period before World War II, Cagney became cherished as a representative immigrant cultural force in Hollywood film, the assimilated Irish-American with his brogue intact.

Film noir reflected the deferred traumas of the Great Depression and required a shift from aspirational virtuous upper-class heroes to realistic working-class anti-heroes. These reformed gangsters began appearing between 1938 and 1941, a prewar period of economic recovery that enabled an unconscious hunger for reflection on recent experience after a decade of escapism in comedies, musicals, revues, gangster films, and Busby Berkeley musicals. Orson Welles's partner in the Mercury Theater, John Houseman, reflected on this four-year period as "a time of transition between the end of the Great Depression and the beginning of the . . . industrial boom that accompanied our preparations for World War II." Cautious economic hope prevailed as factories were retrofitted for defense industries and unemployment fell drastically. In the months before Pearl Harbor, defense spending surged passed $2 billion a month.[11]

Bogart was the public face of the cultural work actors perform in American life: he was a symbol of the emotional costs of working through the instability and uncertainty of the sacrifices of the so-called Greatest Generation. Audiences chose Bogart's *noir cool* as a transitional mode of survival, a mask over recent trauma. Americans needed noir cool as an artistic mode, first to face up to the sacrifices of the war and then, in its postwar efflorescence, to hold off the fears of another economic depression; this stoic mode also helped to suppress consciousness of the war's mass slaughters and concentration camps. Audiences needed noir cool to face a newly unstable future where Armageddon was suddenly technologically possible. The Bogart persona projected "a man with few illusions but with his own code," as John T. Irwin described it, a man "who knows that finally the game of life can't be won, but still must be played well." In his noir roles, Bogart was neither virtuous nor romantic nor rich, and his projection of deep melancholy was crucial to his success at midcentury, "the price the noir hero paid for the loneliness of going his own way."[12]

Noir's first classics are essentially prewar so the genre cannot have emerged, as current paradigms suggest, in response to wartime anxiety,[13] postwar paranoia, or masculine insecurity,[14] as has been theorized. The genre's formative creators were two young American directors, John Huston and Orson Welles, and two actors, Bogart and Mitchum. It is an American genre, even if was later modified—and codified—by the more complex visions of immigrant Germans, Jews, and Central Europeans. Yet Austrian immigrant director Billy Wilder reflected that he extrapolated this fatalistic outlook from an American context. In effect, noir cool represented a synthesis of three American pop culture archetypes in 1941: the gangster, the cowboy, and the outlaw.[15]

The new genre arrived in seven films I call *emergent noir*, all released between 1940 and 1942, and this chapter contains three case studies of the Depression's aftereffects through theme, subjectivity, and alienation.

First, there is a thematic correspondence between noir and the Depression in *High Sierra* (written by Huston) and *This Gun for Hire* (1942), with Alan Ladd and Veronica Lake. Studios and critics were so perplexed by these films that the rhetoric from both the production (studio) and reception (review) sides reveal the limits of previous categories for identifying this new genre (*noir*) and new sensibility (*cool*). Each of the other five films in emergent noir provides cinematic and historical context for the genre's thematics, visual style, or narrative innovations: *Citizen Kane*, *The Maltese Falcon*, *Casablanca*, *The Glass Key*, and *The Grapes of Wrath*. The third case study is of a film from five years later, *Out of the Past* (1947), when a new existential register revised the themes of emergent noir through Robert Mitchum.[16]

The decade-long economic depression left a searing fear among politicians and businessmen of a moribund economy once the defense industries demobilized. The federal government's rationale for passing the GI Bill in 1944 was to keep potentially unemployed veterans off the streets—hence its official name, the Serviceman's Adjustment Act. Prosperity did not fully arrive until the early 1950s, fueled by the defense industries' buildup for the Korean War. Noir was nearly visually and thematically coherent as early as 1942, so its emphasis on the subjective alienation of its protagonists does not correlate with either World War II or Communist paranoia, nuclear war or male anxiety. All these thematics do come more fully into play in the second phase of the noir genre. (See chapter 7.)

Film Noir as Failure Narratives

Noir cool reflects a search for a recast individuality that invokes violence as a cinematic language of resistance. Typically, a noir protagonist lacks family, history, and roots, not to mention nearly all bonds of affection. Yet each believes in his or her own individual agency and willed potential. The impulsive personal choices of the noir hero distinguishes American noir from the purer fatalism of French poetic realism or heavy-handed social realism. Mark Bould calls this central tension in noir "determinism without predictability." For example, director Fritz Lang defined his cinematic vision in noir as "this fight against destiny, against fate," and in his films, "the *fight* is important . . . not the result of it." To understand

Bazin's suggestion of a "secret harmony" at work toward a start date of 1941 as the birth of this dark cinema, we need to understand the appeal of ennobling failure narratives for a society in transition.[17]

Orson Welles's objective with *Citizen Kane* was to create a "failure story," a narrative in opposition to "the formula of the 'success story,'" by which he meant the rags-to-riches American mythos of Horatio Alger stories. In fact, each emergent noir here manages to spin a story of social failure into a mythic narrative of individual integrity for its edgy protagonists. Even *Casablanca* is a failure story of this type, spun like celluloid gold into the smartest Hollywood ending ever conceived. Noir protagonists nearly always fail in their attempts to exert control over their lives or imagine unconventional lives; they often die trying. These are failure stories in which men attempt to reboot their own meaning and purposefulness by what Richard Slotkin calls "regeneration through violence." It is the *fight* of the protagonist—against anonymity, undignified work, or the cultural shocks of technological modernity—that resonated with audiences groping for new models of individuality.[18]

With *Citizen Kane*, Welles and his cinematic team pioneered all the visual elements of film noir: chiaroscuro, flashbacks, voice-over narration, and documentary style. Film scholar David Thomson analyzed the new cinematic elements pioneered by Welles and his team: (*a*) "high-contrast / high-focus photography" that created a new visual spectrum of darkness; (*b*) "the investigative flashback structure" that brought the past into the present; (*c*) tight and intimate shots that highlighted the "spatial suffocation . . . [and] melancholy" endemic to the genre. This combination of cinematic effects compelled the audience into the sense of entrapment germane to the noir sensibility. Certainly Welles's artistic innovations anticipated *Double Indemnity* and *Murder, My Sweet* (both from 1944), two films usually upheld as noir's first classics.[19] Even before *Kane*, *The Grapes of Wrath* was a proto-noir reflecting the economic anxiety of an uncertain future: it features a sympathetic and symbolic criminal protagonist unrepentant about murder (Henry Fonda as Tom Joad), a priest who has lost his Christian moorings, and innovative chiaroscuro by cinematographer Gregg Toland (a year before *Citizen Kane*). Henry Fonda's expressionless resilience as Tom Joad was an early half step toward the creation of the cool mask as it became part and parcel of noir's stylized framework that reflected a decade of sacrifice, subsistence, and instability.

Raymond Chandler once explained that his iconic cool private detective Philip Marlowe "is a failure and . . . knows it." It was important for the audience to perceive Marlowe as "a dangerous man, and yet a sympathetic man." An iconic postwar noir figure in *The Big Sleep, Farewell, My Lovely,* and *Lady in the Lake,* Marlowe would not have been a convincing character as a rich or successful man. In effect, Marlowe's *social* failure was inversely proportionate to the literary and cinematic success of this rogue figure. Marlowe may have been "extremely immature" due to "inadequate social adjustment," as Chandler once wrote in a letter to a friend, but at least he offered the fantasy of being content within one's limits: "Of course Marlowe is a failure and he knows it. He . . . hasn't any money. A man without physical handicaps who cannot make a decent living is always a failure and usually a moral failure. But a lot of very good men have been failures because their particular talents did not suit their time and place." Marlowe's "particular talents" include physical stamina and street smarts, his comfort within monastic solitude and flawless bullshit detector, as well as a stubborn pursuit of the situational truth. To Chandler, only Bogart was capable of being "tough without a gun," and his edgy violence crowned the paradigm shift in detective novels from the drawing-room model of Sherlock Holmes to the American man of the streets.[20]

Marlowe's cool depended on the tension between his nearly aristocratic self-worth and his choice to be an underpaid gumshoe in a "shabby office" who returns late at night to "[a] lonely house." Marlowe was not only an uncommon common man, as Chandler once described the noir anti-hero, but a man who wore his job like a cross. If true, the value of his life (and his life's work) can only be understood by Marlowe himself: it is a secular version of a religious calling. Marlowe's work is "possibly not the best destiny in the world," Chandler once wrote, but it has dignity since "it belongs [only] to him."[21] For all of his low social status and questionable violence, Marlowe functions as a cultural symbol of secularized righteousness. It is significant that Chandler published his first best-selling novels featuring Marlowe concurrent with the seven films of emergent noir — *The Big Sleep* (1939) and *Farewell, My Lovely* (1940).

Chandler creates Marlowe as a Depression-era character and yet he becomes a postwar anti-hero—he is therefore an exemplary symbolic figure of the transition first to wartime and then to postwar cool. Chandler was aware of the context of Marlowe's appeal. "In the long run I guess we are all failures," he wrote in 1951, "or we wouldn't have the kind of world we have." It is this self-conscious sense of living in a failed civilization that creates the crosscurrents of cool. Since social status and worldly success involved having a wife and family, Marlowe's life must be monastic. Chandler himself was devoted to his wife, a woman fifteen years his senior, but that his alter ego Marlowe "should be married, even to a very nice girl, is quite out or character," he wrote to a friend. "I see him always in a lonely street, in a lonely room, puzzled but never quite defeated." Marlowe must always appear to be *beat-but-not-beaten*, the key trope of cool in Postwar I.[22]

Put into Depression-era context, noir cool emerges as an inquiry into the fallen national mythos of Horatio Alger. From 1868 to 1929, the sustaining myth of American industrial capitalism was upward mobility, as read by three generations of youth in the rags-to-riches, luck-and-pluck novels of Horatio Alger. As author Nathanael West reflected in 1940, "Only fools laugh at Horatio Alger, and his poor boys who make good. The wiser man knows that . . . Alger is to America what Homer was to the Greeks." In a book review from 1945, Richard Wright admitted he "felt ashamed" to have "been so naïve as to derive enchantment" from the Alger myth in his youth. Wright called Alger "an utterly American artist," whose success was due to "the truth of the power of the wish." Alger created the American Dream before it was named, having reduced "the theories of Max Weber's Capitalism and the Spirit of the Protestant Ethic" to a narrative formula that highlighted "their most simple function and fulfillment."[23]

Yet even as the work ethic of the Alger formula rang hollow during the Depression, American audiences could not expunge the myth. Instead, the rags-to-riches narrative morphed into the gangster film in instant classics such as *Little Caesar* (1931) and *Scarface* (1932). In effect, the gangster film grafted a revenge narrative onto the Alger formula: in replacing the virtuous hero of the businessman with a rogue criminal protagonist, the genre provided a vicarious outlet for those who felt cheated of their savings, hopes, and future, without sacrificing the myth of upward social mobility. In gangster films, ethnic immigrants raised their social status using violence to climb a black-market corporate ladder, then lived in high urban style. Noir cool mediated the gangster's ruthless materialism and the temporary lost faith in capitalism and its mythos. To C. L. R. James, the gangster became symbolic of a "national past" emptied of meaning in the Depression. Factory workers tied to the assembly line transferred their admiration to "the gangster . . . who displays all the old heroic qualities" of energy and determination to become an ironic "[and] derisive symbol of the contrast between ideals and reality."[24]

Since French intellectuals did not see any American films during the Nazi occupation, they were shocked five years later to see such dark cinema coming out of Hollywood in 1946. They named it "film noir," a phrase not used by Americans until the mid-1970s. Two French critics published the first study of noir in 1955, analyzing the new genre as "a synthesis of three kinds of film": the gangster film, the detective film, and the horror film. For the first time, "ambiguity and ambivalence penetrated the psychological drama" in Hollywood films through a modern, alienated consciousness. These films were quickly recognized as visual analogues to the philosophy of existentialism that had emerged during the war.[25]

Noir was also a rebellious artistic response to the epic myths of national identity produced by Hollywood during the *annis mirabilis* of 1939: *Gone with the Wind* (Southern myth), *Stagecoach* (frontier myth), *Mr. Smith Goes to Washington* (Midwest heartland myth of virtue), and *The Wizard of Oz* (technology and innocence). In contrast to these nostalgic explorations, the films of noir are reflexive manifestations on the mundane experiences of Depression-era Americans. In his cross-country travels during the 1930s, author Sherwood Anderson noted a pervasive sense of failure among the unemployed men he picked up hitchhiking. Historian Warren Susman summarized the national mood as one of internalized failure. It was a period when "middle-class America [was] frightened and humiliated, sensing a lack of any order," and without any obvious scapegoat, they "often . . . internalize[d] the blame for their fears." The other option was to reevaluate capitalism and democracy or to reveal their "hostility to a technological and economic order they did not always understand."[26] Such a fragmentation of ideology created the artistic conditions for films whose absence of direct social critique is compensated by their cynical, trapped, and isolated protagonists.

Noir's major cinematic innovations were all in the service of subjectivity: *voice-over narration, flashback, subjective point of view, and documentary-style presentation.* This gets to the heart of noir cool's popularity with audiences: first-person narratives brought a sense of immediacy to stories of rootless individuals who were beat but not beaten. The formal innovations of voice-over and flashback, for example, created new formulas of cinematic storytelling "at a time when our old formulations . . . no longer seemed adequate." In the films of emergent noir, audiences rebelled against these archetypal myths by choosing existential meditations on modernity. Since previously, Hollywood had always attempted to create "myths encoded to prescribe [social] harmony," the success of noir's failure narratives "subvert[ed] our screen's imagery," as one noir scholar observes.[27]

◆ ◆ ◆

What if at a given moment certain narrative conventions have been exhausted and a nation lacks cohesive mythic symbols? What if a film industry then dominated by studios and producers was "reluctant to alter or challenge a proven profitable procedure"? Where would new narrative frameworks be found? They would come from young artists tired of obsolete commercial conventions and exhausted artistic formulas.[28]

Two conditions for artistic rebellion existed: a younger generation bored by a form's current conventions and a source of new narratives — hard-boiled fiction, an already popular genre — seeking its cinematic equivalent. *Citizen Kane* reflects the first condition: a young genius of theater and radio is given unprecedented control over his first film, brings a squadron of new faces to Hollywood, and his artistic vision inspires master craftsmen to push the envelope. Set designer Perry Ferguson, editor Robert Wise, soundman James G. Stewart, makeup artist Maurice Siederman, and especially cinematographer Gregg Toland, along with actors such as Welles and Joseph Cotten, all conspired as "a band of compatriots, all given a unique opportunity, a moment against the grain of the factory system, a chance for . . . showing what a movie could be." Wise later became a first-rate noir director and he recalled "the thrill of working" on *Kane*: "Every scene that Gregg Toland shot seemed to be a completely fresh shot. It wasn't just camerawork. It was art direction, acting, and . . . editing as well."[29] Bogart and Huston represent the second condition: an ability to write, shape, and embody new narratives that enable audiences to transgress vicariously while cheering their own survival in (often) unconscious self-reflexivity.

Now I turn to the first two case studies. In both *High Sierra* and *This Gun for Hire*, the protagonist is a sympathetic violent criminal. In both, the anti-hero has a work ethic and a personal code; in both, each character insists on completing a job at considerable personal risk; in both, he wins the love of the female lead—as far as the spectator's gaze is considered—before dying at peace. In both films, the initial bond between the couple is the acknowledgment of shared hard times, and the trust established pays off when the women enable the protagonists to work through their violent pathologies caused by past trauma. Like other modernist artists, noir directors knew their Freudian psychology: both protagonists have recurring dreams that mark the origins of their violence and its so-called repetition compulsion.

In both films, the female partner acts as the redemptive agent—and therapist—that guides the traumatized males away from acting out to the process of working through the pathology. To narrate a traumatic memory requires a witness: for therapeutic catharsis to occur, a person needs an "addressable Other" capable of sympathy or the suspension of judgment; such a person facilitates the process of bringing forth the fragmented memories of emotional strife.[30] This concept works on two levels for these two films. First, each male protagonist encounters a woman who perceives that his toughness is a mask. She witnesses the internalized trauma and guides his therapeutic integration; she is the addressable Other *in* the film. Second, the two noir directors found an addressable film audience of Americans willing to use these films to reflect on their own recent experience.

In short, in emergent noir, the protagonist functions as a symbolic sacrificial hero: for noir audiences, "witnessing" these films became an act of self-reflexivity. These emergent noir films provided audiences with the chance to work through their traumatic experiences of the Depression. As the economy recovered through the buildup of the defense industries, this prewar period (1938–42) provided a window of opportunity for the production of films that darkly illuminated the collapse of the nation's myths and symbols, its lost faith in businessmen and the work ethic, its first bouts of technological pessimism and class war. In the films of emergent noir, a protagonist often copes with some kind of repetition compulsion—often through crime—that allows for a pattern of violent behavior in response to an unarticulated past trauma. The cure can only come from "working through" the trauma: to remember, articulate, transfer it to the therapist, grieve, and finally, process the repressed emotions.

Again, if we approach noir up from the 1930s, the genre's emergence in 1941 makes sense. First, two American auteurs—Huston and Welles—appear as fully formed artistic voices in their debut films. Second, the genre's signature technical innovations distinguish *Kane* and *Falcon* as artistic breakthroughs, while Gregg Toland's innovative cinematography soon becomes a new model. One veteran face and one new actor—Bogart and Ladd—are quickly embraced as new icons of white masculinity in personae that will dominate the 1940s. In addition, in *High Sierra* and *This Gun for Hire*, Ida Lupino and Veronica Lake play semi-autonomous, empowered *femmes* who are not *fatales*. In fact, the femme fatale as a formulaic element of 1940s noir may be overstated. Angela Martin argues that, in eighty films featuring central female characters, only eight are actually *fatale*. In addition, she suggests that women might have enjoyed "the treat of seeing women giving as good, if not better, than they got."[31]

To mark the changes wrought by the Depression on national beliefs and values, American audiences required new iconic figures, innovative narrative techniques, more complex psychological types, and a grittier sense of life's choices. Audiences externalized their Depression-era experiences as validated in these new cool-masked men—in their faces and gazes, in their bodies and attitudes, in their vernacular speech and thwarted dreams.

These forces first became embodied in the Bogart persona, a new synthesis that C. L. R. James called the "gangster–private detective." A new icon of cool often comes from a convergence of disparate types that are "absolutely necessary" to each other in the embodiment of a new style. As an actor, Bogart found a confident new footing in *High Sierra*, a film in which he brought the Hemingway code hero to the screen, a redemptive gangster slipped under the radar of the prudish Hays Code. As James wrote at the time, here was a man "going his own way" without conforming to bourgeois attitudes, a man with dignity but without revolutionary hope, a man "sick of the pretenses of the world . . . but he has to intervene." Or as his biographer declares simply, "Bogart was the essence of cool," with his Postwar I characteristics of "integrity, stoicism, [and] a sexual charisma accompanied by a cool indifference to women."[32]

High Sierra (1941)

The public's experience of familiar B actors like Bogart—who audiences watched age on-screen, and whose off-screen lives were familiar—became reflections of their own experience. Cavell's crucial perception about the studio era is that it provided Americans with shared cultural ground over two generations: "Hollywood was an enormous stock company, America's only successful one, its State Theater." Within the studio system its actors were continuously active in the national imagination such that "the individuality of stars was defined by their self-identity through repeated incarnations." The cultural resonance of studio actors created a collective dreamscape in which "their histories become part of what the movies they are in are about." For Bogart, the pivotal film of his occupational redemption was *High Sierra*, a film that even the studio called "a paradox" and failed to categorize beyond calling it "a gangster story that isn't a gangster story at all."[33]

Originally Paul Muni (*Scarface*) accepted the part of Roy Earle, but when he backed out, Bogart immediately wired producer Hal Wallis: "Dear Hal, You told me once to let you know when I found a part I wanted. A few weeks ago I left a note for you concerning *High Sierra* . . . . I'm bringing it up again as I understand there is some doubt about Muni doing it. Regards, Humphrey Bogart."[34] At that moment (May 1940), Bogart was a B actor often marketed as Warner Brothers' "number one screen gangster" since his role as Duke Mantee in *The Petrified Forest* (1937). In Roy Earle, Bogart saw his chance to break out of his Hollywood typology: Earle's a gangster but a thoughtful, sympathetic, ethical man. There was a certain logic to the sequence since his previous role was as a hard-working, hard-fighting independent trucker in *They Drive by Night* (1940), in which he loses an arm and has a crisis of masculine identity since he cannot work. It also repeated the success of that film's team, director Raoul Walsh and co-star Ida Lupino.

Roy "Mad Dog" Earle (Bogart) is the last living member of the Dillinger gang, and his release from prison is front-page news. Earle receives instructions from his old boss to drive cross-country to a camp in the Sierra Nevadas and take control of a gang to rob a resort in Los Angeles. Earle finds his underlings (Babe and Red) to be substandard thugs, and instead befriends Babe's girlfriend, Marie, and the camp's dog (Pard). The gang pulls off the robbery but an inside tip puts the police on their tail during the escape; Babe and Red die in the chase. Earle goes on the lam with Marie (Ida Lupino), the dog, and the jewels. Cornered in a car chase, Earle climbs up a mountain and holds off the police in an overnight siege broadcast live on national radio as a major media event. He is shot down at dawn without regret or moral closure. This skeletal plot outline shows both why some reviewers considered it a gangster film and why it defied its genre conventions.

Bogart as Roy Earle embodies the transition from criminal behavior that must be punished to the individual resistance of noir's ethical rebel loner. Gangster films of the 1930s featured these genre conventions: urban settings, emotionally unstable ethnic gang leaders (e.g., Irish, Italian), Prohibition frameworks, working-class neighborhoods, and social climbing through violence. Roy Earle is neither ethnic nor urban; he's from Indiana and even visits the old family farm on his cross-country drive to the Sierra Nevadas. In a suit and tie he leans over the fence of the farm and makes conversation with its current tenant, a bewhiskered farmer. "You're not from the bank, is ya?" the farmer suddenly worries. Earle laughs at the irony, then tells the man's sons where to find the best local fishing hole. As it dawns on the farmer that this is "Mad Dog" Earle, his eyes widen; Earle just waves and walks away. The poverty-stricken farmer seems equally terrified of banks *and* bank robbers, a position redolent of Depression-era experiences.[35] In terms of genre conventions, *High Sierra* is not a gangster film.

In the next scene, Earle swerves to help keep another car from going off the road. When they pull over, he meets Ma and Pa Goodhue and their granddaughter Velma, a pre-modern virtuous agrarian family who have lost their farm and are heading to California. They are Dust Bowlers headed West and, seeing Earle's suit and tie, Pa Goodhue assumes he's a slick urbanite. When he finds out Earle's just a Midwestern farm boy, Pa Goodhue is thrilled—"I knew you were one of our kind," he claps happily. The juxtaposition of these two scenes suggests that the Goodhues' current experience mirrors the Earles' uprooting of a generation earlier that led him to the city and to a life of crime in challenging economic times. Earle then lends Pa Goodhue some money on a handshake—establishing their bond—and falls for Velma, who is pretty but has a clubfoot. The scene projects a Capraesque nostalgia for small-town community. Earle later finances an operation to heal Velma's foot but she still refuses his entreaties.

Here are two other Depression-era themes in emergent noir: respect for hard work and the virtue of loyalty in service to romanticized working-class masculinity. The sympathetic protagonist of emergent noir is a worker who speaks the American urban vernacular, resents official corruption, and has seen dignified work—as an aspect of masculine identity—taken from him. The noir hero lives in humble circumstances, has an egalitarian worldview and a personal code of ethics, and carries class hostility toward wealth and institutional justice.[36] In effect, authority figures are assumed to be lying until proven otherwise—"What's *his* angle?" is a noir trope, for example. As Marie asks Earle about the Goodhues, "What's *their* racket?" These tropes apply across emergent noir through hard-earned experience and across occupation: they apply equally to Sam Spade (detective), Rick Blaine (nightclub owner), Tom Joad (farmer), and Charles Foster Kane (newspaper publisher) as for Ed Beaumont (political operative), Roy Earle (gangster), and Philip Raven (paid assassin).

The cool-masked protagonist of emergent noir must be loyal and hardworking, as if to suggest that unemployment was never a matter of laziness or left-wing radicalism. Even as a bank robber, Earle has a work ethic: he's loyal, he executes, and he protects others. For example, after the heist, an ex-cop and middleman named Kranmer offers to split the take rather than follow Mac's original directions for fencing the jewels. Earle is defiant: "I'm still working for Mac and so are you." Kranmer pulls a gun and laughs: "Hand over the box, Earle. Give me any trouble and I'll fill ya full of lead. I'd be reinstated for capturing 'Mad Dog' Earle and probably get a promotion." Earle replies with true disgust: "A copper's always a copper." To Earle, Kranmer is simply an unethical person, whereas he tries to be loyal and fair within his circumstances. The audience is directed to sympathize with Earle: he outwits Kranmer and kills him.

Earle's ethical egalitarianism also extends to women, allowing for historical context. At first, finding Marie with Babe and Red, he mutters bitterly: "Those two will be spilling blood over you before long." But Earle quickly recognizes that Marie's smarter than both men and hedges on his threat to send her away. After Babe hits her (fig. 4), Earle walks her over to Babe's cabin and directs Marie to hit him with his gun. She hesitates, and instead Earle backhands Babe with the pistol, acting as her proxy. That night Marie asks to stay in Earle's cabin on a cot, and he barely notices her disappointment when he goes to bed alone. Later when they're on the lam, Marie yells at Earle for his complacency. When she apologizes an hour later for being out of line, Earle retorts, "Are you kidding? I wouldn't give two cents for a dame without a temper. My folks fought like cats and dogs for years."

The key trope for Earle's redemption in the film is the phrase "to crash out." Its first use in the film is literal: Earle tells Marie of a prison break he was planning. Later that night, Earle writhes in troubled sleep as Marie watches: "Take the gates away," he moans. "I'm crashing out. . . . I'll go back to the farm. . . . Don't hold me back. . . . You can't take it away." As Earle wrestles with his demons, Marie's sympathetic gaze reveals her romantic and redemptive desire. The next morning Marie interpolates the phrase into the breakfast conversation. "I've been trying to crash out as long as I can remember. My old man used to knock us around a few times a week," she tells Earle evenly. "I crashed out just like you did . . . I guess I was [just] never hooked up with a guy who wasn't wrong. Till I met you." Earle listens sympathetically and later he teams up with Marie and Pard to form an unconventional—but cinematically cohesive—family unit of fugitives.

In *High Sierra*, "crashing out" translates simply, abstractly, as individual freedom. To successfully "crash out" means "to be free"—of economic uncertainty and traumatic pathologies, of class distinctions and social stigmas. For Earle, it means to be free of the tag of "Mad Dog"; for Marie, to throw off the stigma of being a taxi dancer and a gangster moll. The trope was woven into the studio PR: "'Mad Dog' Earle . . . battl[es]

Figure 4. Wearing a dead-black suit, Roy Earle (Bogart) inspects Marie's bruises (Ida Lupino) under classic noir key lighting.

a force bullets cannot conquer . . . [he] *crashes out*—at last—to freedom!" One contemporary reviewer caught the existential connection of the phrase "crashing out." Even if Earle's plan winds up being "nothing but a masterpiece of futility," yet and still "he has his woman and his dog." For this critic, Earle maintains his dignity even in death: "In a smashing climax he realizes that's about all that's worth struggling for in all of man's long sad pilgrimage. . . . You'll remember 'High Sierra' and talk about it long after it has faded from the screen."[37]

The trope of crashing out turned *High Sierra* into a full-fledged noir, redolent of existential motifs and modernist self-construction, focused more on subjectivity than sociology, and imbued with the genre's dark vision of entrapment, transgression, and violent death. At the end, Earle is cornered in a car chase and neither panics nor confesses his remorse. The time has come to die the death of the Hays Code since crime cannot pay. Earle parks and runs up Mount Whitney with a gun and some supplies. When the sheriff asks him to come down, he barks a classic

Hollywood line: "Come and get me, copper." Yet despite Earle's defiant attitude, this scene is not a prelude to a shooting spree: he has chosen his death and looks satisfied with it. By way of contrast, a reporter's running commentary prattles on below while Earle's quiet, nighttime vigil seems like meaningful action. Earle plays neither to the media nor the crowd, just hunkers down to survive as long as possible.

Director Raoul Walsh shoots the sunrise over the mountain behind Earle as he wakes up the next morning, as if bathing this new "Bogart" persona in the dawn's early light. With his black collar up and black rifle alongside, Earle seems either blessed by divine grace or living in defiance of the very concept. He yells Marie's name three times and then is shot dead by a marksman. After Earle's death, Marie asks a reporter what "crashing out" means: "It means you're free," he shrugs. The last shot of the film is a soft-lit close-up of Marie whispering "free," a one-word eulogy for Roy Earle.

In the Warner Brothers studio pressbook distributed to theaters to promote the film, the most common adjective used to describe Roy Earle is "strange," a polyvalent term covering "different," "disturbing," and "compelling." This is Bogart's "strangest role . . . as the strangest killer in history," one poster reads, and on another, Roy Earle is dubbed "the strangest man in the strangest of stories." For all its violent rhetoric resonant of the gangster films for which the studio was famous, the marketing for *High Sierra* was moderated by uncharacteristic ambiguity. "He killed . . . and he must be killed!" reads one poster that conformed to the Hays Code. Yet another focused on Marie as a "taxi-dancer, gun-moll, hungry-hearted woman," and yet here was "a dame with more nerve than ten guys." Here's the tagline for the Lupino-Bogart match-up: "A tough dame with a soft heart . . . meets a dreamer with a gun."[38] (See fig. 4.)

In effect, the phrases "a strange man" and "but he isn't beaten" (i.e., beat but not beaten) function as placeholders for "cool," a term not yet in use. Without any language for the double edge of cool—the romantic heavy, the good-bad man, James's "gangster-detective"—the studio threw all kinds of ambivalent rhetoric on posters to distinguish *High Sierra* as a unique gangster film. "Bogart carries a gun, an unsmiling face, and a prison record. . . . But he doesn't admit he's a criminal," read one.

Many posters featured one of two unusually long taglines, each emphasizing Earle's tragic, undeserved fate.

1. He wasn't born to be a hunted criminal. His hands were made for a plow, not a tommy-gun. . . . A *strange* man, yes . . . and a *strange* story.
2. A lone man clings to a rocky crag of the High Sierras. . . . He's cornered, yes . . . *but he isn't beaten!* Because, you see, this isn't what he was born for! He should have had a fireside on a friendly farm, the warm arms of a loving woman. Instead, his strange destiny . . . [is] carved forever on the peaks of . . . HIGH SIERRA![39]

High Sierra was simply an uncategorizable film in 1941.

Film critics fared only slightly better. Bosley Crowther of the *New York Times* called *High Sierra* a gangster film but he noted that Earle was a "gunman who has got some ideas about freedom and the joy of living." Another reviewer noted Bogart's "grim authority" and his "perfection of hardboiled vitality." The critic for the *New York Journal-American* was frustrated by the idea of a non-virtuous hero: "A man who is kind to dogs . . . loves the great out-doors . . . befriends strangers and who plays fair with his associates is, by every . . . standard, a good and worthy citizen. . . . At the same time . . . [he is] a notorious criminal who doesn't hesitate to shoot and kill anyone who stands in his way. *You'll have to figure it out for yourself*" (italics in original). Audiences did: they made it the first hit to establish Bogart as a box-office brand, heralding the arrival of the *ethical rebel loner* as a new archetype of cool.[40]

Whereas the 1930s gangster film was chock full of violence, emotion, and ambition, here the gangster is redeemed as a man with a complex inner psychological landscape. Roy Earle marks the end of the Depression-era gangster since he transcends its typological limitations, paving the way for the cool register and the postwar anti-hero. In addition, the film reversed the roles of "good girl [Velma] and bad girl [Marie]," as film studies scholar Frank Krutnik perceived, since "the former betrays the hero, while the latter remains loyal." In effect, Marie (Ida Lupino) makes some cinematic strides toward a cool female aesthetic—tough, ethical, and mobile, she is a follower after models for dignity and existential freedom.[41]

Why did audiences root for Roy Earle? To quote the contemporary film reviewers, his cool mask was an "unsmiling face" that conveyed "grim authority" and "hardboiled vitality": it represented controlled suffering as a result of hard-earned individual experience. In the scenes shot at the mountain forest camp, Earle signifies noir's post-traumatic subtext through dress alone: Bogart strolls through the bright daylight scenes in a stylish dead-black suit and fedora, darkening every beautiful landscape like a walking indictment of the American dream. (See fig. 4.) But by adjusting his sights to reality and providence (Marie and a bad-luck dog)—and away from nostalgia and innocence (Velma)—the character of Roy Earle performs a symbolic transmutation of shifting expectations for his audience.

Bogart appealed to an older generation as a man redeemed from instinctual urges. Moviegoers had known Bogart for seven years through over forty films: his was less a new face than one marked and scarred by experience. Roy Earle transcends a traumatic past, practices ethical violence, shows vulnerability, treats women fairly, and yet acts with self-confident conviction. Without a vocabulary for complex, interiorized characters, studio marketing simply unified oppositions of good and evil, romantic and heavy, virtue and villainy, to give the people what they seemed to want: "Humphrey is back behind his six-shooter, practicing villainy . . . [but] 'High Sierra' . . . shows him as a heavy with a soft heart."[42]

Roy Earle's complexity was a creative collaboration between Bogart and John Huston, the launch point of a key cinematic collaboration as well as a lifelong friendship. Working as a screenwriter and script doctor for Warner Brothers, John Huston convinced the studio to buy the rights to the novel and then wrote the first draft of the script in three weeks. The film was adapted from W. R. Burnett's *High Sierra*, but in the novel, "Mad Dog" Earle is a brutal man of instincts—a tall, dark, heavy-shouldered "farmer-ape" who cannot control his rages. Huston and Bogart together sculpted Earle into a modern, alienated individual.[43]

Six months later, Huston directed *The Maltese Falcon* and its reputation as noir's first classic depends on the Bogart persona shifting from ethical criminal to immoral detective. Bogart's stock-in-trade was "his individualist stance in the face of the unknown," and it became codified a year later in *Casablanca*.[44] Over this five-year period, the actor

Humphrey Bogart transformed into the global American brand of "Bogart": from a cold-blooded gangster (*The Petrified Forest*) to a sympathetic working-class criminal (in *High Sierra*) to a shady detective (Sam Spade in *The Maltese Falcon*) and finally, to the nation's favorite iconic anti-hero as Rick Blaine, owner of the Café Américain. Bogart carries his brand of noir cool into *To Have and Have Not* and *The Big Sleep* (as Philip Marlowe), then into *Dark Passage* and *In a Lonely Place*. The pair worked together on one more noir classic—*Key Largo* (1946)—then Huston directed one of the final classic noirs of Postwar I, *The Asphalt Jungle* (1950), launching the last icon of noir cool, Sterling Hayden. (See chapter 7.)

Bogart traded his black hat for a white one, inflecting from Roy Earle's tight-lipped convict in a dead-black suit to casino owner Rick Blaine's white tuxedo dinner jacket. In Cavell's terms of a cumulative cinematic biography, this half decade mirrored the audience's awakening to reflection and a renewed search for individuality after the sacrifices of the Depression. In Bazin's terms, *Bogart* functioned as a postwar signifier of existential freedom in France, of "accepting the human condition which may be shared by [both] the rogue and the honorable man."[45] Through a strategic choice of roles, Humphrey Bogart engineered his cinematic redemption over a five-year period, from a typecast killer and gangster to a new American archetype.

Interlude: Hollywood Typology and Literary Noir

Film noir was a genuine cultural phenomenon in terms of how its reception guided production. Hollywood studios then typecast actors and industry conventions prevented them from taking career risks. Neither Paul Muni nor George Raft wanted to risk their box-office appeal as criminals on a strange character like Roy Earle; only Bogart saw the role's potential. In the analogous case of *Double Indemnity*, director Billy Wilder was turned down by all of Hollywood's gangsters and romantic leads for the role of Walter Neff. "It was difficult to get a leading man," Wilder recalled. "Everybody turned me down . . . including George Raft. Nor did Fred MacMurray see the possibilities at first. He didn't want to be murdered, he didn't want to be a murderer. He said, 'Look, I'm a saxophone player [as a type]. I'm making my comedies with Claudette

Colbert." No one predicted the success of *Double Indemnity* nor anticipated its influence. In terms of artistic vision, only "[Barbara] Stanwyck knew what she had," Wilder recalled. Director Edward Dmytryk had a similar experience casting *Murder, My Sweet* (1944), the film version of Raymond Chandler's *Farewell, My Lovely*. After being turned down by all the A-list actors, Dmytryk chose an eager Dick Powell, a song-and-dance man known for his roles in Busby Berkeley musicals then desperate to change his image. In retrospect, it is extraordinary that no leading man wanted to play the iconic detective Philip Marlowe.[46]

Such evidence contradicts the theory that noir was the cinematic projection of a European existential or "left culture" imported through the alienation of German or Jewish émigré directors such as Wilder, Dmytryk, and Fritz Lang. Asked if *Double Indemnity* reflected "an angst pervading Central Europe after World War I," Wilder replied, "I think the dark outlook is an American one." Dmytryk called *Double Indemnity* "very typically American," one obviously "preceded by *The Maltese Falcon*" and fitting "a very American tradition." Asked of the origins of his "fatalistic outlook," Fritz Lang claimed only an artistic perspective "of the human condition" that was "existential" in a positive sense. Asked if "Eastern Europeans . . . brought their own sardonic mood to pictures," Dmytryk admitted to only one cinematic influence on *Murder, My Sweet*: Welles's *Citizen Kane*. This evidence may not be overwhelming, but Wilder, Lang, and Dmytryk were three acclaimed noir directors and all were émigrés from Central Europe. Yet all three recognized the prewar period as foundational to noir and all three viewed the genre as American in mood. Literary noir in combination with Welles's cinematic innovations created a globally influential style during World War II.[47]

In terms of the genre's audiences, noir's resonance and reception depended on a visual style and cityscape that functioned as a virtual space for Americans to project their long-simmering economic anxieties. Noir's street fights, small apartments, and neighborhood dynamics provided a stage set with which to reflect on the massive transformations of the industrial era, letting loose "demons lurking since the predawn of the Industrial Revolution," critic Nicholas Christopher noted, up to and including "the breakneck consolidation of our large cities." Noir was an American genre informed by an organic alienation extrapolated from its popular literature.[48]

The misreading of noir's origins stems from separating the films from their literary sources—the hard-boiled fiction and detective novels of the Depression that were its source texts. In 1930s France, this genre of literary noir was simply known as "the tough novel" or "the American novel"; film noir represented its cinematic adaptation.

This popular genre began in the 1920s with the stories in the pulp periodical *Black Mask*, featuring violent white working-class anti-heroes. Its first recognized literary voice was Dashiell Hammett, rendered through his detectives, the Continental Op and then Sam Spade (in *Red Harvest* and *The Maltese Falcon*, 1930) and its second was Raymond Chandler's Philip Marlowe. Concurrently, James M. Cain's best-selling works crossed over from this readership. Each author presides over encoded forms of class resistance against rampant capitalist greed, bourgeois complacence, and organized crime. There are often multiple villains: corrupt businessmen in cahoots with gangsters, con men and their female partners, policemen on the take. The lack of dignified work bleeds into the allure and thrill of breaking the law and living on the lam. Literary noir provided the new genre with a ready-made framework of atomized disenchantment. "The noir ethos didn't spring out of nowhere in 1940," as critic Michael Walker reflected. "It would be more accurate to say it had been suppressed [in Hollywood] during the '30s."[49]

Noir cool might have emerged ten years earlier but for the Hays Code of 1934, as enforced by the Production Code Administration (PCA). Under the clergy-dominated puritanical leadership of Joseph Breen, all ambiguous sex and violence had to be punished on-screen—every criminal killed or put behind bars, each act of extra-marital sex punished or redeemed. For example, in both versions of *The Maltese Falcon* produced in the 1930s, Sam Spade is rendered as a cavalier urbane gentleman, a man of means: Spade is a supercilious, greedy bachelor in *The Maltese Falcon* (1931) and a huckster playboy in *Satan Takes a Lady* (1936). Both films are more attuned to 1920s opulence than Depression-era grittiness and ratify the dominance of the upper-class WASP protagonists before emergent noir. In addition, the PCA expressly forbade studios to produce films of Cain's works due to their unfaithful wives, unpunished violence, and immoral characters (e.g., *Double Indemnity*, *The Postman Always Rings Twice*). Film noir could not emerge in the 1930s since creating verisimilitude for such hard-boiled characters violated the code's "Victorian principles."[50]

The PCA fenced off literary noir until World War II, at which point an aesthetic shift occurred in American audiences. The violence and gore of wartime newsreel footage toughened the American visual palate, predicating a shift in national standards of sex, violence, and morality. There was also a fortunate coincidence. In late 1941, Joseph Breen took a six-month leave of absence: *The Maltese Falcon* and *This Gun for Hire* slipped through with their ambiguous embrace of sex, violence, and stark realism left intact.[51] By 1944, the relaxation of the Hays Code made possible faithful adaptations of hard-boiled literary source texts. With regard to the popularity of *Double Indemnity* (1944), Cain claimed it had nothing to do with a shift in public taste, "nothing to do with the war or how it's affected the public or any of that bunk." He ignored the earlier films of 1941–42 and said simply that, in 1945, studio producers "have got hep to the fact that plenty of real crime takes place every day." The *New York Times* analyzed this new genre in 1945 as "a growing crop of homicidal films," and Cain said it was only Hollywood pretense with regard to public morality that prevented a Depression-era start date for film noir. "If Billy Wilder . . . had made *Double Indemnity* in 1935," Cain said confidently, "the picture would have done just as well." (The screenplay was co-written by Raymond Chandler, Billy Wilder, and Cain himself.)[52]

The surprising box-office success of *This Gun for Hire* also marked the successful reception of the cool register in film. In Graham Greene's original novel and screenplay, Philip Raven is a hideous, hare-lipped assassin. Yet Ladd's pretty-boy looks and sullen, wounded quality evoked more sympathy and empathy than judgment from film audiences, launching his career as an "angelic killer" who steals Veronica Lake's heart from her virtuous fiancé. Just as Huston and Bogart transformed Roy Earle into an alienated rebel trying to crash out to freedom, so too did director Frank Tuttle and actor Alan Ladd collaborate on the analogous paradoxical character of Philip Raven.[53]

This Gun for Hire (1942)

Alan Ladd was one of the few precursors of James Dean—he was a brooding, young, blond tough who at first reflected the costs of his cool back to young men on the verge of heading off to World War II. The film critic Bosley Crowther caught Ladd's appeal in 1942 with impressive prescience and nearly identified the *pre*-birth of cool in his review of *This Gun for Hire*. Crowther observed the young generation's instant appreciation of Ladd's "tight-lipped violence," his impassive emotional self-control, "his gangster toughness combined with a touch of pathos." What was the appeal of this "sympathetic rebel"?

> *Is it that youngsters see in him some vague implications of themselves?* That is, beyond the obvious romance attached to a handsome tough guy, do they see imaged in him their own insecurities, *a sympathetic rebel against the problems and confusions of modern youth?* And do they find vicarious pleasure in his recourse to violence?[54]

All the elements of cinematic cool are here: the "sympathetic rebel" and his sexual charisma; the combination of toughness and vulnerability; the allure of violence as metaphorical revolt; the self-absorption of teenagers and their need for cinematic icons to dream on. The word "teen-ager" was only first coined in 1935 to refer to swing culture, the first cross-class American youth culture—its music, dances, jazz slang, and fashion styles. Since big bands and studio films appeared on the same programs in movie theaters, film critics in particular were well aware of the swing generation's jazz lingo, habits, and tastes. Ladd was a new face, a tabula rasa for a young generation's mood on the verge of entering the war.[55]

In addition, Alan Ladd and Veronica Lake were an instant star pairing, blank slates written on by the swing-culture youth audiences of emergent noir. As a team for seven films between 1942 and 1948, they were nearly as popular as Mickey Rooney and Judy Garland just before them, and their initial chemistry deserves deeper inquiry. Ladd was a box-office phenomenon in the 1940s: he received twenty thousand fan letters a week and his films were often in the top ten. As for Veronica Lake (fig. 5), so many female defense plant workers wore their hair in her trademark lush blond "peek-a-boo" hairdo that the War Production Board passed an ordinance requiring the workers to wear it short and out of their faces for the war's duration. "I must admit," Lake reflected later, "I was flattered to think I had become that crucial to our war effort."[56]

Ladd's star turn in *This Gun for Hire* came from an opposite set of

Figure 5. A noir sex symbol, Veronica Lake seems to be wearing the mantle of night itself here.

circumstances than Bogart in *High Sierra*. Veronica Lake received top billing, coming off a breakthrough performance in the Preston Sturges hit comedy, *Sullivan's Travels* (1941), whereas Ladd had only landed bit parts until he became an overnight sensation as contract killer Philip Raven (or just "The Raven"). Actor Robert Preston was originally cast as Raven, but the director wanted a new face, and quickly perceived the allure of Ladd's touchy toughness, his combination of scowling resentment and vulnerability. Ironically, Tuttle downgraded Preston to the romantic lead of the good-guy cop, then "rewrote the script to favor [Ladd]."[57]

To see how the wartime moment of 1941–42 forms the cusp of noir cool, we need only look to the similarities of *Casablanca* and *This Gun for Hire*. These two films catch the salient difference between the virtuous upper-class ideal of the tall, handsome Anglo (or WASP) man and the restrained ethical violence of cool-masked masculinity. Just as Ingrid Bergman is torn between the virtuous hero and the cool man in *Casablanca*, so too in *This Gun for Hire*, the camera frames Veronica Lake in love with both the straight-arrow policeman (Preston) and the struggling hitman (Ladd). Like Victor Lazlo, Preston's Lieutenant Crane is too good to be cool and fails to engage his fiancée's imagination or desire, her sympathy or sexuality. In both films, the virtuous man has lost his hold as a romantic lead since surviving the Depression required a grittier set of survival skills. In both films, the romantic lead retains the love of his partner only because the cynical, violent, ethical rebel loner steps aside.[58]

Figure 6. Philip Raven (Alan Ladd) meets entertainer Ellen Graham (Veronica Lake) and they strike up a therapeutic romance.

Tuttle framed Ladd and Lake as a couple more so than Lake and Preston: they have the cute meet, the nascent sexual chemistry, the dramatic courtship, and the tragic romantic ending. As with Roy Earle, critics read the character of Raven as *strange* and found Lake's low-key femininity both startling and off-putting. The *New Yorker*'s reviewer lacked the vocabulary to analyze the *cool* sensibility: *This Gun for Hire* featured new faces ("young and youngish . . . not oppressively familiar"), transgressive roles ("strange roles" leading characters into "bizarre circumstances"), and a fresh mood ("altogether quite a surprise"). If Preston was the ostensible hero's role—and marries Lake at the end—still Ladd thwarts the corporate traitors and received Lake's redemptive gaze (and love).[59]

This Gun for Hire opens in Raven's bare room in a San Francisco boarding house. He wakes up in midafternoon, feeds a stray cat, and roughs up the maid for being intrusive. He puts on the noir uniform of trench coat and fedora, then goes out and efficiently executes a chemist and his secretary. (It is a given here that noir is an irredeemably misogynist genre.) Raven then meets with a heavyset, ghoulish Los Angeles–based nightclub owner named Willard Gates (Laird Cregar), who pays him in marked bills and quickly phones in a robbery to silence him. Gates is an effete, wealthy businessman marked as homosexual and a stock noir villain: he fronts for the owner of a chemical company selling poison gas to the Japanese. Raven eludes the police and hops a train for Los Angeles, vowing revenge, yet he has no unmarked cash. Luckily he winds up sitting next to Ellen Graham (Lake), a singer and magician on her way to headline Gates's club; she is also a recent conscript for the FBI hired to foil Gates's spy ring. (See fig. 6.)

The film first stirs audience sympathies for Ladd and Lake through Depression-era codes. When Graham goes to the bathroom Raven steals a five-dollar bill from her purse then pretends to be asleep when she returns. Graham is a tough cookie of the 1930s—she quickly notices the theft—and simply asks Raven, "Are you that broke?" Ashamed, he returns the money, and Lake offers him a dollar, no strings attached. Raven accepts, a bit embarrassed, and they have a short friendly conversation before falling asleep. When they wake the next morning, his head is on her shoulder, an intimate gesture that foreshadows Raven's trust in the woman who will become his addressable Other. In LA, the police are waiting for Raven, searching for a man with a deformed wrist from a childhood injury. Raven forces Graham to help him escape at gunpoint then attempts but fails to kill her in an alley and she escapes.

The first test of *virtuous hero* versus *cool-masked noir hero* occurs at the villain's house that night. Gates invites his club's new headliner to his mansion ostensibly for dinner but intending to seduce and then kill her. Lt. Crane arrives in a cab, having been tipped off by a friend that his fiancée is in danger; he takes Gates at his word that Graham has left. In contrast, Raven rips a page from the phonebook and gets directions from a scraggly old man out of a portfolio of Walker Evans photographs. "That house is way up in the hills. You can hitch a ride up if you're broke." Raven arrives in a laundry truck and stays hidden when Gates leaves. He knocks out the valet and finds Graham tied up in an armoire in a back room.

Raven lifts Graham out pietà-style and lays her gently on a chaise lounge: she wakes up into a clinch, close in his arms. Thematically, the survival skills acquired from trauma and poverty have already been valorized over institutional authority and wealth. Visually, at this moment, Graham is Raven's girl. Ladd and Lake remain in each other's arms for a terse, knowing exchange that would become characteristic of noir, his flat monotone moderated by her cool contralto.

> *Ladd/Raven*: What's Gates got against you . . . ?
> *Lake/Graham*: Saw us on the train. Thinks I'm your girl.
> *L/R*: Look I'm not gonna hurt you. You treated me OK.
>   But you do what I say. . . . So you're a copper's girl?
> *L/G*: Who told you that?
> *L/R*: He was here looking for you.

In a few, quick strokes, Raven / Ladd's work ethic and grim perseverance are set against the plodding forces of virtue and Gates's greedy treason. The traditional virtuous hero came looking for his tough cookie; the cool heavy found and rescued her. This scene's spare dialogue spoken in subdued tones in a back bedroom of a haunted mansion symbolizes individual suffering kept secret and foreshadows Raven's climactic redemption at Graham's hands.

Meanwhile, the sinister corporate forces of the Depression take form in the aged Mr. Brewster, a malicious, wheelchair-bound millionaire known as Old King Chloride. This depiction of physical impotence combined with economic power correlates with the fall from grace of the businessman-hero during the Depression (e.g., Henry Ford, John D. Rockefeller Jr.). Who can trust corporate power or individual wealth as embodied in monstrous figures such as Brewster and Gates? Simply to frame this rhetorical question is to recognize the implicit logic—and attraction—of Raven's outlaw violence. Raven's actions resonate with James Naremore's framework for the noir protagonist: he has engaged the audience's sympathy as "a victim of Depression-era social injustice" and, once he saves Lake, he can be redeemed as "a champion of democracy."[60]

Noir's thematics and visual style in *This Gun for Hire* rests mostly on an extended twenty-minute nighttime sequence set in the fogbound rail yards beneath Brewster's industrial gasworks. It's early 1942 and the noir matrix has arrived: visually, the fog of consciousness and accompanying key lighting turns bodies into shadows and shifts in facial expressions into emotional revelations; symbolically, there are trains to represent mobility and darkness to represent the unconscious; in terms of gender and sexuality, there's a mysterious, alluring woman; in terms of cool rebellion, there's an easily duped police force outwitted by a sympathetic criminal dressed in fedora and trench coat. Together, Raven and Graham negotiate the noir loner's consciousness while Lt. Crane and the police stand outside, blind and impotent, waiting for the fog to lift and hoping Raven will not murder Crane's fiancée. Yet at no time does Lt. Crane attempt to rescue his fiancée on his own.

The film's primary tension resides in the growing intimacy between Graham and Raven through their therapeutic relationship: in this scene, this relationship replaces the latter's "acting out" (by killing) by accessing the origins of his trauma. Graham asks Raven not to kill Gates and Brewster in revenge but instead to get a signed confession stating they are selling poison gas to the enemy, creating "Japanese breakfast food for Americans." Raven at first refuses, all the while obsessively rubbing his deformed wrist, freshly cut from barbed wire. Graham bandages his arm and notices his appreciation. "You're a funny guy. You like that but you can't say that you do." Raven snaps back, "That's sucker talk. You're trying to make me go soft," the noir anti-hero says, pulling away, "and I don't go soft for nobody."

This line echoes Rick Blaine's iconic line from *Casablanca*, "I don't stick my neck out for nobody," which is also a front, a pose, the mask of cool. Just as Ilse Lund invokes patriotism to sway Rick Blaine, Ellen Graham makes a similar plea to Raven to assist in the war effort.

Lake/Graham: Why don't you stop thinking about yourself?
Ladd/Raven: Who else is gonna think about me?

Raven remains stolid but the camera frames their exchange as a conversation between equals—not lovers or victims, not Girl Scout and bad boy, not therapist and patient. Lake keeps her voice calm and low, without recourse to traditional feminine markers of sentiment, tears, or histrionics. Raven's responses have no trace of pity or remorse, nor of heroic or tragic grandeur.

This is the *cool* register and it was new to movie audiences as an emotional mode. The *New Yorker* praised Lake's laconic slow burn in an amazing phrase: "Whether it is simply her lackadaisical hair-do or the exquisite effect she suggests of *a wink combined with rigor mortis*, the poor child's graces are alarming." The critic compared her sexual charisma—those languid, controlled movements—to the aesthetic of the *danse macabre*, an eroticizing of death. *Life* magazine chose *This Gun for Hire* as its movie of the week, and its critic, too, admired Lake's ability to moderate any man's desires, whether to "cool the fevered brow of a sick man . . . [or] produce a fever in a well man." For Ladd's side, the *Los Angeles Times* critic was prescient: "Preston is overshadow[ed] by the new young man on the screen." Audiences rooted for Raven's redemption—just as they had Roy Earle's—and again some critics threw up their hands. "Despite he is a hard-bitten criminal[,] Ladd in his role gains sympathy," wrote one critic. "*Maybe that offends the morals code*, but it's a fact anyway." Fans preferred Ladd's cool mask over Preston's company-man persona. In 1946, Ladd reflected that *This Gun for Hire* was the film that first "brought me a flock of fan letters, convinced Paramount that I could do stellar parts, and really started me on my way."[61]

As a term, "cool" was then only in circulation among African-Americans, yet it is the word everyone reaches for now to describe such noir heroes. Naremore calls Ladd a "coolly lethal dandy," while Ladd's biographer invoked his cool on page one: "He was aloof, self-sufficient, occasionally lonely, and sometimes outside the law. His aura was one of *great cool*, of a forceful, masculine presence with a strong undercurrent of violence and heavy sex appeal. . . . That's how the fans who went to the movies in the 1940s saw Alan Ladd." As with Bogart, Ladd was not a typical leading man; Raymond Chandler famously called him "a small boy's idea of a tough guy." By Hollywood standards, Ladd was a short (five foot five), blond, eager pretty boy, more likely to be cast as a lifeguard or beach frat boy than a hard-boiled protagonist. Ladd's biographer duly notes the contradiction of "a small, shy, self-effacing, moody young man" whose youth and strategic silences set him apart "on screen as a hard, cynical, sexy, self-contained tough guy." Again, this points up the audience's demand for a grittier masculinity in the early 1940s. In short, the audience elevated Ladd to stardom rather than the studio.[62]

This Gun for Hire was made for $500,000 and grossed $12 million, making Ladd an overnight sensation. "No need to hail Ladd as a comer," wrote the *Hollywood Reporter*. "He has arrived in one jump." Audiences saw in Ladd's stylish emotionlessness a redeemable white criminal, "a different kind of mugg," one critic suggested, "smooth and with even a parlor manner." Until 1942, it was rare to cast a fair-haired, seemingly educated young WASP or Anglo-American as a violent criminal. One critic cited "the killer's laconic nontalkativeness"; *Variety* called attention to Ladd's "still ferocity" and lack of emotion. By and large, critics read Ladd as racially redeemable. "He seems to be a rather agreeable killer, his felt hat pulled down at a frivolous angle, his mouth only a trifle sullen," as the *New Yorker* critic described him. The *Life* reviewer was surprised that "the festering bitterness of a killer who hates everything" could come from a "green-eyed, sandy-haired young American"—in other words, from a white man and not an ethnic Other. In the *New York Times*, Bosley Crowther admired Ladd's "tight-lipped violence" and found in him a younger cinematic brother for Bogart. "Mr. Ladd is a new sort of gangster—a moral gangster. There is despair in him."[63]

As with *Casablanca*, the studio solution for the female lead's ambivalent desire was to allow the cool heavy to win the romantic screen battle of masculinity while the virtuous hero takes the woman home. This ambivalence is depicted in an odd, unmarked hospital room in the film's final scene, a cross between a dream state—set against black walls—and something like heaven's waiting room. Ladd lies in delirium on a couch with several bullets in him awaiting Lake's absolution. He looks up at her with boyish hopefulness: "I did all right for ya?" Lake smiles and nods in response, an action that releases Ladd—literally—into eternal bliss. He dies peacefully, and Lake suddenly turns away, imploring Lt. Crane to "hold me, just hold me."

In Ladd's next film, he was cast as the ethical gangster Ned Beaumont in the screen adaptation of Dashiell Hammett's *The Glass Key*, the film for which Paramount tested out the new phrase "romantic heavy." On the back of a studio promotional still, the caption reads that Alan Ladd, "pictured here[,] . . . is styled a 'romantic heavy,' a sort of combination of George Raft and Robert Taylor because both women and hard guys admire him." In combining the gangster's violence with traditional sexual charisma, the romantic heavy appealed to both men and women. The studio instantly promoted Ladd to "Hollywood's rogue's gallery"—on par with Bogart and Edward G. Robinson—yet he radiated a youthful ambiguity. As the studio noted, "Alan combines romantic qualities with his ability to portray a sinister type of role." For the first two French critics of the genre, Ladd became "part of noir mythology" by introducing a new type, the "angelic killer." They fairly rhapsodized over this charismatic young white rebel with his "slight frame . . . docile baby face . . . limpid eyes . . . [and] gentle, unobtrusive features."[64]

In retrospect, with regard to Veronica Lake and Ida Lupino, the lack of focus on female cool characters was a missed opportunity. The flat affect of both actors—their cool—was germane to their sexual charisma. American women aspired to Lake's laconic self-control and men were thrilled by her smooth sensuality. The *New Yorker*'s reviewer caught this quality in 1942: "When she smiles, as she does perhaps twice in this film, hearts can be heard to break . . . throughout the loges . . . and the tougher element upstairs have to shout their ecstasy." In her memoir, Lake claimed modestly to have been merely a Hollywood type: "Veronica Lake as Everyman's mistress." Yet she sells herself short. Female characters that exhibited individual style, economic independence, cool compassion and self-reliance were the dramatic flip side of the tough cookies of prewar's screwball comedies. And they were rare in post war noir.[65]

Noir Cool, 1942

For cool characters to resonate with audiences, their masking of emotion had to signify the control of one's inner intensity—including rage and pride—and its cost. Without this muted despair, the cool mask would register neither style nor personal suffering for its audiences. Instead, the flat affect and unemotive violence would connote brute stupidity or coldness, a void or a vacuum, a *lack* of consciousness. Without cool, such blank dispassion conveys a warped, withdrawn pathology: a zombie's unconsciousness, the bare life of an automaton, the mechanical workings of a wind-up toy soldier. Roy "Mad Dog" Earle and Philip Raven die not only as moral retribution for breaking the law—the death required by the Hays Code—but also because there was no place for them in the prewar American cultural imagination.

Bogart and Ladd burst forth fully formed as embodiments of cool, the major postwar American vernacular mode of masculinity. In their hard-boiled masculinities, in their insistence on individual agency, in their attempts to work through the loss of belief in American mythos with female partners—Roy Earle and Philip Raven found a place in a new collective dream of the wartime moment. Americans were apparently sympathetic to the subdued ethical violence of the failed, cornered, violent men of emergent noir, and it represented a shift in aesthetics, taste culture, and even morality. As film audiences vicariously groped toward reflections of their own traumatic experiences, they required new faces and a new emotional register. Heroic masculinity was conscripted into World War II as much from the *noir cool* side of human nature—the heavy's dark side—as from the traditional hero's virtuous side.

These two films—*High Sierra* and *This Gun for Hire*—reveal a new matrix of post-Depression cross-class cool masculinity. First, there is the concession of individuality and rational intelligence to the former ethnic gangster. Second, there is a battle for the beautiful woman between the virtuous hero and the romantic heavy. Third, there is the demonization of the wealthy businessman—Gates and Brewster—now rendered as frail, effete, and corrupt. Fourth, there is the framing of policemen and institutional justice as either ineffective or corrupt (Kranmer and Preston, or in *Grapes of Wrath*). As the bottled-up feelings from economic anxiety rose to the surface, audiences responded to violent, sympathetic loners who found crime *had* to pay when free market forces did not provide dignified work. In the films of emergent noir, the United States has yet to enter the war and the women are rebels in their own right.

Five years later, the baton was passed from Bogart to Robert Mitchum, starting with *Out of the Past* (1947), one of the genre's masterworks. "Mitchum *was* film noir," Martin Scorsese once said. On-screen, he was the ethical rebel loner incarnate, a man of mystery, "dangerous, strong but guarded," and yet always "unconvinced by the actions of those around him." Off screen, Mitchum ignored nearly all rules, codes, and social norms; rather, he was a fearsome, seductive rogue whose reputation was only burnished by a famous 1948 bust for marijuana possession. For maverick director Jim Jarmusch, Robert Mitchum projected "that odd sense of someone smoldering on the inside but so damn cool on the outside."[66]

Robert Mitchum's Existential Cool in *Out of the Past* (1947)

Screenwriter and novelist Daniel Mainwaring had *The Maltese Falcon* on his mind when he adapted the screenplay for *Out of the Past* from his novel, *Build My Gallows High*. Mainwaring's twist on the noir formula was to have the detective play the sap, the fool, the fall guy—a man who "tossed ethics out the window" for a woman, then "double-crossed his client and helped her to kill his partner." It marks the difference between the Bogart persona and Mitchum's, between emergent and postwar noir.[67]

In the original film treatment, Mainwaring distilled its noir situation in three short sentences: "There was a guy named Markham . . . a private detective with a sense of honor. His credo was: 'You can't touch pitch and stay clean.' Even men without honor trusted him." The word "pitch" here refers to the pure darkness of the femme fatale and Markham falls in love "with his dream of her." In other words, Mainwaring flipped the script of *The Maltese Falcon*. In *Falcon*, Sam Spade sends the woman he loves to prison for killing his partner both to serve his code of ethics and to maintain control of his desires. In *Out of the Past*, PI Jeff Markham watches his paramour shoot his partner dead and realizes he will always be her fool.[68]

Bogart wanted the role of Markham but director Jacques Tourneur insisted on the younger, taller, and more physically intimidating Mitchum. "Mitchum was younger, more deadpan, [and] more serenely hopeless than Bogart could ever be," David Thomson once suggested of the actor's lack of moral conviction. The character of PI Jeff Markham (Mitchum) is sharp, cynical, and charismatic, a working-class man risen from the streets with every survival skill except self-motivation. He has a reputation for honesty yet takes a job from a sadistic gangster just for the money. Markham possesses the ethical loner's code of the Depression-era detective yet without his moral righteousness: his desires obscure the truth of a situation, and he resists neither sex nor greed. Studio ads did not pretend otherwise, as this one in *Life* attested: "Mitchum's a private detective, a little on the shady side—who makes a buck wherever he can find it." Mitchum was a far better choice than Bogart to play a detective who winds up dead in a double suicide after being outsmarted by his femme fatale.[69]

The film opens in the idyllic small mountain town of Bridgeport, Nevada, and we quickly learn from small talk at the local diner that gas station owner Jeff *Bailey* has a mysterious past. We find him fishing with his younger girlfriend, Ann Miller, planning their future together while he evades questions about his past. On return to his garage, a thug from his former life appears and summons Bailey to the Lake Tahoe home of his former gangster boss. That night, Bailey picks up his girlfriend dressed up in a trench coat and fedora—the noir detective's uniform—and invites her to take a ride. In a few quick opening strokes, the film has highlighted archetypal oppositions at the core of the American cultural imagination: small-town community versus rootless modernity, pastoral innocence versus urban ambiguity, the past versus the future. "You wanted to hear about my past," Bailey says, as he holds the door for her against a dark, portentous sky, "well, tonight's the night." (See fig. 7.)

In the car, a velvety chiaroscuro drapes them in their symbolic roles: the man veiled by his dark past and the wholesome girl next door with the redemptive light in her eyes. It is an organic framing for a pitch-perfect voice-over and flashback. Driving on a dark, isolated road, Jeff Bailey tells a story about a former self, Jeff *Markham*. He speaks of himself in the third person, "Now our friend Markham was living in New York," Bailey says, and the scene fades into the office of syndicate boss Whit Sterling (Kirk Douglas). Mitchum narrates an adventure without judgment or regret: he tells his innocent girlfriend about living on the lam, about deceiving his partner, about his paramour's murder of said partner. He tells her of their final separation and of his move to Nevada three years earlier.

Whit Sterling hires Markham to find his girlfriend: she stole forty grand and shot him four times, yet he wants her back. Mitchum follows the trail of Kathie Moffett (Jane Greer) to Acapulco and there falls in love with her like a death wish. They spend weeks having a torrid affair, as if Sterling's sword of Damocles was not hanging over their heads. "I don't know what we were waiting for," Mitchum confesses to his current girlfriend while driving. "Maybe we thought the world would end. Maybe we thought it was a dream and we'd wake up with a hangover in Niagara Falls." We are definitely in the postwar world now, driving on unstable ground between escapist fantasy and the larger unreality of Armageddon. *Maybe we thought the world would end.*

As a PI, the self-possessed Mitchum seems bored with the human race: even obvious lies do not ruffle his reptilian aplomb. One studio promotional photograph called Mitchum a "Cool Customer" as he listens to Kirk Douglas offer him the assignment that will ruin his life.[70] (See fig. 7.) "You just sit there within yourself and listen while I talk," Douglas says admiringly of Mitchum's half-dead slouch, "I like that." Mitchum responds offhandedly: "I never learned anything listen to myself talk." Even the femme fatale wonders about his otherworldly nonchalance: "You're a curious man. You never ask me any questions." And at the climactic moment when Jane Greer pleads, "Won't you believe me?" Mitchum responds with his most iconic line: "Baby, I don't care." Mitchum's persona projects a cooled, stoic inner life: he has made his choices and will take the consequences without rationalizing them.

As in *This Gun for Hire* and *High Sierra*, this is a trauma narrative, or rather, a post-traumatic one: Jeff Markham is a past self that Jeff Bailey cannot shake off; in effect, they are light and dark selves unintegrated into his present life. The addressable Other of noir cool remains the Woman, in this case, an ideal symbol of virtue—the only possible redemptive agent in a world without God. Bailey tells her everything, hoping to pay a small penalty for his transgressions and then to return to Bridgeport to marry her, cleansed of his past sins. For Jeff Markham / Bailey, the past ledger reveals the Depression-era city filled with its gangsters and guns,

Figure 7. "Mitchum was *cool* . . . . He had his own outlook on life and didn't let anyone interfere with it" (actor Harry Carey Jr., recalling working with Mitchum on *Pursued* [1949]).

shadows and artifice, erotic and esoteric temptations. Yet he imagines a future ledger full of bright sketches of small-town bliss, his own business, and a young family.

Markham's narration suggests he does not even understand his own actions; in effect, he must continue retelling the story in hopes of illumination. Noir is an existential genre in which characters attempt to understand themselves without recourse to conventional morality, family obligations, or social prestige. Noir films also often meditate on the limits of human understanding and free will. Why does Mitchum / Markham take a job he knows smells bad? *He doesn't know.* What was the couple waiting for in Acapulco? *He doesn't know.* Why does he believe Moffett when she's clearly lying? That even the audience knows: his dream has become flesh, and he hopes it will fill the existential void with love, lust, and meaning. After this twenty-minute voice-over and flashback, the rest of the action takes place in the present.

The voice-over is central to noir cool and it is useful to think of it as a secular confession. Unlike a religious confession—where the priest can forgive you—the voice-over is existential in that it is a self-inquiry with one question: can you forgive yourself for your actions? The voice-over represents a symbolic transition from traditional religious morality to living within the absurd—the concept that life has no plan or moral framework—and confessing simply to a lover or a lawyer. The confession is also a way to externalize an inner dialogue—it's self-therapy— such that an individual tries to make sense of his or her past actions. The confession is an internal meditation voiced for cinematic logic, a first step toward the construction of a new identity. It is no surprise that James M. Cain did the first rewrite of the screenplay for *Out of the Past*, as he was a master of literary noir's first-person confessional novels.

The voice-over in *Out of the Past* is both confession and promise: a man tells his backstory to his girlfriend then sends her back home to wait for him with a kiss for their future. This is film noir, so of course his plan immediately fails. On arrival at Sterling's palatial home, he finds Kathie Moffett (Jane Greer) back in the gangster's fold. She has signed an affidavit claiming that Mitchum murdered his partner (not her) and now Sterling orders him to steal a briefcase in San Francisco as penance for his past affair. Mitchum knows he is being set up and he does have a counterplan; yet his fate has been thrown back in with a femme fatale who has always managed to outsmart him.

If you're mired in "too much past," how can you build a wholesome future on incomprehensible choices? How can a man be worthy of a good girl when he's "too old and too beaten around the edges"? And how can this nostalgic dream of small-town satisfaction compare with "a streamlined femme fatale," a woman as sleek as a new car yet operating on her own impulses? *Out of the Past* both continues and transcends the framework of trauma and redemption of emergent noir. The film's only dream of the future is the past—the idyllic pastoral dream of Bridgeport, Nevada, lived out with a pure, wholesome girl at your side, an angel of nostalgic redemption. In contrast, Jane Greer plays Kathie Moffett as the devil of an unethical future, a woman willing to commit any crime to gain control of her own life and desires. Greer/Moffett double-crosses Mitchum/Bailey a few times, arranges for the death of Sterling's right-hand man, and then kills Sterling himself in cold blood.[71]

Many critics found the film difficult to follow due to its flashbacks and plot twists; "too much past" was, ironically, the catchphrase marketed for the film. Such levels of narrative complexity were still new to audiences more comfortable with good guys and bad girls. Bosley Crowther in the *New York Times* threw up his hands: "There have been double- and triple-crosses in many of these tough detective films . . . but the sum of deceitful complications that occur in *Out of the Past* must be reckoned by logarithmic tables." Mitchum's cool mask was as inscrutable as Greer's character motivation, yet Crowther enjoyed the "very sleek" Greer and the cool "nonchalance" of Mitchum, "magnificently cheeky and self-assured as the tangled 'private eye.'" Mitchum plays "a stone-faced ex-detective . . . [in] a colossal frame-up," noted another critic, who admired Jane Greer "in the role of a two-faced beauty whose capacity for deceiving men is utterly phenomenal." For contemporary philosopher Robert B. Pippin, the entire film concerns simply whether "one can ever get 'out of the past' and into a [new] future," a crucial question for post-war American audiences. For this inquiry, American audiences chose Mitchum as their "noir archetype"—that is, "a man [who] lives under a new name, trying not just to hide, but . . . to become this new person."[72]

In 1947, the suburban version of the American Dream had not yet arrived with its balloon mortgages and interstate highways. In 1947, World War II veterans were just starting in college on the GI bill or settling into new union contracts, while troubled vets still haunted the national imagination in films such as *The Best Years of Our Lives*. Within a decade, a new cultural dream of the future arrived and stabilized around the new suburban homestead with its groomed lawn and "populuxe" appliances, with its social dreams of space travel and winning the Cold War, with its accessible fever dreams of leisurely vacations in Vegas and family camping trips. And in 1947, Jack Kerouac began the road trips of which he asked in 1949, "Whither goest thou, America, in thy shiny car in the night?" Back to the past or into the future?

◆ ◆ ◆

With *Out of the Past*, film noir graduated to a more conscious and complex existential mode. The characters here are unknowable to themselves, they are slaves to desire and vice, they make irrational, improvisational choices. . . . *They are us.*

Once the streetwise, self-reliant detective is as much a victim of unconscious desires and social forces as any other *schnook*, we are in an existential situation lacking even the fantasy of the code hero's ethical rebellion. An exchange between Mitchum and Greer toward the end encapsulates the film's fatalism. "I never told you I was anything other than what I was," Kathie tells him (this is a bald-faced lie) but, rather, "you just wanted to imagine [it]," which was true enough. Greer then tells Mitchum her new plan: going back to Mexico, starting over, enjoying their lives as they had once planned. "And I have nothing to say about it?" Mitchum asks. Moffatt stares back, killer to ex-detective: "Don't you see you've only me to make deals with now?" She holds the cards and has her own dream of the past in her sights: to continue the best time of her life, their love affair in Mexico.

It is a striking moment and offers up this rare question of gender relations in film noir: What if the hard-boiled detective met a woman who was his equal? The woman is smart and thinks like a chess player: she can shoot a man standing in front of her without a moment's doubt; she has an equal understanding of artifice, detachment, cool, greed, power, and violence. As the studio sold her character, Jane Greer plays "an innocent-seeming lass who coolly kills several men," and she fights Mitchum to a draw with regard to violence. In the final scenes, Greer doesn't even appear as a sexual object: she is dressed in an oddly stylish nun's bonnet and plain clothes. "You're no good for anyone but me," Moffatt explains in the penultimate scene. "You're no good and neither am I. That's why we deserve each other." Markham agrees, knocks back a hit of bourbon, throws the shot glass into the fire, and while Greer packs, he secretly calls the cops.[73]

As they drive into the night to reenact their past in Mexico, Mitchum

Figure 8. Velvety blackness ensnares fallen detective and femme fatale in their final death drive.

sits in aggrieved silence at the wheel in a parallel scene to his earlier romantic confession. In the pitch darkness with the femme fatale, he sits at an ethical impasse, on a narrow road leading to a temporal nowhere. (See fig. 8.) His past has been emptied of gangsters and debts; his dream of the future lies behind him in Bridgeport. He calmly drives along in a somber existential present, having made a choice yet to be revealed to the audience. For philosopher Slavoj Žižek, Mitchum faces the void of existence itself—the absurd—at the moment Greer outlines her plan. He is nothing but a slave to his desires, he realizes, such that the illusion of free will dissolves. Mitchum's last thought is that he does not want to be beholden to this beautiful new gangster-boss of love.[74]

In an absurd situation, ex-detective Jeff Markham is faced with Camus's original existential question: Why not commit suicide? The unmoored, double-crossed detective chooses a suicide with a purpose, one that retains some personal dignity. When Mitchum called the police, he incriminated himself as a murderer along with Greer. The moment Greer sees the police barricades ahead she shoots pointedly down into Mitchum's groin, the center of his desire. The car crashes into a tree and they die in a half murder, half suicide. As characters, Markham and Moffett represent the death drive and the absurdity of existence during the peak years of film noir.

• • •

The femme fatale was already resonant enough within global popular culture for Simone de Beauvoir to offer an interpretation of "the bad woman" in *The Second Sex* (1949). To Beauvoir, the noir protagonist has an irrational and impossible desire to possess the bad woman's wildness without being captivated by it: "He imagines her as servant and sorceress at the same time."[75] What seems like heightened sexual desire quickly leads to crime and violent passion since it taps a primal desire to control all that is wild and chaotic in the human condition. This kind of passionate Dionysian desire, if given free reign or left unpunished, has the potential to subvert capitalist society and its workaday disciplines. If everyone acts on such desires, then the unspoken pact of work, nuclear family, community, nation, and the nine-to-five breaks down. So the femme fatale must embody temptation—wildness, freedom, and erotic power—and then be defeated. *Out of the Past* offers up the fantasy and then punishes everyone involved.

Out of the Past is the noir most often analyzed by contemporary philosophers as it features the coupling of Mitchum's existential cool with the genre's most complex femme fatale. For Žižek and Fredric Jameson, the film is symbolic of the larger felt powerlessness of any individual in the wake of the revelations of 1945 and under nuclear shadows. Due to this tension, the femme fatale is an agent of resistance that the hard-boiled detective cannot dominate; she comes to represent an encounter with the urge toward self-destruction. For Pippin, the film foreshadows the postmodern era, the destabilizing of modernist concepts such as the authentic self and rationality itself. For example, Jane Greer often implores Mitchum to realize her actions were predicated on self-preservation. She pleads with shiny pearls in her eyes, "I had to do it" or "they made me do it." When they first meet and become lovers, she pleads "won't you believe me?" then later, "don't you believe me?" and then "you *must* believe me." Each successive phrase is inflected toward the demands (and desires) of the moment and, in effect, to the revised *self* of that moment.[76]

By the end of the film we are out of the past of ideological naïveté and modernist authenticity as even our tough men and bad women have been unmasked. We are now fully centered in the postwar ambivalence of 1947. The audience has been stripped of its Depression-era past, small-town nostalgia, and the fantasy of an idyllic return to traditional morality. We are returned to the core existential question: how shall we proceed in the present?

Where would a new ethics of modernity come from? Or would Americans just get in their cars and escape when feeling haunted by purpose or meaning? Until the vision of the future arrived with the prosperity of the mid-1950s, the mask of cool functioned as a romantic ideal: facing the uncertain and absurd present with stylish stoicism and disillusioned engagement. In the 1980s, at a French film festival dedicated to literary noir and gangster films, Robert Mitchum was honored as a "*vrai* existentialist."[77] In retrospect, the late 1940s was a fertile half decade for existential treatises that theorized individual acts of rebellion. Every rebel writer was searching for a philosophical basis to invest the individual with an ethics of existential cool.

Figure 9. Everyone said he looked like Bogart: Albert Camus as the embodiment of existential cool (© Henri Cartier-Bresson/Magnum Photos).

3

Albert Camus and the Birth of Existential Cool from the Idea of Rebellion (and the Blues)

> Each generation doubtless feels called upon to reform the world. Mine knows that it will not reform it, but its task is perhaps even greater. It consists in preventing the world from destroying itself. Heir to a corrupt history, in which are mingled *fallen revolutions, technology gone mad, dead gods, and worn-out ideologies* . . . *this* generation . . . has had to re-establish . . . a little of that which constitutes the dignity of life and death.[1]
> Albert Camus, Nobel Prize Acceptance Speech, 1957

During a visit to the offices of *Vogue* for an interview in New York in 1946, Albert Camus was described by several women as "a young Bogart" — a comparison he heard often and always took as a compliment. In the late '50s, Camus drove a black Citroën on the Left Bank and often wore sharp gangster suits underneath a trench coat. When an admirer called his name, he just waved and kept going, a man "playing his own part in an unfinished movie," one French intellectual recalled. His French celebrity acquired star power as a result of this synergy. When Camus accepted the Nobel Prize in Stockholm in a rented tux, "everyone said . . . he looked like Bogart." He was so taken with the comparison that night — perhaps due to Bogart's recent death — that he had a similar tuxedo custom-made and always wore it to the opening nights of his plays until his own untimely death three years later. French-Algerian journalist Jean Daniel thought of Camus as "Humphrey Bogart young," only with "a more Japanese mask and a more expansive zest for life." His off-hand remark underscores the syncretism of a cross-cultural mask of cool.[2]

Even as a student, friends and classmates recalled Camus's *pudeur*, a French-Algerian colloquialism for reserve and restraint — in other words, his *cool*. His editors characterized him as a paradoxical mix of intensity and relaxation, the hallmark of cool in jazz and noir protagonists. *Pudeur* refers to a quiet, fierce pride and translates to being "unwilling to deliver one's secrets." Camus traced these qualities of "silence and reserve" to his family and its "Castilian pride." His first editor at Gallimard found Camus to be both "direct, penetrating, intensely attentive to you," and yet at the same time, "amused, malicious, full of an irony which was perhaps wicked." This relaxed intensity could be read even from his facial expression — "the half-smile slightly sad and ironical, the lowered eyes" — a fellow *Combat* editor recalled, and yet "the firmness of his expression" always also carried a "heart-rending and winning contrast." Camus's bearing held the tensions of a certain jaded confidence central to existential cool and akin to the ironic stoicism and existential affirmation inherent to Bogart's appeal. Camus even wore a rumpled raincoat in the 1940s, the sartorial uniform of film noir's private detective and a global symbol of midcentury American culture.[3]

Camus was a real-life Bogart figure of noir cool: a charismatic yet low-key intellectual force, he was a master of rhetoric, a freedom fighter, and a womanizer. Born poor in the French colonial outpost of Algeria and raised by a single mother to whom he remained devoted, Camus fought in the French resistance and presided as journalist, editor, and moral voice of the French underground paper, *Combat*, even while writing *The Stranger* (1942). As the anonymous writer of uplifting editorials in *Combat* that kept up morale in occupied Paris, Camus embodied the postwar cool associated with "the underground" as a literal and figurative idea of resistance.[4] After the liberation of Paris, Sartre introduced Camus as a resistance hero — as *the real deal*. Camus was the ethical rebel loner of existential cool.

Sartre also carried an image of American cool during the developmental stage of existentialism: Gary Cooper. Sartre was fascinated with the global influence of Hollywood films and "Cinema as Art" was one of his first public lectures in 1931. In 1939–40, he spent six months in uniform before war was declared, and it was one of the most productive intellectual periods of his life. Sartre mentions Cooper twice in *The War Diaries* (1939–40), journals in which he first worked out many of the principles of his breakthrough philosophical work, *Being and Nothingness* (1943). Gary Cooper was a proto-cool figure in the Hollywood typology: a tall, laconic, frontier figure of moral decency. American men were often imagined as "natural men" in France, more primitive and unconscious than Europeans, and so Cooper was Sartre's anti-type—an instinctual, tall, handsome American in contrast to him, a short, homely, angst-ridden French intellectual. Sartre dreamt of being such a man as Cooper, "handsome, hesitant, obscure, slow and upright in his thoughts," a man slow to anger but ethically confident.

> How I should have liked to boil with great, obscure rages. . . . My
> American worker (who resembled Gary Cooper) could do and feel
> that. I pictured him sitting on a railway embankment, tired and dusty;
> he'd be waiting for the cattle-truck, into which he'd jump unseen—and
> I should have liked to be him.

For Sartre, the Cooper figure was in some way programmed for ethical behavior, an unintellectual being lacking in "acquired grace" yet possessed of "a silent, spontaneous kind." Sartre and Beauvoir even created an imaginary character in their domestic life called "LittleHead-high," a Western frontier character who "thought little, spoke little, and always did the right thing." Here, Sartre's romanticized conflation of Native American and Marlboro Man calls attention to the power of the mythic stereotypes projected by the Hollywood Western. "I should have liked to be him," Sartre wrote of his idealized cool proletarian, Gary Cooper.[5]

Gary Cooper was, for Sartre, a visual analogue for the repression of suffering: the mask of cool. Sartre was already certain in 1939 that it was necessary to maintain a self-possessed front. In *The War Diaries*, he lays out the stoic ideal to which he held himself: "I would see myself at every moment . . . just as if I had passed a test, and was on my way back from bearing the most terrible pain without uttering a word." Sartre sounds like a Hemingway code hero here and he was influenced by the latter's sparse literary style and solitary protagonists. To carry existential cool is to be *self*-authorized through the capacity to suppress everyday suffering and to embrace one's past without judgment of its agents. To be "totally responsible for one's life" is to concede that fate is impersonal and implacable, that life owes you nothing. The world exists outside of you: the existential response is to create a personal morality to live within its subjective givens.[6]

Nor was Sartre alone in his admiration of Gary Cooper's cool. Italo Calvino idolized Cooper for his embodied sense of physical restraint. C. L. R. James advised a friend to pay close attention to the actor's controlled kinesthetic: "See how Cooper walks, the way he holds his body — watch him, watch him closely." A range of intellectuals supports the idea of an emergent *cool* masculine aesthetic in Depression-era America.[7]

Existential cool depends on self-mastery and the conscious rejection of obsolete moral frameworks and master narratives. An existential perspective begins with the rejection of determinism, whether through religion, nationalism, fate, race, or gender. A person must accept the limits of rational control and of a human life, since there will be neither reward nor punishment for one's actions. Existential cool assumes the necessity of self-consciousness and self-creation — that is, of taking responsibility for one's own identity and choices. By definition, existential cool begins with individual rebellion — or in Camus's pity phrase, "With rebellion, awareness is born." In addition, existentialists such as Camus, Sartre, Beauvoir, and Maurice Merleau-Ponty all rejected Cartesian mind-body dualism by opposing existential self-assertion to the absurdity of existence. If experience is subjective, there is neither objectivity nor an ideal rational mind; the brain is embodied, as is all consciousness. As Sartre wrote in *Being and Nothingness*, "how I live" is equivalent to "how I live my body." Camus wrote in a journal, "One tolerates oneself thanks to the body — to beauty. Then the body ages." Such is the human condition and its existential limits, or as Camus wrote in a later notebook, "The body, a true path to culture, teaches us where our limits lie." Existential philosophy invokes self-consciousness through embodied introspection as the locus of existence.[8]

Existential cool was an ultra-rational pose, a philosophical analogy to the noir anti-hero's cool mask, "the pride of [a solitary] consciousness facing the world" without sentiment. Both Camus's and Sartre's journals document a struggle to find a personalized masculine ethics. "We are free-to-suffer and free-not-to-suffer," Sartre wrote in a typical medita-tion. "We are responsible for the form and intensity of our sufferings. It's very easy to be distraught." In Sartrean terms, "cool" translates to authenticity and detachment as contained in what he called simply "a discreet attitude." Discretion paved the way to detachment and then "authenticity requires one to accept suffering, out of fidelity to oneself and . . . the world." This is the upshot of "The Wall" (1939), his short story about prisoners of war, in which only Sartre's alter ego (Pablo) remains stoic facing death; in contrast, one companion becomes hysterical and another commits suicide. Sartre admitted to being disgusted by those who displayed their pain. "I must confess, I have a kind of spontaneous irrational repugnance for people who complain when they are suffering. I wouldn't . . . do so for anything in the world." He repeated this disdain for emotional outpouring three times in a single passage and declared himself always "on the side of those who do not moan."[9]

In effect, existential cool was viable only for men and was often in-voked at the expense of women. Both Camus and Sartre defined mas-culinity in opposition to the lack of emotional self-control in women. Sartre reflected back on his twenties and early thirties as a time he felt it necessary "to keep oneself . . . free-for-his-destiny," and most of all this meant, "asserting this freedom against women." Camus once con-trasted the rich "inner life" he sought to a vacuous "home life"; he would never "succumb to" domesticity since "'bourgeois' happiness bores and terrifies me." If women were framed through family and domesticity as opposed to male identity and autonomy, a woman could not—by definition—be cool.[10]

Ironically, Simone de Beauvoir *was* cool: brilliant and charismatic, self-confident and self-possessed, sexualized and autonomous. As Sar-tre's partner and a woman of independent thought, will, and means, Beauvoir lived in defiance of traditional female roles while taking long-time artistic lovers from author Nelson Algren to documentarian Claude Lanzmann. When Beauvoir wrote in *The Second Sex* (1949) that "woman is Other to man," she drew on her experience with an A-list of existential-ist lovers guilty of ontological sexism (Sartre, Camus, Arthur Koestler). *The Second Sex* was the only seminal work of postwar feminism and its influence on American feminists can hardly be overestimated, from Betty Friedan to Adrienne Rich to Lorraine Hansberry. (See chapter 11.) Susan Fraiman's explicit feminist critique of cool masculinity honors Beauvoir in the title, *Cool Men and the Second Sex* (2003). Beauvoir's novels and memoirs earned every literary prize in France.

Befitting a cool woman, Beauvoir loved jazz and noir: she wrote perceptively about race and jazz in *America Day by Day*; her favorite noir was *The Third Man*. She confessed to a crush on Orson Welles as Harry Lime in that film (see chapter 5) and wrote to Algren of her hope to meet him in her travels. She referred to Robert Mitchum simply as "Mitchum," as if he was a noir brand. She perceived the elements of emergent noir in *The Grapes of Wrath* (1939): "I never saw such a 'tough' picture, in the good meaning of the word." One of her favorite noirs was *Dark Passage* (1946), featuring Bogart and Bacall—she saw it with Boris Vian—and she wrote excitedly to Algren of *The Big Clock* (1949), a first-rate noir written by his friend, Kenneth Fearing. Much more so than Sartre or Camus, Beauvoir was acutely attentive to rebellious artistic expression across media formats, whether in literature, film, or music.[11]

Before the term and concept was named, cool as an emotional mode of stylish stoicism was already part and parcel of modern global consciousness through Hollywood iconography. During a trip home to Oran in 1939, Camus noticed a shift in Algerian youth. Young people performed their modernity by adapting their style and bearing to film stars who represented the toughness and resilience soon to be associated with cool. Teenaged boys smoked, pulled down their felt hats, and clicked their steel-tipped heels to "sound their unshakeable self-confidence." These specific gestures echoed the gestures of '30s Hollywood gangsters, and Camus realized the youths had chosen to "imitate the style, the brashness, [and] the *superiority* of Mr. Clark Gable" (emphasis added). The women wore elaborate makeup and elegant skirts to refract a general nightclub glamor onto the streets. He learned that along the boulevard, the young men were nicknamed "the Clarques" (for Gable) and the women, "the Marlenes," after Dietrich. Camus's eye remained alert to such embodied rebellion a generation later in 1956, when in Paris, he observed "the little punks, dressed up like James Dean . . . their ring fingers arranging their genitals . . . wedged too tightly in their blue jeans."[12]

Camus published *The Rebel: The Study of Man in Revolt* at precisely the historical moment when cool—as word, concept, and cultural matrix—became a key global export of the American century. This is an important cross-cultural convergence. New cultural expression and concepts arise when a younger generation demands them. The first theories of individual rebellion inherent to the concept of cool arose across racial lines and national borders. In the postwar era, Camus's story spills out into a broader postwar French-American cultural exchange that includes Sartre and Beauvoir, Richard Wright and Ralph Ellison, Big Bill Broonzy and the blues.

Existential Cool

From the dire days of the Depression through the Nazi occupation of France, French existentialists drew on American culture for artistic renewal: from Hollywood films, from blues and jazz, and from the so-called American novel (literary noir). When Richard Wright moved to Paris in 1945, his ideas and presence became the source and symbol of race consciousness for Sartre and Beauvoir in developing new theories of race, gender, and anticolonialism. Sartre makes of Wright an exemplary case of an author writing for a "split public" as an outsider-insider able to write for blacks and yet also challenge the "tranquil certainty" of most white readers confident "that the world is white and that they own it." Beauvoir's travelogue of 1947 (*America Day by Day* [1952]) provided first drafts of theoretical concepts that recur in *The Second Sex*, with race as the guiding analogy to her application of "the Other" to women within patriarchy. Beauvoir built her framework "on comparisons not only with American blacks," Sarah Relyea observes, but on the "intellectuals who . . . found no way to challenge the Cold War." For Wright, in return, existentialist philosophy and fiction replaced Communism as his artistic and philosophical lodestar. In addition, the literature and music of African-Americans functioned as a parallel set of existential responses that helped delegitimize the Age of Europe and American triumphalism.[13]

Existentialist writers were the first to theorize the individual as a positive force of what I call *post-Christian imperfectibility*. They admitted the implosion of the West's "worn-out ideologies" as descended from Christianity and the Enlightenment. They confronted the hypocrisy of the ideals of Western Civilization—morality, perfectibility, progress, rationality, equality—and realized they were *white* mythologies. This became clear not only through the mass slaughters of the camps, gulags, and atomic bombs, but through the revelations of racism and colonialism. As Paul Gilroy has shown, Richard Wright's cultural production was crucial in destroying the vestiges of "social perfectibility and progress" as he illuminated "the history of black subordination" within modernity and invoked "the lives of Black Americans [as] emblematic of the struggles of exploited and oppressed human beings in general."[14] Existentialist writers emphasized self-creation outside of ethnic, national, or religious identities, and as a group, they included Chester Himes, James Baldwin, and Ralph Ellison. The only vector of protest left to explore after World War II was the individual.

The implicit challenge of life would be to give style and expression to one's mind and body as it carries one's experience in the public sphere. Such revaluing of limits, sensuality, rationalism, and personal style amounted to a new set of soundings for what John Dewey simply called "mind-body integration" in 1934, building on Henri Bergson and Nietzsche. To carry one's own "philosophical justification," Nietzsche wrote in *The Gay Science*, "*One thing is needful.* — To 'give style' to one's character—a great and rare art!" This utopian ideal of the self-conscious moral rebel was the core appeal of existential cool even if it is now easy to see the weakness in this intellectual formulation.[15]

It is reductive but useful to distill the revolution of existentialism to one word: "situatedness"—it is Beauvoir's term. Human beings needed to "abandon the dream of an inhuman objectivity," Beauvoir insisted, "[since] it is not a matter of being right in the eyes of a God, but of being right in his own eyes."[16] To be human is to be situated in a body and to understand one's experience subjectively, that is, through a person's unique mix of gender, class, ethnic, and cultural aspects. There is no objectivity within human relations, no abstract Truth or Soul, no universal truths. The apocalyptic plight of the postwar world was created by human beings who now needed to take responsibility for its current state and attempt to solve its problems without hoping for transcendence in heaven or the future.

Did an individual matter anymore—a single person's existence? The role of postwar cool was to recuperate the value of the individual in the face of failed collective ideologies, "fallen revolutions, [and] technology gone mad." Could individual purpose be reestablished in a cratered Europe where most people lived on subsistence wages and Communism revealed itself as a cover for totalitarian oppression? In the late 1940s, both Sartre and Beauvoir published philosophical treatises on individual rebellion in the face of the Cold War's polarization. The existential cool of Camus became the model for American rebels, due both to his personal experience and to his moral literary voice. His spare, lyrical, cool prose with its characteristic "laconic brevity" (Walker Percy's phrase) guided readers in a personal search for ethical renewal through secular, rational, activist humanism. This singular combination remains influential on contemporary writers, especially African-Americans.[17]

Yet existentialists *wrote* their new, radically autonomous selves into existence; what would be the analogous process for working-class people? These authors overestimated the time and effort everyday working people could submit to relentless intellectual introspection even for the goal of self-liberation. Nearly all existential exemplars were writers and artists as opposed to scientists or steelworkers. Yet Camus's writings in particular fueled the reformist dreams of a cohort of American rebels in the 1960s, from Bob Moses to Betty Friedan to Tom Hayden. If the function of existential writing was to develop a rebellious inner consciousness focused on social and cultural change, it must be judged successful across race, class, gender, and nation for the following generation.

A Philosophy for *The Rebel*

Existential cool found its philosophical basis in *The Rebel* (1951), the first full-length historical study of individual rebellion. Camus was the perfect figure to theorize a mobile identity for the social rebel: he was unmoored from home, family, and nation. An "internal exile" in France, Camus feared losing touch with his homeland and held tight to his working-class identity—quite unlike Sartre, who was a French intellectual to the manner born, a brilliant student from the École Normale Supérieure. Tony Judt called Camus a "rudderless intellectual" from the frontier of Western colonialism (Algeria), and so it fell on Camus to create a framework of moral action: he was a political outlaw come to the center of empire from its periphery. An exile cannot rely on traditional forms of identity such as family, nation, or religion, and as such, self-invention is inherently necessary.[18]

In *The Rebel*, Camus theorized the act of individual rebellion as ground zero of existential being, as the seminal act of identity itself. This is the first declaration in Western philosophy that to rebel is a fundamental element of human behavior and a moral imperative. He meant it for white European men, of course, but his main claim remains radical. Camus first separated resentment from rebellion by delineating private gripes from public acts. To proceed from a feeling of *resentment* was selfish—gratuitous, emotional, and whiny—while he theorized individual *rebellion* as a public act kinetic with generative potential. "What is a rebel? A man who says no, but whose refusal does not imply a renunciation." Camus theorizes rebellion as a positive resistance—what Sartre might call a "positive negation"—and it is an oxymoron key to understanding existentialism. To Camus, the rebel is "always fighting for the integrity of one part of his being" against social forces over which he has no control.[19]

More importantly, Camus declares an interactive idea of subjective rebellion: "*I* rebel—therefore *we* exist." In other words, *my* rebellion creates the conditions for *yours*: therein lies the *cultural* politics of cool. Camus suggests that any authentic individual rebellion contains ethical and moral substance, even if it is (at first) unconscious or inchoate. In the arts, we have seen how this example worked with Humphrey Bogart and Lester Young. In more political terms, revolutionary potential emerges when an individual defies authority and in doing so realizes there is a limit to the oppression or persecution he or she is willing to sustain. This action often entails an implicit or explicit threat of violence: it is a concrete action equivalent to crossing a line in the sand.[20]

Camus's abstract figure of enacted rebellion is "the slave" who refuses a command, throwing off the master's unquestioned authority and standing up to physical force. "The rebel slave affirms that . . . [he] will not tolerate the manner in which his master treats him." Camus here invokes the abstract philosophical figure of the slave derived from Hegel and he makes no attempt to connect it to historical realities, for example, the nascent political liberation movements among colonial African nations or the then-global impact of the former slaves in the United States. Yet there is a correspondence between Camus's dialogic model of intersubjective action and the call-and-response of African-American blues, jazz, and swing, the dominant global musical forms of the postwar era. Both models displace the Cartesian foundation of being and thought to being and action. Each active mode features an improvisational model of rebel agent and responsive audience. ("*I* rebel—therefore *we* exist.") The blues is itself a genre that presumes the "I" of a given song creates a "we" with a live audience, thus creating a temporary community and providing cultural materials for self-consciousness.[21]

Existential cool was a metaphysical rebellion centered on rejuvenating the individual through a personal ethics. In this way, it was a philosophical analogy to the private code of the noir hero or the jazz musician's creation of a personal sound. When Camus writes that "the metaphysical rebel protests against the condition in which he finds himself as a man," his figure of the rebel translates as a secular version of the soul. To substitute soul in the above sentence, it reads: "The soul protests against the condition in which it finds itself." Here is a soul frustrated by the earthly world, but without a God to run to: "The metaphysical rebel declares that he is frustrated by the universe." Either the rebel must then embark on a path of self-consciousness through social justice and rational action or be resigned to nihilism. "To experience freedom is, above all, to rebel," Camus wrote in a 1939 book review, even before the Nazi occupation of Paris.[22]

There is an important personal context as well. Camus considered his literary works to be acts of rebellion meant to empower the poor, voiceless people who raised him—his mother and extended family, the communities of French *pied noirs* and Arabs in Algeria. Camus was ashamed of neither his roots nor his uneducated background. Poverty was not "a misfortune," he wrote, since in North Africa, "the sun and the sea cost nothing." He was influenced in this attitude by a now-obscure novel by André de Richaud, *La douleur* (1930). He realized that his own reserve—his *cool*—was a defense mechanism masking inarticulate rage. This reservoir of repressed rage could be transmuted into artistic engagement. "My obstinate silences," he recalled, "this vague but all-pervasive suffering . . . my family and their poverty, my secrets, all this, I realized, could be expressed!" Camus felt liberated by literature and believed his texts were "revolts for everyone, so that every life might be lifted into that light." Yet at the center of his body of work, Camus always admitted, was "the admirable silence of a mother and one man's effort to rediscover a justice or a love to match [it]." This autobiographical context is crucial for understanding Camus's oeuvre.[23]

With *The Rebel*, Camus tried to rescue the history of European oppression through a narrative history of individual acts of political rebellion beginning with the Enlightenment and the French Revolution. Instead of an identity based in empire and conquest, Camus created a counternarrative in which "rebellion is the history of European pride." *The Rebel* traces the process for exploding ingrained ideologies and it is a history of discounting the claims of powerful elites — denying the idea of divine right to monarchs, repudiating aristocratic frameworks of privilege and breeding, revealing the hypocrisy of virtue as a mask for brute political power. There is the revolution of reason and science against the dogma of organized religion; the rise of political consciousness against monarchy; and then the testing of limits against defrocked moralities, from Danton and Sade to Marx and Lenin. The narrative arc of *The Rebel* sidesteps to account for the legacy of the early Socialists (Saint-Simon, Fourier) then registers the advent of Hegel's historical utopianism and Marx's "scientific messianism." In the middle passage between theory and practice in Marxism (1848–1917), Camus offers profiles of key anarchists and nihilists, traces the emergence of trade-union socialism, and then narrates the ramp-up to the Bolshevik revolution. There is also a concluding chapter on the role of literature and art in building revolutionary consciousness (e.g., the surrealists, modernist authors).[24]

For Camus, Dostoyevsky was the prophetic figure of this transition as well as his authorial model of philosophical inquiry. The character of Ivan Karamazov marks the shift from nineteenth-century romantic rebellion to an objective of social justice. "With Ivan, the tone changes," Camus reflected, and "God, in His turn, is put on trial." Early nineteenth-century romantic rebels were nationalists and nature worshippers, communalists and transcendentalists. They sought a fusion with cosmic forces, whether of nature, God, or humankind — for example, the Herderian folk or Emerson's Oversoul. Ivan refuses the salvation of the Church in *The Brothers Karamazov* and chooses a nihilistic hedonism, drawing a line in the sand against moral and political authority. For Camus, Ivan's inchoate defiance is "the essential undertaking of rebellion . . . replacing the reign of grace by the reign of justice."[25]

Camus's metaphysical rebel is Ivan Karamazov's heir, one who now must focus on the possibility of achieving social justice without God. Unlike Dostoyevsky, Camus did not allow himself the respite of spiritual grace but instead replaced it with a quasi-sacred ideal of social justice. "When the throne of God is overturned, the rebel realizes that it is now his own responsibility to create the justice, order, and unity . . . within his own condition." This is a distilled version of Camus's brand of existentialism. As Ray Davison sums up Camus's literary project, "His dominant aim is to create a new race of men and a new [kind of] Christ figure."[26] Camus always tried to hold the line against Ivan's nihilism, as when the latter famously declares: "Everything is permitted" (often quoted as "If God is dead, then everything is permitted"). The inevitable drift toward nihilism haunted Camus's plays (*Caligula* and *The Possessed*) and his novels (*The Stranger* and *The Fall*) just as secular sainthood lay at the opposite pole of his fiction (*The Plague*, *The First Man*).

Sartre and Beauvoir also felt compelled to theorize the relevance and potential of individual rebellion in the late 1940s. Sartre's abstract figure of rebellion was a working-class white male who realizes he must "demand the liberation of all his class." Sartre's angry young man could only acquire political consciousness as directed by intellectuals; without such shaping, he will often choose a racial scapegoat to retain his white privilege and superiority. What this figure needed was "a theory of violence as a riposte to oppression," along the lines Sartre first mapped out in *Anti-Semite and Jew*, his earliest treatise of anti-racism. Anti-Semitism was simply "a poor man's snobbery," Sartre wrote in a deft analysis of racism as the underpinning of fascism and populism. To create revolutionary consciousness in such a young man, "his oppression [must] be explained to him," and intellectuals needed to provide a buffer against both working-class male violence and strict party-line obedience.[27]

In Sartre's extended essay on the subject, "The Philosophy of Revolution" (1948), he contrasted the figure of "the revolutionary" to a superficial rebel. A rebel "stands alone" in false consciousness with "an anarchistic, individualist freedom," whereas the revolutionary attaches himself to a historical movement and works "for the liberation for [of] the oppressed class." For Sartre, authentic feelings of rebellion must lead to political action through Marxist revolution. Sartre equated freedom with socialist revolution such that individual rebellion was *only* valid as a "revolutionary act" leading to Communism. For Sartre, revolution had to supplant egoism; for Camus, inchoate political rebellion had to displace resentment.[28]

Beauvoir carved out some middle ground between Camus's rebel and Sartre's revolutionary in her key philosophical treatise, *The Ethics of Ambiguity* (1947). As with Camus's rebel, an individual first had to wrest an existential freedom for him- or herself apart from political ends and ideological transcendence. "To *will* oneself free," Beauvoir writes, "is to effect the transition from nature to morality by establishing a genuine freedom on the original upsurge of our existence." This key phrase—"the original upsurge of our existence"—both riffs on Sartre's "existence before essence" and establishes a keynote of existential freedom that owes as much to Freud as Marx. First, one must strip down social and cultural conditioning to find subjective *being* (the "original" upsurge); second, a person must self-authorize his or her own existence through constant introspection. "No behavior is ever authorized to begin with," Beauvoir declares and so "*existentialist ethics* is the rejection of all the previous justifications which might be drawn from the civilization, the age, and the culture; it is the rejection of every principle of authority" (emphasis added). By definition then, individual rebellion requires the rejection of authority. But then what? And with whom? And for what reasons? Beauvoir left this question open-ended, while Sartre only pointed to the potential of global Marxist revolution led by the USSR.[29]

Why was there so much philosophical attention to individual rebellion in the postwar era as the active essence of a new consciousness? In France, the revelation of the gulags and the Nazi-Soviet pact had compromised the dream of Communism, while American materialism, racism, and self-righteous imperialism offered little vision of social democracy. For Camus, the Scylla and Charybdis of postwar values were Marxism and Christianity. He envisioned only a partial victory, "the acceptance of a relative utopia that leaves some chance of human action" since this was "the only real possibility." Sartre was more dogmatic and dualistic: he called on youth to "choose between materialism and idealism . . . there is no third way." Materialism meant U.S. dominance while idealism was associated with the Soviet Union. In effect, this meant casting one's vision with the USSR and hoping to reign in its excesses. Beauvoir worked through these debates as a novelist in *The Mandarins* (1954), a roman à clef in which Sartre, Camus, Arthur Koestler, and herself (among others) confront an ideological crisis after learning of the existence of the Russian gulags.[30]

All of this focus on the individual rebel attests to the felt political impotence of intellectuals in the face of a Cold War standoff and the brute fact of nuclear weapons. "The new era . . . now opening had never been foreseen in books," Henri Perron reflects in *The Mandarins*. "What . . . was the good of a solid political background when weighed against the brute face of atomic energy?"[31] The existentialist writers were all tormented by their irrelevance, especially after their failed attempt to organize a nonaligned socialist-democratic party in the late 1940s—the Rassemblement Democratique Revolutionnaire (RDR)—with allies such as Wright, Koestler, and Merleau-Ponty. Beauvoir wrote to Nelson Algren of her dashed hopes after this movement of Leftist writers (the RDR) had attempted "something important, really in a revolutionary mind, really on the left wing, against communism, but now it does not hope much [*sic*]. . . . We see nothing to do in politics, in fact. . . . Everybody feels it. This is why everybody is so sad . . . young men in France now . . . drink too much, do silly things, not knowing what to do."[32] The existential question on the table concerned powerlessness: what would replace God, law, or nationalism as an order of ethics, morality, or social justice?

Take the example of *The God That Failed* (1949), the best-selling Cold War anthology in which the "god" of the title referred to Communism. In this compendium, seven former Communist partisans recalled and recanted their allegiances to party-line collective despotism. Of the seven, Wright, Koestler, and André Gide were integral to the world of Paris intellectuals; in many ways, their public confessions signaled the failure of left-wing ideologies, the irrelevance of Christianity, and the moribund myth of Enlightenment progress. In effect, the seven sections point to the individual writer as the only remaining agent of political change. "[I] should never again express such passionate hope," Wright concluded about politics and revolution, but instead, "I would hurl words into this darkness and wait for an echo."[33]

The famous break between Sartre and Camus was actually due to their philosophical argument over rebellion—in fact, it was over *The Rebel*. In 1951, Sartre commissioned a review of *The Rebel* in his journal, *Les Temps Modernes*. The review was a comprehensive attack on Camus as an intellectual, a philosopher, and a political agent. It was both a political act and a hatchet job, although not simply an act of personal vengeance: Sartre truly thought *The Rebel* was a puerile work of philosophy. Yet Camus's work was more a hybrid of philosophy, sociology, and political history, and he once described it as his intellectual autobiography. Camus told a friend late in life that *The Rebel* "was the one [book] he held most dear," the work that best held out a positive sense of rebellion "for [those of] us who are wrestling with nihilism."[34]

Sartre's loyalty to the Soviet Union as the saving grace of a socialist future tainted his philosophy of revolution and his influence among postwar American readers. Sartre's current legacy concerning existential rebellion derives more from his original theories of racism and postcolonialism, as well as his relationships with Frantz Fanon, the Négritude poets, and Marxist revolutionaries in France's former colonies.[35] His salient contribution to theorizing rebellion lay in encouraging individual rebels to create counternarratives and counterhistories. Winners may write history but revolutionaries create practices that "destroy the very notion of [traditional] right, which they see as a product of custom and force." Sartre defended the Communist party and the Soviet Union as late as the late 1970s, three decades after Camus had already thrown state Communism onto the pile of historical oppressors requiring overthrow by all rebels.

Camus never forgot the lesson of Dostoyevsky's critique of Communism—that society was unlikely to be sustained through utopian ideals of working-class solidarity or an equitable distribution of wealth. With impressive prescience, Dostoyevsky imagined the rise of a nihilistic totalitarianism from Marxism in *The Possessed* through the character of Stavrogin, a dandy and anarchist revolutionary who is something of a proto-punk anarchist. Camus was obsessed with the character of Stavrogin: he quotes him as early as *The Myth of Sisyphus* and worked throughout the 1950s to adapt *The Possessed* for the stage. To Camus, Stavrogin was a metaphysical rebel frustrated by his own nihilism yet unable to find any rational belief system. His play revolved around the central question of his personal philosophical search, as first raised in *The Plague*, itself an allegory of the Nazi occupation: "Is it possible to become a saint without believing in God? That is the sole concrete problem worth considering nowadays."[36] Camus's Stavrogin is a figure of nihilistic coldness rather than of existential cool: his aggressive indifference hides an antipathy for both God and the secular god of revolution that failed. Stavrogin stands as Camus's last literary figuration of a character holding out for an individual ethics against both a complacent bourgeois society and a corrupt state. The acclaimed Paris production of *The Possessed* in 1959 was Camus's last artistic act before his untimely death in an auto accident.

As Camus distilled it, rebellion is "the secular will not to surrender" — to an oppressive society, to a degrading existence, or to social approval. If we insert the word "individual" here, we get a four-word phrase that distills Camus's existential project: the secular individual will. The question of a post-Western ethics is implicit: What sustains and validates an individual's will to existence or meaning if there is no agreed-on morality guided by religion or God, no allegiance to nation or legal code? In retrospect, Camus's theory of the individual rebel as a catalyst of social change has worn well as an example of "the power of the powerless," to use Vaclav Havel's resonant phrase. Camus's novels and essays retain their power as literary texts and inspirational works of meditative philosophy. And it is significant that his works and theories have been taken up, in particular, by African-Americans.[37]

Interlude: Race and The Rebel

> Albert Camus once said that *racism is absurd*. Racism introduces absurdity into the human condition. Not only does racism express the absurdity of the racists, but it generates absurdity in the victims. And the absurdity of the victims intensifies the absurdity of the racists, ad infinitum. If one lives in a country where racism is held valid and practiced in all ways of life, eventually, no matter whether one is a racist or a victim, one comes to feel the absurdity of life.
>
> Chester Himes, *My Life of Absurdity*[38]

Camus's work has enjoyed a new currency in the past generation both for his life of witnessing and his quest for a moral path of individual integrity through rebellion. His work has been valorized across several fields, from social historian Tony Judt to trauma theorist Dori Laub to sociologist Orlando Patterson. For Judt, the author of the comprehensive history *Postwar* (2005), Camus was "a reluctant moralist," the only intellectual who had "the courage to make the elementary points" of a new humanism during the "age of gas ovens and concentration camps." His theory of rebellion has proven adaptable even to groups then absent from his analysis. Elizabeth Ann Bartlett applied Camus's theories to her concept of "rebellious feminism," a pragmatic political philosophy for women, "a workable ethic" as well as a "guide, a way to act . . . a way to live decently in the world." During his postwar exile in Paris, Chester Himes pointed out that race and racism are constituted within the absurdity of black existence, something philosophers such as Charles Mills have only recently theorized. Novelist Charles Johnson points to Camus as a model for the philosophical novel. In Danzy Senna's novel *Caucasia*, a black scholar traces his existential angst to the social construction of race, a lie of white Western culture that ingrains "existential angst" into every black life on the order of "the myth of fucking Sisyphus." As Darryl Pinckney recently put it, "Race is an unasked-for existentialism."[39]

Orlando Patterson, the most influential scholar of race of the past two generations, calls *The Rebel* both "an immensely moral work" and "a great philosophical work." Patterson translates Camus's central aphorism into African-American terms: instead of "I am—therefore we exist," he substitutes "I rebel morally—therefore *our humanity* exists." By "our humanity," Patterson means the equality of African-Americans achieved, first, through moral rebellion and, second, through that recognition, "*all of* our humanity." His meaning is simple: Western culture has always reserved the concept of equality for white Europeans and any renewed sense of a global humanity ("our humanity") must start from an individual demand for social equality. Camus's influence on Patterson, a Jamaican-American, is fundamental. It dates back to his first novel, *The Children of Sisyphus* (1964), in which three workers push garbage carts around a slum—their metaphorical boulders—and discuss the absurdity of their oppressed lives due to imposed racial definitions. It continues up through his magisterial studies on *Freedom in the Making of Western Culture*, in which Patterson illuminates the symbiotic relationship of freedom and slavery, an insight dependent (in part) on Camus's theorization of existential freedom.[40]

Patterson delineated two intertwined elements of "existential rebellion" in *The Rebel* as applied to African-Americans. There is a negative aspect—the affirmative negation—in an individual's "refusal to make peace with" the status quo. Yet such repudiation has to avoid the slippery slope to nihilism and generate positive social change through moral autonomy. Patterson calls this "creative defiance" at the level of the individual—the inner drive to transform both "the physical world as well as man's inner world." Once defiant, an individual is unfit for the status quo, "unable to make its peace with *that which is* for the sake of that which *ought to be*." With self-awareness comes the realization of social justice for all, a transformation for which a person stands "ready to defy the forces of man, of nature, of history—yes, even of God—in order to reach out for . . . the realization of hope and ideal." Patterson believes African-Americans have succeeded at the first stage of existential rebellion as a group—refusing to make peace with the absurdity of a hypocritical racist society—but not yet at the level of moral autonomy.[41]

Patterson then critiques Camus by pointing to a key precedent for his abstract figure of the slave: Frederick Douglass. Just before being broken in mind and spirit by the slave driver Covey, Douglass famously turned to fight his oppressor and wrestled him to a draw. The dawning of his physical equality leads directly to Douglass's famous affirmation of existential manhood: "You have seen how a man was made a slave; [now] you shall see how a slave was made a man." Patterson draws the obvious connection from Douglass to the line in the sand of *The Rebel* while Lewis Gordon has anointed Douglass the first black existentialist in his study *Existentia Africana*. As Patterson observes, "Camus uses the rebel slave as a paradigm of the existential rebel . . . a slave who has conformed all his life suddenly says 'no.'" For Patterson, the slave refuses "[for] no other reason than . . . [that] sooner or later an inherent sense of dignity demands to be released," and, by way of example, he offered that "Frederick Douglass's account [is] the classic real-life instance."[42]

Patterson implied that individual African-American acts of rebellion have already helped create the conditions for imagining "our [global] humanity" outside of white, Western frameworks. There are obvious moral and aesthetic exemplars—Muhammad Ali, Martin Luther King Jr., Angela Davis—as well as Richard Wright's influence on Beauvoir's *The Second Sex*. There are the repercussions of the civil rights movements on all social movements of the 1960s: Betty Friedan wrote *The Feminine Mystique* spurred by the civil rights movement, while the Mexican-

American civil rights movement (La Raza) and the American Indian Movement (AIM) followed closely on the African-American pursuit of equality through a mix of protest and legal struggle. In addition, the global artistic influence of jazz, soul, funk, and hip-hop have provided the cultural platforms to give voice to oppressed peoples around the world, from reggae (Bob Marley, inspired by New Orleans rhythm and blues) to Afrobeat (Fela Kuti, inspired by James Brown) to South African township music.

For Camus, rebellion was a European act by definition—due to the Western emphasis on the individual—yet here is Frederick Douglass providing a textbook declaration of existential freedom in a letter to William Lloyd Garrison in 1853:

> I have no end to serve, no creed to uphold, no government to defend; and as to nation, I belong to none. I have not protection at home, or resting-place abroad. . . . I am an outcast from the society of my childhood [that of slaves], and an outlaw in the land of my birth.[43]

Ironically, like Camus, Douglass was a journalist, publisher, editor, and freedom fighter. The omission of Douglass from *The Rebel* points up the invisibility of African-Americans—and race more broadly—within postwar existential discourse as does the absence of his fellow Parisian, Richard Wright. Frederick Douglass's existentialism echoes forward a century to Wright's postwar declaration: "I have no religion in the formal sense of the word. I have no race except that which is forced upon me. I have no country except that which I'm obliged to belong. I have no traditions. I'm free. I have only the future."[44]

Richard Wright's Existential Blues in Paris, 1945–50

In 1945, Richard Wright analyzed the resistance of African-American men in an eerie correspondence to existential theories in France. Chicago's black men were partially liberated by the Great Migration out of the U.S. South, and he wrote of their attitude in an unpublished journal entry: "We are like white men in that there is a limit to what we'll take; a limit when we'll say that we've had enough; that life is not worth it under certain conditions." He hoped to map out a theory of consciousness for the oppressed to combat the liberal paternalism of Gunnar Myrdal's *An American Dilemma*. He wrote up a proposal for an anthology by African-American writers to illuminate the "inner personality, the subjective landscape of the Negro."[45]

Wright was a member of the Communist Party for seven years and a staunch believer in intellectual rigor, Marxist ideology, and revolutionary class consciousness. Marxism had freed Wright from a racial identity invested in a narrative of oppression and victimization; without its ideological frameworks, his fiction lacked philosophical intent. Ralph Ellison recalled Wright's confession to him of the time: "Really, Ralph, after I broke with the Communist Party [in 1942] I had nowhere else to go." Nor could he carry off his literary synthesis of Communism, naturalism, and sociology. Wright turned to theorizing the role of the individual for social change and he wondered, "What was the danger in showing the kinship between the sufferings of the Negro and the sufferings of other people?" He had always believed that psychological detachment was a form of individual progress; he now focused on theorizing a path to existential freedom *through* racial consciousness rather than through class solidarity. During this transition, Wright invoked "cool" in a way that documents its early usage among African-Americans. When a party operative called him "a fool" for leaving the party, Wright felt anger well up within him and then thought to himself, "*Keep cool . . . Don't let this get out of hand.*"[46]

This transitional moment is preserved in Wright's novella, *The Man Who Lived Underground* (1944), an existentialist literary noir. An African-American man is framed for a crime he did not commit but he cannot prove his innocence. He escapes into the sewers from where he occasionally emerges to watch people, but cannot free himself. For Wright, the novella was a productive failure at best, an initial attempt "to invent a new order of language, of concepts to use." The work left him in a state of anguish due to grappling with an inchoate personal philosophy outside of his now-discarded frameworks.

In a key journal entry, Wright expressed his frustration in a one-sentence existential manifesto: "What I must do is find a new language for the way I see life, *a language which is immediately understandable by everybody*, but yet which says *what I feel and I alone feel*. God, what a task."[47] How can a writer create a sense of subjective rebellion that is universal in application? What "order of language" will serve such a task? This reflection mirrors similar statements made by Camus right up to the religious irony of the exclamation, "God, what a task."

The upshot of Wright's epiphany reflects his belief—and that of his friend, Chester Himes—that a black man lived an existential life in practice due to the absurd framework of race. C. L. R. James once visited Wright's home in France and he was impressed to see an entire shelf of Kierkegaard's works. Wright pointed to them and said: "You see those books[?] . . . Everything that he writes in those books I knew before I had them."[48] Yet it was only after moving to Paris that he made the connection between his experiential existentialism and its philosophical frameworks. Wright was galvanized by reading Sartre and Beauvoir in the waning months of World War II and realized "that existentialism was all about him[self]." He wrote with excitement to Gertrude Stein, "Nothing like it [their writings] exists anywhere on earth today. . . . New York was buzzing over existentialism." Wright traveled back and forth to Paris for two years then moved there permanently in 1946 with his wife and daughter. There he universalized his search for rebellion, wondering in a journal what kind of larger rebellion was relevant to the postwar era, "when guns and gas and atoms stand ready to disintegrate the world and the people on it."[49]

After moving to Paris, Wright and his wife Ellen became good friends of the first existential couple. After a few social visits, Wright wrote in a journal entry from 1947 of their shared intellectual perspective: "Sartre is quite of my opinion regarding the possibility of action today, that it is up to the individual to do what he can to uphold the concept of what it means to be human. The great danger in the world today . . . is that the very feeling and conception of what is a human being might well be lost. He agreed. I feel very close to Sartre and Simone de Beauvoir." One midsummer morning, Wright read a thematic issue of *Les Temps Modernes* on freedom featuring articles by Sartre, Beauvoir, and Camus. "How those French boys and girls think and write," he wrote in his journal. "How keenly they feel the human plight."[50] Sartre returned the favor when the journal published an excerpt of *Black Boy* in 1947. Beauvoir told him the excerpt was "a great success" and that "there were very good reviews in the newspaper." In the same letter, she thanked him for being her guide in the United States: "It was owing to you I felt at home in New York."[51]

When Wright read *The Stranger* that year, it rejuvenated his fiction. He read it slowly, "weighing each sentence," admiring Camus's prose, narrative style, and characterization, and how he infused fiction with "a philosophical point of view." A year later, Wright published his only overtly existential novel, *The Outsider* (1948), a title that carried a double-edged tribute: it is an allusion to Camus's *The Stranger* (the better translation of which is "The Outsider") and to the protagonist, Cross Damon, a racial outsider. Early in the novel, Cross Damon wishes to break free of his life and find a community of fellow rebels, just as Wright had in Paris: "Were there not somewhere in the world rebels with whom he could feel at home, men who were outsiders not because they were born black and poor, but because they had thought their way through the many veils of illusion? But where were they? How could one find them?" Wright lived among such rebels in Paris and never returned to the United States to live. Yet the discourse of this intellectual cohort did not change his evaluation of humanity or global politics.[52] "I have no panacea to offer," he wrote as part of his author biography for a publisher in 1953. He continued: "Rejecting Communism, I have embraced neither fascism, nor Socialism, nor Catholicism, nor Nihilism, nor God, nor the so-called cause (whatever it is!) of the Western World. My consciousness is in[stead] filled with awe and pity at the confounding spectacle of a global Cold War that is rapidly sapping the lingering vestiges of man's humanity."[53] Wright soon found new ideological motivation by documenting the rising independence movement in Ghana (then the Gold Coast). This was the last political movement to inspire him with hope, and he captured the rising racial, anticolonialist consciousness in *White Man, Listen!* (1957).

Wright encountered existentialism at a fortuitous moment, when he, too, was trying to create through literature a model of ethical individuality. Yet all theories of individuality were written by and for white, Western philosophers and intellectuals that figured the black man as Other. So Wright's interest in the self as a detached mode of being necessarily involved additional obstacles of recognition and subjectivity. By 1953, after six years in Paris, he saw himself as a black man *within* Western cul-

ture and his objective was to inscribe his experience into Western consciousness. "The break from the U.S. was . . . with my former attitudes
as a Negro and a Communist," he reflected back on his move to Paris.
"I was [now] trying to grapple with the big problem—the problem and
meaning of Western civilization as a whole and the relation of Negroes
and other minority groups to it."[54] Wright's existentialism illuminates a
postwar matrix of race, feminism, existentialism, and cultural politics in
Paris that prefigured the civil rights, women's, and student movements
of the '60s.

◆ ◆ ◆

Wright's friend Ralph Ellison believed his one-time mentor had traded
in his African-American cultural birthright for some high-concept intellectual porridge in Paris. Ellison criticized Wright's existential fiction
(such as *The Outsider*) for having lost connection with the working-class
existentialism of the blues and the resources of African-American culture
more broadly. Yet the early bond of these two authors in part touched on
the need for cool among African-American writers.

In 1941, a then-unpublished Ellison wrote a revealing, vulnerable letter to Wright about his mask of cool, an homage to the senior author's
work. He kept his bitter feelings "underground" and out of his writing—
otherwise his rage against white oppression might tear him apart. These
feelings were "caged by rigid discipline" to enable him to think and write
with clarity.

> I have learned to keep the bitterness submerged so that my vision
> might be kept clear. . . . I know those emotions which tear at the in-
> sides to be free and memories which must be kept *underground*, caged
> by rigid discipline lest they destroy. . . . Usually we Negroes refuse to
> talk of these things.

Ellison's method of "staying cool" was to suppress destabilizing memories and emotions. Wright's earliest works signaled nothing less, for
Ellison, than "the emergence of the American Negro as a Western individual" in *Uncle Tom's Children* (1938) and *12 Million Black Voices* (1941).
These two works provided a corrective of individual consciousness to
the survivor mentality of racial solidarity. "You write of the numbness

which our experience has [often] produced," he wrote to Wright, admitting he could only mete out his ideas by a slow "thawing" of emotion.[55]

As with jazz musicians, this flat emotional affect of cool presumed an artistic relationship with a broader racial community. Ellison allowed his feelings to escape only "drop by drop through the trap doors of the things I write," or else he might personally "lose control." Then he would be just one more African-American man stereotyped as angry or emotional in a culture that valued self-control and rational analysis. As he eloquently put it at twenty-eight: "I have had to rigidly control my thawing, allowing the liquid emotion to escape drop by drop through the trap doors of the things I write, lest I lose control; lest I be rendered incapable of warming our frozen brothers."[56]

Yet a decade later Ellison believed Wright had lost himself, his art, and his culture by casting his lot with the alien philosophy of existentialism. In an exchange of letters with his intellectual comrade, Albert Murray, both men maintained that Wright failed to understand the existential irony of African-American music and ritual—in particular, of the blues. "Wright goes to France for existentialism when [any] Mose, or any blues, could tell him things that would make that cock-eyed Sartre's head swim," Ellison wrote in 1953. "Mose" was then a slang term for a black everyman, and Ellison shared the belief that racial exclusion had produced an organic existential response. Murray responded to Ellison with equal frustration: "So now he's hep to Camus' *The Stranger* [. . . ?] That was the very first thing I said to myself." Murray then indicted Wright's work in exile with some colorful backhand praise for French intellectual pyrotechnics:

> Look man, you can lose your hat[,] ass and gas mask farting around
> with them damned French cats if you don't know what you're doing . . .
> but I just caint [*sic*] help saying that *that* oscar [Wright] looks more and
> more like an intellectual parasite to me everyday, a sort of [a] white
> man's NEW NIGGER.

For Ellison, both *The Outsider* and James Baldwin's *Go Tell It on the Mountain* were "interesting examples of what happens when you go elsewhere looking for what you already had at home." In contrast to Camus and Sartre, Ellison favored the activist humanism of André Malraux or

"Unamuno . . . without the religious framework." Murray would later indict Wright's novels as "social-science fiction" since they were often polemical and based in sociological frameworks. Ellison and Murray were proud modernist fiction writers and focused their work on individual experience and innovative narrative techniques.[57]

To Murray and Ellison, Wright sold short the philosophical capacity of jazz, blues, dance, and ritual. Regarding Wright's frustrations as to "what order of language" will guide a new theory of individuality that might include African-Americans, Ellison and Murray thought that language already existed in jazz and blues. Both musical forms provided the African-American cultural source materials that Ellison and Murray mixed with the modernist approaches garnered from James Joyce, Thomas Mann, and Hemingway to develop a "blues aesthetic" for American literature.[58]

In 1947, the Serbian-American poet Charles Simic became obsessed with the blues while growing up in Belgrade, a time when "one could go to jail for listening to American music," due to the Soviet Union's ban on blues and jazz. The ten-year-old Simic was captivated by the full range of the genre's artists, from Bessie Smith and Louis Armstrong to lesser-known figures such as Ida Cox and Victoria Spivey. He wore out many of his records: he found blues to be an existential form that transcended any boundaries of its context and aesthetics. "Like all genuine art, the blues belong to a specific time, place, and people which it then . . . transcends." For Simic, blues was the most important lyric poetry of the twentieth century, since its performers testified in the moment to daily existential affirmation. "The reason people make lyric poems and blues songs is because our life is short, sweet, and fleeting. The blues bears witness to the strangeness of each individual's fate." A blues song often begins "wordlessly in a moan [or] a stamp of the foot" and then proceeds rhythmically and lyrically, pausing with "a sigh or a hum," while the performer "seeks words for that something or other that has no name in any language," and yet "for which all poetry and music seek an approximation."[59] (See chapter 5 and the section titled "Confronting Absurdity with the Existential Blues," below.)

For Ellison, French existentialism was a philosophical outgrowth of the literary existentialism inherent in the alienation of the Hemingway code hero and the bluesman; these intellectual preoccupations were distinctly American, having emerged organically from the rebellion against puritanical values following World War I. In Hemingway's writing, Ellison found the valorization of the individual in opposition to corrupt society and hypocritical morality. In unpublished lecture notes of the mid-1940s, Ellison analyzed Hemingway's most existential short story, "A Clean Well-Lighted Place" (1926). In this story, the waiter is something of a Sisyphus character, doing his regular round of work and trying to live within its meaninglessness. "*Nothingness* in Hemingway [was a theme] long before the French Existentialists came along with their neat talk of the absurd. . . . Here again Americans in seeking to define their own situation have not followed Europe but blundered where Europeans were soon to discover themselves propelled." In this story, Ellison located the thematic and literary framework that influenced the later philosophical turn: "[It is] a world without religious values, and whose traditional values had been abused to the point that Hemingway could no longer believe in them." To Ellison, Hemingway's accomplishment was his literary revolution through technique and voice. Hemingway's style provided a format for "the delineation of a philosophical attitude," as delivered in "a statement of disillusionment given style."[60]

In such a world, the only authentic life comes from the inside out, from the ethical center of the individual. For this, one needs a code to adhere to as if it was a sacred text, and this is what the Hemingway code hero provided to his readers: a self-directed man with a private ethical code. And this "individual morality" had to be put to the test regularly, similar to Sartre's daily testing of himself to prove he could repress suffering. For Ellison, the Hemingway code modeled a way to "liv[e] with courage before the certainty of death, and usually violent death."[61]

Ellison's perception here grasps the American novel's appeal for Camus and Sartre: "The code takes on a religious aspect, in that it is a search for values in a world without religious sanction." Such is the spiritual wealth of ragged inner peace earned by the hard-boiled protagonists of literary noir. Ellison called this "the despair beyond riches"—an evocative phrase that neatly compresses Kierkegaard and Hemingway into the unconscious artistic power of noir cool as a counterforce to American materialism. Well ahead of the intellectual curve, Ellison perceived Hemingway's influence on French existentialist authors, a useful entry point into the influence of literary noir on existential narratives.[62]

Existentialism and Literary Noir

> [In the 1930s], *the American novel* took its place, together with jazz and
> the movies, among the best of the importations from the United States.
> America became for us the country of Faulkner and Dos Passos, just as
> it had already been the home of Louis Armstrong . . . [and] the Blues.
> Sartre, "American Novelists in French Eyes" (1946)[63]

The roots of existential cool are in literary noir: drawn from Hemingway's code hero, from Hammett's and Chandler's detectives, and from
the desperate agents in the hard-boiled novels of James M. Cain and
Horace McCoy. In 1946, the French publisher Gallimard introduced the
Série noire, a series devoted to French translations of literary noir, the
American novel of Hammett, Chandler, and Cain. The primary translator of these works was jazz impresario Boris Vian, who wrote a best-
selling noir himself about racial passing, *I Spit on Your Graves* (1946).
Independent from one another, Hemingway, Hammett, and Cain had
developed the language of literary noir: its rat-a-tat prose; an active,
propulsive narrative voice; the journalistic depiction of violence and
corruption; a defiant consciousness for its first-person narrators. From
these writers, French authors learned to present a series of actions without reflection or psychological setup. "Many of the rules we observed in
our novels were inspired by Hemingway," Beauvoir told *Life* magazine at
Sylvia Beach's apartment in 1945. André Gide and Camus favored Hammett novels and Faulkner's only noir, *Sanctuary*; Beauvoir even read
Mickey Spillane. More generally, French readers were drawn to Horace
McCoy and Raymond Chandler.[64]

The violent, hyper-masculine tough novels were told in a stark,
stripped-down, modern urban American vernacular. This language reflected the authors' collective experience as journalists, ad copywriters,
soldiers, corporate managers, and private investigators. Hemingway
was a journalist (as was Cain), and his telegraphic prose owed much to
his apprenticeship at the *Kansas City Star*. Hammett wrote ad copy for
newspapers in California, then worked for the Pinkerton security force
for a decade. Raymond Chandler worked as an office manager for a ty-
coon in Los Angeles during the 1920s' oil boom there. These jobs gave
the authors access to an emerging, evolving set of American jargons:

of journalism and the street, of advertising and corporate culture. The American novel was the first to absorb the jargons of power, public relations, and popular culture, essentially, creating a vivid modern prose that mixed the profound with the profane. In effect, the American novel modeled the use of the vernacular as literary language to render tragedy and irony within working-class lives.[65]

It was easy to miss the hard-boiled style of Camus's *The Stranger* in the original British translation of the Cold War era, but the debt became clear in the first American translation. Here's how Meursault narrates the opening paragraph: "Maman died today. Or yesterday maybe. I don't know. I got a telegram from the home. 'Mother deceased. Funeral tomorrow. Faithfully yours.' That doesn't mean anything. Maybe it was yesterday."[66] This could be the opening of Chandler's *Farewell, My Lovely* or Hammett's *Red Harvest*, with its terse, blunt sentences, tough-guy tone, and a character "ostensibly without consciousness," as translator Matthew Ward reflected. This opening also highlighted the existentialists' rejection of sentimentality and social bonds as embodied in women, a keynote of noir cool. What could be a more challenging canvas of emotion from which to project your detachment than a mother's passing?[67]

By Camus's own admission, Cain's *The Postman Always Rings Twice* (1934) was a major influence on *The Stranger*. David Madden has shown how "the American method" of literary noir directed Camus to the innovative prose and structure of his first novel. There was the hard-boiled language of action that provided authorial rebellion against literary wordplay or modernist virtuosity. There was the aesthetic infusion of the grammar of violence that made of the protagonist Meursault an analogy to the noir anti-hero. There was the protagonist's seizing of sensual and sexual pleasure, the central figure as drifter, the raw, primal masculinity, and especially, the first-person narration as testament to one's own subjective truth.[68]

Camus's greatest debt to Cain is for the narrative structure of the confession: it is a literary device emblematic of a symbolic transition from conventional morality to living within the absurd. In *Postman*, Frank Chambers confesses to God and makes of his girlfriend Cora an angelic figure he hopes will redeem him in the afterlife. In contrast, *The Stranger* can be read as Meursault's confession to the reader, where the audience functions as his only judge. In both cases, the immediacy of first-person narration and the format of the confession makes a jury of their readers. *Is the man guilty?* It is for the reader to decide and the confessional format created an audience compelled by the alienation and rebellion of the anti-heroes of literary noir. In fact, the germ of *The Stranger* can be found in Camus's journal of 1937: "Narrative—the man who does not want to explain himself. He dies, alone in *being conscious of his truth*—Vanity of this consolation."[69]

In fact, all of Camus's novels are confessions—*The Stranger, The Plague, The Fall*—and all can be said to follow up on the Cain model (e.g., *Postman, Double Indemnity, Serenade*). In Camus's novels, the protagonist never confesses to an authority figure. Dr. Rieux's confession is an act of witnessing of *The Plague*: he narrates the daily life of the quarantined city of Oran in dispassionate prose and calls himself a historian. Jean-Baptiste Clamence is a "judge-penitent" in *The Fall* and confesses to an unnamed, unknown companion as a stand-in for all of Western culture. Meursault only breaks his code "as supremely indifferent" to life and death once, and that's to scream at the priest who wants to take his confession. Camus's protagonists neither feel guilt nor do they capitulate to church, custom, law, or capitalism. In effect, as Walker Percy observed, "it is the judge, all judges, who are guilty [instead]."[70]

Literary noir provided a new template for existentialist narratives. The weight of the novel's significance was the protagonist's search for his own subjective truth, even unconsciously, and featured the quick decisions and passionate action of solitary, often violent male characters. Camus and Sartre saw the characters in the American novel as elemental creatures—active, primitive, instinctive—and all the more available for their infusion of philosophical ideas. The noir anti-hero is engaged with the *negative* aspect of Camus's existential rebellion, the repudiation of the status quo—consider Jake Barnes, Sam Spade, Philip Marlowe, Frank Chambers. To Camus, "[in] the 'tough' novel of the thirties and forties," American authors "reduced man to elementals or to his external reactions and to his behavior."[71] These authors created personae that were part monastic, part immoral, and part misogynist in their demonization of women.

In literary noir, the protagonist's *cool* functions as an artistic rendering of individual rebellion in opposition to traditional ideas of social status, economic success, or bourgeois morality. As Beauvoir told a surprised group of American critics in 1947, French writers thought it was better to question human destiny through these rogue agents than "through the babblings of inferior disciples of Proust." Even when narrated in first person, the hard-boiled American novel kept "the hero's subjectivity in the background." The protagonist's values were "implied through silences," Beauvoir reflected, and in this way, the American novel managed to "express . . . inner life with the greatest truth and depth." Beauvoir was shocked to find that many American intellectuals and journalists disliked hard-boiled fiction. "In the American novels we like," she wrote in 1947, "reality is described through strongly felt convictions involving love, hate, and rebellion. Life is revealed . . . through the hero's consciousness." There was neither authorial command nor moralizing and no overt social critique. It was for the reader to figure out.[72]

The first-person existential confessions of Cain and Camus renewed stoicism in new narrative frames—novels of action across a range of psychological and philosophical types. A crucial connection between American literary noir and existentialism is the focus on death as the only remaining narrative structure for measuring secular success. John T. Irwin's study of noir puts its existential quality right in the title: *Unless the Threat of Death Is behind Them* (2006). If life is existence without external meaning, then an individual's conduct can only be "assessed in this world and by . . . limited human means," Irwin observed. He quotes Sam Spade as representative of this noir philosophy: "I'm not heroic. I don't think there's anything worse than death." Joyce Carol Oates is right to note that this "fable of the man under sentence of death" is an old formula.[73]

Yet there are always *emotional costs* to noir cool and the daily solitary confrontation with mortality: alcohol abuse, unbearable loneliness, the objectification of women. The inherent hyper-masculinity of literary noir was central to its transatlantic translation and its philosophical overlay. There is an internal satisfaction to living one's own masculine code, and the social reward is an admiring audience of readers for a literary romance of pure existential freedom.

Both Camus and Sartre opposed the self-mastery of rational individuality—the hard-boiled ideal—to feminized emotional weakness in their earliest works. In Camus's *Caligula* (1938) and *A Happy Death* (1936–38), the protagonists are unemotional and solitary to the point of pathology, and each stakes his own authenticity on divorcing himself from interpersonal attachment, especially from women. In Sartre's "The Wall" (1938), Pablo projects a calm defiance in the face of torture and imminent execution affirmed in opposition to his cellmates who break down from anxiety or panic.[74] In *Outline of a Theory of the Emotions* (1939), Sartre subjected emotions to phenomenological analysis, as if to control a threat to the rational ideal. Both authors seek to transcend emotional affect while inhabiting a stoic ideal of rational control. Anne-Marie Solal caught the similarities in Camus's and Sartre's first published novels (*The Stranger, Nausea*): both works feature anti-heroes whose triumphs are based less in action than in confronting "the absurd" and responding with "indifference, distance, [and] aloofness." Both authors are invested in what she calls "savage individualism."[75]

With *The Plague*, Camus redirected literary noir into a more sophisticated framework and style reflecting the rational choices of each character and the narrator's underlying humility. The protagonist Rieux is Camus's ideal rebel. His choice to stay and practice medicine within the plagued city enables the survival of many others, and his egalitarian form of leadership creates the hope for a future community based on ethical individual choice. Rieux's narrating consciousness models a certain rational, existential cool, alternating between first-person plural ("Our actions were futile," "we could not continue this way") and third-person objective ("Rieux went to Tarrou and asked"). Yet *The Plague* has the same tragic flaw as the philosophy of *The Rebel*: Rieux is a secular saint. Dr. Rieux acts as doctor, witness, historian, and journalist, and although he has desires and doubts, he remains an ethical rebel loner without a dark side. Rieux requires no payment, no ego stroking, no social recognition; his actions are for neither earthly nor heavenly reward; he wears no halo, provides no answers, and refuses the mantle of leadership. Camus creates Rieux as a model of the intellectual galvanized into an awareness of being, responsibility, and solidarity as and against apathy, materialism, and the will to power. Rieux does not judge any character's choices, regardless of their contribution to society (or lack thereof), since without a traditional moral framework for good and evil, there is no basis on which to judge. Yet Rieux also represents the central problem of idealism within existentialism: How many people are capable of acting as secular saints within the pressures of a job, a marriage, and children?[76]

There was another influential existential cool figure of the era who narrated an intimate knowledge of despair, violence, and alienation, as well as his daily wrestling with the dark side. This was a figure Camus never imagined and one new to Western consciousness. He was African-American, usually a man (but not always), carving out a new musical space of individuality, a flesh-and-blood *ex*-slave who had drawn a *song-line* in the sand. European audiences (in particular) found an accessible Other in the bluesman that allowed for an affirmation of life from a separate artistic framework built expressly as survival technology against anomie and despair. The bluesman was no saint, and his strength lay in celebrating transient joys and setbacks. In short, his organic existentialism and artistic confessions reflected a struggle for survival against white European and American oppression itself, a necessary stage of change for listening to the Other.

Confronting Absurdity with the Existential Blues

To make a point: compared to Sartre's *Being and Nothingness*, one might define blues as being *from* nothingness. To W. C. Handy, the musical form of the blues, born only at the end of the nineteenth century, came "from nothingness, from want, from desire." It was an upsurge into existential definition against dominant white American society by a people considered "socially dead"—that is, denied participation, recognition, and equality as American citizens. It was a genre that traded in tragic, ironic affirmation and marked a shift from a collective musical form of resistance signifying freedom in a religious sense (spirituals) to a genre reflecting an individual's confrontation with modernity, oppression, and transience. Amiri Baraka marked it as ground zero of modern cultural defiance to white dominance in *Blues People*: as a musical form that emerged in the 1890s, "blues [was] one beginning of American Negroes," he wrote, since it represented the first "relation of the Negro's experience in this country in *his* English." Blues is composed of first-person subjective, rhythmic meditations and the genre established an ethnic vernacular poetics that marked "the Negro's conscious appearance on the American scene."[77] Significantly, these first claims for the blues as black existential music appeared in the postwar era and not, say, during the Harlem Renaissance.

Even more than film noir, blues is a popular form of existentialism: an accessible, democratic art form focused on sex and violence, desire and imagined freedom. As Handy wrote, "The blues came from the man far-thest down. . . . And when a man sang the blues, a small part of the want was satisfied from the music. The blues go back to slavery, to longing." The most prolific songwriter of Chicago blues, Willie Dixon, initially thought of blues as good-time party music until he encountered men who were "moaning and groaning these really down-to-earth blues," and then he "began to inquire about 'em . . . what the blues meant to black people." As Dixon immersed himself in Chicago's South Side clubs, he realized that blues gave blacks a way to think out loud, to reflect on their experience within a supportive, collective situation. The blues "gave them consolation to be able to think these things over": in other words, in singing a given line over and over—in blues tropes such as "how long has this been going on?" "you let me down," "the sun is gonna shine in my backdoor some day"—it was a way of "sing[ing] to themselves." When singing out loud, this action "[let] other people know what they had in mind and how they resented various things in life." Dixon here echoes Wright's reflections about the dignity of black Chicagoans.[78]

In public performance, blues functioned as a form of existential group therapy through individual artistic reflection. As Charles Keil showed in *Urban Blues* (1966), the blues singer functioned as an emotional conduit for its in-group audience, a secular leadership that rivaled the preacher or minister. The singer gave voice and eloquence to repressed emotions by naming them, inhabiting them like an actor, and in turn, making the listener feel less alone. "Blues laughter," Ellison called it, then eloquently defined it is as "an impulse to keep the painful details and episodes of a brutal experience alive in one's aching consciousness, to finger its jagged grain, and to transcend it."[79] This is art created to help work through trauma: recall, relive, reconsider, engage, work through it; Toni Mor-rison calls it "re-memory." For African-Americans in the postwar era, blues was rarely an escapist form of party music, even in its up-tempo modes: it was instead a communal ritual of musical therapy and critical engagement.

Blues was a new art form of the twentieth century, created by and from the experience of Americans of African descent, and born out of great suffering, social exclusion, and the *blues aesthetic*. In several postwar essays, Ellison designated blues as "classical vernacular music," a phrase that seems like an oxymoron but instead demystifies the form.[80] Ellison argued for blues as part of an embodied African-American existential matrix of music, dance, humor, irony, and laughter. Blues was a distinctively African-American philosophical "attitude toward life which looks pretty coldly and realistically at the human predicament, and which expresses the individual's insistence on enduring in face of his limitations."[81] This is in stark contrast to the utopian vision of the American Dream with its emphasis on a lack of limits in life and its vision of individual freedom from social obligation or collective responsibility. These were two aspects of a hyperindividualized sense of freedom that black Americans could hardly afford to invest in before the civil rights movement. Rather, for Ellison, blues as a musical genre "is in itself a kind of triumph over self and circumstance."[82]

Now I'll bring together blues and existentialism as concurrent, disparate philosophical practices of existential cool. For Camus, "the absurd" is a starting point for confronting meaninglessness and a God-less existence, for accepting one's life without the consolation of religion or ideology. In his foundational work, *The Myth of Sisyphus*, he theorizes absurdity as a positive *negative* term suggesting a courageous, rational, personal philosophy; in other words, Camus did not mean that the struggle to create meaning was pointless. To live *in*—or *with*—the absurd was to acknowledge the arbitrariness of all authority and then yearn for meaning or unity through relationships with others. Since life has no transcendent purpose, and there is "no order, pattern, or reason . . . in the world" from which to create freedom for everyday affirmation, an individual chooses between "miracles or absurdity," religion or self-creation. Camus certainly wanted to believe human beings could create greater social purpose through rational means and collective values. As he once scribbled in frustration at the questions of journalists, "I do not believe in God *and* I am not an atheist."[83]

Famously, Camus reinterpreted the myth of Sisyphus as a worker's uplifting daily struggle. If you do the same kind of work every day, you're pushing a boulder up a hill; if every day you *choose* to do it again, then you must try and find either joy or meaning in the work, in the *why* of doing it. Camus concluded the essay with a counterintuitive declaration: "We must consider Sisyphus happy." Sisyphus's boulder is analogous to a workweek without leisure as compensation. The challenge for any worker is to keep up his or her spirit while doing the repetitive work of modernity.[84] This is the kind of tragic affirmation that blues singers and musicians provided for their audiences: the challenge of maintaining one's spirit in an oppressive and absurd society.

The archetypal existential blues that approximates the myth of Sisyphus is T-Bone Walker's "Stormy Monday" (1947). A chestnut of the postwar era, the song is simply about getting through the proletarian's workweek. (In this song, "the eagle" is a slang term for paper money and payday.)

> They call it Stormy Monday,
> but Tuesday's just as bad. (2×)
> I say they call it Stormy Monday,
> but *Tues-day* is. . . . just as bad.
> Wednesday's worse, and Thursday is oh so sad.
>
> The eagle flies on Friday,
> and Saturday I go out to play.
> I say the eagle flies on Friday
> And Saturday I goes out to play.
> Sunday I go to church, then I kneel down and pray
>
> Lord have mercy,
> Lord have mercy on me.
> Lord have mercy, my heart's in misery.
> Crazy about my baby, yes, send her back to me

To hear any blues singer perform this song, it's clear there is no religion in the last verse and little belief in the transcendence of love. B. B. King defines the song as simply "the true-life story of a workingman." If there is any meaning to be found in life it is fleeting and transitory, enjoyed in the moment, and buoyed by an ironic striving for meaning or temporary satisfaction. Blues laughter is an aesthetic of irony at the heart of the musical form, encouraging listeners to grapple with the random cruelties of life, then to stomp their blues away through music, dance, and the temporary community created in live performance. This is Albert Murray's theory of the blues ritual in *Stomping the Blues*, a work focused on the swing and postwar eras. The combination of lyrical melancholy, driving rhythm, and the call-and-response of instrumental interplay creates temporary absolution from *having* the blues, a phrase that connotes both existential anomie and absurdity.[85]

T-Bone Walker captured the therapeutic existentialism of stomping the blues away (ritually speaking) in another song from the same year, "T-Bone Shuffle" (1947). The first verse concerns relaxation, pleasure, and joy, "Let your hair down, baby / Let's have a natural ball"; this is the escapist aspect of music, dance, and drinking. The second verse begins with an existential given—"You can't take it with you / that's one thing for sure"—and then Walker brings in the punch line of blues laughter: "There's nothing wrong with you, people / that a good T-Bone shuffle can't cure." This is an ironic, humorous message for *black* listeners, a group whose existential problems certainly trumped those of most white Europeans and Americans in Jim Crow America. Among postwar black audiences, T-Bone Walker was a blues avatar on par with Lightnin' Hopkins, Muddy Waters, and Howlin' Wolf. B. B. King recalled the guitarist and songwriter as "too cool for words," and as someone who, with his sartorial style and sly, virtuosic guitar licks, first made him "want to *be* cool."[86]

In 1959, Richard Wright eulogized the bluesman Big Bill Broonzy, a fellow Mississippi-to-Chicago artist of the Great Migration with whom he felt a special kinship. Broonzy was part of a cohort of expatriate blues musicians with a strong enough European fan base—along with Sonny Boy Williamson, Champion Jack Dupree, Washboard Sam, and pianist Memphis Slim—to have left an important musical legacy in England, France, and Germany. Yet Broonzy came of age with the first generation of Delta blues musicians and reinvented himself in Chicago in the 1930s through cosmopolitan jazz influences. In this way, he was an avatar of modern adaptation for African-Americans of the Great Migration. He reinvented himself again in the postwar era as an itinerant folk-blues musician and became famous throughout the world, "[in] Tokyo, Rome, Calcutta, Cairo, Paris, London, Hamburg, Copenhagen—all the tense, worried cities of the earth," Wright wrote, "[that] are filled with the blues of the black men and woman of America." For Wright, the uneducated, untrained Broonzy enacted a sophisticated folk-philosophical mode with the simplest materials: an acoustic guitar, his voice, his experience, and a natural bent for storytelling.

Broonzy was a contemporary of Lester Young, and as men raised in Mississippi, they were shaped by the terrorism of lynching and convict labor. Like Young, Broonzy rarely spoke out directly on racism due to social conditioning. Yet Broonzy wrote a few iconic blues songs of social protest. He wrote "Black, Brown and White" in 1945 with its chorus drawn from a vernacular black expression about employment: "If you're white / you's all right / if you're brown / stick around / but if you black? / oh, get back, get back, get back." No record company would publish it. The song addressed both color-coded racism and job discrimination at a time when record companies did not record songs of overt racial protest. "Why do you want to record such a song?" producers asked him. "Nobody would buy it," he recalled.

To take another example, Broonzy wrote the song, "When Will I Get to Be Called a Man?" in 1928 and was unable to record it until 1955 when he moved to Europe: "I was never called a man and now I'm 53 / I wonder when will I be called a man / or do I have to wait 'till I get [to be] 93?" This song echoes forward to Bob Dylan's "Blowin' in the Wind" (1963)—"How many roads must a man walk down / before they call him a man"—and Dylan, a blues singer first and foremost, probably knew the song. When Broonzy first began performing the song in public, he noted the difficulty of speaking about his Mississippi upbringing.[87]

> I'll say yes [I grew up there] but I'm mad and don't like to talk about it, because I was born poor, had to work and do what the white man told me to do, a lot of my people were mobbed, lynched and beaten . . . [If] the white man wanted [a black man's] wife or his best horse, he had to give it up . . . he paid me what he wanted to give and I had to take it.[88]

Here Broonzy invokes his own situatedness as an indirect critique of universal human rights or abstract individuality. The thematic questions of existentialism inflected differently for African-Americans and oppressed peoples around the world.

Wright speculated that it was precisely Broonzy's "not-belongingness" that allowed Europeans to participate in this unfamiliar music ritual:

Wright portrayed Broonzy as both an exotic visitor and a holy fool. Here Broonzy was, "poor, black, filled with wanderlust, possessing no rights that others were bound to respect," so the audience was free not to take him seriously. That left Broonzy "free to tell what life meant to him, how it felt to be alive. He was free to be more daringly truthful and universal in meaning than even he knew." Wright also compared Broonzy to poet Countee Cullen, collapsing high and low culture: "And what a poet was Big Bill! He recorded some 350 songs about love, cotton fields, railroads, river banks, and the crowded slums where black men worked, loved, drank, fought, sang, and died." When he was a young man, Broonzy struggled self-consciously with a choice between religion (preaching) and music (blues) as rival paths to cultural leadership as a "race man," to use a term of the time. As he wrote of the struggle in his 1955 autobiography, "'I'm trying to lead people and tell them the right way and don't know how and what is right myself.'"[89]

The blues is a form of existential practice in which mobility functions as a trope for existential freedom. As Wright wrote about the genre's social functions, "the blues [was] despair transmuted into sensuality, sorrow made rhythmic, defeat measured in the jumping cadences of triumph."[90] If Broonzy walked a "lonesome road" accompanied by "only the blues, a haunting sense of estrangement, an ill-at-easeness in the face of life, and a bottle of whiskey to keep him company," as Wright eulogized him, it was perhaps these very qualities of estrangement and discomfort as moderated by alcohol that hit the postwar zeitgeist. Wright wondered, "How was it that this untutored man gave voice to that feeling of sorrow that has gripped us all? Was it because he was rejected, lived outside of the normal boundaries of society? If so, from where did he get the confidence to holler in song?"

Broonzy, too, embodied a certain existential cool that had a global impact. The singer and guitarist influenced the shift from the Delta blues to rock and roll in two distinct ways. First, he was Muddy Waters's mentor in Chicago, and Waters honored Broonzy with the term "cool" for his guidance: "Big Bill was my mainline man. . . . I met some real good cool people . . . [but] Big Bill, now, he was big name *but cool.*" To Waters, Broonzy was relaxed and confident in his manner without putting on airs, the opposite of someone who acted like "the head-tall man," a colorful Delta vernacular term for arrogance. (Waters was a pallbearer at Broonzy's funeral, along with Studs Terkel.)[91] Second, Broonzy's live performances in postwar Britain exerted a formative influence on the rock and rollers of the British invasion—Eric Clapton, Pete Townsend, and Keith Richards. Broonzy was the first Delta blues musician many of them saw on TV or heard on record, and each emulated his guitar playing and vocal style.[92]

In contrast to how Ellison and Murray analyzed the blues, Wright considered Broonzy more of a folk artist and blues an unsophisticated, unintellectual musical form. Yet Wright was eloquent in his eulogy: "So long, Big Bill. Be content that we are warming our hearts over the low blue flames of your songs—songs that make us feel so melancholy that we are joyful, and yet somehow humble. How much richness Big Bill Broonzy gave us out of his poor, hard life! . . . 'lord, I ain't got no money / but I'm the happiest man in town!'" Outside of the intellectual and artistic frameworks of Europeans, Broonzy's folk wisdom became what Wright called a "strange and dubious wealth" for him to distribute. In his essay "Richard Wright's Blues," Ellison wondered at the racial irony of Wright, an African-American writer who could not imagine a black character (in fiction) as complex as *he* himself was as an author.[93] In another postwar irony, Camus could not imagine a man like Wright: an African-American who found more intellectual grist for his rebellion in European existentialism than in jazz or blues.

Coda: Camus's Existential Rebels

In effect, a soft version of existentialism became the de facto philosophy of the hip American underground in Postwar I with Camus as its literary avatar and the individual black musician as its symbol.[94] Camus theorized absurdity, suicide, and rebellion, while providing accessible critiques of capitalism, colonialism, and Communism. Camus's literary style was fluid and concise while keeping a neutral and dispassionate tone, a convincing formal technique reflecting the author's implicit detachment. In books of essays published in the late 1950s, Camus established a lyrical sensibility: measured and evocative, balancing sensuous detail with intellectual distance. There are meditations on friendship and café life, descriptions of the sun and sea, invocations of homesickness and cosmopolitanism. Yet there is always a guiding ethical narrative voice, a person taking pleasure in simple sensual and existential experiences. This balance of vulnerability and restraint mediates his political essays and his search for meaning. For these reasons, Camus's literary work remains widely read as opposed to Sartre's. His prose itself expressed a cool aesthetic.[95]

There was always in Camus the joy of living in one's body even if one is condemned to freedom within an absurd existence. Such pleasures are particularly on display in his one major posthumous work, aptly titled *The First Man* (1992). In this work, Camus renders his Algerian childhood in lyrical strokes that take into account his family's poverty, the sensuality of sun and sea, and the fractured relationships of the French, the Arabs, and the *pied-noir* class. Here was a man living in the world rather than emphasizing the Western intellectual canard, "the life of the mind," as he considered over three decades an embodied philosophy for the ethical rebel loner.

How can we measure the influence of existential cool on postwar Americans?

The existential cool that rebounded back from France found resonance in the United States with intellectuals, artists, rogue leftists, college students, theatergoers, and self-conscious rebels. These were the readers of William Barrett's perennial used-bookstore classic, *What Is Existentialism?* (1947), of Camus's novels and essays, of Sartre's philosophy and plays, and later of Paul Goodman's *Growing Up Absurd* (1960). Four of Sartre's plays were adapted for Broadway in the late 1940s— *No Exit* (1946) by John Huston and Paul Bowles, then *The Flies* (1947), *The Respectful Prostitute*, and *Red Gloves* (1948)—and Sidney Lumet directed Camus's *Caligula* (1960), with a score by Beat jazz musician David Amram. The public profile of existentialism allowed for a cult of personality around Camus and the super-couple Sartre and Beauvoir. African-Americans wrote the first existential fiction in the United States—Wright, Ellison, Himes, and Baldwin—while white existential authors such as John Barth, Walker Percy, and William S. Burroughs started publishing in Postwar II. In terms of an organic American existentialism, in addition to jazz and noir, the blues disseminated further into American culture through radio and records: blues, soul, jazz, and rock and roll.

Yet Walker Percy called attention to existentialism as an *un-American* philosophy in the eyes of the WASP upper class, and much of America's middle class, in an unpublished essay, "Which Way Existentialism?" As a philosophy, it was "militantly anti-scientific" and "militantly atheistic" for a power elite that saw itself as "custodians of science and . . . custodians of religion." For American technological and managerial elites, existentialism was an impenetrable mishmash of self-actualization and nihilism. Yet even as such social elites remained invested in dreams of technological progress and military power, the spiritual crisis of the world wars and its mass slaughters generated a cohort of widely read *Christian* existential philosophers of varying outlooks: Rollo May, Paul Tillich, Thomas Merton.[96]

In his Nobel Prize speech, Camus declared that his generation could claim a negative victory of defiance and self-affirmation, of "refusing . . . nihilism." It was enough, he reflected, that his generation "forge[d] for themselves an art of living in times of catastrophe in order *to be born a second time*." This new "art of living" would require rebirth into a post-Western world: to refigure and configure new qualities of individual dignity applicable to all members of the human race, including the newly rebellious colonized peoples, women, and other oppressed groups. In the 1960s, cultural leaders around the world—in America, those George Cotkin called "Camus' rebels"—took up this challenge. The same can be said for Wright's influence on Beauvoir, Sartre, and Frantz Fanon, as well as Ellison, Himes, and Baldwin.

With regard to Camus and Wright as literary rebels, one might say of each man: *he* rebelled and *they* now existed.

Figure 10. The badass nobody knows: Billie Holiday responds to a drug possession charge in a mink coat and shades in 1949.

4

Billie Holiday and Simone de Beauvoir

Toward a Postwar Cool for Women

She was, for her time, the voice of Woman.

Ralph J. Gleason, "Billie"[1]

How, in the feminine condition, can a human being accomplish herself? . . . How can she find independence within dependence?

Simone de Beauvoir, *The Second Sex* (1949)[2]

Duke Ellington proffered the supreme compliment on her: "Billie Holiday is as a person, [and] as a musician, the *essence* of cool." What made Holiday cool if she lacked control in her personal life and seemed a victim of larger forces? Ellington was referring to "cool" as it has always signified among African-Americans: the self-possession and self-expression of a person's art as embodied in an original, signature performance style. She was cool in her capacity to inhabit complex emotional states from within a physical state of relaxation. Perhaps most importantly for postwar audiences, Holiday was cool in her self-possession: she walked to the stage of every club and concert hall with the stately elegance of a trained dancer or born aristocrat. "She was one of the first singers that did not emote, no bouncing around, sang very quietly, snapped [her] right hand . . . and tapped her feet very quietly," jazz drummer Specs Powell recalled, such that "her whole attitude was very cool [and reserved]." Cassandra Wilson, her most important contemporary jazz heir, bemoans that Holiday is "seldom acknowledged as a musical genius" for her innovative minimalism: the ability to "make soft sounds and still have a powerful impact," a key element in, for Wilson, "the true 'birth of cool.'"[3]

Holiday stood at center stage and transformed superficial Tin Pan Alley ditties into short stories seemingly born of her own experience. To classical composer Ned Rorem, her artistry was without precedent in transforming song into "pure theater," experience distilled into emotional self-expression: "It's not real life," he wrote. "It's a concentration of life." Her artistic creativity gained aesthetic power from a stagecraft of economy: she swayed subtly while singing, barely moving a muscle, belying the emotional histrionics associated with African-Americans. "When she was on stage in the spotlight she was queenly and absolutely regal," producer Milt Gabler reflected. "The way she held her head up, the way she phrased each word and got to the heart of the story in song." In 1940, she helped make Café Society in Greenwich Village the first successful interracial club for "free thinking people," a venue first known as a "'liberal club' patronized by 'New Dealers.'" The café's owner, Barney Josephson, recalled that "Billie always knew just what she wanted to do with a song."[4]

By 1946 Holiday was already billed as "the greatest jazz vocalist" on Norman Granz's popular Jazz at the Philharmonic concert tours, and audiences experienced a certain emotional catharsis through her transmutation of blues into something of a jazz chanson. "Billie was the vestal virgin, with fifty million scars," fellow vocalist Marie Bryant said of her friend. "She got to love suffering. . . . This woman was only feelings." As historian Eric Hobsbawm has distilled her effect on audiences, "Suffering was her profession; but she did not accept it."[5] Despite her emotional travails, as a jazz musician, on stage, and in her art, she was adjudged *cool* by nearly all jazz musicians.

In 1947, Billie Holiday's status as a global icon was well-established enough that Simone Beauvoir made sure to go to a club she called "Billie Holiday's Place" on Fifty-Second Street during her American tour that year. There was no club by that name—it was probably the Three Deuces—but it speaks volumes about her impact that Beauvoir graced the club with Holiday's name. Beauvoir left this evocative fragment about her short visit: "A sparse audience is listening to a tepid band, waiting for Billie to sing. She is there, she smiles. She is very beautiful in a long white dress, her black hair straightened by a clever permanent and falling straight and shiny around her clear brown face. Her bangs look like they've been sculpted in dark metal. She smiles, she is beautiful, but she doesn't sing. They say she's on drugs and sings only rare now."[6] Blues and existentialism share an artistic mix of resignation and affirmation, of reality and lyricism. At this historical juncture just before Beauvoir began writing *The Second Sex*, Holiday had already given voice to the range of women's experience. Through both artistic resonance and intellectual analysis, Holiday and Beauvoir created conversations—both public and internal—for the experience of "the Woman as Other to Man."

Holiday was a working-class woman self-taught in her art form from records, then mentored by jazz masters in the "rolling academy" of big bands, in particular, of Count Basie's with Lester Young. Holiday understood herself more as an improvisational jazz artist than a singer, or as the music industry's idea of a singer. "I don't think I'm singing. I feel like I'm playing a horn," she often said. "I try to improvise like Les Young, like Louis Armstrong," she said in an early interview from 1939. "What comes out is what I feel. I hate straight singing. I have to change a tune to my own way of doing it."[7] Here was a personalized mode of resistance communicated through a stylistic mix of yearning, confession, resignation, affirmation, and survival. There was no shared language for feminism in the postwar era, and Holiday provided a resonant emotional range of responses for her female listeners. The grain of Holiday's voice was a far cry from the gospel shouting of Sister Rosetta Tharpe, Bessie Smith's blues power, or any jaunty swing-era girl singer. In contrast to such singers, "one word from Holiday is worth a thousand pictures," as jazz critic Will Friedwald put it.[8]

By the late 1940s, Holiday sang mostly for white audiences, and she was framed as a tragic figure through abusive romantic relationships and the public's knowledge of her heroin addiction and arrests. Albert

Murray lamented that, for these audiences, "her singing . . . came to represent the pathetic sound of an attractive but wretched woman crying in self-pity." Even now, quick sketches of Holiday foreground "Strange Fruit" and "My Man" as vocal reflections of Holiday's tragic persona. This was magnified further by her autobiography *Lady Sings the Blues* (1956), which emphasizes and mythologizes her suffering from racist and sexist oppression while it fails to illuminate her musical artistry. Jazz critic Whitney Balliett caught the dissonance of the memoir between its emphasis on "her pitiable life" and its dismissal of the "unique, beautiful, and indestructible kind of jazz singing" she created.[9]

Yet for six years (1937 – 43), Holiday's playful exuberance and controlled emotional flow helped create a genre of chamber jazz in small ensembles backed with the likes of Lester Young, Teddy Wilson, Count Basie, Lawrence Brown, and Benny Goodman. Despite the acclaim among all jazz scholars and aficionados for these recordings, they barely exist in public memory today compared to the pathos of Holiday's later recordings. Her reputation remains as the tragic victim, a framing that obscures her artistic achievement and represents a certain kind of aesthetic sexism and racism. Unlike the male jazz musicians whose heroin addictions burnished their outlaw cool (e.g., Charlie Parker, Chet Baker, Art Pepper), Holiday's addiction only drew pity and the ongoing persecution of the Federal Bureau of Narcotics through Harry Anslinger.[10]

Holiday's model for creating a singular artistic voice from personal experience and cool understatement still rains down on American song whether in jazz or soul, from Sinatra and Etta James to Diana Ross and Nina Simone to Diana Krall and Cassandra Wilson. From listening to Holiday, the Jewish teenager Hettie Jones heard her own postwar need for voice: "I wanted a tone like that, like a sure bell, and to sing . . . on my own line in my own good time." Jones wanted to learn Holiday's "genius approach to craft" and to use it as a model, as did many Beat bohemians. Jones recalled one Village poet going up to Holiday's car after a reading at the 7 Arts Gallery to say, "Thanks, Lady. Just . . . thanks." As postwar jazz chronicler Ira Gitler mused, "She was a demi-goddess to us. I [still] haven't heard anyone to equal her singular personality and approach to a song." Holiday is even—quite deservingly—in the Rock and Roll Hall of Fame.[11]

Cool: A Masculine Sign of the Times

Billie Holiday was a streetwise tough as a Baltimore teenager and was already known for her love of singing even before coming to New York in 1929. In her career, she exercised a great deal of control over her songs, her accompanists, and her recordings, even long after her heroin addiction. She always said she crafted her musical hybrid of jazz and blues by combining Bessie Smith's vocal power and self-expression with Louis Armstrong's swing and rhythmic nuance. In addition, she fought and drank as hard as Bessie Smith and had Armstrong's melodic imagination. Often when a boyfriend hit her she punched him right back, according to her friend Carmen McRae. More than once, she beat up racist sailors who called her a "nigger bitch" with a bottle outside the Onyx Club on Fifty-Second Street, according to eyewitnesses. She was opinionated and impolitic about other musicians and despised imitators, much like Lester Young. "I can't stand copycats," she once said about Ruth Brown in *Downbeat*, and about Count Basie's band in 1950, "tell the truth I'm ashamed of them" for their decline and for "how great it [the band] used to be." Holiday once mooned an audience at Café Society in an evening gown for no apparent reason except general frustration: it was just a way of "saying 'kiss my black ass,'" according to the club owner.[12]

Simone de Beauvoir wrote that women were in a state of *becoming*, of emergence. If Woman was the Other of Man, recognition of that tension—of her inferior social status and unlimited potential—was not only a necessary beginning but a philosophical manifesto. After all, French women only got the vote in 1944. Beauvoir transformed all ideas of gender in *The Second Sex*, a magisterial work with no precedent. Beauvoir was probably a better young philosopher than Sartre—their professors thought so—and her body of work may turn out to be of more lasting *social* import. Her novels and memoirs were best sellers in postwar France, and she may have created the opposition of self and other still credited to Sartre.[13]

Both Beauvoir and Holiday were defiant young artists and bisexual women in their early twenties. Holiday rolled as an equal on the bus with the Count Basie Orchestra in the late 1930s, shooting dice, drinking, and carousing. Beauvoir was a free-thinking novelist and philosopher, living

with Sartre and taking all manner of lovers. During the Nazi occupation
of Paris, Beauvoir began to craft a new ethics: it owed a larger debt to
Heidegger's concept of the Other and her friend Merleau-Ponty's concept of embodiment than to Sartre's work. Similarly, "Billie [always]
went her own way," Barney Josephson recalled. "She was . . . a free soul
who did what she liked," leaving the club as often with a man as a woman,
smoking hash in a cab while driving around Manhattan.[14]

So why does public memory and artistic history still ascribe the two
women as either tragic and vulnerable (Holiday) or literary and secondary (Beauvoir)? Holiday was beloved by all black jazz musicians and
writers, including Miles Davis, and was held up as a postwar voice of
African-American resistance and historical suffering by everyone from
James Baldwin to Malcolm X to (more recently) Angela Davis.[15] The keynote of her performance style was the cool aesthetic of a relaxed attitude
and, in addition, she often wore a mask of cool. She is, quite simply, one
of America's greatest artists.

So why don't Holiday and Beauvoir come to mind when we think
of cool?

Cool was a postwar masculine aesthetic, and its paragon figures are
ethical rebel loners. Cool is based on *self*-authorizing: its characteristics are independence, rebellion, and a capacity for violence. Lacking
autonomy and agency, the female caretakers of homes, husbands, and
children could hardly resonate in a similar manner in the cultural imagination. In addition, the dominant artistic genres that carried cool into
American and global consciousness—jazz and film noir, philosophy and
literature—were dominated by male authors and critics. Holiday wore
a mask of cool, yet it was only perceived by African-Americans. "She
was shrewd . . . like an urchin is shrewd who's going up the street and
has to get some food," Marie Bryant recalled. "But inside you're vulnerable. It's a role you assume." Yet the dominant society recognized neither her resilience nor the transmutation of suffering into a cool vocal
aesthetic.[16]

When amateur sociologists began constructing a canon of postwar
cool in the 1980s, it focused almost entirely on men. Cool connoted a
certain rogue artistic masculinity in Gene Sculatti's *The Catalog of Cool*
(1982), Roy Carr's profiles in *The Hip: Hipsters, Jazz, and the Beat Generation* (1986), and Lewis MacAdams's *Birth of the Cool: Beat, Bebop,*

and the American Avant-Grade (2001). Gwendolyn Brooks's "We Real Cool" (1959) was the only contemporary feminist riposte to the era's African-American hyper-masculinity and her concise seven-line poem anticipates the millennial feminist critique of cool in Susan Fraiman's *Cool Men and the Second Sex* (2003), bell hooks's *We Real Cool* (2003), Marlene Connor's *What Is Cool?* (1995), and in particular, the sociological study by Richard Majors and Janet Billson, *Cool Pose* (1993). In contrast, the critique of cool for white men depends on their appropriation of black culture: Andrew Ross's long essay, "Hip and the Long Front of Color," Ingrid Monson's "The Problem with White Hipness," or bell hooks's "Eating the Other."

In crucial ways, Holiday and Beauvoir promulgated their own myths of passivity and deference to men in their memoirs and texts (whether literary or musical). Beauvoir always deferred to Sartre's superior intellect and declined to call herself a philosopher while he was alive. And so it is that a French philosopher chose to stand by her man rather than to claim her own intellectual inheritance as a rogue free agent. Billie Holiday was raised among pimps and prostitutes such that she carried the dynamic of male violence and female dependence into her own love life, idolizing "nightlife strongmen . . . from whom she demanded protection." She brought autonomy and authority to her music, but in her personal life, she had a psychological need to be dependent and dominated by a man. From starkly different backgrounds, Beauvoir and Holiday still mythologized their lives as beholden to a dominant man, whether an intellectual or a street hustler.[17]

The emphasis on drugs and victimization in *Lady Sings the Blues* has long been blamed on the racism of her co-writer (William Dufty), yet we now know Holiday was a willing co-conspirator in the projection of a tragic damsel in need of rescue by powerful, often violent men. In *Wishing on the Moon,* biographer Donald Clarke revealed Holiday's early ambition as a jazz singer (at twelve and thirteen) and her youthful rounds on the streets of Baltimore. Interviews with her Baltimore crowd revealed Holiday's story of immaculate artistic conception in 1933 to be a fairy tale rescue of a damsel in distress that placed producer, impresario, and musical scout John Hammond in the role as white knight. In *Lady Day*, Robert O'Meally suggests that, when she dated "fast hustlers" as a young teen, she was always seeking men with her dreams of upward mobility rather than to serve white people (like her mother) and with the freedom of her jazz musician father, Clarence Holiday.[18]

Lady Sings the Blues might be better understood as a narrative illuminating the singer's subjective sense of vulnerability after a decade of addiction and the death of her mother. By 1943, Holiday had already recorded some of the classic music of the twentieth century. After 1945, her best friends from the Basie band often kept their distance rather than to become entangled in her junkie rounds—trumpeters Harry Edison and Buck Clayton, and most importantly, Lester Young. (Young and Holiday did not speak for fourteen years.) By the time of *Lady Sings the Blues*, it was "as if, in the face of her pitiable life," Balliett wrote in the *New Yorker*, "her art were not an inestimable feat."[19]

Yet even in the midst of her addiction, Holiday never poured out her emotions in song but, rather, through the "elegant inventiveness" of her musical technique, she generated subtle pathos through "cool understatement," as Albert Murray observed. Pianist Teddy Wilson was the leader on many of Holiday's best early chamber jazz sessions and assessed Holiday's art as an organic projection of her subjective modes: "Her singing, in a very integral way, was a reflection of her whole psychology, her experience." Holiday enacted a form of artistic introspection and, in effect, performed the process of mediating experience into self-knowledge. Trained in the blues, her performances partook of something close to group therapy as conducted by a social artist.[20]

Two images of Holiday point up the distance between her public image among white Americans and her artistic street cred among African-Americans. Holiday appeared in a single Hollywood film—*New Orleans* (1947)—in which she played a jazz-singing maid. She hated wearing the maid's costume, and her resistance in the film is apparent: she is sullen and uninterested throughout *New Orleans*, except when she is singing. Holiday's style was innovative and influential—furs, matted hair, fit-and-flare dresses, the gardenia in her hair—and seemed an emanation of a personal glamor. Being seen on the screen as a maid was humiliating. This is a woman who, on being arrested for heroin possession in 1949, came down to the police precinct in a mink coat and shades, creating an iconic photo of a badass woman for Postwar I. (See fig. 10.)

Jazz drummer Specs Powell was eighteen when he first encountered the new postwar "cool, reserved attitude" in Fifty-Second Street clubs, and in retrospect he distinguished between the pose and the artistry. "Anybody who carried this attitude was very worldly, and to an eighteen-year-old boy this was something—[a] very slow-moving matter-of-fact way of looking at life." Yet some people affected this world-weary front where others carried themselves with the confidence of their artistic ability: "Billie never affected anything. She was authentic." To tap dancer and raconteur Honi Coles, Holiday was very young but "very cool, very gentle," and "she had *that* confidence," which others described as "her style and her arrogance," the same qualities in men often ascribed as cool.[21]

Yet so hermetic is the fusion of masculinity, rebellion, and cool that only now can we begin to sound out the tenor of a postwar women's cool.

Beauvoir

In the aftermath of the Holocaust, artists, politicians, and philosophers began to deconstruct obsolete ideas of fixed racial identities and genetic predispositions. If the case study was "the Jew," as Beauvoir first acknowledged Sartre's *Anti-Semite and Jew* (1946), it soon extended to "the black," "the Indian," and "Woman." Beauvoir (fig. 11) considered the problem under the influence of Richard Wright, whose understanding of being Other as a black man (a racial Other) in the United States provided a lens for writing about women (Woman as Other). Women were raised for dependence on men, who did not recognize equal humanity across gender lines. Any individual woman was constantly "being reduced to what she was" (*only* a woman) or, more to the point, to being framed by specific subsets of feminine traits defined by men.[22] *The Second Sex* went even further: Beauvoir declared the individual human being a "historical idea" and argued that every person is constantly redefined by other humans. In so doing, she quietly declared intellectual war against all hierarchies of race or gender and paved the way for considering a "relational self" against modernist ideals.[23]

"Woman is not a fixed reality but a becoming," Beauvoir wrote in *The Second Sex,* "that is, her *possibilities* have to be defined." Neither Beauvoir nor Holiday represented themselves as heroic rebels in their own work. In effect, their lives and works are a simultaneous testament to

Figure 11. Simone de Beauvoir on the streets of Paris, 1945 (© Henri Cartier-Bresson/ Magnum Photos).

existential rebellion and the oppression of women. They defined the possibilities in their time through their lives. To their credit as artists, they represented the subjective lives of women within realistic frameworks rather than offering assertive, empowered women in literature and music.[24] And yet without individual defiance, without the rebel drawing a line in the sand . . . no *cool*.

Social conditioning allowed no space for a woman's individual rebellion. "In particular, the attitude of defiance, so important for boys, is unknown to [girls]," Beauvoir wrote. Straitjacketed within conventional frameworks of femininity, girls were discouraged from participation in sports or intellectual contests and conditioned to suppress individuality and anger. To take one fascinating example, author Annie Dillard grew up in Pittsburgh as a tomboy and loved playing tackle football with boys: nothing girls did in the early 1950s rivaled the sport's demand of will, skill, improvisation, and physical exertion. Then one day in 1952, during a blizzard, she and one of her football buddies were pummeling a passing car with snowballs. A man in his twenties stopped his car in the street and chased the two kids ten blocks through the neighborhood's streets, alleys and backyards. When she was caught, she felt no fear: in fact, she felt as if she'd won an Olympic title. What could the man do? There was no punishment that mattered. The chase itself was a challenge and an honor. Reflecting back at the age of forty she wrote without irony, "Nothing before or since had ever required so much of me."[25]

During adolescence, there was an emphasis on sports and violence for boys, Beauvoir showed; for girls, there was only preparation for marriage. Girls were conditioned to find satisfaction through a man, not her own acts. Such conditioning was reflected back through popular culture. In music, a blueswoman or jazz singer was seen as more an erotic figure (to men) than an artist engaged in moral introspection or social protest. In film noir, an independent woman with a criminal's savvy was a femme fatale (to men), not a figure of resistance acting out a quest for abstract freedom. Beauvoir distilled the difference:

> At about thirteen, boys serve a veritable apprenticeship in violence, developing their aggressiveness, their will for power, and their taste for competition. . . . [Yet] at this moment the little girl renounces rough games . . . in many countries, most girls have no athletic training. . . . They are banned from exploring, daring, pushing back the limits of the possible.[26]

It bears repeating: without defying limits and social conventions . . . no cool.

Beauvoir pursued and analyzed the intersections of race, cool and jazz more than any other existentialist besides Boris Vian. In the late 1940s, Beauvoir attended concerts featuring Louis Armstrong, Mezz Mezzrow, and Sidney Bechet, all of them with euphoric young audiences. The Armstrong concert she describes as "maybe the best thing I heard or saw since years," and it was "full of screaming . . . young people mad with enthusiasm"; she singled out the "wonderful pianist" virtuoso and bandleader, Earl Hines. New Orleans jazz was the soundtrack for the liberation of Paris from Nazi occupation in Beauvoir's *The Mandarins* (1954), and the novel features a jazz singer who might be based on Billie Holiday, an expressive singer entangled with an unfaithful man to the point of emotional paralysis. Then in 1947, Beauvoir took a four-month solo trip to the United States that produced *America Day by Day*, a memoir in which race is a major theme and jazz a preoccupation.[27]

In New York, Richard Wright introduced Beauvoir to a community of jazz and race scholars who took her under their wing in clarinetist Mezz Mezzrow's Harlem apartment. Mezzrow had just published the underground classic memoir *Really the Blues* (1946), one of the first respectful, insightful analyses of black music and culture in Chicago; Beauvoir had heard Mezzrow in concert in Paris. Mezzrow's co-writer was Bernard Wolfe, an intellectual gadfly and former secretary to Leon Trotsky whose cultural criticism was published in *Les Temps Modernes*. Wolfe introduced Beauvoir to Ernest Borneman, an astute German anthropologist and jazz critic, whom she called "my best friend in New York."[28] The Swedish sociologist Gunnar Myrdal often tagged along—his magisterial work on race, *An American Dilemma* (1941), was as influential on Beauvoir's *Second Sex* as Wright's works and friendship. Mezzrow, Wolfe, and Borneman together provided Beauvoir with ways of seeing (and hearing) jazz as the soundtrack of American rebels inasmuch as this coterie of intellectuals "passionately love jazz and . . . hate American capitalism, racism, [and] puritanical moralism."[29]

It would be hard to imagine a better set of teachers in the late 1940s, and Beauvoir was a quick study. Sitting in a half-empty club on Fifty-Second Street—the "Jazz Street"—Beauvoir listened to New Orleans clarinetist Sidney Bechet and, in a single long paragraph, showed her understanding of the in-group social function of jazz for African-Americans. Her epiphany came less through musical analysis than by observing the effect of Bechet's solos on a black female cook:

> Bechet could not dream of having a public worthier of his genius than the dark-faced woman in the white apron who appears from time to time at a little door behind the platform. She's probably the cook, a stout woman in her 40s with a tired face but big, avid eyes. With her hands resting flat on her stomach, she leans toward the music with a religious ardor. Gradually, her worn face is transfigured, her body moves to a dance rhythm; she dances while standing still, and peace and joy have descended on her. She has cares, and she's had troubles, but she forgets . . . [them], forgets her dishcloths, her children, her ailments.

Without a past or future she is completely happy: the music justifies her difficult life, and the world is justified for her. She dances . . . with a smile in her eyes that's unseen on white faces, in which only the mouth expresses gaiety.

Beauvoir ascribes to the woman a working-class life with its attendant cares, yet appreciates the temporary transcendence of the woman's response. Her description is not racial but individual—"a stout woman . . . tired face . . . big, avid eyes"—and grants this kitchen worker both agency and subjectivity. This is a realistic depiction of the era's ethnic gestures inasmuch as one can see them mirrored in the performance of jazz singer Ivie Anderson as a maid in the Marx Brothers classic, *A Day at the Races* (1937). In that film, Anderson similarly has her hands on her stomach while leaning into the music until starting to "dance while standing still" and being transfigured by the music.

By describing the woman as "completely happy" while listening, Beauvoir was assigning neither an essentialist nor a primitivist notion of racial naturalness in describing the woman's reaction. Rather, she intuited the way in which jazz is a *situational* art form. It is a dialogic ritual created *in* the moment, *for* the moment. Beauvoir extends to this anonymous woman the ultimate compliment: "Looking at her, we understand the greatness of jazz even better than by hearing Bechet himself." Her description echoes forward to James Baldwin's analysis of the function of music for African-Americans. "Music is our witness, and our ally," Baldwin wrote. "The beat is the confession which recognizes, changes, and conquers time."[30] Bechet's effect on this woman was the primary objective of jazz at midcentury: musicians strove to evoke an emotional response in others without themselves becoming excited or "playing hot." In so doing, jazz musicians created a space for personal and social change in others.

Billie's Existential Blues

Blueswomen created the first body of American feminist literature in the 1920s, for which they rarely receive the proper credit. This is due to an artistic and even academic racism that derives from a hierarchy of literature over music and a refusal to recognize African-American women as

artistic pioneers. In the 1920s, a cohort of blueswomen sang of independent, sexualized women on the road inhabiting an impressive range of
women's experience, including sexual desire, racism, freedom, anomie
and transience, lesbian relationships, female rivalries, domestic abuse,
and vengeance against oppressive husbands. In *Blues Legacies and Black
Feminism*, Angela Davis found precedent for her own brand of revolutionary politics in blueswomen's songs, creating a genealogy from Ma
Rainey to Bessie Smith to Billie Holiday.[31]

Blues was a poetic language of emancipated thought during the Great
Migration, with particular application to the lives of African-American
women. Blueswomen were the conduits for musical urbanization and
they embodied the tensions of modernity and tradition with their innovative brand of jazz-infused blues. It is little known today that Bessie
Smith was the highest-earning, best-known, and most race-conscious
African-American singer of the 1920s. Her songs offered a new narrative of female empowerment and, in addition, of racial pride and black
consciousness. For much of her life, Smith performed only for African-
Americans—for "her people," as she said—and only twice for white
audiences in the South. Holiday built her artistry on this pioneering
generation of singers, in particular through Bessie Smith's example.
She agreed to sit for photographer Carl Van Vechten in 1949 only after he proved his bona fides by showing Holiday his portraits of Bessie
Smith.[32]

Blueswomen almost never sang of domestic life: there are no husbands, housework, or children in the blues of the 1920s and 1930s.[33]
Bessie Smith's persona depends on a sexualized, autonomous woman
ready to hit the road at any time, and yet her songs acknowledge emotional states of pity, revenge, dependence, and social protest. In Smith's
"Young Woman's Blues," she leans over in bed to find a kiss-off note from
her man saying "no time to marry, no time to settle down." Rather than
bemoan her fate or cry—as nearly all white singers would have done
in the '20s—the singer's first response is one of liberation rather than
victimization: "I'm a young woman / and ain't done runnin' round." Her
second response proclaims social equality and racial pride in her dark
skin: "I'm as good as any woman in your town / I ain't no *high yeller*
[light-skinned] / I'm a deep killer brown." Then she sets out on the road

and, akin to Walt Whitman, she deftly invokes language to mirror a traditionally masculine sense of freedom:

> I ain't gonna marry, I ain't gonna settle down
> I'm gonna drink good moonshine
> and rub these browns [black men] down
> See that long lonesome road
> Lawd, you know it's gotta end—
> And I'm a good woman
> And I can get plenty men

In blues as a genre, mobility is a metaphor for freedom, especially for women. Bessie Smith was a conduit for the Great Migration and its possibilities, and, more generally, blueswomen were the first female cohort to render this modernist sense of emancipation. What did the teenaged Eleanora Fagan (i.e., Billie Holiday) hear in the grain of Bessie Smith's voice? She heard a deep contralto voice, clear enunciation, and vocal lines punctuated by the growls, moans, and yells of subjective experience. She heard the sound of a woman who was not a fixed reality but a becoming.

Bessie Smith was well-known as the greatest blues singer in the nation when Holiday was in her teens. Smith sang as if music offered ritual solace and momentary triumph over the absurdity of life. She stood regally on stage and rang out in songs that alternated in power and poignancy: she could command an audience to silence and evoked responses of gospel enthusiasm (e.g., "you tell it, sister," "that's right"). Rather than use a megaphone in large halls—as most singers did before microphones—Smith depended on "the volume of her natural voice." According to blues scholar Paul Oliver, this choice proved both "the inadequacies of her lesser rivals" and her ability to process subjective experience into self-expression. Oliver described Smith as singing "with her whole body—passionately, powerfully, subtly swaying," an artist "giving the impression of great strength barely held in control."[34]

The *cool aesthetic* registers exactly this tension: great power held under aesthetic control and artistic will. For two generations, music writers and scholars believed blues singers simply poured out their emotions in song until Charlie Keil and Albert Murray put the lie to this trope by analyzing the ritual aspects of blues performance. For example, Bessie Smith shouts the same (seemingly) spontaneous interjections in alternate takes of her recordings. She understood her role as a social artist and the artistic effectiveness of giving "the impression . . . her work was *ex tempore*," as Oliver reflected, "and required neither rehearsal nor practice." Audiences chose certain singers and musicians to act as emotional conduits since they had proven their merits as masters of stagecraft and self-awareness. For Oliver, this is "the 'art that conceals art.'"[35]

When James Baldwin moved to France in 1948 he took only his typewriter and two Bessie Smith records. In Smith's "Backwater Blues," written about the Mississippi flood of 1927—which she witnessed—Baldwin heard an existential blues aesthetic: "What struck me was she was singing about a disaster that had almost killed her and she had accepted it and was going beyond it. There's a fantastic kind of understatement in it. . . . It's the way I want to write." Baldwin then isolated a single line of the song as exemplary of a cool minimalist statement. "When she says, 'my house fell down / and I can't live there no more,' it's a great sentence, it's a great achievement."[36] Bessie Smith's musical influence runs down through the past century, from Billie Holiday to Dinah Washington, from Mezz Mezzrow to Bob Wills (both of whom saw her live), from James Baldwin to Janis Joplin (who worshiped her), from Irma Thomas to Lucinda Williams.

Cool is the projection of self-possession with one's vulnerability just visible enough to show the emotional costs of the stance. Cool requires emotional self-control and stands for the aesthetic expression of detachment. A blueswoman or bluesman *performed* individual freedom onstage: he or she was a radically free individual in this moment. Lionel Hampton recalled about Bessie Smith: "What she sang was so relaxed, the stories she sang became so true—this was reality."[37]

Jazz vocalist Betty Carter said something similar about Billie Holiday—"she was only free when she was singing"—and then elaborated on this meaning of freedom. "Everything else didn't mean much [to her] except that it led up to the moment when she stepped out on that stage and became what we all wanted but only she could give us. She was free then, and everybody knew it."[38] Holiday was working within an ethnic ritual of social artistry, representing *her people* on stage such that she "became what we all wanted." Within her vocal artistry was pain and suffering, affirmation and survival: she gave the gift of dignity, acceptance, and freedom. Regardless of the image white audiences had of Holiday, she retained these qualities within African-American and Beat communities until her untimely death in 1959. She had brought Bessie Smith's legacy forward.

Off stage, neither Bessie Smith nor Billie Holiday masked their emotions. Smith was more comfortable drinking moonshine in an alley with street people than on a concert stage like Carnegie Hall. Holiday was just as open with her life and equally egalitarian in terms of her compatriots: she often walked around naked in her apartment, unashamed and uneroticized, no matter who visited. As her long-time pianist and accompanist Bobby Tucker once reflected, "One of her best friends might be the attendant in the ladies room and this would really be a friend and this friend wouldn't take back seat to the First Lady or the Queen of England."[39]

As Malcolm X eulogized her, "Lady Day sang with the soul of Negroes from the centuries of sorrow and oppression." When he was still a pimp and thief in the early 1940s, Malcolm Little was friends with Holiday and often went to see her at the Onyx Club:

> We took a taxi on down to 52nd Street. 'Billie Holiday' and those big photo blow-ups of her were under the lights outside. Inside, the tables were jammed against the wall. . . . Her white gown glittered under the spotlight, her face had that coppery, Indianish look, and her hair was in that trademark ponytail. . . . She did the one she knew I always liked so: "You Don't Know What Love Is."

That night, Holiday sat down with the then-troubled hustler and his girlfriend Jean. She sensed something was wrong, but he played it cool only to regret it later. "Billie sensed something wrong with me. She knew that I was always high . . . and she asked in her customary profane language what was the matter. . . . I pretended to be without a care, so she let it drop. . . . That was the last time I ever saw her." This encounter probably pre-dates Holiday's heroin addiction, and yet twenty years later Malcolm X still mourned her, a woman and artist with a "heart as big as a barn and that sound and style . . . no one successfully copies." Malcolm X highlighted the subtext of racial pride and black consciousness in Holiday's music: "What a shame that proud, fine, black woman never lived where [or when] the true greatness of the black race was appreciated!"[40] American culture can claim Holiday for her artistic achievement and for the cool aesthetic she developed from the original model of blueswomen.

Toward a Cool Female Aesthetic

Both Beauvoir's analysis of the social conditioning of girls and the proto-feminism of blueswomen through Billie Holiday shed light on how to rethink postwar cool away from its inherent male mavericks. Billie Holiday was an original artist and the co-creator of the cool aesthetic in jazz, along with Lester Young. As for Beauvoir, a generation of feminist scholars have put her into intellectual context: she was the only existential figure to produce a cohesive theory of ethics and her work influenced Sartre's at key points, more than either admitted while he was alive. Both women were among the greatest artists of the twentieth century. As Frank Sinatra told *Ebony* magazine in 1958: "Lady Day is unquestionably the most important influence on popular singing in the last 20 years."[41]

A cool female aesthetic starts in the 1920s with Bessie Smith and extends to Mae West, who appropriated her persona in part from blueswomen. It includes maverick artists such as Dorothy Parker, Georgia O'Keeffe, and Louise Brooks.[42] In 1930s films, it re-begins with Barbara Stanwyck carving out a new American type as a sexually independent ingénue in pre-code films like *Ten Cents a Dance*, *Illicit*, and *Baby Face* (1931–33) before she goes on to outfox and outthink a detached cool character such as Walter Neff (Fred MacMurray) in *Double Indemnity* (1944). Stanwyck, too, played down her intelligence and independence in nearly every film, yet like Beauvoir and Holiday, she was always as smart as she was sexy, often steely and scheming, an onscreen survivor who reflected the range of women's lives.[43] (See fig. 12.)

The cool women of Postwar I include Lauren Bacall and Anita O'Day, avatars of noir cool and jazz cool, respectively. Bacall was the rare woman considered cool and tough onscreen; O'Day was one of the dominant jazz voices of the era and self-identified as a "hip chick." James Agee perceived the new cool register in Bacall's persona, hailing her as "the toughest girl Hollywood has dreamed of in a long, long while." Agee described

Figure 12. Barbara Stanwyck's steely boldness radiates out from a classic noir background in a promotional photo taken two years before *Double Indemnity*.

her film presence as the combination of "a dancer's eloquence of movement, a fierce female shrewdness, and a special sweet-sourness."[44] Bacall's unsentimental contralto was analogous to the vibrato-less register of Lester Young's saxophone. Bacall married Bogart in 1945, and they starred together in four classic noirs, where her resilience and physical grace moderated his grizzled cynicism (*To Have and Have Not, The Big Sleep, Dark Passage,* and *Key Largo*).

Anita O'Day was a jazz singer whose streetwise style shifted the idea of the "girl singer" or "canary" to the *hip chick*. Raised in the Depression and toughened by poverty, O'Day broke into show business by winning walkathons and dance contests. As the star vocalist of Gene Krupa's band, she was the model for Barbara Stanwyck's streetwise jazz singer in *Ball of Fire* (1941), the first cinematic portrayal of a hip woman from the jazz world. O'Day's art and style transgressed race and gender norms in influential ways: (*a*) she created a professional look for women—a black sports jacket and short skirt; (*b*) she broke the color line on American stages by singing duets with the trumpeter Roy Eldridge; and (*c*) she was a heroin addict who spent two short stints in prison such that she drew crowds hoping to see this outlaw woman. O'Day was neither proud nor ashamed of her addiction.[45]

O'Day's confident artistry was made possible by the mask of cool, no less than for her fellow jazzmen. O'Day reflected on her parents' bad marriage as the source of her stoicism in her frank memoir of jazz and addiction, *High Times, Hard Times*. "Like a turtle, I developed a hard shell to protect myself," she wrote. "I might be vulnerable, but I learned how to hide my pain with a flip remark or a hard-boiled attitude," she recalled with some pride. "I hardly ever cry," she continued, since "the only thing crying accomplishes is to make you sick." O'Day's emotional struggle did not come from racism—nor did her hard shell—yet she, too, channeled her repression into jazz and heroin, until "the price of being a hip, swinging chick . . . became too great to pay."[46]

A genealogy of postwar female cool awaits further analysis and its own full-length study. The cohort would include Bettie Page and noir novelist Patricia Highsmith, jazz vocalists Lena Horne, Dinah Washington, and Abbey Lincoln, and noir actresses Gloria Grahame, Veronica Lake, and Ida Lupino.

Figure 13. Harry Lime (Orson Welles) faces off against his childhood friend Holly Martins (Joseph Cotten) in *The Third Man* (1950).

5

Cool Convergences, 1950

Jazz, Noir, Existentialism

How is Thelonious Monk's "Round Midnight" *not* a noir theme? Composed in 1945 and an instant classic, it evokes the strange allure of dark romantic melancholy like a four-minute short film. "'Round Midnight" actually *sounds* like a man walking around at midnight along sleek, empty, rainy streets, lamppost-lit, conscious (and also unconscious) of his desires, aware and yet unaware he is searching for a bar full of night people to echo back his alienated sorrows.[1]

Or what about the grain of Billie Holiday's voice? The strands of yearning and affirmation—and of hurt and experience—in her narrative vocal style could have carved a natural soundtrack into the genre's nightclub scenes. Imagine Holiday singing "Trav'lin Light" or "You Let Me Down" over the opening credits of *Out of the Past*, *Double Indemnity*, or *The Killers*. Talk about foreshadowing.

Jazz producer and critic Ross Russell wondered if jazz musicians were America's only organic existentialists.

This chapter presents a series of evocative convergences of the three expressive arts of postwar cool: on noir and existentialism, jazz and ex-

istentialism, and noir and jazz. My theory of cool in Postwar I appears
in the final section.

The Third Man: The Cold War Noir

As soon as it is formed, the skin of History peels off as film.[2]

André Bazin (1946)

Noir cool's postwar consciousness arrived with *The Third Man* (1950), an
international production shot on location in occupied Vienna. Cynical,
transitional, and liminal—even self-consciously philosophical at times—
The Third Man is narrated in present tense by a British inspector. There
are no flashbacks; this is our fragmented postwar world. The film is a
cinematic apotheosis for an existential half decade—a synthesis of Italian neorealism and Cold War realpolitik, of French poetic realism and
Hollywood studio production. If the *cool* sensibility was ideologically
inchoate in '40s noir—an aesthetic without content embodied in certain
personae—*The Third Man* reveals the genre's self-awareness. The film
was also the rare noir to enjoy commercial success and critical acclaim:
it was awarded the Grand Prix at Cannes; Carol Reed won the New York
Critics Circle Award for best director; Robert Krasker received an Oscar for cinematography. For all of *The Third Man*'s noir style, Krasker
probably earned the Oscar for shooting much of the film with a tilted
camera—on an angle—as if the world itself was askew and lacked any
stable moral angle for narrative grounding.

The Third Man concerns a black marketeer named Harry Lime afoot
in an occupied city rendered as both labyrinth and open-air prison to reflect the destitute state of postwar Austria and much of postwar Europe
by association. Austria experienced World War II much like a colony
and remained occupied until 1955. Absorbed by Nazi Germany in 1938,
thousands fled Austria before an occupation that reduced the Jewish
population from twenty-two thousand to two hundred. When Russian
troops drove the Germans out in 1945, the so-called liberation included
a notorious campaign of rape and plunder that continued into the period
of occupation.[3]

As a capital of empire that gave birth to much modernist art and
thought, from Freud to Wittgenstein, Vienna serves as a metaphor for

the end of the age of Christian Europe and its empires. The setting casts audiences back to the first implosions of empire in World War I (the Austro-Hungarian and Ottoman empires), and Vienna is in rough parallel to occupied Berlin three hundred miles northward. During noir's crucial half decade, the British Empire began to crumble (India, 1947; Republic of Ireland, 1948) as did the French (Indochina and Algeria); the seeds of revolution took root throughout Africa and Asia (especially in China); and Europe's historical Other—the Jews—were now cast out, exterminated or redirected to Israel (founded, 1948). As a joint British-Austrian production written under Hollywood auspices, *The Third Man* seems self-conscious of these convergences and offers up an end to the master narrative of Europe itself.

The film also figures as a bookend to the 1940–42 moment that produced *Casablanca* and *Citizen Kane* and it is indebted to both films. *The Third Man* pointedly mocks simplistic American morality—good guys versus bad guys, heroes and villains—and works as a film negative to *Casablanca*'s patriotic notes of Allied unity eight years earlier. "What *Casablanca* was to wartime optimism, *The Third Man* was to postwar anxiety," Frederick Baker declares in his documentary, *Shadowing the Third Man*.[4] The film is also something of a sequel to *Citizen Kane*, with Orson Welles and Joseph Cotten reprising their roles as charismatic genius and hero worshiper. These three films could hardly be more iconic: *The Third Man* sits at number one on the top one hundred of the British Film Institute, just as *Kane* and *Casablanca* remain number one and number three, respectively, on the top one hundred of the American Film Institute. In addition, *The Adventures of Harry Lime* was a popular BBC-produced radio show (and later TV series), and it was imported to the United States in 1951–52. In many ways, James Bond is an Anglo-American hybrid of Rick Blaine and Harry Lime.

As a film shot mostly at night, *The Third Man* is a pitch-perfect noir: slick streets, documentary style, key lighting, rich chiaroscuro, snappy repartee, doppelgangers, shadows literal and metaphorical. In the style of documentary realism, Krasker's camera dignifies every exhausted, haggard Austrian face against a background of rubble and hardscrabble apartments, half-burnt cars and bombed-out sites (including the old Gestapo headquarters). Carol Reed seamlessly mixed in local Viennese extras with great Austrian character actors to create a city full of lost, ghostly figures wandering the ruptured ground of this ruined capital of empire.

The source text for the film is Graham Greene's *The Third Man*, a novella written to be filmed and narrated in tart humor by the solitary, hard-boiled Inspector Calloway. The opening sequence features a voice-over by Calloway describing the four occupation zones over a montage of black-market street transactions. Vienna is "simply a city of undignified ruins," Calloway reports. "The Danube was [only] a grey flat muddy river." These illicit street transactions resemble the opening montage of the Arab bazaar in *Casablanca*, as if Vienna is no more or less than a colonized city where everything is negotiable and for sale, including human beings. There are no vestiges of the glamorous Vienna, in either its modernist phase or the romantic era of Strauss waltzes. Calloway is the civil authority in the British zone, and his everyday life mirrors the Cold War as he steers a middle path between the naive, half-drunk American GIs and the secretive, thuggish Russians. As witness and narrator, Calloway's literary errand is truth telling, the compelling aesthetic ideal that marks noir's ethical rebel loners. In Greene's novella, Calloway declares to the reader: "It is as accurate as I can make it—I have tried not to invent a line of dialogue." At each turn, Calloway weighs the motivations and angles of each character: "[if] there are too many 'ifs' in my style of writing . . . [then] it is my profession to balance possibilities, human possibilities."[5]

For Calloway, there's no Civilization to uphold, no Progress on the horizon, no History worth holding onto: *The Third Man* visually renders the end of empire. In the novella he narrates a nighttime taxi ride that slides past "the half-destroyed Diana baths" and the "enormous wounded spire" of St. Stephen's cathedral, symbols of a city and a faith in ruins. There are only the streets to be policed—"the rusting iron of smashed tanks which nobody had cleared away"—and the act of witnessing to sustain him. The skyline is dominated by the enormous Ferris wheel in the Prater amusement park, "the Great Wheel revolving slowly over the foundations of merry-go-rounds like abandoned millstones."[6] The film's pivotal scene takes place on the Great Wheel in the Russian zone: it is symbolically both a wheel of fortune and a symbol of Greene's cyclical view of history, as indebted to Spengler's influential *Decline of the West*. Stoicism is the default philosophy for noir's ethical rebel loners like Calloway, and it's no wonder: a mere half century after its apex, Vienna is an urban corpse.

Yet the noir figure here is not Calloway but Harry Lime (Orson Welles), a charismatic racketeer. Welles does not appear until an hour into the film, then, amazingly, steals it at first glance in an iconic noir shot. Standing hidden in a doorway, a sudden light from an overhead apartment hits Lime full in the face. For five held seconds, Lime is chiaroscuro itself: the moon of his face appears suspended in the dead of night while his broad body blends into the doorway. Krasker shoots the doorway at an exaggerated thirty-degree angle, as if only Lime is aligned with the off-kilter moral geography of postwar Europe. The dramatic thrust could not be more startling: Lime had been presumed dead until this moment, and this apparition shocks his old friend Holly Martins and filmgoers alike. In this instant of his illumination, everyone realizes his death was faked and covered up. Then the light switches off and Lime disappears, as if into smoke.

Holly Martins is the film's naive protagonist, a childhood friend of Lime's and an unemployed writer of pulp Westerns. He comes to Vienna at Lime's invitation to join him in a business venture but arrives only to find his friend dead. He attends Lime's (fake) funeral after trying to dig up the facts of the (fake) car accident that killed him. Lime is the rebel cool figure of Martins's youth; when Inspector Calloway tells him Lime ran a black-market operation distributing tainted penicillin, Martins punches him in the jaw. Martins then begins his own investigation, looking for a "third man" at the car accident, yet he is woefully unfit for the role of detective: he can't hold his alcohol or keep his mouth shut. As with the virtuous heroes of his Westerns, Martins never questions his own motives or values. "He thinks he [always] has . . . God or virtue on his side," as one film scholar puts it.[7] Yet Calloway slowly convinces Martins of Lime's penicillin racket, and we watch this vain, virtuous man struggle first with issues of loyalty and morality, then with friendship and betrayal.

Harry Lime was something new in film noir—an *un*ethical rebel loner, a truly existential criminal. Consider the dark-side cool of this hustler, a man working a racket in tainted penicillin yet with a twinkle in his eye and a complex half smile. In his study about the film, Rob White wonders about Lime's jaunty, wistful persona: "[What] is that expression? . . . A smirk, a leer, a wistful grin, a bitter smile? It *is* a picture of confident self-possession—but is there anxiety and torment in it too? There could be nothing behind that look *or* . . . a lifetime's worth of disillusionment." "That look" is the mask of cool snugly fit over *realpolitik*. Lime's expression projects "confident self-possession," yet in split-second breaks, we are given sneak peaks into the "anxiety and torment" necessarily suppressed to pull off this performance. Is he a fallen hero or an anti-hero, a rogue hustler or a charismatic murderer?[8]

Harry Lime's mask of cool covers the sacrifice of morality that enables him to rationalize his black-market dealings. "What might he have seen?" White asks, and then, "What has Harry Lime lived through?" The artistic objective of noir remains self-reflexivity for its audience: What have *I* lived through? What do *I* think about what I've just lived through? Did Harry descend into nihilism due to the revelations of European civilization's shadow over two generations of world wars and the hypocrisy of its supposedly rational view of human nature or Enlightenment values? Did he become disillusioned "brought on by experiences during the war," and descend into self-interest as survival? "Is he a devil or a cherub?" White wonders.[9]

White's study of *The Third Man* takes its epigraph from Camus's *The Myth of Sisyphus*: "There is no sun without shadow and it is necessary to know the night." The figure of noir cool puts a face on a generation of experience that allows audiences to reflect on their own traumatic experiences. "Maybe, despite his ebullience and sparkle," White concludes, "the darkness of despair is on him." There is also the shadow of colonialism, the collateral damage of the building of empires. Here, the *uneth-ical* rebel loner has given into moral darkness in order to survive with style, and yet he is loved for it. Despite the film's revelations of Lime's crimes, "Audiences loved Harry Lime for his suave wit, his cockiness, his unbending desire to live well and resourcefully."[10] Orson Welles carries off noir cool's ethical ambiguity with enough panache to enchant even Beauvoir. How is the audience supposed to feel about Lime? The question remains moot even now: noir directors do not play to the virtuous chords of conventional morality.

So to measure the import of postwar anxiety we turn to the virtuous American, Holly Martins. When the old friends meet again, Lime comes around a corner whistling his theme song just below the Prater Wheel. In a scene filmed exactly as written, Martins excitedly awaits his boyhood hero hoping to hear his criminal activity is a misunderstanding while childhood memories swirl in his mind. Why was he filled with "fear and excitement?" "*Life had always quickened* when Harry came, came just as he came now, as though nothing much had happened . . . came *with his amused, deprecating, take-it-or-leave-it manner*—and of course one always took it" (my italics).[11] This is the *double*-edginess of the noir cool figure: a person who brings drama into one's static life of compromise and to whom the acolyte is in thrall.

Lime and Martins then have their only conversation in the film, a famous exchange that takes place as they ride on the Great Wheel. Holly wants to hear Harry proclaim his innocence, but instead Lime evades the facts and invokes the Nietszchean *übermensch* defense. At the apex of their booth's climb, Harry points to the "dots" below, humans telescoped to the size of ants. "Would you really feel any pity if one of those dots stopped moving forever? If I offered you twenty thousand pounds for every dot that stopped, would you really, old man, tell me to keep my money?" After evoking this nuclear subtext, Harry proves to be an old-school hustler in the P. T. Barnum mode: "the governments call them 'the people' or 'the proletariat' and I call them 'the suckers' and 'the mugs.' . . . It's the same thing." Yet despite his cynical worldview, Lime speaks with such wit and nonchalance—such style and hypnotic flow— that the audience remains charmed and roots for his survival. When the two men step off the Wheel, Harry extends to Holly an opportunity to join his penicillin racket and to send a message through an accomplice if interested.[12] It's Mephistopheles tempting Faust in the key of noir.

Then just before Lime departs, Orson Welles—the actor, in character—improvises a final flourish that contains a startling insight into the entire notion of "civilization." It is akin to a virtuosic cadenza at the end of a jazz solo:

> In Italy for 30 years under the Borgias they had warfare, terror, murder, bloodshed—but they produced Michelangelo[,] . . . da Vinci and the Renaissance. In Switzerland they had brotherly love . . . [and] 500 years of democracy and peace, and what did they produce? The cuckoo clock. So long, Holly.

Lime here becomes the resilient voice of capitalism: *greed is good*. The creative destruction on which free markets thrive fosters drama, progress, art, history, civilization itself. Lime harkens back to the Renaissance to justify the upheavals of modernity and his own choices. Again, the implication is Nietzschean: that Holly Martins's herd morality is the rule of cowards, a set of strictures made only for suckers and simpletons, prigs and rubes. Or to reduce it to a noir credo: *Don't be a chump, Holly*.

Finally, between Lime and Martins is "the girl," Anna Schmidt—a Hungarian actress holding an illegal passport to keep from being reclaimed by the Russians and put behind the Iron Curtain. Inspector Calloway uses Anna to tempt Martins, turning this cynical, existential woman into a damsel in distress to suit the needs of his investigation. Anna also serves as a symbol of the fate of Central Europe in the twentieth century—the "bloodlands," as Timothy Snyder calls them—all of those countries traded "between Hitler and Stalin." From Czechoslovakia and Poland to the Balkans and Baltic nations, these populations endured exile, forced migration, totalitarian government, and ethnic cleansing. At one point, when Martins worries that Anna will be deported, she acts nonplussed: "Oh, perhaps something will happen first . . . perhaps there'll be another war, or I'll die, or the Russians will take me." Numbed by recent experience, Anna repudiates naive distinctions of good and evil, as when Holly goes to her for solace and to persuade her of Harry's perdition. "For heaven's sake stop making him [over] in your image," she shouts. "Harry was real. He wasn't just your friend and my lover. He was *Harry*."[13]

The noir imagination often invokes doppelgangers to integrate Jungian ideas of the unconscious, of self and shadow self. The similarity of the friends' names—Harry and Holly—make their obverse apparent, and Anna even calls Holly "Harry" a few times by mistake. Holly is a sunny writer of Westerns—"honest, sensible, sober Holly Martins," Anna calls him—while Harry is a liminal figure, a hustler literally living underground. Holly strives to be virtuous and rational, yet he is self-righteous and naive; Lime is charming, elusive, and ambiguous, but he is hip, cynical, and playful. In an ingenious twist, the sunny hero is here trumped by his own shadow in the audience's minds: Reed and Greene here illuminate noir cool's inquiry into the lost power of the good (or virtuous) man.

The final blow to Martins's hero worship occurs when Calloway takes

Holly to a children's ward full of the victims of Lime's tainted penicillin. What follows is a negative epiphany: the end of a worldview. In the no-vella, Calloway narrates Martins's silent grief:

> If one watched a world come to an end, a plane dive from its course, I don't suppose one would chatter . . . and a world for Martins had certainly come to an end, a world of easy friendship, hero-worship, confidence. . . . Every memory . . . was [now] simultaneously tainted, like the soil of an atomized town.

Greene depicts Martins's paralysis with images of failed technology— planes falling, radioactive soil in an "atomized town"—as a metaphor of lost faith in one's nation and civilization. The personal and the geo-political come together here with both fission and *frisson*. In noir, there's only one decent thing to do at such a moment. "I . . . poured out two large doubles," Calloway tells the reader. "Go on . . . drink that," he says to Martins, and to the reader, "he obeyed me as though I were his doctor."[14]

This is the crucial Cold War moment of geopolitical critique for Greene and Reed. Both author and director believed the self-righteousness of American power was a dangerous framework for a global empire. The cultural arm of this blind patriotism was the genre of the Western: in effect, *The Third Man* makes a case for noir as realpoli-tik in comparison to the morality tale of the Western, as symbolized by Martins. Visually and cincmatically, if the Western trafficked in wide-open desert landscapes, then its shadow was the occupied city with its dark streets and repressed darker aspects of human nature. Early in the film, Martins stands up to Calloway's indictment of Lime: "You take that back," he hollers drunkenly and initiates a bar brawl. Calloway snipes back: "This isn't Santa Fe, I'm not a sheriff and you aren't a cowboy." Reed and Greene surely had John Wayne and John Ford on their minds: *The Third Man* opened in 1950 alongside John Ford's "cavalry trilogy" in which John Wayne embodied American triumphalism (*Fort Apache, She Wore a Yellow Ribbon*, and *Rio Grande*, 1948–50).[15] Five years after *The Third Man*, Greene published *The Quiet American* (1955), a novel that indicted America's arrogant virtue in taking over the French role in Vietnam. In this way, *The Third Man* proved quite prescient.[16]

The film ends with a one-shot denouement that sits in cinematic judgment of American innocence. After Lime is shot and killed in the sewers that have been his hideout, there is a second (real) funeral for him. Anna refuses to speak with Martins but he offers her a ride home then waits by his car. The camera looks up the road from behind Holly and remains still as it watches Anna approach from a distance. She walks purposefully toward and then past Holly without a glance. The screen fades into a still photograph, leaving Martins abandoned, paralyzed, and bereft. Holly betrayed Harry for the right reasons but at a cost he cannot measure. The camera remains planted: Martins fades into the background less as a shadow than as a specter—an empty suit, a husk to be blown to the four winds. Anna leaves Holly's tone-deaf chivalry to fade into the closing credits, a sepia photograph of an obsolete morality in a new post-Western world.

The opposite of global empire is the underground, the imagined space of a free mind imprisoned by convention. Greene and Reed were both compelled by the perspective of a sympathetic criminal living underground.[17] The noir anti-hero is a rebel ethical loner who gives range to his dark side as a social protest. Rather than being too good to survive in this world, he is punished with a memorable cinematic death, a symbolic punishment for stealing an expanded notion of freedom. The last shot of Harry Lime focuses on his fingers gripping a sewer grate from below as the blood flows out of him. As with Roy Earle on his mountain, Harry Lime shakes the bars of his cage and "becomes a symbol of generalized existential tragedy."[18]

This is the underground as postwar metaphor. Postwar cool figures are repressed selves made artistically manifest in fugitive characters living in sewers or narrating from basement rooms, confessing crimes that make them feel alive, or blowing bittersweet signature solos in smoky nightclub caverns. Postwar cool also partakes of émigré directors from the Austro-Hungarian Empire (Billy Wilder, Otto Preminger) projecting their lost worlds through deep shadows that cast Southern California in the chiaroscuro of German expressionism. There are no heroes and villains, just survivors among those in power, living between allegedly free markets and the black market. Or as Lime puts it when he laughs at the possibility that Martins would betray him: "You and I aren't heroes, Holly. The world doesn't make heroes anymore."

This new postwar mode of human behavior—the register of noir cool—modeled the inclusion of sun and shadow, good and evil, ideals and hypocrisy. Rather than a fantasy of human perfectibility or future enlightenment, this new philosophy of the pulsating day-to-day yin and yang would require the return of the repressed. A post-Western mindset still awaits the *re*integration of the shadow selves—the Others— excluded from the sunny civilizing errand of the Age of Europe. Yet the task began in Postwar I with an existential outlook open to the perspectives of Others after centuries of self-serving narratives of civilization, colonialism, and racial superiority.

Neither the United States nor England was yet willing to engage in such geopolitical reflection in 1950. For this reason, Harry Lime outlives the film and becomes a figure suspended in time, a hybrid Anglo-American anti-hero. Although Lime is an American in *The Third Man*, the British embraced him as a countryman: he quickly became an Anglo analogue for Philip Marlowe in the popular radio drama, *The Adventures of Harry Lime* (or *The Lives of Harry Lime* in the United States, 1950–52). For the radio show the writers created a prewar Harry Lime along noir lines, yet added a playboy component: he was now an ethical rebel loner comfortable with physical violence, a rogue to charm even the most virtuous women, a one-man intelligence network doing the right thing by unethical methods. The radio show played off his unethical behavior with a light touch and his globe-trotting became a fantasy of the dashed vision of empire in postwar England. As with the films of emergent noir, Harry Lime's past is left to the imagination and falls across the Depression, the war, and the blasted, impoverished state of postwar Europe. Within the tradition of noir cool, Lime looks back to the detectives of emergent noir, inherits the charismatic gangster personae of James Cagney and French actor Jean Gabin, and anticipates the figure of James Bond.

The ambient noir sensibility of *The Third Man* also extended to sound by way of Anton Karas's solo zither compositions. "The Third Man Theme" is one of the most memorable in film history: compelling, iconic, and elegiac, it is a *memento mori* for lost empires and a lost modernist capital. The film score stayed atop *Billboard*'s charts for ten weeks and the film's theme was the number three song of the year, just behind Nat King Cole's "Mona Lisa." If Thelonious Monk had only recorded and improvised on the theme—of if the young Miles Davis had rendered it on muted trumpet—then *The Third Man* might have been the perfect storm of these three postwar cultural forms, a smoking gun of Cold War cool.

Jazz and Noir

In retrospect, jazz is conspicuous by its absence in noir. The presence of jazz in the classic noir era exists more in the background swing beat of nightclubs with interracial clientele (*To Have and Have Not, The Killers)* or in the big band dance music of upscale nightclubs (*Gilda*), or in a torch-singer's rendition of a ballad (*Dark City, Roadhouse, The Racket*). Jazz sometimes simply signifies as sex, as when a soulful saxophone solo smokes its way out of the orchestral soundtrack to signal a sexual act or a "bad" woman. The torch singer is usually a "canary"—in jazz musicians' slang, she looks rather than sounds good—rather than an improvising jazz vocalist such as Anita O'Day or Lee Wiley. Of course, she was nearly always white. The sole African-American canary is Mattie Comfort in *Kiss Me Deadly* (1955), a girlfriend of Duke Ellington's for whom he composed "Satin Doll" (1956).[19]

David Butler kicks off his study *Jazz Noir* with a humbling admission. He expected the genre's soundtracks and scores to be suffused with jazz but to his surprise, there were few. There was no bebop or hard bop, few solos, and almost no black Americans in the cityscapes.[20] There are a few exceptions: the nightclub scene with African-American musicians soloing in *DOA* (1950); the upbeat swing scene in a black club in *Out of the Past*; the thunderous sound coming out of a club in *The Set-Up* to mirror the beating a boxer takes for not throwing a fight. There is a sprinkling of saxophone riffs we now associate with that feeling of late-night existential lonesome, nearly all played by white jazz musicians due to the Jim-Crowed musicians' union, the American Federation of Musicians. There are the jazz-influenced scores of white arrangers and composers such as Henry Mancini and Elmer Bernstein (e.g., *The Big Combo, Walk on the Wild Side, Phantom Lady, Man with the Golden Arm, The Sweet Smell of Success, Touch of Evil*). In the late 1950s, a few maverick filmmakers commissioned soundtracks from jazz musician-composers such as Miles Davis (*Lift to the Scaffold*, Louis Malle), Charles Mingus (*Shadows*, John Cassavetes's first film), Duke Ellington (*Anatomy of a Murder*, Otto Preminger), and John Lewis (*Odds against Tomorrow*, Robert Wise). Yet these films all appear at the tail end of the classic noir period and were not influential on the sight or sound of the noir aesthetic.

In addition, historians and scholars rarely write about jazz and noir together when evaluating postwar American culture—as if African-Americans and Euro-Americans grew up in different Americas with little overlap. Bogart and Orson Welles were serious jazz fans and both saw Ellington's *Jump for Joy*, the play meant to take the figure of "Uncle Tom" out of American theater. Mitchum once said he was a lost "scrawny kid" until someone gave him a saxophone to mess around with and he began to find himself (fig. 14). In 1941, Welles pitched to Ellington the idea of "the history of jazz as a picture" to be called *It's All True*—they would co-write and co-compose—then spent two years of his creative peak trying to make this aborted film. At the same time, Lester Young was obsessed with Westerns and identified with Jesse James as a man shot down by imitators. Miles Davis found his musical phrasing in part through the radio voices of Sinatra and Orson Welles. As Richard Wright wrote in 1940 of the impact of African-American culture in the American century: "Our music, jokes, and dances go where we cannot go." The most potent arenas of overlap existed in the nation's popular culture—music, film, radio, theater—specifically because artists always ignore genre and boundary lines.[21]

So why do we associate film noir with jazz?

First, jazz and noir were artistic sites of "cool" as that word first signified: underground, mysterious, secret, oblique, subterranean. These two genres provided a pop-cultural framework of resistance, an alternative mode of being-in-the-world that rejected both corporate workaday conformity and the blind patriotism enfolded into Cold War consumerism. Very few writers caught the jazz-noir connection. Jazz scholar Ross Russell actually wrote literary noir in the 1930s and he compared Raymond Chandler to Charlie Parker directly: "I feel the same way about Chandler as I did about Bird. Both worked within a 'popular' medium and created an art, a major art as far as I am concerned." Another exception was German jazz critic and anthropologist Ernest Borneman, who compared the authors of literary noir to jazz musicians in 1952, both groups "like prophets . . . read in secret but rarely praised in public." As Beauvoir's best friend during her American travels, Borneman noted that jazz and noir were more respected in France and the United Kingdom than in

Figure 14. Mitchum took up the saxophone as a "scrawny kid" and here he jams at a backstage party during the shooting of *The Racket* (1951).

the United States. "America's few genuine pioneers of art—the jazzmen and the 'tough' writers—had to go abroad before they dared hope for recognition at home."[22]

Second, film noir was rife with cries for individual dignity made by artists who toed neither the patriotic nor the corporate line. Jazz and film

noir were vehicles for inchoate social protest, on the one hand, and a repudiation of nihilism on the other. Jazz musicians protested nonverbally
and sonically with solos that included cries and moans and screams; directors cast narrative visual spells of individual defiance lacking any overt
left-wing critique. Many classic noirs were directed by central European
directors featuring gritty American actors in the roles of outcasts trying
to find an ethical middle way. When McCarthyism slowly encroached
on a supposedly free society in the early 1950s, jazz and noir were ready-
made forms of underground cultural resistance.

Third, noir protagonists are nearly all alcoholics and repair to local
bars to self-medicate, find clues, figure things out, and cool their existential pain with music. As a mental escape plan, alcohol abuse was to
the noir protagonist what heroin was to the jazz musician. Some kind of
jazz often plays in the background of these bars as the up-tempo surge of
mellow soothing, even if it's some pallid swing or a background singer.
These bars usually have an eclectic cast of working-class Americans, a bit
on the shady side: there are businessmen on the make, small-time gangsters and loose women, divorced average Joes and JoAnnes, traveling
salesmen, corrupt cops, grifters, and informants. (See, for example, *The
Killers*, *The Big Heat*, *The Racket*.)

Fourth, noir cool seems to require the detective or protagonist to be
beaten up badly at least once, whether by a cop or a criminal. The beating created a bond with the audience: this is a common man, an average
man, a man without connections, a man who has suffered, a man who
has been beaten and yet pulled himself up by his bare hands (rather than
his bootstraps). The jazz musician plays his subjective truth every night
at a club. The private detective returns to his shabby apartment every
night to reflect on his monastic life and ethical code. To be "beaten up"
was a cinematic translation of being "beat," that crucial postwar vernacular term meaning exhausted and wrung out. The beatdown of the detective was analogous to the real life of black jazz musicians, nearly every
one of whom was beaten up by a policeman without justification, often
for being in a car with a white woman. (See chapter 9.)

There are two short noir scenes in which jazz serves as the soundtrack
of working-class African-American life in neighborhood nightclubs, and
these exceptions prove the rule. In *Out of the Past* (see fig. 15) and *Kiss Me*

Figure 15. At a local jazz club, PI Jeff Markham (Robert Mitchum) tries to get information from Kathie Moffatt's maid, Eunice (Theresa Harris).

Deadly, cool, edgy sleuths display their street cred at these clubs. They scout for information from black informants, who are treated with rare postwar dignity in these films.

In *Kiss Me Deadly*, PI Mike Hammer limps into a black jazz club he frequents and the fast-talking hip young black bartender quips, "Hey man, you sure look beat. You look real lean, real *wasted*. What's got you, man? It looks like you in it." Hammer simply orders a bottle of bourbon and shares it with him. (See fig. 16.)

Then Hammer turns to listen to Mattie Comfort singing "I'd Rather Have the Blues" (fig. 17), a Nat King Cole hit of the era. One crucial line of the song hits Hammer where he lives: "I'd rather have the blues / than what I've got."[23] He inhales the music and then listens to this cosmopolitan black woman sing about something worse than the blues: "I feel so mean and fraught," Hammer hears his thoughts echoed back, "the web has got me caught." The camera stays on Comfort for a while then shifts into the mirror where it holds jazz singer and detective in balance as if on a set of scales.[24]

To riff on June Christy's 1954 hit of the same name, "something cool" emerged in postwar American culture that still calls to authors, directors, and musicians. Novelist Robert Coover recently distilled the detective genre to its literary DNA in a novella simply called *Noir* (2010). Detective Philip M (a.k.a. "Mr. Noir") hangs his hat at a local jazz club called the Woodshed (a.k.a. "the Shed"). The Shed is a dive bar and "tea pad," as well as the venue for jam sessions run by a jazz pianist known as Fingers. To Philip M, the Shed is the funky oasis he deserves: "Homeless, you feel as much at home in here as anywhere," he reflects. What makes the Shed an outcast's home? "It's the beat, the melody, the melancholy, the music." It's carved right into his table, the most precise, profound quote about the existential power of music: "'You are the music while the music lasts,' it says on the scarred tabletop." This famous line from T. S. Eliot's *The Four Quartets* (1941) fits the fleeting dialogic ritual

Figure 16. In *Kiss Me Deadly* (1955), PI Mike Hammer (Ralph Meeker) receives some distressing information at his regular local jazz club from the bartender (Art Loggins) and torch singer (Mattie Comfort).

Figure 17. The original "Satin Doll," actress Mattie Comfort sings "I'd Rather Have the Blues" at a black nightclub in *Kiss Me Deadly* (1955).

of jazz musicians and their audiences, of artists capable of keeping you musically alive when you're not so sure about yourself. For Philip M, the music and the Shed supplant his self-loathing: "The place itself is filthy, smoky, gloomy, rank. *It's you.*"[25]

Fifth, by the mid-1950s, jazz musicians began to claim their music was vernacular *American* art—that is, made in America by American artists—just as Raymond Chandler claimed detective fiction was true literature in the *Atlantic Monthly* in 1944. For Chandler, the noir detective must be "a complete man and a common man and yet an unusual man . . . the best man in his world and a good enough man for any world." He must be a man of integrity and individuality, hip to the street and to social difference. Duke Ellington defined jazz as a musical form that was "essentially Negro music," with open spaces for "the elaborations [of] self-expression." Such openness makes jazz quintessentially American in its approach but with an African-American difference. And yet any musical form is accessible to any person willing to learn its chords, tonalities, and practices. As drummer Max Roach spoke of the artistic imperative of jazz musicians: "Ours are individual voices listening intently to all the other voices, and creating a whole from all of these personal voices."[26] Jazz is a musical form at once individual and social.

In the 1950s, drummer Art Blakey gave some version of the following speech about jazz as vernacular American art every night at Café Bohemia or the Village Vanguard. The confident hostility here partakes of the Black Arts Movement of the late 1960s but the speech was rhetorically the same in a gentler tone:

> Jazz is known all over the world as an American musical art form. . . . No America, no jazz. . . . We're a multiracial society here . . . [and we] are the product of a multiracial society. So what difference does it make? Our parents were slaves, so you don't know whose grandmother was bending over picking cotton when the slaveowner walked up behind her! There was nothing we could do about it. Otherwise we wouldn't be all the different colors of the rainbow.
>
> We are here, we are the most advanced blacks, and jazz comes from us. When we heard the Caucasians playing their instruments, we took the instruments and went somewhere else . . . This is our contribution to the world, though they [Whites] want to ignore it. . . . It couldn't come from anyone but us."[27]

Jazz came from taking the instruments of Western culture and going "somewhere else" in terms of musical form and social function. The instruments were only the hardware: African-Americans wrote entirely new software. In effect, they *over*wrote the cultural possibilities of music and deconstructed high and low culture by creating a music that was artistic, emotive, individual, and (at times) spiritual.

Jazz and noir were organic and contemporary American art forms, shared genres of cultural resistance. Significantly, in nearly all of the retro-noir that harkens back to the postwar era, jazz is the soundtrack of Los Angeles across ethnic and racial lines: in Walter Mosley's Easy Rawlins novels of postwar black LA (*Devil in a Blue Dress*), in James Ellroy's *LA Quartet* (including *LA Confidential*), and in the Zoot-suit themed works of Luis Valdez and Thomas Sanchez. The literary fascination with postwar LA suggests that it is an era we still need illuminated, a dark, underground seam of the American Dream that remains unintegrated. In addition, in numerous homages and parodies of noir, a soulful saxophone riff often introduces the detective to create a texture of existential urbanity: to name only three, Garrison Keillor's character Guy Noir from *The Prairie Home Companion*, Steve Martin as Philip Marlowe in *Dead Men Don't Wear Plaid*, or Captain Picard's fantasy as PI Dixon Hill on the holodeck in *Star Trek: The Next Generation*. Sometimes the detective receives his own jazz intro, and if not, he will hear a saxophone riff in his head as soon as the femme fatale enters, as if the sax is the sound of sex itself.[28]

Given the state of ferment within jazz in 1945, jazz musicians should have been the natural composers of film noir, of a dark cinema concerning individual struggle against overwhelming social forces. Many redolent compositions of bebop, hard bop, and cool jazz were four-minute mini-concertos with memorable, whistleable themes: consider John Lewis's "Django," Miles Davis's "Something I Dreamed Last Night," Cannonball Adderley's "Dancing in the Dark." If not for the Jim Crowing of the film industry and the musicians' union, jazz might have signified as a musical return of the repressed in Hollywood film, a new *sounding* created by the descendants of ex-slaves to artfully consider an emerging post-Western era.

Being Cool from Being Colonized: Jazz as Sonic Existentialism

The handwritten first draft of Norman Mailer's "The White Negro" was entitled "Dialectic of an American Existentialist." Its salient perception across racial lines was that each black person knew "in the cells of his existence that life was war, nothing but war." This is also the major theme of both Chester Himes's *If He Hollers Let Him Go* (1945) and Ellison's *Invisible Man* (1952), novels narrated by smart young black men as they are bullied in public—in all non-black spaces—by police, guards, co-workers, employers, and even waiters. "No Negro can saunter down a street with any real certainty that violence will not visit him on his walk," Mailer wrote. "The Negro has the simplest of alternatives: live a life of constant humiliation or ever-threatening danger."[29] Mailer's friend James Baldwin wrote that Harlem was a place where nearly every "Harlem citizen, from the most circumspect church member to the most shiftless adolescent," could spin "a long tale . . . of police incompetence, injustice, or brutality," an experience he had "witnessed and endured . . . more than once." As Richard Wright wrote in "I Choose Exile" from Paris, "Born in America, I could never, with my black skin, hope to meet America's prime racial requirements of first-class citizenship as long as the atmosphere of Anglo-Saxon racial jealousy prevail[ed]."[30]

White remained the color of power and domination, of virtue and citizenship: to be American required being white, by law, by social practice, and in the national imagination. Himes's novel about wartime black shipyard workers in Los Angeles starts off by showing the gauntlet of insults any black person might run on an average commute to work such that the narrator (Bob Jones) concludes: "The white folks had sure brought their *white* to work with them that morning." As Wright, Baldwin, and Ellison had shown him, Mailer perceived that African-Americans had been "living on the margin between totalitarianism and democracy for two centuries."[31] In a key postwar parallel, Mailer's reference to war as an apt metaphor for a black person's life independently occurred to French intellectuals during the Nazi occupation of Paris.

Existentialism crystallized through the experience of the Nazi occupation of Paris: for the first time, white, Western intellectuals were treated as non-white peoples had always been treated by oppressors. French men were rounded up at will, silenced and sent off to convict labor, shot without trial, and forced to listen to the master-race claims of their oppressors in radio speeches. In Sartre's famous essay, "The Republic of Silence" (1944), he reflected how "every day we were insulted to our faces and had to take it in silence." The insults appeared every day in print and in watching one's fellow citizens humiliated. "Everywhere—on the walls, on the screens and in the newspapers—we came up against the vile, insipid picture of ourselves our oppressors wanted to present to us." Under such circumstances, each Parisian had to make "authentic choice[s]" every day, as "exile, captivity, and especially death . . . became for us the habitual objects of our concern." The individual life was suddenly a war in Paris and survival paramount within what Jean Guéhenno called "our artificial prison" in his *Diary of the Dark Days*, a journal he called nothing but "prison stories." This journal was an existential testament to writing itself as a response to the strain of maintaining dignity in the face of spiritual oppression: "Our defeat may be definitive and I wonder what our lives will be like in this prison. Prison for life, at least for people my age." The response to such overwhelming social and political forces was to apotheosize the individual. As historian Mark Mazower recognized in *Dark Continent*, "the experience of occupation had a powerful effect on the development of existentialist thought."[32]

Such an everyday set of "authentic choices" within a daily life of insults and threats was second nature for African-Americans. Isn't an "open-air prison" an apt term for the Deep South during the Jim Crow era? Do you choose smiling obedience (Uncle Tomming), sullen withdrawal, coded protest through music, or outright defiance (violence)? Do you choose migration or local political resistance? Do you suppress your rage and the internalization of insult? Do you work in the black markets of prostitution or gambling away from the white man's boot heel? Do you choose liberty or death? This was simply everyday life under the oppressive terror of the segregated U.S. South in the Jim Crow era. The main difference between prison and many jobs in the Deep South was mobility. As blues singer Big Bill Broonzy said, "The only thing different between a levee camp [job] and a prison farm . . . is that you can go from one levee camp to another."[33]

Herein lies the crossroads of the cool mask for the expressive arts of black Americans (music) and French existentialists (literature). How do you preserve individual dignity within oppression, terrorism, and a daily diet of insults? "All France, all Europe is in prison," Guéhenno wrote about the Nazi occupation. "All over the countryside . . . the green men stand on guard with their legs spread and their eyes in a vacant stare." Guéhenno used the words "prison" and "prisoners" 125 times together to render the occupation of Paris during wartime. His journal was a form of artistic practice and self-assertion to remind himself he had a voice: "Since we were in prison, we had to live like prisoners and at least hold onto a prisoner's honor: fully appreciate our servitude, the better to find an intense, living freedom inside ourselves."[34]

This is a pitch-perfect European analogy to Ellison's definition of the blues, except that blues was played in public as a form of critical engagement. Ellison famously defined the blues as "an autobiographical chronicle of personal catastrophe expressed lyrically." In many ways, jazz subsumed the blues to become a statement of grappling with a (relatively) new freedom outside of the open-air prison of the U.S. South. As Sidney Bechet once said about its emergence in New Orleans, jazz is about "all that freedom, all that feeling a man's got when he's playing next to you . . . all that waiting to get in for your own chance, freeing yourself."[35]

For African-Americans, social protest to the daily oppression of the racial order had always come through music rather than literature, politics, or philosophy. "The music had to say what we could not say out loud," as Duke Ellington once said. The blues were a form of sung protest and defiant self-assertion, as Big Bill Broonzy and Memphis Slim discussed in a rare recorded conversation in 1949. "I've known guys that wanted to cuss out the boss," Broonzy said, but instead, "I've heard them sing those songs—sing words, you know—back to the boss . . . [from] behind the wagon, hookin' up the horses." Memphis Slim replied: "Yeah, blues is a kind of revenge."[36] Blues is a form of encoded prison stories, rendered in first person, combining suffering and survival.

Within jazz and blues are encoded methods of speaking and conversation—of speaking up and speaking out—against invasive racist ideologies invested in social humiliation. All African-American musics serve this function, but jazz musicians were the first to function as public intellectuals within the ethnic community across economic class. Jazz was a *non*-verbal method of conversation and social protest. Beginning with bebop, African-American musicians transformed this daily war into artistic self-expression. (See chapter 9.) "Jazz was an expression of improvisation, spontaneity and imaginative response to given situations that cannot be controlled," one cultural historian reflected on the Cold War.[37]

Postwar jazz was *sonic* existentialism. It was the individual's sound of survival at a time when social and racial progress were moribund, Europe was in tatters, and nuclear apocalypse was imaginable—especially after Russia's first A-bomb test in 1949. Yet despite the ubiquity of jazz in postwar Paris and a vital African-American expatriate community, French intellectuals were then unable to perceive jazz as an embodied philosophical act.

Today a cultural historian like James Campbell easily links jazz and existentialism in postwar Paris: jazz was a "freedom music" communicating "defiance and protest" while projecting a "rude and erotic" individuality. If "man simply is," Campbell reflected back to the Left Bank,

"[then] the black jazz musician was *man-simply-is* par excellence, improvising his freedom nightly." Yet despite their affection for jazz, Sartre
and Camus suggest no such connections in their visits to New York jazz
clubs. In 1946, Sartre did not name any of the bebop musicians he saw
but he considered this post-swing jazz as "speaking to the best part of
you, the toughest, the freest, to the part which wants neither melody nor
refrain." At the end of the night, the music left him "a little worn out, a
little drunk, but with a kind of dejected calm." Camus admired a swing
pianist's "rhythm, force, and precision," and wrote in his notebook: "Impression that only the Negroes give life, passion, and nostalgia to this
country which, in their own way, they have colonized." Both authors
convey a sense of the music's existential vitality as well as its centrality
to American art, identity, and subterranean politics. Yet neither names a
musician or refers to individual artistic achievement—as Vian did, with
Parker, Miles, and Gillespie—on an analogous level to other art forms.[38]

The failure to historicize jazz with other art forms remains a conse-
quence of an entrenched (white) Western linkage between rationalism,
suffering, and individuality as set against the stereotypes of African-
American physicality, emotional abandon, and natural instinct. Mailer's
ridiculous declaration that "jazz is orgasm" in "The White Negro" forever
tainted an essay that still holds keen insights about postwar anomie and
the impact of black culture on national life through jazz, slang, style,
and embodiment. Yet it was difficult for African-American writers to get
passed the romantic racialism of Mailer's famous essay. Ralph Ellison
repudiated Mailer's "belief in the hipster and the 'white Negro' as the
new culture hero" since it depended on "the same old primitivism crap":
an aspiration to black "cocksmen possessed of great euphoric orgasms
[who] are out to fuck the world into peace, prosperity, and creativity."
Albert Murray was stupefied that he had to explain to a white poet "that
jazz represented CONTROL not abandon, as did all forms of American
Negro dancing."[39]

Instead, jazz and blues are forms of what Murray calls "survival technology" and their musical objectives are to affirm individual, racial, and
group identity simultaneously. Black vernacular culture insists on a ho-
listic, organic celebration of mind and body through joy, humor, celebration, and sexuality: these are artistic objectives tied to existential affirmation and enfolded within dialogic public rituals. For big bands, this

artistic tension played out publicly on the dance floor within the ideological crisis of work during the Great Depression, as a joyous band of musical *workers* played up-tempo, enlivening songs to rejuvenate national morale one night at a time. To see men and women enjoy and take pride in their work—as performed in public for the physical pleasure of its audiences—goes to the heart of the popularity of big bands not only for Americans but also in global culture. From Prague to Paris, and even for youth in Soviet Russia and Nazi Germany (as in *Swing Kids*), swing-era jazz contained the portable cultural elements of New World African modernity. These cultural elements developed by African-Americans functioned as democratic acts of survival technology for all participants.[40]

James Baldwin suggests that jazz remained encoded in the postwar era because it was still difficult for African-Americans to stare straight into slavery and reckon with their past; in effect, the musical form carried history and its wounds without re-memory. Consider that it was equally hard for white Westerners to stare directly at the legacy of World War II—its concentration camps, nuclear slaughter, and Russian gulags. Germany was probably the second most technologically advanced country in the world, yet it used its industrial power to methodically murder millions through the methods and efficiency of Fordist mass production. In addition, Germany's actions (and the dropping of the atomic bombs on Japan) signaled the failure of the Enlightenment and proved there was no relationship between technological advance and social progress.

This central existential problem was best framed by Mailer in the often-forgotten opening paragraph of "The White Negro":

> Probably, we will never be able to determine the psychic havoc of the concentration camps and the atom bomb upon the unconscious mind of almost everyone alive in these years. . . . We have been forced to live with the suppressed knowledge that . . . we might . . . be doomed to die as a cipher in some vast statistical operation . . . a death by *deus ex machina* in a gas chamber or a radioactive city.[41]

Along with the implosion of classical Western values went the utopian socialist and Communist hopes that had buoyed a century's worth of political rebels. Mailer ticked off these failures in an early draft of the essay: "revolutionary consciousness," "impotent bureaucratisms," "the perverted example of Stalinism," "trade-union mediocrity," and "compromised right-wing socialism." In its place there was only triumphalist consumerism—in Mailer's words, "the Cold War prosperity of the Fifties"—a vacuum of moral and political authority that he called only "a false solution."[42]

To be conscious and brave enough to stare recent history in the face was to understand that advanced industrial society had proven as murderous and savage as any non-Western or pre-industrial empire. Europeans and White Americans had to begin reckoning with the fact that those non-white peoples once designated as savages or heathens were equally human while the "white race" was equally primitive. The savage mass slaughters of Auschwitz and Hiroshima were planned and carried out by men proud of their achievements, whether of purifying their Aryan tribe to rule the world for a thousand years or of expressing technological dominance. As Mailer continued: "The Second World War presented a mirror to the human condition which blinded anyone who looked into it. . . . Tens of millions were killed in concentration camps out of the inexorable agonies and contractions of super-states founded upon the always insoluble contradictions of injustice." In other words, God was dead and religion delegitimated.

Western culture had bet its values on an unconscious assumption that there was an inherent virtue to technology and its myth of progress. The white, Western world equated scientific progress with a world bent to a machine-built will and a blind eye set on a utopian future featuring "an economic civilization founded upon the confidence that [even] *time* could be . . . subjected to our will."[43] To Mailer's thinking, any individual now had to face the fact that he or she was equally capable of murder, equally capable of taking joy in violence and sadism (*pace* My Lai or Abu Ghraib). If that were true, then being "civilized" was a fraudulent white mythology. Humans now had the fate of the planet in their own hands, and it was hard to bet on a future of peaceful coexistence, moral perfectibility, or social progress.

Camus addressed this problem in *The Fall* (1954). "Ah, this dear old planet!" the protagonist Jean-Baptiste Clamence moans aloud. "All is clear now. We know ourselves; we now know of what we are capable." Clamence calls himself a "judge-penitent": his role in the novel is both to judge Western Civilization and to exist in a state of penance for its crimes of colonialism, social injustice, inequality, racism, and genocide. The character of Jean-Baptiste—John the Baptist, that is—represents the call for a new, secularized moral order to reboot the society since it is "the last chance of Western Civilization."[44]

In short, if French or Euro-American audiences felt an analogous alienation and anomie to African-Americans in nuclear anxiety and the Cold War, they failed to recognize or theorize these responses with any kind of solidarity. They may have found it readily enough in the emotional communication (the "cry") of African-American jazz musicians, blues shouters, and soul singers, yet they kept its content of survival and affirmation at arm's length since it was the music of the Other. Baldwin believed that Euro-Americans fear emotional outpouring and so reserved their white privilege to experience it vicariously through the Other. In this way, such emoting remains excluded from Western self-definitions of rational white self-control. The emotive cry of a jazz musician is thus "somehow seen as curious and prurient by those outside [the group]," saxophonist Archie Shepp once wrote, echoing Baldwin.[45]

Herein lies the historical correspondence of jazz musicians, French existentialists, postwar youth, and liberal intellectuals and writers. Existentialism was a theory of individual response to both religious hypocrisy and the randomness of the universe, both the failures of European superiority and the collateral damage of corporate capitalism. Jazz represented an artistic and nonverbal struggle against repression: its soundings of freedom came from an oppressed people against a dominant white society that functioned at times as a police state. This nonverbal art form, as played live, made of the audience a sounding board and forced their empathy. Mailer interpreted the emotional communication of a jazz solo simply: "I feel this, and now you do too." It was a dialogic ritual, "a communication by art."[46] In the choice between feelings of shame or confronting the Other, jazz split the difference and forced members of the dominant society to reassess the men behind their cool masks.

Sartre may have been unable to hear the existential racial protest in jazz but he sure could see it in the literature of négritude when he first read the works of French Caribbean poets. These black men wrote about white colonists with the same resentment, anger, and revenge any oppressed people would feel, and Sartre felt exposed. His shock still rings through the stunning opening paragraph of his introduction to Léopold Senghor's first anthology of négritude poetry in 1947, *Black Orpheus*:

> What were you hoping, when you removed the gags that stopped up these black mouths? That they would sing your praises? . . . Here are black men standing, men looking at us, and I want you to feel, as I do, the shock of being seen. *For the white man has*, for three thousand years, enjoyed the privilege of *seeing without being seen*. He was pure gaze. . . . *The white man . . . white as day, white as truth, white as virtue*, lit up Creation like a torch. . . . These black men look at us today and our gaze is driven back into our eyes.[47]

In a single sentence here, Sartre mapped out the entire symbolic system of whiteness and blackness. If white people thought of themselves as being "white as day, white as truth, white as virtue," the opposite was cast as associations for blackness: whiteness is equated with the light of day against the blackness of night and the darkness of human nature; whiteness is equated with truth such that black men live in delusion or false consciousness; whiteness is equated with virtue as and against the blackness of sin and vice. These poems from the French colonies were blowback, the return of the repressed. Sartre had the cultural courage to understand the declaration of cultural war on the color line.[48]

To Sartre, the négritude anthology was a shock to the system, a revelation of Western culture's shadow evil in colonialism. These poems represented a third blow to French identity after the Nazi occupation and their powerlessness during the Cold War. Sartre wrote that the French were "already feeling our dignity crumbling beneath the gaze of the Americans and Soviets," but at least they still felt like "divine-right Europeans." Yet here were black writers shaking the Western door with "poems [that] shame us," and in addition, poems that "were not written for us." To Sartre, these poems represented "a gaining of awareness" for black men and an act of artistic rebellion against their oppressors. For Sartre, the objective of these poems was quite obvious: it was to "force those who, for centuries, have . . . reduce[d] him to the animal state, to recognize him as a human being."[49]

The same was true for jazz musicians: in effect, jazz was the first global musical form of nonverbally talking *back*—and talking *black*—to dominant white society. Yet there is a key salient difference to jazz as opposed to literature: in jazz, the artist *is* the agent of change itself, the very document of change. The live communication *fuses together* the art and the artist—they are inseparable, part and parcel of one another, and yet also interacting with the band and the audience in real time. There is no separation of art and artist, as there can be with painter and canvas, author and book: your sound *is* you.[50]

As Baldwin wrote of the postwar artistic moment, jazz was an existential genre that made it possible for a musician to "bear witness" to slavery through its ingathering of blues, spirituals, and voices while also sustaining the collective ethnic identity of Americans of African descent. "It is a music which creates . . . the response to that absolutely universal question: *Who am I? What am I doing here?*" With the support of other musicians, the soloist gives that night's testimony. Just as blues songs rarely made overt reference to racism, jazz needed to be abstract such that its content "not be 'de-coded.'" If the encoded protest was conscious, the music would not then be able to fulfill its social function as a nonverbal "description of black circumstances." Jazz was at first an in-group artistic form with therapeutic import and an objective for helping "overcome" history. The *cry* of the jazz musician, adapted from gospel and blues vocalists, enfolds the social history of African-Americans. For saxophonist Archie Shepp, any given solo can tap the source of "an inexplicable pain that need never be explained to its initiates."[51]

Then why was jazz so popular with white intellectuals of the postwar era? Ralph Ellison was of two minds about this question, starting with the fact that the soloing jazz musician represented a new artistic figure in Western culture. For Ellison, "[jazz] originally was [a] mose signifying at other moses," meaning it was an African-American art form with only in-group meanings. Yet the aesthetic power of jazz transformed the perception of African-Americans: "Like any real work of art," he wrote to Albert Murray, "jazz made a helluvalotta white folks want to *be* mose." If some of these progressive people confused the artistry with biology and aspired to *be* black, that was "simply because jazz is art and art is the essence of the human."[52] Ellison also thought there was a ritual of guilt involved. He believed the new intellectual interest in jazz among college students and liberals arose as Euro-Americans became more aware of the nation's everyday racism and its shameful past such that it tainted proclaimed ideals of freedom and democracy. At any given jazz gig, audiences watched African-Americans transmute individual protest and struggle into musical cries, moans, and flights of imagination. The objective of the soloing musician was to create a complex, affective musical statement of great emotional range while staying cool and relaxed in body and mind.

Euro-Americans needed the dialogic ritual of jazz at a time of spiritual crisis in which white identity was not sufficient for survival. In "The Price of the Ticket," an essay that harkens back to the postwar moment, Baldwin wrote that without white identity to cover their existential dilemma—"the ticket" needed to secure first-class citizenship and economic success—whites would find themselves in need of similar kinds of cultural sustenance inherent to the music rituals of African-Americans. Baldwin insisted further that "white people are not white," but only "delude themselves into believing that they are," based on "an American superstition" about its cultural forebears being solely of "the Old World, or Europe." Without nationalism and white privilege, Baldwin suggested, Europeans and Euro-Americans would face the same challenge of ongoing self- and collective reinvention at work in black music.[53]

What if postwar intellectuals then only beginning to understand their own feelings of exile, their own need for de- and reconstruction, were drawn to a musical form ontologically created to produce identity on the wing since they were assuaging their own feelings of anomie? What if the public display of expressive, improvisational individualism by jazz musicians suggested artistic pathways to fill a "need [or lack] in white culture," to invoke musicologist Christopher Small's phrase?[54]

What if jazz was indeed *sonic existentialism*?

Recently, drummer and bandleader Ahmir "Questlove" Thompson of The Roots reflected on the legacy of jazz on global culture in the postwar era: "Jazz . . . forced the mainstream to see black musicians as virtuosos with complex ideas and powerful (and recognizable) emotions. How are you going to treat someone as less than human, in any way, once they've been so deeply human in full view?"[55]

To riff again on the last line of Ellison's *Invisible Man*: And who knows but on the lower frequencies, they spoke for you?

Lester Young Redux: The Sisyphus of Jazz

In an unpublished folder of notes labeled "Lester and Alienation" from the mid-1950s, jazz critic Ross Russell referred to Lester Young's nightly labors as Sisyphean in nature. If "life is absurd . . . [and] man must seek solutions," he wondered, was it possible that a jazz musician's nightly challenge of creating a new solo for the same songs was one public model of this problem *and* its solution? "Jazzman as Sisyphus," he speculated, such that "each solo performance requires improvisation, i.e., new treatment of theme—cf. to rolling stone up the hill." The boulder is symbolic of the jazz musician's many challenges, first and foremost "the Burden of Improvisation," since each must push it up the hill in public (i.e., improvise live). Yet, to Russell, the boulder also symbolized the black jazz musician's occupational hazards: long nights of travel, second-class citizenship, and police harassment, as well as the need for drugs to provide stimulation and escape. "They must live from solo to solo, also club to club, one night stand to one night stand, [especially] the eminent ones, who have ideas and create."[56]

Russell wondered: "Are jazzmen a body of professionals who are all (or mostly) existentialists?" This is a sociological question for which he takes Young as his only example. "He had been born into an alien [white] culture, apprenticed to a trade that was a function of show business, doomed to ever recreate a new solo line." And yet his victory is that the solo line is his alone, an artistic fingerprint stamped within the daily challenge of maintaining dignity and an individual humanity. The jazz musician is condemned to freedom on the bandstand even as he is immersed in the absurdity of his job and his race: "[Within] the freedom that jazz afforded within its strict discipline . . . he had been doomed to forever endlessly create a new melodic line to every solo . . . no matter how familiar the theme."

There was this satisfaction: to express one's own distinctive experience—to tell *your* story in a self-defining sound, a tonal portrait—through an alternation of humor, weakness, joy, disappointment, and pleasure. If Russell was saddened and confused by Young's inconsistent performances in the 1950s, he still understood Young's motivation for pushing the musical boulder up the hill: "What kept him going was a faith in what he was doing, despite his waning powers, despite his lack of support." Young had more support than Russell knew, since the latter knew little of his personal life or periods of domestic happiness.[57]

Russell was the only postwar intellectual to suggest explicitly that jazz musicians were America's organic existentialists. The primary challenge of existentialism is to admit and then confront the intellectual fact that the purpose of existence is at best unknown, at worst pointless, and absurd without God or religion. In existential terms, every human being must figure out how to bring dignity to the quotidian aspects of life, his or her everyday mundane work. This leaves each person to create his or her own freedom, a notion that is seemingly liberating but actually terrifying. If every person needs a private ethical code, how do you go about creating one?

In *Stomping the Blues*, Albert Murray theorized that all African-American music works as public ritual involved in modeling existential affirmation in the face of adversity. For each musician, the challenge is "the most fundamental of all existential imperatives . . . reaffirmation and continuity in the face of adversity." This is the motivating force behind both the self-dialogue of creating one's sound and the performer-audience relationship. For Murray, the existential success of *any* art form lies in its ability to revive, compel, and rejuvenate individuals, "for what is ultimately at stake is morale . . . and what must be avoided by all means is a failure of nerve." The primordial problem is having the blues, "when you wake up with the blues there again . . . all around your bed but also inside your head as well, as if trying to make you wish that you were dead or had never been born." To this problem, an art form must create a space for resistance rather than resentment, "because the whole point is not to give in and let them get you down."[58]

Murray also theorized "the break" in jazz, a short four-bar solo where all the other instruments fall out. The improvising musician faces a chasm of silence and emptiness that he or she must now make meaningful and personal: it is an act of existential affirmation through self-expression. The break is "the Moment of Truth" for jazz musicians and "that disjuncture that should bring out your personal best." In essence, Sisyphus's boulder is equivalent to the audience at a live performance: the musician's job is to take them up the mountain to where they can see the light and live another day. When the musician successfully crosses over the chasm, he or she takes the audience along, an act of individual leadership with collective implications. This is one of Murray's ideals of "heroic action," the translation of the archetypal hero of literature into improvised music.

In effect, *existential cool* in postwar jazz and blues can be defined as *the stylization of artistic statements of resilience*.[59] "Lester saw life as absurd," Russell speculated, imagining Young's perspective on life over long observation. "Night clubs, cities, ghettos, the jazz press with its sophomoric enthusiasm . . . all this was not so much a nightmare as an absurdity." Young certainly saw racial oppression as a nightmarish imposition onto everyday absurdity. In his existential melancholy, Young fascinated nearly all postwar white jazz critics, from Nat Hentoff to Whitney Balliett to Jack Kerouac. Yet Young delineated the racial nightmare from a broader absurdity in the last interview of his life in Paris. Asked about racism by François Postif, he answered: "It's the same way all over, you dig? It's fight for your life, that's all. Until death do we part."[60] Young drank himself to death in the late 1950s and yet rarely expressed self-pity for his choices. One might say he chose his form of suicide in alcoholism—like a good existentialist—since he certainly knew the logical end of drinking two fifths of gin a day.

"What is jazz?" This question was once put to drummer Jo Jones, one of Young's closest friends and a true griot of the music.

> *What is jazz?* . . . All jazz musicians express themselves through their instruments and they express the types of persons they are, the experiences they've had during the day, during the night before, during their lives. There is no way they can subterfuge their feelings. . . . When he brings his experiences onto the bandstand, he projects his feelings amongst the audience and he can either have them going out of the place smiling or in frowns.[61]

Jazz is emotional communication: each solo is an artistic transmutation of personal experience processed into sound. Yet it is an act of both self-expression and social outreach. "The listener [is] the one all us musicians are trying to reach," Gil Evans explained. "If we can reach him emotionally, he becomes part of the music. . . . Reaching is what counts."[62]

If the postwar jazz musician publicly embodied an artistic method of overcoming this adversity, then the attraction for white audiences of the public, improvising African-American individual in a destabilized post-Western world becomes apparent. Listening to the beautifully sad ballads of Lester Young in his last years, one hears a record of his daily experience and the emotional costs of his attempt to share them. Albert Murray compared Young's later sound to the "somewhat painful but nonetheless charismatic parade-ground strut of the campaign-weary soldier who had been there one more time and made it back in spite of hell and high water."[63]

This ethic of emotional communication is the primary objective of jazz in performance and musicians pass down its importance through the generations. Willie "The Lion" Smith explained it to a young Duke Ellington in the late 1920s, and Art Blakey recalled Thelonious Monk's indoctrination: "When you hit the bandstand [it] . . . is supposed to lift from the floor, and the people are supposed to be lifted up too.'" Then Blakey inscribed this ideal onto two generations of Jazz Messengers, and of the best ones, he said, "they just lift the bandstand up[,] they have this power." Bassist Charlie Haden passed it onto Ornette Coleman's son, the drummer Denardo Coleman, in his teens: "He was always on a mission to lift you up."[64]

In the mid-1950s, Lester Young explained the difference between virtuosic improvisation and emotional communication to his young drummer, Willie Jones III. "You have good technique, Lady Jones, but what's your story?" Jones was confused by the question. "What do you mean?" he asked.[65]

"I mean, a musician is a philosopher and a scientist," Jones recalled Young's explanation, "and he uses the science of music to project the particular philosophy he subscribes to. So you have good technique, *but what's your story*?" That's the existential part, to narrate your experience in a signature sound that reflects your nature.

Young then alerted Jones to a second, *social* challenge of the jazz musician: to unify audiences in a ritual of temporary community. Jones asked him how do you do *that*? Thirty years after the exchange, he still recalled Young's answer. "Go down to the audience, see what the plumber is thinking, [and] what the carpenter is thinking," Young advised him, "so when you go up on stage you can help tell *their* story."[66] Again, this shows the resonance between jazz and existential rebellion, the affirmation of individual dignity without recourse to morality or national purpose.

The jazz musician's transmutation of suffering into soloing created the conditions for the listeners' potential awareness. Young's phrase "[to] tell *your* story" was a concise measure of the jazz musician's artistic objective at midcentury. Such a phrase is similar to the implicit collective therapy of the blues. Lester Young helped transfer this blues ethos to jazz, and it resonates deeply with the implied action of the Camusian rebel: *I rebel—therefore we exist.* This is a first step toward creating a broader, pluralistic canvas of existential cool at midcentury.

A Theory of Postwar I:
The Mask of Cool Supplants the Mask of Virtue

The origins of cool are grounded in the performance of relaxed calm to cover the loss of belief in Western civilization. Cool was and is an expressive matrix of transition—it was an emotional mode based on "keeping it together." The mask of cool serves self-presentation through its stylistic elements: in other words, through *the aestheticizing of detachment.* As facial armor, the cool mask registered traumatic experience without emotional affect. It reflected a period of withdrawal among postwar artists, rebels, and audiences that marked the consideration of the possibility— even if unconsciously—of an end to classical Western tradition. For the postwar generation that existed from 1945 to 1965, Western civilization lost its sustaining power as a coherent historical bloc reflecting a shared set of European and American values.

In the first decade following 1945, any universal ideal of classical human values or social equality lay buried in the atavistic tribal genocides of advanced technological society in concentration camps and bombed-out cities. In the wake of delegitimated authority and obsolete artistic ideals, young jazz musicians and B movie actors wore a blank, cooled facial expression to cover the depth of this loss. At nightclubs and movie theaters, intellectuals and rebels of all kinds were pulled into the gravity of their evocative, mysterious detachment. For college-age audiences, the search for a recast individualism after Auschwitz and Hiroshima can be located in an emergent structure of feeling signaled by the mask of cool.

In jazz, noir, and existentialism, the mask of cool was the sign of rebellion through withdrawal. Musicians, actors, and writers communicated a besieged individuality through the cool mask as they groped for ethical renewal after a period of social failure—whether for Euro-American men (the Great Depression), African-American men (white supremacy), or French existentialists (the Nazi occupation). For all three groups of artists, cool was a sign of masculinity in transition. Within these misogynist genres, women were often cast as sexual relief (the jazz vocalist), figures of temptation (femme fatales), or emotional hysterics. The mask of cool unified the affinities of these concurrent artistic forms around the search for new masculine modes of subjectivity and identity in the face of modernity, trauma, mass society, technological encroachment, and geopolitical crisis.

In *Cool Rules*, two UK sociologists reflected that cool emerged in the postwar era as "a new secular virtue." If so, what virtue did it displace?[67]

The mask of cool supplanted *the mask of virtue*. Virtue presumes the indoctrination of a class ideal through the inculcation of traditional ideals, creating an instinctive call to self-sacrifice for the sacred cause, religious or national. Virtue is a social class value based on tradition and gender roles: a man embodies republican virtues or Christian virtues; a woman is virtuous with regard to sexuality, family, and propriety. Virtue is even more hegemonic for its subconscious encoding. Hemingway repudiated the language of virtue in these famous lines from *A Farewell to Arms* (1929): "I was always embarrassed by the words sacred, glorious, and sacrifice. . . . I had seen nothing sacred, and the things that were glorious had no glory and the sacrifices were like the stockyards at Chicago. . . . *Abstract words such as glory, honor, courage, or hallow were obscene* beside the concrete names of villages . . . the names of rivers."[68] From the Great War to World War II to Vietnam, working- and middle-class men began to realize they were often cannon fodder for upper-class elites.[69]

Virtue has also always been a racial value: it is *symbolically* white and associated with being pure, clean, innocent, righteous, and civilized. As such, it is integral to the self-image of white Europeans standing against what they believed to be a planet of primitive, darker-skinned peoples. "White" virtue remains encoded against the revealing phrases of "black magic" or the "black market," against dirt and darkness, against the blackness of sin and vice. The symbolic repudiation of a racialized white virtue takes shape publicly through the example of the jazz musician's quiet stylistic rebellion. Jazz musicians rejected the racial order by hiding their eyes behind shades, crying out in individual protest artfully rendered, "talking black" in public while creating the nonverbal in-group conversation of jazz. The jazz musician as black Orpheus faced off against racial inscription and state-supported oppression.

In direct contrast to the class ideal of being a virtuous man or woman, *being cool* mandated a singular, original, introspective mode of being-in-the-world. The cool aesthetic became compelling precisely because the old order had been rendered hypocritical and corrupt by those politicized (or hip) enough to notice. Gone are the nineteenth-century bourgeois ideals: family name, local community, national character, religion, a professional occupation that speaks one's values. "Cool" supplants the aspiration of being good through moral frameworks; it replaces the vacuum with an abstract prize—to be cool—representing self-creation and inner direction, as maintained at social cost by alienation or rebellion, and rewarded only by like-minded souls.

Postwar cool involved the projection of authenticity and autonomy: it functioned as the outward sign of inner rebellion. It arose as a new model of identity for a mobile, unstable, technological society, a society in transition and soon to be morally and metaphorically on the road. White youth so desperately needed a call to these primal elements of self-assertion that they crossed racial lines to grab what they needed musically, from jump blues and bebop to rhythm and blues, soul, and rock and roll. These genres answer the unasked question of youth culture: what makes you feel glad to be alive? African-American music was the answer in every decade of the twentieth century, up through funk and hip-hop. In 1955, *Billboard* magazine was shocked to admit that rhythm and blues—that is, black music—continued to be popular across racial lines and it must be reconsidered as music that was not simply "'poor taste' or [a] 'passing fancy' of youth as sales and airplay doubled from the previous year."[70]

In short: cool was the public face of survival. Being cool signified the rejection of innocence, optimism, virtue, technological advance, and the myth of progress as markers of identity. The cool mask was posttraumatic, but it valorized rational despair in its artists and audiences, demanding introspection or reflection concerning the dark side of every individual's nature concerning violence, impulsive desire, or criminality. The mask of cool affirmed survival for audiences whose belief systems had been shattered by the events of the first half of the twentieth century and the revelations of 1945.

A GENERATIONAL INTERLUDE

Postwar II (1953–1963)
and the Shift in Cool

Cool joined the aesthetic to the political. Cool was a militant act.
Lewis MacAdams, *Birth of the Cool*[1]

After a long apprenticeship with Beat poet Gregory Corso, Lewis Mac-Adams interviewed all the living figures of New York's postwar scene for his evocative oral history, *Birth of The Cool: Bebop, the Beats, and the American Avant-Garde* (1999). Born and raised in Dallas, MacAdams recalled the first time he heard the word "cool"—in its modern context—on a rhythm and blues radio show in 1952. Abstract and inchoate at first, the mythic repercussions of the concept unfold from then until now: "What did I mean, then, when I thought that the Beats were cool? I had no idea. I just liked *the feeling* when I said the word. *'Cool' meant not only approval, but kinship.* It was a ticket out of the life I felt closing in all around me; it meant the path to a cooler world."

A "cooler" world is one where the "hip" cats recognize each other through nonverbal codes and where the "squares" don't matter at all. It is a utopian fantasy akin to the hobos' Big Rock Candy Mountain or what Thomas Pynchon once called "a doper's dream." It is an ideal bohemia—this cooler world—a floating community of kindred spirits equally supportive of individual innovation, vision, self-excavation, and self-liberation. MacAdams suggests this new American bohemian ideal first became established by jazz musicians at Minton's, the iconic Harlem jazz club, where during World War II, "cool became an allegiance, a code."[2]

In Postwar II, for the first time, the term "cool" became a password for something akin to *generational desire*. An iconic figure of cool catalyzed youth culture organically: something inchoate was communicated through new artistic ideas, styles, language, and gestures as it took embodied form in new artists. One conceptual precedent was the zeitgeist—the spirit of the age—but the German philosophical term predates any necessary consideration of media and demographics in modernity. Gene Sculatti provided a useful definition in *The Catalog of Cool*. In popular culture, a new figure registers as cool when he or she appears on the national stage "resembling nothing that had come before . . . an incomparable icon of fresh style," Sculatti wrote about the generational resonance of Bob Dylan, as postwar cool inflected toward its next stage in the early '60s.[3]

By the mid-1950s, *hip* and *cool* were separate modes, although the concepts have long since become conflated. Marlon Brando and Sidney Poitier and Johnny Cash and Miles Davis and William Burroughs were cool; Dizzy Gillespie and Allen Ginsberg and Norman Mailer were hip. To be hip was synonymous with being considered "worldly-wise, enlightened, sophisticated." This is the definition of hip in a dozen or so postwar glossaries of African-American slang left by streetwise authors from Mezz Mezzrow to Zora Neale Hurston to William Burroughs. Mailer called himself "The Philosopher of Hip" during the five years he spent grappling with these two African-American philosophical ideas (1955–60). The original meaning of "hipster" meant "a person who is knowledgeable and resourceful," as well as a jazz devotee.[4]

In contrast, to be cool was associated with detached composure as well as artistic achievement. Cool was defined as "restrained and relaxed" in *The Jazz Lexicon*, and in terms of artistic action, "[as] sizable achievement within a frame of restraint."[5] Cool was a rogue sensibility carried off with a certain hard-fought grace and personal style. To understand the cultural work of postwar cool requires linguistic recuperation and an analysis of a generational shift in the concept from Postwar I to Postwar II in the early '50s. Only then can we analyze the more familiar cool canon of Kerouac, Brando, Sinatra, Miles Davis, and James Dean.

In Postwar II, both cool and hip were underground anti-heroic concepts and ideals, a social and linguistic fact often ignored in ahistorical discussions of these concepts.[6] When the cultural rebellion inherent to cool failed in the early 1980s, its meanings, connotations, and nonverbal gestures devolved into commodities, into rebellion as style. Thomas Frank called this "the conquest of cool," but his influential study might have been better titled "the conquest of hip."[7] His study of advertising starts in the 1960s, and his historical erasure of a generation of foundational meanings continues to block a deeper understanding of this key American cultural concept. To be considered cool was the supreme compliment of American culture from 1940 to 1980 and remains high praise today.

Hip and Cool: A Quick Overview

After World War II, to be hip meant you knew what was *happening*, you were streetwise, you had that "up-to-the-minute awareness then known as hip," as Duke Ellington recalled.[8] You were hip *to* something new: a certain musician, an underground film, marijuana, existentialism; you were hip to racism, police brutality, imperialism, blind patriotism, the hypocrisy of national drug policy. The knowledge gained through this new cultural thing (or understanding) turned you on, it galvanized your spirit; the new awareness of how society functioned at street level lit up your mind. Hip people were attuned to innovative artistic vibrations, whether intellectual, cultural, sexual, or interpersonal. Call it "kicks" and write it off as self-indulgent. Call hip an engaged intellectual inquiry and it refers to improvising your life as it goes along.

To be hip required three steps of engagement: first, *to want* to be where the action is, second, *to know* where the action is, and, third, *to be* where the action is. Certainly "the action" is an abstract concept but not to those who were hip. As late as 1964, when the concept had reached full diffusion, even the Beach Boys sang, "I'm gettin' bugged driving up and down the same old strip / I gotta find a little place / *where the kids are hip.*" This is the opening line of the hit "I Get Around" and it's clear that "hip kids" were tolerant, open-minded, creative young people. Hip kids believed in a floating community of cool-minded people out there for them to find. The next year, in "California Girls," the Beach Boys sang that "East Coast girls are hip"—in other words, they were the national leaders of women's style.

"Hip" was the opposite of "Square": "the Squares" were static individuals, set in their ways, obedient of authority and social custom, observant of social structure and behavioral norms. The iconic hip jazzman Dizzy Gillespie elaborated on the difference in his autobiography. He defined a hip person as someone "'in-the-know,' 'wise,' or one with 'knowledge' of life and how to live." In contrast, a square "accepted the complete life-style . . . dictated by the establishment" and, quite pointedly, "rejected the concept of creative alternatives." Here were the real dangers to society of postwar squareness: "[A Square was] apathetic to, or actively opposed to, almost everything we stood for, like intelligence, sensitivity, creativity, change, wisdom, joy, courage, peace, togetherness, and integrity."[9] A square was someone who thought and lived *inside* the box. In other words, the hip saw themselves as social progressives opposed to the conservative squares, who guarded the status quo. Hip translated as both awareness and open-mindedness, and specifically to experimentation with sex, drugs, and jazz. Hip people mocked national pieties and common platitudes such as the common Cold War rejoinder to dissent, "if you don't like it here, move to Russia."

The hip person often took pride in his or her openness and called attention to it, setting one's self against the staid, pious, practical squares. As Muddy Waters sang to a woman in "I'm Ready" (1954), "I know you feel like I ain't nowhere / [but] I'll prove to you baby / that I ain't no square." He's hip, he's *going* somewhere, and he promises to take the woman to where the action is. Mailer published an esoteric chart of "The Hip and the Square" (fig. 18), opposing the philosophical positions of the two imagined groups, from "romantic versus classic" to "Negro versus white."[10] In evocative poetic comparisons such as "midnight versus noon" and "obeying the form of the curve versus living in the cell of the square," Mailer creates visual and sensory oppositions in terms of the body: hips are curves and cells are square. Here, Mailer's extension of the definitions in the hipster glossaries adds to the evidence of postwar

THE HIP AND THE SQUARE

I. The List

Hip	Square
wild	practical
romantic	classic
instinct	logic
Negro	white
inductive	programmatic
the relation	the name
spontaneous	orderly
perverse	pious
midnight	noon
nihilistic	authoritarian
associative	sequential
a question	an answer
obeying the form of the curve	living in the cell of the square
self	society
crooks	cops
free will	determinism
Catholic	Protestant
saint	clergyman
Heidegger	Sartre
sex	religion
wedeln	rotation
the body	the mind
rebel	regulator
differential calculus	analytic geometry
Schrodinger's model of the atom	Bohr's model of the atom
Wilhelm Reich as a mind	Wilhelm Reich as a stylist
Marx as a psychologist	Marx as a sociologist

Figure 18. Norman Mailer's list of "hip" versus "square" from *Advertisements for Myself* (1959).

writers and musicians to reveal a consensus as to the meaning of hip as it came out of jazz culture between 1930 and 1965.

In addition, Mailer's writings on hip are literally unthinkable without his introduction to marijuana in early 1955. His philosophy of hip first came to mind during his first experiences of being stoned; he declared hip to be nothing less than "the liberation of the self from the Super-Ego of society." Against the superstructure of superpowers, against the fortress mentality of Cold War *realpolitik*, against centralized industrial practice . . . there was the feeling of being stoned, of a dismantling of logical systems. For Mailer, "this is how the war of the Hip and the Square begins." Against the very concept of traditional moral virtue, "hip" suggests a libertarian freedom of the individual. Once in touch with your hipness you reject your square past, sometimes comically, like Mailer, who wrote that hip was a "primal battle" of self against bourgeois morality. To Mailer, "the only hip morality" was immediate gratification, "to do what one feels whenever and wherever it is possible."[11]

Hip was a matrix of emotional energy: it was a quest for primal feeling and vitality as and against the seeming *ill*-logic of middle-class bourgeois complacency on the ground and the nuclear threat overhead. Hip was about exploring the experience of one's physical body—as *well* as the mind—through sex, drugs, music, dance, experimentation. A person could find hip kindred spirits through style, cultural tastes, and even body language. "A catlike walk from the hip was Hip," Mailer wrote, perhaps thinking of Marlon Brando's well-known exaggerated hip-centered walk, while "a bearlike walk from the shoulder" was square.[12]

The Beats were hip, by and large: searching for kicks, happenings, vitality, rejuvenatory energies. They wanted their energy to be infectious, revolutionary, incendiary. It's all metaphors of heat, speed, burning. "We just have to go Go GO," as Moriarty tells Sal Paradise throughout *On the Road*. Kerouac recalled that everyone at the Six Gallery premiere reading of "Howl" just began chanting "Go! Go! Go! Go! Go!" In Tennessee Williams's play *Orpheus Descending* (1958), the hip Carol Cutrere shouts at the cool Val Xavier, "I just want to live, live, live, live, live!"[13] (See chapter 10.) To be "hip" was to be a first responder to new cultural trends and icons.

In contrast to this consensus on hip, "cool" was such a new term it didn't appear in any of the early glossaries of jazz slang. Yet by 1963 it was the "protean word" of jazz culture in the dictionary of postwar bohemia, *The Jazz Lexicon*, with two pages of meanings that included new phrases such as "be cool," "cool it," and "I'm cool."[14] In his novel *The Sound* (1960), for example, Ross Russell wrote about a hip blond named Zaida who "wore her hair Veronica Lake style," and spoke the jazz argot. "Her vocabulary was riddled with the new jargon. *Cool, crazy, hassle— dig, gone, gassed* . . . The secret language passed among them like a kind of black-market currency." In the same novel, a jazz drummer named Hassan always passed along the same advice: "You just have to know where you stand and play it cool. Play it cool, that's the main thing, man, play it cool, *play it cool*!" The importance of the African-American jazz vernacular as a postwar underground lingua franca cannot be overestimated and "cool" itself was something "close to the heart of his [the jazz musician's] philosophy." In *How to Speak Hip* (1959), Del Close, a pioneer of improv comedy, said offhandedly: "Most of the language of hipsters comes from jazz musicians."[15]

The word "cool" crossed over through Beat writers attuned to jazz and new slang. In John Clellon Holmes's *Go* (1952), the narrator identifies "cool" as a new word gaining currency: cool meant "pleasant, somewhat meditative, and without tension," and young adults were acting "cool, unemotional, withdrawn." That same year, William Burroughs designated "cool" as part of "the new hipster vocabulary" and defined it as "an all-purpose word" for anything that met aesthetic approval and, in addition, "any situation that is not hot with the law." To be cool was inherently anti-authoritarian and opposed to legal norms—in other words, in quiet rebellion against "the heat" or the cops.[16]

At the individual level, *cool* was a quest for existential stillness, relaxation, and self-control. A cool person projects a calm center through economy of motion and has an implied intensity. Lester Young's inflection of saying "I'm cool" or "I'm cool with it" still means to be relaxed or safe in a given situation and in one's own style. These meanings began with jazz and remain in jazz, even today.[17]

The cool person does not explain the content of his or her rebellion. This is a salient difference between being hip and being *cool.*

Instead, an icon of cool leaves behind an artistic vapor trail, a legacy that becomes for others a flag of future rebellion. For MacAdams, the example set by a trio of martyrs in 1954–55—Charlie Parker, Jackson Pollock, and James Dean—triggered "the age of cool." "Bird lives" was scrawled on subway walls after his early tragic passing; Pollock and Dean projected what Lewis MacAdams calls "the myth of tragic cool . . . that cool was a caged thing waiting to be freed."[18]

Cool was an emotional mode projecting authenticity and integrity in a quest for spiritual balance whereas hip was a streetwise philosophy. "Hip" and "cool" were not interchangeable terms. You were hip *to* something new; you were cool *with* something, like breaking the law for an ethical reason or doing drugs as an emblem of freeing your mind.

Cool was a myth of embodied personal power and autonomy—a "caged thing" waiting to be freed. Cool was a revitalized romantic myth for a new bohemia and a coalition of social rebels. It was strongest when the myth turned tragic, as it has been applied to self-destructive artists (Bird, Pollock, and Dean in Postwar I or, later, Hendrix, Morrison, and Joplin).

Yet this "caged thing" ready for rebellious flight—what is it that Beat youth found so resonant in this myth? Was it a romantic fantasy of boundless freedom? Or was it an existential problem of individuals grappling with apocalypse and godless absurdity? Were iconic cool figures new models of personal integrity once embodied in prophets and presidents, businessmen and inventors? Or were they simply charismatics in the religious sense, that is, individuals of immense personal magnetism? Was it simply the dream of an "authentic self" in a modernist sense? Or was it the psychological residue of a world globalized by fears of Armageddon and socially atomized by nuclear families unmoored from community networks? Or was it simply the discontent of an emerging affluent society?

The only answer can be yes, yes and yes, yes, yes, and yes. *Yes.*

Cool was and remains a myth for rebels seeking an innovative cultural charge from iconic artists who embody social change and project a deep grace borne from introspection and experience. Such an artist rebels and a new cohort exists.

The Generational Shift

Modes of cool overlap for different generations. Every generation has a different cultural imagination and its distinctive relationship to society takes shape through icons of cool as they reflect economic and social factors. Just as social change is rapid in a technological consumer society, so, too, cool figures on-screen and onstage. The combination of a group once called "the Silent Generation" (born 1928–45) and the oldest of the boomers (1945–50) became galvanized by a new set of cool figures to be analyzed in the second half of this work. In effect, the continuum of cool registered a change in masculine affect—or more precisely, a shift in desirable masculinity within a newly prosperous consumer society.

Cool is a fluid concept. In the 1950s, Americans experienced the kind

of once-in-a-century prosperity that created a new economic class: teenagers. Even though it was first coined in 1935, Depression-era youth had
neither disposable income nor the emerging space of freedom of postwar youth, with its suburbs, cars, and full employment. In 1945, the *New
York Times* published "A Teen-Ager's Bill of Rights," as if a new kind of
citizen had been discovered. Within ten years, this new class demanded
cultural rights (so to speak): they wanted to see their lives represented
on the screen. James Dean was their man, yet this white, middle-class,
suburban teenager would have been seen as nothing more than a sullen,
whining pretty boy before 1950, a kid to be knocked around and toughened up by gangsters. In contrast, British youth of Postwar II chose their
avatars of cool from urban blues and from rock and roll without regard to
race (e.g., Elvis, Muddy Waters, Chuck Berry, Duane Eddy), while German youth rioted at Marlon Brando films, in particular, *The Wild One*.[19]

In Postwar II (1953–63), two crucial new elements informed the
cool aesthetic for this younger generation: (1) the excavation of emotions, rather than their suppression, and (2) the value of improvisation
and spontaneity. In contrast to the repression of emotion, this element
of vulnerability within bravado signaled an alienated cool relative to the
singular combination of Cold War tensions, social prosperity, and nuclear anxiety. Through the unmasking of masculine bravado, passion and
instinct breathed out: as with Freudian analysis, the unconscious was
liberated until its contents might become conscious. Within an artistic
form, this worked as an inward turn for Beat writers, method actors,
rock and rollers, and jazz musicians—that is, a cool aesthetic as embodied by Marlon Brando, James Dean, Elvis Presley, Jack Kerouac, and
Miles Davis.[20]

In Postwar I, the outer shell of noir cool had been impassive, edgy,
stoic, darkly calm. Its inner ideal was subjective truth: there was a modest sense that self-knowledge and personal ethics might still be hard-won
from experience. Noir cool represented survival with style, something
akin to existence with dignity. Even for its criminal protagonists (as in
Double Indemnity), noir was an exploration of an individual's darker side,
tested out through criminality and existential will. It was an apolitical
position recuperated from failed belief systems, whether capitalism and
Christianity, or Communism and imperialism.

Yet there is more continuity to these artistic figures than a radical cultural break. Brando, Kerouac, Mailer, and Davis were all born in the mid-1920s, and their key personal experiences and artistic apprenticeships took place in the late 1940s. Brando's early stardom on Broadway, Kerouac's cross-country trips, Miles Davis's first phase, and Norman Mailer's early fame—all take place between 1947 and 1951. Brando was influenced by actors such as George Raft, Cary Grant, and Paul Muni; Elvis was influenced by Sinatra and Dean Martin; playwright Lorraine Hansberry was influenced by Beauvoir and Paul Robeson. Kerouac wrote the sacred scroll of his road trips in 1950, even if *On the Road* was not published until 1957. Yet if it had been published in the late 1940s, it might have faded into obscurity as a hobo's fever dream. As Louis Menand rightly observes: "*On the Road* is not a book about the nineteen-fifties. It is a book about the nineteen-forties."[21]

This new modality of cool was due in large part to the onset of national prosperity in the 1950s during one of the greatest economic boom decades in U.S. history: median family income increased 30 percent and home ownership rose 50 percent; oil and food were both cheap; there was low inflation and low unemployment in concert with increased productivity and sustained technological advance. All areas of industry expanded, from electronics and pharmaceuticals to food processing and leisure. In many ways, such prosperity was viewed as virtue earned for the righteousness of an American democratic system "that had triumphed over depression and fascism," one historian wrote, "[and] would sooner or later vanquish Communism."[22]

In Postwar I, cool was a marker for outcast masculine figures of failure, real-life and fictional. The rogue male protagonists of film noir, the rebels-*with*-causes in existential narratives, African-American jazz musicians in Jim Crow America—all were framed as solitary, autonomous men, without families, histories, or social networks of any kind. These figures could not be measured as successful in any conventional sense of social status, wealth, recognition, or influence. As the Depression-and-wartime generation felt more secure in prosperity, they made the stoic, urban avatars of noir cool obsolete.

Instead, at the turn of the '50s, the new postwar genre of police procedurals inflected film noir into narratives supporting authority and the justice system, such as *Dragnet*. Gone were the solitary private detectives and charismatic rogues; they were replaced by paternalistic urban policemen chasing slick gangsters and psychopaths. Retro-noir novelist James Ellroy calls these films "public-service noir, crime-does-not-pay noir," a genre in full force and effect in Postwar II.[23]

In effect, the cool of the Depression and wartime generation moved out West to Las Vegas and re-formed around the romantic image of Frank Sinatra. In fact, the original "Rat Pack"—a term coined by Lauren Bacall—referred to Humphrey Bogart *and* Frank Sinatra, the original co-leaders of two dozen Vegas habitués who dedicated their leisure hours to "the relief of boredom and the perpetuation of independence," as Bogart once told a syndicated columnist.[24] For the wartime generation, the prosperity of the 1950s displaced their attraction to the ethical rebel loner's noir cool.

In Postwar II, two generations of cool coexisted side by side. For the wartime generation, the cool of jazz and film noir trickled down through popular TV shows such as *Peter Gunn* (1958–61), where the detective's home base is a jazz club (Mother's) and the jazz musicians are his friends. Actor Craig Stevens plays Gunn as a cross between Cary Grant and Bogart, a suave, WASP playboy with little doubt about right and wrong. The same basic setup existed in the less successful (but aptly named) *Johnny Staccato, Jazz Detective.* John Cassavetes played the title character, a streetwise white ethnic (Italian) jazz pianist whose home base is a club called Waldo's. As with *Peter Gunn*, a number of episodes focus on the underground slang and social withdrawal of Beat artists and musicians. In both shows, jazz is the soundtrack and backdrop for an American existential underground. In fact, Cassavetes took the role to raise money to make an independent film about race and jazz, *Shadows* (1959). Both the wartime and Silent Generation had jazz foundations, swing and bebop, respectively: the Rat Pack's swinging bacchanalia of independence emerged from a big band model; the self-affirmation of bebop's soloing influenced the rebel cool of Brando and Kerouac, Miles Davis and Sonny Rollins.

"Cool" continued to be the password of a search for a broader scope of human behavior, both more tolerant and more adventurous. What were the goals in Postwar II? First, the avoidance of any virtuous moral code of good guys and bad guys continued, whether stemming from puritanical origins, legal repression, or a new awareness of white oppression. Second, icons of cool continued to subvert the Christian-derived assumptions of American dualism, the binary assumptions of good and evil. Here were the poles of the cultural imagination: obedience/sin, virtue/vice, white/black, good girl/bad girl, light/darkness, heterosexual/homosexual, male/female. In Postwar I, as we have seen, the tension and ambiguity of cool required contradictory terms, such as the "good bad man" or "the romantic heavy." In Postwar II, the assertive attack on these traditional values simply became the new parameters of cool itself.

The Cool Constant in Capitalism

There is one constant of cool across generations: *You don't own me. You're never gonna own me.* Cool is an honorific bestowed on radical, rogue, free agents who walk the line of the law — that is to say, mavericks with a signature style. They transgress social norms and a generation loves them for it. In both postwar phases, cool functioned as *an alternative success system* dependent on generational needs.

A cool icon projects a charismatic self-possession independent of social approval, state obedience, or the nine-to-five of corporate capitalism. In a consumer society where social prestige is based on wealth and material goods, cool emanates from symbolic individuals who project this simple ethos: you don't own me.

Cool does not and will not have a boss. As Elvis sang in "Trouble," a key song in *King Creole* (1958): "I don't take no orders / from no kind of man."

The cool aesthetic became compelling precisely because the old order had been rendered hypocritical and corrupt by those politicized (or hip) enough to notice. As conferred by others, cool became the prize for self-creation and inner direction, as maintained at social cost by alienation or social failure and as rewarded by peers, youth, and principled isolation.

The opposite of virtue is vice, and the cool figure straddles the opposition of good guy/bad guy or good girl/bad girl or hero/villain. The cool figure always has prior experience with vices through gambling, violence, sex, drugs and alcohol, gang life, or the streets. The cool figure is familiar with desire, temptation, primal needs, deception, and hunger.

In fact, a cool icon often persists in such hedonism or escapism until self-destructing.

Of course, "cool" is also simply a symbolic term for the romantic ideal of the rebel as projected onto artists, musicians, public figures, cinematic icons, and even fictional characters. Dashiell Hammett once called his detective Sam Spade "a dream man," an idealized composite of the private detectives he worked with at the Pinkerton Agency. Spade was the kind of man each of those operatives "would like to have been," and what a few imagined they were in their own minds. Yet Hammett so effectively hit the zeitgeist of urban masculinity that even a tough cookie like Dorothy Parker swooned for Sam Spade: "I went mooning about in a daze of love such as I had not known for any character in literature since I encountered Sir Lancelot."[25]

Parker's admission gets to the heart of how icons of cool shift over time. Sam Spade was noir cool: he was a cynical, modern, de-commissioned urban knight, the tough romantic protector of situational truth and kinetic individuality. He maintained an aura of authenticity through interior reflection, moral ambiguity, a round-the-clock work ethic, and a modest, urban lifestyle. The wartime generation embraced a romantic fantasy of such solitary, alienated men from 1930 to 1950 rather than virtuous heroic policemen or brilliant scientists.

In contrast, postwar youth elevated wild, emotional, sexy men as their avatars of social change. Here's what the two generations had in common: they chose romantic figures to embody cool, which has since become an American myth for the fantasy of individual power through one's integrity. For every generation, that integrity is measured against different social, cultural, economic, and political forces.

In short, the concept of cool was in a state of becoming. Cool has since evolved into an outlaw sensibility for a consumer society.

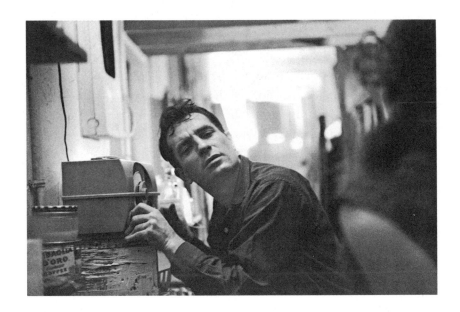

Figure 19. Jack Kerouac tries to tune into a signal just out of reach (© John Cohen, Courtesy L. Parker Stephenson Photographs, NYC).

6

Kerouac and the Cool Mind

Jazz and Zen

I've been thinking about *cool* for the past week almost to the point of a theory.

> Jack Kerouac, Letter to Neal Cassady, 1950[1]

O [Buddha,] Noble Prince of the Sakyas!
Your coolness!

> Jack Kerouac, *Some of the Dharma*, 1955[2]

In a 1950 letter to Neal Cassady, Kerouac confessed to being obsessed with the new concept of cool. A long-time habitué of jazz clubs since his college years, Kerouac perceived that, for jazz musicians, cool signaled a more cerebral, deliberate, and relaxed mode of being in the world. Kerouac opposed the "cool mind" to the "raw mind" and did not see himself within this new modality: "A raw mind and a cool mind are two different minds. The *raw mind* is . . . associated with the physical life, whether athletic, work or just beat. The *cool mind* is the intellectual emphasis[;] the physical counterpart of it is a kind of gracefulness . . . that is almost effeminate."[3] Kerouac and Cassady sought the "raw mind," the kind of primal, natural response to living in the world associated with youthful enthusiasm and the primitive. Kerouac's tradition was the Whitman-esque: he sought an organic, instinctive, uncivilized response to experience. Kerouac was interested in cool as a new philosophical cast of mind, a new attitude in the New York air, perhaps also "that sound of the night which [be]bop has come to represent for all of us," as he wrote of the year 1947.[4]

In *On the Road*, Kerouac wrote about African-American culture as if it expressed both sides of this dialectic, the instinctive and the cerebral. In terms of the raw mind, Kerouac romanticized the community bonds and good times (or "kicks") he perceived among Mexican immigrants and African-Americans. While walking around with the existential blues in a black neighborhood in Denver—"I felt like a speck on the surface of the sad red earth"—Sal Paradise has a fantasy of belonging to a different ethnic group, a counterforce to his "white ambitions" of social status and economic success. He watches a pick-up softball game with a multiethnic crowd cheering the "strange young heroes of all kinds, white colored, Mexican, pure Indian," and wishes his childhood was full of "boyish, human joy like this" rather than his "college, big-time, soberfaced" ambitions. He equates whiteness with materialism and so fantasizes about life in a different skin ("wishing I were a Negro") since "the best the white world had offered was not enough ecstasy for me, not enough life, joy, kicks, darkness, not enough night." As Dean Moriarty tells him, "We know time—how to slow it up and walk and dig and just old-fashioned spade kicks, what other kicks are there? *We* know." Yet a few chapters later, with regard to the cool mind of jazz musicians, Kerouac provides a quick, insightful summary of jazz history through its African-American avatars, Louis Armstrong, Lester Young, and Charlie Parker. There are also extended riffs in Kerouac's *Visions of Cody* on the tone and style of Lester Young, Charlie Parker, Flip Phillips, Roy Eldridge, Dizzy Gillespie, Billie Holiday, and Coleman Hawkins. Kerouac traced jazz as a modern art to Young since "it was Lester started it all, the gloomy saintly serious goof who is behind the history of modern jazz and this generation like Louis his, [and] Bird *his* to come and be."[5]

Kerouac deserves his own chapter for five reasons. First, he pursued "cool mind" through jazz and Zen Buddhism in two of his least analyzed works, *Mexico City Blues* and *Some of the Dharma*. Second, he was the literary herald of a cultural shift toward improvisation in artistic method and spontaneity in life.[6] Third, he was pivotal in the redirection of the concept of cool as a synonym for rebellion for the '60s counterculture—in particular, through his worship of Neal Cassady, later the driver of Further, the bus of the Merry Pranksters. Fourth, much of white bohemia and teenaged boomer youth thought Kerouac was cool and many people still do. Fifth, Kerouac's literary practice was shaped by jazz, noir, and existentialism. He referred to himself as a "jazz poet," recorded three undervalued poetry and jazz albums with musicians, and created a new literary approach he called "bop prosody" (or bebop prose). His six-year experiential inquiry into Zen Buddhism was the culmination of his quest for an American type of up-Beat spiritual existentialism and included an album of poetry and jazz called *American Haikus* (1958).

Finally, Kerouac's first novel was a literary noir co-authored with William Burroughs in 1944, *And the Hippos Were Boiled in Their Tanks*. Though *Hippos* was written in 1944, it wasn't published until 2008 due to the authors' promise to their friend Lucien Carr, the autobiographical protagonist of the novel's events. *Hippos* is a roman à clef of *the* pivotal event of early Beat history. David Kammerer, a thirty-five-year-old man, had romantic designs on the twenty-one-year-old Carr, a young writer who introduced Ginsberg, Kerouac, and Burroughs to one another. In a still-mysterious encounter, Carr stabbed and killed Kammerer either in self-defense (Kammerer stalked him) or because Carr himself was conflicted sexually. As depicted in the recent film *Kill Your Darlings* (2013), this murder bound them as an artistic gang of young men. The police arrested Ginsberg, Kerouac, and Burroughs as accessories to the crime.[7]

Hippos is narrated in alternate chapters by the seedy, brilliant, amoral Nietzschean detective Will Denison (Burroughs) and the melancholic wandering merchant seaman, Mike Ryko (Kerouac). *Hippos* reads like early demos from two new narrative voices: Burroughs's voice of detached nihilism, Kerouac's of existential lament. Both of them were then writing "in the style of Raymond Chandler, hardboiled," Allen Ginsberg recalled.[8] The detectives and gangsters of literary noir were the cutting edge of pop-cultural cool during the Depression-era youth of the Beats so it was natural to graft the crime onto the genre. "I was fascinated by gangsters, and like most boys my age, I wanted to be one," Burroughs reflected, while his own analyst diagnosed him as "a 'gangsterling'—a 'gangster wanna-be.'"⁹ In contrast, Kerouac was a blue-collar, working-class union man, a merchant seaman seeking spiritual uplift. This convergence of Beat writing, hard-boiled fiction, and alienation fit the wartime moment like a new glove. *Hippos* was "[a] combination hard-boiled murder mystery and existentialist lament on the meaninglessness of modern life," as one Kerouac scholar reviewed it. "Think Dashiell Hammett meets Albert Camus."¹⁰

Hippos romanticized New York's gangsters, thieves, hustlers and addicts yet it also contained the seeds of Kerouac's beat-to-beatific utopian re-envisioning of American culture. After a night of bored adventuring in Times Square—playing pinball and watching peep shows—Mike Ryko finds his only joy on the jukebox. He drops a nickel in the slot and plays Benny Goodman's "The World Is Waiting for the Sunrise." This phrase would have made a fitting epitaph for Kerouac's gravestone: he was a writer trying to find the hope in apocalypse.¹¹

Here I excavate the generational appeal of Kerouac's quest for cool in the postwar era. "Who wouldn't want to wake out of a nightmare?" Kerouac scribbled in *Some of the Dharma*, echoing James Joyce's modernist question of the century. In jazz, Kerouac heard African-American musicians artistically waking out of *their* long historical nightmare. In Zen Buddhism, he found an ancient method for controlling the mind—first, cleansing the mind and then *cooling it*.¹² This *cool*-ing of anger and desire by emptying the mind remains central to cool as an emotional mode. If Kerouac aspired to "raw mind" over "cool mind" in 1950, he nonetheless spent the decade on a conscious quest for the cool mind via two non-Western artistic foundations, jazz and Zen Buddhism. Ginsberg dedicated *Howl and Other Poems* (1956) to Kerouac as both "the new Buddha of American prose" and the creator of a "spontaneous [be]bop prosody."¹³

According to Sam Charters, a friend of Kerouac's and a groundbreaking postwar scholar of jazz and blues, Kerouac often said that one crucial meaning of his term "the Beat generation" was that it was the generation that discovered "the beat." Charters recalled Kerouac often saying some version of the following: "The Beat generation is the one that's with the beat in jazz [itself]. They're the ones who hear the beat, and feel the beat, and that's why they're the beat generation." This is the artistic logic for the spoken word albums he made with jazz musicians Steve Allen, Al

Cohn, and Zoot Sims. In *On the Road*, Sal Paradise marks the year 1947 as a time when "bop was going like mad all over America," in transition "between its Charlie Parker Ornithology period and another period that began with Miles Davis."[14]

What did readers find in Kerouac's work besides a trigger for new adventures, an affirmation of vernacular American culture, and a guide to road-tripping? Kerouac's appeal remains simple: he was a seeker modeling a quest for spirituality through the creative process, literary practice, Buddhist methods, and African-American music. It was a search for a cool mental space or what Ken Kesey later called the "search for a Kool place."[15] Kerouac failed at this quest, dying early of alcoholism and embittered, but succeeded by creating literary works that still find a global youth audience outside the college canon. Readers then and now find in Kerouac's work a *post*-Western search for meaning and aesthetics afoot in the postwar era.

Jazz as Artistic Method

Kerouac's first phase came from jazz—as an African-American musical and spiritual practice of self-excavation, as a sign of a revitalized masculine individualism, and as an aesthetic of the cool. A jazz solo is, by definition, a spontaneous composition. This essential improvisatory practice was, for Kerouac, the basis for his manifesto of literary style, "Essentials of Spontaneous Prose," his playful, exuberant epic work of poetry, *Mexico City Blues*, and his Benzedrine-driven novel-on-a-scroll, *On the Road*. The icon for Kerouac's jazz-based philosophy was Neal Cassady, whose nonstop verbal style was an equivalent influence on his bebop prose. Kerouac found in the jazz objective of crafting an original sound the artistic imperative of stripping off layers of imitation to find a literary voice borne of experience and signature stylistic gestures.

As late as 1962, he distilled his writing philosophy to one sentence riffed from a hit jazz song from 1939: "It ain't whatcha write but the way thatcha write it," a paraphrase of Jimmie Lunceford's swing hit from 1939, "T'Ain't What You Do (It's the Way That You Do It)." In short, Kerouac believed literary voice and prose style carried ideas and personal philosophy more effectively than did formal eloquence, exposition, or narrative structure. As a writer, he wanted from jazz what Hettie Jones called "its genius approach to craft" (not its blackness) and took from its musical example a method for learning how to "sing on my own line, in my own good time."[16]

The experiential aspect of Kerouac's philosophy became concretized in *the road* itself on which he was Neal Cassady's rider. Cassady turned the automobile into a technological chariot for youthful religious pilgrims. Throughout *On the Road*, Cassady cheerleads jazz musicians through their solos—"yeah yeah yeah man" or "Go go go," he shouts at Slim Gaillard, George Shearing, and a few anonymous musicians. Cassady used language with the kind of raw enthusiasm Kerouac perceived in jazz solos: a continuous spontaneous stream of language broken up by artistic phrasing and cadence. In Cassady's rambling verbosity, Kerouac found a vernacular American voice that combined the jazz solo with frontier masculinity. It swung Kerouac's literary style away from his derivative imitation of Thomas Wolfe in his first novel, *The Town and the City* (1950). For Cassady, life was an ongoing set of escalating up-tempo riffs in an endless jam session that he enacted through a propulsive hedonism, whether speeding down highways or conning his way into multiple simultaneous dalliances with women. Kerouac later brought this raw enthusiasm to the iconic first reading of "Howl," yelling "Go Go Go" to inspire the crowd. Ginsberg always claimed that "Howl" itself was indebted to "Jack's spontaneous method of composition."[17]

In his short literary manifesto, "Essentials of Spontaneous Prose," Kerouac codified the jazz solo as the model for his literary practice. A solo is not an outpouring of emotions; it requires long apprenticeship and mental discipline. Only through long hours of practice can a musician create a coherent artistic statement spontaneously. With the solo in mind, Kerouac began writing long, unpunctuated prose narrative, bypassing formal literary conventions. He realized, he had to burn off the husk of an experience to get to the kernel of a personalized artistic statement through structured improvisation:

> WRITING . . . You'll never know what you wanted to say about something till you're scribbling furiously into it, reaching the center, then scribbling out again. This is BLOWING, accidentally and actually finding your center.

In jazz, such blowing is not "accidental" but part of the essential method. When jazz musicians "blow," they surf into the core of a given composition's melodic or harmonic framework with the intention of creating a new musical statement on the bones of the old. In a letter to Malcolm Cowley, Kerouac clarified his method as favoring the potential revelation of emotional depth over craft: "If it isn't spontaneous, right into the very sound of the mind . . . [then] we get what a man has hidden, i.e., his craft, instead of what we need, what a man has shown, i.e., *blown* (like jazz musician)." Kerouac also found a Zen analogy for the jazz practice in the Surapama: "You must learn to answer questions spontaneously with no recourse to discriminating thinking."[18]

Kerouac absorbed the dialogic nature of performer and audience from his regular visits to jazz clubs. His first wife Edie Parker recalled, "We went up to Minton's [the Harlem jazz club] so often they wanted us to open a charge account."[19] In one of Dean Moriarty's monologues in *On the Road*, Moriarty explains how a jazz musician works toward transcendent moments in live performance.

> Here's a guy [soloing] and everybody's there, right? *Up to him to put down what's on everybody's mind.* He starts the first chorus, then lines up his ideas . . . and then he rises to his fate and has to blow equal to it. All of a sudden somewhere in the middle of the chorus he *gets it—* everybody looks up and knows; they listen; he picks it up and carries. Time stops. *He's filling empty space with the substance of our lives.*[20]

Kerouac here repeats the core of Lester Young's philosophical advice to Willie Jones III with regard to the interactive nature of live performance ("up to him to put down what's on everybody's mind") and the objective of galvanizing the audience.

Toni Morrison described her jazz-influenced literary practice a generation later in more formal terms. When writing the novel *Jazz*, she reflected, "I thought of myself as like the jazz musician, someone who practices and practices and practices in order to be able to invent and to make his art look effortless and graceful." The challenge and reward of public improvisation comes from artistic courage or "the willingness to fail . . . because jazz is [a public] performance." This is the inherent drama of any live jazz performance since a musician does not "have the luxury of revision that a writer has; you have to make something out of a mistake, and if you do it well enough it will take you to another place where you never would have gone had you not made that error." In contrast to Kerouac's literary objectives, for Morrison, the jazz solo was a model of "thrift," of what (and when) to conceal and reveal. A jazz musician always "conveys that he has more but he's not gonna give it to you. It's an exercise in restraint, a holding back. . . . That sense of knowing when to stop is a learned thing." In other words, spontaneous art has the excitement of immediacy, the potential for revelation, the looseness of experimentation, and the danger of failure. In jazz, it requires an immersion into musical structures since, during a solo, ideas are instantaneous and associative yet arranged spontaneously through subconscious knowledge of structures.[21]

Even Norman Mailer understood that soloing in jazz was a new artistic form of risky existential performance, "something which is constantly triumphing and failing," and that the thrill of it for players and listeners came from experiencing "the effort merely to keep musically alive." Once while watching Dave Brubeck solo, Mailer realized the pianist had "wander[ed] into a musical cliché" and nearly panicked. Then he watched and listened as his bandmates helped him out by feeding him chords and ideas to lead him back into the song's structure. Mailer found the process "thrilling to see" and realized then how a musician takes an idea, "plays with it, investigates it, pulls it apart, attempts to put it together into something new . . . and sometimes succeeds, and sometimes fails." Mailer found in this aspect of soloing a key aspect of manhood since with each solo a musician "left his record of defeat at that particular moment."[22]

Unfortunately, Kerouac applied the jazz practice of improvisation to his literary method with more success than he did in his fictional representations of musicians. A jazz solo is a second-nature meditation on certain chord changes, an individual nonverbal statement declared in musical language. A jazz solo happens in real time and it is affected by the musician's mood and mental state, but it is never a matter of raw emotion; it has as much to do with restraint as expression — this is a key factor in a jazz musician's cool. Yet in *On the Road*, Kerouac describes long solos at jazz clubs as if they are great strings of yay-saying affirmations with Cassady cheerleading "*Go Go Go.*" In this sense, Kerouac equates jazz

solos with raw mind in his fiction, and this mistaken perception is analogous to Mailer's artistic racism when he declared that "jazz is orgasm."
At the time there were indeed rhythm-and-blues saxophonists known as
"honkers and shouters" who sprung wild bursts of sound on their horns
in seemingly raw, lusty, goatish pleasure. Yet these are not the musicians
Kerouac highlights in *On the Road*.

Jazz practice requires the shaping of emotional response from a calm
center as manifested in conversation with other musicians and mediated
by the audience. To create a personal sound in jazz requires constant
interrogation of an individual artistic voice in order to project a sophisticated subjective consciousness. These are Kerouackian ideals. Had he
continued his inquiry into jazz as an art form, his literary work might
have become tighter and more thematically focused: such distillation
of a narrative artistic voice was common to the jazz musicians he worshipped. To be fair, there were then few theories of African-American
musical practice or analyses of African aesthetics to consult. Without
such texts to support his inquiry, Kerouac was tempted by an older,
more venerable spiritual tradition. Zen Buddhism offered him a philosophy of active moral (and mental) action and, more importantly, the
possibility of a measure of grace akin to his Catholic upbringing.

Kerouac's detractors and worshippers—then and now—continue to
misunderstand his artistic objectives. His detractors mock Beat ideals
and deride its artists' prized value on intuition, the irrational, and the
unconscious. This value is captured in the famous phrase, "first thought,
best thought," often attributed to Allen Ginsberg but which is instead a
pithy Zen phrase of his Buddhist teacher, Chögyam Trungpa. Beat critics
consider this phrase a sign of an immature poetics based on unedited outpouring and excess. Yet Trungpa's original phrase was not "first thought,
best thought" but, rather, "first mind, best mind," and it was more aspirational than prescriptive. The phrase stands for the clarity of mind sought
by Buddhists through meditation and the illusion of desire; it is nearly
synonymous with the ideal of spiritual balance in West African cool.
Through training, Zen Buddhists aspire to a mind sharpened equally
by rational thought and spontaneous action; certainly it did not mean
emotional reaction. In fact, Ginsberg preferred Kerouac's playful phrase,
"Mind is shapely, Art is Shapely," to "first thought, best thought."[23]

Both Trungpa and Kerouac refer to the Zen ideal of a well-trained mind. This ideal dates back to at least the sixth century and represents an adept's objective for simultaneous thought and action. It is not meant to idealize the primordial or the unconscious in the sense of, say, creating spontaneous romantic poetry inspired by the Muse. Whatever Kerouac's literary limitations — and he had many — his works are not simplistic, as the pejorative dismissals of John Updike and Truman Capote had it. (Capote on Kerouac: "That isn't writing at all; it's typing.") Kerouac brought together Zen concepts, jazz practice, blues poetics, and European modernist ideals into a new synthesis for American literature.[24]

Zen Cool

The ideal consciousness in Buddhism is the empty but conscious mind that shares in the so-called transcendental void: Kerouac used "cool" to designate this state of mind in *Some of the Dharma*. If the objective of Zen practice is to find "a cool Void," Kerouac wrote in his journal that he would make of his mind "the cool pool of emptiness." In some cases, "cool" represents the cessation of rational thought and mental noise entirely. When Kerouac wrote "Nirvana is cool," he meant to make the concepts equivalent. In other words, to be in a state of Nirvana is to enjoy a cool, composed mind: "Nirvana means being able to find a cool mental space no matter what the situation."[25] If it is now common to use terms such as "being Zen" when one is still in a given environment, or if it is now more common to understand African-American cool as an "Afro-Zen" mode, Kerouac intuited this culture concept as an ideal state of spiritual balance from his engagement with both jazz and Zen.[26]

Between 1953 and 1956, Kerouac kept an elaborate two-columned journal full of poems, anecdotes, epiphanies, copied-out sutras, and internal dialogues concerning the role of Buddhism in what he hoped would be a coming revolution of consciousness. He called it *Some of the Dharma*, and the work remained unpublished until 1997. However, it was among the five or six manuscripts Kerouac's literary agent attempted unsuccessfully to sell throughout the 1950s, including *On the Road*. In other words, Kerouac thought this thousand-page packet of journal scraps — revealing his daily personal wrangling with issues of consciousness — was a central work in his oeuvre.

For Kerouac, the embodiment of American Zen was Gary Snyder, the

Pulitzer Prize–winning Buddhist poet and essayist, who he fictionalized as Japhy Ryder in *The Dharma Bums*. Snyder was a practicing Buddhist and a translator of classic Chinese texts before Kerouac met him. He was the Zen guru of the Beats at the same time that Alan Watts popularized Buddhism for middle-class Americans in best-selling books and magazine articles of the late 1950s. Snyder had studied with Watts for a while but thought him "square." "He was cool in relation to the people around him," Snyder once said, referring to "middle class, needy" Americans, but he was "never actually cool." Then Snyder added with a wink, "[and] you *know* what I *mean*, as the Big Bopper says," invoking the rock-and-roll classic "Chantilly Lace" for those hip and in-the-know.[27]

In Postwar II, Kerouac imagined himself as a new kind of American pilgrim, a combination of Walt Whitman, Zen monk, and Christian mystic. As he wrote in the opening pages of *Dharma Bums* (1959),

> [I was] very devout in those days. . . . I really believed in the reality of charity and kindness and humility and zeal and neutral tranquility and wisdom and ecstasy, and I believed that I was an oldtime *bhikku* [pilgrim] in modern clothes wandering the world . . . in order to turn the wheel of the True Meaning, or Dharma, and gain merit for myself as a future Buddha (Awakener) and as a future Hero in Paradise.[28]

Kerouac saw himself as an avatar of a democratized, Americanized Zen Buddhism, "a future Hero in Paradise" to be judged by Buddhists of the future. Kerouac's hope to "gain merit" or heavenly credit for his wanderings was a misreading of Buddhism but he carried forward the original engagement with the religion as first embraced by Emerson, Thoreau, and Whitman.[29] In Allen Watts's famous 1956 essay, "Beat Zen, Square Zen, and Zen," he famously called out the Beats as being "too self-conscious, too subjective and too strident" in their Zen practice.[30] If that was an accurate rendering of many Beats other than Snyder, Kerouac represented something else—that Buddhism has always been in transition and might be changed by its encounter with the West.

In Zen Buddhism, Kerouac found religious legitimation for the qualities of spontaneity and naturalness he theorized as "raw mind." He valued Buddhism as an alternative consciousness to Christian guilt, dualism, original sin, and deferred gratification, not to mention the complicity of institutional Christianity with everything from slavery to nuclear weapons. To Kerouac, Buddhist texts were literature, scripture, and Talmudic commentary all rolled together: "I find no [priestly] assemblage to compare with the monks of the Surangama Sutra," he wrote. Yet he did not sit *zazen* with any regularity nor study with a master. He never stopped trying to grasp intellectually what Buddhist texts insist *cannot* be grasped intellectually. And he never conceded the notion of spiritual merit as a form of grace.[31]

In effect, Kerouac attempted to take the devotion of Zen practice and apply it to writing. He took to heart two Zen ideals: (1) the "empty, marvelous mind" and (2) the higher value of a spiritual experience rather than its formal rendering. He learned these concepts in part from reading D. T. Suzuki—the postwar Zen mentor of everyone from Watts to Thomas Merton. Kerouac must have understood the parallels of jazz and Zen from reading Suzuki's *Introduction to Zen Buddhism*: "Copying is slavery. The letter must never be followed, only the spirit is to be grasped." In addition, Suzuki's message was of a joyful existentialism: "Zen never explains, but only affirms. Life is fact and no explanation is necessary or pertinent. . . . To live—is that not enough? Let us then live, let us affirm! Herein lies Zen in all its purity and all its nudity as well." In such ways, Zen mirrors jazz as a form of affirmation and self-excavation from a calm center, even if with different objectives in mind.[32]

Kerouac's devotional five-year study of Buddhism under Snyder laid the critical foundation for his best work after *On the Road*. From *Some of the Dharma* he distilled his exuberant and undervalued work of poetry, *Mexico City Blues*; his second most popular novel, *Dharma Bums*; and two years later, an American sutra, *Scripture of the Golden Eternity* (1960). When Ginsberg called Kerouac "a new Buddha of American prose," he meant it as gratitude for starting him down the path toward his own (deeper) engagement with Zen. On the last page of *Dharma Bums*, Kerouac expressed his gratitude to Snyder from the solitude of his mountaintop outpost: "[I] thank you forever for guiding me to the place where I learned all."[33]

In *Dharma Bums*, Kerouac tells Snyder that he is particularly interested in two of the four noble truths of Buddhism: "the first . . . *All life is suffering*," and "the third, *The suppression of suffering can be achieved*."[34]

He tells Snyder that he "didn't quite believe [it] was possible then"—that there was a method to suppress emotional pain or an escape from desire and anxious thought. Kerouac's aspiration to these two truths resonates with the objectives of postwar cool: self-mastery and de-sacralized individuality. Yet it was alien to Kerouac's Catholic upbringing and challenged his core belief in the fallen state of human beings and original sin. At the outset of the novel, Ryder/Snyder refers to Smith/Kerouac as a "bodhisattva" ("'great wise being' or 'great wise angel'") and perceives his spiritual gift to be "sincerity" of action.

In retrospect, Kerouac's personal dialectic was to have a daily Whitmanesque barbaric yawp of joy and a daily portion of Catholic suffering. In all his works, Kerouac cannot reconcile his twin desires of passion and prayer. Yet it is precisely the tension between this constant quest for calm and his inability to find satisfaction that still makes his work compelling reading for restless youth.

To his credit, Kerouac chided himself for his failure of discipline in *Some of the Dharma*—for his alcoholism, his melancholy, his lack of self-mastery. Here's an introspective entry:

> DON'T LAUGH, I'M A BIG DRINKER, I'm trying to find some expedient means to stop drinking . . . [it makes] me forget the above wisdom . . . little fool [that I am] . . .—I want DRY STRONG HAPPINESS instead of all this WET WEAK UNHAPPINESS (hangover)—
>
> Drinking like that ruins my physical strength, mars my morning joy, breaks the back of my resolves, blurs my clear reflection. . . . I should sacrifice the few remaining pleasures . . . of strong drinking to my vow to emancipate all beings— (325)

Kerouac's brutal honesty—his melancholy and self-reflection—has always been a factor in his appeal and his frank introspection here is endearing. It is analogous to Sal Paradise's existential despair as it works like a shadow inside Dean Moriarty's neurotic hyper-momentum in *On the Road*. Near the end of *Some of the Dharma*, Kerouac confronts his sojourn in Buddhism as a moral failure: "*I'm not a Buddha this trip . . . face it . . . [I'm just] a veritable crone of ideas . . . because of sensuality, drink, involvement in the ideas and antagonisms of men.*"[35]

In short, Kerouac was serious about Zen Buddhism but was never a practicing Buddhist. In contrast, he rejected core aspects of institutional Christianity and yet he was always a serious Catholic. In a given journal entry in *Dharma*, he might repudiate Christianity: "Catholic Dualism is behind the error of Western Civilization with its war of machines, each machine claiming [to be] the 'Good.'" Yet the next day, he was back to Catholic iconography: "Buddhism is the understanding of the Angels—My life ambition [is] to be an angel looking back on life in the world."[36] Midway through *Dharma Bums*, Snyder challenges Kerouac: "You really like Christ, don't you?" "Of course I do," Kerouac replies, "a lot of people say he is Maitreya, the Buddha prophesied to appear after Sakyamuni." Yet there are no angels in Buddhism and the very concept is antithetical to the religion. In Zen Buddhism, the iconic figures are human beings, not deities, up to and including Buddha. Nirvana and Heaven are not analogous. So at the end of *Dharma Bums*, Snyder predicts Kerouac will wind up "kissing the cross" on his deathbed like one of his friends who "spent his life as a Buddhist and suddenly returned to Christianity in his last days." This was a prescient remark.[37]

Kerouac spent his entire life searching for a cool mental space for affirming life, a place of spiritual balance, and an artistic method to write from a calm center. He never found the strategic silence central to either Zen cool or the African aesthetic of the cool. He could grasp it intellectually, but the noise of his desires, emotions, and self-flagellation always intruded. "Obtaining Nirvana is like locating silence," he wrote, and he never achieved this stillness of mind.[38]

Kerouac's spiritual dilemma lay in his constant hope for epiphany, illumination, and vision: as he confessed, "man[,] I wanta be enlightened by actions."[39] Immersed in Zen Buddhism, Kerouac sometimes turned on his former artistic passions, writing on one day that "jazz is simpleminded noise" or, on another, that literature was an egotistical, irrelevant pursuit. Yet he always came back to both artistic forms. He recognized the need for a Zen master or guru to guide him to "right conduct," yet Kerouac could never submit himself to such a discipline, nor even to Suzuki himself (whom he later met). Yet in his only synthesis of jazz and Zen—*Mexico City Blues*—we can locate the meaningful failure of Kerouac's Buddhism.[40]

The Zen Bird of "The Great Historic World Night"

In February of 1955, Kerouac dreamed that he entered "the Halls of Nirvana" and there among the Buddhist monks sat Charlie "Bird" Parker, the artistic genius of the bebop revolution. He transcribed this dream in a journal entry entitled, "The Dhyana [Meditation] of Complete Understanding." Walking through the hall, Kerouac has an epiphany about the work and humanity of Buddhist monks. "Sages and Saints are real men," he realizes—neither gods nor angels, that is—and their work involves making "astounding discoveries of the Mind." Then he suddenly spots "Charley Parker," and as if reliving the dream, he writes, "I . . . see a Chinese Saint with Bird Parker's face." This saint has "Bird's quiet virility and leadership and [his] faint smile among the cats and *arahats* (perfect souls)." Here, Kerouac perceives Parker from the perspective of African-American jazz musicians—that is, as a cultural leader, artistic exemplar and jazz saint.[41]

Mexico City Blues is a modernist epic poem and a singular synthesis of jazz and Zen as Beat philosophies. *Mexico City Blues* starts off with this epigraph, a word of advice from Kerouac on how to listen to the poetry: "I want to be considered a jazz poet / blowing a long blues in an afternoon jam session on Sunday." In its final four page-long choruses, Parker rises from its pages as a serene, cool American Buddha who blows a brutal wave of blues forward on his alto saxophone as if to irradiate the future from apocalypse. Parker is a deity of cultural fertility here, the conduit for African-American musical practice and aesthetic power: *Bird dies, Bird lives, Bird rises.* Kerouac sets himself up as a cultural John the Baptist, a medium for cool as it emerges from black jazz culture. At the exact same moment that Elvis is crossing over African-American expressive culture in rock and roll, Kerouac invokes Charlie Parker as his saint at the crossroads of jazz, Zen, and cool.[42]

Mexico City Blues combines the improvisatory artistic practices of Zen and jazz to create a joyful poetry of serious whimsy. Kerouac attempts to combine Japanese and African-American poetic traditions by finding the modernist space between haiku and blues. He was serious about the convergence, as his poetry and jazz call-and-response session called *Haikus and Blues* (1959) attests, with jazz saxophonists Zoot Sims and Al Cohn.[43] Kerouac also left an intact manuscript called *Book of Blues* that was published posthumously in 1995. Kerouac knew his African-American musical forms: these poems were—like blues—more distilled and on point than the jazz poet's looser improvisations here.

In *Mexico City Blues*, Kerouac found an appropriate modal form to contain his nonstop verbosity: one poem per page. He envisioned each riff of language as a single "complete poem written filling in one notebook page . . . usually in 15-to-25 lines, known as a Chorus." Each of the book's 242 numbered poems functions as an improvised chorus of a single, epic jazz solo, although sometimes the "ideas . . . roll from chorus to chorus," just as in a jam session.[44]

In any given chorus, Kerouac stretches words into strings of phrases that walk the line of sense and nonsense. It is as if he heard Joyce's *Finnegans Wake* through Whitman's free verse then strung his ideas onto the fluid musical solos of Young or Parker. These poems affirm life and language most when read aloud: their sense is in the sonics of verbal pyrotechnics. For example, take the end of the "130th Chorus," a meditation on self-doubt. The jazz poet wanders into an American literary hall of mirrors, a place "Where I am not sure [who I am]." He wonders what tradition he slots into, whether here, "I am [Thomas] Wolfe," or perhaps

>Whitman Free
>Melville dark
>Mark Twain Mark
>   Twain
>   where I am
>   w i l d
>Where I am Mild

(130)

Kerouac is split in half between light and dark American romanticism—Whitman and Melville—and thus marked twain, that is, walking the line between wild and mild. Only in his poetry can he blow to the center of false dualities and come out cool. In one way, this is the proof of his jazz manifesto's pudding—blowing out through language to find the center—and in another, it is central to the nonduality of Zen Buddhist thought.

Or take the entire "115th Chorus," a seemingly nonsensical cultural remix with allusions ranging easily from Baudelaire to street junkies, from Buddhism to the A-bomb, from *vaqueros* to existential despair.

115th Chorus

LANGUID JUNKEY SPEECH WITH LIDDED EYES
So bleakly junk hit me never.
Must be something wrong with the day.
"How you feel?" — "Um — Ow" —
Green is the wainscot, wait
For the vaquero, 1, 2, 3 —
     all the faces of man
     are [con]torting on one
     neck

Lousy feeling of never-get-high,
I could swallow a bomb
And sit there a-sighing,
T's a Baudelairean day,
Nothing goes right — millions
Of dollars of letters from home
And the feeling of being,
Ordinary, sane, sight —
     Arm muscles are tense
     Nothing ever right
You cant feel right
     Hung in Partiality
        For to feel the unconditional
        No-term ecstasy
        Where, of nothing,
          I mean, of nothing,
          That would be best

It is a depressing day. The jazz poet could eat an A-bomb and sit non-plussed as he belched a mushroom cloud. Even the junkie can't get high off his horse (heroin) — "so bleakly junk hit me never [before]." As usual,

Kerouac wishes he could just feel right—in other words, just *to be*: "the feeling of being, / Ordinary, sane." As ever he is caught between being and nonbeing. As always, he is looking for the cool space, "the unconditional / No-term ecstasy / . . . of nothing." If he could only reach that place of what Hui-Neng calls "no-thought," well then, "That would be best."[45]

The choruses of *Mexico City Blues* are like tiny black rubber balls that Kerouac kicks into corners and bounces off the walls. In the capricious "116th Chorus," Kerouac suddenly stops and just writes "Music" in the center of the page to shift the theme. "It's an Aztec Radio," he declares, as if to suggest that music is crucial to any civilization as a form of primal emotional communication. Then to close out the chorus, he spins a nice little arabesque on the phrase "jazz singer":

> The Great Jazz Singer
>   was Jolson the Vaudeville Singer?
> No, and not Miles, me.

In invoking the question of who is "the Great Jazz Singer," Kerouac first alludes to the film *The Jazz Singer*. In its climactic moment, Al Jolson rebels in blackface against his Jewish father (a rabbi) by singing a peppy, rhythmic version of '20s jazz. Then Kerouac calls Jolson's music by its real name, vaudeville.[46]

Then he wonders, who is the real jazz singer and who the vaudeville singer of his own generation? The former might be Miles Davis—in the sense that any musician with a distinctive voice is a vocalist. But who is the real vaudeville singer? That's Kerouac himself: "not Miles, me." Is this an admission to his own love and theft of African-American culture, a claim to literary blackface? The ambivalence of "No, and not Miles, me," certainly suggests this possibility.

After 238 such choruses, Kerouac finds his hybrid soul in the fusion of jazz and Buddhism in the climactic final five choruses: "Charley Parker Looked like Buddha," the "239th Chorus" begins, "[and] was called the Perfect Musician" (241). This begins a poetic eulogy for Parker, who had only just died of a heart attack (with complications) on March 12, 1955; "Bird Lives" sprouted as graffiti all over New York at the time, mostly from the hand of Beat poet Ted Joans.

Kerouac first attests to the cool serenity of Parker on the bandstand:

And his expression on his face
Was as calm, beautiful, and profound
As the image of the Buddha
      ... the lidded eyes,
The expression that says "All is Well" (241)

Parker's sound "had the feeling of early-in-the-morning," a joyful noise, "like the perfect cry / of some wild gang at a jam session." Moreover, Bird's artistic innovations of speed, harmony, and tempo reflected post-war American culture, its cars and its arms race: "Charley burst / His lungs to reach the speed / Of what the speedsters wanted." The "239th Chorus" ends with a simple declaration: "A great musician and a great / creator of forms / That ultimately find expression / In mores and what have you." In other words, the innovations of jazz trickle down into American music, style, and language.[47]

Kerouac's elegy to Bird rolls into the next chorus (the 240th) with a jazz truism then considered artistic blasphemy: "Musically as important as Beethoven, / Yet not regarded as such at all." To some people this is a radical thought even now, the equivalence of a jazz genius with a classical composer. Credit Kerouac with depicting Parker as a great artistic leader at a specific moment of spiritual crisis. "Proud and calm," he recalls Bird on the bandstand, "a leader / of music / In the Great Historic World Night." Parker wields his only weapon against oppression and history, "wail[ing] his little saxophone, / The alto, with piercing clear / lament / In perfect tune & shining harmony." He describes the power of Bird's musical call when it finds audience response:

And soon the whole joint is rocking
And everybody is talking and Charley
      Parker [is]
Whistling them on to the brink of eternity.

This chorus ends with a playful, dreadful vision of Bird as Pied Piper of the Apocalypse: "And like the holy piss we blop / And we plop / in the waters of / slaughter/ And white meat, and die / One after one, in time." Yet this chorus is less Armageddon than death as rebirth: it is ground zero for the jump-starting of a post-Western culture. That the audience "plops in[to] the waters of slaughter" contextualizes the poem in the ideological paralysis of the Cold War. That the audience is "white meat" dying "in time" suggests either apocalypse or baptismal rebirth into a post-Western era that will demand the kind of non-dualistic, non-theistic philosophies Kerouac sought. That we die separately and yet "in time" implies that even death has its own musical groove.[48]

The jazz poet rolls again into the "241st Chorus" singing with Bird: "And how sweet a story it is / When you hear Charley Parker / tell it," as if even Apocalypse can be artistically rendered. Here he first mentions Bird's heroin habit as it led to his early death of a heart attack and bleeding ulcer—yet Kerouac neither dwells on it nor judges him. (And how could he, as an alcoholic?)[49]

At the end of the "241st Chorus" Kerouac offers Parker an apology: he is ashamed to have been so easily fooled by the mask of cool, the racial performance of calm defiance. "Charley Parker, forgive me — / Forgive me for not answering your eyes —" It is a declaration of white guilt that recognizes the long-suffering struggle behind African-American cool. Kerouac again invokes Parker as an American Buddha, a medium through which clarity of mind might emerge in the future. "Charley Parker, pray for me — / Pray for me and everybody / In the Nirvanas of your brain / Where you hide, indulgent and huge." Too late Kerouac realizes that Parker hid his consciousness somewhere white people could not reach.[50]

Kerouac then elevates Parker to sainthood: "No longer Charley Parker / But the secret unsayable name." His hope is that Parker will be evaluated by otherworldly moral criteria, since his new "unsayable name . . . carries with it merit / Not to be measured from here." Kerouac peeks into a future where Bird will receive his due as a music god rather than condemned as a heroin addict, two sides of the same introspection. Then he ends: "Charley Parker, lay the bane, / off me, and every body."[51]

With Parker as his exemplar, Kerouac proposes a synthesis of the African aesthetic of the cool and the Buddha's half smile. A year earlier in his *Dharma* journal, Kerouac had written that "the Silent Eternal Smile of Buddhahood is a *Mental Smile*—not a Lip-Smile—Buddha[-]ship is a silent Eternal Mental Smile!"[52] Parker's "faint smile" is the outward sign of inner Zen grace, the symbol of self-mastery according to the third Noble Truth, the suppression of desire and suffering.

If "Budda-ship is a silent Eternal Mental Smile," then I suggest this convergence: the mask of cool is an insolent version of a Buddha-type smile, born of a stoic turn in the African-American struggle for social equality.[53] Many white critics saw Parker as a diffident junkie or an idiot savant yet nearly all black jazz musicians experienced Parker as a maverick artist, a defiant rebel, and an intellectual, despite his heroin addiction and sleazy behavior. Parker always had his mask of cool pulled tight as if it was a set of facial blinds. Kerouac proves himself one of the few white writers able to see through the mask or (at least) to reflect on his own ignorance.

In three choruses, Kerouac unifies jazz and Buddhism in a literary hybrid form that speaks to the Cold War moment: here he references the atomic age and white American *dis*-ease; implores Charlie Parker to save the society and accept his proxy apology for racial oppression; invokes Parker's name as talisman for a post-Western future. In the ultimate chorus of *Mexico City Blues*, without referring to Bird by name, Kerouac brings back the idea, from the "239th Chorus," that the artistic impact of someone like Parker "ultimately find[s] expression / In mores and what have you." Kerouac suggests a method for finding a cool space in one's own mind through musical self-excavation and Zen silence:

> The sound in your mind
> > is the first sound
> > > that you could sing
>
> If you were singing
> > at a cash register
> > > with nothing on yr mind —

There is a common archetypal image of Zen mind: "the mirror with no stains." Here Kerouac redirects its connotations for a technological civilization: the mind as a clear, metallic reflective surface, still and yet active, alive to the rejuvenation by song. This image is accessible to any kid with a boring job: what if your mind was at peace even while flipping burgers?

What if even then you heard in your mind the signature song that calms your mental landscape? That would be a cool space to inhabit during the everyday work world.[54]

Mexico City Blues is the purest statement of Kerouac's dialectic: equal parts jazz yawp and cooled Buddhist mind. It is an epic poetic cycle that mixes the modernist model of stream of consciousness with postmodern pastiche. Allen Ginsberg read much of it aloud to Chögyam Trungpa on a long car ride and the monk "laughed all the way as he listened." The next day he told Ginsberg, "I kept hearing Kerouac's voice all night." Kerouac recorded the choruses on Parker accompanied by Steve Allen on piano on *Poetry for the Beat Generation* (1960). They were the only choruses on that album extrapolated from *Mexico City Blues*.[55]

A half century after *On the Road*, Kerouac continues to gather readers because his quest was emblematic of the then-dawning post-Western, post-Christian age. Kerouac learned this from Gary Snyder, who once reflected on the demand upon the individual in Zen: "There is one side of Buddhism that clearly throws it back on the individual—each person's own work, practice, and life. Nobody else can do it for you; the Buddha is only the teacher."[56] This is the subtext of much of Kerouac's literary oeuvre: the search for unconventional teachers, the rendering of spiritual explorations, an individual quest for meaningful work through writing.

And yet Kerouac remains something of a scapegoat in literary studies even now; in 1972, Allen Ginsberg put it down to the ignorance of cultural critics. In *Mexico City Blues*, Ginsberg maintained, "Kerouac wrote with great sophistication on Buddhism," while his critics were ignorant of these "ancient and honorable texts"—nor were they willing to do the research to assess Kerouac's work.[57] Since literary critics then knew little of African-American music, Zen Buddhism, or the aesthetic of the cool, they could not see these artistic practices or concepts at work in Kerouac's prose. If his detractors lacked an aesthetic foundation to understand his artistic objectives, postwar youth understood it at the intuitive level; in other words, his stylistic innovations were so subtle that they were read as artless (by critics) and unobtrusive (by young readers). As with the populist accessibility of blues, Kerouac subsumed his experimentation into a conversational style. If critics thought of him as an artistic primitivist, it is more precise to say he *was* a primitive—proudly so, as possessor of a "raw mind"—who was never able to channel his spiritual yearnings into a cool mental space.

Allen Ginsberg had been a practicing Buddhist for nearly a generation when he called out Kerouac's critics in 1972. He listed the literary innovations and thematic ideas Kerouac brought into common usage: "spontaneous speech, the use of drugs on the side, marijuana and psychedelics, the preoccupation with American Indians, the second religiousness . . . the interest in black music . . . the sense of a Fellaheen subterranean underground nonofficial existence." To Ginsberg, Kerouac had mastered a "body of poetics" intellectuals did not know or respect. "The tradition . . . in Kerouac is the black blues. It wasn't until the '60s . . . that it got to be accepted as a major art form with . . . intellectual distinction." More than jazz or Zen, Ginsberg credits the literary success of *Mexico City Blues* to Kerouac's knowledge of the blues, a misunderstood art form until Baldwin, Ellison, Samuel Charters, and Amiri Baraka analyzed its workings in essays and books between 1959 and 1964. "The intellectuals said that it [*Mexico City Blues*] came out of no tradition, [but] they were not smart enough or learned enough to know the tradition, or sensitive enough to understand it." Kerouac's *The Book of Blues* contains many successful blues poems and shows he understood the poetic form. Yet American literary and cultural critics had "no ideas of this as literature, the true literature of America [at the time], and it was," Ginsberg said.[58]

Cool and the Post-Western Era

In the sixth century AD, the Zen teacher Bodhidharma declared Buddhism available to anyone willing to work on their minds: Kerouac annotated this fact with pride in *Some of the Dharma* by writing, "There is no difference between a Buddha and an ordinary person." Kerouac traded the word "citizen" for "fellaheen," an Arabic term for peasants. This was an unfortunate choice and redolent of his primitivism, yet it was a marker of his egalitarianism:

> Buddhism is a Fellaheen thing.—Fellaheen is Antifaust Unanglosaxon Original World Apocalypse. Fellaheen is an Indian Thing, like

the earth. Jean-Louis [Kerouac] the Fellaheen Seer of New North
America.—The Unfaust, the Antichrist . . . Unsquare, Ungothic.

Kerouac imagines a new kind of pilgrim working against the false consciousness of Anglo-Saxon superiority, stodgy Christianity, racial hierarchy, and the myth of progress ("Antifaust") in a positive vision of an
"Original World Apocalypse." In an emerging post-Western era, Kerouac
imagines apocalypse as a rebirth for a "New North America" that honors the earth itself and the continent's indigenous peoples. He imagines
a hip ("Unsquare") vision that casts off European fears ("Unsquare,
Ungothic").[59]

"WESTERNERS ARE SO IGNORANT OF ENLIGHTENMENT," Kerouac
said, thereby leaping into the post-Western abyss with a single pun.
The subtext here is Buddhist enlightenment, of course, and he quickly
enfolds the pun into an indictment of postwar nuclear anxiety: "They
[Westerners] are like some scientist slaving day and night in his laboratory to invent a new kind of grief." Here lies the core of postwar existential dread: what is the West without its myth of technological progress?
In retrospect, was it only a set of once-warring tribes that came together
to colonize the planet's peoples and environment under the sign of
progress? And hadn't the conceptual edifice been destroyed by the dual
whammy of the atomic bomb and the ethnic slaughters by Germans and
Russians?[60]

The literary success of the Beats was due in part to their calling out
of the West's dysfunction: the division between its claimed religious
precepts and its immoral actions, between its soapbox morality and
pragmatic capitalism, between its abstract Enlightenment values and
its seeming technological death wish. In another pun from *Dharma*,
Kerouac trades Western rationalism for an alternative Buddhist
method. "Buddhism is a system of Mind Control," he writes with wry
inversion—meaning to have control over one's own mind as opposed to
brainwashing.[61]

In addition, Kerouac understood jazz and Zen as embodied democratic philosophies. Following Whitman, he believed that democracy
had a spiritual dimension and referenced his one political treatise in
Dharma: "'For I say at the core of democracy, finally, is the religious

element,' WHITMAN, DEMOCRATIC VISTAS." Kerouac was also drawn to Zen sutras as a writer since they shared with Whitman's poetry the accessibility of colloquial language and concepts evoked by everyday images of nature and work.[62]

By the late 1950s, Kerouac's vision was loosely post-Western as it might inform a new American grain. His writing sat squarely within the Western and American literary traditions but it had become inextricably infused with non-Western arts, music, forms, ideas, practices, and language. Here's a set of four meditative fragments compressed into a mere quarter-page of *Some of the Dharma*.

1. "'COMPARISONS ARE ODIOUS,' says Doctor Johnson and that's the end of St. Augustine";
2. "[Jazz pianist] Teddy Wilson playing China Boy—cant get it played [tonight], no time";
3. "THE DIAMOND SCRIPTURE . . . The Lordship of the Buddhas is a vehicle—you gotta have somethin' to ride, a raft to cross over in";
4. "A Chachacha on radio, from Cuba, I remember my wine walks to Cathedrals in narrow nightstreets of Fellaheena—I remember Holy Marijuana warming my brain with Visions of . . . the HOLY SNOW— transcendental freedom of the mind, among the sweet Indians of Mexico."[63]

This list brings together the following artistic practices with equivalent rhetorical weight: (1) fifth-century spiritual autobiography, eighteenth-century English literature (Enlightenment); (2) African-American jazz, improvisation as an artistic method; (3) canonical Buddhism—a ninth-century Sanskrit text—riffed on in the American vernacular with a reference to *Huck Finn*; (4) Afro-Cuban music (cha-cha-cha), primitivism, romanticized Native American philosophy. This range of influences appears throughout *Some of the Dharma*: Buddhist texts copied out and riffed on; a few haikus and jazz allusions; short quotes from Joyce, Shakespeare, Balzac, Proust, Whitman, Yeats, and Dickinson; critiques of Céline, Freud, Buber, Spengler, and Einstein. All are invoked in Kerouac's search for "transcendental freedom of the mind."

In 1959, Gary Snyder challenged Kerouac to write a sutra of his own, and the result was *The Scripture of the Golden Eternity*. It is a unique sixty-six-stanza American Buddhist text usefully understood as a long, ten-minute jazz solo. Kerouac opens with a theme connecting the personal to the transcendental, "Did I create that sky?" and he answers yes, but only inasmuch as it is a conception of his own mind. He then plays with the notion of the sky as heaven for ten stanzas, mixing the natural and the cosmic, before moving from the heavens to Heaven itself. He takes a quantum leap past the sky at this point to mediate on the concept of God (in His Heaven) by declaiming the deity's many names: "A God, a Buddha . . . an Allah, a Sri Krishna, a Coyote, a Brahma, a Mazda, a Messiah."

At the climax of the sutra, Kerouac suggests a reorientation of the American gods with Coyote as Earthmaker and anoints him the prevailing spirit of the nation's future. In stanza 63, Kerouac has Coyote announce a coming transformation after which all beings "will be transformed . . . their words and their bodies . . . will all change." Then Kerouac-as-narrator faints: this is a shrewd narrative move. He allows himself a near-death experience in his backyard (stanza 64) only to awaken and see the sky, heaven, and the world anew as if reborn into this post-Western world. Again, the song title from Benny Goodman provides the trope for his hopes: "The world is waiting for the sunrise." In Kerouac's work, the sunrise is opposed to the mushroom cloud.[64]

There was a single question for which both jazz and Zen Buddhism provided an artistic method for Kerouac: how can a writer create a calm center to allow the artistic statement to manifest while keeping the ego and superego at bay? His first artistic method was bop prosody, the improvisational flow as personalized statement in the long, fluid jazz solos of bebop. His second was Zen Buddhism's stripped-down aesthetic of simplicity as an implicit critique of Christianity, rationalism, and technological worship. To put it bluntly: Kerouac knew he was up a nuclear shit-creek without a worthy literary paddle. To reckon with the loss of Western ideals, he aspired toward the vernacular eclectic mix of American culture, guided by both the "elegant simplicity" of black music (to invoke Toni Morrison's phrase) and Zen Buddhism.

In Postwar II, Kerouac recognized as Western "philosophy's dreadful murderer, Buddha," and he aspired to the religion's empty, cool mind. "AWAKE MEANS MIND-EMPTY," he wrote in all caps. Kerouac considered writing itself a medium for his own spiritual redemption: "From Writer

I'll go to Realizer," as he imagines this karmic transformation. Kerouac failed this ideal, but his attempts remain compelling literary documents of a multicultural reimagining of American literature.[65]

Zen Cool: A Postwar Sounding of Philosophical Fusion

> Buddhism is atheism that became religion . . . a Renaissance originating from nihilism. Unique example, I believe, and priceless to reflect on for us who are wrestling with nihilism.
>
> Albert Camus, *Notebooks 1951–1959*[66]

Buddhism and existentialism share so much conceptual ground—including the timing of their impact on the postwar West—that it is puzzling how rarely connections are made between them. Both Buddhism and existentialism are systems of mind training that jettison God, fate, and destiny. Both systems pursue an abstract ideal of cognitive freedom in that each insists on individual independence and critical thinking. If existentialism has an initial stage of dread due to the realization of one's aloneness, Buddhism insists on a first stage of clearing your mind of all previous thoughts. If Sartre claims we are condemned to freedom, Hui-Neng insists on a sudden awakening into "no-thought" (in the *Platform Sutra*) before any authentic relationship can exist between action and knowledge. If Sartre claims one must first lose hope and fear, present and future, Trungpa says one begins with hopelessness.[67]

Both systems provide a method for liberation from social and political dogmatism and both methods found adherents in the postwar spiritual crisis. The monk Thomas Merton reflected in 1968:

> The impact of Zen on the West [struck] . . . with its fullest force right after World War II, in the midst of the existential upheaval, at the beginning of the atomic and cybernetic age, with Western religion and philosophy in a state of crisis and with the consciousness of man threatened by the deepest alienation.

Merton understood the appeal of Zen and he left an incisive account of the Buddhist challenge to traditional Christianity in *Mystics and Zen Masters* (1972). Zen offered "modern man" a religious practice that was "non-doctrinal, concrete, direct, [and] existential," with an emphasis on confronting life as lived—and felt, and experienced—rather than through moral abstractions often revealed as hypocritical.[68]

Zen monks created sutras about philosophy of mind as early as the sixth century. In "Treatise on Faith in the Mind," attributed to Seng-ts'an, there is a question that runs throughout early twentieth-century philosophy: "If you work on your mind with your mind, / How can you avoid an immense confusion?" This echoes forward from Kierkegaard to Heidegger to Sartre, yet such questions were already a full millennium old and ingrained in Buddhist thought. Snyder describes the intellectual riches of the tradition simply: "The Buddha-Dharma is a long, gentle, human dialog—2,500 years of quiet conversation—on the nature of human nature . . . and practical methods of realization."[69]

In the late 1970s, Gary Snyder drew a straight line through the rebellions of the twentieth century leading from Marxist revolution to Zen Buddhism. He traced the thinking rebel's spiraling movement, and as each failed to produce social change, a new search for other philosophical methods. The quest began "from the dialectic of Marx and Hegel," then led to "the dialectic of early Taoism," and then it was "another easy step to the philosophies and mythologies of India." In between came Freud and psychoanalysis, the "concern with deepening one's understanding in an experiential way." From this dead end for social change Snyder declared that, beginning in the '60s, many people began to find "in the Buddha-Dharma a practical method for clearing one's mind of the trivia, prejudices and false values that our conditioning had laid on us." Simultaneously, it provided a method for "penetra[ting] to the deepest nonself Self," and it ran concurrent to other exploration such as "yoga, Shamanism, [and] Psychedelics." Zen Buddhism appealed to apolitical rebels weary of psychology, surrealism, phenomenology, and Sartrean ideas of freedom.[70]

Camus imagined that even the gods envied Buddha for his "wisdom and . . . stone-like destiny." How did Buddha achieve this ideal of cool detachment? Camus imagined that he "stifled in himself desire and will, fame and suffering." When Camus meditated on the ephemeral qualities of all life, this cool stone stood in judgment—but then he realized even stone does not last and cried out, "'Oh, to be nothing!'" This passage evokes both Buddhism and his dream of existentialism, both of them philosophical methods that aspired "to revolt against desire and pain."[71] As early as 1939, Buddha was one of Camus's models of detachment and self-control: "Sakyamuni in the desert . . . squatting motionless with his eyes on heaven." Camus was ambivalent with regard to Buddha's unnatural equilibrium but compared it positively to the quality of cool, hard stone in the desert city of Oran, his hometown.

When Kerouac analyzed the "emptiness" of Buddhism, he created several analogies with Sartre's "nothingness." Kerouac declares the potential of Zen: "Let me lay it out as simply & concisely as I can:—All things are empty . . . in three ways, as Things of Time, as Things of Space, as Things of Mind."[72] Yet the void in Zen is more akin to a cloudless sky than a bloodless stone or bottomless well. The "nothing" of which Zen speaks refers to neither nihilism nor detached withdrawal. Merton perceived the concept as "in no sense negativistic or pessimistic" and delineated it from Sartre's sense of nothingness as abstract, unattached existence. To Merton, Zen had "no relation with the néant [or *nothing*] of Sartre," and he considered its practices not only more generative but the more superior (and practical) philosophical stance.[73]

Cool is an ideal mode of spiritual balance with roots in African cultures. For Gary Snyder, meditation is itself a *practice* of cool—of cooling the mind—and thus of simple being without striving for any effect. Meditation quiets the mind and mutes hyperactive mental activity. It connects human beings to animals, "all of whom/which are capable of simply just *being* for long hours of time." Snyder considered meditation "a complete natural act," and wondered why more people did not aspire toward this state. "It's odd that we don't do it more, that we don't, simply like a cat, *be* there for a while, experiencing ourselves as whatever we are, without any extra thing added to that." The goal of Zen Buddhism remains the satisfaction of simple being, of *be*-ing—"simply like a cat, [to] *be* there for a while"—and as such it crosses paths with the postwar mask of cool in that effort or exertion should be hidden. "There is no place in Buddhism for using effort," Alan Watts wrote of his Buddhist apprenticeship. "Just be ordinary and nothing special."[74]

For Merton, Zen Buddhism's appeal was strongest when embodied: meeting Suzuki brought about his understanding. "One cannot understand Buddhism until one meets it, in this existential manner," Merton wrote, "in a person in whom it is alive." A Zen monk aspires to be "miraculously natural without intending to be so" and can only be so—or just be—when he or she "has lost affectedness and self-consciousness." Such a monk must be non-materialistic, uninterested in grace, aligned in thought and action: "a spirit of this kind comes and goes like the wind."[75] In Postwar II, Suzuki was the kind of spiritual leader (and being) to whom Kerouac aspired: the everyday Zen monk without affectation or self-doubt, as natural as a cloud passing over and then dissolving.

• • •

Robert Thurman, the first American Buddhist monk ordained in the Tibetan Buddhist tradition, recalled Suzuki's postwar influence on American culture as a "cool, inexorable, inner revolution." If Zen was a slow wave breaking over popular culture, then poet Lewis MacAdams's analysis of Thurman's phrase "inner revolution" makes sense as a like-minded community of people: "a social transformation based on individual transformation."[76] This is a useful framework for cool as it moved out from the postwar era to its generational iteration in the 1960s. In contrast to the devaluation of cool as a concept today—and to its commodification— postwar cool concerned the potential for self-transformation through risk, introspection, transgression, and the romantic potential of an ideal bohemia.

Kerouac's favorite scripture was the Diamond Sutra, which emphasized "The Middle Way"—of moderation and balance—as the right path. Kerouac aspired to this ideal of spiritual calm but failed to achieve it even for short periods as he lacked personal discipline. He found in Lester Young's self-expression and existential affirmation an embodiment of jazz cool long before he engaged these ideas intellectually.[77] He found in Snyder's Zen practice a combination of psychological ideal and philosophical practice that approximated the secular sainthood he sought. Kerouac's objective was precisely this kind of "cool, inexorable inner revolution," one that reinforced the ideal of cool as a concept "indifferent to privilege, dogma, and attachment, *in* but not *of* the world."[78] These thematic hopes still pervade cool as an emblematic phrase for the postwar aspiration of transcendent balance and aesthetic detachment.

Figure 20. Frank Sinatra recording at Capitol Studios in 1956 for one of his concept albums drawn from the Great American Songbook (© Herman Leonard Photography LLC).

7

From Noir Cool to Vegas Cool

Swinging into Prosperity with Frank Sinatra

You own them body and soul.
You're not gonna own me.

Edward G. Robinson as Victor Scott in *Illegal* (1955)

In Postwar II, newly middle-class nuclear families were a new domestic front that caused a major inflection in the register of noir cool. As the postwar generation of veterans settled into suburban security, the ethical rebel loner gave way to the tough police captain, a kind of urban sheriff. This new character was an enforcer of a restored moral order, his toughness due to solitary leadership and sacrifice rather than to any abstract quest for personal dignity or situational truth. This social sea change in the national imagination reflected both a new, confident sense of prosperity and American triumphalism as felt through full employment and global hegemony. Buoyed by the economic engines of the Korean War, the Marshall Plan, and the nuclear arms race, the United States then produced 75 percent of the world's goods. Such global domination allowed corporations to grant generous contracts to labor unions and created the kind of widespread (white) middle-class prosperity the nation has not known since.[1]

This noble cop-protector presided over the reinstatement of traditional morality and enforced the law on the outskirts of the suburban postwar homestead. While they raised children, the wartime generation chose psychological protection from an unreckoned past through John Wayne and the Western (genocide, slavery) and from Cold War global anxieties through paternalistic police captains in TV shows such as *Dragnet* and *Naked City*. With the Duke out on the frontier re-staging Manifest Destiny, the police force patrolled the urban wilderness with the latest technology to keep the streets safe. The police force stood in for technological progress as well as the liberal dream of rational society with the *deus ex machina* often coming through scientists in the police lab or new national networks of surveillance. Films focused on a democratic labor force of beat cops who kept the streets clean through hard work, ubiquity, and efficient bureaucratic organization. Meanwhile, the markers of *social* progress came through a steady flow of new products and gadgets into the home, the daily guarantors of convenience and pleasure (e.g., cars, phones, television, washer/dryers, stereos). Technology penetrated the cultural imagination as an abstract vision of networks and control focused on nuclear energy, giant computers, and the lab.

Frank Sinatra became the primary avatar of cool renewal for the wartime generation and shifted its cultural imagination from past to future with the onset of national prosperity. Sinatra, Dean Martin, and the Rat Pack embodied a hedonistic twist on the Horatio Alger story, swinging coolly in an artificial city built for middle-class escapism. Here were great singers who brought style, depth, and fantasy to American song while "livin' the dream"—to backdate a phrase. Yet this choice represented continuity as well as escapism. Sinatra was a jazz singer par excellence and his vocal synthesis blended Italian and African-American vocal styles and musical practices. In effect, he created an urbane blues style for a nation of immigrants. Sinatra embodied the triumph of the immigration saga yet the romantic yearning in his voice harkened back to the emotional costs of urban modernity and its inchoate nostalgia for community, whether ethnic, urban, or collective. To journalist Pete Hamill, the "one basic subject" of all Sinatra's vocal performances was "loneliness." As a fellow second-generation immigrant, Hamill analyzed

Sinatra's cool schematic as double-edged: "His ballads are . . . strategies for dealing with loneliness; his up-tempo performances are expressions of release from that loneliness."[2]

For the wartime generation, Sinatra's hedonistic cool came through a romantic soundscape meant to accompany leisure and domestic life in contrast to Bogart's solitary bravado. This passing of the *cool* torch (so to speak) was obvious enough to the generation that lived through it. Contemporary music chronicler Arnold Shaw wrote in 1968: "If Humphrey Bogart stands forth as the existential man, viewing life with a sense of detached irony but living with courage . . . Sinatra is the archetype of the romantic man, raging against the human condition." Bogart symbolized the resilience of living through the Depression and war, surviving with style and stoic humor in an unstable era. Sinatra was compelling through his dual embrace of streetwise bravado and open-hearted romance. Sinatra's projection of gritty reality was set off against his jazz vocal artistry and he walked "the fine line between pathos and bathos." Sinatra's multiple personae fit several American myths. He was both a national cultural leader and a Horatio Alger with a second act. He was both a cultural CEO (the so-called Chairman of the Board) and yet a rebel outsider (an Italian-American in a WASP nation). In a nation liberated from wartime obligation, Sinatra represented "a great paradox" to historian Douglas Brinkley: "tough and tender, the hard-luck boy from Hoboken who made it to the top." And as for Pete Hamill and his second-generation white ethnic men, "Sinatra created a new model for American masculinity."[3]

Like most new models, Sinatra's cool was actually a synthesis of disparate aspects into a new style of masculine rebellion. Las Vegas represented the transmutation of the Prohibition matrix into an extralegal zone on the Western frontier. The Rat Pack was the wartime generation's hip elite and mirrored other groups of men enacting "the flight from commitment" to suburban normalcy, whether through a *Playboy* lifestyle, weekend motorcycle gangs, or bohemian communities such as the Beats.[4] If Sinatra was a naturalized American culture hero, the Rat Pack was a twist on World War II infantry units, with its variety of regions and ethnicities represented. In addition, Rat Pack cool had the advantage of newly interconnected media networks of celebrity through film, television, concerts, and Vegas. In effect, the Rat Pack's pleasure principle was original enough—in its sex, booze, music, adventure, and group hijinks—to establish the archetypal posse for both rock-star cool and hip-hop gangsta lifestyle. Rappers have name-checked Sinatra as the O.G. or "Original Gangsta" since the 1990s, creating a black-Italian gangster noir ideal that draws parallels between these ethnic urban communities across generations. To cite just one example, Jay Z's tribute to Sinatra on "Empire State of Mind" combines the latter's "New York, New York" with "My Way."

Sinatra did not create this matrix by himself: Dean Martin played an equal role in shifting a generation's ideal from the solitary consciousness of Hemingway's existential cool to the swinger's playboy bacchanalia. "Dino" Americanized the Italian concept of *sprezzatura*, an analogy for "cool" that suggests effortlessness in artistic creation. Martin was equally ubiquitous for the wartime generation: as a popular crooner, actor, and off-stage lothario; in his comic turns in Westerns or in spy films as Matt Helm; and (later) in his long-running top-ten NBC variety show. To his audiences, Dean Martin had it all—sex, money, fame, and women—and projected a charismatic nonchalance of not giving a damn about any part of it from within a jocular alcoholic haze.[5]

Why did the cultural pendulum swing so far from noir cool? The noir sensibility survived in the shadow side of Sinatra's persona: in a late-night urbane romantic style repurposed for the obligations of the nuclear family as leavened by a fantasy of alcoholic hedonism. The wartime generation settled into the suburbs and raised children. They fed their nostalgia on big bands and Rat Pack fantasies; the significance of "cool" as a mode of authentic stylish rebellion shifted to a new young generation. With the temporary evisceration of economic uncertainty came a rejuvenation of national confidence and American triumphalism. The sudden prosperity after the Korean War manifested in the casting off of noir's ambiguity and the restoration of traditional Christian morality in the cultural imagination.

As a representative example of the shift in noir cool, the private detective had become such a nostalgic trope by 1953 that even Fred Astaire and Frank Sinatra were detectives that year. In the radio drama *Rocky Fortune* (1953–54), Sinatra played a temp worker who stumbled onto crimes while on assignment. To play Fortune, Sinatra thickened up his Italian Jersey accent to project urban swagger, yet despite a popular lead-in following *Dragnet*, the show was short-lived. Yet in the next two years, Sinatra infused the Rocky Fortune aspect into his Vegas persona, a mask of cool unlike his public image as a skinny crooner and teen idol from the 1940s. "He *had* to put on this shield of swagger, bluster and masculinity," biographer James Kaplan reflected. "He was a little man . . . who grew up at a time when Italian-Americans were just a half step above African-Americans [in terms of ethnic prejudice]." This was another step toward constructing a newly tough ethnic masculinity.[6]

That same year, Fred Astaire played detective Tony Hunter in "Girl Hunt: A Murder Mystery in Jazz," the featured vignette in the acclaimed musical *The Band Wagon* (1953). In his midnight walks, Hunter stumbles onto a series of murders involving a tall blond, a jazz trumpeter, and an elusive "Mr. Big." Actress Cyd Charisse danced the roles of both Astaire's helper and good girl ("The Brunette") and the bad-girl femme fatale ("The Blonde"). As the gangster moll, Charisse vamps her way into Astaire's encrusted heart with some pelvic *va-va-va-voom* timed to thunderous big band riffs. In a nice twist on the formula, the villain (Mr. Big) turns out to be The Blonde cross-dressing as a man: in this way, Charisse dies in Astaire's arms as the femme fatale yet also walks off with him as The Brunette.

The moral and sexual schizophrenia here of good girl / bad girl represented the tensions of female sexual desire, a subject directly addressed in a production number, "Two Faced Woman." Cyd Charisse danced with two separate troupes of women: good girls in white, bad girls in red. Charisse declared herself to be *both*—both "a little bit of boldness and / a little bit of sweetness"—and sexually speaking, both "a little bit of coldness / and a little bit of *heat*ness." In effect, she staked a claim to being a cool woman, the good-bad girl of a detective's dreamworld, "a little bit of wrong and right." Yet fittingly for the '50s, there was no room for such a woman in American society: the number was cut from the film. "With my dual nature," as Charisse sang, "I don't belong."

Even Philip Marlowe had lost his edge. Raymond Chandler grudgingly agreed with a friend's critique of his longest novel, *The Long Goodbye* (1952) that Marlowe "had become Christ-like and sentimental." In this meandering work, Chandler's longest and most personal novel, Marlowe can barely tolerate the loneliness required of his private chivalric code. He sleeps naked with a woman for the first time and has a close,

Figure 21. PI Tony Hunter (Fred Astaire) dances with his assistant, "The Brunette" (Cyd Charisse), in "Girl Hunt: A Murder Mystery in Jazz."

homoerotic friendship with a character named Terry Lennox. In a telling bit of self-reflexive projection, Marlowe befriends an alcoholic author bored with the formulaic nature of his best-selling novels. Chandler admitted that he found writing the novel a chore since "the hardboiled stuff was too much of a pose after all this time." On the last page of *The Long Goodbye*, his friend Terry confesses his own emptiness yet also seems to be speaking to Marlowe's exhaustion with the mask of cool: "An act is all there is. There isn't anything else. . . . I've had it, Marlowe."[7]

Consider this existential dilemma: Chandler wonders whether he had exhausted the narrative energy of Philip Marlowe. Six years later in *Playback*, his final novel, Chandler simply rehashed old themes and stuck a symbolic title on it about writing mechanically. The novel ends with Marlowe getting married and settling down, something Chandler once said was antithetical to the character. In Postwar II, the ethical rebel loner no longer walked the rain-spattered streets of the American unconscious, a shift in noir cool observable through mainstream popular culture.

Police Procedurals and the End of Noir Cool

Film noir lost *its* narrative energy by the mid-1950s and morphed into police procedurals and heist films. The crime procedural began in the late 1940s and revolved around the workings of a single police precinct. Its emphasis was on process, system, and technology—in other words, on crime solving—rather than moral ambiguity, existential dilemmas, or individual agency.[8] "In *Dragnet* it is always the system that wins," as one scholar has distilled the message of the genre; the cliché of "Just the facts, Ma'am," sums up the return to a reliance on puzzle solving in the crime drama.[9] In retrospect, these shows seem like public relations infomercials for American police forces and the genre did not launch a single major figure of cool. Born in 1945 as a literary genre that heralded methodical police work and technological progress via the lab, the police procedural remains a vital force in popular culture. Americans still turn to this predictable, satisfying narrative formula in the face of geopolitical instability, whether in the Cold War or in the wake of 9/11 and global terrorism. It is arguably the dominant television genre today (e.g., *Law and Order, CSI*).[10]

In the postwar police procedural, there is an everyday struggle to revitalize the moral order and it codes for the fight against Communism. Led by white, WASP leading men dressed in suit and tie, the genre defaulted to an ingrained cultural opposition of vice-ridden city versus virtuous small town. The national syndicate is usually run by slick, urbane, ethnically inflected racketeers (usually Italian) who run the city via payoffs to cops and politicians. The hero is often an upstanding family man who works overtime and emerges victorious over amoral criminals. Apparently, making society safe again for good hardworking Americans was not a job for bourbon-swilling misanthropic anti-heroes but rather for normal, average, virtuous men. Both "normalcy" and "average American" were common—and quite positive—postwar tropes.[11]

With *Dragnet*, the police procedural carried forward the noir style while restoring the notion of a traditional virtuous hero. *Dragnet* helped commit a genre takeover: as a prototype, it inflected noir toward the morality tale, moved crime to residential neighborhoods (or the suburbs), and reinstated the opposition of good guys and bad guys as a moral framework. *Dragnet* was a major entertainment franchise: it was a hit radio drama for a decade (1947–57), it ran for seven years as a TV series, and spun off three feature films. With its mechanistic, moral flattening of nocturnal cityscapes into suburban or small-town homogeneity, *Dragnet* promoted the police as the protectors of home and nuclear family against rogue agents. Iconic detectives were rare in film noir after 1950, although there were more than a dozen radio dramas featuring private investigators. Across media formats, there were fewer liminal anti-heroes and more righteous policemen along stricter moral lines.[12]

Instead of the noir protagonist's voice-over confession of his dark desires and willful quest for agency, there was now a righteous, stentorian voice of authority explaining the unambiguous forces of law and order. There is a symbolic shift over a three-year period (1949–52) in which *Dragnet* coexisted on the radio with the hit drama *The Adventures of Sam Spade*. In 1949, Dashiell Hammett's name was struck from *Sam Spade*'s credits due to his prewar Communist affiliations and his leadership of the Civil Rights Congress, which was declared a Communist front in 1947. *The Adventures of Sam Spade* was cancelled in 1951. The social critique of film noir faded away in conjunction with the cultural forces of anti-Communist paranoia and repression.[13]

Visually, this transition can best be experienced in the early films of director Anthony Mann, a pioneer of the police procedural within film noir in *Railroaded* (1947), *T-Men* (1947), *He Walked by Night* (1948), and *Border Incident* (1949). Mann's films are concurrent with the first incarnation of *Dragnet* and signal a shift in American tastes concerning law and order, moral autonomy, and the benevolent state. In each film, the tone is set by a formal voice-over so campy it is now hard to take seriously. Yet Mann's films remain recognizably noir due to John Alton's expressive cinematography. Alton lights each face in his own distinctive brand of chiaroscuro portraiture, dignifying cop and criminal, barkeep and bystander, migrant worker and immigrant fruit seller. Alton's visual aesthetic blends the styles of street photographer Weegee with those of Walker Evans; it meliorates Mann's law-and-order zealotry with a vestigial Depression-era populism.[14]

The original trailer of *Crime Wave* (1954) makes for a representative example of noir's moralistic and systemic turn. First we are given a panoramic view of Los Angeles in broad daylight and then the camera settles on Sterling Hayden sitting high above the city on a rock. "Sims, LAPD," Hayden proclaims. "Murder is my business and midnight is my beat." By day, Hayden declaims, Los Angeles is a beautiful, staid, nearly ideal city, but at midnight, it's all murder and mayhem. There is, however, no need for citizens to worry while they sleep. By night, as soon as a violent crime occurs, "the word goes out along the city's vast network of communication . . . [that] a killer's loose in a city."[15]

The city is transparent to the police force, "stripped naked" of its hiding places such that "there's no escape." The metaphoric wheels of justice transmute visually into the quite-real white-walled tires of police cars, rolling out inexorably after any criminal who dares to foist his dark plans on good Angelenos. If that seems like purple prose, here's Hayden's voice-over: "The wheels of the law's machinery grind hard and the long arms of the department stretch out[,] girdling the city, drawing the steel net tighter and tighter." Fusing natural and mechanical metaphors, the law is figured as both inexorable machine and omniscient spider. The moral of this story is clear: that pesky criminal fly hasn't got a chance. The subtitle of *Crime Wave* was *The City Was Dark*, implying that, once the criminals are caught, Los Angeles returns to its natural state of illumination.

The shift from the ethical rebel loner to the paternalistic cop is the endgame of noir's moral ambiguity and *Crime Wave* has a lens in both worlds. Hayden's Lt. Sims is a bullying middle-aged police lieutenant who rides roughshod on a paroled ex-con to flush out two thieves who have killed a cop. Sims is a solitary middle-aged autocrat with no life outside his job; he walks the LA streets like he owns them. Director An-dré De Toth knew what he wanted from Hayden as the grizzled, sadistic Sims. "For the cop, I needed somebody that walked the line between en-forcing the law and breaking the law, that had enough strength to survive in either sphere, but not completely tied up in knots inside, someone who has a warm spot inside." This is a distillation of the social function of the noir cool figure. Warner Brothers originally cast Bogart for the role of Lt. Sims but De Toth insisted on Hayden, and the studio penalized the director by cutting his budget in half. For De Toth, Bogart was already "bigger than life," while Hayden had a "certain rumpled dignity" that was less heavily iconic and formulaic. Hayden first attracted notice in the genre as the sympathetic muscle in John Huston's heist film, *The Asphalt Jungle* (1950), and he was the only new noir cool figure of Postwar II. Retro-noir author James Ellroy calls Hayden "film-noir's poet-brute."[16]

The film's protagonist is a redeemable ex-con named Steve Lacey (Gene Nelson), a reformed thief with a new wife and a good job. Lacey is a crack aircraft mechanic, a skillful getaway driver—he's good with machines, a postwar man—and he prefigures James Dean in his black shirt and jeans. Two escaped convicts kill a cop then hole up in Lacey's apartment, holding his wife hostage to coerce him to be their driver in an upcoming bank robbery. Throughout the film Lacey talks tough and bides his time, searching for an exit strategy from the thieves holding his wife while he is constantly bullied by Sims. Hayden stalks Nelson—"I'm just waiting for you to screw up"—and yet carries the edge of an older brother figure. Visually, Nelson resembles a younger Hayden enough that the latter seems to envy the reformed thief's youth and his beautiful wife. (See fig. 22.)

In a key speech, Hayden explains how to walk the line between de-sire and morality, between vice and virtue. "You know, it isn't what a man wants to do, Lacey, but what he has to do. Now you take me. I love to smoke cigarettes, but the doctors say I can't have them. So what do I do? I chew toothpicks. Tons of 'em." Given the ratio of toothpicks to cigarettes—tons to packs—it's apparent that Hayden enforces the law as a method for containing his own desires. In the promising future offered up by postwar prosperity, deferred gratification is the new normal.

In the end, it turns out, society always had a strategy for helping Steve Lacey reform. By playing the role of tormentor, Sims was protecting

Figure 22. Sterling Hayden (*right*) was the only new icon of noir cool, post 1950.

Lacey while using him as bait to catch the convicts. The robbery was a setup—the police knew about it the whole time: the tellers are undercover cops. After the arrest (fig. 23), Hayden throws Lacey and his wife in the back seat then speeds off. The couple clutch each other, expecting the worst—to be thrown in jail or beaten up—yet Sims just pulls over at a trolley stop. Hayden grumbles out just three short lines: "I want you to go home. Back to your three rooms, your job, your grocery bills, taxes, babies, and all the other hazards of life on the outside."

In other words: go on and be good consumers (that's *your* job); leave the bad guys to the police (that's *their* job). These lines were unthinkable in the noirs of Postwar I, and the speech symbolizes the postwar shift from a rhetoric of citizens to one of consumers. "Go on, go home," he orders them. The couple is so terrified that Sims has to physically pull them out of the car. "Next time, Lacey, call me. A cop's job is to protect the citizens. . . . If you need help, call me." Lacey asks if this is some kind of joke. "What are you waiting for, haven't you got a home?" The

Figure 23. Sterling Hayden (Lieutenant Sims) arrests Gene Nelson (Steve Lacey) in *Crime Wave* (1954) as if to toughen him up for noir cool.

couple moves away slowly. "Go on, there's your bus. Beat it outta here before I run you in." And so the parolee is redeemed by the tough love of the noble cop-protector, Postwar II's emblematic symbol of a caring, bureaucratic society.

The film's thirty-second final shot amounts to a eulogy for noir cool. Having restored order and sent the couple home, Hayden / Sims leans against the corner of a bank wall, tall, solitary, and haggard in his crumpled hat. He shakes out a cigarette that is broken at two points, as if neither he nor the cigarette had been straight, new, or clean for a long time. Hayden lights it and takes a slow first drag, and his pleasure spreads into his first smile of the film. Then he takes a second drag, slowly, even more satisfied, but then suddenly frowns and flicks it away, and in one and the same motion, takes a toothpick out of his pocket and dangles it out of the side of his mouth. He then leans there content, detached and solitary, a man coolly leaning (literally) on the edge of desire and self-control, of alternating affinities for generosity and sadism.

A final note on how the second phase of cool plays out in *Crime Wave*. Early in the film, a police bulletin goes out for Steve Lacey that makes it seem the cops are looking for a movie star: "blond, blue eyes, six feet tall, thirty-two years old . . . but looks younger . . . white shirt, chinos." In retrospect, the physical resemblance between Gene Nelson and Sterling Hayden was a visual harbinger suggesting a cultural need for cool embodied in younger actors unencumbered by association with wartime experience. Before *Crime Wave*, actor Gene Nelson had been a dancer in musicals; this was his first dramatic role. The film reads as a boot camp for cool with Hayden passing on this new emotional mode that required grittiness, nonchalance, stoicism, and emotional masking, as if the subtext was a single question: "Can you take it, pretty boy?"

Crime Wave is less prophetic than right on time. Like Steve Lacey, the cool avatars of Postwar II needed to be more handsome but less hypermasculine, more vulnerable and less embittered than Bogart, Mitchum, Ladd, and Hayden.

◆ ◆ ◆

I now turn to three pairs of emblematic noirs to narrate this moralistic turn for the wartime generation: *Naked City* and *Side Street*; *The Racket* and *The Big Heat*; *Illegal* and *Kiss Me Deadly*. The end of noir cool can be seen in the lack of menace or ethical ambiguity in once-iconic noir actors such as Bogart (*The Enforcer*), Mitchum (*The Racket*), and even Edward G. Robinson (*Illegal*). It can be seen in films where the femme fatale is redeemed, such as *The Racket* and *The Big Heat*: in both, gangster molls are domesticated from the urban lowlife of bars, gangsters, and sex. In half of these films, there is a Christian subtext: a noble police captain shepherds weak, redeemable men and women back to the side of the angels. In the other half, there is a technological subtext: justice is an efficient machine and the rogue cop is a vessel of the rule of law. Here we see the rise of a neoliberal ideology that combines or conflates technological rationalism with a neo-Christian ethos.

With the nation's social institutions reinstated as righteous and redemptive, even Bogart could not find a cool modality in a noir like *The Enforcer* (1950), a film that introduces the Mafia style of assassination. Bogart plays a district attorney confused by a series of murders that lack motive; they are committed by hired assassins. As District Attorney Ferguson, Bogart wears a bowtie and spends more time at his desk than on the street; he literally walks around too much. Bogart yells a bit and cuffs a criminal now and then, but it's old hat; like Philip Marlowe, he is no longer convincing as a resilient existential tough guy staking out his personal dignity. If the film's gritty cityscape, flashbacks, and overuse of shadows mark it as noir, it is still just a formulaic police procedural focused on protecting an informant from the syndicate before trial. Within a system of justice even Bogart is rendered uninteresting.[17]

There are three dominant metaphors in the cops-and-villains game of the police procedural: the machine of justice, the virus of crime, and the hunted man. Justice has become a problem-solving *system* enacted through technological networks and efficient, methodical productivity. Crime is broadly rendered as either a social plague spreading through the city or as germ-carrying individuals to be quarantined. Unlike the sympathetic criminals in the noirs of Postwar I (e.g., Roy Earle, Philip Raven), here the criminal is a hunted man who must be exterminated like a rat.

These three overarching metaphors are often mixed and matched. The syndicate can be figured as a demonic machine that also rots the body politic from the inside. If a film opens by focusing on a crime syndicate, the rogue policeman is figured as an antibody to fight an infection threatening to destabilize the body politic. For example, in both Fritz Lang's *The Big Heat* and John Cromwell's *The Racket*, the crime machine controls the city by night through payoffs, murder, and collusion; still its penetration of urban life suggests a slow plague by day that rots politics—and the police force—from the inside through lazy bureaucrats. This selective survey of police procedurals renders a shift in the national imagination that reflects the same renewed desire for triumphant, virtuous white men then fueling the Western, the most popular genre of the postwar era across all media.

Naked City (1948) and *Side Street* (1950)

There is an underlying existential question to Jules Dassin's *Naked City*: What does it mean to be an ordinary man in a metropolis? Or more to the point, how can one find individual dignity and social purpose as part of the urban masses? Filmed in quasi-documentary style, an impersonal voice narrates the detective work of the New York Police Department (NYPD) in methodical detail. The work of the police is seen as representative of factory work: it is dignified despite its repetition, and the social purpose of each man is to be a worthy cog in a morally righteous system. Combining the metaphors of the machine and the military, the film synthesizes the division of labor with the chain of command. *Naked City* offers its American audience a pragmatic, nonreligious framework of social purpose and function: every person is an important unit in urban society. Its reward was two Oscars (cinematography, editing) and a nomination for best screenplay.[18]

Naked City was filmed on location in New York City—then a rarity—and Dassin mixed actors with ethnic locals in the search for the murderer of a blond model, an itinerant jewel thief. The police force cranks into action like a human assembly line: beat cops gather evidence, the lieutenant checks out leads and interviews suspects, individual cops show initiative and reveal their character traits. On their return to the precinct, a wise Irish lieutenant assesses the information, asks for and considers each one's hunches, then redirects them efficiently to their next task for the NYPD. *Naked City* at first feels like government propaganda. Yet as influenced by Italian neorealism, the policemen mix as equals with locals and its populism seems genuine: in any given scene, a policeman may go into a candy shop or jewelry store, pass kids diving off the docks or playing street games, watch as construction workers lower a beam or dig into the ground. We hear emanations of conversations from people at the crime site or from telephone operators. The film mediates the central tension of mass society—that is, between the individual and the collective—in order to fight a common enemy.

The level of intelligence increases every step up in the chain of command, from each beat cop to young Jimmy Halloran to Detective Lieutenant Dan Muldoon: the rational quality of a policeman's thought, his level of maturity, his sense for compassion, and even his capacity for joie de vivre. In so doing, the film endorses the core Horatio Alger aspects of American mythology: social mobility is real, virtue rises, hard work will be rewarded, America is a meritocracy open to immigrants. Jimmy Halloran in particular represents the postwar future since his home life and work life are intertwined. He performs a civic duty at the domestic level with a new home in the suburbs, a young, beautiful wife, a sexualized relationship, and a young son. The film revels in the hierarchical nature of corporate society as a stabilizing force allowing each individual enough wiggle room to gain a viable freedom within a democracy full of surveillance.

Dana Polan's perceptive analysis focuses on the film's tone of "sunny normalcy," as Hollywood attempted to ideologically reinforce the rewards of routine and even automation. In a society where everyone was replaceable and factory jobs constituted more than 30 percent of American jobs—the word "automation" became prevalent only in the late 1940s—this film is the flip side of the same year's *Death of a Salesman*. The film embraces the sheer repetition of modern life—its boring, plodding jobs—by underscoring the importance of the system. Someone has to do these repetitive jobs, and the film models an attitude adjustment to the nine-to-five job.[19] In contrast to Willy Loman, each young cop in *Naked City* hits the streets like a charged battery. Repetition is a trope, but the film offers several comforts: first, that any worthy job involves variations on a theme, not just boring repetition; second, that a man's reward is leisure and freedom, as with Halloran's home and family; and third, like factory work, all the piecemeal contributions create a collective product, let's call it a cleaning product—it hunts out the human grime hiding in the corners of society. And on a propaganda level, this cleaning product—as manufactured by the police force—uncovers, let's say, the "truth" of a given situation.

There is also individual dignity within an affirmation of ethnic identity. *Naked City* features a righteous, compassionate authority figure in detective Muldoon, a working-class man risen through the ranks and proudly, distinctively Irish. The nation first embraced its melting-pot identity in World War II, led by President Roosevelt, and such proud ethnic pride was new to Hollywood films. Muldoon is a widower in a modest, small apartment and sings Irish songs with a gentle brogue as he prepares his breakfast. He is a New Yorker with sympathy for its citizens and a certain humility about his role. The film marks the mainstreaming of a new national self-image as a nation of immigrants (the melting-pot model) rather than assimilation dominated by WASPs (the Anglo-conformity model).[20] Still the tensions of ethnic immigrants within a WASP-dominant society remain fraught. The murderer is a brute, heavy, lower-class immigrant (Ted de Corsia) and he lives in a crowded, ethnic

neighborhood (the Lower East Side) where he hides in a dirty, swelter-
ing apartment. The people in the neighborhood are filmed as if they are
"the masses," in need of direction and incapable of autonomous action.
Naked City carries a tense ambivalence about mass society in its mix of
optimistic, melting-pot populism and its suspicion of the uncontrolled
masses.

Naked City was also a long-running TV drama (1958–63), second
only to *Dragnet* in its small-screen success. The show starred the film's
two major characters, Detective Jimmy Halloran and Lieutenant Dan
Muldoon: it was populist in its thrust, unapologetically urban, and assumed an urban working class with middle-class values. It had a famous
closing tagline: "There are eight million stories in the Naked City. This
has been one of them."

◆ ◆ ◆

You're just not used to prosperity.
Joe Norson to his pregnant wife in *Side Street* (1950)

Anthony Mann's *Side Street* (1950) can be thought of as one of those
eight million stories of the naked city as viewed from the lofty perspective of a social elite. The opening credits and final scene are composed of
aerial shots that look down as if from Heaven on the steeples of skyscrap-
ers: it was innovative cinematography then and remains much-imitated
since. These establishing shots contributed to an artistic reinforcement
of postwar society as a surveillance system. The camera became the
conduit of a benevolent, omnipresent God on watch from a heavenly
perch, waiting to help the weak and tempted man. This conceptual
framework was reinforced at street level, where the police functioned
as a benevolent occupational army. There's always a beat cop around in
this film—checking into bars, hanging out on a corner, driving around
the docks. Sociologist C. Wright Mills presciently wrote that the nation
never demobilized after World War II, transmuting its centralized armed
forces into the military-industrial complex. Films such as *Side Street* and
Naked City manifest a *visual* transfer from military forces to an urban
police force.[21]

Joe Norson is a good man sorely tempted, a combat veteran who still
hangs out with his former sergeant, a beat cop downtown near city hall.

Living with his parents after a couple of failed business ventures, Norson's daily round is all Depression-era urban cityscape: crowded streets, bars, small apartments, office buildings, loading docks, jazz clubs. In an attempt to break out of his working-class life as a Manhattan mailman and bestow luxury on his pregnant wife, Norson steals thirty thousand dollars that come into his hands. After this theft from a small-time syndicate, Norson's settled domestic life becomes set against the second-story violence and double dealing of philandering businessmen fronted by a gang of thieves. Yet this average Joe is quickly gripped by conscience and wants to return the money, only it is stolen from *him* by a bartender.

For much of the film, Norson plays detective and tries to locate the bartender and the money: since his investigation parallels that of the police, it reveals his own toughness and innate decency. The film has several scenes on Wall Street—including a car chase finale, shot from above—that reinforce the economic subtext that it takes wealth to have respect. All the while behind the scenes, Captain Walter Anderson of the NYPD efficiently oversees his network of detectives and beat cops as they gather clues that will eventually redeem Norson.

The final scene provides a striking example of how existential thought maintained a toehold even in police procedurals. When Norson is caught, the righteous voice-over of Captain Anderson explains that everything is under control since justice is inexorable for the good man: "This is the story of Joe Norson: no hero, no criminal, just human—like all of us. Weak, like some of us, and foolish, like most of us. Now that we know some of the facts, we can help him. He's gonna be all right." This is a unique speech since the moralizing is minimal: this average Joe is "just human," weak and sometimes foolish, "like all of us." Joe Norson needed to be reminded that he's a key cog in the social machinery, a role that brings with it certain historical and economic obligations.

Captain Anderson delivers his short speech on Wall Street in front of Federal Hall, next to the statue of George Washington that commemorates his swearing-in here in the nation's first capital. As Norson is taken away in a squad car, the bells of Trinity Church ring from just down the block. His wife presses her beatific face against the car window, a symbolic promise to wait for her wounded man to return and help in his healing process. The moral of the story echoes that of *Crime Wave*: even a city as large as New York can function as a benevolent, sympathetic machine, manufacturing daily redemption for any worthy average Joe through the virtuous efficiency of good, normal, straight white men like Captain Anderson, forever watching from above.

The aerial sequences that open *Side Street* are a signature of Mann's visual aesthetic to project the omnipresence of technological surveillance and visually reinforce the righteousness of the system. American justice is efficient and relentless: it is a machine built out of punch-card facts yet capable of compassion. This is a logical outcome—yet also a fantasy—of wartime America: the mobilization and training of millions, the breakthroughs of radar and satellite communication, the compression of space through air travel, and the early use of computers. The fairness of the system is embodied in superrational agents of a technological utopia, policemen aided by the scientists in the lab; it is underscored by the loyalty and hard work of bureaucrats and clerical workers.

Noir Cops: *The Racket* (1951) and *The Big Heat* (1953)

Due to his iconic work in Postwar I, Robert Mitchum best embodies the shift from noir's trapped protagonists to its noble cop-protectors. In John Cromwell's *The Racket* (1951), Mitchum plays Captain McQuigg, a veteran police officer who insists his precinct remain honest, drawing a line against political corruption while continuing to be circumspect about the city's nightlife. McQuigg has an ongoing rivalry with the city's reigning gangster Nick Scanlon (Robert Ryan) that stems from their childhood. At the film's outset, their rivalry is amplified by the new moves of a national syndicate heralding its "efficiency" since it favors regular payoffs through routine corruption rather than the old-school urban model of gang control through brute force and intimidation.

Mitchum's ethical rebel now only heralds the loneliness of command: his stoicism is less a matter of surviving with style than it is of the wages of sacrifice and service. McQuigg runs his precinct along military lines, even holding inspections, and he is happily married, with a newly pregnant wife. He claims to run the only "clean" district in a Midwestern metropolis, and "cleaning up" is the dominant metaphor here for purifying an urban metropolis. "Our job is just to make sure our house is clean," McQuigg reminds his rank and file during an inspection, while his wife reinforces the metaphor the next scene as he leaves for work: "You get on with your cleaning and I'll get on with mine." When a car bomb nearly kills Mrs. McQuigg it only reinforces their shared battleground.

Even as a police lieutenant, Mitchum still wears the noir uniform of trench coat and fedora. Like Sterling Hayden in *Crime Wave*, he channels his desires into his authority to pressure others to conform. But unlike Hayden, his victory is tied to his domestic life: in effect, the McQuiggs domesticate the Cold War into a model of the postwar moral order through their separate spheres. This message is doubled in a subplot featuring a righteous beat cop named Johnson, also happily married and with a pregnant wife. Johnson kills racketeer Nick Scanlon to prevent him from breaking into the precinct jail to silence their key witness but loses his life in the process. Shortly after, Mrs. McQuigg comforts Mrs. Johnson and the martyred policeman's sacrifice reinforces the role of the nuclear family as heroically embattled against all social plagues, whether racketeers or Communists.

In a new twist of the genre, the redeemable figure here is the femme fatale, a gun moll of racketeer Nick Scanlon named Irene Hayes, who becomes a rare figure, a bad-girl-*gone-good*. Elizabeth Scott plays a torch singer who holds center stage for two entire scenes (and two entire songs) in a dark nightclub where salesmen and straying husbands dream of her promiscuity. Scott exaggerates a certain educated diction to signal the audience that she's no hard street thug but a fallen woman by mistake, a night owl waiting to be brought into the light of day. Since she has a long association with Scanlon's gang, McQuigg puts her in jail for her own protection. Through prison bars she confesses her emotional turmoil to a naive reporter who falls in love with her. In the penultimate scene, with McQuigg's blessing, the reporter walks her home just before dawn, a symbolic meeting that closes the gap between a toughened good boy and a chastised bad girl.

Mitchum / McQuigg disowns any pride in his rogue individuality despite his steely leadership: rather he insists that he's just a carburetor within the engine of justice. "Justice . . . is a kind of machine," he explains to his wife in the final scene, "a slow machine." Even if corrupt politicians "are always throwing sand in it, getting it out of gear," the system of justice always rights itself. "It's a daily struggle keeping those gears oiled and clean," he says, suggesting that this is precisely the dirty work of clean, decent policemen everywhere. With existential good humor he concludes, "Tomorrow it starts all over again." Then he gets into his car with his wife at dawn to drive home. If evil is now represented as a syndicate—something collective and bureaucratic—so, too, must good be thus imagined. These metaphors of network and surveillance lead easily to the robotic cops of *Dragnet* patrolling our dark desires while encased in the nation's favorite mobile machines: cars.

The final shot of *The Racket* (1951) is almost comical: an automatic street-cleaning machine follows the noble cop and his wife down the streets as they drive home. The machine of justice has exterminated the syndicate and purged the city of its social plague as carried by its dirty criminal agents.

♦ ♦ ♦

Much like *The Racket*, Fritz Lang's *The Big Heat* (1953) features a city rife with organized crime and police corruption while an honest beat cop gets squeezed in the middle. When a police sergeant commits suicide, Dave Banyon (Glenn Ford) uncovers evidence of collusion with the city's leading racketeer, an Italian-American named Lagana. Lagana has the police commissioner and several councilmen on his payroll and runs the city through his right-hand man, a vicious psychopath named Vince Stone (Lee Marvin), one of the most brutal criminals in the genre's history.

Ford's investigation begins at the Retreat, Stone's hangout, a jazz club he enters with visceral distaste as if it's the first circle of hell. Ford runs afoul of Stone immediately, knocking him off his stool after he hits a woman. He then interviews the club's jazz canary, a B-girl named Lucy Chapman who was having an affair with the now-dead sergeant. Later that night she is found dead, and Ford is pulled off the case due to Lagana's intervention. The following day, Ford's wife trips a car bomb meant for him and dies. Bereft, traumatized, and homicidal, Ford brings his five-year-old daughter to a friend's house, where she is cared for by a cadre of his fellow veterans. He moves into a downtown hotel room possessed of a righteous fury and he becomes outspoken about the police force, accusing all other cops of cowardice.

The real noir figure here is not Ford's vigilante cop but Gloria Grahame as Debby Marsh, Stone's girlfriend. At once playful, bored, observant, vain, saucy, and dissatisfied, Grahame makes a grand entrance. The phone rings and she tells the district attorney, "I always like to tell

Vince you're calling. I like to see him jump." She is enamored of Banyon at first sight, when she sees him knock Stone down. She offers to buy him a drink at the Retreat but Ford refuses: "I don't take anything from something owned by Vince Stone." "That's not nice," she replies, genuinely hurt.

Ford invites her to his hotel room for an interview and ignores her as she flits ditzily about, making drinks and enjoying herself. She slowly realizes that Ford actually wants to interview her rather than seduce her: he means business without any sexual payoff. We see it dawn on her that Ford is some kind of a good man, with motivations outside of gratuitous power plays and self-interest. So Grahame begins to question Ford in return, conducting her own inquiry into the sources and values of a good man's ethics; she is also compelled by Ford's grief and love for his wife. Over the course of the film, Grahame finds an introspective streak, sobers up, and repudiates her criminal life.

The drama of Grahame's emerging self-awareness triangulates Lee Marvin's brutality and Glenn Ford's vigilante fury. In an iconic noir scene, Marvin throws hot coffee in Grahame's face, disfiguring her left cheek with burns. Grahame becomes a literal liminal figure—a rare good *bad* woman, noir's version of the "two-faced woman" of Cyd Charisse's playful song from *The Band Wagon*. Grahame is half burned and half beautiful, half rough and half smooth, forever scarred by her choices. The act creates the conditions for her existential freedom at the cost of her life. At one point, Ford mutters that he'd like to murder a certain cop's widow for withholding information; Grahame talks him out of it. If Ford's social function is to retain his virtuous core, he must resist the darker desires of murder and vengeance, proving himself worthy of being the town's protector. So it is Grahame who performs the culminating violence required of the noir anti-hero: she shoots and kills the sergeant's wife to get evidence to incriminate Lagana, the corrupt officials, and the crime syndicate.

Grahame and Ford thus redeem each other. In effect, Grahame sacrifices herself so that Ford can maintain his moral compass. At the end, Stone / Marvin begs Ford to kill him but he can't enact personal vengeance: in effect, Grahame reinforced Ford's ethical core. In return, he redeems Grahame as she lies luminously passive on the living room floor. Ford places a mink coat under her head: "You and Katie would have gotten along fine," he says, reassuring the bad girl of her social equality such that she dies redeemed. Instead of solitary existential individuality, we are back to old-school Catholicism: each individual is capable of good *and* evil, and each is in need of community fellowship to stay morally strong. This is symbolized both by Grahame's half-smooth, half-burned two-face and Ford's regression from moral cop (and good man) to amoral vigilante.

In Postwar I, Ford had played Johnny Farrell, the elegant front man of a stylish casino caught up in an unholy romantic triangle in *Gilda* (1946). All three pursued sex, alcohol, gambling, and money with a vengeance, disowning their past traumas and choices. "I was born last night," Johnny Farrell toasts the trio, "and I'm no past and all future." In Postwar II, Ford enacts the new archetypal role: heroic protector of the suburban homestead, the new site of American values. If *The Big Heat* had been made in the 1940s, Ford, Mitchum, or Bogart would have killed the Lee Marvin character to reinforce his toughness and survival skills. Yet here, in contrast, Ford embodies the rule of law as if a vessel of righteousness.

These four films all end with a return to the quotidian, with each man back on the job for Monday morning. In Postwar II, noir audiences embraced individual men husbanding a traditional morality from within the support of their nuclear families. Police procedurals end with everything returned to the status quo in contrast to earlier noirs that ended with death, disillusion, or a certain dark nihilism.

The End of Noir Cool, 1955: Lewis Allen, *Illegal* and Robert Aldrich, *Kiss Me Deadly*

The year 1955 marks the end of the line for noir's ethical rebel loner.[22] In *Illegal*, Edward G. Robinson plays Victor Scott, a popular district attorney who falls from grace after sending an innocent man to the chair. Hounded from public office, he switches sides and becomes an equally successful—if morally ambiguous—criminal defense lawyer. During a successful defense of a low-level thug, he comes to the attention of the local syndicate boss (Frank Garland). Garland offers to put Scott on retainer, but he sidesteps the offer, knowing full well the extent of the gangster's stranglehold on the city's politicians. Scott refuses in the key of *cool*: "You own them body and soul. . . . You're not gonna own me."

This is what cool offers in its various embodiments, sometimes in strategic silence, often just in subtext, and even across generations: *You own everyone else, but you'll never own me.*

Illegal marks the symbolic end of this noir figure. Scott is an uncharismatic, aging lawyer with a workaday briefcase and a department store overcoat. When he falls from society's *good* graces, he becomes a skid-row bum in an unconvincing, melodramatic turn of events unworthy of the genre's grittiness. His only close relationship is with an old friend's daughter, his legal assistant, and he is blind to her adulation. In fact, he dies on the courtroom floor to prove her innocence, having taken poison to win a case. Much like Bogart, the gritty, streetwise Edward G. Robinson had outlived his usefulness for its original audience. Perhaps Scott should have married his assistant, settled down, and had a family.[23]

In contrast, *Kiss Me Deadly* is an existential nightmare with global implications. Loosely based on a Mickey Spillane novel, the screenplay was transformed from the source text by noir screenwriter A. J. Bezzerides and director Robert Aldrich into a noir that repudiates individual agency in the Cold War, signaling the end of the genre's classic phase.

Mike Hammer is a sleazy young PI with no private code beyond narcissism. He stalks adulterous partners for divorce cases and spends his spare time skirt-chasing or giving orders to his beautiful assistant. One night he is hailed by an attractive woman on an empty road and stumbles onto a nefarious espionage operation that revolves around a stolen, locked suitcase containing a "whats-it" (the term used). Hammer opens the strongbox and beams of blinding light pour out, searing his forearms with burns. When the film's humorless police captain sees the burns on his arms in the next scene, he addresses Hammer as if he's a child. "I'm going to say a few words . . . fragments, really," and then measures his words as if casting a magic spell: "Manhattan Project, Los Alamos, Trinity." Hammer's face empties of color. "I didn't know," he says contritely.

The "whats-it" of the postwar era is. . . *nuclear fusion*! Due to cultural lag, this is one of the first representations of nuclear energy in Hollywood film, and it comes a year after Godzilla first terrorized Tokyo. In the last scene, an injured Hammer is held captive at a beach house when a young woman opens the suitcase, setting off a raging inferno rendered visually as the flames of hell. His secretary manages to find him, and they run together into the ocean where they helplessly watch the conflagration. The visual associations for the fire run from Hiroshima to the Bikini Atoll, from Hell itself to the symbolic dark side of Southern California's beaches.

Once nuclear apocalypse has become part of national consciousness, no ethical rebel loner can contain larger social forces as a romantic standard-bearer for cool integrity. *Kiss Me Deadly* marks the end of classic noir: its private detective is an amoral, unethical playboy played for a sap; his female assistant saves his life; and he narrowly escapes death from nuclear fusion.

The last figure of noir cool was not exactly an actor: rather, he walked the line of insider and outsider while *singing* the line of a new masculine register. Frank Sinatra set off his Jersey-gangster front with warm, romantic yearning, another inflection of the mask of cool. With a stable economy and a stable enemy in the USSR, the wartime generation could finally afford to relax a bit . . . and to take a vacation in that worry-free liminal zone, Las Vegas.

Frank Sinatra and Vegas Cool

If it was once said that Billie Holiday was like "an actress without an act," Sinatra was an actor *with* an act: his persona was of a successful, lonely artist, hard-boiled on the outside but with a romantic soul. In his iconic version of "One for My Baby (and One More for the Road)," Sinatra tells an imaginary bartender two things about his act. First, he may want to be vulnerable but has to play it cool: "I could tell you a lot / but a man's got to be true to his code." Second, he confides that he's a blue-collar poet, a romantic for the nonliterary: "You'd never know it / but buddy I'm a kind of poet / and I've got a lot of stories to tell." Sinatra's persona of the mid-1950s was every-workingman: he gave voice and words to the noirish urban soundscape left behind for the suburbs. Sinatra projected emotional depths in nighttime confessions with enough global appeal to influence genres from bossa nova to hip-hop. Like Brando and Elvis, Sinatra combined swagger and vulnerability, charisma and romantic humility. And across generational lines, women seemed to desire a bit more emotional depth in their postwar men.

The migration of noir cool to the irrigated neon fantasy of Las Vegas was mediated by Sinatra's midcareer rejuvenation, as the once-skinny wartime teen idol was reborn as a new kind of American songster in the dual personae of swinging lothario and world-weary raconteur. Sinatra was at first a big band singer with trombonist Tommy Dorsey's orchestra, but in the late 1940s, he began to personalize a romantic world that led popular music away from big bands and swing dancing. But Sinatra hit the skids between 1949 and 1952: lovestruck with his own femme fatale (Ava Gardner), his voice became thinner and strained, lacking in precision and passion. Incredibly, he was barely able to get a record contract with Capitol in 1952.[24]

By the time he recorded his classic mid-'50s records, Sinatra's voice had a burnished edge redolent of loss, yearning, and loneliness, of failure and resurrection. The Rat Pack Sinatra came out of a personal response to romantic trauma and career failure, and he enacted a self-transformation with a voice now "protected . . . with the armor of the stoic." Sinatra's comeback began in earnest with an Oscar-winning performance as the Italian-American soldier Angelo Maggio in the iconic World War II film, *From Here to Eternity* (1953). Slowly, his records began to sell again. One last time, he followed Ava Gardner to Europe, begging (unsuccessfully) for a reconciliation. On his return, the singer and actor "transformed himself into the Sinatra who wore a hat," journalist Pete Hamill recalled. He reinvented himself as a playboy and a swinger, a man whose main companions were men but yet "[a] man with a lot of women." Sinatra slowly crafted one of the most influential cool personae of the twentieth century. "The message was there in the music, the attitude, even the hat: he had come through a dark, hard time, and he wasn't ever going back to the darkness."[25]

Sinatra now inhabited the mask of cool full time: the ethical rebel loner in public, the existential romantic cynic in song. Sinatra was admired and emulated for embodying the emotional mode of cool: for suppressing his emotions to keep his personal darkness at bay. He appealed to a newly middle-class suburban society with a haunted urban past. Sinatra even acquitted himself well in mid-'50s noirs such as *Suddenly* (as an assassin [see fig. 24]) and *Man with the Golden Arm* (as a heroin addict). Sinatra's life and songs and film roles all blurred together as if on an ongoing nonstop tour. Sinatra made two films a year and appeared constantly on variety shows on TV; his best-selling albums floated out of radios and new hi-fi record players. Sinatra was a constant cinematic

Figure 24. Sinatra played an assassin hired to kill the president in *Suddenly* (1954), one of the ways he toughened up his image in the early 1950s.

presence as a song and dance man (e.g., *Guys and Dolls*, *High Society*, *Pal Joey*), the omnipresent hero of the American night, and the nostalgic embodiment of the swing era. Led by Sinatra, Rat Pack cool should be considered the flip side of John Wayne's heroic violence for the wartime generation.

In particular, Sinatra was the avatar of cool for white ethnic immigrants, the descendants of the Ellis Island migration. Sinatra's rebirth signaled the acceptance of white ethnics (e.g., Italians, Jews, Poles, Irish) as full citizens as he insisted on retaining his Jersey accent edged with ethnic pride. His experience of ethnic prejudice toward Italians stung him his whole life. Even Dean Martin, for example, Anglicized his given name from *Dino Paul Crocetti*. Big band leader Harry James wanted Sinatra to change his name to "Frankie Satin" in the '40s and, as he told the story, "'I said no way, baby. The name is Sinatra. Frank fucking Sinatra." Sinatra sang with his ethnicity and regional identity intact at a time when most performers changed their names and expunged their roots.[26]

To vocal effect, Sinatra code-switched: his speaking voice was coarse, tough, streetwise Jersey-Italian yet his warmer singing voice carried lyrics with a sweetened, educated, enunciated diction. Swing trombonist Milt Bernhart recalled that Sinatra sang "with the grace of a poet, but when he's talking to you, it's [straight up] New Jersey. It's remarkable." Sinatra worked on this unmarked, unaccented American voice consciously in his teenage years, and it reveals his early ambition to be a national cultural force. He started by imitating the voices of Hollywood actors he admired—Cary Grant's formal elegance, Clark Gable's frontier masculinity, Bing Crosby's hip jazzbo urbanity—and then practiced the diction of formal standard English. "I talked one kind of English with my friends. Alone in my room, I'd keep practicing the other kind of English." Sinatra's vocal style was his own synthesis of swing-era jazz phrasing, streetwise bravado, Hollywood masculinity, and African-American blues-based storytelling. To Hamill, he created "the voice of the twentieth-century American city."[27]

Sinatra's experience with ethnic prejudice made him a diligent advocate and lifelong fundraiser for civil rights. In his wartime big band days with the Dorsey orchestra, Sinatra often declined to stay at any hotel that refused to house black band members. In 1945, he went on a tour of high schools having problems with racial tension and gave speeches on integration. A teenaged Sonny Rollins witnessed Sinatra's appearance at Benjamin Franklin High School in response to an early episode of busing that sent Harlem students to this heavily Italian neighborhood.

Frank Sinatra . . . came to the school and he gave a concert at the audi-
torium. He admonished the kids for fighting, especially the Italian kids.
He said, 'Cut it out and learn how to be good neighbors.' Then Nat
'King' Cole came and he put on a concert. It was . . . really great and it
worked. The animosity stopped. We learned that you don't have to love
everybody but you don't have to kill them either. I wound up becoming good friends with some of the Italian kids.

Sinatra had less success with this strategy at Froebel High School in
Gary, Indiana, where students went on strike rather than share their
school with black students in a steel town with blue-collar jobs. He was
treated like a celebrity and the girls swooned a bit, but he made no impact on the school or its tensions. A decade later, Sinatra broke the color
line in Las Vegas, boycotting segregated hotels and casinos, and he later
headlined several benefits for Martin Luther King Jr.[28]

The felt discrimination for Italians in Sinatra's adolescence also
alerted him to the transmutation of suffering into artistic creation. From
Billie Holiday he learned how to turn raw experience into poetic storytelling in song: "What she did was take a song and make it hers. . . . All
the jerks . . . [and] all the nights strung out on junk. All the crackers
who treated her like a nigger. They were all in her music. . . . She made
them her story." Through Holiday's example, Sinatra sang the American
Songbook as if the songs were great literature, showing how to delineate
vernacular songcraft from pop-chart fodder through jazz method and
practice. Sinatra actually helped *create* the American Songbook through
his selection and elevation of certain songwriters.[29]

Yet Sinatra learned his aesthetics of detachment—his *cool*—from
Bing Crosby's voice and Tommy Dorsey's jazz phrasing. He found
Crosby's vocal style "so relaxed, so casual," it seemed to be an extension of his very personality—autonomous, authentic and organic—
since "you never saw the rehearsals, the effort, the *hard work*."[30] From
Crosby's example, Sinatra distilled jazz into an accessible and populist
gospel of romance that brought something "bent and weathered" to the
once superficial popular song. Robert Christgau summed up his influence across all genres: he "naturalized and nationalized" four decades
of jazz by drawing equally on the phrasing of Billie Holiday, Crosby, and

Tommy Dorsey, and in so doing, "he turned English into American and American into music."[31]

Sinatra's iconic album *Songs for Swingin' Lovers* (1956) is useful as a case study to reveal his reimagining of jazz cool for Postwar II. Most of the songs work off a mid-tempo jazz bounce that floats Sinatra into romantic fantasies focused on the rejuvenating power of a given woman, with his masculinity punctuated by supercharged big band riffs. The album kicks off with "You Make Me Feel So Young," a song celebrating self-renewal with sophisticated ease, as if Sinatra's in love with not only a new woman but God and country as well. "I'm hip that I'm the slave / and you're the queen," he sings in typically enamored fashion, flattering everywoman's power over any man on songs such as "I've Got You Under My Skin" or "Too Marvelous for Words." Sinatra sings about missing women, dancing with women, women watching over him, women refracted by the moon—that special woman without whom a man's life is not worth living. Playing call-and-response with horn sections, Sinatra's songs mediated between domesticity and boredom for a generation staking out the new suburban homestead. For women, this once-adored teen idol had grown into an amorous stranger in the night. For men, those testosterone-boosting ka-*powie* brass riffs kept that libido swinging while the songs provided a language and a range of moods for romancing wives (and even mistresses). Now heading families, the wartime generation neither lived nor drank in the noirish part of town. Instead, their lives were reflected in Sinatra's nostalgic tapestry of being young at heart within escapist romantic fantasies, whether flying to the moon or Monterey.

Famously, Nelson Riddle's orchestrations brought a musical and melodic lightness to Sinatra's music, leaving the brawny industrial power of the big band in the past. Sinatra's swing sensibility now seemed as mobile as the American populace, whether out for pleasure drives or camping trips or heading to Vegas. Sinatra swung into the crest of each swing groove and emerged light on his feet in every verse, often on a bed of strings with only the occasional trumpet fill. Miles Davis and Quincy Jones both adapted Riddle's example for their own musical voices. To Miles Davis, "Riddle['s] backgrounds are so right that sometimes you can't tell if they're conducted," and each orchestration gave Sinatra "enough room" to work with the orchestra. Quincy Jones compared

Riddle's musical aesthetic to "Ravel's approach to polytonality," and echoed Davis's emphasis on how he sculpted out musical space for Sinatra to fill with his voice.[32] There were few actual jazz solos on Sinatra's records: these were stories in a swing soundscape and any listener could follow the bouncing ball while emulating these hopeful, swinging lovers.

Perhaps the best indicator of the overlap of cool for the two postwar stages are the *Billboard* album charts of 1956: *Songs for Swingin' Lovers* dueled for dominance with Elvis's first album (*Elvis Presley*) throughout the latter half of the year. Even as rock and roll stormed the charts, Sinatra had three number one and five number two albums between 1956 and 1960.[33] This also makes for an important comparison regarding various genres of black music. As with Elvis, Sinatra's relation to African-American culture is complex: his vocal art depended on jazz and swing developments created by black musicians; he is considered among the greatest jazz singers by both musicians and African-American audiences; he has retained his street cred all the way through hip-hop. Like Elvis, Sinatra remains a Euro-American avatar of an African-American-based musical idiom such that historian Douglas Brinkley has called Sinatra "the personification of Norman Mailer's 'white Negro' for every generation since World War II." To make his ethnic persona even more complex, Sinatra was a civil rights advocate who told *Amos 'n' Andy* jokes on stage in the 1960s and allowed Sammy Davis Jr. to play an Uncle Tom figure within the Rat Pack.[34]

By 1960, Sinatra and Dean Martin were "the old guard" of cool while a younger generation chose a set of new icons. Elvis tried to play Vegas in 1956 and flopped badly: the wartime generation at leisure was not his audience. The cultural generations split: Elvis "was the voice of youth, the Dionysus of Spring," as Nick Tosches mythologized the generational schism. His "incendiary fire" was wild and explosive in contrast to the "laid-back *vecchia guardia* candlelight" of Sinatra and Martin, their "old-guard twilight." Elvis's debt to Sinatra was not common knowledge in the late 1950s nor was the fact that "Dean was Elvis's idol" (one of them, anyway). An early rapprochement took place on a 1960 TV special when Elvis and Sinatra performed "Witchcraft" together as if burying the hatchet of Sinatra's hostility toward Elvis *and* rock and roll. In the mid-1970s, Dean Martin went to see Elvis in Las Vegas, and Elvis sang "Everybody Loves Somebody" as an homage.[35]

Rat Pack cool hit its first peak in the original *Ocean's Eleven* (1960), when a reunion of the Eighty-Second Airborne Division decides to commit a "commando raid" on five Las Vegas casinos. Its target audience was clear—the veterans of World War II—and cool masculinity is the axis of their collective midlife crisis. As Danny Ocean, Sinatra appeals to his buddies' outlaw sensibility from their army experience: "Why waste those cute little tricks that the army taught us just because it's sort of peaceful now?" It's time to get rich: that is, after all, the American Dream. Yet after hearing the plan, Dean Martin (as Sam Harmon) calls them out of their fantasy: "This isn't a combat team—it's an alumni meeting. Any of you liars want to claim you're half the guy you were in 1945? Can you run as fast, or think as fast, or mix it up as good? *I* sure can't. . . . Go try to catch lightning in a bottle if you want to, Danny. Don't try to catch yesterday." Peter Lawford (as Jimmy Foster) responds by calling him a coward. "You'd be surprised, Sam. Some guys can get older without turning chicken." Of course Martin goes along—loyalty trumps doubt—and the heist succeeds but the money goes up in smoke. That's as it should be, symbolically: in contrast to film noir, the stakes here are neither life and death nor individual dignity. Their lives are good and stable; they're just bored.

There's even some good swing music in the film: Dean Martin sings "Ain't Love a Kick in the Head" with Red Norvo on vibes and a veteran combo. Sammy Davis Jr. tosses around jazz slang in a scene concerning some new high-tech infrared glasses. When one of the thieves is frustrated by how to use them, Davis simply says, "Cool it, man" (meaning: *relax*). And when the same man makes a sexual joke about using the glasses on women, Davis says, "I'm hip" (meaning: "I'm already thinking along those lines").

Sinatra is also a cusp figure of cool as the concept mediated ethnicity in Postwar II. Sociologist Herbert Gans captured Sinatra's appeal for Italians as an ethnic culture hero of the American Dream in 1962. Gans interviewed an Italian-American gang in New York known as the West Enders and summarized their feelings about Sinatra:

> Sinatra is liked first because he is an Italian who is proud of his lowly origin . . . [and] he is willing to admit and defend it. . . . He has become rich and famous, but he has not deserted the peer group that gave

him his start. Nor has he adopted the ways of the outside world. Still a rebellious individual, he does not hesitate to use either his tongue or his fists. . . . He shows scorn for those aspects of the outside world that do not please him, and does not try to maintain appearances required by middle-class notions of respectability.[36]

This is an apt distillation of postwar cool in 1962: rebellious, tough, independent, scornful of social convention; pride in class, ethnicity, and origins, and thus true to one's roots within fame; acting with integrity and style on a situational basis. Sinatra was a world-famous celebrity but he had neither forgotten his roots nor sold out.

In the early '60s, Sinatra recorded three best-selling albums with his favorite big band, the Count Basie Orchestra: *Sinatra-Basie, It Might as Well Be Swing*, and *Live at the Sands*. The Basie band's buoyancy, fluidity, and torque challenged Sinatra to swing harder than on the Riddle arrangements and his voice finds a new depth even on standards such as "Nice Work If You Can Get It" and "I'm Gonna Sit Right Down and Write Myself a Letter." It was an important jazz marriage and a swan song for the postwar swing soundscape. On the eve of the March on Washington in 1963, the most musically influential big band of the wartime generation provided an ideal showcase of integration with an Italian-American artist who was a favorite of nearly all African-American jazz musicians.[37]

Cool is *perceived* authenticity in any era. In Postwar II, cool was the sign of vulnerable, confident masculinity: if Sinatra was the concept's most senior exponent, this mix of street cred and charisma, adaptability and vulnerability was also central to the appeal of Brando, Dean, and Elvis. Sinatra's bravado lies on the cusp of the two postwar phases, a cultural shift that reflected his personal losses and the adaptation of the mask of cool to the Rat Pack Sinatra of public memory. As biographer James Kaplan perceived, "His greatest performance was as himself."[38]

Coda: The Generation Gap of Cool

In 1966, journalist Gay Talese profiled Sinatra as the cultural president of the wartime generation. He was an idealized rogue figure beloved as Hollywood royalty and feared as "Il Padrone"; he represented the rugged individualist as American artist and yet there was still "something of the boy from the neighborhood" to his appeal. Most of all, at fifty, Frank Sinatra seemed to be in the prime of his life and in control of every aspect of it: music, films, family, women. "He does not feel old, he makes old men feel young, makes them think that if Frank Sinatra can do it, it can be done," Talese wrote of his symbolic leadership, "not that they could do it, but it is still nice for other men to know, at fifty, that it can be done."[39]

Sinatra embodied both liberal democracy and the leisure society: he was the American Dream, an immigrant once bullied as un-American due to his Italian heritage and now a civil rights advocate. He was the wartime generation's avatar during the 1960s, a time "when the very young seem[ed] to be taking over, protesting and picketing and demanding change." He was also the *Playboy* man as first envisioned by Hugh Hefner only a decade earlier, "the man who can do anything he wants . . . because he has money, the energy, and no apparent guilt." His story was America's history and Sinatra was a resilient survivor, "a national phenomenon . . . the champ who made the big comeback, the man who had everything, lost it, then got it back." Sinatra was a global public face of the American century, "the embodiment of the fully emancipated male, perhaps the only one in America."[40]

So it was logical for Hollywood studios to tap Sinatra to resurrect the symbolic role of the noir detective for the wartime generation in the late 1960s. Sinatra played PI Tony Rome twice (*Tony Rome, Lady in Cement*) and also a gritty NYPD detective in *The Detective*.[41] In *Lady in Cement*, Sinatra tells his philosophy to the hired muscle and a femme fatale: "play it cool." Yet at this point the solitary detective was more a playboy than an angry rogue figure, and Tony Rome was more an American cousin to James Bond than a son of Sam Spade. The last gasp of postwar noir cool came in the early '70s when Robert Mitchum played Philip Marlowe in a remake of *Farewell, My Lovely* and Elliott Gould transformed Marlowe into a dissipated countercultural anti-hero in *The Long Goodbye*. In effect, the archetypal detective re-emerged as if to impose postwar morality on the emerging counterculture, the swan song of the noir species of lone wolf.

The end of noir cool dovetailed with its inflection toward the young rebels of Postwar II, with its younger generation of romantic idealists taking their cues from the margins—whether through jazz or drugs, rhythm and blues or road-trip adventures. Still there was more overlap with the cool of Postwar I than is generally realized. Two months after *The Big Heat* hit the big screen, Marlon Brando and his biker gang tore up a complacent California town in *The Wild One*. Brando's bikers are violent, wild, and irrational: their rebellion abhors and then displaces the cultural vacuum of Plainville, California, a staid town that won't even defend itself. The same year *The Racket* was released, Jack Kerouac typed out the literary scroll of *On the Road*, a kind of hip Western (with cars) about Neal Cassady, a Denver delinquent who embodied the endgame of the American frontier.

On the last page of *Some of the Dharma*, Kerouac plucks Sinatra's voice out of the air: "'Don't let the blues make you bad,' sings Frank Sinatra." The date of the journal entry is March 14, 1956, and Sinatra's bluesy ballad, "We'll Be Together Again," was probably on the radio. Sinatra lived long enough to unite the once-opposed generations in appreciation of his transfiguration of American popular music. Sinatra inflected noir cool toward its unmasking, toward the loneliness as haunted by the ghosts of modernity, toward colonizing the "wee, wee hours" with the cool aesthetic of intoxicated romanticism.

Bob Dylan recently recorded a tribute album to Sinatra's art, *Shadows of the Night* (2015), and in an interview, Dylan recalled Sinatra's presence in the 1960s from his generational perspective: "He had this ability to get inside of the song in a sort of a conversational way. Frank sang to you—not at you. . . . I never bought any Frank Sinatra records back then. But you'd hear him anyway—in a car or a jukebox. Certainly nobody worshipped Sinatra in the '60s like they did in the '40s. But he never went away." As Talese's article shows, the wartime generation still idolized Sinatra—even if the boomers did not. In the 1960s, Sinatra was their model for aging gracefully, or rather, *coolly*, in America.[42]

Figure 25. Marlon Brando rebrands American cool as a rebel's search for existential meaning on the road in *The Wild One* (1953).

8

American Rebel Cool

Brando, Dean, Elvis

In 1957, Jack Kerouac called attention to the inward turn of Hollywood's cool masculine aesthetic in a short sentimental ode, "America's New Trinity of Love: Dean, Brando, Presley":

> Up to now the American Hero has always . . . killed Indians and villains and beat up his rivals and *surled*. He has been good looking but never compassionate. . . . Now the new American hero, as represented by the trinity of James Dean, Marlon Brando, and Elvis Presley, is the image of compassion in itself.[1]

The grouping of Dean, Brando, and Presley was common enough at the time — often as juvenile delinquents[2] — but this is Kerouac's proto-hippie tribute to a new secular trinity. For Kerouac, Brando's look of "searing compassion" was the leading edge of secular renewal for American culture. He identified a shift away from the *surled* (surly) bravado of gangsters, detectives, and cowboys to young anti-heroes who turned themselves psychologically inside out, at times exploding with emotion, as if imprisoned by a repressive society. Such introspection and adventure required alternating bouts of cool and self-doubt rather than steely self-reliance. Any search for inner direction required testing one's limits and social conventions: Brando and Dean created a new cultural circuit with an audience galvanized by their ambivalence, vulnerability, and sexuality. At the same time, Elvis crossed over the existential imperatives of African-American music and dance to give European and white American youth the cultural permission to find sources of self-affirmation outside their racial boundaries.[3]

The cool of the ethical rebel loner shifted in Postwar II to young men who revealed the tensions of inner life. It was still a mask but one the actor strategically shattered: neurosis was no longer suppressed but expressed, a sign of how deeply psychoanalysis had penetrated artistic and intellectual communities. In social context, the actor's grappling with ethical issues might be read as modernist politics run through popular culture: the authentic (or *real*) self in conflict with a repressive society. For Beat youth, it read as adolescent aspirations to authenticity. For some critics, it was gratuitous self-absorption; for others, an existential revelation of the long night of the soul struggling for freedom through self-knowledge. It may have only been the artistic discontent of an affluent society. Nevertheless, in Postwar II, cool remained the sign of alienation, autonomy, and survival along a postwar continuum from jazz and noir. As film scholar Lee Server pointed out, Robert Mitchum's "brooding, darkly sexual characterization" in *Pursued* and *Out of the Past* "anticipate[d] . . . the style brought to the screen by Marlon Brando and . . . Elvis Presley."[4]

And yet there *was* something new to this rebellion—namely, the rejection of all male authority through any and all father figures. Incredibly, neither Brando nor Elvis ever played a character with an on-screen father. James Dean spent all three of his films battling with oppressive, passive, and presumptive fathers, even if his friends thought "the toughness . . . a pose," and a "carefully calculated" one at that.[5] Kerouac used the term "lackadaddy" in *On the Road* as emblematic of the absence that sets the Beats on the road. In that novel, their nostalgic search is for Dean Moriarty's father ("Old Dean Moriarty the father we never found")—an old railroad brakeman, broken-down drifter, and sometime hobo.[6]

The idea of the lost father was poetically expressed in the slang term "daddy-o," a hip term of affection crossed over from African-American slang. An emblematic term of '50s rebels, "daddy-o" at once demoted the value of the patriarch and elevated your friends into fraternal camaraderie. In effect, this poetic act recalibrated the all-male peer group as the rebel rival faction to the nuclear family, whether in a biker gang or an artistic group (the Beats, jazz musicians). Fathers may have known best in postwar sitcoms but they were weak or absent in narratives of cool rebels. Lacking Daddy . . . *we're on the road*, the mobile rebels seemed to proclaim, wrapped in leather jackets and searching for both purpose and kicks. Daddy-O was also the name of a legendary, influential black jazz DJ heard by a huge swath of middle America, Chicago's "Daddy-O Daily" (real name: Holmes Daylie).[7]

Brando, Dean, and Elvis all wore leather jackets and drove motorcycles—two objects that still confer cool on its bearers— translating psychological mobility into an abstract ideal of freedom and self-liberation. Brando drove his own Triumph Thunderbird into a generation's imagination in *The Wild One* (1953). James Dean referred to himself as "H-Bomb Dean" in his excitement over "a red '53 MG" he bought after moving to Hollywood. "My sex pours itself into fast curves, broad slides and broodings. . . . I have been sleeping with my MG. We make it together." After he bought a silver Porsche Speedster, Dean showed some talent behind the wheel and told film producers he cared more about racing cars than acting.[8] Kerouac wrote the dream of speeding on the road in a Benzedrine-driven frenzy with Neal Cassady behind the wheel as a lothario hedonist and daredevil highwayman. *On the Road* crowned the new automotive ideal and fueled the dreams of young baby boomers.

Kerouac even wanted Brando to play Dean Moriarty in a film version of *On the Road*. "I'm praying that you'll buy *On the Road* and make a movie of it," Kerouac opened a 1958 letter to Brando. Then at work on a screenplay of his novel, Kerouac volunteered to introduce Brando to Neal Cassady: "You play Dean and I'll play Sal." For Kerouac, it was a natural fit due to their common approach to improvisation: he hoped they could help "re-do the theater and the cinema in America, give it a spontaneous dash, [and] remove pre-conceptions of 'situation.'" Improvisation within artistic discipline was "the *only* way to come on [now]," he wrote, "whether in show business or life." The two men had never met, and yet Kerouac signed off with characteristic familiarity: "Come on now, Marlon, put up your dukes and write [back]!"[9]

Being "on the road" was a simple metaphor for an inchoate existential search starring the rebel protagonist as stylish avatar. In 1958, John Clellon Holmes insisted that the road was less "a flight than a search" to the Beats, a spiritual quest by which to find answers to the question, "how are we to live?" Such slacker male outsiders resonate deep in the American male grain, whether riding the raft with Huck and Jim in the past or riding shotgun with Han Solo into the future's frontier. This romantic ideal is embedded in rogue fantasy figures shrugging off work and domesticity, whether travelin' light up the river or heading west to the frontier. Were the Beats just latter-day hoboes carrying forward the Depression-era generation's rogue outsiders with a spiritual overlay and their own set of wheels? Was it just a philosophical pose to cover resistance to domesticity, family, and materialism, this early "hipster cool" of the 1950s?[10]

With *The Wild One*, Brando's motorcycle and leather jacket became consonant with cool itself: it projected the stylish, controlled power of the rebel. Biker style became symbol and statement: the leather jacket as a second skin, a sleek shell; the motorcycle as a vehicle for channeling anger into motivational fuel for adventure, speed, self-liberation, and quick escapes. Sitting atop an engine symbolizes the transmutation of mechanical power into testosterone. Brando was both Hollywood's own Hell's Angel and its redeemable angry young man. Since postwar American films and music dominated global popular culture, Brando's biker image fueled rebellion across Europe. Youth gangs in Germany and Italy rioted at showings of the film, channeling their frustration at Europe's continuing poverty and desolation into sullen, aggressive masculinity. "Brando raised the image of the outsider to the level of myth, transcending time and place," as historian Richard Pells reflects on his European influence in *Modernist America*.[11]

Cool is a matrix that changes according to generational desire. For historian Louis Menand, the Beats were *un*cool by definition since they were "men who wrote about their feelings." Yet this was precisely the *ground* of cool as it shifted to Postwar II: actors, writers, and musicians whose artistic display depended on their artistic performance of inner emotional upheaval. One key reason for their star power was the influence of women on "eroticizing the rebel" in films featuring Brando, Dean, and Elvis—as midwives to a cool that excluded them.[12]

Brando Breaks the Mold

> Marlon's the most exciting person I've met since Garbo. A genius. But I
> don't know what he's like. I don't know anything about him.
> Director Joshua Logan, on working with Brando in *Sayonara* (1957)[13]

What Bogart was to the first postwar phase, Brando was to the second: the arbiter of cool. The differences in their personae reflect a change in aesthetics and attitude from the wartime generation to the first boomers and Beat youth. From *A Streetcar Named Desire* (1951) to *The Wild One* (1953) to *On the Waterfront* (1954) to *The Fugitive Kind* (1959), Brando's cool yoked together defiance and vulnerability, the side-glances of thwarted hope with kinetic explosions of righteous anger. The symbolic passing of the cool baton occurred at the 1952 Academy Awards, where Brando was pointedly denied the best actor award for *Streetcar* even as the film's three other stars all won in their categories. Instead, the Oscar went to Bogart for his performance in *The African Queen*. In effect, the now-tamed renegade was acknowledged for playing nice in an autumnal romance while now Brando's cool was inchoate and dangerous. Even Elvis was in awe of Brando: after bumping into him at the studio commissary while filming *King Creole* (1957), Elvis exclaimed to a friend, "Oh my God, I shook hands with Marlon Brando!"[14]

In the five years between his star turns as Stanley Kowalski in *A Streetcar Named Desire* onstage and then on-screen (1947–52), Marlon Brando redirected the keynote of postwar cool—its aestheticizing of detachment. Brando inflected cool toward a mask of iconic aloofness barely covering deep reserves of resentment and kinetic energy, "the American male who cares so deeply he must pretend not to care at all," as biographer Patricia Bosworth put it. James Dean was nineteen years old when he saw Brando in his first film role as a paraplegic war veteran in *The Men* (1950), and Brando's kinetic brooding hit him like a revelation. When Dean saw *The Wild One* three years later, his Brando worship kicked into a higher gear: he moved to New York, bought a motorcycle, took up the congas, poured himself into a T-shirt and leather jacket. Dean hung out in the same cafés and dives and on the same streets, following his idol, "inscrutable, dangerous, irresistible [Brando]—a fresh aggregation," as one Dean chronicler described the transference.[15]

Brando was a major artist—not just a great actor—and effectively the co-author of his films, according to directors from Elia Kazan to Bernardo Bertolucci. "No one altogether directs Brando," Kazan explained, "you release his instinct and give it a shove in the right direction." Brando was like Charlie Parker: once the ensemble had the theme, he was off running the changes and everyone else just had to keep up. Kazan would give Brando a goal for a scene "and before I'd [be] done talking, he'd nod and walk away. He had the idea, knew what he had to do, and was . . . ahead of me. His talent in those days used to fly." It happened first in rehearsals for *A Streetcar Named Desire* on Broadway in 1947. Brando thoroughly reshaped the character of Stanley Kowalski into a sympathetic figure, all the while adding phrases and shifting rhetorical emphasis, playing with objects and reorienting the choreography. Producer David Selznick thought Brando was ruining the play and brought Tennessee Williams down from Provincetown to demand that Brando stick to the text. Williams was awed and told Selznick simply, "Let him play it that way, it's better." Brando revealed "a new value" in his play, Williams wrote to his agent, a new American mood. "He seemed to have already created a dimensional character, of the sort that the war has produced among young veterans."[16]

Brando's *lived* sense of acting forced his co-actors into a state of high-level awareness and instinctive response. Brando's impact on the craft of acting reached beyond his own character immersion and included "his ability to draw other actors into his own sphere of unreality . . . [to make] them play the scene his way." Like jazz, acting is a collective enterprise, especially in live theater. As Kim Hunter (Stella) said of *Streetcar* on Broadway, "Some nights he made terrible choices but they were always *real*. That's why it was such a challenge." Brando's friend Maureen Stapleton upbraided Brando while filming *The Fugitive Kind*, "Marlon, you're a genius; I'm not. I can't fill those pauses. . . . I could make dinner in all that space."[17] When Hollywood columnists called Brando "the Valentino of the bebop generation," they reinforced the centrality of improvisation and phrasing to both jazz and method acting. Brando regularly improvised lines and gestures onstage and on-screen, up to and including the iconic line from *On the Waterfront*, "I coulda been a contender, Charlie."[18]

This new rebel cool was shaped by the desires of young women: female libidos needed this bad-boy rebel persona to break away from

Freudian associations with fatherly masculinity and the restrictive nuclear family. From the static authoritarianism of President Eisenhower to the insular patriarchy of the postwar nuclear family as reinforced in *Father Knows Best*, *Make Room for Daddy*, *Ozzie and Harriet*, and even *Bachelor Father*, American culture was awash with images of tolerant, moral, half-detached fathers. Good boys resembled miniature fathers too much, conforming and workaday, obeying the rules to ensure a good future. Where's the fun or thrill or youthful exploit in that? In the benevolent paternalism of Postwar II, there was no room for female sexuality for mothers or daughters: Daddy was democracy's king. A new darker youthful masculine style surfaced on-screen that radiated sexualized energy in polar opposition to monolithic paternalism. To say "OK, daddy-o," to any authority figure was to mock this oppressive image with offhand insolence. As the Coasters sang on "Charlie Brown" (1959) about rebel cool versus domesticated authority: "Who walks in the classroom, *cool and slow* / Who calls the English teacher, Daddy-O?"

Brando's body was a new masculine frontier, the canvas on which '50s masculine style became enacted for rebels in two iconic looks. First, he sexualized "the earthy proletarian male" as the source of youth style. In 1947, he took the stage as Stanley Kowalski in a ripped, dyed T-shirt and tight blue jeans, a look conceived by designer Lucinda Ballard and modeled on the Con Edison ditchdiggers in midtown Manhattan. Ballard washed the jeans dozens of times to make them tight and faded. When Brando put them on, he literally jumped with joy when he looked in the mirror. Eight years later, James Dean wore a pair of prewashed Levi's for *Rebel Without a Cause*, which the cast and crew called "Dean's Jeans," an indicator of the early resonance of this youthful style. Then in *The Wild One* (1953), Brando sat astride his motorcycle in a white T-shirt, leather jacket, and rakish cap that became the rebel's uniform of global culture in the second half of the twentieth century. Throw in rockabilly's pompadours and jeans on Elvis and Johnny Cash, and the decade's still-resonant rebel styles are nearly complete.[19]

Brando was a sexualized Sisyphus of the soul, a mythic and metaphysical rebel with no real precedent in the Hollywood typology, a fresh icon. He was a turn in the spiral of noir's anti-hero, a mythic existential seeker trying to exorcise his demons. Brando represented a new cool synthesis—neither cowboy nor gangster, neither romantic leading man nor rogue villain. "[In] movie mythology, he was a two-faced Janus — half-good, half-bad," film critic Rene Jordan observed. "He was brutal-tender, offensive-defensive, menacing-vulnerable."[20] *Ambivalence* was Brando's strong suit, according to Elia Kazan, one of the era's most acclaimed directors: he yoked together seemingly opposite qualities of feeling. Brando's assets were silence, improvisation, presence, and great stillness: he had the relaxed intensity of a jazz musician — able to go from rest to artistic explosion in a millisecond — yet he was impenetrable to even his closest friends. James Dean embodied a similar paradox: assertive defensiveness or tentative empathy.

Brando was a new inflection of the romantic heavy or good-bad man, with Dean as his youthful acolyte. Brando thought of Dean as "just a lost boy trying to find himself," but they remain tied together in history by their social diffidence. "I'm trying to get past the layers to the roots," Dean once said. So he riffed Brando's modal sulk — "his slouch, his jeans, his loaded silences and sullen expression" — and created a global model of youth revolt, frozen by his death at the moment of creation.[21] Dean's softer vulnerability has long since carried more cultural influence than Brando's unnerving intensity but they are still the public faces of "controlled rage that made being 'cool' the strategy of survival," in the judgment of postwar historian John Patrick Diggins.[22] Compared to the trench coat and fedora of noir cool, jeans and leather jackets were evidence of street savvy and automobility, earthy in spirit but ready to roll at any time.

A certain ambiguous sexuality was crucial to the generational turn: both Brando and Dean were considered beautiful (not handsome) by men *and* women; both men were gay icons and had bisexual relationships; both men manipulated women on- and off-screen based on their emotional needs for attention and control.[23] As film scholar David Thomson eulogized Brando's beauty in his obituary: "He was amazingly beautiful — there is no other way of saying it, or denying its vital thrust in what happened. He had huge eyes, a wide, deep brow, an angel's mouth, with the upper lip crested. . . . He could speak softly, like breathing . . . but he was as male as a wild animal; hunky, husky, sensual, and incoherent or rhapsodic, depending on which style worked best with the young woman of the moment."[24] The elevation of the new masculine trinity to iconic status depended on their physical beauty being read as the outward sign of an inner grace.

Brando versus Hollywood

Brando's threat was also structural to Hollywood's economy: through him, the actor as creative force stole power away from the studios. This was a revolution analogous to professional athletes becoming free agents a generation later. "It was still a producer's game," Kazan reflected about '40s Hollywood, a sentiment echoed by Alfred Hitchcock's words, "the Producer was king."[25] Brando's disdain for fame and Hollywood glamor struck at the foundation of the studio system since he ignored its blandishments and yet still received constant press coverage. During his first year in Hollywood (1950), he once brought a seventeen-year-old girl up to the studio office for a meeting with several producers as if he was just stopping by. She was dressed down in ballet slippers and jeans but Brando introduced her around as his girlfriend while she was "tongue-tied" and terrified. She understood Brando's intentions: "it was really [about] 'Fuck you, fuck your decorum, fuck your businessmen's mentality.'" If method acting itself was a challenge to studio control, Brando's steady antagonism of convention and hierarchy cemented his reputation in the public mind.[26]

Warner Brothers was savvy enough to understand Brando's appeal as a rebel and to adapt its corporate advertising accordingly. "Brando is an Individualist," ran the headline of an article in the *Streetcar* pressbook, a tabloid sheet directing local theaters in their marketing. Brando was "a rugged individualist" as well as "an eccentric," so the studio rhetoric ran, since he rejected special treatment and "failed to conform from the very beginning with the accepted convention of a theatrical star." The studio capitalized on the actor's repudiation of star power, fame and privilege—his very incorrigibility—as part of the Brando brand. Meanwhile, Brando refused to indemnify himself to any single studio or to sign on for a film that did not interest him. "He won't sign any long-term Hollywood contracts," the studio copy ran on, and he would only "do a picture . . . when the part interest[ed] him." As a star, Brando lived like a bohemian and traveled light: "[He] lives in a glamorless walkup, wears loafers and t-shirts, and eats in cafeterias."[27]

In films and in everyday life, Brando proceeded as if he was against authority as a *concept*. Brando's knee-jerk antagonism to all male authority made him the crucial transformative Hollywood actor of this phase.

More than one director said he needed something "to be dissatisfied" about, "either the script or the director or somebody in the cast."[28] This was due in part to a lifelong fight with a distant, bullying father: his artistic energy came from channeling this rage as mentored by his surrogate artistic parents, Stella Adler and Elia Kazan. Gratuitous defiance was the true Brando gestalt. In his daily life, Brando was equally expressive and repressed, wearing shades day and night for reasons analogous to jazz musicians.[29]

Brando also effected a victory in a generational war within the *art* of acting: he elevated improvisation, physicality, instinct, and character immersion as superior to oratory, static choreography, and the word (the script). In effect, there was a triangulated postwar battle between the method acting of New York's Actors Studio, the Hollywood naturalistic style of Bogart or Gary Cooper, and the aristocratic British style of Laurence Olivier. The Hollywood style was based on national myths, fixed genres, and typology, such that an actor became a role-player as the girl next door, the gangster, the tough guy, the sidekick, or the good mother. In contrast, for method actors, the script is only a starting point to develop an individual character; their framework comes from Freud and the unconscious, not mythic identification or virtuosic oratory. For method actors, the play becomes a script for a nightly conversation (on-stage) or a set of experiments (on the movie set); its success is determined by moods, improvisation, group dynamics, and interpersonal relationships. It is analogous to jazz as a conversation among musicians: both ensembles play the changes of the written score/script differently every night. This is a far cry from the classical British model with its emphasis on speech-driven, well-rehearsed professionalism as inherited from the stage.[30]

For Brando, subtext was everything: he believed overt hostility was simplistic—artistically speaking—and this also contributes to the continuity of a cool aesthetic in Hollywood films. Brando admired the restraint of his studio predecessors, in particular, Cary Grant, George Raft, Spencer Tracy, and Paul Muni. He admired Spencer Tracy for "the way he holds back, *holds* back," as if cooling his temper, "then [he] darts in to make his point, [then] darts back." He admired Muni for his silences— how he coolly flipped a coin in *Scarface* and rarely said more than five words—and Muni was the rare studio actor from whom Brando took advice. In fact, Brando regretted making *The Wild One* since it pimped gratuitous or obvious rebellion; he refused to work with the director again. In his theatrical minimalism and off-stage mystery, Brando built a new wing onto cool. As director Joshua Logan said of Brando on the set of *Sayonara*, "I don't know anything about him."[31]

Brando also pioneered the kind of character research that actors like Robert De Niro later became famous for: how to physically manifest a character's subjective consciousness. In his very first film, *The Men*, Brando lived with paraplegic war veterans in a hospital wing and learned their habitus: he lived in his wheelchair all day and developed an athletic physical style of manipulating the wheelchair with angry urgency; he learned the veterans' attitudes and coping mechanisms; he socialized and drank with them. For *The Wild One*, he lived with a motorcycle gang and riffed some of his best improvised lines from its members, including the iconic "Whaddya got?" in answer to "What are you rebelling against?" In *On the Waterfront*, the entire cast hung out with dockworkers in Hoboken, New Jersey, and the union workers came to respect the actors' work ethic as they all endured one of the town's coldest winters.

As for *The Men*, one night, Brando was out drinking with the paraplegic veterans at a bar in Van Nuys, California, when a woman came in and began to preach about the power of the Lord to heal the sick. Brando slowly, arduously raised himself up on his arms and expertly pantomimed the thrill of regaining the feeling in his legs. Then he jumped on the bar and did an Irish jig while the veterans played along, cheering his miraculous recovery. The woman ran out of the bar and all the veterans fell out laughing. If the method insists on imagining life within a character's body—while on a given job or in a given marriage, shaped to a wheelchair or a Harley—Brando brought the physicality of acting to a high interpretive level.[32]

Young audiences find their own yearning manifested in embodied form, not in explanations; certainly the tensions of a person's emotional life can often be read more clearly on the body than from the script. Brando's sudden explosions, his seeming narcissism as he played with objects, his mumbling of lines as representative of self-doubt—all of these were innovations of craft. In each film, Brando revealed an individual suffering from unresolved spiritual conflicts, and then he enacted the unfolding of a psychological resolution. Method acting depends on theater at the speed of consciousness and it represented a paradigm shift in the art itself, a revolution of young actors against entrenched craft values. The artistic ideal is not to get the scene *right* but to enact its lived tensions in the moment. In his book *The Hip*, Roy Carr reflected that Brando, Dean, and Paul Newman, as "[the] new young method actors[,] made everybody else on the screen look like they were phoning in their lines." Here was an intersection of Beat ideals and Hollywood rebellion, a link John Clellon Holmes made when calling the Method "the acting style of the Beat Generation."[33]

Brando's triumphs in *Streetcar* and *On the Waterfront* also reflected the new cultural confidence of the American century. Seen through this vernacular framework, Camille Paglia claims Brando "brought American nature to American acting and American acting to the world."[34] This is historical hyperbole, given the previous global influence of Hollywood's genres and stars, yet it points up the revolutionary nature of method acting. Humphrey Bogart often insulted Brando's beat style as simply a lack of class. "I came out here [to Hollywood] with one suit and everybody said I looked like a bum," Bogart reflected. "Twenty years later, Marlon Brando came out with only a sweatshirt and the town drooled over him. That shows how much Hollywood has progressed." Yet Bogart himself adapted his dramatic practice to the method style even if he never admitted it. Working with Katharine Hepburn in *African Queen*, the actors often ignored the script: "We just got the general idea and talked each scene out overlapping one another, cutting one another off, as people do in everyday conversation." When Bogart worked with actress Kim Hunter (Brando's co-star from *Streetcar*), he once exclaimed with professional joy, "By God, we winged it!"[35]

The Rise and Fall of Brando's Cool

How can we measure Brando's impact on masculinity as a new type of cool icon? Let's look closely at the iconic scene of *Streetcar*, the "Stell-*luh!*" scene. Stanley Kowalski hits his wife in a drunken rage; she runs upstairs to her friend's apartment. Overwhelmed by guilt, Brando first *cries* all alone in his apartment—Bogart and Mitchum did not cry—then drops to his knees as if beseeching God for forgiveness. Then he darts outside and screams at the pitch of wretchedness. Only *then* does he famously shout for Stella. She ignores him at first. But he howls in pain until his voice breaks and his contrition registers in his wife's ears. She slowly becomes entranced by his deep remorse as heard from upstairs. Stella (Kim Hunter) then drifts away from her neighbor and languorously floats down the staircase. As she hits the bottom step Brando drops to his knees and they melt into each other like statuary. Here is the difference of Postwar II cool: crying strengthens rather than lessens Brando's masculinity.

This is a new era of masculine cool in which *the body* becomes the new axis of existential affirmation. In effect, desire and sexuality are established as human rights to be claimed against obsolete moral and aesthetic standards. Standard markers of identity—class privilege and ethnic difference—are suddenly up for grabs. "He's common," Blanche says to Stella in summary judgment, and "I suppose he is," Stella remarks lightly, a happy traitor to her social class. Stella tells Blanche that her husband sometimes smashes things up when he's angry, and Blanche is horrified. "Once Stanley smashed up all the light bulbs in the house," Stella muses. "Didn't that upset you?" Blanche asks, wide-eyed. "I was sorta thrilled by it," Stella says, with a leering curl to her lip. At this moment, a gay playwright captures the punk thrill of destroying a repressive social order, striking a blow against moral norms and artistic gentility.

Streetcar revels in such class, ethnic, and cultural tensions during a pivotal moment of social change. As late as the 1960s, American society encouraged immigrants to assimilate through Americanization, a socialization process often called "Anglo-conformity." Starting in the early 1920s, veterans' organizations put considerable social pressure on immigrants to identify as "100% American" without any ethnic markers. In *Streetcar*, Blanche often refers to Stanley as a Polack until he explodes: "People from Poland are called *Poles*, not Polacks. . . . And I'm one hundred percent American. A veteran of the Two Hundred Forty-First Engineers." During World War II, President Roosevelt first began to champion the idea of the United States as a nation of immigrants against the white supremacist philosophies of Nazism, the U.S. South, or domestic nativism. It was only in the postwar era that the ideal of the melting pot took shape within an upper-class society still dominated by WASPs. The national pride in diversity—that is to say, ethnic pride on the contemporary model of multiculturalism—did not emerge until the late 1970s.

As shaped by Brando, Stanley Kowalski is a raffish, slovenly, working-class Polish-American veteran lording it over an upper-class white Southern girl to the manor born. "When we first met, you thought I was common, common as *dirt*," Kowalski reminds Stella during an argument. "And you showed me a picture of a house with columns [where you grew up]. And I pulled you down off those columns. And you *loved* it." Yet tearing down Blanche's pseudo-aristocratic ideals raises a fraught social dilemma: where will we find new values and ideals? What if so-called mass culture leads only to bread or circuses, or the allure of violence? For better or worse, postwar popular culture was becoming a battlefield of social values.

Streetcar rides on these interrelated subtexts: civilized versus savage, upper class versus lower class, highbrow versus lowbrow, white privilege versus ethnic Other. Blanche condemns Stanley as a vulgar beast in thrall to "brutal desire" and refers to his poker-playing buddies as "this party of apes." She accuses Stella of forsaking civilization itself: "There's art, there's poetry, there's music.... Don't hang back with the brutes." Freud theorized that so-called civilization and its arts were only a thin veneer covering primal emotional urges for sexuality, dominance, and violence. Just as the violence of the age proved him right, so too, did *Streetcar* reveal such an urge to dominance. When Kowalski rapes Blanche, it signifies cultural civil war as well as the rage of class consciousness.

Yet within this struggle, Brando somehow managed to represent *both* civilized and savage, *both* highbrow artist and lowbrow brute, *both* American celebrity and quasi-Socialist, *both* white Westerner and defiant Other. Williams, Kazan, and Brando caught the first postwar phase in all its ferment in 1947 with *Streetcar*, and five years later the film version kicked Postwar II cool into national gear.

Kazan believed Brando's next iconic performance—as Terry Molloy in *On the Waterfront*—to be the finest by a man in film history. Kazan points to the roiling guilt on Brando's face as Molloy sits with Edie (Eva Marie Saint) at the bar and realizes his role as an accessory in her brother's murder. Slowly, Molloy starts to internalize how his violent act hurt this particular woman; slowly the hubbub of the bar recedes, leaving a "depth of guilt as well as tenderness on Brando's face [that] is overwhelming." To Kazan, such acts were the "small miracles" of Brando's acting choices, as was his iconic scene with Rod Steiger. "What other actor, when his brother draws a pistol to force him to do something shameful, would put his hand on the gun and push it away with the gentleness of a caress. Who else could read 'Oh, Charlie!' in a tone of reproach that is so loving and so melancholy and suggests that terrific depth of pain? I didn't direct that; Marlon showed me . . . how the scene should be performed."[36] And his improvisational choices could be lightning fast. At one point, Brando picks up a glove Saint drops and he first puts it on his own hand before returning it; this subtle visual gesture deepens the audience's sense of their growing bond. Yet it happened in a flash, Kazan recalled, "just as it might have [happened] in an improvisation at the Actors Studio." In Molloy's embodied tensions and ambivalence, Brando balanced "the tough-guy front and the extreme delicacy and gentle cast of his [Molloy's] behavior."

Truman Capote analyzed the actor's meteoric rise in a profile for the *New Yorker*, "The Duke in His Domain" (1957), describing the actor's synthesis as a gritty combination of "plain bad boy and sensitive sphinx." Capote recalled the buzz around Brando a decade earlier during the Broadway rehearsals for *Streetcar* and going down to the theater to find Brando in a white T-shirt and jeans lying asleep on stage with a copy of Freud's *Interpretation of Dreams* open across his stomach. Capote first assumed he was just a stagehand—such a romantic conflation of enlightened worker and average Joe was probably crucial to Brando's early appeal. Capote highlighted the aesthetic tension between his "squat gymnasium physique" and his facial expression, which was "so very *un*tough" as to suggest "an almost angelic refinement." In the mid-1950s, Brando often dressed like the biker outlaw he made famous in *The Wild One*, preferring "motorcycles to Jaguars," and for his sexual encounters, "secretaries rather than movie starlets." By 1957, Brando dressed in a retro gangster style that Capote called an "outlaw chic" derived from "the prohibition sharpie—black snap-brim hats, striped suits, and somber-hued George Raft shirts with pastel ties." It was as if his role as Bat Masterson in *Guys and Dolls* (1955) had stuck. To Capote, Brando admitted to having a short attention span ("seven minutes is my limit"), a hunger for spirituality (yoga, Buddhism), and an impenetrable loneliness.[37]

Then Capote laid out a psychoanalytic theory about Brando, locating his appeal within the paradox of "wounded indifference" that came from a textbook oedipal childhood. Raised middle class in Nebraska and Illinois, young "Bud" Brando was torn between a rigid businessman father who "was indifferent to me," Brando said, and a brilliant, charismatic and frustrated alcoholic mother who was "*everything to me* . . . a whole world." Brando's mother was an actress in local theater, talented and beautiful, but with a crippling addiction to alcohol that left her unable to break off an unhappy (and abusive) marriage. His father was gone for weeks at a time and Bud Brando often carried his mother home passed out drunk from bars twenty miles away. In response, young Brando attached himself to surrogate families, without gratitude or contrition. Yet he was a neighborhood star—a good mimic, a daredevil, fun to be around, charismatic, attractive to girls and boys. He was thrown out of high school for a range of pranks and then later expelled from Shattuck Military Academy for insubordination, despite the boycotts and protests of his fellow cadets. In the summer of 1942, rather than go straight home after being expelled, he rode the rails and stayed in hobo camps—listening to their stories and slang, learning how to avoid cops and how to bum meals.[38]

Brando traced his "indifference" to women and success to his failure to intercede in his parents' dysfunctional marriage. In his early twenties, Brando invited his mother to New York for a weekend and begged her to leave his father. "My love wasn't enough," he said in a tone Capote describes as "wounded bewilderment." Instead, she cried and drank all weekend within her standard pattern of powerlessness as Brando watched her "fall apart like a piece of porcelain." He claimed to snap out of his parents' emotional vortex that weekend. "I stepped right over her. I walked right out. I was indifferent. Since then, I've been indifferent." Capote was surprised at how easily the adult Brando revealed the emotional pain of his childhood, yet he had witnessed a rare and revealing moment (and one Brando regretted). "Brando has not forgotten Bud," Capote wrote. "The boy seems to inhabit him, as if time had done little to separate the man from the hurt, desiring child."[39] Fifteen years later, the wound was still fresh enough for Brando to insert it during an improvised monologue of *Last Tango in Paris* (1972). In response to a younger lover's question about his past, Brando slowly metes out a dozen words: "My father was super-masculine . . . and a drunk." Then he pauses and adds, "my mother was very poetic . . . and also a drunk." In an interview later that year, Brando confessed that he probably punished women throughout his life as revenge against his mother.

If Brando's cool drew on both noir cool and his deep reading of existentialism then it was also his own personal neurosis writ large. The key question remains: why did Brando's artistry find instant generational resonance as the *new* ethical rebel loner? It may be this simple: Brando did not know what he wanted out of life, women, or himself. Rejected from military service in World War II due to a trick knee, he embodied a Beat cool that resonated with the so-called Silent Generation. He spoke a "bop lingo" with friends and played bongo drums while learning jazz and African dance in the Katherine Dunham dance company. (Brando can be seen beating out a conga rhythm on a cigarette machine in *The Wild One*.) On-screen, Brando played a tormented soul searching for connection who usually finds temporary resolution with a woman. In his off-screen romantic life, he had many girlfriends and also a neurotic need to control women. According to his friend Maureen Stapleton, Brando gave each woman his full attention until such time as the idea of love or emotional attachment was raised and then he broke off contact. By the late '50s, Brando often spent his New York nights at jazz clubs with stars of his own magnitude: Juliette Gréco, Ava Gardner, Marilyn Monroe. Miles Davis recalled that Brando and Gardner were often at the Café Bohemia during his residency there in 1957.[40]

Why was wounded indifference so attractive to '50s youth? Such cool indifference kept faith with inner hopes while outer rebellion struck at the unsatisfying materialism of suburban complacency. Brando was indifferent, sensual, and stylish: beautiful and controlled on the outside, but hurt and wounded on the inside, and it tells. He played every character as if his decisions at every moment *mattered*—to the character, to Brando's artistic choices, to the audience's empathic responses. He was a walking indictment of consumer society who was also always performing a personal indifference drawn from his childhood's emotional fragments. The wound had to be poked, the hopes tweaked, the rage for living exposed. Kinetic and unreliable, explosive and subdued by turns, Brando yoked these opposites into redemptive narratives of individual characters undergoing a trial by *new* fire.

In short, images of beautiful men suffering inner torment offered secular passion plays for a younger generation. Such sudden eruptions of emotion were startling for Hollywood films. It was as if the audience "has overheard a confession" in *On the Waterfront*, John Clellon Holmes wrote in "The Philosophy of the Beat Generation" (1958). If adults saw in Brando and James Dean only "leather-jacketed motorcyclists and hip-sters 'digging the street,'" Holmes insisted their films represented a Hol-lywood form of existentialism. In *On the Waterfront*, Brando "so interi-orized the character" that, despite the larger social forces in conflict—of class, religion, and power relations—Holmes perceived Terry Molloy as simply "a single human soul caught in the contradictions and absurdity of modern life." The lack of ideological content was central to the appeal of such characters for their young audiences. Holmes made a key per-ception about the Postwar II generation and its rejection of collective ideologies: "This [current] generation cannot conceive of the question in any but personal terms."[41]

Brando's cinematic power lay in the kinetic promise of new begin-nings: the liberatory energies of therapeutic man. His '50s films were also something of a swan song for the dream of the Popular Front. Brando's artistic and intellectual awakening occurred in postwar New York City, courtesy of a cohort of disappointed Leftists still hoping to unmask corporate capitalism through the ideal of art as communication. Elia Kazan called it "the common-man movement" and traced its ori-gins to three things: the Great Depression's leveling of social class, the underlying socialist politics of the era, and arts programs such as the Works Progress Administration. To Kazan, Brando was invested, like him, in "the surge of hope and confidence and determination that took over from the Great Depression" and carried forward into the 1950s from "the anti-monopoly-capital movement . . . of the thirties and forties."[42] The significant seven years' difference between Brando and James Dean represent a shift from the continuities of such utopian common-man ideals to postwar prosperity and its discontents.

In retrospect, Brando's artistry reflects the *failure* of existentialism within the creative life. As a philosophy, it offered a clearing ground to reject obsolete moral standards and ideological frameworks yet it pro-vided no method for converting such liberated energy into political fer-ment. Brando's career is a case study in the inability for protest-based art to create social change. By the mid-1950s, Brando claimed he would only work in films with a social message: this was his reason for mak-ing *Viva Zapata* (about the Mexican revolution), *Teahouse of the August Moon* (about bigotry in the U.S. Army), and *Sayonara* (about an inter-racial marriage). His films after 1958 represent a roll call of anti-bigotry statements—*The Fugitive Kind, The Chase, Burn*—that reflect his active role in the civil rights movements and his desire to be artistically relevant, a catalyst for social and political change.

For all these reasons, Brando lost his way in the 1960s. He was a high-profile spokesman for civil rights, Native American causes, and fair housing, and yet he found no way to align his liberal politics with an artistic vision. Along with his close friends James Baldwin and Harry Belafonte, Brando participated in a televised postgame roundtable after the March on Washington to plan further action.[43] In 1968, he was deeply affected by the assassination of Martin Luther King and the subsequent killing of Black Panther Bobby Sutton two days later, allegedly during an ambush by the Oakland police. He gave a short, impassioned, improvised eulogy for Sutton that suggests his impotence. There is a certain desperation here with regard to the potential of any individual to effect change, especially concerning the structural problem of race:

> It's up to the individual to do something to force the government to give the black man a decent place to live, a decent place to bring his children up. That could have been my son lying there. . . . and I'm gonna start right now to inform white people about what they don't know. The Reverend said *the white man can't cool it because he's never dug it.* And I'm here to try to dig it because I myself as a white man have got a long way to go and a lot to learn.

One can hear his voice break during this soliloquy as if he has long since realized that empathy in one's art rarely translates off-screen to the real world of economics, markets, and government. "I haven't suffered as you've suffered," he said to the black crowd. "I'm just beginning to learn the nature of that experience. And somehow that has to be translated to the white community now." Brando broke off his speech and just said, "Time's running out for everybody. . . . That's enough talking." By the late '60s, Brando could no longer hold onto the postwar notion that social change begins with the individual's will to protest. This speech remains contemporary a half century later.[44]

Brando's life is also a case study in cool as it intersects with generational desire. After his comeback in *The Godfather* and *Last Tango in Paris* (1972), Brando repudiated acting as a worthy artistic enterprise. "A movie star is nothing important . . . Freud, Gandhi, Marx—these people are important," he often said when interviewed.[45] "In a funny way, I never was an actor," he said after *Last Tango*. "I never really knew what I wanted to do . . . [and] I acted because I was trained to do nothing else to make a living, but now I think it's coming to an end." This was a prophetic statement. In *Apocalypse Now* (1975), Brando muttered incoherently, in character, about the meaning of a life's work; then for three decades, he received enormous sums for insignificant parts in minor films. Once while watching *Streetcar* with a girlfriend he said, "Oh, God, I was beautiful then. But I'm much nicer now." Three generations of actors are indebted to his model—including the entire cast of *The Godfather* (all of them his artistic sons), but also Johnny Depp, Sean Penn, and Mark Ruffalo. Yet for three decades Brando remained a recluse, seemingly happy with family, friends, wealth, and a quiet life.[46]

The last two minutes of *Last Tango in Paris* are a series of close-ups of Brando's face as he tries to set it into an everyday mask that can face the camera: he tries a smile, a sneer, a goofy expression, exasperation, a snarl, the mask of cool. He cannot hold any look for more than a moment: he cannot look the camera in its mechanical eye. Brando simply had no authentic self left to believe in, no pose of control, no state of rest, no mask of cool. This two-minute close-up is Brando's true swan song, the last time he exhibited what Kazan called the "nakedness of soul" as a dream of existential vitality. It was as if Brando was kept aloft in the postwar by the zeitgeist itself, until it shifted and he drifted to shore two decades later, alone and bloated, a used-up spirit.

The Eternal Young Rebel: James Dean

> They wore what he wore.
> They walked as he walked.
> They played the parts they saw him play
>   and they searched for the answers
>   they thought he was asking for.
>   Robert Altman and Stewart Stern, *The James Dean Story* (1957)

James Dean remains cool icon number one, the first name on teenagers' lips when the elusive quality comes up.[47] Dean is the romantic image of

American-style youthful authenticity, the archetypal figure of cool in its "live fast, die young, leave a pretty corpse" division. He is postwar cool's Keats or Rimbaud, and his death echoes forward in time to Joplin, Morrison, and Hendrix and then to Kurt Cobain. Dean's androgynous beauty and sudden, tragic demise propelled his sexual persona into the future such that young white male actors now seem born into Dean's slouch and half-squinted gaze. There is a recent documentary called *Born Cool*, a popular college poster with "4EVR COOL" imprinted on an iconic photo, and an ongoing debate about Dean's sexuality. The title of Dennis Stock's book of Dean photos is simply *American Cool* (2013). He is sometimes referred to simply as "the epitome of cool."[48]

Dean's cool retains its cultural power because the late '50s constitutes a certain start date for a middle-class American-style suburban youth culture that remains structurally intact even today. This is the emergent period of television and fast food and shopping malls, of driving as a rite of passage and the norm of the nuclear family. Drinking and joyriding, bored violence and clueless parents and political apathy—all still mark the suburban round in film, TV, and music. As director Nicholas Ray said of *Rebel Without a Cause*, "I wanted to make a film about the kids next door . . . middle-class kids," by which he meant white suburban kids. During Postwar II, the United States produced much of the world's popular culture and spread the global styles of Westerns, rock and roll, and blue jeans to the still-recovering economies of Europe and Japan.[49] Teenagers of Postwar II remain a global archetype, and the image of James Dean, who never grew up or grew old, now lives in this surreally eternal pop-cultural present.

Dean made only three films and died after the first was released (*East of Eden*), leaving his legions of fans to simply applaud in tribute every time he appeared in *Rebel Without a Cause* and *Giant*. He instantly became a conduit for this first teenaged cohort's dreams of itself. On-screen he was an abstractly normal—if beautiful—young man, the visual symbol of the first automotive generation of suburban kids. Unlike Brando, Dean's characters are neither embedded in political or ethnic tensions nor aligned with a social class. Dean's half-squinted look resonated with the anxieties of white teenagers in a society at once prosperous and paranoid, globally dominant and sexually repressed. If such self-doubt now seems endemic to adolescence, the whole idea of being a teenager, as a psychological stage, was a postwar creation. A mid-1970s documentary of the actor was entitled *James Dean: The First American Teenager*, and as one biographer defined Dean's appeal, "He made adolescent defiance heroic."[50]

Dean is the good-bad *kid* rather than the good-bad man. He carries the charge of a lost boy rather than that, like Brando, of an angry worker or veteran—yet he projects integrity and lacks cynicism, responds through the experience of the character, and longs for a better society. One promotional poster underscored the dilemma of Jim Stark (Dean) in *Rebel Without a Cause* as the good kid yearning to find the moral path of the virtuous man as he walks the line of adolescence:

> HE'S BAD. HE'S GOOD.
>
> HE'S WILD. HE'S GENTLE.
>
> HE'S A KID. HE'S A MAN.
>
> HE'S JIM STARK, IN THE YEAR 1955.

Dean was a cross between Montgomery Clift's tragic sensitivity and Brando's passionate intensity. Dennis Hopper often said of Dean (whom he worshiped) that he had "Marlon Brando saying 'fuck you' in his left hand and Monty Clift saying 'help me' in his right." Dean even occasionally signed his letters, "from Jim (Brando Clift) Dean." William Zinsser caught Dean's appeal for his generation in his review of *East of Eden*. "He has the wounded look of an orphan trying to piece together the shabby facts of his heritage. . . . You sense badness in him, but you also like him." In contrast, film critic Bosley Crowther of the *New York Times* mocked Dean for imitating Brando: "He scuffs his feet, he whirls . . . he sputters, he leans against walls . . . he swallows his words . . .—all like Marlon Brando." Yet starting with *Rebel*, critics perceived that Dean began carving out his own style of getting "inside the skin of *youthful* pain . . . and bewilderment."[51]

Robert Altman's documentary, *The James Dean Story* (1957), was released only two years after the actor's death, and he interviewed Dean's family, friends, and fellow actors. Co-written by Stewart Stern, the screenwriter of *Rebel Without a Cause*, the film frames Dean as the public face of a generation cut off from postwar American triumphalism. In his hometown of Fairmount, Indiana, Dean was shown to be at once shy and driven, stubborn and hardworking, fearful and adventurous. He harbored crippling feelings of abandonment: his mother died when he was nine; his father left him with relatives and stayed in California. He moved to New York and joined the Actors Studio, had his talent recognized, and then almost quit the first time he received harsh criticism. In Hollywood, he was miserable at first and sabotaged romantic relationships "cause I'm mean and I'm really kind and gentle," he wrote to a girlfriend, "and things get mixed up all the time."[52]

The melodramatic voice-over of Altman's documentary is telling: "They searched for the answers they thought *he* was asking for." Dean's closest friends believed he could neither give nor accept love but rather his talent was in being "able to expose the emotion on-screen that he couldn't in real life." In so doing, Dean provided catharsis for his audience. He was "a hero made of their loneliness," we are told and out of his short life came "a legend woven from their [the generation's] restlessness." Dean was a reckless, confused young man of twenty-four when he crashed his cherished silver Porsche Spyder. "I'm trying to find the courage to be tender in my life," Altman quotes Dean in the film's final elegiac note.

Dean's cool remains universally adaptable to late adolescence since it is based as much on Dennis Stock's black-and-white photos of Dean on the streets of New York as on his three films. In his short career, Dean managed to project a persona simultaneously small-town rural (Indiana childhood, *East of Eden*) and hip urban (still photos from New York), middle-class suburban (*Rebel Without a Cause*), and mythic Western (as Jett Rink in *Giant*). His characters are caught between self-fashioning and the need for social approval: each is a neurotic loner seeking love, direction, and acceptance from parents, on the one hand, and from his object of romantic desire, on the other. As biographer David Dalton reflected, Dean was "the poet of what it's like to be young, lost, or alone."[53]

Dean was an actor of great promise and all but typecast in his three roles, yet ironically he wasn't cool in any of them. Not in *East of Eden* as Cal Trask, an eccentric, introverted, high-strung, and unloved younger son tortured by abandonment. Not really as Jim Stark, although he looks cool a few times in *Rebel Without a Cause*, usually when smoking and in jeans. He plays a teenager begging for authority figures to teach him how to do the right thing. He develops a certain cool in *Giant* as the savvy maverick oil-rigger Jett Rink, a marginalized poor white fighting against an oil-rich rural elite and in love with the refined, beautiful Elizabeth Taylor. In all three films, his cool depends on redirecting the passionate interest of the woman with the highest social status to his thoughtful, vulnerable sensitivity. In all three films, Dean covets the alpha male's woman and either steals or redirects her erotic gaze. Yet his character lacks any alternative idea for what to do with these victories. In *Rebel*, all he can imagine is that he and Judy and Plato should treat each other better. "Why do we do this?" is the question at the core of Dean's appeal. *Show me what I'm fighting for* or, at least, *how to do the right thing*. Otherwise, *lackadaddy*, you've taught me nothing about social values or ethics.

Off-stage, Dean was charismatic but also not especially cool. He drove sports cars with reckless skill, bounded around with endless energy, and had passive homosexual relationships with influential men to help further his career. He followed Brando around or crashed his parties such that Brando once turned and yelled "Be yourself!" at him; Dean only giggled. The young actor was disliked by many older Hollywood professionals, for whom his need for love and approval was transparent, and his closest friends thought he desperately needed therapy. Elia Kazan cast Dean as Cal Trask in *East of Eden* after an audition in which Dean drove him perilously around on his motorcycle. Kazan disliked Dean as a person and actor but he came away thinking Dean *was* Cal Trask: distracted and cocky, alternately arrogant and obsequious. "His face was very poetic," Kazan recalled, "and full of desolation."[54]

Dean's cool was more of an act than a mask, according to his friends; it was a coping mechanism for the roller coaster of his everyday emotional strife. According to his friends, Dean was in a state of constant self-monitoring, as if watching himself in his own movie. Many of his friends thought him dangerously neurotic, including Leonard Rosenman, Barbara Glenn, and Dennis Stock, whose photographs helped create his iconic bearing and gestures. Rosenman, a composer and older-brother figure to Dean, said his "bad boy pose was carefully calculated" and called his "toughness" an act, while Barbara Glenn said the same of his "'I don't give a damn' attitude."[55]

In short: Dean's real-life personal confusion was little known, but his cinematic confusion was compelling. It signaled a shift in cool from being an implicit critique of social conformity to cool as a commodity with its own exchange value.

As Altman's narrator intones about Dean in 1957: "He seemed to express some of the things they couldn't find words for: rage; rebellion; hope." And yet rage *for what*, rebellion *for what*, hope *for what*? By Postwar II, icons of cool embodied generational questions of meaning on-screen that were inaccessible to parents or media. Dean even appropriated a photo of Albert Camus off a paperback, perhaps to enhance his own intellectual credibility. In one of Stock's most iconic photos, Dean consciously mimicked Camus walking in the rain in Paris, peacoat collar up, cigarette dangling from his mouth, stylishly hunched against the rain and traffic. It is not known whether Dean read Camus, but he sure knew an image of cool when he saw one.[56] (See figs. 9 and 26.)

Case Study: *Rebel Without a Cause*

The talk is jive.
The walk is swagger.
Don't call him "Kid."
Don't dare!
    Warner Brothers promotional poster for *Rebel Without a Cause*[57]

James Dean is the whole show in *Rebel* as the disaffected Jim Stark, a new American icon framed in the nation's colors: red (jacket and lips), white (T-shirt), and blue (eyes and jeans). Stark is the outsider, the new kid in town, the rogue agent of change. As such, Dean's body becomes a new patriotic symbol: he is both an erotic object and a quasi-sacred one. Director Nicholas Ray frames Dean as much as a Christ figure as a cool rebel, between Natalie Wood's eroticizing gaze and the homoerotic crush of Plato (Sal Mineo). When Dean is hurt, the film verges on becoming a passion play: in the final shot, the camera focuses on his chest wounds like stigmata, hovers over the bloody cuts on his hand after the break-in, and casts a final, silent blessing on him through the appreciative expression of Plato's black maid. If not for Dean's yearning and occasional emotional explosions, *Rebel* would be a maudlin teen melodrama of feckless parents and clueless youth. The film, often boring,

Figure 26. James Dean invokes Henri Cartier-Bresson's iconic shot of Albert Camus (see chapter 3) to seem existential cool in Times Square (© Dennis Stock/Magnum Photos).

offers Natalie Wood miscast as a gang leader's gal and features a musical score more *West Side Story* than rock and roll.

The key masculine trope in the film occurs when Stark is called a "chicken" or a coward: he rises to the opening knife fight with Buzz only when the punks taunt him with their call of "bawk, bawk-bawk-*bawk*." He shrieks "I'm *not* chicken" and joins the fight—yet when he knocks the blade from Buzz's hand, he's still willing to walk away. When his mother asks why he agreed to the drag race, Stark says it was "a matter of honor . . . they called me a chicken." Like any cool rebel, Dean needs to prove he doesn't avoid fighting from fear but because he wants to understand the motivations for this macho posturing. We learn in the film that Stark got into fights in the last town as well; now he must have adult direction or he will go crazy. "Jimbo, you can't be idealistic about things your whole life," his father says and Stark shouts back, "Except for yourself. *Right, Dad? Except for yourself.*" In this scene, Dean becomes a lodestar of youthful desire by illuminating how little parents had to offer to navigate the postwar world. Yet, unlike Brando and Elvis in their films, here Dean actually receives useful guidance and fatherly advice from the police captain (played by Edward Platt).

The key scene for understanding the film's resonance comes just before the drag race. Buzz (Corey Allen) and Jim Stark (Dean) share a cigarette overlooking the edge of the bluff, where the cars will plunge into the ocean. "I like you, you know that?" Buzz says, surprised. Stark replies: "[So] Why do we do this?" Buzz takes a drag and spreads his arms wide in the night air. "Well, ya gotta do *something*, now don't you?" This is the film's best line, and it is akin to Brando's "Whaddya got?" Nicholas Ray lets it hang in the night air, a smoke ring on the edge of their purposeless lives. Then the scene breaks and they're in their cars dueling over Natalie Wood as they prepare for their fight to the death with stolen cars.

In effect, Buzz is an alpha male who has created a rite of passage to secure his status leaving Stark to squint unhappily at being complicit in the head-butting ways of macho men. For all of Buzz's biker violence, he represents traditional, competitive masculinity, and his clumsy death in the drag race suggests such performances of cockiness are (perhaps) becoming obsolete. In effect, Jim Stark steals his woman by enacting a new kind of inquisitive masculinity. In this scene, screenwriter Stewart

Stern suggests men will always create new arenas for honor if traditional rituals fade. Stern was a veteran of World War II and he conceived of the teenagers in *Rebel* as "soldiers without an enemy."[58]

In a consumer society, what is the drama and pleasure of everyday life? What are the social values to uphold? The studio worked Stern's theme into at least one poster: "These kids are checking their weapons for an affair of 'honor.'"[59] Stern's real questions in *Rebel* concern honor, manhood, and virtue, just as in a noir or a Western. Stern drew on his wartime experience for the film's homoerotic relationships (he claimed they were "not sexual but romantic") and grafted wartime solemnity onto the affluent society.

The studio's posters reveal that it was casting about for a message of connection for a younger generation. One poster combined Dean's popularity from *East of Eden* with the rebel sensibility of juvenile delinquency: "James Dean! Juvenile Delinquent! Just Dynamite!" Another poster showed Jim Stark, Buzz, and the other gang members in leather jackets walking up the police steps and wondered: "Maybe the police should have picked up the parents instead!" As in *The Wild One*, the adult men seem cowed by youthful violence and mothers simply wring their hands. *Rebel* offers up the good-bad kid as a cultural leader looking for a middle path between conformity and gratuitous macho violence.[60]

Stern's screenplay sets up two opposing poles for the teenagers—apocalypse and suburban boredom—through two scenes at the local planetarium. In the first, the students look up at the dome of constellations and listen to a solemn narration warning of an imminent nuclear apocalypse. They're all bored and the subtext is transparent: if human beings are insignificant in the cosmos, how and why would *teenagers* matter? One studio poster attempted to connect the personal and sociological to the apocalyptic: "Jim Stark—from a good family—*what makes him tick. . . . like a bomb?*"

What everyone in *Rebel* wants of Jim Stark is nothing less than to figure out how to act like a man in a technological, consumer, suburban society. That kind of pressure would tear anyone apart. In effect, the new father figure in the suburban landscape is the angst-ridden rebel himself. When Jim, Judy, and Plato escape their parents and break into an abandoned mansion, all they can imagine is a romantic fantasy of playing house, of becoming a more supportive and loving nuclear family. "Is this what it's like . . . to be in love?" Wood asks enraptured, equating Jim's integrity with maturity and experience. Then Plato ratchets it up a notch: he says he wishes Jim was his father. In effect, the icon of cool has become a cultural leader in a society where traditional authority figures have lost power.

The message resonated with a cautious generation seeking meaning and purpose outside of their daily lives as structured by family and society. "He was not what they wanted to be," John Clellon Holmes wrote of James Dean in 1958, but instead "*he was what they were*. He lived hard and without complaint . . . [just] going fast." And so Dean's rebellion in *Rebel* is more oedipal conflict than social critique. To Holmes, Dean's audience saw him "looking over the abyss separating him from older people with a level, saddened eye" and finding little to emulate. In the face of their seeming passivity, he chose youthful enthusiasm, "eager for love and a sense of purpose," and until then, on-screen, "living intensely in alternate explosions of tenderness and violence."[61]

In Dean's disaffection in *Rebel*, there is a shift from the postwar recuperation of individuality as it might lead toward social purpose to making a fetish of the self. Dean carves out some middle ground between punk anarchy and the paternal police captain, yet he draws attention only to his own image. Herein lies the future of cool: the implication that the self is the last object of meaning and purpose in consumer society.

Elvis: Rebel Erotics

You can't be a rebel if you grin.

Elvis Presley, 1956

Elvis Presley was something of a pop genius: in the midst of high-energy performances he still recognized when something he'd done had the slightest effect on audiences. If a given spontaneous kinetic movement or vocal embellishment received a response, he integrated it into his next performance of that song or sometimes even the next number, according to his bandmates. Elvis studied the desires of the girls who screamed for him, the moves of the actors he idolized, and his own synthesis of the Southern musical mix. He consciously built his persona as his fame increased, as this revelatory response to a reporter's question made clear in 1956:

> I've made a study of Marlon Brando. And I've made a study of poor Jimmy Dean. I've made a study of myself, and I know why girls, at least the young 'uns, go for us. We're sullen, we're broodin', we're something of a menace. I don't understand it exactly, but that's what the girls like in men. I don't know anything about Hollywood, but I know you can't be sexy if you smile. You can't be a rebel if you grin.[62]

I don't understand it exactly, Elvis says as if with a wink, but rebels are what '50s girls want. Elvis was a good boy, even a mama's boy, until he started singing: he was a working-class truck driver with a sweet girl-friend he planned to marry. *I've made a study of myself*, he says, and then rejected his shy Southern sweetness for an electrifying, kinetic persona since "you can't be a rebel if you grin." As one young female fan said, "He was just one big hunk of forbidden fruit."[63]

Elvis was the most influential American rebel and white Negro of Postwar II. Raised in Memphis and Tupelo, Mississippi, he absorbed the vocal style, rhythms, and stagecraft of rhythm and blues while also sexualizing the willfulness of self-liberation from his cinematic idols, Brando and James Dean. "Elvis had the nuance of cool down pat," Greil Marcus wrote of Elvis's synthesis of swagger and sneer, black style and kinesthetic vitality. Presley's first recordings under the direction of producer and engineer Sam Phillips featured an innovative sound aesthetic with stripped-down instrumentation accented through echo, slapback, and distortion. Elvis gave white teenagers an access point into the existential affirmation of African-American cultural dynamics, and "the will to create himself . . . was so intense and so clear," Marcus observed.[64]

Elvis was the rebel incarnate but his artistic vision came from Sam Phillips, who was a Southern Beat by any measure of artistic iconoclasm. As a producer and recording engineer, Phillips had two overriding artistic objectives: "extreme individualism" (in an artist's sound) and "perfect imperfection" (as a production ideal). He insisted on authentic self-expression, vernacular culture, and improvisatory artistic creation—for example, Elvis was in the studio for two days before Phillips heard what

he wanted in a throwaway take of "That's All Right, Mama." A sharecrop-
per's son like Johnny Cash and Carl Perkins, Sam Phillips's artistic objective was to midwife a music that had the vitality, rhythmic complexity,
and spiritual uplift of the music he heard African-Americans sing in the
fields and churches of his hometown of Florence, Alabama, a small town
near Muscle Shoals. In this cradle of interracial American music, Phillips learned of African-American musical practices—its improvisations
and rhythmic foundations—from a blind black man who lived with his
family, Silas Payne, who he called "Uncle Silas" when he was a child. "He
taught me rhythms on his knee, and he sang me songs that he made up in
his head about molasses and pancakes."

Phillips at first recorded only blues singers and thought he caught
lightning in a bottle when he recorded Howlin' Wolf in 1951, an artist he
considered the most profound of his experience. But he soon learned
there was a hard racial boundary in terms of what white Southerners would claim as their own music; he sold Wolf's contract to Chess
Records in Chicago. In this sense, Wolf was the main source of Phillips's
infamous statement, "If I could find a white man who had the Negro
sound and the Negro feel, I could make a billion dollars." Phillips opened
the Memphis Recording Service looking to attract anyone with a distinctive personal style culled from subjective experience. By 1956, he had
effectively shaped the distinctive musical visions of Elvis, Johnny Cash,
Carl Perkins, and Jerry Lee Lewis at Sun Records. He probably created
rockabilly single-handedly and has as much right to the title Peter Guralnick gave him—"the man who invented rock 'n' roll"—as anybody. "You
don't have to be an outcast to be a rebel," he often said.[65]

Just as Little Richard, Chuck Berry, and Fats Domino crossed over
onto the (white) pop charts in the mid-1950s, so too Elvis, Jerry Lee
Lewis, and Carl Perkins crossed over to the rhythm and blues (black)
charts, shocking Southern musical networks and *Billboard* but not Phillips, for whom their success was the culmination of his vision. Having
number one hits on the rhythm-and-blues charts meant these songs
were assessed by black listeners as effective, innovative artists within
an African-American musical tradition. This was only logical as these
white working-class men were inspired and influenced by the black vocal styles, rhythms, hip slang, and musical practices all around them in
church (gospel), on streets (blues), and on the radio (rhythm and blues).

A Memphis writer reported that even Sam Phillips didn't know how to categorize Elvis: "He has a white voice, sings with a Negro rhythm, which borrows in mood and emphasis from country styles." In just three years, between 1954 and 1957, songs on the pop charts by black artists rose tenfold, from 3 percent to 30 percent, and that doesn't include the white artists recording with Sam Phillips and working within the African-American tradition.[66]

Elvis was at first called the Hillbilly Cat, a phrase that nearly translates as "the white Southern Negro." In the postwar black vernacular, a "cat" was a cool man and a term of admiration. Jewish songwriters Jerry Leiber and Mike Stoller, who wrote several of Elvis's biggest hits of the mid-1950s, were called "cool cats": they claimed black culture as their artistic métier from long-time immersion in the black neighborhoods of Baltimore and New York, wrote iconic rhythm-and-blues hits, and managed The Coasters. For Carl Perkins or Jerry Lee Lewis to shout "Go, cat, go" in a song or on stage was to invoke a call for improvisational performance through a black cultural term. Elvis recalled that when people initially heard his first records, "a lot of people liked it and you could hear folks around town saying, 'Is he, is he [black]?' and I'm going 'Am I, Am I?" Elvis was first heard nationally on the radio singing live from the *Louisiana Hayride*, and his voice launched the musical dreams of many fifteen-year-old boys, from John Lennon and Paul McCartney to Bob Dylan and Paul Simon. The first time Simon heard Elvis, he recalled, "I thought for sure he was a black guy." In Memphis itself, Howlin' Wolf thought of Elvis as one of the first white blues singers: "He *started* from the blues . . . *he made his pull from the blues.*" B. B. King's simple, generous theory about Elvis's success—"his own interpretation of the music he'd grown up on"—was based on its reception: "Blacks are a small minority. The white majority . . . want their heroes and heroines to look like them. That's understandable."[67]

Elvis was readymade for Hollywood films as the vehicle for rock-and-roll rebellion. Camille Paglia called Brando and Elvis the "supreme sexual personae" of the 1950s, a phrase that points to the fusion of sexual charisma and cool: "an icon who has entered our dreams and transformed the way we see the world." Brando's ability to inhabit the corners of his "profound complexities" gave him a vast artistic palette such that he exposed his own insecurities in every character, whether drifter,

worker, revolutionary, or soldier. Paglia considered the symbolic importance of Keith Richards naming his son Marlon, an act that symbolized
the connection of Brando's "wild, sexy rebel" persona with rock and roll
and Elvis, highlighting the appeal of figures who galvanized a generation
through "bolts of barbaric energy."[68]

"Elvis films" were a genre unto themselves since his celebrity was
built-in, but it was always Presley's plan to join the ranks of Brando and
Dean. While shooting his first film in Hollywood, *Love Me Tender* (1956),
Elvis wound up filling Dean's shoes with much of the cast of *Rebel Without a Cause*, hanging out with Natalie Wood and Dennis Hopper. In his
third film, *King Creole* (fig. 27), Elvis snagged a role intended for James
Dean that mixed teen angst with film noir. Studio publicity described the
character as a "troubled New Orleans youth who seeks to rise above his
environment," a working-class kid just trying to succeed. The film opens
with Elvis picking up on the street cry of "crawfish" from a black female
vendor, first singing with her, and then taking the song over. In effect,
we watch the music literally crossover on-screen from black bodies to
white ones. During the filming of *King Creole*, thousands of girls followed
the film crew "from the French Quarter to . . . Lake Pontchartrain," a
five-mile distance, and Elvis needed constant round-the-clock police
protection from his fans. The studio noted that "their shouts of 'we want
Elvis' could be heard for miles," and more than once, Elvis was spirited
by police "over two and three rooftops to . . . safety."[69]

In iconic bad-boy narratives of the 1950s featuring Brando, Dean, or
Elvis, wholesome young women lavish care and adoration on this iconic
trinity, in effect ratcheting up their cool capital: in *On the Waterfront*
(Eva Saint Marie for Brando) and *The Fugitive Kind* (Joanne Woodward
for Brando), in *Rebel Without a Cause* (Natalie Wood for Dean) and *King
Creole* (Carolyn Jones for Elvis), and even in *On the Road* (Marylou for
Sal and Dean). In his study of postwar *Rebels* (2005), Leerom Medovoi
theorized the three new intertwined elements of the female gaze that
burnished the young rebel's cool. First and foremost, the man is the
erotic object of desire in these films, not the woman. Second, when
the female characters minister to the rebel's wounds, they eroticize and
glamorize his defiance. Third, the rebel girl does not try to domesticate
the man but, instead, joins him in social rebellion, as if going off to join
the Resistance. In her attraction to the bad boy, the rebel girl validates

Figure 27. Elvis plays a singer resisting organized crime's control of New Orleans bars in *King Creole* (1958), a rare convergence of noir cool and Beat cool.

his attitude: she becomes his partner and secular confessor. "Precisely because she finds his rebelliousness attractive," Medovoi writes, the woman "enjoin[s] his defiance of their domesticated parent culture."[70] The woman witnesses the rebel's psychological trauma and helps him work through it, akin to the films of emergent noir. Cool women were scarce in the second postwar phase but "rebel girls" directly shaped the

Beat generation's desire for Brando and Dean, and through Elvis, for rock stars in general.[71]

The process of eroticizing the rebel was as pivotal to Elvis's success as it was to the appeal of Brando and Dean in *On the Waterfront* and *Rebel Without a Cause*, respectively. In the former, just after her dockworker father warns Edie to stay away from Terry Molloy (Brando), she defends him: "He tries to act tough . . . but there's a look in his eye." Kazan understood Saint's role as an addressable other, a hybrid of confessor and romantic partner: "[Yes,] a man can, no matter what he's done, be redeemed—particularly if he has a sympathetic young woman as his confessor. She's better than a priest, but does the same job."[72] Natalie Wood offers a similarly redemptive gaze for James Dean as she cradles his head in *Rebel Without a Cause*. Robert Altman caught this aspect of Dean's appeal in a voice-over of a shot of listless teenaged girls: "Because he died young and belonged to no one, every girl could feel he belonged to her alone."[73]

Even *The Wild One* depends on this relationship in a more macabre fashion, in terms of the relationship of Johnny Strabler (Brando) and the sheriff's daughter, Mary Murphy. After the opening sequence of gratuitous destruction, Mary becomes the town prize—the smart, moral girl in the tight sweater—for whom the rebel is willing to redeem himself. The indifferent Brando shifts from anarchic nihilism to goal-oriented vulnerability, from aloof diffidence to engaged struggle. The battleground is Mary's body, and by extension, her potential sexual power. With his biker gang wreaking havoc on the town, Johnny courts Mary: in this split narrative, the seduction and conquest of the sheriff's daughter is equated with the seductive, episodic distraction of the road. Film critic Rene Jordan analyzed this rebel narrative through sexual conquest that also works as Freudian rebellion: "Not only does she resist him [motivation], she is also the sheriff's daughter [rebellion], and the Brando character takes his revenge on the figure of authority by defiling the female he most cherishes." This was Brando's specialty, the displacement of the oedipal battle of father-and-son onto rebel-versus-authority-figure.[74]

The rebel girl sees through the young man's shell yet remains bound by traditional gender roles so she can only midwife the cool of Postwar II. One black cultural analyst of cool once distilled this narrative to describe his parents' courtship in the early '60s: "Girl meets bad boy. Bad boy rubs girl wrong. Girl learns boy has depth beyond what the world can see. . . . Nothing in Brenda's life so far had been half as thrilling . . . here was someone so special that the world couldn't take him."[75] When the male character is so unique that "the world couldn't take him," there are two meanings: first, that he is too good (or conflicted) for the world and second, that in a fight, this rebel could take on the world and win or be a martyr for an important cause (like her).

When postwar girls screamed and cried for Elvis, they were trying to burst their skins and bust out of the domestic traps society had set for them. Memoirs of '60s rebellion nearly always mention the static boredom of mainstream culture overseen by the image of President Eisenhower. Then along came Brando, Dean, Elvis, Jerry Lee Lewis, Chuck Berry: rebel masculinity on the big screen and the big stage, sweating and brooding, pelvic popping and duckwalking. Bob Dylan once said about Elvis, "Hearing his voice for the first time was like busting out of jail." Imagine how it was for girls with few sexual outlets to hear such two-minute rocking seductions as "Don't Be Cruel," "Lonely Avenue," and "All Shook Up," or for the good girls, "Love Me Tender" and, most pointedly, "(You're So Square) Baby, I Don't Care."[76]

In 1956, Elvis barnstormed across the black-and-white television landscape and even the seven-year-old Bruce Springsteen recalled the shock of this new cool icon. The observant child had never seen anyone remotely like Elvis—his knowing sneer, his brilliantined black hair, his loosely intense, manic, half-dancing stage persona. Elvis's rogue style startled the future rock star into early self-awareness. He told an interviewer in 2010: "A child wants nothing but to upset the world, and there it was being done. It's like sort of tearing your house apart and reconfiguring it according to your dreams and your imagination. You knew that this man was doing that." After Elvis's death in 1977, Springsteen pondered the message of this rock god, as both myth and cautionary tale. In concert, he wondered aloud why a man with such gifts and artistic power let it all dissipate into frivolous tragedy. After a concert in Memphis in the mid-1970s, Springsteen tried to jump the wall of Graceland but was stopped by the guards. "Is Elvis home?" he asked. Springsteen often told this story in concert; it may be apocryphal, of course, but it

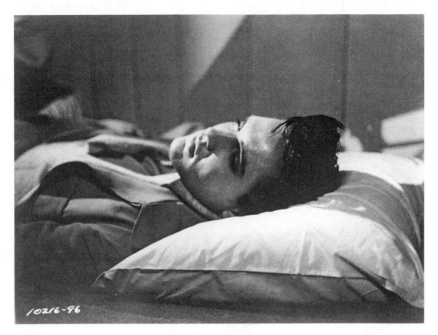

Figure 28. For rebel girls everywhere: a defiant Elvis temporarily laid low in *King Creole* (1958).

was no less important for its constant retelling. Without irony, thirty years later, Springsteen said simply: "He was actually the forerunner for a new kind of man."[77]

Coda: Cool-by-Example

Art critic Dave Hickey contrasts *cool-by-example* to *cool-as-irony* within a framework of citizenship. *Cool* gathers force organically from an original artistic example without drawing attention to itself or invoking "fancy justifications" for its message. By playing a certain artistic game with sufficient style and originality, an artist creates a dialogic relationship with an audience. *Cool-by-example* is often communicated through physical grace of bearing and depends on an assumption of egalitarianism and a lack of hierarchies. *Cool-by-example* emerges from "one's own embodied authority as a citizen." In contrast, *ironic cool* is a rhetorical strategy used by the powerless who accept the status quo and throw eggs from behind the barricades. "Irony is a way of eluding the wrath of your superiors; cool is a way of not imposing on your peers."[78]

Both Brando and Dean were excellent mimics and they studied passersby to create a grammar of physical gesture absorbed from the hip street life around them. This was similar to Bogart's studying the vernacular and physical gestures of working-class Americans during the Great Depression and Lester Young's directive to younger musicians to go into the audience and understand their everyday dreams and anxieties. The cool rebel sounds out the yearning of a public as it searches for innovative strategies of individuality and dignity for a given generation.[79] An original artistic vision impacts a specific field by first establishing an unofficial, underground relationship with an audience, "a discourse of peers and citizens," as Hickey calls it.

A hero restores order to society; an anti-hero remains unsatisfied and alone as the credits roll. Such an ending inheres to *On the Waterfront*, *Rebel Without a Cause*, *Giant*, and *King Creole* (among other films). Brando and Dean had a great deal in common as middle-class Midwestern loners with vexed relationships to both idealized mothers and absent, bullying fathers. In response, they were manipulative rogues offscreen and shared a fear of emotional commitment. As Stewart Stern said about his friendship with Dean: "He could woo you, make you think you were his best friend, and then he'd disappear just when you needed him most."[80] Yet on-screen, Brando and Dean projected rebellion and yearning made manifest in an oblique masculine style that created the new keynote of cool.

Three iconic musicians of the 1970s invoked Brando's example for walking cool on the streets as an indictment of American triumphalism. On his first album, Springsteen name-checks Brando as a model for how to walk tough on the streets ("I could walk like Brando / right into the sun") in a song that opposes the mask of cool to the mask of virtue, "It's So Hard to Be a Saint in the City." David Bowie saw behind Brando's mask to his existential core in "China Girl" ("I feel a-tragic like I'm Marlon Brando"). Neil Young imagined sitting around with Marlon Brando and Pocahontas to plan a confrontation over the brutal treatment of Native Americans in "Pocahontas."

An anti-hero registers *cool-by-example*, or to riff on Camus' formulation, *rebellion for-others*. A new icon rebels and a generation begins to exist. This holds even more true for Elvis, since his example leads so clearly to the '60s pantheon of rock-and-roll rebels—Dylan, the Beatles, the Rolling Stones. "Before Elvis, there was nothing," John Lennon famously said. "If there hadn't been an Elvis, there wouldn't have been the Beatles." Elvis was the rupture in the social fabric, the agent of change we now register as cool. Paul McCartney said something similar: "When we were kids growing up in Liverpool, all we ever wanted to be was Elvis Presley." The proof is in the musical pudding: the Beatles covered "That's All Right Mama," his first hit on BBC Radio in 1964 with McCartney doing a pitch-perfect rendition of Elvis's vocal. The Beatles always showed off their mastery of the '50s rock-and-roll canon on these live BBC performances, covering multiple songs by Little Richard, Carl Perkins, and Chuck Berry, but this is the rare song performed with note-by-note reverence.[81] And of course, the Beatles were also leather-jacketed *wild ones* on the Brando model during their early nightclubbing days in Hamburg and Liverpool.

In such ways, cool-by-example gets passed on to the next generation. Or consider Bob Dylan (born 1941), whose favorite films were typical for the next Midwestern generation of teenagers: *East of Eden*, *The Wild One*, *Rebel Without a Cause*, and *The Fugitive Kind*. As the cultural child of Brando and Dean, Elvis and Johnny Cash, the Beats and Miles Davis, Hank Williams and Big Joe Williams, Dylan created the next cool synthesis from every aspect of Postwar II.[82]

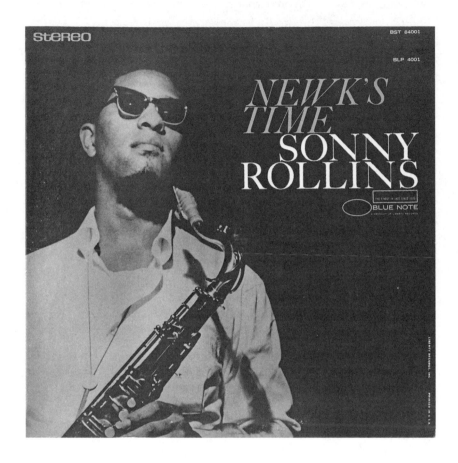

Figure 29. "Cool was defiance with dignity." Sonny Rollins captures the quiet revolution of *the mask of cool* on the cover of *Newk's Time* (1957).

9

Sonny Rollins and Miles Davis Sound Out
Cool Individuality

In 1960, journalist George W. Goodman, then an aspiring jazz musician, heard Sonny Rollins playing in his apartment building with a sound so brutal and powerful that it "came through the wall[s] like shots from a nail gun." At the time Goodman idolized Rollins and secretly thought of him as "Mr. Cool." The honorific stood for Rollins's tenor sound and complex thematic solos, his commitment to jazz as protest, his cold-turkey cure of heroin, and to "the man himself" as the embodiment of cultural rebellion. Before Malcolm X and Stokely Carmichael, Goodman reflected, "the young lions of jazz were our cultural revolutionaries—rebellious, angry, but always cool." To "be cool" meant you were in control of yourself; in addition, "playing it [jazz] with authority meant you were at home in your own skin." Goodman's generation of New York men were "in awe" of jazz musicians and even their heroin addiction "enhanced the gritty existential mystique that . . . James Dean and Marlon Brando were [then] projecting for white America." Reflecting back to this period, Goodman declared that, in 1960, "cool was defiance with dignity."[1]

In Postwar II, the relationship of jazz, individuality, existentialism,

347

and cool converged into an organic urge toward racial equality. The most intellectual white jazz critics—such as Nat Hentoff, Whitney Balliett, and Martin Williams—wrote of these musicians as cultural leaders during the cultural self-doubt of the Cold War. To Williams, "the experience of feeling unworthy is fundamental" to understanding the twentieth century after its revelations of human nature; the "old gods" had been lost. The avatars of a renewed individuality came from a "people who have been told . . . they are unworthy" through an art form equally invested in finding one's own voice while in dialogue with others. "It is as if jazz were saying to us that not only is far greater individuality *possible to man* than he has so far allowed himself, but that such individuality, far from being a threat to a cooperative social structure, can actually enhance society."[2] In this sense, cool was the sign of a cultural black-market search for what was "possible to man" in contrast to the felt powerlessness of postwar alienation. Jazz was a publicly performed art form that "exalts the individual finding his own way" while the musician also helps maintain the collective groove and drives the conversation.

In short, histories converged.

Jazz musicians were organic existentialists in that they established an artistic model that was part modernist, part blues aesthetic, and part Afro-diasporic. They were modernist in their rejection of traditional and popular approaches to expand the possibility of the art in formal, theoretical, and stylistic ways. In positing an individual artistic search for authenticity against a corrupt society, each hoped to lead the masses toward higher self-consciousness. Yet nearly all black jazz musicians were also conscious culture bearers of the role of music in the historical struggle of African-Americans for social equality. As drummer Kenny Clarke recalled of the subtext of their musical protest, "If America wouldn't honor its constitution and respect us as men, we couldn't give a shit about the American way."[3]

Under the sign of cool, the rebel was reframed as a productive critic of society, a concept that crossed over into public culture first through jazz musicians. A rebel creates new pathways that disarm obsolete conventions, illuminates new social possibilities, and triggers the notion of expansive individual potential. The cool mask was a shield: it kept out the oppressive white gaze while enabling public artistic expression. As James Baldwin once said about how Miles Davis effectively deployed the mask, "Miles's disguise would certainly never fool anybody with sense, but it keeps a lot of people away, and that's the point."[4]

For these reasons, Postwar II witnessed a singular outpouring of literature about jazz musicians. There was Baldwin's "Sonny's Blues" (perhaps the best short story on jazz), Mailer's "The White Negro," Ellison's canonical essays on jazz, Kerouac's artistic manifesto of "bop prosody," and an outpouring of poetry about jazz musicians, from Frank O'Hara's famous eulogy for Billie Holiday ("The Day Lady Died") to albums of jazz and poetry by Langston Hughes and Kenneth Rexroth.[5] In terms of novels, John Clellon Holmes's *The Horn* (1958) follows protagonist Edgar Pool—a composite of Lester Young and Charlie Parker—in his dying days. Ross Russell's *The Sound* (1961) features Red Evans, a thinly veiled portrait of Charlie Parker. (Its original title was *The Hipsters* and its alternate title, *The Sound Was Cool*.)[6] In Julio Cortázar's *The Pursuer* (1959), Parker is fictionalized as Johnny Carter, a man who repudiates his biographer's attempts to reduce his music to rational analysis. Louis Armstrong is the sleeper hero of *Invisible Man*'s "Prologue" and (as shown above) Charlie Parker is the sleeper hero of Kerouac's *Mexico City Blues*.

Jazz musicians have never, before or since, occupied such prominence in the literary or cultural imagination. The jazz musician was the emblematic postwar cool figure while the concept of "cool" itself was a cryptic term associated with an artistic underground inhabited by African-American musicians. "The jazz musician—significantly, the saxophone player—had surfaced as the culture hero of the new generation," Russell wrote of Parker.[7] For Kerouac, Lester Young was the "cultural master of his generation," and he meditated on the debt Neal Cassady owed to Young's model: "what mysteries as well as masteries" did Cody learn from Young, Kerouac wrote in *Visions of Cody*, "what door-standing influence has Cody gained [from him]?"[8]

As an art form, the jazz difference was in modeling conscious, direct emotional communication in real time between an individual and an audience; as such, it may be without precedent among Western artistic models. Jazz historian Marshall Stearns described this jazz revolution in the *New Yorker* in 1954: "Jazz leads from rigidity toward mobility. . . . It is anti-Puritan and inimical to all regimentation [e.g., fascism]. It may be in the groove, but you can hop in and out of it."[9] Such an undeclared conceptual framework can be extrapolated from the literary works of Baldwin, Ellison, and Albert Murray and was certainly implied by Mailer, Ross Russell, Kerouac, and Beauvoir.

The emblematic power of the word and concept of "cool" remains enshrined in postwar African-American jazz compositions: in Postwar I, Parker's "Cool Blues," Young's "Just Cooling" (which translates now as "Just Chilling"), Monk's "Let's Cool One," Count Basie's "Stay Cool," and Erskine Hawkins's "Keep Cool, Fool"; in Postwar II, Horace Silver's "Cool Eyes," Ray Brown's "Cool Walk," Sonny Clark's "Cool Struttin'," Fats Navarro's "Everything's Cool," Howard McGhee's "Cool" and "Cool Fantasy," and Oscar Brown Jr.'s comic monologue, "But I Was Cool." By the late 1950s, "cool" became a lyrical attractor suggesting a charismatic style of emotional self-control, as in the phrase "playing it cool," June Christy's hit "Something Cool," and Etta Jones's "Cool, Cool Daddy." There are few jazz compositions with "cool" in the title in the 1930s.

Then as now, the word "cool" could be ascribed to anything positive but its deepest connotation was of a relaxed physiological state, a mode of psychological balance. "*Cool* is a word he likes," Ross Russell observed of Charlie Parker's frequent use of the term in his biography, *Bird Lives!* "It denotes all good qualities, and *situations under control.*" Russell was the founder of Dial Records—on which Parker recorded his best work—and he recalled Bird at rest, listening to playbacks of a studio recording: "He breathes slowly and deeply, and has the air of a man not about to hurry. The physical man is satisfied and quiescent—*cool.*"[10] If a black person was comfortable in a given environment, then he or she was safe and relaxed; if in a public situation with white people, an African-American projected cool composure or emotional self-control. As Lester Young shaped the term, "cool" meant being relaxed with style.

There was an equally important aesthetic side of jazz cool: melodic minimalism, with the challenge of creating a compressed artistic statement. These were the musical values of the subgenre of "cool jazz," and it was perceived as a whiter, West Coast form. Its original avatars were Lester Young, Miles Davis, and Gil Evans, but its key crossover figures were Stan Getz, Gerry Mulligan, Art Pepper, and trumpeter Chet Baker. Baker was a charismatic Californian rogue and heroin addict often called the "James Dean of Jazz" due to their resemblance. He initially copied the sound of Miles Davis but soon translated the latter's muted lyricism into his own ethereal, off-beat style. Like Parker, Baker was a singer and icon of cool with a clear preference for living and playing while high. "Everything becomes beautiful and pure, serene and pleasant," Baker said first about marijuana. "The nerves are relaxed, worries fade away. . . . Time takes on new meaning." Once addicted to heroin, Baker embodied the dangerous ease of antisocial detachment yet it only enhanced his image. "His blasé attitude seemed like the soul of cool," an Italian newspaper wrote of Baker and his comrades Mulligan and Art Pepper, heroin addicts all.[11] The "cool musicians" are a new breed, "musicians whose emotions are controlled and ordered," Lillian Ross wrote from the Newport Jazz Festival in 1954. The cool aesthetic crossed racial lines and was applied to swing musicians Teddy Wilson and Milt Hinton as well as George Shearing and Stan Kenton.[12]

A jazz musician creates a personal aesthetic value system through a signature sound in an artistic practice that rejects all notions of correct form or racial definition. In Postwar II, jazz's objectives were an organic method for reaching a space of existential cool. Here I will show, first, how a jazz musician develops a signature sound and, second, how this artistic practice correlates with the pursuit of subjective truth. In an early work of existentialism, Søren Kierkegaard declared two methods necessary to self-excavation without illusion. The first is "persistent striving" through introspection and the second is ascribing a higher value to "*how* it is said" rather than "*what* is said." In other words, Kierkegaard called for a philosophy in which personal style and depth create more effective self-knowledge than formal artistic content.[13]

The Jazz Musician in the Postwar Imagination

Cool is the master trope of African America, according to the concept's first theorist, Robert Farris Thompson.[14] It is also the emblematic concept of cultural transmission from a pan-African set of cultures as transmuted into African-American culture. Due to this long historical movement and its American environment, cool had to be rendered through individuality. In *Clawing at the Limits of Cool*, Farah Jasmine Griffin and jazz musician Salim Washington stated the contemporary resonances of a distinctively African-American cool: "Keep in mind that within African America, 'coolness' . . . is something rather like a moral category . . . *what is revered is the person* who *is* cool, who brings the virtues of this attribute to all of his or her undertakings." Their exemplary figure is Miles Davis as he embodied the attributes of a cool person: "Being cool involves being relaxed, unruffled, quick-witted, reluctant to use aggression, and, most of all, able to follow one's own path. *Coolness celebrates individuality.*"[15]

Thomas Pynchon focused on this meaning of cool in a key scene in his first novel *V.* (1963), a work concerning the search for meaning among an ensemble cast of Beat slackers in Greenwich Village. Only one of them is a real artist: the alto saxophonist McClintic Sphere. Sphere is an amalgam of two jazz innovators and composers, Ornette Coleman and Thelonious Sphere Monk. In the novel, Sphere regularly plays at the V-Note, a reference to the Five Spot, an East Village club that drew artists, Beats, bohemians, college students, and the likes of Leonard Bernstein to their gigs.[16]

McClintic Sphere works out the only postwar bohemian ethos that Pynchon leaves unmocked in the novel: "Keep cool, but care." Sphere comes up with this four-word mantra during a short soliloquy to his girlfriend Paola, and it works as a verbalized riff. First, Sphere admits to Paola that he had been just "blowing a silly line," showing off his mastery of current hip licks. He then repudiates religion, determinism, God, progress, romantic love, and other people as inadequate resources for *being cool* in the Cold War: "Nobody is going to step down from heaven and square away . . . Alabama, or South Africa or us and Russia. There's no magic words. Not even *I love you* is magic enough. Can you see Eisenhower telling Malenkov or Khrushchev that? Ho-ho." Then Sphere has an epiphany and thinks aloud: "Keep cool but care." It is the climax of the solo: the phrase crystallizes a personal philosophy. He turns it around a few times, then tells Paola poignantly: "If my mother was alive I would have her make a sampler with that on it [for me]."[17]

This moment constitutes an unironic epiphany concerning the relationship of the self to others. As the scene ends, Sphere is singing to the Berkshire trees, "Flop, flip . . . Once I was hip." He has traded his *hipness* for a deeper existential *cool*. But even cool has its limitations: it's detached, diffident, isolated, and hyper-masculine. So keep cool *but care*, Sphere realizes.[18]

Bassist and composer Charles Mingus remembered the moment he gave up hip technique for cool self-excavation, a real-life epiphany that echoes Sphere's.

> For a while I concentrated on speed and technique almost as ends in themselves. I aimed at scaring all the other bass players. . . . Then one night (when I was eighteen or nineteen) all this changed. . . . It was suddenly *me*; it wasn't the bass any more. Now I'm not conscious of the instrument as an instrument when I play."[19]

Mingus here refers to the instrument as an extension of his creative process in real time and then of a changing self, a self-in-process. "I'm going to keep on getting through and finding out the kind of man I am through my music. That's the one place I can be free." Mingus grappled with issues of rage his whole life and, as a bandleader, acted like a marine sergeant. "Even in public . . . he'd yell at you in the middle of a solo to stop playing just licks and get into yourself," one Mingus band member recalled. "Christ, he had more confidence in what we were capable of than we had." Mingus required of others what he demanded of himself: "I'm trying to play the truth of what I am. The reason it's difficult is because I'm changing all the time."[20]

Racial and cultural blinders continue to block the recognition of jazz as the central American model of expressive individuality, even if African-American authors have long since made the connection. James Baldwin's exemplary model of artistic practice was the jazz musician: "I really helplessly model myself on jazz musicians and try to write the way they sound." He compared the primary aesthetic objective of the jazz musician to Henry James's ideal of literary practice, "perception at the pitch of passion." For Ralph Ellison, "each solo flight, or improvisation" of the jazz musician created "a definition of his identity as individual, as member of the collectivity and as a link in the chain of tradition." Toni Morrison claims that she has always been "chasing the musicians" and that, as mentioned earlier, for an artistic work to qualify as "black art," its achievement "must look effortless. . . . It must look cool and easy." Western culture has always valorized literature over music yet Morrison, Baldwin, and Ellison (and the Beats) aspired to the self-excavation and social engagement of jazz musicians.[21]

In New York, Chicago, San Francisco, and Los Angeles, jazz was the soundtrack and artistic model for fellow artists—method actors, transgressive comedians, Beat writers, abstract expressionists—and jazz clubs were their meeting ground. Comedian David Steinberg recalled that Lenny Bruce "was influenced by the jazz musicians of the time. . . . He would improvise around ideas." When Bruce took an idea or phrase and deconstructed it from many angles, listened to and shifted along with the crowd's response, he employed a jazz method of spontaneous improvisation in public. It was simultaneously a self-dialogue, a monologue, and a conversation with the audience. Albert Goldman claimed Bruce "fancied himself an oral jazzman [and] his ideal was to walk out there like Charlie Parker, [and] take that mike in his hand like a horn." Bruce often hung out with pianist (and fellow heroin addict) Hampton Hawes, "and when we were both low on bread," he wrote, "we'd meet someplace and tie up together."[22]

Bohemians, artists, and intellectuals were drawn to the ambience, edginess, artistic individuality, and liberal racial politics of jazz clubs such as the Five Spot, as Hettie Jones recalls in her indispensable memoir of postwar Village life.[23] Jones heard Monk and Ornette Coleman as artists analogous to abstract expressionists. "When you opened the door the music rushed out, like a flood of color onto the street." Archie Shepp, Don Cherry, and others were regulars in her home with her husband (Amiri Baraka—i.e., LeRoi Jones, at the time of their marriage) and to her ears, jazz was "technically the most interesting I'd ever hard, and the hardest to play. All I wanted to do at the Five Spot was listen." In addition, the Five Spot was an intellectual oasis from apocalypse: "I remember a whole lot of laughter at the Five Spot. . . . I think of us trying to laugh off the fifties, the pall of the Cold War, the nuclear fallout—right then, the papers were full of it—raining death on test sites in Nevada. I think we were trying to shake the time. Shake it off, shake it up." In her memoir, the Five Spot functions as a Village cornerstone of postwar Beat life, a place where half steps toward an interracial bohemia occurred among the regulars, "all of us there—black and white—were strangers at first," and an artistic flowering occurred across racial and artistic boundaries. For Hettie Jones, "the young black musicians I met didn't differ from other aspiring artists."[24]

One journalist delineated three audiences in attendance at the Five

Spot watching Thelonious Monk and his quartets: jazz fans, college students, and novelty seekers all in search of this weird character, Monk. An autonomous and mysterious figure—profound and confident, racially proud and diffident—Monk had an original artistic vision and a public mask consisting of slang, shades, and a variety of hats. "Every night I heard a new sound, or heard sound a new way," Hettie Jones said about hearing Monk at the Five Spot. In addition, the bebop generation practiced a sullen stagecraft that fit the expectations of a guilt-ridden audience and they were heard as sounding out an underground rebellion of the marginalized and disrespected.[25] All these factors contributed to Monk's cool only a generation after swing musicians referred to venues like the Cotton Club as plantations.

Through jazz, improvisation spread throughout the arts. Gillespie, Parker, and Monk were profiled in the *New Yorker* and *Harper's*, in the *Atlantic Monthly* and *Saturday Evening Post*. Miles Davis was named one of the nation's best-dressed men by *Esquire*, as "an individualist who favors skin-tight trousers, Italian-cut jackets [and] seersucker coats."[26] Art Blakey compared his various line-ups of the Jazz Messengers to the Actors Studio: training grounds for young artists to hone their skills before live audiences.[27] Lewis MacAdams considered the key message of John Cassavetes's independent film *Shadows* (1960) to be that "race has been subsumed in the desire to be cool" in Greenwich Village.[28]

In addition, African-Americans were embattled victims of police brutality and institutional violence. Nearly every major black jazz musician was beaten up in this period, unprovoked, by a white policeman: Dizzy Gillespie, John Coltrane, Monk, Mingus, Art Blakey, Ben Webster, Bud Powell. Most were beaten up when policemen perceived them in social situations with white women. Incredibly, Miles Davis was beaten up under a marquee with his name on it in 1959; just as incredibly, he sued the NYPD and won. Due to his celebrity, Miles Davis was a page-one headline—and in fact, his assault was the only one ever reported. Yet legal redress through the courts was in its infancy for African-Americans and militant self-defense would have simply resulted in more police brutality. For jazz musicians, there was only the individual act of artistic rebellion through cultural politics, racial consciousness, and in-group ethnic style.[29]

Langston Hughes once ascribed the origins of "bebop" as a musical response to police brutality and oppression through his iconic folk character, Jesse B. Semple, in a column for the *Chicago Defender*. "Every time a cop hits a Negro with his billy club, that old club says 'BOP! BOP! . . . BE-BOP!" Then the beaten man yells in pain, "Ooool-ya-koo!" and the "Old Cop just keeps on [hitting], 'MOP! MOP! . . . BE-BOP!" Since "Ool Ya Koo" was an actual bebop composition of Dizzy Gillespie's, this is an encoded statement about cool and violence. "That's where Be-Bop came from," Semple states, then elaborates:

> [It was] beaten right out of some Negro's head into them horns and saxophones and piano keys. . . . [And] that's why . . . white folks don't dig Bop. . . . White folks do not get their heads beat *just for being white*. But me—a cop is liable to grab me almost any time and beat my head— *just* for being colored. (italics in original)

This column echoes Duke Ellington's claim in 1931 concerning jazz as a protest music in the Jim Crow Era: "What we could not say openly, we expressed in music."[30]

Cool was defiance with dignity. Walking the streets unafraid was part of a jazz musician's cool. Musicians raised in Harlem such as Sonny Rollins, Jackie McLean, and drummer Art Taylor often spoke of the regal bearing and confident resolve of the neighborhood's resident jazz musicians. "Men like Basie, Ellington, and Hawkins . . . by carrying themselves with pride, *just by acting like men* . . . influenced younger guys like me," Rollins reflected about the early 1940s. Then in Postwar II, their swing-era models were supplanted by Parker, Gillespie, and Monk: "All the guys I grew up with [in Harlem] wanted to be jazz musicians . . . because they were the coolest cats around." Rollins reflected in 2011 that "Dizzy was my great [first] inspiration" and that his first experience of bebop made him feel "that's what I wanted to do . . . to play like Charlie Parker." A decade later, he completed his training under Monk's tutelage, and he has said of that time, "I consider Monk my guru . . . so does Trane." In his short novel, *The Subterraneans* (1958), Kerouac wrote of seeing "Thelonious Monk sweating leading the generation with his elbow chords, eying the band madly to lead them on, the monk and saint of bop."[31] Bebop's innovative breakthroughs took place from 1943 to 1950 and its musical practices transformed jazz and African-American culture in Postwar II.

Bebop was a generational call to African-American individuality.

Bird and Diz and the Bebop Transformation

The bebop generation was an artistic cohort as important to global music as the Impressionists were to art or the Romantic poets to literature. In rejecting the big band format indebted to collective swinging and social dance, Parker and Gillespie redirected jazz to individual development and formal musical advance. Once bebop displaced big band music, a professional swing-era trumpeter, for example, could no longer find his musical bearings at a jam session. Becoming a jazz musician had suddenly became "a self-actuated quest" under African-American leadership, and jazz itself "a virtuoso's music." As Ishmael Reed reflected in 2008, "Bebop was my generation's hip-hop. . . . We dressed like bebop-pers. . . . Bebop musicians didn't walk. They came at you, dancing. . . . Beboppers were sharp, and we were their acolytes."[32]

Yet bebop was also a launching pad for a global exploration of new musical possibilities. Over fifteen years, this generation sought theoretical and experimental approaches to improvisation and harmony, while requiring a high benchmark of musical knowledge and compositional structures. They experimented with new paths for integrating every aspect of music: harmony, rhythm, melody, orchestral arrangement, and musical timbre. They studied classical and non-Western musics, and through extensive collaboration and daily improvisational practice, developed musical practices that included instantaneous artistic communication, distinctive harmonies, and a sophisticated internal rhythmic sense. The result was several overlapping musical movements over a single generation. After bebop, in rough order, came cool jazz, hard bop, soul jazz, modal jazz, and free jazz. Concurrently, jazz musicians pursued the first soundings of a global music by first, integrating the rhythms, scales, and timbres of Afro-Latin musics (through Gillespie, Mongo Santamaria, and Tito Puente) and second, through Indian and African music—the ragas, dense percussive textures and polyrhythmic explorations of John Coltrane, Eric Dolphy, Art Blakey, Max Roach, and others. In effect, these musicians became "their own music theorist[s]," Ingrid Monson reflects, and in so doing, this cohort "maximize[d] their aesthetic agency."[33]

Jazz scholar Scott DeVeaux has shown that bebop was a paradigm shift carried off through the "transformative example" of Parker and Gillespie. Nearly every musician of the generation received direct support and encouragement from "Bird and Diz," whether of African-, Euro-, or Latin American heritage.[34] DeVeaux applied Thomas Kuhn's model of paradigm shifts point by point to the wartime moment, starting with bebop's "reconstitution of the field from new fundamentals." Bebop had all the "symptoms of the revolution": "The youth of the revolutionaries; the startling, unexpected nature of the new insight; the specter of an older generation clinging to the old paradigm . . . [and] finally, the triumph of the new paradigm and the recasting of the field in its image."[35] Swing-era musicians rejected bebop as did white audiences who heard it as abrasive and unmelodic. Cultural historian Eric Lott described the bebop aesthetic as a "willfully harsh, anti-assimilationist sound." In its lightning solo runs, fast rhythms, and angular harmonies, one could hear the first soundings of black nationalism.[36]

Charlie Parker's infamous heroin addiction also played a role as a marker of defiance, resistance, and racial consciousness. Pianist Hampton Hawes reflected on Parker's choice to stay high all the time:

> He hated the black-white split and what was happening to his people, couldn't come up with an answer so he stayed high. Played, fuck, drank, and got high. The way he lived his life was telling everyone[:] You don't dig me, you don't dig my people, you don't dig my music. . . . Didn't answer to nobody but himself . . .'cause [then at least] when you go, you go down alone.[37]

As much a heroin addict as Parker, Hawes explained its allure with cryptic precision concerning despair and hopelessness: "Well, shit, we ain't no super race." Hawes' claims may be a series of rationalizations for drug addiction, but there is a great deal of testimony from jazz musicians as to Parker's intelligence and political consciousness. "He was the first out on the frontier," Hawes recalls of his influence on Los Angeles in the mid-1940s, "and gave birth to all of us."[38] Bebop was "the music of revolt," jazz critic Leonard Feather observed, and its main artistic effect was to "reassert the individuality of the jazz musician" against the collective machine of the swing-era big band.[39]

Tenor saxophonist Don Byas was asked in 1970 if his turn to bebop in the 1940s had been a form of social protest.

> I'm always trying to make my sound stronger and more brutal than ever. I shake the walls in the joints I play in. *I'm always trying to sound brutal without losing the beauty*, in order to impress people *and wake them up* . . . . That's protest, of course it is. My form of protest is to play as hard and strong as I am.[40]

Two key phrases here fit in with Camus's existential ideas of art and rebellion: (1) Byas's "I" assumes an audience—a *we*—with an objective "[to] wake them up"; (2) he is also constantly searching for a personal musical ethic and self-aware of projecting his subjective experience, "to sound brutal without losing the beauty."

Poet Amiri Baraka's first intellectual epiphany happened at a Parker performance in a nightclub in Newark. Baraka wondered about the innovative "staccato rhythm and jagged lines" in Parker's soloing and "the breakneck speed" of his solos. "It was a burst of magic to me. I didn't know what to make of it. . . . It was blue and pink and white . . . a blue that shattered into many unknown moods. Moods unknown to me. *Different modes of thought* . . . . The music was magical and it covered me over and *turned me into myself.*" Parker provided Baraka with a bebop conversion experience that quickly set him wondering about the thwarted struggle and bourgeois aspirations of African-Americans. Bebop was the new soundtrack for a generation of young black intellectuals and the germinating force of *Blues People* (1963), Baraka's groundbreaking study of the social functions of black music. "What was Bebop?" Baraka asked in his autobiography. "Bebop. A new language a new tongue and vision for a generally more advanced group in our generation. Bebop was a staging area for a new sensibility growing to maturity. And the Beboppers were blowing the sound to attract the growing, the developing, the about-to-see." Baraka also wondered about the individual musicians and "the sound itself. . . . Why were they sounding like this?"[41] There were four main reasons.

First, the bebop turn was practiced by a tight band of musicians that Sonny Rollins called "a brotherhood." These musicians were a group of angry young artists creating, with each solo, a personal and ethnic identity denied by the dominant culture. In the case of white musicians, each was able to carve out individual artistic space in jazz unavailable in other forms. This musical cohort was also socially and aesthetically aware: they created art for economic scraps, all the while bouncing new ideas, sounds, and approaches off of their small, devoted audience. Rollins reflected back from the vantage point of the late 1990s: "We were really a brotherhood back then. It is gone now, but . . . back then . . . there was a smaller, more intelligent audience. Everybody knew everybody else; everybody played the same clubs. . . . Now it is no longer a small group of people with a mission. . . . Then you played for the love of it and didn't expect to get anything [i.e., money]. And we didn't get anything."[42]

Second, there was the accelerated tempo of technological change and increased mobility through new roads and highways—W. T. Lhamon Jr. has theorized "speed" as the "cultural style" of the 1950s. With bebop came the aesthetic challenge of velocity and acceleration to keep pace with culture: musical thinking had to be done at a breakneck pace yet also at the highest harmonic level. Dizzy Gillespie once recalled how Parker would be "at a tempo way up there and he'd 'cram' something [in at] . . . triple the tempo that he was already playing," to which Miles Davis responded that "it made you [and the band] play a little bit faster." Examples of such triple-timing in solos can be found in iconic Parker compositions such as "Ornithology," "Salt Peanuts," and "KoKo." In each, Parker improvises across melodic, harmonic, and rhythmic structures "at velocities that extended the intimidating relationship of thought and action." This was one of Parker's central contributions to postwar culture.[43] All music became "faster and more dissonant," historian Robin D. G. Kelley reflects, as jazz became "the perfect accompaniment to the new atomic age." Jazz critic Stanley Crouch considered Parker's virtuosity a model for musicians to take "control of the present." As Miles Davis recalled about bebop, "That whole movement was conducive to [the] acceleration of everything."[44]

Third, there was the existential challenge of being black in the Jim Crow era. James Baldwin's "Sonny's Blues" is the story of two brothers, one a teacher and the other a jazz pianist and heroin addict. When Sonny quits shooting up, the world seems so raw that he is paralyzed by fear on the bandstand and then rescued by the drummer (Creole), who sends him coded musical messages of encouragement to utilize musical ideas as exploratory expressions of communication. Sonny tries to solo at first but can't, reflecting a severe lack of faith in himself. "He and the piano stammered, started one way, got scared, stopped," his brother narrates, "started another way, panicked, marked time . . . then seemed to have found a direction, panicked again, got stuck. And the face I saw on Sonny I'd never seen before." Creole then steers the band into a blues pattern, and Sonny suddenly feels grounded enough to cast off and explore his musical ideas. His brother realizes right then that "the blues . . . were not about anything very new," but what Creole and Sonny had done instead was "*keep* it new, at the risk of ruin . . . [at the risk of] madness and death, in order to find new ways to make us listen." Sonny finally finds his stride and plays a solo so personal it makes his brother recall holding their late mother's face, and he cries. Baldwin here implies that the existential core of jazz and blues was one of survival and affirmation. "For, while the tale of how we suffer . . . and how we triumph is never new, it must always be heard," the narrator concludes. "There isn't any other tale to tell[;] it's the only light we've got in all this darkness."[45]

Fourth, during an apprenticeship period, a jazz musician of any ethnicity becomes immersed in jazz as an embodied musical form of modernity. By "modernity" I mean two things: (*a*) the acceptance of rapid social change, and therefore the inadequacy of traditional, folk, and national musics to reflect and engage a global, technological society; and (*b*) an artistic form that is portable, embodied, interactive, and engaged with an audience in mind. In addition, jazz is a modernist musical form that was created from the ground up—by a once-despised, denied, oppressed, and persecuted ethnic group—that became a liberating force, part and parcel of an Afro-diasporic consciousness. "One of the deepest lessons of Afro-Modernism," Monson writes, "is that it is possible both to be honest about one's [ethnic] origins and to cultivate the knowledge and expressive means to become something more than the sum of one's social categories."[46]

Interviewed at the age of eighty, Sonny Rollins proudly pointed to his steady maintenance of his own existential integrity over the years. "The thing I'm most proud of is . . . listening to my inner self. . . . If I'm straight with the guy in the mirror, that's all that matters."[47] To get it together and keep it "straight" with one's self in the postwar era required shutting out the gaze of dominant white society, as illustrated on the cover of Rollins' *Newk's Time* (1957). (See fig. 29.) The inward turn of bebop required an outward mask that was cool, tough, and impassive, enabling the public performance of deep self-excavation, an artistic act more post-Western than postmodern.

Signature Sound and Subjective Truth

With bebop, jazz became codified as an artistic system for the development of subjectivity. The musical form had a good start: there is no proper way to play an instrument in jazz, since its success depends on emotional communication rather than correct form. The crucible of the art is "the individuality and personal inflection of the jazz musician's tone," as defined by composer and jazz scholar Gunther Schuller. Any musician dedicated to "the life" is measured by this accomplishment, a creative process requiring years of emotional self-excavation. This is the essence of jazz artistry for Schuller since its "communicative power lie[s] in this individuality, which comes from inside the man; indeed a jazz musician without this individual quality is not a jazz musician in the strictest sense." For Ellison, the criteria for graduating from journeyman to master artist was the "power to express an individuality in tone." Art Blakey declared simply, "If you can't identify yourself on a record, you're in trouble."[48]

At midcentury, this was simply known as the musician's *sound*. "The underlying task, the core of the task, is sound," Miles Davis told one critic. "Sound is your very own voice. . . . Sound is in charge of your person. . . . You are your own sound."[49] Coleman Hawkins, the co-creator of the tenor saxophone's voice, put it this way: "Sound is *it* . . . . The whole thing is sound. Lester Young didn't change any conception of tenor playing," he said, taking a potshot at his rival. "It was his *sound*, that's all."[50] Duke Ellington composed with each band member's musical parameters present in his mind. "I write to each man's sound. A man's sound is his total personality."[51]

Jazz critic Ben Ratliff summed it up this way: "Every musician . . . needs a sound, a full and sensible embodiment of his artistic personality,

Figure 30. With his shades on in the recording studio, Miles Davis coolly considers the last take (photograph by Aram Avakian. © Aram Avakian Jazz Photo Collection).

such that it can be heard . . . in a single note." He then contrasted a trio of iconic sounds: "Miles Davis's was fragile and pointed, Coleman Hawkins's was ripe and mellow . . . Coltrane's was large and dry, slightly undercooked, and urgent."[52] If Ratliff here sounds like a wine taster he still manages to convey the aesthetic objective of unifying style, sound, and person in jazz.

All this points to why jazz was the central governing artistic form of cool. If the cool figure exhibits a public composure suggesting an internal harmony, and jazz's aesthetic objective concerns the integral creation of individuality, sound, experience, and style, then jazz is an artistic practice concerned with expressive individuality grounded by emotional self-control. Evidence for the total diffusion of this artistic ideal can be found in nearly any interview of a jazz musician over the past three generations.

Alto saxophonist Charles McPherson provided an accessible example of this concept during one of *Downbeat* magazine's famous blindfold tests. McPherson listened first to "Bossa De Luxe" and interrupted: "This is Jackie McLean on alto. I know Jackie's style and his sound. *Everyone has a sound*, just like everyone has a recognizable voice. Someone calls you on the phone, you answer and you know who it is by the voice."[53] A jazz musician's sound is a personal combination of tone, timbre, accent, cadence, and stylistic choices, as well as identifiable melodic, harmonic, and rhythmic signature moves. McPherson extended this elegant conflation of speaking voice and musical voice throughout the session. During Frank Morgan's version of "Nefertiti," McPherson first guessed Art Pepper, then corrected himself: "No, it's not him. Is this Frank Morgan? There was something about . . . his upper register playing." As he listened to "Street Blues," McPherson quickly identified the altoist: "It's Ornette Coleman. . . . I recognized Ornette's sound. *There it is again: the voice.*" Finally, in "Topsy," McPherson heard an artistic sound from his apprentice years: "I'll bet this is Lee Konitz. If not, it's someone very much influenced by him. . . . He's light, airy, and his approach is very different from mine. It's delicate, more ethereal. *It's his saxophone voice, and that's the way he is as a person*—quiet, doesn't talk much, doesn't talk loud. You are what you are."[54]

Vocalist Betty Carter started out in Lionel Hampton's swing-era big band in the late 1940s, and like so many others, she experienced a musical epiphany on first hearing Charlie Parker. She then went on to develop perhaps the most unique vocal style in jazz history. "Everybody wants a sound," Carter reflected on her journeywoman years, and her analysis of this process is both pragmatic and imbued with the hard humor of what jazz musicians simply call "the life":

> You've got to think about the club owner, the audience and yourself. That's the art of being an artist. Then if you want to be an individual, you've still got to be unique on top of that. It takes time. . . . *You have to really inquire into yourself* . . . . A lot of musicians out there should be bookkeepers. . . . Some musicians really ought to be composers or arrangers.
>
> To know what you're all about, you've got to keep working. . . . You've got to find yourself, where you're at. . . . Maybe you want to be out front, but you're not qualified. *You should know this about yourself.*

Carter here triangulates the artistic parameters of art, audience, and the marketplace. Only after knowing the music *and* the business *and* the audience does the deeper, interior artistic work begin, the next level when you "really inquire into yourself."[55]

A musician's sound is thus profoundly individual: it stands for the musical qualities of one's instrumental voice, the projection of one's personality, and the expression of a unique aesthetic. Most importantly, it is a reflection of the musician's lived and felt experience. Lester Young often expressed this idea in interviews: "Every musician should be a stylist. I played like [Frankie] Trumbauer when I was starting out. But then there's a time when you have to go out for yourself and *tell your story*. Your influence has already told his."[56] To "tell your story" means both that you must have a story to tell—you must be "sayin' something," as musicians say[57]—and that you must create a distinctive artistic and narrative voice to tell it in. At first, you imitate someone else ("you have a model, or a teacher") but then, you have to "start playing for yourself," Young explained. "Show them that you're an individual."[58]

Take the challenge of finding an original sound for a trumpeter like Dizzy Gillespie or, five years later, Miles Davis. In the late 1930s, Louis Armstrong was the then-tyrannical artistic force on the trumpet while Roy Eldridge was the key swing-era innovator. Gillespie started out imitating Eldridge, but gradually developed his own voice through an emphasis on speed, his aesthetic delight in the upper register, and an affinity for Latin American rhythms. Drummer Kenny Clarke observed Gillespie in this period: "It's *how* you play it. . . . Are you gonna play like Coleman Hawkins . . . [or] Louis Armstrong? Or are you gonna get your own creation? . . . Dizzy's contribution was to create his own sound."[59]

The younger Miles Davis started out imitating Gillespie, but found that the latter's virtuosity did not fit *his* musical strengths: lyricism, succinct phrasing, and a melodic sense of timing. Gil Evans, Davis's co-creator of cool jazz, recalled the young trumpeter's challenge in finding his sound: "Miles had to start with almost no sound and then develop one as he went along, a sound suitable for the ideas he wanted to express." Davis found artistic footholds in Freddie Webster's buttery tone, Clark Terry's phrasing, and Lester Young's melodic intelligence. So he began to play "fast and light—and [with] no vibrato," taking as his artistic model the human voice. He attached a mute to his trumpet to help approximate its nuance and vulnerability: "People tell me my sound is like a human voice and that's what I want it to be."[60]

The development of a signature voice was especially liberating for bassists and drummers since their function in big bands was limited to supporting soloists, keeping steady time for dancers, and propelling the ensemble. Listeners may be unaware of a bassist's or drummer's sound or style, but the musicians know. Kenny Clarke's style was called "dropping bombs," a wartime reference to how he challenged soloists with disruptive bass drum accents. As Gillespie recalled, such accents first angered swing-era soloists more used to rhythmic support. "Kenny's style of drumming, with 'bombs' . . . in the bass drum and regular rhythm in the cymbals . . . furnished just the right amount of support [for me]. . . . A lotta people didn't like them. . . . He infused a new conception . . . into the dialogue of the drum [and soloists], which is now *the* dialogue."[61] After Clarke, Max Roach and Art Blakey extended the solo dimensions of the drum throughout the postwar era, bringing in African and Latin rhythms, artistic fills and cymbal filigree. At the same time, the bass emerged as a solo instrument in the hands of Jimmy Blanton, Oscar Pettiford, and Nick Fenton, while Charlie Christian created the sound of the electric guitar.

Or take the artistic vision of Thelonious Monk, who fundamentally changed how anyone can play (or hear) the piano through a stylistic array of accents, silences, fragments, and dissonances. Monk and Bud Powell deconstructed the familiar lyrical and stride modes of jazz piano, often ignoring the piano's role of "comping" (playing supporting chords behind soloists).[62] To pianist Hampton Hawes, Monk's groundbreaking style was simply self-extension: "Monk plays it strange and beautiful because he *feels* strange and beautiful."[63] As there were no formal schools for jazz, the new message was disseminated at nightclubs and in musical salons at the apartments of Gillespie, pianist Mary Lou Williams, and arranger Gil Evans.

Finally, take the experience of popular Argentinian saxophonist, Gato Barbieri, at the end of Postwar II. Following the artistic revelations he experienced listening to Coltrane and Ornette Coleman, Barbieri "wanted very much to be a black jazz musician." But by the late 1960s, he wanted his sound to include his own cultural roots, the story of another "part of the world where there is great oppression." Barbieri found the answer first in folk rhythms but especially in listening to tango musicians, who he found, "tell their stories [with] the same power, feeling, and spontaneity" as jazz musicians. As with Mingus, Barbieri's goal was to make his saxophone an extension of thinking and being: "[to] be able to express what is in me through the horn as naturally as the act of walking, of breathing." He wanted to eliminate the interference of rational consciousness in the creative process: "The way it is now, you have each thought and then you . . . execute it. My dream is to eliminate that step . . . so the music will flow instantaneously . . . [and] other people will respond to it as naturally."[64]

Finding one's signature musical voice required an apprenticeship within a set of core African-American musical practices that form the foundation of jazz: "swing, call-and-response patterns, vocalized timbre, 'blue notes,' improvisation." To master this musical grammar translates to what DeVeaux calls an "ethnicity of jazz" that is African-American. Of course there are major jazz artists of every ethnicity and nationality, yet an apprentice musician finds a sound world by embedding him- or herself in blues, spirituals, and work songs; moreover, each of these genres has its own aesthetic and gestalt, just as in European classical music. "These [African-American] musical markers of ethnicity are usually treated as *essentials*," DeVeaux asserts.[65] This is one reason the term "jazz" was disliked and often avoided by black jazz musicians; most used the term "music" or "our music." Duke Ellington once told Gillespie he should have called bebop "Negro music." Then any musician would have to say, "I play Negro music" (or African-American music), as if it was an explicitly classical, national, or ethnic genre.

Yet even if jazz is an African-American artistic form, its practices can be adapted and reshaped to any musician's subjectivity. "I've always felt that the music started out as black," (white) guitarist Jim Hall reflected, "but that it's as much mine now as anyone else's. I haven't stolen the music from anybody—I just bring something different to it." Trumpeter Rex Stewart compared (white) baritone saxophonist Gerry Mulligan to Louis Armstrong: "He has soul, and he plays and talks like a man who enjoys life and people. I felt a kinship with him right away. If a man doesn't feel him, he must be dead." Musicologist Tim Brennan invokes the fraught term "authenticity" to refer to a musician immersed in a given tradition, who has mastered its canon and values, and who consciously acts as a representative of its form. By this definition, Jim Hall and Gerry Mulligan are certainly *authentic* jazz musicians.[66]

Of all postwar artists, it was the poets who best understood the self-excavation involved in the creation of a signature sound through personal experience and rendered through improvisation. In "For Miles," Beat poet Gregory Corso praised the trumpeter's achievement: "Your sound is faultless / pure & round / holy / almost profound / Your sound is your sound / true & from within / a confession." In "Walking Parker Home," Beat poet Bob Kaufman imagined "brain extensions seeking trapped sounds" in Parker's mind, "Ghetto thoughts / bandstand courage / solo flight." Kaufman tried to imagine how a musician fills space with voice, sound, and experience: "Heroin nights of birth / and soaring / over boppy new ground. . . . Cool revelations / shrill hopes / beauty speared into greedy ears." In "Art Pepper," Edward Hirsch focused on the jazz musician's symbolic action: "Playing solo means going on alone, improvising," he offers at first, then inverts the riff: "It's the *fury* of improvising, of *going it alone*." South African poet Keorapetse Kgositsile distilled jazz practice in seven words—"How you sound is / who you are"—in his poetic homage, "Art Blakey and the Jazz Messengers."[67]

Patricia Spears Jones implored Miles Davis to blow us all into being through his horn in "The Blues of This Day (for Miles Davis): "What we want is to be brass. / The horn-scratched voice blown through." In "Lester Young," Beat poet and trumpeter Ted Joans meditated on Young's artistic leadership: "Sometimes he was cool like an eternal / blue flame," but then again, sometimes he was "preachin' in very cool / tones." In every case, "he [Young] knew what he / Blew, and he did what a prez should do," leading the jazz nation as a "prez should." Joans affirmed Young's cultural legacy in the last line: "Angels of jazz—they don't die—they live . . . / in hipsters like you and I." Joans invoked "hipster" here in its positive postwar definition, "one who is interested in the latest trends and tastes, especially a devotee of modern jazz," one current until the early 1990s.[68]

Odes to Young, Parker, Davis, and Coltrane were common in both the Beat and Black Arts Movements. For postwar poet Ed Sanders (later of The Fugs), the jazz musician was the Promethean artistic figure for the Beats. In a poetic tribute to their artistic legacy, Sanders offers this verse: "The Beats taught us / about the thrill / of the *Spontaneous Solo*," and then he acknowledges its origins, "[since] they took fire / from those thrilling / bebop / lonerhood / tremble zone / spontaneous / saxophone solos / on West 52nd."[69] For poet and jazz scholar Lorenzo Thomas, the jazz musician was "the leader of rebellion against postwar conformity" for all bohemians "and the spiritual agent of the politically powerless."[70]

In the swing era, jazz musicians were social artists involved in a public ritual of spiritual uplift; in the postwar era, the jazz musician's role was focused on a type of self-assertion that was closer to Camus's ideal of existential freedom. The result was a melding of the personal and the political, of self and ethnicity, of aesthetic and racial awareness—as all these intertwined aspects of freedom became explicit in albums like Rollins's *Freedom Suite* (1958), Max Roach's *We Insist: Freedom Now Suite* (1960), Art Blakey and the Jazz Messengers' *The Freedom Rider* (1961), and in Mingus's compositions, such as "Fables for Faubus" and "Freedom." Bebop musicians simultaneously spoke to American and Afro-diasporic futures, at once redefining "*freedom* in jazz . . . [as] that feeling of improvised musical self-determination," Ingrid Monson reflected.[71]

Even that most famous literary riff of existentialism—"to be or not to be"—became a trope in postwar jazz. The title of Dizzy Gillespie's indispensable autobiography is *To Be, or Not . . . to Bop*. Poet Al Young paid tribute to Lester Young's final year when his former exuberance had "Cooled, the jazz 'To Be or Not / to Be'—withdrawn, a whisper" (in

"Prez in Paris 1959"). In "Am/Trak," a poetic meditation on the relationship of Monk and Coltrane, Amiri Baraka breaks up the national train service ("Amtrak") into "[I] Am" and "[on] Track," equating existential affirmation with spatial mobility. He heard in Monk's solos, "A *why I'm here* / A *why I ain't*." To Baraka, Monk had turned the piano into a melodic drum, or as he translated it onomatopoetically, "Pink pink a cool bam groove note air breath." Meanwhile the younger Coltrane "clawed at the limits of cool / tryin' to be born" through Monk's guidance.[72]

In "Am/Trak," Baraka dubs Monk's musical philosophy "street gospel intellectual mystical survival codes." I parse that Beat riff as a six-word poetic skein distilling *existential cool* into a philosophy. Cool was a secular urban survival technology equal parts street- and worldly wise, both encoded and open-ended.

Interlude: Sonny Rollins under the Williamsburg Bridge, 1958–1960

The early 1950s was a rough period for Sonny Rollins. He did a stint in prison for drug possession (heroin), lived on the streets and in the Chicago subway system, worked as a janitor, and finally checked himself into the Public Service Hospital in Lexington, Kentucky. "I really went into the Lion's Den and came out alive." Rollins then kicked heroin and experienced what Kierkegaard called a transformation from the aesthetic to the ethical sphere—an explicit commitment to something outside one's self that marks an end to a past self. By 1958, Rollins was one of the music's premier tenor saxophonists: he single-handedly created the format of the piano-less saxophone trio on *Saxophone Colossus*; enjoyed an artistic peak experience with the Clifford Brown/Max Roach Quintet; recorded classic albums with Monk and Miles Davis. Yet he slowly turned further inward. "Rollins became a penitent of sorts," Goodman recalled, "incorporating the artist's solitary confrontation with self and complete immersion in music as if they were both the ends and the means of a devotional calling."[73]

In the liner notes of *Freedom Suite*, Rollins declared that mainstream American culture was dependent on the creative production of African-Americans. The love and theft of black music and culture added an extra ironic burden to racial oppression: "America is deeply rooted in Negro

Figure 31. Sonny Rollins, mid-solo, 1959 (Institute of Jazz Studies, Rutgers University).

culture: its colloquialisms, its humor, its music. How ironic that the Negro, who more than any other people can claim America's culture as his own, is being persecuted and repressed, [and] that the Negro, who has exemplified the humanities in his very existence, is being rewarded with inhumanity."[74] But just after *Freedom Suite*, Rollins felt he had lost his artistic footing due to many factors: fame, jazz critics, and the death of his close friend, trumpeter Clifford Brown. He also experienced pushback from club owners for both demanding higher pay and for his cultural politics: "I was what you would call an uppity nigger or whatever. . . . This was for acting up and asking for [decent] money."[75] Rollins disappeared from the scene and did not record or perform in clubs for two years.

Instead, every night Rollins played under the Williamsburg Bridge, often alone but sometimes with fellow saxophonists Steve Lacy or childhood friend Jackie McLean. These musicians had a simple artistic objective: "I went to practice the rudiments of my instruments—to get more proficient," Rollins insisted, "that sort of thing." Lacy echoed these craft objectives: "What I was doing. . . . was just plain work," said the (white) saxophonist. "We [were] just trying to find out about ourselves musically." The origin of the idea—and its rationale—was surprisingly pragmatic. Rollins had a small apartment on the Lower East Side and "felt guilty because I'm a sensitive person and I know that people need quiet in their apartments." One day he was out walking on the bridge and realized it was "a private place [where] I can blow my horn as loud as I want." Moreover, there was a lot of competition in that soundscape: "the boats . . . the subway . . . coming across, and cars, and I knew it was perfect." Rollins and his friends would stylize and replicate the sounds of the boats and the cars, then work on boosting their sound over the industrial noise. "I've seen Sonny blow some of those tugboat flats [and sharps] and have the tugboat answer him," Jackie McLean recalled.[76] According to Lacy, Rollins often overpowered the entire urban soundscape: "On the bridge there was this din, a really high level of sound from boats and cars and subways and helicopters and airplanes. Sonny played into it. I couldn't hear myself but I could hear Sonny." Lacy was in awe of Rollins's determination as they practiced "fingering, intonation, tones, scales, intervals." Drummer Art Blakey simply said, "I've never seen a man that determined."[77] When he re-emerged in 1962, Rollins released one of his finest albums, *The Bridge*.

Asked once by a fellow musician whether he plays for himself, other musicians, or the public, Rollins declared, "I'm playing for the music [itself]. . . . It's all done for the music first, regardless of what it costs me. . . . In other words, I'm playing and thinking about trying to get the music across and nothing else." Ellison once wrote that the relationship of musician and instrument was analogous to "the monk for the cross." Timothy Brennan considers the work of nearly all Afro-Latin musics a form of "secular devotion." Art Blakey called his jazz units "The Messengers" in reference to the prophet Muhammad (often called "The Messenger") and the emotional substance of the band's messages. Rollins, Blakey, and Coltrane (among many others) have often declared jazz to be a spiritual vocation.[78]

Rollins read deeply in Eastern philosophies throughout the 1950s and 1960s, yet his devout practice has always been jazz. "I've been religious at times . . . [but] every time you try to say, yes, this is it, there is a God or there is a reason . . . there might be a circumstance in life which could shake that. I haven't met anyone who really knows anything about religion. No one knows. I would like to believe."[79] Camus wanted to believe, too, but could never find a religious system adequate to his needs. In effect, Camus's devotional practice was literature just as Rollins's was jazz. In short, Rollins was then and remains a postwar existential artist.

John Clellon Holmes, *The Horn* (1958)

The Horn was the only postwar jazz novel to grasp the music's artistic breakthroughs within both the American cultural grain and African-American experience. Early on, Holmes hones in on the saxophone as the symbol of African-American cool. Young Walden Blue stares at his saxophone, knowing it was

> an emblem of some inner life of his own . . . to Walden the saxophone was, at once, his key to the world in which he found himself, and *the way by which the world was rendered impotent* to brand him either failure or madman or Negro or saint.[80]

This is a striking perception across racial lines of the late 1950s: that the musician's sound reflects his complex interiority; that through persistent

striving, "he found himself"; that the self-excavation "rendered impotent" the white gaze. The instrument is Blue's vehicle of subjective truth,
and "truth" is a keyword throughout *The Horn*. In effect, this is Holmes's
translation of Sartre's idea of being "condemned to be free" and the need
to create individuality from personal experience and self-accounting.
Holmes remains an undervalued source of Beat writing and postwar history: he wrote the first two essays defining the Beat generation for the
New York Times, the first Beat novel (*Go*, 1952), and Kerouac coined the
term "Beat Generation" in his apartment.[81]

  The Horn is an innovative roman à clef and a meditation on the American artist through the postwar jazz world: it features characters based
on Parker, Monk, Gillespie, Billie Holiday, and Lester Young. *The Horn*
is dedicated to "Kerouac, who talked," and its wealth of specific detail
could only have come from someone who spent many postwar nights in
jazz clubs. Holmes claims he was a fan of big band swing until forced to
make "the arduous transition . . . to bop with the help of Jack Kerouac
and Bird in 1948." Despite the scarcity of good jazz novels in its golden
age, *The Horn* sold few copies and quickly fell out of print—nor has it
ever received the attention it deserves from readers, jazz scholars, literary critics, or historians.[82]

  Holmes wrote the first draft in three creative bursts between 1952
and 1955. In the first section he wanted to capture Lester Young's artistic
contribution to jazz and American culture. He wrote the second in a state
of exhilaration, following an epiphany that "the quintessential American
artist was the black jazz musician." The novel lay unfinished for more
than a year until he wrote its third section as therapy "for coping with
the death of Charlie Parker in 1955." Holmes was aware of his inadequacy
"to deal with black experience and black music," but he decided to roll
the dice on his artistic vision, "to go with my love for both, and let the
flaws justify themselves by my passion and sincerity." All the characters
are African-American, and his objective was to capture the power of the
music, the "beauty, lift, [and] swing wrestled out of sordidness."[83]

  Each chapter focuses on a single jazz musician and begins with an
epigraph from an author of the American Renaissance. The symbolism
was clear: these musicians provided the postwar response to Emerson's
call for American poets, just as Melville, Whitman, Dickinson, and Poe
had first "defined . . . the situation of the artist here." Holmes is the only

writer to link jazz musicians back to the American Renaissance: Edgar Poole (Young) and Edgar Allen Poe, Walden Blue and Thoreau, Georgie Dickson (Billie Holiday) and Emily Dickinson, Wing Redburn (Parker) and Melville, Junius Priest (Monk) and Hawthorne, Curny Finnly as "both Dizzy Gillespie and Mark Twain." "I wanted each of these characters to represent an American writer . . . [but also] to represent a particular kind of jazz musician," Holmes reflected in 1976. "The novel as it evolved . . . was to be about the American-as-artist."[84]

Edgar Pool (Lester Young) is a swing-era tenor saxophonist whose relentless quest for his own sound became the model for bebop musicians. One night the younger saxophonist, Walden Blue, cuts Pool on the bandstand, an artistic slaying of the father in jazz. The older man is shocked out of his mask into the reality of his own mortality and debilitation. His physical health begins to decline, and the novel's action is triggered: a range of jazz musicians realize their debt to him and recall their first meeting. "He was everybody's evil father," reflects Wing (Bird): it was Pool's "obsession with his sound" that led to the inward turn of jazz practice and from which "the irreverent furor of bop had come." Holmes frames these musicians as "furtive minnesingers," making of their music an analogy for the praise song of Catholicism. He renders jazz musicians as outcast monks performing their spiritual practices in public every night, as if their artistic introspection contributed to social and cultural morale.

Pool models each jazz musician's route to existential self-possession. Geordie (Holiday) recalls that Pool alone "had possessed himself"; he was "embittered, but full of his peculiar, isolated truth." She often meditated on how Pool alone created himself through his sound, "pursu[ing] the years in lean and tireless communion with himself." At one point, Pool shows up at a recording session so incapacitated nearly all the musicians refuse to play with him. Yet when his turn comes to solo, Pool steps up and plays three respectable choruses—"fragmented, arduous, spaced with poignant and terrible intervals"—and the other musicians are "astounded . . . by the curiously undefeated . . . will to endure in the splashed and quivering figure."[85]

In certain ways, Holmes asks and answers key questions about jazz for the acolyte reader. *What is a solo in jazz?* "[It is] a true confession flung up bravely once against a world that had small use for truth; a fragment of a man, and of his life, and thus . . . holy." *How were jazz musicians seen in American society?* Pool realizes "he had spent his life like a moody fugitive among sensation hunters [audiences], enunciating what seemed to him just then . . . a rare and holy truth in the pits of hell." *What could an empathetic listener hear in a jazz musician's sound?* Experience and humor and survival and affirmation, the travails of one human being and his particular cast of mind. Here is Holmes's lyrical description of Pool's sound:

> [His saxophone] had a singularly human sound—deep, throaty, often brutal with a power that skill could not cage, [and] an almost lazy twirl on the phrase ends: strange, deformed melody. When he swung with moody nonchalance . . . [you] would hear a wild goose honk beneath his tone—the noise, somehow, of the human body, superbly, naturally vulgar. . . . And then out of the smearing notes, a sudden shy trill would slip, infinitely wistful and tentative.

Pool's sound was his nightly narration of his life in his own voice. Holmes gives each character's sound (and story) equal attention, granting each a single chapter (a "Chorus") in which we hear about the moment each musician heard Pool's message as an epiphany, a call to artistic arms.[86]

Jazz musicians were playing the unwritten cultural changes in American life and the future social equality of African-Americans. It was a hidden transcript, the improvised musical score of the street. "Jazz was a kind of growing Old Testament of the Negro race," the narrator imagines, "and of all lost tribes in America, too—a testament being written night after night by unknown, vagrant poets on the spot." The music was a living quasi-sacred text with Pool figured as "a sort of Genesis," a creation myth, even if that role rightfully belonged to Louis Armstrong or Jelly Roll Morton. Yet culturally, Pool is figured as one beginning of a modern African-American individuality: defiantly repudiating the dictates of Jim Crow obedience while self-driven on an "inevitable and irreducible" journey. Pool is a first emanation of the modern self working to create a new secular gospel, "sound[ing] the bittersweet note of Ecclesiastes, ironical in his confoundment." More than any other black musician, Lester Young's sound compelled *white* critics and musicians to consider jazz as a modern art form. Ross Russell called Young's tenor saxophone style "the first modern sound in jazz" since he eliminated the overt rhythmic drive of the solo and substituted a melodic propulsion that soared over Count Basie's orchestra, "a pure sound, luminous, almost without vibrato, heard as a feather floating over other sounds in the dancehall."[87]

The character of Junius (Monk) mirrors the trajectory of postwar cool as Holmes narrates the character's experiential arc from his early self-expression, signature style, and masking to the appropriation of these signs across racial lines. First, cool is a mask of self-protection achieved through sunglasses: "His eyes were shielded from the world by a huge thick-framed pair of dark glasses." Even without the glasses, "his face . . . reflected nothing that he saw, as if everything 'out there' was just . . . a dream." On the bandstand, Junius played in a state of rapture, "commun[ing] with the music, as if he were alone there, but gave no hint of what it cost him in either agony or joy." Junius played like a self-confident artist and he neither indulged in Uncle Tomming nor in showmanship: "He played, but he would not perform."

Yet Junius lives a simple neighborhood life, taking care of his mother, joking with the guys on the corner. Holmes mocks the hipster romanticism that turned Junius into a mysterious, exotic Other and imagines that hipsters might be "astounded had they tracked him down" only to find him living in a "rambling, commonplace apartment over the grocery store." Both jazz musicians and hipsters appropriated Junius's rebellious style such that in the process, "what had been an individuality disappeared behind the uniform eccentricity of the dark glasses and berets . . . and Arabic names." His point is simple: how a human being copes with these challenges will be what comes out of his instrument. As Junius (Monk) wonders: "Who knew . . . what reality was for another man? Who could say?"[88]

When a young pianist named Cleo cares for Pool during the last week of the fallen idol's life, he gets his first taste of mortality and "fear[s] that the audacity and devotion necessary to go on repeating [his solos] might come to seem like sickness or obsession." What saves the two of them from despair is Pool's legendary humor as when he acknowledges that he is just the society's holy fool:

Man. . . . Who's that . . . got a goddamn suitcase in his hand, like he's always running late for a bus, coming from no place and going somewheres else? Man, who *is* that? . . . Like, lady, that's a musician . . . and he probably got a change of socks, and his razor, and a coupla rubbers, and two sticks of tea . . . with his reeds. . . .

That man is a musician, and he's just transporting his horn from one place to another like usual, and probably don't own nothing else in the goddamn world. . . . I mean, that man don't *live* anywhere, he only *sleep*. I mean, that man is God's own fool, now ain't he?

The jazz musician is "God's own fool" for doing his Sisyphean labors without reward. Yet within the existential repetition of the jazz life, the musicians had created a space to speak one's subjective truth. Cleo then has his first existential epiphany about the social and racial pressures of life. He learns "what *they* could do to a man and to his truth" and how a man could be broken, "what could happen to anyone."[89]

The novel ends with Pool's death on the bandstand and his final words, "Celebrate. . . . Listen, listen." Young Cleo mourns him deeply and reflects on these three words: "What had he [Pool] meant, if not that the music, *theirs*, had always been a celebration of—Of what?" In a rare failure of imagination in the novel, Holmes lists a series of unsatisfactory symbols of Americana—the light on rooftops, the design of beer cans, automobile graveyards—to reflect Cleo's contemplation of his mentor's deathbed message. A better answer to "of what?" might have been *a celebration of black music, which was their survival*. The novel ends with Cleo roaming the city writing on "subway wall[s], 'The Horn Still Blows.'" (This is an allusion to Ted Joans's scrawling of "Bird Lives" on subway walls after Parker's death.) Then Cleo understands the final word on the death of jazz icons: "It does not matter what carried them off. Once they blew the truth."[90]

In the late 1980s, tenor saxophonist Archie Shepp, a radical black nationalist of the post-bebop generation, contributed a glowing foreword to a reissue of *The Horn*. He admitted he did not know and could not tell the author's race or ethnicity from the text but cared only about its message. "Edgar Pool is the 'icon' itself," he wrote. "Though he is subjected, as is his entire race . . . he stands among those few that defined a new status for himself through his life and his art, and in so doing, for his entire people."[91]

For African-Americans, self-determination was interdependent with social equality and race consciousness—this makes jazz's sonic existentialism a shot across the bow for a post-Western world. The reshaping of any abstract idea of transcendent humanness would require white, Western eyes to recognize the equal humanity of the Other. In *The Horn*, Geordie Howe (Billie Holiday) recalls that she once felt nostalgic for her rural South Carolina home until Pool read her the riot act:

> You always thinking *back*! And what're you thinking back to? . . .
> Colored diners, colored buses, even colored crappers. . . . 'Yassah,
> no'm' . . . Back o'town, tip yo' hat, move along. . . . Baby, I think back
> to *that*, and I go goofy. . . . You brush their coat or pour their booze or
> play the music for 'em, but you don't think back! . . . Play *your* music,
> baby, make *your* money, and be no one's '*nigra*' any more."[92]

In short, the only space for African-American individuality lay in the future. The road there was paved with notes and personal tones, with playing "your music, baby," from your cultural resources, past experiences, and inner pain, the self-affirmation and re-memory of every jazz solo. Cool was the sign of disavowing the need for recognition by white people as well as the repudiation of the deferential disciplines of the U.S. South and Uncle Tomming.

In 1979, Holmes called jazz "the illegitimate child of our 'peculiar fate' as black and white Americans," a phrase he adapted from Ralph Ellison by way of Henry James. Beat writers are often damned by scholars for appropriating African-American culture and yet they did not shrink from their debt to the artistic methods, practices, and exemplars of jazz and blues. They saved their own artistic lives through immersion in jazz's artistic and social implications, in the music and clubs and interracial friendships of Beat camaraderie. They then attempted to explain it to a wider, whiter audience. It is a fate still unspooling through the mythos of cool.

Coda: Cultural Rebellion Triggers Political Rebellion

James Baldwin observed that whenever music made by African-Americans originally *for* African-Americans found an audience outside of its in-group, the meanings of its songs, rhythms, and sounds changed.

This is equally true of keywords and concepts. "Cool" reached total global diffusion two generations ago without any sense of its original and still distinctive meanings in African-American culture. Its initial importance and resonance inhered to its meaning of "defiance with dignity." Cool may have crossed over as a password for rebellion and became diluted, but as a myth, then and now, "cool" still stands for the reconfiguring of individuality for a post-Western era under the original countercultural sign of African-American music.

Sonny Rollins inflected cool in evocative ways as a challenge to postwar myths of American triumphalism. Rollins wore a cowboy hat and holster on the campy cover of *Way Out West* (1957), for which he recorded "I'm an Old Cowhand (from the Rio Grande)" and "Wagon Wheels," to put black people in the frontier past. Two years later, he started wearing his hair in a Mohawk to acknowledge the suffering of Native Americans. "No one copied him," said Hettie Jones, recalling his bold stylistic and musical statements, "for years he stood alone." In a 1961 *Playboy* interview conducted by Alex Haley—Miles Davis's first with an African-American journalist—Davis invoked "Uncle Tomming" four times as the mode of behavior he most detested. White people demanded from black musicians "that you not only play your instrument, but entertain them, too, with grinning and dancing." In the postwar era, jazz musicians replaced "grinning and dancing" with virtuosity, mystery, detachment, and an aloof stare. The cool revolution was a form of cultural politics that preceded the political action of the civil rights movement.[93]

The modern usage of the word and concept of "cool" emerged from 1940s jazz culture, and yet many scholars of cool ignore jazz (and even noir) or give only lip service to this foundational cultural matrix.[94] Their reticence is due in part to anxiety from treading on what some scholars perceive to be African-American intellectual property and in part, simply, to artistic and aesthetic racism. Scholarship on Beat writers still often glosses over jazz without any declaration that it is the art form which provided the artistic model for this body of literary work. Kerouac, Ginsberg, Holmes, and Baraka declare this explicitly—this omission, too, is an example of artistic and aesthetic racism. More generally, postwar scholars have abdicated their responsibility for understanding the artistic methods, practices, and social history connecting the two artistic forms.[95]

In the face of leftist ideological failure, a surprising "new man" appeared that few Europeans or Euro-Americans imagined existed. Jazz musicians developed a music embedded in European musical structures yet according to African-American musical and performative practices that dovetailed with modernist ideas of self-invention. In American terms, the jazz musician was, in effect, a public model for the recuperation of the Whitmanesque experiential imperative of artistic leadership that dates back at least to Emerson's "The Poet."[96] The African-American jazz musician was the existential rebel in American life, coming from a non-Western tradition in direct tension with social and artistic convention.

Cool was the postwar sign of this development. In jazz, on-stage, in public—the mask of cool functioned as a weapon of self-defense that allowed for the creation of a *sound* as personal conception. If "cool" as a word was a sign of spiritual balance, cool as a mask represented the recognition of despair and its overcoming for the purpose of artistic creation. The individual jazz musician faced an existential challenge to which jazz provided an artistic process of engagement: subjective truth as a pathway of rebellion, racial consciousness, and the defiance of victimization; persistent striving, in that the process involved the intertwining of self, art, and style—how it is said as an expression of experience versus the what of proper musical form. Just in the past generation, African-American scholars have begun to theorize an "Orphic mode" of self-affirmation and self-validation in modernity through "the agency of sound" in African-American music, especially as it influenced literature more generally.[97]

The history of twentieth-century arts and popular culture will remain elusive and incomplete without an understanding of the model and impact of African-American musics. As musicologist Susan McClary once laid out this achievement, "one of the most important facts about culture of the last hundred years . . . [is] that the innovations of African-Americans have become the dominant force in music around the globe—universal in ways [even] Kant could not even have begun to imagine."[98] Jazz and blues are the foundational existential genres of these innovations.

Figure 32. Cool Val Xavier (Marlon Brando) and hip Carol Cutrere (Joanne Woodward) shake up a small Mississippi town in Sidney Lumet's existential film, *The Fugitive Kind* (1960).

10

Hip versus Cool in *The Fugitive Kind* (1960) and *Paris Blues* (1962)

Sidney Lumet's *The Fugitive Kind* (1960) represents existential cool as a myth for rebels—that is, a myth for activating the potential for social change, one consciousness at a time. An often overlooked film in Brando's oeuvre, *The Fugitive Kind* features a hip woman and a cool man at large in a small racist Southern town (fig. 32). Based on Tennessee Williams's play, *Orpheus Descending*, the film reveals how much existentialism had penetrated American intellectual and artistic life. The "fugitive kind" is an American rebel version of either Sartre's free man as defined in his play *The Flies* (1943) or as akin to Camus's Dr. Rieux in *The Plague*. Significantly, Lumet's next project was directing Camus's play *Caligula* on Broadway with music provided by the Beat jazz musician, David Amram. The film was shot on location in the small town of Milton, New York, where Brando was so mobbed by fans the cast feared for his safety and their own.[1]

Hip and cool are here set against a very *square* postwar background, rural postwar Mississippi. The protagonist is a drifter musician carrying the name of two saints: Valentine Xavier (Brando) wears a snakeskin jacket and carries a guitar he calls "my life's companion" slung across his

Figure 33. Val Xavier (Brando) listens to a sentence of exile from a New Orleans judge and promises his years of hedonism are at an end.

back. In the opening scene, a contrite Xavier stands before a judge in New Orleans for charges of vagrancy and disturbing the peace—for playing his guitar on the street for a party. We learn that his years in New Orleans were spent indulging his dark side: parties, substance abuse, playing for others. Xavier assures the judge he is now through with his hedonistic life and promises to leave town if freed (fig. 33). He drives north in the pouring rain, and his car breaks down in a small, unnamed racist town where he upsets the social order by liberating (and arousing) the town's oppressed and repressed women. In existential terms, the film begins with Xavier rejecting Kierkegaard's "aesthetic stage" (hedonism and pleasure) to embark on the deeper "ethical stage" (purpose and self-validation).[2]

The film also sets up Xavier as a "white Negro," a man heavily influenced by African-American music and culture: in the opening scene, he proudly shows the judge the many engraved autographs on his battered guitar—Bessie Smith, Leadbelly, Blind Lemon Jefferson, Woody Guthrie, Jelly Roll Morton, King Oliver (fig. 34). Xavier embodies the existential spirit of blues and jazz as he improvises a new stage of life. Xavier's cool ancestry descends directly from blues musicians and ramblers—the South's persecuted transient agents of freedom—as it partakes of both Beat rambling (Guthrie, Jelly Roll Morton) and what might be called

Figure 34. Val Xavier (Brando) as troubadour and "white Negro" holding a guitar with the prop signatures of Billie Holiday, Bessie Smith, Leadbelly, Woody Guthrie, W. C. Handy, Louis "Satchmo" Armstrong, Ma Rainey, and Hank Snow.

the blues counterculture (Bessie Smith, Leadbelly).[3] To the town's white male elite, Xavier is unfathomably Other. He is also a sexual magic stick, a walking phallus: a snake in the garden, a musician in the backroom, an outside instigator. The hypersexualized aspect of the white Negro is here in Brando's black-and-white countercultural hybrid. Albert Murray once called this racialized aspect of the postwar white imagination the "hot fat injection" as based in the fear of miscegenation and represented by "the cult of Marlon Brando (which includes Brando himself)."[4]

Val Xavier is thus figured here as a culturally mixed-race *black-and-white* Orpheus descending with a battered guitar in his hand and the dominant society's hellhounds on his trail. He is a secular fallen angel, a Whitmanesque version of a Christ figure, a white symbol of civil rights—a tormented white bluesman and ethical rebel loner. Carrying the symbolic name of a tortured saint, Xavier suggests these questions: *Who is this man? Are you interested in his inner torment and quest for meaning and social change?* Will it alter your individual consciousness?

The example of Xavier's rebel individuality threatens the white male elite from the first night he arrives in town and is given shelter by the sheriff's wife, Vee (Maureen Stapleton). She allows him to sleep in a makeshift prison cell in their house, a cell emptied only that very night by an escaped black prisoner who has just been hunted down and killed by the sheriff's posse. Here again, Xavier symbolically displaces the danger of the black man—as a white Negro—and he, too, is caged for the night. Yet before locking him up, Stapleton shows him her paintings, which feature dynamic, violent bursts of color in pastoral landscapes, Gothic churches and upthrust crosses towering over dark fields of cotton. Later in the film, Xavier helps her understand the motivation for these paintings:

> X: Before you started painting, it didn't make sense [*he intones quietly*].
> M: *What* didn't make sense? [*she wonders*].
> X: Existence [*he whispers*].
> [*She pauses, stunned.*]
> M: That's right. [*She shudders.*]
> X: Lynchings, beatings [*he continues in a deep, low whisper*], you've been a witness and you know. [*He pauses.*] We both seen these things and we know.

Her mouth hangs open: she has seen the light through the illumination of this secular double saint, Valentine Xavier.

The film's hipster is Carol Cutrere (Joanne Woodward), a rara avis in postwar Hollywood film: a hip female character equal to the cool man she chases. A smart, sharp, feisty eccentric, Cutrere searches for thrills full time. She is a former "church-bitten reformer" but now joyfully taunts the town's squares, wearing her sexual desire on her sleeve. A progressive bohemian, Cutrere drives a roadster, dresses like a thrift shop Southern flapper, and cares for the town's lone black figure (Uncle Pleasant, a conjure man). Cutrere embodies the joie de vivre of the Beat generation in defiance of the nearly fascist control of the town's white male elite (fig. 35).

Brando plays Xavier as a tormented soul—furtive, homeless, pursued by demons, a fugitive searching for a peaceful harbor. Xavier is alienated, ethical, inner-directed. He doesn't care what anyone thinks about him and falls in love with his employer, an older, unhappily married woman, Lady Torrance (Anna Magnani), who runs the local general store since her husband is bedridden. The budding romance of Xavier and Lady is the main storyline of the film and sets up the primary conflict: her crippled husband is the leader of a white supremacist group akin to the Ku Klux Klan or a White Citizens' Council.

Cutrere is a hip, Beat woman who defines herself *against* squares; she must act in spite of others to feel alive and know her identity. In contrast to Brando's lizard-like cool, Woodward is a pinball waiting to be popped into play on a more complex board or, at least, into a society where she can make a difference. Cutrere recalls meeting Xavier at a party in New Orleans and she stalks him like a new species, eroticizing this rebel with the hope of joining forces in collusion. Cutrere survives as a rogue agent in the town only because she is the scion of the town's wealthiest family; yet by decree of her older brother and the sheriff, she can neither drive in the county nor sleep inside the town limits. So she hangs at the juke joints and roadhouses, drinks, screws around, and defies the local authorities.

A key exchange in Williams's play delineates hip from cool. When Cutrere enters Lady's general store to talk with Xavier, two older women stop their conversation. Cutrere asks Xavier what they've been saying about her.

Figure 35. Carol Cutrere (Woodward) salaciously brags to a friend about being with "that New Orleans boy" at a Mississippi roadhouse.

X: Play it cool [*he says quietly*].
C: I don't like playing it cool! What are they saying about me? . . .
X: If you don't want to be talked about, why do you make up like that?[5]

Cutrere possesses the defiance of a cool rebel but channels this energy into hedonism: she thrives on an enthralled or spiteful audience. Xavier remains unmoved by her high-octane hip enthusiasm, preferring the older, exotic Magnani in the role of Lady, whose broken spirit resonates with his own. In a noirish scene at a local cemetery, Cutrere gets on her knees to show her appreciation, and yet Xavier lifts her off the ground, rejecting even this offer. A bright light shines behind them as if suggesting a higher philosophical mode of action. Existential cool sometimes entails the sacrifice of basic desires.

Going Juking with Hollywood's Only Female Beat

The key scene that highlights Cutrere's hip vitality in contrast to Xavier's existential cool occurs at a roadhouse, and it is one of the most significant (and overlooked) scenes of Beat rebellion in film history. After Xavier and Cutrere get drinks, some instrumental rhythm and blues plays on the jukebox while Cutrere makes a phone call. The lesbian owner walks up to Xavier and asks them to leave on the orders of Cutrere's brother, who sits at a table, an embittered drunk. Cutrere refuses at first, but Xavier insists and guides her to the door. "I'm going, I'm going," she says to the owner while glaring at her brother. "There are plenty of other jook joints on the Highway. Mr. Xavier," she says, turning to Brando, "would you like to go jookin'?"

Then an older barfly asks, "What do ya mean, *go jookin'*?" What follows is an impressive improvisational meditation on the word "jook-ing"—or "juking"—a Southern term for going dancing or clubbing or just drinking in "juke joints." Woodward gives a bravura ninety-second answer as she walks the perimeter of the bar and flirts with several men. It takes place in one long shot and, along with a raucous rhythm-and-blues saxophone, the backdrop accentuates the continuous energy flow sought by postwar hip seekers. In addition, "juking" and "jukebox" and "juke joints" are all African-American vernacular terms—originally descended from the Wolof language—and represent another influential aspect of postwar black culture.[6]

"What's *jookin'*?" Cutrere bumps the man playfully. "That's when you get into a car . . . and you drink a little bit," she says, and steals an older man's beer, takes a swig, hands it back, "and then you *dr-r*-ive a little bit"—she moves on to the dancefloor and hugs a slow-dancing couple while doing a jig—"and then you stop and you dance a little bit with a

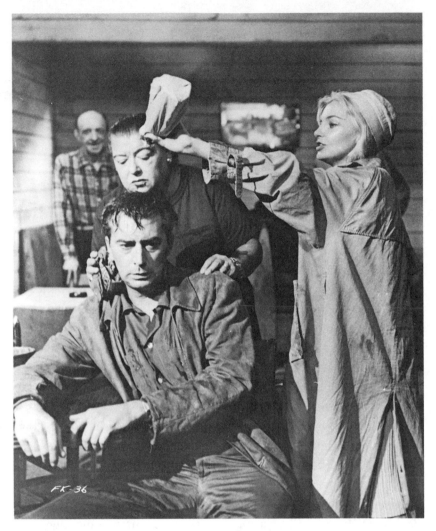

Figure 36. Carol Cutrere (Woodward) pours beer on her brother's head during her bravura ninety-second riff about the joys of "going jukin'."

jukebox." She continues her tour of the bar's denizens. "And then you *drink* a little bit more, and then you *d-r-rive a* little bit more," she says as she knocks off a man's hat, "and [then] you stop and dance a little more to another jukebox." She pours some beer on one man's head and continues; she now has the entire bar enraptured. (See fig. 36.) "And then you stop dancing"—she pushes one man away playfully—"and you just drink and drive." She ruffles a man's shirt, and his date burns her with a hostile gaze. "And then you stop driving"—she pulls up a chair—"and you *ju-u-u-ust* drink." She pauses, drinks from a bottle in a paper bag, becomes melancholy for a few seconds. "And finally you stop *drink*-ing," she yells and throws the beer bottle over her shoulder, breaking the window. There is dead silence in the bar.

"Well, what d'ya do then?" an older man asks.

"Well that depends on who you're jookin' *with*," she yells excitedly and kicks up her legs, her skirt falling open, and a saxophone suddenly explodes as if the view up her skirt has set free the bar's collective desires.

At that moment, her drunken brother stumbles over and slaps her hard across the face. Incredibly, Cutrere slaps him back with equal intensity.

Xavier steps in and pulls her away by one arm (fig. 37) as if she is made of paper. "Can't you see he's drunk?" he whispers to her. "He can take care of himself," Cutrere shoots back straining to land a second shot, her eyes wild with passionate anger. Her brother then collapses to the floor, more in emotional shock from the public slap than its physical force.

"He can't take care of anything," Xavier says. "Come on," he adds, and pulls her toward the door.

Cutrere turns to address the bar as if it is a national assembly: "This country used to be wild," she says. "Now it's just drunk." This is a scene worthy of *On the Road* in its celebration of rebellious hedonism and sexual desire as social critique of a staid, repressed culture.

Cutrere and Xavier then drive away in her roadster in silence and, in the stillness, Woodward's raw, hip energy refracts against Brando's detached cool. Driving into the dark rural Southern night, Xavier asks Cutrere a question that illuminates the contrast between hip and cool at the turn of the 1960s:

> *X*: Why do you make such a crazy show of yourself?
> *C*: [*half joking and with pride*] Because I'm an exhibitionist. [*Pause.*]
>   I want people to know *I'm alive*; don't you want people to know
>   you're alive?
> *X*: I just want to live, I don't care whether they know I'm alive or not.
> *C*: Well, I want to be *noticed* and *seen* and *heard* and *felt*.

Figure 37. Xavier pulls Cutrere away after she slaps her brother in the face and knocks him back into his chair.

This scene is faithfully adapted from the play. Yet it omits Cutrere's key final declaration to "Live, live, live, live, live!"[7]

Fifteen seconds of screen silence follows. The central difference between Cutrere and Xavier—between hip and cool—has been established. Cutrere thinks they are two wild adventurers who should take to the road together. Xavier seeks only a cave to lick his wounds and to become comfortable in his own skin.

In contrast to Carol Cutrere's romanticizing of this charismatic fugitive, Xavier's epiphany in New Orleans was almost Buddhist in nature. He realized his suffering was related to the pursuit of desire and that his hedonism was a flight from ethical consciousness. Now Xavier wants only a place to land and yet he knows he will not find one. Following this scene, he focuses on his relationship with Lady and they fall in love.

The *cool* difference also figures into the film's title metaphor as woven into a speech Xavier gives to Lady (Magnani). The inflection point of their relationship occurs during a short soliloquy when Xavier compares himself to a legless bird that cannot land. Until this moment, Lady thought of Xavier as a drifter gigolo with disarming eccentricities, but now she begins to see him more as a strange angel and her salvation.

Xavier starts off his poetic rumination with an anti-capitalist metaphor: "There are two kinds of people . . . the buyers and those who get bought." Then Brando pauses, paces, shifts the weight to the other hip. "No, there's a third kind," he mumbles. "It is a bird with no legs that has to stay aloft all the time since it literally cannot land. They have to live their whole lives on the wing and sleep on the wind." Brando caresses these words as if it is both Xavier's life story and his own, allowing Lady to bear witness to whatever trauma brought him to his present impasse.

The "fugitive kind" lives in social exile as a self-authorized human being and disrupts unethical social practices wherever he goes. This legless bird is condemned to freedom—in other words, to flying without hope of landing. A fugitive of this kind is literally out-*cast*, a person at large, on the run or on the road, a symbolic criminal fleeing one figurative prison after another. "None of us really ever knows anyone else," Xavier concludes. "We're all doomed to solitary confinement." That is as existential a line as exists in Hollywood film. It is also the central conceit of a distinctively American existential cool: the fugitive kind revises Camus's metaphysical rebel for an American cultural imagination invested in freedom through mobility and rootlessness.[8]

The film then returns to Xavier's role as a white Negro and makes of him a symbol of civil rights and Southern oppression. Lady's husband tells the sheriff to lead a group over to surround Xavier at his job. The posse circles him like dogs, and one man rips Xavier's shirt off. When they are interrupted by two customers, the sheriff takes Xavier outside and tells him to leave town. The sheriff tells Xavier of a road sign at the county line that says "'Nigger, don't let the sun go down on you in this county.' That's all it says, it don't threaten nothing. . . . Well, son! You ain't a nigger and this is not that county, but son . . . imagine that you seen [that] sign." Such signs were still common in the "sundowner towns" of the Jim Crow South. In the play, Williams's stage directions suggest the scene be played "casually, like the performance of some familiar ritual." In other words, the white Southern men threaten Xavier with lynching, the cathartic ritual of white supremacy.[9]

The climax of the film revolves around Xavier and Lady rebuilding her father's wine garden, a symbol of her rejuvenation. Lady's father died in a suspicious fire that burned down the original wine garden fifteen years earlier; bereft, she married her husband for security. On the gala opening day of the new wine garden, she learns her husband set the first fire to kill her father so she would become dependent on him. The same posse sets fire to the resurrected wine garden built by Lady and Xavier.

When Xavier attempts to put out the fire, the sheriff's posse turns fire hoses on him, forcing him backward into the conflagration in a manner foreshadowing events of the civil rights movement. As a sexual rival and an agent of change, Xavier must be eliminated. This lynching ritual has Brando-as-white-Negro as its sacrificial victim.

The morning after the fire, Carol Cutrere stands with Lady outside the burned-down wine garden holding Valentine Xavier's snakeskin jacket as if it is a saint's relic. She takes up his death as an object lesson and provides a short eulogy that harkens back to the end of *High Sierra*: "There's something still wild. Still free in this world."

To be free and cool requires leaving one's repressive hometown (or family) to seek a floating community of rebels. Carol Cutrere is hip in her hometown against the squares; to be cool, she will have to leave and find an objective other than scoring points against her oppressors. Until then, the town is a prison and she is a convict rapping on the metal bars with a tin cup.

The film's message translates Camus's *Rebel* for Hollywood audiences: now it's up to you. *He rebelled . . . now how will you exist?* The question is self-reflexive for Cutrere in this final scene.

Cutrere gets the last word in the film—"wild"-ness—and it echoes out in Beat tones that define the rebel cool of Postwar II. Wildness connotes freedom, the road, animal grace, untamed human passion, even creative destruction. Ginsberg's "Howl" is a tribute to wildness as a necessary element of the search for meaning: to create something new requires destroying order, whether artistic, social, or political. There is also the example of Brando and his motorcycle gang in *The Wild One* (1953). When a rebel says no before knowing why, it may involve a violent or self-destructive act (i.e., taking drugs, criminality) or an explosion of anger against others. In *Jailhouse Rock* (1957), Elvis's girlfriend and manager accuses him of playing romantic games with her. "That ain't no tactics," Elvis drawls, half apologetically. "It's just the beast in me." In the most famous quote from *On the Road*, Sal Paradise confesses that he admires *only* the wild ones. "The only people for me are the mad ones, the ones who are mad to live, mad to talk, mad to be saved, desirous of everything at the same time, the ones who never yawn or say a commonplace thing, but burn, burn, burn, like fabulous yellow roman candles exploding."[10] "Wildness" is the opposite of being tamed through the status quo or the carrot of social mobility. Brando, Elvis, Neal Cassady, Sinatra, Miles Davis—all are wild and untamed. Each echoes forward the central unspoken premise of every cool icon: *You don't own me; you're never gonna own me.*

If *The Fugitive Kind* had been called *The Rebel Kind*, the resonance of cool and existentialism would be even clearer in this striking collaboration of Brando, Woodward, Lumet, Camus, and Williams. Here the secular saint Valentine Xavier rebels and the women of the town exist. The film represents an inflection point of cool as it pivots on the Beat values of wildness and creative madness into the social protest and counterculture experimentation of the 1960s.

Sidney Poitier in *Paris Blues* (1962)

Sidney Poitier would have been a major icon of cool if his confident masculinity did not threaten Hollywood conventions of racial typology and underlying fears of miscegenation. The *New York Times* nearly defined him as cool just after his star turn in *The Defiant Ones* in 1959: "There is a deep-grained integrity about the man that somehow gives his screen image added dimension and the breath of vitality." Integrity, depth, vitality—such qualities combine the relaxed intensity of Postwar I with the wildness of Postwar II. Poitier's acting trademark was "the cool boil," the suppressed dynamite of a "powder keg never exploded," such that "racial frustration" could be marked and yet leave white audiences assured that "blacks would eschew violence and preserve [the] social order." Poitier's blackness made it impossible to correlate his artistic rebellion along the Brando-Dean-Elvis axis and he has little purchase in the dominant public memory of '50s rebellion. Yet *Ebony* magazine named Poitier one of the "25 coolest brothers in history" in their 2008 cover story, "The Genius of Cool," due to his "sleek, self-assured elegance" and his embodiment of what Jelani Cobb calls the "Negro Zen" of the black cool aesthetic.[11]

Poitier's breakout role was as a diffident teenager among juvenile delinquents in an unstable high school in *Blackboard Jungle* (1956). In his first two scenes, Poitier projects a smoldering dissatisfaction in rebel cool style against an untested teacher: cigarette dangling from his mouth, white T-shirt with its sleeves rolled up, each kinetic movement relaxed and stealthy. As his biographer assessed Poitier in this key cinematic moment, "He is, in a word, cool."[12] Glenn Ford plays the idealistic teacher, Mr. Dadier (*doddy*-yay), and the students quickly inflect it to "Daddy-O," the mock authoritarian term for square father figures. Yet Ford soon redirects Poitier's cynical defiance into productive channels, and the black teen's reward is a certain social equality as granted by the humanist teacher. To the credit of both actors and director Richard Brooks, the film manages this intergenerational diplomacy with dignity and without any Uncle Tomming; still and all, it reinforced the limits of black possibility on- and off-screen.

To producer and director Stanley Kramer, Poitier was Brando's only peer with regard to an artistic palette "from pathos to great power," yet there were simply no roles for black rebels in postwar films. Film critic J. Hoberman has called Poitier "Hollywood's version of Jackie Robinson," the emblematic black actor in films *about* race in an integrationist moment. In more blunt assessments of the early '60s, *Variety* called him "a useful Negro" and a *New York Times* columnist called him "a showcase nigger." When Harry Belafonte started a production company in 1959 to create better opportunities for African-American actors, he dismissed Hollywood's sole message of paternalistic assimilation—"where brotherhood always wins in the end"—and invoked Poitier as his main example: "Take my good friend, Sidney Poitier, he always plays the role of the good and patient fellow who finally wins the understanding of his white brothers." Poitier's roles served Hollywood's liberal agenda as a cultural arm of the civil rights movement and his stellar family life enhanced the integrationist agenda. *Variety* singled out Poitier as Hollywood's one-man team on this social issue: "We don't have race films, we have Sidney Poitier films."

Yet in an anomalous film of the early '60s, *Paris Blues* (fig. 38), Poitier played a relaxed bohemian jazz musician just before his most famous films as a black super-gentleman—*Lilies of the Field, To Sir with Love*, and *Guess Who's Coming to Dinner*.[13] In the source novel by Harold Flender (*Paris Blues* [1957]), a working black American jazzman named Eddie Cook enjoys his bohemian life in Paris and struggles with an interracial romance. With this in mind, Duke Ellington signed on to create a score for a film he hoped would reflect the polyglot Parisian community, including its African-American expatriates, gay men and women, and interracial couples. However, the studio disemboweled every aspect of this vision: the producers elevated a minor white character from the novel, Ram Bowen, as a Beat anti-hero and the film's protagonist; one producer decided against interracial romances and cast two couples along racial lines; the early rushes of integrated audiences at the existential caves of Paris were whitewashed to exclude people of color. *Paris Blues* ended up as a formulaic film about an angry young man featuring a white sex symbol (Paul Newman) with a black sidekick (Sidney Poitier) set to a swing-era jazz score by Ellington and featuring Louis Armstrong.[14]

Newman and Poitier play bohemian jazz musicians enjoying Paris until they encounter Joanne Woodward and Diahann Carroll, schoolteachers stretching their prim wings. Newman is a hip trombonist and well-known composer who helps divorcée Joanne Woodward cross over from *squaresville* while Poitier is a cool alto saxophonist who defends his expatriate life against Carroll's accusations of racial apathy. As a subplot, Louis Armstrong plays Wild Man Moore, a jazz legend who mentors Newman and, as well, an Uncle Remus figure played off against Poitier's low-key cool. By film's end, Woodward softens Newman and they come together as a hip couple seeking new adventures: "This little chick and

Figure 38. Sidney Poitier practices for his role as expatriate saxophonist Eddie Cook in *Paris Blues*, 1961.

me," Newman says proudly, "we're gonna make it together big in New York." Meanwhile Carroll compels Poitier to return to the United States to fight for civil rights, ending on a Hollywood major chord: two beautiful actors as cool exemplars of the civil rights movement. In effect, the resonance of the postwar mask had raised consciousness through its critique of normalcy, racial oppression, and American triumphalism such that even schoolteachers in Hollywood films now sought personal and social change.

In many ways, jazz is the subject of the film's first half, and the music breathes the air of bohemian Paris. Newman acts hip, speaks jive, and dismisses the squares. On jazz, he literally echoes Lester Young's musical ideas and slang: "I live music—morning, noon, the whole night. Everything else is just icing on the cake, ya dig?" (Woodward responds: "I dig.") Neither man expresses much interest in the two unhip women at first, and Poitier explains to Woodward why she should find another crush: "You are a day person. We are the night people, and it's a whole different world." The couples start to mesh halfway through the film: Poitier and Carroll take to the streets for lyrical scenes of Parisian romance as if their future together spells an inevitable end to the jazzman's hip life. This gives Poitier an opportunity to display his primary Hollywood role, balancing "mass appeal and political viability." The film sidesteps the Uncle Tomming noted in the novel, where Eddie Cook honors Moore's musical legacy but rejects his minstrelized persona: "Wild Man Moore was . . . a white man's Negro, a handkerchief-head Negro," he thinks in the novel. "Moore could have done so much for his people."[15] When Newman takes advice from Wild Man Moore, there is no sense of jazz's impact, its African-American roots, or its existential protest.

In addition, Poitier has to massage Newman's hurt feelings twice, as if the *white* musician's suffering for his art—*jazz*, that is—trumps Cook's experience of racism. Newman's character, Bowen, is an abrasive, arrogant, charismatic bohemian artist yet he is fairly unconvincing as a jazz musician, due to a failure of imagination on either Newman's part or the director's (Martin Ritt). When Newman mimes his trombone solos, he fakes sensitivity rather than improvisation and shows no awareness of the ensemble or its conversation. In contrast, Poitier's solos are vividly imagined in terms of physical gesture and timing. As a character, Eddie Cook is cool just living in Paris with a good job and away from American racism. Bowen remains a defensive rebel, sensitive and domineering yet beloved by fans and women. Newman plays Ram Bowen as if he is the Fast Eddie Felson of jazz: either he's the greatest young player in the game or this jazz thing just ain't worth his time.

Joanne Woodward is the constant in these two films illuminating hip versus cool (*Paris Blues* and *The Fugitive Kind*) and she alone embodies the female Beat of Postwar II in Hollywood film. In contrast to her role in *The Fugitive Kind*, Woodward here redirects the Beat anti-hero's narcissism, and the couple wind up together as lovers, returning to conquer New York City. The happy ending reprises the couple's romantic pairing in a rural Mississippi setting in *The Long, Hot Summer* (1958). In both films, Newman is the iconoclastic rebel and Woodward the dissatisfied independent woman inflecting the rebel-girl role of the 1950s toward greater partnership even as she eroticizes the rebel. In both films, this real-life married couple walk into the cameras in their final shot as if going off to trail blaze a cooler future.

In effect, at film's end, Newman and Woodward are hip, while Poitier and Carroll are cool. Poitier's cool artistic persona may be obvious to contemporary audiences but he remains locked out from the rebel canon. "I am artist, man, American, contemporary," Poitier said defining his self-image. "I wish you would pay me the respect due." In *Paris Blues*, Poitier channels his frustration into charming Diahann Carroll, who in turn, radiates an alluring maturity and elegance. Poitier and Carroll were in the midst of a torrid long-term love affair at the time, and their fraught desire shines through the elegant couple's pleasures and fights in *Paris Blues*. In fact, it may be the first film in Hollywood history to end with a long passionate kiss by a black couple. Their intelligent conversations about artistic and personal choices—bohemian satisfaction versus racial obligation—constitute a high point of postwar adult black romance and sexuality. In consonance with her character, Diahann Carroll actually hosted fundraisers to support the Student Non-Violent Coordinating Committee (SNCC) in her Greenwich Village apartment during the filming of *Paris Blues*.[16]

In playing Eddie Cook, Poitier's love of Parisian freedom makes an evocative bookend to Miles Davis's dilemma of 1949. More than a decade later, American society was still held hostage by its racial caste system and choices along the Hollywood-Washington axis. For example, when Sammy Davis Jr. campaigned with his friend Frank Sinatra for John F. Kennedy during the presidential election of 1960, both Sinatra and Kennedy pressured him to defer his marriage to his Swedish fiancée (May Britt) until after the election to prevent racial backlash; Davis acquiesced and yet he was still dropped from the inaugural program. Miscegenation still scared the pants off American politicians and audiences (and voters) in Southern states, and Americans more broadly. It was ingrained in the political forces arrayed against social equality.[17]

In 1960, Poitier was the only A-list African-American actor in Hollywood: he was "the first of his race to reach the top of the Hollywood ladder solely on the basis of acting ability," one film critic wrote meaning, in particular, that "Poitier does not dance or sing." Yet Poitier shrugged off his achievement as important only if it made social equality and African-American success possible. This, too, recalls Camus's value on rebellion-for-others rather than fame or personal success. Poitier realized many blacks of the time saw in his success "a certain kind of extension of themselves in terms of . . . their hopes and dreams," a variation on the *West African* sense of cool, the relationship of the individual to the spiritual morale of the community. Yet in Poitier's own mind, he was just a working-class cat working hard in his artistic field. "As I see myself, I'm an average Joe Blow Negro. As the cats say in my area, I'm out there wailing for us all."[18]

Here again is jazz's contribution to postwar cool. The idea of "wailing for us all" roots Poitier's rebellion in song and individual voice, in solo and nonverbal protest, in defiant rebellion with community intentions.[19]

Poitier finally had a chance to remove his mask of cool in Lorraine Hansberry's *A Raisin in the Sun* (1961), a film with an all-black cast. As Willie Lee Younger, he describes his Uncle Tomming as a chauffeur to his mother, but at home, unmasked, the audiences sees and feels his frustration, naïveté, shame, and anger, an actor "lithe and electric" in his everyday life. In revealing this frustrated search for social mobility to unaware white American audiences, Poitier "emit[ted] the lightning of an angry, violent man who dreams of smashing the chains of his economic enslavement," the *New York Times* observed at the time.[20]

In both postwar phases, cool was an artful, suppressed violence—a cultural concept emitting an underground pulse. Poitier's artistry and supernatural composure seem even more impressive in retrospect, given current Hollywood racism. Poitier was the first African-American nominated for best actor in a leading role (*The Defiant Ones*, 1958) and the first to win it five years later (*Lilies of the Field*, 1963). No African-American was nominated again in a leading role until 1999, thirty-six years later.

Figure 39. Lorraine Hansberry at home, 1960 (National Portrait Gallery, Smithsonian Institution. © David Attie).

11

Lorraine Hansberry and the End of Postwar Cool

Lorraine Hansberry remains mostly known and misunderstood as the author of *A Raisin in the Sun,* a play itself misunderstood as a paean of middle-class aspirations.[1] After her tragic early death of pancreatic cancer in 1966, her husband and executor, Robert Nemiroff, collated Hansberry's plays, essays, and letters into an influential book and theatrical production called *To Be Young, Gifted and Black*, after a phrase she invoked in an early speech for civil rights. *To Be Young, Gifted and Black* was then the longest-running off-Broadway play of 1968–69 and a national bestseller. Her close friend Nina Simone wrote and dedicated the song "To Be Young, Gifted and Black" to Hansberry, her political mentor; Aretha Franklin made it the title track of an acclaimed, iconic album of black consciousness three years later. Inexplicably, there is no major biography of Hansberry a half century after her death, and she remains little more than a footnote in historical and artistic analyses of the postwar era or the 1960s.[2]

Hansberry was cool on her own terms: she was an ethical rebel loner and public intellectual with a singular artistic vision. She wrote the text for *The Movement* (1963), a book-length photo-essay focused on the

work of (and in collaboration with) the Student Nonviolent Coordinating Committee. She wrote the first anticolonialist play by an American, *Les Blancs* (*The Whites* [1961])—in response to Jean Genet's *The
Blacks*—a work too radical to be produced for a decade. She wrote the
first two-hour TV drama on slavery, *The Drinking Gourd* (1960), which
was canceled in anticipation of lost advertising and Southern pressure.
She wrote short plays attacking existentialism as a form of literary paralysis and an acclaimed Broadway play about the political paralysis of
white bohemians, *The Sign in Sidney Brustein's Window* (1964). To reread *Raisin in the Sun* now is to find an ensemble play shot through with
social protest: it contains thematic conflicts with regard to feminism,
class consciousness, Uncle Tomming, Beat Generation self-expression,
gender politics, African revolution, segregation, and social inequality.
Raisin was the first Broadway play by an African-American woman, and
her screenplay for the 1961 film was a first as well.[3]

As a playwright, civil rights activist, and feminist, Lorraine Hansberry represents the end of existential cool and the onset of a period
of participatory social change often just called "the '60s." Born in 1930,
Hansberry considered symbolic individual rebellion and artistic alienation empty by the mid-1950s. "I am of the generation which grew up
in the swirl and dash of the Sartre-Camus debate of the postwar years,"
she wrote, and reflected that her close friends yearned for Communism,
settled for nihilism or "turned to Zen, action painting, or even . . . Jack
Kerouac." Her work repudiates political passivity and serves as a clarion call for social protest; she had no use for romanticizing the rebel.
To Hansberry, even "[the] Koestlers and Richard Wrights . . . left us
ill-prepared for decisions . . . about Algeria, Birmingham or the Bay of
Pigs."[4] A bisexual woman married to a Jewish man, she was not beholden
to any single ideological position: she was an old-school humanist with
her eyes on the prize of social change. A true public intellectual during
the civil rights movement, Hansberry's writings and civic engagement
with regard to race and gender make her an overlooked postwar cultural force.

Hansberry called out the Beats in particular for creating a hollow
rebellion full of gratuitous pleasure without political objectives. "I am
ashamed of the Beat Generation," she told a college audience in 1961.
"They have made a crummy revolt, a revolt that has not added up to

a hill of beans." She considered their literary works a distraction, and their artistic circles had "proven no refuge for true revolutionaries. I accuse them . . . of having betrayed Bohemia and its only justification."[5] For Hansberry, all artistic statements needed to aspire toward political consciousness without overt ideological content. In other words, true bohemian life could only be purposeful as an urban garden for nurturing such ideas. Her artistic heroes were playwrights—Shakespeare and Seán O'Casey, whom she called "[a] warrior against despair and lover of humankind."[6]

Hansberry's cultural politics were equally influenced by the unlikely pairing of Simone Beauvoir and W. E. B. DuBois, as both informed her then-radical positions on race and gender. She called *The Second Sex* "[the] work which has excited and agitated me more than any other single book that I can recall out of my adult experience." She read it while living in Harlem, where she quickly became an editor for Paul Robeson's *Freedom*. She was DuBois's research assistant for one of the first seminars on African history and prepared some of his lectures. She made clarion calls for racial and gender equality, met and conversed with Malcolm X, and famously told off Attorney General Robert F. Kennedy in an integrated room full of experienced activists. She was a public voice for civil rights and an early supporter of gay rights; her best friend was James Baldwin.[7]

Hansberry even openly debated—and rebuked—Norman Mailer for his racial ideas in a 1961 exchange in the *Village Voice*, unearthed here for the first time. In respectful essays, she called out Mailer for making an abstraction of an entire people and for the irrelevance of his primitivism, especially in light of the wave of anticolonialist revolution that made 1960 "The Year of Africa" at the United Nations. Mailer was so impressed with Hansberry he offered to debate her and Baldwin at Town Hall in New York with all proceeds to be donated to the legal fund of the Freedom Riders.[8]

Hansberry's relation to postwar cool is fourfold. First, she rejected the individual male rebel anti-hero as a politically impotent stance and instead supported literature that raised political consciousness. Second, she rejected Beat and existential cool, then called out by name Beckett, Camus, Mailer, and Richard Wright as artistic failures. Hansberry used the term "social artist" to define herself as a writer and rejected works marked by "all this Camusian guilt." Third, she rejected the white male romanticizing of black culture and tagged their discourse as "the new paternalism" since it lacked any real exchange with African-Americans themselves. And yet, she suppressed her early left-wing politics and writing—and her homosexuality—to cut a less controversial public figure (much like Betty Friedan). Fourth, her body of work is equally divided between the power dynamics of race and literary responses to existentialism. Since the intersections of these aspects of her work are so little known, I will examine each aspect in turn.

The Making of an Organic American Rebel

Hansberry's intellectual and artistic development in the Harlem of the 1950s was in marked contrast to the legendary bohemian community of writers, actors, and jazz musicians five miles south in Greenwich Village. Her class consciousness had its origins on the South Side of Chicago where her father was a successful Republican businessman, yet life there remained segregated and circumscribed. "I was known as—a 'rich girl' . . . [and] my mother sent me to kindergarten in white fur in the middle of the depression; the kids beat me up; and I think it was from that moment I became—a rebel."[9]

She grew up within the struggle for social equality and civil rights. Her father, Carl Hansberry, was a college-educated Republican businessman and the secretary-treasurer of the Chicago National Association for the Advancement of Colored People (NAACP) in the late 1930s. He was the plaintiff in two important cases that struck down restrictive racial covenants in housing, including *Hansberry vs. Lee* (1940), a key legal precedent for *Brown vs. Board of Education*. DuBois and Langston Hughes were frequent visitors to the Hansberry home. Her uncle, William Leo Hansberry, was a scholar of African history and a professor of Africana studies whose students included future African leaders Kwame Nkrumah and Nnamdi Azikiwe. (There is even a college named after him at the University of Nigeria.) In short, Hansberry grew up within a counternarrative to American triumphalism and Western dominance yet placed herself within an insurgent artistic tradition of authorship.

Hansberry attended the University of Wisconsin for two years but left due to boredom and, a short time after, sent an enthusiastic letter to a college friend of her life in Harlem. She was writing short articles for left-wing newspapers and "all the little journals of the working-class" while working as a typist and receptionist. In effect, Harlem provided the education she desired: "See only foreign movies, no plays hardly, attend meetings every night, sing in a chorus, eat all the foreign foods. . . . [I] go for long walks in Harlem and talk to my people about everything on the streets, usher at rallies, make street corner speeches in Harlem." Her racial consciousness was already so pronounced she was making "street corner speeches" like Malcolm X and writing articles about oppressed African-American women. She concludes the letter with charismatic verve: "Spirit: Happy and defiant."[10]

The FBI opened a file on Hansberry in 1952 due to her left-wing activities—her editorial work for Paul Robeson's journal *Freedom* and her attendance that year at the Intercontinental Peace Congress as a delegate for the *Daily Worker*. She is described as "active in various Communist front groups," such as the Labor Youth League and the People's Rights Party, and the file notes her association with the *National Guardian* and *New Challenge* magazine. She taught "Public Speaking for Progressives" at two schools considered Communist fronts, the Jefferson School and Frederick Douglass Educational Center. Hansberry probably considered herself a Communist (or at least a fellow traveler) until 1957 or so, and FBI reports on Hansberry continued for the rest of her life.[11]

For *Freedom*, she wrote articles calling for realistic representations of African-American life in Hollywood films and for a series on "the history of the Negro woman." She often indicted the mainstream media for its ignorance of non-white American lives. In one article, she asked rhetorically, "What is it exactly that we Negroes want to see on the screen?" She then suggested three changes for Hollywood studios. First, create films that showed black Americans as "a people who live and work like everybody else, but . . . must battle fierce oppression to do so." Second, produce more social-issue films about racism so "the world knows who our oppressors are and what lies at the root of their evil." Third, hire directors who create films for "our young writers and actors" to represent African-American culture and give "expression to our sorrow, songs and laughter, to our blues and our poetry." In effect, these are the three things for which *Raisin* was most celebrated.[12]

As a measure of her growing intellectual confidence in 1956, Hansberry responded combatively to the *New York Times* coverage of the

Montgomery Bus Boycott in a published letter to the editor, "What's New about the 'New Negro'"? Countering the newspaper's claims to the genealogy of King's nonviolence—"Gandhi and Jesus"—Hansberry claimed his "methods [were] founded upon a historical tradition of . . . Negro leaders like Frederick Douglass and W.E.B. Dubois." She rejected the newspaper's term "the New Negro" in three distinctive ways: by situating it in the slave trade—"the New Negro actually arrived in 1619 on the first slave ship"; by creating a long narrative from slave rebellions to the "fifty thousand people in Montgomery"; by rejecting the self-serving white "myth of 'endurance' [passivity] of colored folk the world over." She placed the boycott in line with the "rise of . . . colonial peoples" (global context) and as part of a long struggle of "agitation and protest in behalf of equality" (national context). Yet Hansberry remained a patriot, convinced the boycott heralded a "[new] epoch of that multi-colored individual—the 'New American.'" This rare vision of a multiracial, multi-ethnic, and multicultural American self harkens back to Walt Whitman and Jean Toomer.[13]

The same year, in an unpublished article called "Notes on Women's Liberation," she spoke of her frustrating experiences when raising the analogous oppression of women and blacks. Even left-wing men and women would always "get defensive" and quickly protest in predictable ways: "these are entirely different questions," one would say, or "you must not equate [the two]," or else, she would be called a man-hater. She always formed her responses in structural terms with an eye toward social change. On race, "few Negroes . . . hate all white people," she wrote, but nearly all of them "hate *white supremacy*." On gender, she wrote that men should be "supremely insulted" that women were thought essentially superior in "compassion, understanding—and of all things love." She wrote with idealistic enthusiasm that men should be embarrassed for being considered inferior in empathy or spirituality. Instead, men should reject such gender polarities as "the great slander of the ages and take our [women's] hands—truly as *comrades*." She imagined a society invigorated by the liberated energies of women: "Freed—who can only guess what stores, what wealth she can give humanity: wealth which will be the product of her centuries of humiliation, exploitation, degradation and sheer slavery." At the bottom she left the following time stamp: "Signed: Lorraine Hansberry Nemiroff 11/16/55."[14]

Hansberry wrestled with her own homosexuality in the fifties: she wrote a few anonymous articles in favor of gay rights for *The Ladder* and meditated on the critical perspective of oppression after reading André Gide's *Corydon* and rereading Beauvoir's "startling chapter on lesbianism." In an unpublished article, she quoted an unnamed "intimate friend" yet seems to be speaking of herself. The friend declares herself "a Negro; a woman; an artist; a communist and a lesbian." From living at the bottom of the social hierarchy, she asserts that "'I am, in one, all the world's most oppressed—or . . . despised—divisions. Jesus!—what I could tell the world!" Here she reveals the costs of suppressing her sexuality and hostility. Hansberry believed that being openly homosexual would result in immediate marginalization of her literature and activism. As she reflected, "In the US I can think of no crucial section of the population which takes the question of homosexuality seriously—either as a problem or a cause."[15]

In autobiographical fragments she gropes toward principled stands yet suffers from typical youthful feelings of powerlessness with regard to gender and nuclear anxiety. In one journal entry, she discussed the social conditioning of women along the lines Betty Friedan would take up seven years later in "this precious society where all women are reduced to the status of home furnishings to be appraised like something to buy on billboards, calendars, theater marquees and in their own bedrooms." When depressed, she found rejuvenation in reading Beauvoir. "And then I read Simone in frustration again and slept. And then I arose and sat and stared and read Simone again and wished that I could drink when it is this bad." Or she would wonder aloud as if a self-appointed spokeswoman: "It is as if I can hear my whole generation crying out: what is to become of us . . . and humanity around us?" This is a question she directly addressed in her post-*Raisin* plays, and there is even a certain Beat romanticism here: "How dare they destroy and mutilate our world . . . and our dream of beauty."[16]

On March 1, 1959, just two weeks before the Broadway premiere of *A Raisin in the Sun*, Hansberry delivered a groundbreaking speech revealing a sudden intellectual confidence and a new convergence of artistic and political ideas, "The Negro Writer and His Roots: Toward a New Romanticism." It was a call to social consciousness among writers of the African diaspora at a conference sponsored by the American Society of

African Culture, an organization that promoted African heritage. This speech makes clear that *Raisin in the Sun* only scratched the surface of a deeper intellectual project built on a foundation of artistic craft, Marxist analysis, and anticolonialist politics.[17]

"The Negro Writer and His Roots" is a manifesto on the writer as social artist. Hansberry argued against the fetishized idea of the romantic individual artist since "all art is ultimately social" and to think otherwise is a form of self-delusion. She considered literature that reified despair or absurdity as both self-indulgent and antisocial, in particular that "there is a uselessness in the beat." She called for an inquiry into the *cause*—"let there be magnificent efforts to examine the sources of that anguish"—for which black writers had a special role. She called on her audience to either disregard or repudiate the nation's "ridiculous money values" and to create a personal objective: what is the "social statement" of your work?[18]

She advised each black writer to repudiate the "white supremacy" of school curricula and instead become "the prime observer[s]" of U.S. society. To start with, there were many white-supremacist narratives to discredit: that "the African continent" was a place to catch slaves and lions; that the Civil War was fought over states' rights and not slavery; that African-American music is about sex and sensuality. For their resources, Hansberry pointed to the vernacular culture of language and music: the African-American English vernacular she simply called "the speech of our people" with its "tones and moods . . . that the African tongue prefers"; spirituals, jazz, and especially blues, "[that] sweet and sad indictment of misery." African-American life should be written about by black writers rather than by Norman Mailer, whom she singled out as someone taken seriously as an interpreter of African-American life and culture. Yet Mailer was using black music to project his own "confused and mistaken yearnings for a return to primitive abandon" when he wrote something ridiculous like "jazz is orgasm." Instead, jazz was "the tempo of an impatient and questioning people."[19]

For Hansberry, these were the battle-tested vernacular strategies of black Americans, the survival techniques of a people used to repel the despair of racial oppression and now, potentially, to assist a languishing Western culture. "*Despair*? Did someone say 'despair' was a question in the world? Well, then, listen to the sons of those who have known little else if you wish to know the resiliency of . . . the human spirit! *Life*? Ask those who have tasted of it in pieces rationed out by enemies! . . . Perhaps we shall be the teachers when it is done. . . . Out of the depths of pain we have thought to be our sole heritage in this world."[20] Hansberry scoffed at nuclear anxiety and the Cold War as the end of Western civilization since she felt instead the rise of the peoples of the African diaspora. In 1959, black music from jazz to blues to soul to rock and roll was providing popular cultural affirmation, just as it had for two previous generations of American youth. Hansberry did not make this connection for this audience, yet it was precisely these cultural resources culled from African-American musical practices that gave expressions of hope and possibility to twentieth-century global youth at moments of existential crisis.

This would be a daunting project for any writer or intellectual, such a "vast task of cultural and historical reclamation." Hansberry laid out a blueprint, linking global oppression to Western history to motivate the writers, linking Roman slavery to the Nazis to the civil rights movement.

> Not only yesterday when Spartacus rose against the Romans. . . . Or when the Jews of Poland rose in the ghetto—but today. . . . Who could match the epic magnitude of fifty thousand Negroes in Montgomery, Alabama, walking their way to freedom, and doubt the heroism of the species? Or the nine small children who insisted on going to school in a town called Little Rock?[21]

To start the project would "reclaim the past if we would claim the future."

Hansberry viewed the white West as a global minority that had lost direction and confidence, opening up an opportunity for black writers and people of African descent to raise new hopes for global humanity. "The truth is that a deluded and misguided world-wide [white] minority is rapidly losing ground," she addressed the writers in her speech. The following year, seventeen African nations declared their independence and the United Nations named 1960, "The Year of Africa." For Hansberry, this was a moment to link "together forever" the people of the African diaspora and here she spoke of the shared "destiny and aspirations of the African people and twenty million American Negroes" five years before Malcolm X. In the speech she referenced an anecdotal conversation with an African-American intellectual who asked why she was "so sure the human race *should* go on?" Her answer to this question was always the same: "[Because] man is . . . the only creature who has . . . the power to transform the universe." Yet she was no naïf full of "idyllic possibilities" based on "innocent assessments" of human nature but, rather, a woman familiar with the postwar era's "racial and political hysteria" (McCarthyism, civil rights struggles), its "lynching and war," its daily life under "the worst conflict of nerves in human history—the Cold War."[22] Yet she retained her faith in civilization (broadly conceived) and believed "the human race does command its own destiny."[23]

For this shift, Hansberry claimed to be "more typical" of the global political temperament of 1959 than most Americans since she offered the advantageous perspective of being "a black woman in the United States in the mid-twentieth century." This rhetorical gesture mirrored Allen Ginsberg's declaration of insurgency in the poem "America" about his personal potential for rebellion as an unemployed gay Communist man: "It occurs to me / I am America." Ginsberg's poem also contained an evocative critique of the Cold War, racism, American advertising and even "Asia . . . rising," such that he drew a line in the sand in the last line: "America I'm putting my queer shoulder to the wheel." For all Hansberry's abstract criticism of the Beats, she never refers to Ginsberg, the main activist of the group, but invokes Kerouac as a straw man. She might have found in Ginsberg a fellow advocate in his affirmative critique of beauty out of materialism, in his affirmation of homosexuality, or in his attempts to build community from poetry, say in "Howl" or "Sunflower Sutra."

That said, "The Negro Writer and His Roots" anticipated black power, the Black Arts Movement, and Malcolm X's rise to national recognition. Each of its many salient points appear elsewhere in Hansberry's work, whether in essays, speeches, plays, or interviews. Yet the speech was not published in any form until 1981, as if it would taint her legacy with its radicalism. After the success of *Raisin*, Hansberry successfully suppressed her Communist activism and instead acted the part of playwright and activist within an apolitical framework.

On the eve of *Raisin*'s debut, Hansberry declared her radical politics through this artistic manifesto for writers of African descent. Yet in her plays, she never indulged polemical speeches or partisan politics. I speculate that she learned this literary lesson through her close readings of

Beauvoir's work. She dashed off rich, perceptive responses to both *The Second Sex* and *The Mandarins*, and in her response to the latter, Hansberry found the germ of *A Raisin in the Sun*.

Hansberry and Beauvoir

In 1956, three years after reading *The Second Sex*, Hansberry experienced a series of epiphanies on reading Beauvoir's *The Mandarins*, a roman à clef of Sartre's circle. She wrote an excited, unpublished four-page letter to her husband that marked her shift from party-line Communism to individual ethical activism. *The Mandarins*, as she wrote to her husband, "just *might* be the most important novel of the entire postwar period." Yet she found it hard to sympathize with the Beauvoir figure (Anne Dubreuilh), a committed activist who has many affairs. Rather she identified deeply with Henri Perron (Camus), an ethical person unable to take sides in the Cold War once he learns of the Soviet gulags in 1945. To Hansberry, here was a portrait of "an honest, militant leftist who . . . understands what he sees and cannot be fooled or misled." In the novel, Perron's dilemma concerns whether to publish reports of the Soviet gulags and labor camps, and thus to betray the Communist party and the French Left, or to publish the reports and let go of the dream of revolution. "For a long time I have known I was unhappy about *being* unhappy about the 'new' USSR," she wrote. "Now all of a sudden I know why." The novel crystallized Hansberry's inchoate feelings about the Cold War. "Henri Perron . . . is me," she wrote.[24]

She then praised Beauvoir with impressive intellectual self-confidence: "this DeBeauvoir chick is a fine intellectual . . . because she questions everything, including reality." Like the best existential works, *The Mandarins* posed questions that forced Hansberry to rethink her own moral assumptions—it was "intellectually brutal," she wrote—and the novel's ideas went to "the very essence of my future ability to go on living in this fucking world." The novel forced her to reflect on her youthful values, which she found to be simply "the vague social mores of my time." Yet Hansberry had enough literary self-confidence to indict *The Mandarins* as a boring novel, entirely lacking in literary style. She judged Beauvoir "a brilliant and genuine intellectual, but . . . no artist at all."[25]

Ironically, the Perron character is based on Camus yet Hansberry was unaware of the connection. Hansberry used Camus as a straw man for her crusade against existentialism as a literature of despair yet bracketed off Beauvoir from its implications due to her revolutionary writings about gender. Yet Hansberry never mentions a single specific work by Camus: she seems to have judged him solely on his Algerian politics. If she had read *The Plague*, she might have found it lined up with her philosophical position of action; if she had read *The Fall*, she might have found it supported her vision of the West's decline and malaise.

In 1957, Hansberry wrote an important but unfinished essay on *The Second Sex* that posed the question of why this radical work—"732 pages of revolutionary treatment of the 'woman question'"—had failed to stir up a women's movement. Even if a woman was "a free and autonomous being" due to independent economic means or attitude, she still "finds herself living in a world where men compel her to assume the status of the Other." She blamed it on many factors: the fear of being perceived by men as hostile to "discussions of motherhood and marriage"; the influence of *Playboy* and other "male sex publications"; the superficial arguments of "the tabloid sheet[s]"; the "alleged 'lesbianism'" of Beauvoir; the relative freedom American women enjoyed. In terms of oppression, Hansberry compared an American woman to "a slave prior to the Civil War," one incapable of understanding "intellectually the nature of his bondage." The community of "American woman intellectuals" was small and unlikely to read about "their problems in the alien idiom of a scholar, [and] a thinker" like Beauvoir. Here she anticipates the need for a Betty Friedan–type to awaken American women and to write of "the problem that cannot be named." If American women refused to fight for freedom and equality, they allowed men to think of "woman as [solely the] body of woman."[26]

Hansberry still considered herself a Communist at this point and declared the oppression of women in terms of class consciousness. Women were "twice oppressed," she told Studs Terkel in a 1959 interview: "Obviously the most oppressed group of any oppressed group will be women, who are twice oppressed."[27] She compared women abstractly to "the Negro, the Jew, [and] colonial peoples" and offered up that it was neither natural for women nor advantageous for society to maintain the current gender order. No person would choose a secondary role by choice and thus "it must necessarily be imposed on her—by force." She predicted that once women recognized their secondary status, they would be "forever in ferment and agitation against their condition and . . . their oppressors." To awaken political consciousness she referred to the success of women's rights activists around the world: "It is woman herself who has wrought the changes in her condition: she has demonstrated and gone to jail; chained herself to the capitol gates . . . for the right to vote, own property, and later[,] divorce laws." Hansberry created a multiethnic historical tapestry of rebellious American women, from "the peasant girls off the ships from Ireland and Poland set loose in the industrial chaos of our social order . . . [to] the black slave woman . . . [to] the Jewish woman finding liberty in picket lines." Hansberry was frustrated with the lack of feminist consciousness in the women she knew and therefore "her emergence into liberty is, thus far, incomplete, primitive even." Yet she girded herself with the knowledge that "Beauvoir insists [what] woman desires is freedom."[28]

In effect, Hansberry's unfinished essay reveals her intellectual understanding of Beauvoir's crucial philosophical concept of *situatedness*. It is the parent idea of postwar subjectivity, inasmuch as each individual is situated in and filters all experience through a specific set of biological and cultural factors; it is opposed to any universal idea of humanness within an implicit norm of the white male. Equally important, situatedness invokes the individual body as the locus of lived experience: each person is born into a certain body, a certain era and environment. "The body is not a *thing*, it is a situation: it is our grasp on the world," Beauvoir wrote in *The Second Sex*, "[and] the world appears different to us depending on how it is grasped."[29]

Hansberry revealed her debt to situatedness in her standard opening for public speeches. She made neither a universalist appeal to equal humanity nor a liberal call for color blindness but rather insisted on the strength of subjective experience.

I was born on the South Side of Chicago. I was born black and female. I was born in a depression after one world war, and came into my adolescence during another. While I was still in my teens the first atom bombs were dropped on human beings at Nagasaki and Hiroshima, and by the time I was twenty-three years old my government and that of the Soviet Union had entered into the worst conflict of nerves in human history—the Cold War.[30]

Race, gender, geography, childhood, politics, historical *mentalité*: Hansberry situates herself within her body, her racial identity, and her country. This is also an early benchmark for declaring the personal as political (and vice versa) in the 1960s.

Hansberry felt it equally crucial to provide the same situatedness (or specific context) for her characters. Writer Julius Lester reflected that Hansberry's work depends on "a thorough probing of the individual within the specifics of culture, ethnicity and gender."[31] In *Raisin*, the Youngers are "a Negro family, specifically and culturally," Hansberry told Studs Terkel, and not only black but a "specifically Southside Chicago [family]," neither from nor equal to a similar working-class family from New York or Detroit. For Hansberry, only by accentuating the specific could writers create solidarity such that "universality . . . emerges from [the] truthful identity of what is."[32]

With regard to the Youngers, Hansberry's four-page letter responding to *The Mandarins* also contained the germ of *Raisin*. The novel crystallized an internal debate she had been having on the political choice of "truth versus expediency." Until reading *The Mandarins*, she was always on the side of absolute honesty. Yet she had recently hurt her mother by "attack[ing] the morality of my brothers," men who were more conventionally bourgeois than Hansberry. She regretted her actions even if "every living word I said was true and my passion . . . justified." Of what value was it to hurt her mother in service to her own political perspective? She recalls this familiar ethical dilemma: "Which is more ethical: to denounce false illusions or to encourage an aging and good human being to enjoy peace of mind?" She resolves to choose the latter and "never [to] say such things to her [mother] again."[33]

Here is the core of *Raisin in the Sun*: How do the children of a strong, conventional mother find a way to rebel against society without being ingrates? In her consideration of this personal conundrum, Hansberry found an original artistic answer by crafting ensemble plays such as *Raisin* rather than works that revolved around a rebel protagonist. In each of her plays, Hansberry lays out the fraught social dynamics of a family or a social group, showing the complexity of each character. Her method forces each member of the audience to extrapolate his or her own reading of the social issues at stake. For example, nearly every critic thought Walter Lee Younger was the play's hero, yet Hansberry's hero was Joseph Asagai, the Nigerian boyfriend of the younger daughter, Beneatha Younger. Asagai is only a supporting character but he voices Hansberry's political and philosophical positions on race, colonialism, and the need for a global perspective. The ensemble play was Hansberry's natural artistic métier: the result was a misreading of *A Raisin in the Sun* for audiences conditioned to consider only the success or failure of a heroic (or anti-heroic) male protagonist.

Rereading *A Raisin in the Sun*

Raisin in the Sun is autobiographical in that a black family moves into a white neighborhood after being offered money to stay in the ghetto. Three weeks after the Hansberrys moved to Washington Park on Chicago's South Side, their new home was attacked by brick-throwing white mobs; one brick nearly hit then eight-year-old Lorraine. In an unpublished fragment, Hansberry recalled a white policeman telling her mother, "Jesus, these people wouldn't have bothered you no-ways if you was in your [own] neighborhood." She recalled anger rising into her mother's voice and she "heard thirty years of being a Negro come out." Her mother asked the policeman why, in the previous three weeks, no one had welcomed her to the neighborhood or even smiled at her on the porch. "I have a good family, my husband works hard . . . my children are clean and well-mannered . . . but they are [just] . . . *niggers* . . . *niggers* . . . *dirty niggers* [to all of you]." Her mother started screaming at the policeman and he responded quietly: "They just wanted to frighten you." Her mother replied: "I can think of no better way to frighten a mother than to just miss murdering her baby." This fragment figures directly into the play's ending as the Youngers are offered a large sum of money to rescind their bid on a house in an all-white neighborhood. "You may tell them that . . . *we are not moving*," Mrs. Hansberry told the policeman. "What else but fight, this is our house."[34]

    Raisin in the Sun is a play about the generation gap featuring a long-suffering matriarch (Mama) surprised at the urgency of her children's frustrations and desires. The Youngers are a working-class black family living in a small Chicago apartment. They are symbolically trapped within the de facto segregation of housing, jobs, and education. Mama's eldest son (Walter Lee) hates his Uncle Tom job as a chauffeur, hangs out at a jazz club, and hopes to open a liquor store to be his own boss. Her daughter (Beneatha) is an atheist feminist black leftist: she claims there is no God, dates an African immigrant intellectual, takes guitar and dance "to express herself," and plans to go to medical school. Mama and her son's wife, Ruth, just want a new home.

The plot of *Raisin* concerns spending the insurance money left by the recent death of the family patriarch. Mama has reserved one-third of the funds for a down payment on a house, and Walter Lee convinces his mother to let him invest the rest in a liquor store rather than keep waiting on The Man. Walter Lee gets hustled out of the money, causing a family crisis since Beneatha needed the money for medical school. An all-white neighborhood association then offers Walter Lee ten thousand dollars. He is sorely tempted but turns down the money in favor of the family's needs and the Youngers move to a neighborhood where they are unwanted. White critics at the time, including Nelson Algren and other major writers, focused only on the ending and criticized its bourgeois aspirations. Yet the critics were silent as to the equally significant thematics of what Robert Nemiroff called "the (then yet unnamed) feminism of Beneatha," or the "purely *class* aspirations" of Walter Lee.[35]

In the scene that sets up the play's central emotional conflict, Walter explains to his mother the psychological oppression of work on the Uncle Tom model. Confused by her son's sullenness, Mama says to him: "I'm looking at you. You a good-looking boy. You got a job, a nice wife, a fine boy, and—"

"A job, Mama, a *Job*?" he brusquely cuts her off. "I open and close doors all day long. . . . I say, 'Yes, sir; no, sir; very good, sir; shall I take the Drive, sir? Mama, that ain't no kind of *job* . . . that ain't nothing at all." Walter hits on an effective image: "Sometimes . . . I can see the future stretched out in front of me—just plain as day. The future, Mama. Hanging over there at the edge of my days. Just waiting for me—a big, looming blank space—*full of nothing*."[36] Mama is familiar with the feelings he describes—emasculation and racism—yet she is disturbed by both his impatience and his belief in the liberation of economic success.

Something has changed. . . . You something new, boy. In my time we was worried about not being lynched and getting to the North . . . and how to stay alive and still have a pinch of dignity too. Now here come you and Beneatha — talking 'bout things we ain't never even thought about hardly, me and your daddy. You ain't satisfied or proud of nothing we done . . . that you had a home; that we kept you out of trouble till you was grown; that you don't have to ride to work on the back of nobody's streetcar — You [are] my children — but how different we done become.

In response, Walter only mutters — twice — the defining phrase of the generation gap: "You just don't understand, Mama, you just don't understand."[37]

This exchange distills the postwar rebellion against the social deference of Uncle Tomming as it produced an existential imperative to create the mask of cool. Nearly a generation after Lester Young's underground cultural revolution, Hansberry transmuted cultural politics to artistic ferment on the Broadway stage that reflected the civil rights movement. Mama's generation of the Great Migration wanted a job and "a pinch of dignity," but her children want full equality and the end of masking in front of white people. For Walter Lee, it is a time to enact the first step of Camus's *Rebel*: to draw a line in the sand to protect what is left of his individual dignity. He can no longer play stupid before "The Man," a term so new his mother has never heard it. "What man, baby?" she asks. "*The* Man, Mama. Don't you know who *The Man* is? . . . *The Man*. Like the guys in the streets say — The man. Captain Boss. Mistuh Charlie . . . Old Captain Please Mr. Bossman." African-Americans created the now-ubiquitous term "The Man" and originally it meant "The White Man," a slippage so obvious it didn't then need to be verbalized.

In the mid-1960s, comedian Dick Gregory paid tribute to the survival skills of those men and women — like Mama Younger — who had to Uncle Tom (and Aunt Jemima) to protect their lives and their families. "Sure, Tomming was good once upon a time. That's how we got here. The old folks knew that was the only way they could raise you. What we call Uncle Tomming today was nothing but finesse and tact then. The old folks had to scratch their heads and grin their way into a white man's heart."[38] A preponderance of oral testimony supports the effectiveness of Tomming in the U.S. South: white Southerners were shocked to find that their seemingly happy maids and servants attended NAACP, Congress of Racial Equality (CORE), or Student Non-Violent Coordinating Committee (SNCC) meetings at night. Tomming was still in force and effect in 1960 until the civil rights movement brought an end to this masquerade.

Hansberry handles these scenes with skill and nuance: she clearly understood the survival strategies of masking, cool, and encoded language as derived from slavery. In her television drama about slavery, *The Drinking Gourd*, the male slave Hannibal explains that acting the fool is a version of work stoppage: "Every day that I can pretend sickness 'stead of health; to be stupid 'stead of smart, lazy 'stead of quick—I aims to do it. And the more pain it give Marster and the more it cost him—the more Hannibal be a *man*!" Here Hansberry equates black masking with black manhood—more precisely, she equates the self-defense of masking with the suppressed potential of black manhood.[39]

As for cool, the only place Walter Lee Younger finds peace is at a jazz club called the Green Hat. Only here does Walter see black men working in public with dignity to create something original and their own. "You can just sit there and drink and listen to them three men play and you realize that don't nothing matter worth a damn, but just being there." He has a special kinship with the alto saxophonist since when "he blows . . . he talks to me," and this is probably a reference to alto saxophonist Charlie Parker. Hansberry loved a short story by Ralph Matthew that opposed Parker (Bird) to the racist politician Theodore Bilbo. At the story's climax, Bilbo and Bird yell at each other from across a valley in an existential battle of racial equality: "Bilbo is on one mountain shouting [at Bird], *you aint* . . . and Bird is on the other, blowing his saxophone, answering in a million notes: *I am*!"[40]

Black Orpheus is rising. In one spirited scene, Beneatha wears a Nigerian headdress and dances to Yoruba folk music on the record player. Walter Lee stumbles in drunk and mocks his sister for listening to such primitive tribal stuff. But then he starts dancing around, as if to an emerging racial and ethnic pride. "I'm digging them drums," Walter says, and then half in jest, he shouts "I am much warrior!" Beneatha encourages him to get past his mockery and he sings, "Me and Jomo . . . That's my man, Kenyatta . . . THE LION IS WAKING . . . OWIMOWEH!"

Brother and sister then trade Yoruba words and Walter shouts like a man rejuvenated: "OH, DO YOU HEAR, MY BLACK BROTHERS!" Walter's wife, Ruth, is shocked to see this side of her husband. "[They are] telling us to prepare for the GREATNESS OF THE TIME!" Walter yells.

When the song ends, Beneatha takes off her African headdress to reveal her new Afro—a "natural," as it was first called. Her bourgeois date for the evening is shocked and calls her eccentric. Beneatha shouts at him, "I hate assimilationist Negroes!" He demands she define the phrase and she does: "someone who is willing to give up his own culture and submerge himself completely in the dominant, and in this case, *oppressive* culture!"[41] Yet Beneatha remains a faithful daughter within her rebellion. When Mama wonders, "Why should I know anything about Africa?" Beneatha explains their African heritage and brings her next boyfriend, the Nigerian Joseph Asagai, to the house.

Walter Lee may be the protagonist of *Raisin*, but Beneatha is in an equivalent state of rebellion, and Mama changes along with them. Beneatha was an autobiographical character—"Beneatha is me, eight years ago," Hansberry told Mike Wallace in 1960—but her own favorite character was Joseph Asagai, the play's "true intellectual."[42] Asagai claims he represents the embodiment of progress in Nigeria, the rise of oppressed peoples mixed with the best of medical science and technology. Yet he foresees in revolution the potential for just as much brutality as liberation: it is Asagai who speaks Hansberry's philosophy of revolutionary independence in a late scene. He predicts to Beneatha that he is just as likely to "be butchered in my bed some night by the servants of empire," as by the revolutionary resistance, "my own black countrymen." He proposes marriage to Beneatha and asks her to return with him to Nigeria. She refuses and yet the proposal itself symbolized a bridge between African-Americans and the newly independent African nations along the political lines Malcolm X called for five years later.[43]

James Baldwin claimed the play's success and power was due to its very accessibility since it brought black audiences to Broadway to see their lives revealed. "I had never . . . seen so many black people in the theater . . . [because] never before, in the American theater, had so much of the truth of black people's lives been seen on the stage." For Julius Lester, Hansberry's gift was to "see the extraordinary in those who society had decreed ordinary. The Younger family *is* black America."[44] One deleted scene illuminated the role of popular black music in the Youngers' everyday life. Walter walks in from work singing the jump blues song "Cherry Red," a hit for Big Joe Turner in the early 1950s. He sings, "Make love to me, Mama, 'til my face turns cher-ry red!" Walter's good humor then so pervades the apartment that Beneatha and Ruth join him in a cappella renderings of popular African-American singers: Ruth imitates Sarah Vaughan and Lena Horne, Beneatha sings and clowns as if she's Pearl Bailey, and then Walter Lee finishes off crooning like Billy Eckstine, Johnny Mathis, and Nat King Cole.[45]

In striking retrospective confessions, three major African-American writers and activists of the 1960s—Amiri Baraka, Julius Lester, and poet Kalamu ya Salaam—each apologized for marginalizing Hansberry's work within the Black Arts Movement. Ya Salaam gave three explicit reasons:

1. She was middle class when the movement concentrated on the "authenticity" of the experiences of poor and unemployed black Americans.
2. She was married to a white man and was therefore automatically rejected. . . . She "co-habitated with the enemy."
3. The truths she told were complex truths that could not facilely be categorized as "black" or "white."[46]

Hansberry's artistic protest was implicit and collective rather than explicit and individual. Ironically, Hansberry was a Marxist feminist and black nationalist well ahead of the radical turn and yet she was considered a middle-class liberal.

It was precisely Hansberry's faith in the adaptive potential of Western civilization that has since marginalized her work. Rare among American writers, Hansberry perceived a direct relationship between the upsurge of colonized peoples and the characteristic malaise of the existentialist and Beat writers. She proposed that a separate war was under way: the battle for African-American social equality as emblematic of all non-white peoples. Hansberry brought the jazz musician's underground fight for social equality through artistic self-assertion—in sound, slang, and stylistics—into mainstream cultural discourse. Her crossover success at the time deepened with her successful adaptation of *A Raisin in the*

Sun into a popular film with Sidney Poitier and Ruby Dee reprising their original Broadway roles. The *New York Times* praised Hansberry's dialogue for its balance of "the heart-piercing eloquence of poetry" with "the bloodletting slash of knives." In no uncertain terms, the reviewer described *Raisin* as the first film to represent an African-American family through "the ring of authentic conversation and the authority of truth."[47]

So why isn't *A Raisin in the Sun* celebrated as part of the postwar cultural upsurge leading into the 1960s, along with "Howl," Elvis, Miles Davis, *The Wild One*, "The White Negro," and *Rebel Without a Cause*? First, Hansberry rejects individual rebellion as gratuitous resentment or a fetish. The play celebrates neither a generational break from society nor the rejection of authority or parents. Despite its mainstream acclaim, most intellectuals rejected *Raisin* as soft-peddled middle-class materialism. Second, white intellectuals found her work too bourgeois while black writers thought it insufficiently revolutionary and assimilationist. Nelson Algren reviewed *Raisin* as a feel-good play for liberals that presented African-Americans as decent, hard-working people lacking in opportunity. Stanley Kauffman charged, in the *New Republic*, that it was "a facile vaudeville of 'true' characteristics intended to prove that 'they' are just like 'us'": that said, he had to admit "the [black] audience around me enjoyed itself thoroughly." African-American critics such as Harold Cruse thought *Raisin* left audiences satisfied that another troubled family had joined the middle class.[48]

Hansberry was confused by the critics focus on the family's bourgeois values and the insistence on more overt social protest. "The fact of racial oppression, unspoken and unalluded to . . . is [shown] through the play," she responded to such claims; she thought the play was fairly persuasive in showing that blacks "are discriminated against brutally and horribly."[49] Finally, the better known film disemboweled the play's African-American cultural materials: producer Samuel Briskin cut every instance of black vernacular ("there are too many 'jive' expressions"), all references to African politics, a scene where Walter Lee Younger watches a black Muslim soapbox orator, and all specific references to discrimination. Instead of the play's black director, Lloyd Richards, the film was directed by Daniel Petrie, and "Columbia [Pictures] whitewashed the Youngers."[50]

Hansberry versus Mailer, 1961

In May of 1961, Norman Mailer reviewed a new play for the *Village Voice*, Jean Genet's *The Blacks: A Clown Show*, and in two essays, provided a little-known sequel to his ideas of race from four years earlier in "The White Negro." Hansberry wrote an essay repudiating the romantic racialism of both authors, "Genet, Mailer, and the New Paternalists," that was gracious toward their intentions. Mailer was impressed enough by Hansberry's style and argument to respond with a third article, conceding a few points while describing both his own and Hansberry's essays as "brilliant, elegant, jazzy, cheap, prideful, solemn, sloppy, and finally—not integrated." This is the only open debate between Mailer and an African-American writer and it was fittingly triggered by a play of masquerade—*The Blacks*—concerning race and colonialism, rage and revolution.[51] Mailer's three articles here also represent one of the last times he wrote about "the Negro" as an abstraction, possibly because Hansberry bested him in the exchange.

Hansberry called Mailer "a good and decent man" and commended Genet for his critique of a sick civilization, but they were paternalistic in their concerns: white men quick to interpret African-American life who had little knowledge of that ethnic group's actual lives. Hansberry's political belief began from an economic standpoint: for African-Americans, a decent life meant getting out of the ghetto to access decent education, health care, job opportunities, and other advantages of middle-class values. As an American author, she was an anomaly in a period in which writers were often anti-bourgeois and equated such values with conformity. Ironically, Hansberry believed in Camus's version of the rebel: that a person draws a line in the sand for reasons of human dignity that later connect to larger social or political rebellion. If there was no larger cause to a person's subjective rebellion, it was simply gratuitous resentment, her implicit charge against white paternalist writers.

"The White Negro" was maligned then and now for Mailer's primitivist association of vitality with black men, in particular through jazz, street style, violence, and African-American slang. Mailer made "the Negro" his symbol of masculine rejuvenation as this figure was implied to be a young black man. Yet Mailer's primitivism was always tied to an existential vision of Western and American decline: white men were failing all over the world, individually and collectively, with black men on the verge of ascending to political power. If the West was failing, resurrection lay with the black oppressed who retained their anger and animal vitality.

In the first essay, Mailer declares the attraction for his generation of attacking obsolete Western values: "So long as it grows, a civilization depends upon the elaboration of meaning . . . as it dies, a civilization opens itself to the fury of those betrayed by its meaning. . . . The *aesthetic act* shifts from the creation of meaning to the destruction of it."[52] Mailer heard a "sentence graven" into the voices of the black actors of *The Blacks*: "'White man, I want to kill you. Ofay, you die.'" For both Mailer and Genet, "the Blacks" were the best potential revolutionary agent to bring down Western civilization. They were affirmative destroyers attempting to make common artistic cause with the oppressed. In effect, Mailer's projection of anger onto African-Americans was a proxy for his own frustration with the complacency and McCarthyism of the 1950s. "As cultures die, they are stricken with . . . mute implacable rage," he wrote, expressing his own anger as if masked in a militant kind of blackface.

Hansberry accused both writers of dressing up their personal revenge fantasies in black drag. Convinced of the "brooding hatred" of people of color, Genet and Mailer were "wedded to the blackness" of outlaw resistance to romanticize social change. To Hansberry, oppression was "not a condition sealed in the loins by genetic mysteries," but a condition of social and political dominance. For Hansberry, the failure of Genet's play was that "the oppressed remain unique . . . the blacks remain the exotic[,] 'The Blacks.'" She indicts the new paternalists both for their attraction to destruction and for setting up blacks as their proxy barbarians. For Mailer, *The Blacks* was an artistic work suggestive of "the central moment of the twentieth century[:] the passage of power from the Whites to those they oppressed."[53] Hansberry finds these racial reversals romantic and unrealistic: "We sense that *they* shall be disappointed if the blacks really do give more attention to building steel mills and hydroelectric plants throughout Africa than to slitting a few hundred thousand . . . throats." And she excoriates Mailer for finding rogue masculinity in a ghetto that African-Americans want to escape: "blues or no blues[,] negroes of all classes . . . want the hell out of the ghetto."[54]

Genet's play features a kangaroo court of blacks—wearing white masks—as they assess the murder of a white woman; it has been called a "postmodern minstrel show."[55] As the play progresses, underlying hatreds, psychological oppression, class performance, and racial identity itself are on trial. In effect, the whites are put on trial for colonialism. For Mailer, its artistic success lay in its provocation as an "explosive play . . . about the turn in the tide, and the guilt, and horror in the white man's heart." Mailer welcomed the coming revolutionary redemption on American soil: "The survival, emergence and eventual triumph of the Negro during his three centuries in America will [be] . . . considered by history as an epic equal to the twenty centuries the Jew has wandered outside. It will be judged as superior if the Negro keeps his salt." Yet Mailer worried that black Americans would choose security and assimilation over struggle and individuality. He despaired of the dissipation of the rogue element of black culture: "The Negro knows he need merely ape the hypocrisies of the white bourgeoisie and he will win." Of the thrill of black revolution, Mailer wrote that "it is possible that Africa is closer to the root of whatever life is left than any other land of earth." Yet he envied even the black squares since their star was rising as part "of a militant people moving towards inevitable and much-deserved victory."[56]

To Hansberry, *The Blacks* was just "a conversation between white men about *themselves.*" The play could not raise consciousness about social equality since it failed to dramatize the lives of real-life black people either in the United States or Africa. Rather, the play simply aired "some of the more quaint notions of white men," representing a failure of imagination and empathy. The white paternalists romanticized "the damned," as Hansberry called them, "prostitutes, pimps, thieves" and other marginalized characters. Each writer simply sent up "a lament . . . much concerned with the disorders of a civilization" and replaced it with the vitality of agents of change at the bottom of the social hierarchy.[57] This artistic choice illuminated their loss of faith in Western culture. In response to *The Blacks*, Hansberry wrote *Les Blancs* as if to show how it's done. *Les Blancs* remains an insightful play about revolution in a fictional African nation that registered the shifting politics of colonial independence through a range of characters.

Hansberry was confused by the primitivism in "the best of [white] men" and of their inability to see people of color within universal notions of humanity. She had an ethnic, *non*-racialized view of the human condition inasmuch as she believed everyone enjoyed sex, music, and spontaneous interaction. She explained that black people often expressed admiration for the sensual vitality of Italians or Puerto Ricans, ethnic groups who "really know how to live." To Hansberry, Mailer had "fabricated . . . [a] mythology concerning 'universals' about twenty million 'outsiders'" without any insider knowledge of that group's everyday life. Mailer did not "call his essay 'The Hipster' or 'The Outsider' or 'We Who Might Swing,'" Hansberry pointed out, "he called it: 'The White Negro.'"[58]

In a humorous exchange, Hansberry accused Mailer of caring too much if blacks thought *he* was Hip (with a capital *H*). Mailer's response was modest and defensive. "When it comes to being Hip, I am not the Ace of Spades. Merely, a decent honorable club fighter. The ten of diamonds. But the middle of the deck can have a long mind and a tough imagination." Then Mailer repudiated Hansberry's implicit warning concerning his knowledge or expertise about African-Americans, but it was a specious claim. "Let nobody tell me I am not entitled to imagine what the Ace of Spades is like." It is any writer's right to imagine a person of any ethnicity or gender, such as Mailer claims here of, say, a working-class black man. Yet Mailer's insistence on using the term "spade" here—he also refers to Hansberry as a "Lady Spade"—presumes an insider status he does not inhabit. As Hansberry notes, Mailer was swept up in his own romantic premise—of the hipster as a white Negro—and "lock[ed] himself in it," enthralled that his "philosophy fitted his premise."

In his second essay, Mailer employed the metaphor of disease to present the hipster as something of a positive cancer. A healthy body will reject authoritarian control instinctively since "cancer is a rebellion of the cells," and the rejection begins with "the entry of the knife"; this is an allusion to "the knife-like entrance of jazz" he attributes to both jazz and violence in "The White Negro." To Mailer, this is the underlying purpose behind the artistic resistance of the rebel: it is "the therapy of the surreal artist, of Dada, of Beat." Rather than contribute "to a collective meaning," there is instead sullen hostility and "the impulse to destroy [which] moves like new air into a vacuum." The philosophical impetus is analogous to the "positive negation" of Camus and Sartre—trying to create a critical mass of cells to exit the dying body politic and start anew. Sartre had written an epic biography of Jean Genet (called *Saint Genet*),

a literary act analogous to "The White Negro" since Sartre publicly admired the notorious hipster gay convict. Mailer thought of Genet as a
minor author and evaluated his literary works as a "fag's art"—as if only
heterosexual men had the artistic courage and toughness to write a cohesive literary work.[59]

For Mailer, the West's decline was due to the state's objective of de-
feating "the animal" aspect of the individual. Here is the essence of what
he variously called the id, the rebel, the hipster, or the Negro. "What is
at stake in the twentieth century is not the economic security of man. . . .
It is, on the contrary, the peril that they will extinguish the animal in us."
Mailer offers the animal's physical grace, instincts, and scrappy survival
skills as *the* human line in the sand against bureaucracy and the death
drive, mechanization and social engineering, concentration camps and
nuclear weapons. "The philosophy of hip" represents Mailer's theory
of individual rebellion such that he champions its role in destabilizing
middle-class complacency.

Mailer's ideal hipster was then embodied in American rebel cool
as it walked the color line: Sinatra's gruff gangster street persona; Elvis crossing over African-American rhythm, physical gesture, and sexuality; Brando's charismatic existential angst; Miles Davis's fierce cool,
romantic lyricism, and aesthetic tensions. In retrospect, Mailer's omission of Elvis from his iconic essay—the most influential white Negro
in history—reveals the intellectual insularity of his argument. Instead
Mailer invokes Frank Sinatra to make an odd argument about the relative *artlessness* of African-American music and culture. He confidently
asserts that "the greatest entertainers in America have been Negro, and
the best of the Whites [such as] Sinatra" built on their musical innovations and performances, "exhibiting their obvious and enormous debt
every time they make a sound." Yet he draws the line at artistic creation.
He compliments black singers for "the richness of intimate meaning they
bring to a pop tune" but does not name a single African-American vocalist, musician, or actor. This lack of recognition—this invisibility—was
the impetus for the mask of cool among jazz musicians at the outset of
the postwar era. If even the most thoughtful of white writers could not
imagine a black person of equal complexity and artistic capacity, then it
creates the cultural logic for jazz musicians to withdraw into heroin and
their own artistic cohort.

Neither Hansberry nor Mailer mentioned that jazz drummer Max Roach, a key figure of the bebop revolution, composed the score for *The Blacks*. Roach's next project was *We Insist!* (1960), the first jazz album to confront the history of slavery from the vantage point of the African diaspora. During the most symbolic track, "All Africa," Roach's wife Abbey Lincoln reads off the names of more than fifty tribes, validating an African heritage that had been suppressed in the Americas and, in turn, resonating with *Raisin* as the return of the repressed in American society.

Hansberry and Existentialism

Hansberry considered the entire discourse of existentialism immature, including the concept of absurdity. She distilled it in a line for her character Sidney Brustein: "The 'why' of why we are here is an intrigue for adolescents; the 'how' is what must command the living."[60] She called out by name Camus, Sartre, Wright, and Mailer for romanticizing a rebel from "the damned" as a figure for social redemption. She considered existentialist narratives to be a form of egotistical self-absorption and yet it was influential enough to require repudiation: she gave special attention to *Waiting for Godot* and Camus. In retrospect, it is significant that many postwar African-American writers considered existentialism little more than sophistry (e.g., Ellison, Murray, Himes, Baldwin).

To Hansberry, existential authors were simply "incapable of imagining *its* frailty"—the frailty of the *absurd*—and so they had failed to provide artistic leadership for everyday people struggling for personal dignity and political freedom. The most important theme for writers was "man's oppression of man," she wrote, but oppression was a universal problem, not "a unique question where white people do not like black people."[61] The works of her literary heroes such as Shakespeare and O'Casey always provided both the resonance of everyday reality and elements of affirmation, both "the recognition of . . . man's defeat and triumph in the face of absurdity."[62] To Hansberry, existential despair was a given daily challenge and writers had a social responsibility to gird readers for battling meaninglessness with artistic illumination.

To Hansberry, *Waiting for Godot* was the ultimate statement of artistic impotence and she wrote two distinct, direct responses to the play. The direct parody was a short story entitled "The Arrival of Todog"

(*Godot* backwards). Two insecure tramps meet on the road, then greet an aristocratic traveler whose servant has run off. One tramp carries a secret folded message: he opens it and reads one word, "Todog." The trio is shocked: it turns out "Todog" is the last name of all three travelers. They cry out in fear; what can this mean? How could they all be related? Why were they named? The message to the reader is clear: if there's no external guidance, and no God to impose moral justice, then they share the same road and the same path. They must solve their own problems without recourse to morality or *deus ex machina*. The final image features the three tramps dancing and singing an existential tautology: "We are here because we are here because we are here." This short, witty piece shares the core of existential thought—that we are alone and condemned to freedom without God or destiny—but mocks its philosophical pretensions as a form of literary (and social) paralysis.[63]

Her second response was a one-act play concerned with the artist's role to combat existential anomie, *What Use Are Flowers?* It is a post-apocalyptic work in which an English professor goes into exile as a hermit in the forest to escape humans and the nuclear age. When he leaves the forest, he finds only a small group of illiterate, feral, mostly white children. While escaping "man's inhumanity to man," he missed the atomic bombs that left these children orphaned and without guidance. He realizes he has a choice, now, between despair and utility: he chooses to teach the children language, fire, art, music, and beauty before he dies. The play combines elements of *Rip Van Winkle*, *Lord of the Flies*, and *Godot*; it achieves a certain poignancy through the man's horror, guilt, and sacrifice. Here is Hansberry's artistic ideology in somewhat didactic form: writers must be social activists who model existential affirmation and artistic resonance. If they do not, a cultural apocalypse awaits. In a 1962 letter, Hansberry described the action of the play as a challenge to the apolitical, escapist hermit to transmit "his knowledge of the remnants of civilization which once . . . he had renounced." She hoped audiences would come away "with some appreciation of the . . . cumulative processes which created modern man and his greatness and how we ought not go around blowing it up."[64]

There has been oppression and gratuitous violence in every era and Hansberry saw nothing special in the nuclear age except that writers were paralyzed by it. "What serious person . . . who has ever studied

the history of the human race can buy this stuff about 'the destructive-
ness hanging over our age' [i.e., nuclear war]. What in the name of God
was hanging over . . . the Crusades? or the Civil War?" The main theme
for writers of all eras was "man's very real inhumanity to man" such
that the writer's job was to present "the infinite varieties of the human
spirit," Hansberry wrote, as it "hangs *between* despair and joy"—this
was "the supreme test" of his or her skill. Hansberry felt it was an authorial obligation to celebrate everyday joy and beauty—as in *What Use
Are Flowers?*—one of the aspects of literature she shared with Kerouac
and the Beats in terms of addressing postwar audiences. The salient difference between Hansberry and the Beats was that she believed in the
writer as a self-conscious social leader rather than a cultural rebel. "The
ages of man have been hell. But the difference was that artists assumed
the hell of it and went on to create figures in battle with it rather than be
overwhelmed by it."[65]

Finally, in a short, fictional vignette written as a dialogue between
"He" and "She," Hansberry attacked the intellectual worship of Camus
among white intellectuals. In the dialogue, *He* is a Jewish-American intellectual living in Greenwich Village and the argument starts when he
mocks *She* (Hansberry) for using black vernacular phrases. "Please don't
get folksy!" he says, shutting her down. "I utterly *loathe* to hear the way
you colored intellectuals are always affecting the speech and inflections
of the Negro masses!" *She* snaps back at his hypocrisy considering how
his "first-generation self" so often spices up "colorless standard English
with old worldisms [in Yiddish]." *She* further defends her code-switching
to the African-American vernacular due to the "literary strength in its
vitality, [and] its sauciness," and for its joyful self-expression among intellectuals who "lovingly use the idiom and inflection of our people."[66]

The climax of the essay involves a debate over Camus and the human
condition. "When are you going to produce a Camus?" *He* asks, forcing
the woman to represent her entire race. *She* responds that Camus is only
the symbol of the white West's self-absorption and its racial hierarchy.
"When Camus writes of man he means[,] subjectively, Western man,
as you do. That is the worst provincialism abroad in the world today."
She then presents a litany of African nations undergoing a revolutionary transformation through "Western industrial achievement" and the
visions of African leaders such as Jomo Kenyatta, Kwame Nkrumah, and

Ahmed Sékou Touré. "Africa and Asia and American Negroes . . . are in their most insurgent mood in modern history." *He* responds by expounding on the achievements of Western civilization, at which point *She* stops listening and begins to drift away on her own thoughts.

She instead tunes into the music in her mind, imagining a hallelujah chorus filled with activists and musicians. Instead of Camus's rudderless ethical vision, *She* considers the affirmative vernacular resources of African-American music and starts tapping her foot to this internal music as created by "a band of angels of art hurling off the souls of twenty million." This is an image of musical tradition built on and within an entire culture, the relationship of individuals to their community, not romantic rebels in exile. The front line of the band of angels included Paul Robeson, James Baldwin, Lena Horne, Ralph Ellison, Harry Belafonte, and Sammy Davis Jr. Then came the folk singers Odetta and Josh White, then "Sister Eartha [Kitt]" and Pearl Bailey. Last came the jazz musicians: "On and on they came, Sarah [Vaughn] and the Duke [Ellington] and Count [Basie] and Cannonball [Adderley] and Louis [Armstrong] himself, wearing the crown that Billie [Holiday] gave him before she died. Oh, yes, there they were, the band of angels. . . . And the golden waves rose from their labors and filtered down upon the earth."[67]

Just as *He* elevated Camus as his intellectual symbol, *She* countered with a black "band of angels" who had created a century's worth of artistic strategies that forced the white West to dance to its tune. In the early 1960s, the soundtrack of this global revolution was African-American music as it came through jazz, blues, gospel, soul, and rock and roll, from Armstrong and Basie and Ellington to Holiday and Adderley. This music was so important to twentieth-century existential affirmation it was white-faced for crossover consumption, from Paul Whiteman ("the King of Jazz") to Benny Goodman ("the King of Swing") to Elvis ("the King of Rock and Roll"). This is what Paul Gilroy means when he refers to African-American musics as "the counterculture of modernity," a counter (as well) to white writers like Mailer, who still viewed it through a veil of primitivism. These were modernist, innovative, Afro-Western forms created by self-conscious social artists in rituals of community leadership. Hansberry lists the musicians since they, too—as much as the writers—embody her ideal of the social artist.

The Sign in Sidney Brustein's Window (1963)

Hansberry's second Broadway play remains largely unknown and yet *The Sign in Sidney Brustein's Window* (1963) was as radical in its way as *Raisin,* and not just because it featured a nearly all-white cast. Actress Shelley Winters declared simply: "It is not a play *about* our time . . . it *is* our time." The play revolves around an extended family in Greenwich Village—a couple, their intellectual friends, and the wife's sisters—and all the characters are trapped or paralyzed within their own ideological boxes.[68]

Sidney Brustein is a Jewish intellectual living in Greenwich Village who slowly realizes the paralysis of his existential withdrawal and eventually decides to manage a local political campaign to reconnect to social goals. Before this epiphany, he assumed "the system" was rigged and immutable so he found pleasure where he could, dressing up his wife as a simple, mountain girl or praying with his liberal friends to "Father Camus."[69] One night at the Brusteins, they all gather to invoke "absurdity" as if it must be exorcised: "Oh, who's afraid of Absurdity! Absurdity! Absurdity! Who's afraid of Absurdity!" three characters sing. "Not we, not we, not we!" Brustein takes pride in his tolerance and hipness, and through him, Hansberry indicts bohemian elitism and any abstract ideal of rebellion.[70]

Hansberry expressed her hostility to Brustein's hip elitism by giving the best speeches on the theme to the play's sole racist character, an uptight white middle-class suburban wife named Mavis. In a climactic scene, Mavis tells Brustein that her husband has been having a long-standing affair and she has had one herself. Sidney is shocked by her sexual tolerance. Mavis responds, "Don't you know, Sidney? Everybody is his own hipster." Mavis suggests she might experiment with new beliefs if shown more compassion by the progressive rebels; she wonders why hip people harbor so much enmity for squares trapped in social conventions. "How smug it is in bohemia," she begins; if she can't "expect understanding from artists" and intellectuals, where would she find it? Certainly not in traditional religion, Mavis points out as she indicts Sidney and the existentialists, "since you have all so busily got rid of God for us."[71]

Hansberry turned a mirror on the liberal left, and her husband sent this report of the audience: "It is a play for [real] people. They come, they laugh, they take sides, they participate: it is their play and it speaks for them. . . . Let us hope now that the intellectuals surprise us with the depth to rise to their level."[72] A few critics loved it but most were baffled as to how to categorize the play or communicate its complexity. However, the night it was to close, a week after opening, Broadway veterans produced a theater miracle when they refused to leave; right then and there, they began to raise funds to keep the play going. The group was a who's who of the theater: Marlon Brando, Sammy Davis Jr., Mel Brooks, Lillian Hellman, Mike Nichols, Ossie Davis and Ruby Dee, Paddy Chayefsky, and Arthur Penn. This group took out full-page ads in the *New York Times* testifying to a play that evoked visceral responses from audiences, and their efforts kept the play on stage for nearly three months.

Raisin and *Brustein* have more in common than meets the eye. The Youngers are trapped in a small apartment by a system of bias and economic oppression; the Brusteins are intellectuals trapped in a small apartment within their own alienation and narcissism. *Raisin* ends with the implied political awakening of African-Americans in general and Walter Lee Younger in particular. *Brustein* ends with the political reawakening of a disaffected liberal along with three sisters trying to shake off the psychological oppression of patriarchy.

If bohemians and artists were truly hip in the jazz or streetwise sense—aware, tolerant, open to alternatives—their identity would not depend on a reverse elitism based on mocking the squares or making straw men of bourgeois conventions. If Hansberry made straw men out of Kerouac and Camus for her intellectual arguments, it was not out of a sense of superiority or reverse racism. Rather, she flipped the script of cultural entropy toward a surging collective rebellion among black Americans that she hoped would undo the legacy of racism and redeem American ideals.

In effect, the cultural rebellion of the postwar era helped generate the conditions for political protest and social change. Just within civil rights, three quick examples come to mind: from Beauvoir came Hansberry, from Sartre came Frantz Fanon, and from Camus came Robert (Bob) Moses, the civil rights leader. Yet the concept of cool did not converge with political protest but instead remained with the individual cultural rebel as it became inflected by a new generation looking for different answers after the assassination of President John F. Kennedy.

Coda: Hansberry's Vision of Radical Democracy

Hansberry worked her entire life on an unfinished opera libretto called *Toussaint*, in honor of her childhood hero, Toussaint L'Ouverture, leader of the Haitian Revolution; she offered it in tribute to "slaves who made themselves free." As early as 1958, before *Raisin*, she left a "note to readers" that distilled the objective of the writer as social artist through the prism of revolutionary action.

> L'Ouverture was not a God; he was a man. And *by the will of one man in union with a multitude*, Santo Domingo [Haiti] was transformed . . . — the French empire, the western hemisphere, the history of the United States—therefore: the world. Such then is the will and the power of man. Perhaps that is the secret of the greatness of humankind.
>
> Signed "LH NYC Dec. 1958."[73]

Hansberry was a romantic populist, and this is her philosophy in a bottle: "the will of one person in union with a multitude" can change society. This dovetails with Camus's theory of the rebel as a slave who says no in an affirmative gesture of rejection to generate the rebellion of others.

Yet despite the sophisticated racial and gender analysis in Hansberry's journals and essays, there are no rebel heroines in her plays. The protagonists were always men since they were the social agents capable of transformative action: Walter Lee Younger, Sidney Brustein, Toussaint L'Ouverture. Like Beauvoir and Billie Holiday, Hansberry was realistic about the limitations of the national imagination for women in the public sphere even as she constantly worked as an activist.

In 1963, Hansberry wrote a letter to Lena Horne thanking her for marching with Medgar Evers, an action proving that "the real [American] drama has moved from Broadway to Mississippi." The following year, Hansberry wrote the nearly forgotten text for a collection of explicit photographs of police brutality and black resistance to white Southern rage, *The Movement: Documentary of a Struggle for Equality* (1964). She mentored her neighbor Nina Simone about politics—"it was always Marx, Lenin and revolution—real girls' talk," Simone recalled. Hansberry tried to will herself back to health from cancer for the movement: "I must get well. I must go down to the South. I've been a revolutionary all my life, but I've got to go down there to find out what kind of revolutionary I am." Hansberry spoke at all manner of civil rights protests and events right up until she passed away of pancreatic cancer on January 12, 1965.[74]

The cultural work of postwar cool had peaked by 1960, and Hansberry's responses to the Beats, existentialists, and African-American writers signaled the end of an era of symbolic self-expression. Brando, Camus, Kerouac, and Elvis had all completed their best work and the generation spurred by *The Wild One* and *Rebel Without a Cause*, by *On the Road* and *The Plague*, by "Howl" and "All Shook Up" required a new inflection. There had now been twenty years of rebel defiance, icons of individuality alternately squinting at and raging against seeming conformity to an arms race masked as normalcy, Communist paranoia masked as democracy, and white mythologies masked as history.

In 1960, the first sit-ins by African-American college students in North Carolina marked a shock to the generational system about American triumphalism with regard to freedom and democracy. In *The Movement*, Hansberry wrote that "there has been virtually no institution of Negro life, from the churches to the blues, which has not had a fundamental preoccupation with freedom."[75] Most leaders of the counterculture cut their rebel teeth in the civil rights movement and those who did not soon experienced the apocalyptic scare of the Cuban Missile Crisis, the assassination of a popular youthful president, and the first defiant political statement proffered by college students to the U.S. government.

The concept of cool itself was now on the cusp of change.

Figure 40. Paul Newman during the filming of *Paris Blues*, 1960 (© Herman Leonard Photography LLC).

Epilogue

The Afterlives of Postwar Cool

In 1960, Norman Mailer evaluated the Democratic nominee, John F. Kennedy, as an embodiment of the postwar cultural imagination and as a political analogy to both Brando and Sinatra. Mailer framed John F. Kennedy as postwar cool incarnate: "[Kennedy] carried himself with a cool grace . . . indifferent to applause, his manner somehow similar to the poise of a fine boxer. . . . There was an elusive detachment to everything he did." The youthful candidate seemed conjured from "the long electric night with the fires of neon leading down the highway to the murmur of jazz," the postwar underground as mapped out by cooled romanticism. At that year's Democratic Convention, one writer nudged Mailer and said, "Well, there's your first hipster . . . Sergius O'Shaugnessy born rich." He meant that a forty-four-year-old young man from a once-oppressed and excluded ethnic minority — an Irish Catholic — had come up through his own version of sex, drugs, and jazz to be on the threshold of the presidency. In addition, Kennedy and Sinatra were good friends and shared a cultural cohort as ambitious children of white ethnic Catholic immigrants surging against the nation's WASP elite. Sinatra campaigned tirelessly for Kennedy and he was the official organizer and emcee of the televised gala thrown on the eve of his inauguration.[1]

In this famous 1960 *Esquire* essay, "Superman Comes to the Supermarket," Mailer reflected on a schizophrenic American imagination in the first half of the twentieth century, a country living a "double life" with "two rivers" of consciousness surging against one another, "one visible, the other underground." Social and economic transformations had split off the American elites of business and politics from those hopes and myths that now carried the nation's "subterranean river of untapped, ferocious, lonely and romantic desires." Starting in the Depression, there was a slow collapse of capitalism's hold on the imagination through factory work and world wars and, with it, the self-conscious recognition that humans were disposable and "as interchangeable as commodities." There was also an astonishing growth in destructive power in just two generations: the shift from rifles and machine guns to aerial war and nuclear weapons. Yet in the face of these transformative social and technological forces, America kept "the dynamic myth . . . that every man was potentially extraordinary," a myth that Mailer did not realize would carry forward through the single word, *cool*.[2]

To Mailer, American popular culture had created a new niche kind of hero worship such that every person could now choose "his own archetype," whether it was "Cagney, Flynn, Bogart, Brando, or Sinatra." The American cultural imagination now depended on masculine figures that could "fight well, kill well . . . love well and love many," he wrote. Such cultural icons had to "be cool, be daring . . . be wild, be wily, [and] be resourceful." Mailer suggested that Hollywood had turned the nation's frontier myth inward and reflected it back across the country. "The film studios threw up their searchlights as the frontier was finally sealed," Mailer wrote, turning the horizontal dream of "the conquest of land" into a myth of consciousness, "a vertical myth." That myth had now split into two rivers, of square and hip: the myth of tradition and manifest destiny, represented by John Wayne and the Western genre, and the underground hopes of American bohemia. Mailer bemoaned the lost opportunity of the 1950s when "America's need . . . was to take an existential turn, to walk into the nightmare, to face into that terrible logic of history."[3]

John F. Kennedy had a movie-star quality, a beautiful wife, and a heroic military past; he projected an aesthetic detachment that combined elements of noir cool, jazz cool, and existential cool. Kennedy was the rare political figure who captured "the secret cultural imagination of a people," Mailer wrote, and his victory over the well-meaning intellectual Adlai Stevenson for the nomination—and then over the uncool Richard Nixon—marked a sea change at the symbolic level.

Mailer captured the composite meanings of postwar cool just as it surfaced in American politics: "Like Brando, Kennedy's most characteristic quality is the remote and private air of a man who has traversed some lonely terrain of experience, of loss and gain, of nearness to death, which leaves him isolated from the mass of others." This description fits many of the figures in this book as their cool left its mark on audiences and artistic acolytes: Lester Young, Humphrey Bogart, Robert Mitchum, Albert Camus, Charlie Parker, Miles Davis, Sonny Rollins, and Frank Sinatra, and although Mailer ignored the women, Billie Holiday, Anita O'Day, and Barbara Stanwyck.[4]

I offer here a final definition of cool—fully formed as of 1963—as it became part of the American self-concept: *cool is a subconscious method for negotiating identity in modernity through popular culture.* Since the 1920s, the shared habitat of American society has been its popular culture, and, in these zones of imagination, young people navigate their own desires—that underground river—through icons of music, film, and television. It's the actors, singers, and musicians on the walls of teenagers' bedrooms, the obsessive listening to favorite albums or viewing of films. It has to be subconscious since cool can be a synthesis of two or three archetypes and, as well, has to defer any obvious imitation in striving for identity, individuality, or subjective truth. Mailer came close to naming this process in 1960, even if he invokes the obsolete term "hero" instead of the more abstract, elusive "cool": "A hero embodies the [personal] fantasy and so allows each private mind the liberty to consider its fantasy and find a place to grow. Each mind can become more conscious of its desire and waste less strength in hiding from itself." And besides, hero worship is so, well, *uncool.*

In short: cool had become a process by which iconic rebels carve out new strategies of individuality and cultural space for a new generation. When such a rebel embodies inchoate feelings, young people invoke the term: "he's cool" or "she's so cool" or "now that's cool" or just *"Cool!"*

Cool is the designation for inchoate yearnings taking embodied form in new icons: what follows is a slow cultural gestation in individuals and generational cohorts. When black college students held the first sit-ins of the civil rights movement in North Carolina, they jumpstarted the transition from cool's underground cultural rebellion to overt political action and social change.

From Postwar to Countercultural Cool

The myth of cool should be understood as rebellion-for-others: the potential for a lone charismatic individual to generate social change by galvanizing an audience through symbolic artistic or public acts. In the final act of postwar cool (1960–63), cool crossed over through Beat literature (Kerouac and Ginsberg), jazz icons such as Miles Davis and Sonny Rollins and Art Pepper, actors Steve McQueen or Paul Newman, and most importantly, through rock and roll. The tempo of social change continued to be grooved through African-American music and the hybrid Southern culture that gave birth to rock and roll, from Ray Charles and Chuck Berry to Carl Perkins and Johnny Cash.

At the time, the affirmative existential strategies of African-American culture were so little known—and so taboo to white American consciousness—that rock critic John Lydon could write in 1970 of his rock-and-roll coming of age: "You could not say why you loved it and you could not think of it as black."[5] As a word and concept, "cool" itself had these unspoken connotations until around 1980. As cool crossed over from African-American culture in the 1960s, its in-group signs and styles became the lingua franca of white American youth—in music and language (slang), in clothing and hairstyles, in dance and (later) in drug use. In addition to Elvis films, the odd novelty such as the musical comedy *The Girl Can't Help It!* (1956) also captured the new genre's excitement, as it did for the Beatles: the film featured Little Richard and Fats Domino at their peak, rockabilly stars Gene Vincent and Duane Eddy, and a glamorous Abbey Lincoln singing the aptly titled "Spread the Word" (and "spread the gospel") in a diva's red gown.

The idea that rebellion-for-others is projected as well *through* individual style found its most salient and emblematic artistic expression in Johnny Cash's "The Man in Black" (1971). Cash started wearing black in the late 1950s and it took him fifteen years to explain his unconscious stylistic choice. Wearing black at first had no symbolic meaning, Cash once claimed; it was just the only color all the band members owned. Still I doubt the band would have worn powder-blue tuxedos on stage if that was the only color they owned in common. In other words, wearing black *felt* right to Cash in some way, aesthetically and psychologically. It was a statement of self-expression reflecting an inchoate individual sensibility open to social resonance.

In the song, Cash claimed to "wear the black for the poor and the beaten down," as they lived on the "hungry side of town." He wears the black "for the prisoner" in jail long after having paid his debt to society—the implication being that he's "a victim of the times." When will Cash wear a different color? Only when "we start to make a move to make a few things right"—note "we" as a society or nation—will Cash "wear a suit of white" or "wear a rainbow every day." In the meantime, he chooses "to carry off a little darkness on my back" for empathy's sake. The last line of the song is a pure reduction of Christian symbolism as filtered through cool's dark side: "'Till things are brighter, I'm the Man in Black."

To wear "a suit of white" suggests purity, innocence, an absence of dirt; to wear white "tell[s] the world that everything's OK." A suit of white suggests a so-called solid (square) citizen—an upstanding figure of virtue adhering to social mores and traditional morality. Cash will not wear white by example: it's a personal and social lie, given a society where "things need changin' everywhere you go." He chooses to reflect the dark side of feeling, of society, of desire; he embodies *music noir* (so to speak). The Man in Black symbolizes the postwar rebellion against being blindly patriotic in a *love-it-or-leave-it* mode (to use a phrase of the time) or through the knee-jerk anti-Communism of Postwar II.

The mask of virtue partakes of whiteness, privilege, and the power of elites, whereas the mask of cool represents thwarted choices, silent defiance, social injustice, class conflict, and black Orpheus rising. To wear black suggests solidarity for the excluded, marginalized and oppressed in American society. Cash's "Man in Black" is his signature stark version of stylish stoicism: it is indebted to the noirish vision that came out of the Great Depression, Cash's personal encounters with his own dark side (drugs, alcohol, violence), and his apocalyptic Christianity. When Cash played concerts at prisons—as he often did—he sang as an equal and was heard as one. As if only by the grace of God was he on the free side of the prison bars.

The color of black often factors into rebellion so it deserves further analysis. For example, Juliette Gréco was called "the gamine in black" long before Cash, and she claimed her all-black dress code was simply "a blackboard on which audiences gave full rein to their imagination."[6] Why else would black so often be associated with cool detachment if not as the projection of a dark side awaiting illumination and redemption through validation? Black is the color of Bogart's suit in *High Sierra*, the color of eyes hiding behind shades, the dominant color of the Left Bank's existential caves, the default dress code of Beats and bohemia then and now. Just as "film noir" originally meant "dark cinema," wearing black suggests an awareness of the dark side of human nature.

Wearing shades also projects this combination of mystery and self-defense, blacking out one's eyes to block the invasive presence of authority. Black speaks to the shadow self, suppressed desires, excluded Others. Black is kinetic potential and creates mystery through style, shades, and attitude: the viewer will need to inquire further on that which has been cast into darkness. To riff on Marshall McLuhan's terms, wearing shades creates a muted kind of illumination.[7]

Black is possibility. It is the color of darkness in a society suffused with Christian symbolism of light and dark, and it is, not coincidentally, the dyad of racial polarity, the construction of racialized morality. Black is the dark hope for redemption once the repressed is reintegrated.

Of course, black is also the color of mourning. Many of the avatars of postwar cool passed on at the end of the postwar era:

James Dean, 1955
Humphrey Bogart, 1957
Lester Young, 1959
Billie Holiday, 1959
Raymond Chandler, 1959
Boris Vian, 1959
Albert Camus, 1960
Richard Wright, 1960
Dashiell Hammett, 1960

Ernest Hemingway, 1961
Gary Cooper, 1961

The logic of my end date here reflects both the death of these icons of cool and the most transformative postwar death of all: the assassination of John F. Kennedy. The response of the boomer generation to that death fueled the next generation of countercultural cool, pivoting along the Beat path. Postwar meanings still inhered to cool—and its cultural layers still remain with the term—but the concept itself was set to change.

In the mid-1960s, the mask of cool exploded out of its black and Beat phases into shards of rainbow colors. The inflection of rebellion moved away from African-American culture toward a new counterculture and its emphasis on drugs, a value on personal authenticity, and an earthier lifestyle. If its catch phrases and slang still came from the African-American vernacular—"do your own thing" and "let it all hang out," "uptight" and "outasight"—the new value was on being transparent and "out-front" with yourself and others. So-called mind-expanding drugs from marijuana to LSD led to a new social value on interconnection and a critique of masking as being repressed and inauthentic. In 1964, Marshall McLuhan noted a shift in the term "cool"—or in a "cool attitude"—from detachment to "a kind of commitment and participation in situations that involve all of one's faculties."[8]

Tom Wolfe caught the change in San Francisco in 1965. Wolfe was familiar with the cultural impact of black culture as measured through the influence of the African-American vernacular on colloquial speech—the "hip vocabulary"—and he easily tossed around its central terms "dig," "man," "uptight," and "later." Here Wolfe seems happy to wave goodbye to the postwar cultural break represented by African-American protest, language, and music:

> The whole old-style hip life—jazz, coffee houses, civil rights, invite a spade to dinner. . . . It was all suddenly dying . . . even among the students at Berkeley. . . . Negroes were no longer in the hip scene, not even as totem figures. It was unbelievable. *Spades*, the very soul figures of Hip, of jazz, of the hip vocabulary itself, *man* and *like* and *dig* and *baby* . . . and *split* and *later* . . . . All that good elaborate petting and pouring soul all over the spades—all over, finished.[9]

For white New Journalists such as Wolfe and Mailer, the cutting edge of popular culture had shifted from black culture to the counterculture and the latter took *cool* with them, which led to the historical erasure of the postwar era from many contemporary analyses of the concept. Wolfe seems exultant to learn that hip and cool are now centered around LSD and white hippies; his casual racism here (e.g., "spades," "petting and pouring soul all over [Blacks]") reflects a cultural tolerance long since wiped out by the ongoing racial tensions of the past half century. The timing of Wolfe's dismissal coincides with the rise of black nationalism, black power, and the Black Arts Movement. By the midsixties, the deeper aspects of hip and cool split along racial lines.[10]

With this emergence came the three branches of cool that remain: the classic noir cool of Bogart and Mitchum as carried into the present by (first) Paul Newman and Steve McQueen and (more recently) by George Clooney; African-American cool, from Miles Davis to Jimi Hendrix, then Prince to Samuel L. Jackson, then Jay Z to Barack Obama; countercultural cool, from Ken Kesey to Patti Smith to Kurt Cobain to Matthew McConaughey. Here is a parting set of historical reflections on cool on the cusp of "the '60s" and then a final pitch forward into the present moment.

The Cultural Necessity of Black Cool

In an obscure memoir entitled *Death of an Uncle Tom* (1967), an English professor named William H. Pipes traced the shift in his own racial consciousness during the two decades covered here. Pipes grew up within the oppressive constraints of Jim Crow—"born on a Mississippi plantation and educated at Tuskegee Institute"—at a time when Uncle Tomming was a crucial self-defense mechanism. Pipes defined an Uncle Tom as someone who "plays the role of something less than a man" by acting entirely along the lines "expected of him by the white man." There seemed no other way to avoid prison or violent beatings in the Deep South except by this masked mode of "survival by accommodation." By 1967, Pipes lived and taught at Michigan State University and claimed to be motivated by "simply a desire that the Negro be granted his constitutional rights as a man." By then, political rebellion had supplanted cultural rebellion as the leading edge of racial pride. The claims of black intellectuals in the landmark book *What the Negro Wants* (1944) had come to fruition—due to the authors' then-radical claims for social equality, this was a book all white liberal intellectuals refused to support and nearly every press refused to publish. Authors included Langston Hughes, W. E. B. DuBois, and Mary McLeod Bethune. Much had changed in a single generation.[11]

We need only look at two Hollywood films featuring Louis Armstrong to understand why cool was a form of cultural politics necessary for the transition to social protest. Not only in *Paris Blues* (1962) but also in *High Society* (1956), Armstrong played an avuncular, desexualized, Uncle Remus figure, as both Lester Young and Bernard Wolfe invoked this folksy black figure. In the Br'er Rabbit stories and Disney's *Song of the South* (1946), Uncle Remus functioned as the nation's primitive natural man: by definition he was excluded from modernity and the national value of individualism. In these two films, Armstrong dispenses uplifting music and good spirits from an ever-smiling, ever-laughing disposition. In the plot of both films, Armstrong musically midwifes the careers and romances of *white* cool icons Paul Newman and Frank Sinatra, respectively. In both films, Armstrong smiles from inside a character that has no past, no love interest, and no family. In fact, I submit here that Armstrong may be the original Magical Negro of Hollywood films.

Bernard Wolfe wrote a prescient article in 1949 about the structural racism of American society that lay behind the oppressive smile inherent to the masking of Uncle Tom or Uncle Remus. "It is *the white man* who manufactures the Negro's grin. The stereotype reflects the looker ... not the person looked at; it is born out of intense subjective need." Wolfe's analysis was original enough to be translated and published in Sarte's *Le Temps Moderne* and Frantz Fanon footnoted it in his first theoretical work on racism and masking (*Black Skin, White Masks*). When Simone Beauvoir saw Disney's *Song of the South* in San Antonio in 1947, she quickly perceived the function of the Uncle Remus character in white racial consciousness. "The white public smiles smugly at the image of Uncle Remus, the old black retainer with the innocent, childlike soul." She admired the film's live-action animation but the racism ruined her cinematic experience. "The animated drawings inserted into the film do not compensate for the . . . disgust provoked by this insipid story in Technicolor . . . the idyllic countryside [can] hardly conceal the hatred, injustice, and fear in which they are rooted." Beauvoir learned of this type of emotional masking from Richard Wright and anthropologist John Dollard: she called it "the black person's double face" and wrote that it was "expressly meant for whites."[12]

As for *High Society*, Bing Crosby plays a jazzbo aristocrat and narrates a swan song for the kind of aristocratic nonchalance he passed down to Sinatra. Wealthy, aloof, detached, in a fog of smoke and martinis, Crosby's cool here owes a larger debt to European models of sangfroid or upper-class reserve than to American cool by way of defiant alienation. As jazz contemporaries, Armstrong and Crosby had a mutual admiration society dating back to the late 1920s. Yet the two men could not be social equals or friends due to the strict segregation of Hollywood films so here Armstrong serves as a talisman of the roots of jazz and authenticity—as *flava* (so to speak), as the musical *help*—rather than as an equal character in the events of *High Society*.

As mentioned before, the source novel of *Paris Blues* concerned two *interracial* couples, and yet the film reinscribed Jim Crow conventions. The studio's political pragmatism was then standard Hollywood practice: Southern theaters would not show films representing social equality (or romantic desire) between whites and blacks. In this way, Southern audiences had a cultural bloc on national media just as they had a political bloc in Congress until 1964. MGM could not afford to alienate American film audiences by taking a stand on such issues; not for another five years would *Guess Who's Coming to Dinner* (1967) introduce an interracial marriage to film audiences. In *Paris Blues*, Armstrong mentors Paul Newman's character, the familiar young (white) man with a horn, and not Poitier; Hollywood remained in Uncle Remus mode, decades behind the hip ambience and progressive listeners of urban jazz clubs. Armstrong and Lester Young both grew up in the Deep South within the mandatory practices of Uncle Tomming but it was Young's quiet revolution through the mask of cool that liberated Miles Davis, Charlie Parker, Dizzy Gillespie, John Coltrane, Art Blakey, and Sonny Rollins.

Only an independent film could register the cultural politics of cool in the early 1960s. Actor Ivan Dixon and jazz vocalist Abbey Lincoln starred as newlyweds in *Nothing but a Man* (1964), a film set in a small Alabama town where Dixon is fired for trying to unionize black railroad workers.

The film was written and directed by Michael Roemer, a German-Jewish immigrant whose family escaped Nazi Germany when he was eleven years old. In traveling through the South with his cinematographer, Roemer recognized in its strict segregation the kind of state-sponsored terrorism he found familiar from Nazi Germany. The film won two awards at the Venice Film Festival but barely made a ripple in the United States until its re-release in 1993. It was Malcolm X's favorite movie.[13]

After losing his job on the railroad, Dixon winds up working in a gas station where whites complain every night about his surliness. First, an old white man complains to the owner about his attitude—he is disrespectful and does not call him "sir." Second, a car full of white teenagers pulls in and begins to order him around. They provoke him, call him racial epithets, and make insulting sexual statements about his wife. Dixon doesn't react, not even to say "yes sir"; he just pumps gas. "You must think you're white," the driver spits at him. When Dixon just keeps wiping the windshield with a blank look, the driver says: "Real cool, ain't he? Just like we ain't here."

Abbey Lincoln embodies jazz cool with a performance of relaxed intensity that seamlessly combined grit, grace, and silent protest. To a contemporary critic, her preternatural composure here can be seen as an embodiment of *itutu* (Yoruban for "mystic coolness" or spiritual balance) as Lincoln seemed "so poised and radiant that you'd almost believe she could single-handedly rewrite the code of early-1960s, segregated America." Yet this is Alabama in 1964 and the steady dignity of Lincoln and Dixon only meet with the rage and hostility of white supremacy. The strength and purpose of the actors' dignified defiance harkens back to West African associations with strategic silence for community change. Lincoln was married to bebop drummer Max Roach, and on their groundbreaking album, *We Insist!* (1960), the two musical artists created the first radical indictment of American slavery in American musical history with songs like "Drivaman," "Freedom Day," and "All Africa." The recording subsumed slavery within a renewed affirmation of African heritage, similar to Hansberry's strategy in *A Raisin in the Sun.* On "All Africa," Lincoln chants and calls out the names of two dozen African tribes, starting with "Bantu / Zulu / Watusi / Ashanti," and then attests to how music carries memory and struggle: "the beat / has a rich and magnificent / history / full of adventure, / excitement / and mystery." Some of it is bitter, she sings, and some of it sweet, but "all of it part of the beat."

The influence of jazz in terms of individual voice, subjective truth, and blues aesthetic has since pervaded many artistic forms, in literature as well as music. In 1964, jazz became as central to the artistic practice of Japanese author Haruki Murakami as it had been for Kerouac a generation earlier. "Practically everything I know about writing, then, I learned from music. . . . My style is as deeply influenced by Charlie Parker's repeated freewheeling riffs, say, as by F. Scott Fitzgerald's elegantly flowing prose. And I still take the quality of continual self-renewal in Miles Davis's music as a literary model."[14] When Murakami saw Art Blakey and the Messengers in Tokyo in 1964 he was "thunderstruck"—all he wanted to do was "write like playing an instrument." Murakami adapted the jazz method of artistic practice for telling his literary story:

> Whether in music or in fiction, the most basic thing is rhythm. Your style needs to have good, natural, steady rhythm . . . [and] I learned the importance of rhythm . . . mainly from jazz. Next comes melody— which, in literature, means the appropriate arrangement of the words to match the rhythm. If the way the words fit the rhythm is smooth and beautiful, you can't ask for anything more. Next is harmony—the internal mental sounds that support the words. Then comes the part I like best: free improvisation. Through some special channel, the story comes welling out freely from inside. All I have to do is get into the flow.[15]

In 1960, the combination of rhythmic power and personal statement was equally influential through blues avatars such as Muddy Waters, Lightnin' Hopkins, and John Lee Hooker. An individual blues musician embodied existential affirmation, communicated the blues as a model of social protest, modeled the blues as a conduit to democratic cultural production, and proved the blues to be the artistic parent of rock and roll. White bluesman Charlie Musselwhite called Lightnin' Hopkins "one cool operator" after seeing him for the first time in the early '60s in a club in Gary, Indiana. Musselwhite was at first excited by the opening act of J. B. Lenoir and his soul-style band, complete with a full horn

section. "I was wondering who Lightnin' was [that he was] going to follow J.B. and keep this joint jumping by himself." Meanwhile, Lightnin'
Hopkins just sat at the bar drinking, apparently unconcerned, and after
a short break, he walked onstage with just a drummer, plugged in his
amp, and hit the first chord. "Lightnin' had on his shades and a dark
suit with white socks," Musselwhite recalled. "He pulled up a chair and
[just] . . . tore the house up. The place went wild! *The place went wild!* It
was one of the coolest things I ever saw." Guitarist and songwriter Dave
Alvin saw Lightnin' Hopkins several times at a nightclub when he was
very young. "He just exuded cool and confidence and authority," Alvin
recalled. Hopkins wore a sharkskin suit and sunglasses on stage ("the
shades were always there") and Alvin was awed: "I was twelve or thirteen years old, [and] I didn't know there were transcendental men, but
that was what you got."[16]

Like the *sound* of a jazz musician, Hopkins's blues aesthetic was personal and existential, his self-presentation minimalist and understated,
his lyrical communication infused with subjective experience and a musical space reflecting the cool inner place. The existential cool of Hopkins
relies on this African-American musical tradition: one man on-stage able
to command modern audiences with only the most basic elements—one
voice, three chords on his guitar, and himself as a document of survival.
Blues concerns mythic transformation and autobiographical experience
rendered through poetic lyricism. David Ritz recalled that "Lightnin'
had the soul-nourishing gift of molding pleasure from pain, turning brutal experiences into beautiful stories."[17] White musicians and audiences
learned and internalized such musical practices and existential cool at
bohemian cafés, at the Newport Folk Festival, and on records, a crucial
crossover cultural process nearly erased from public memory and recently revivified in Dennis McNally's *On Highway 61: Music, Race, and
the Evolution of Cultural Freedom* and John Milward's *Crossroads*.

The password for "cultural freedom" in the 1960s was "cool" and the
crossover of the concept was fully disseminated by 1965. Richard Wright
first declared cultural war on the racial order in 1938 with his epigraph
"Uncle Tom is Dead!" and by 1956, British journalist J. C. Furnas—in a full-
length study, *Goodbye to Uncle Tom*—revealed that African-Americans
had made of the term "a hissing and a byword," and that many "would
rather be called 'nigger' than 'Uncle Tom.'" The Uncle Tom mask was not

an abstract, literary, metaphorical, or theoretical construct: it was perhaps the single most important black defensive weapon in an undeclared race war, which could and did explode in the faces of African-American men on a regular basis. The repudiation of Uncle Tomming was the first triumph of cool.[18]

In a 1961 *Playboy* interview with Alex Haley, Miles Davis repudiated Uncle Tomming as the most detestable mode of African-American behavior. "Uncle Tomming got started [during slavery] because white people demanded it. Every little black child grew up seeing that getting along with white people meant grinning and acting [like] clowns." Davis was quite conscious of cool as embodied rebellion and of the subtext of his fierce stare. "I ain't scared of nothing or nobody. I already been through too much. . . . I just say what I think, and that bugs people, especially a lot of white people. When they look in my eyes and don't see no fear, they know it's a draw." This is a declaration of social equality at a level of masculine battle.[19]

Davis's cool was a nonverbal public declaration of defiance; but in private, he took down his mask. Quincy Jones recalled that Davis's "gruff exterior" had "more bark than bite" in public, and it projected forward to hip-hop culture. In the 1990s, Jones reflected back to jazz musicians in the 1940s. "All the beboppers did that [back then]. . . . The beboppers invented what the rappers are trying to do now. You know, be cool, the underworld, subculture language, the body language, the lifestyle. You had to be cool." Of Miles Davis, Quincy Jones declared simply "I saw through his shell . . . and it was a shell." Many jazz musicians who played with Davis (across the racial and ethnic spectrum) echo this sentiment.[20]

Postwar black cool paved the way for a new form of cultural currency through two separate modes. First, as conveyed through music, it was a revolution in individuality through self-expression and artistic voice. The Beats redirected this aspect from jazz to the counterculture and literature through Kerouac and Cassady, the Beat road addicts. The second was as a self-defense system: cool was (and is) performative, theatrical, and embodied; its space was the public sphere or the stage, and its intended audience was the Euro-American public. This rejection of everyday social exchange signaled rebellion against a racial and social order still held hostage by Southern politicians and national fears of miscegenation until the mid-1960s.

These meanings of cool are still vital among African-American men: for example, Ta-Nehisi Coates calls the masculinity lessons he learned growing up in 1980s' Baltimore "sacred texts like Basic Game and Applied Cool"; or there is The Roots' advice about style, street cred, and personal conduct in the song, "Stay Cool." Musically, cool remains associated with a relaxed, stripped-down, textured, swinging American groove originally created and exemplified by bands such as Count Basie and Duke Ellington, then streamlined in small combos led by Billie Holiday or Frank Sinatra. Afro-Cuban jazz pianist Bebo Valdés called it the "midtempo bounce," and gave as an example Sinatra's 1960 hit, "Nice 'n' Easy." Valdés waxed poetic about its exemplary slow groove: "Nobody can play music like that except in America, that kind of swing, that time. It's impeccable. The most difficult thing in the world is to play slowly and keep time. When I listen to this, I see American black people dancing." This kind of midcentury evocation of jazz's global influence remains one of the most resonant soundings of American cool.[21]

Paul Newman and the Complex Fate of Noir Cool

Broadly conceived, the noir sensibility created a permanent change in iconic American masculinity: the mask of cool supplanted the mask of virtue as the aesthetic sensibility of American heroism. Whether it's Jason Bourne or Easy Rawlins (Walter Mosley's PI) or Jack Bauer (*24*) today, the heroic badass remains a solitary, cynical, lone wolf, familiar enough with his dark side and ethical anger to commit violent criminal acts on behalf of a nominally democratic system of justice. Noir cool drew on cultural precedent in the Western outlaw, the hobo, and the proletarian worker; it still often speaks in either a working-class vernacular or with unquestioned (and unracialized) street cred. Every generation finds iconic male actors to inhabit this mode, whether rogue cops or spies, all of whom are variations on the theme, from Clint Eastwood to Tommy Lee Jones to Matt Damon to Denzel Washington.

Coming out of the Great Depression, the noir anti-hero was deputized in the cultural imagination to judge an individual neither by social or economic class nor by dress, residence, or circumstances. "He assumes that everybody is dappled with virtue and vice, especially himself," columnist David Brooks wrote of this essential aspect of the genre.

Sam Spade and Philip Marlowe were "moral realists," Brooks reflected, and they modeled for a generation the balancing act of recognizing everyday political corruption while dispensing ethical judgments about individuals and their actions.[22] The *noir anti-hero* was convincing and realistic because exemplary and existential: he was no better than the criminals; he did not believe in aristocracy or breeding; he made no moral judgments based on virtue. The message was clear: there was no such thing as a criminal type, just individual human beings who committed crimes for any number of reasons, the rich and well-bred as well as (sometimes even more than) the lower class or ethnic Others feared by white Americans.

Up until 9/11, there were always rogue individual detectives (either PIs or cops) in one-hour dramas on the noir model, especially in the '70s and '80s. Following the example of Clint Eastwood in the *Dirty Harry* franchise, there were several charismatic rogue detectives for the small screen's weekly serial: *Columbo, Mannix, Cannon, Barnaby Jones, Rockford* (and *The Rockford Files*), and even *Hart to Hart*. But beginning with *Homicide*, and especially after 9/11 with *CSI*, the police procedural became ascendant. The "hero" of the crime procedural is now often a combination of technology and teamwork (i.e., the lab, DNA testing). The working ensemble of the police procedural is a paradigmatic utopian dream of American society and remains the meat of prime time, as in the many variants of *CSI* and *Law and Order*. Even when a show focuses on a maverick investigator (as in *The Closer* or *The Mentalist*), it's still the technology—rather than the individual human being—that is indispensable. (The rare exception features a quirky genius like *Monk*.) Yet since the operational framework is cooperation and depends on a team, these shows have not elevated a single figure into the cool echelon, whether actor, female detective, or ex-hip-hop musician (e.g., Ice T, LL Cool J). These contemporary procedurals owe a larger debt to *Dragnet* than *The Big Sleep*. So then what is noir's legacy to this dialectic of rogue detective and problem-solving police force team?[23]

One answer can be found in the career of Paul Newman, the "King of Cool," as many obituaries called him in 2008: Newman's longevity meant he was the last major actor associated with the postwar meanings of cool such that nearly every eulogy invoked the term from around the world. For example, here's the first line from the obituary of Israel's *Haaretz*:

"Paul Newman, the Oscar-winning superstar who personified 'cool' as the anti-hero of such films as *Hud, Cool Hand Luke* and *The Color of Money* . . . has died, aged 83." Newman was heir to Brando's charismatic angry young man in films such as *The Hustler* and *The Long, Hot Summer* but he became a transitional figure who embodied the countercultural tensions of dissent, from *Cool Hand Luke* to the roguish villains of *Butch Cassidy* and *The Sting* (a Western and gangster film, respectively). As the key Hollywood cool male icon between the postwar noir and counter-cultural rebellion, Newman (fig. 40) connects the present moment back to his early adoration and emulation of Brando.[24]

Having stamped Hollywood with a broader twentieth-century cool masculinity, Newman was something of a secular cultural saint when he died: he was seen as equally rebellious and solid, ethical and irreverent, an institution of cool and a philanthropic entrepreneur. Nearly all eulogies associated Newman with the concept of cool: from "Paul Newman: An Icon of Cool Masculinity" (*San Francisco Chronicle*) to "Cool Hand Paul" (Maureen Dowd, *New York Times*), from "Cinema's Cool Hand" (*The Australian*), to "World Mourns 'King of Cool'" (*Reuters*), from "Schwarzenegger Remembers Newman as 'Ultimate Cool'" (*San Diego Union Tribune*), to the A&E documentary (*Paul Newman—Hollywood's Cool Hand* [2005]). Even President George W. Bush claimed to be "drawn to Paul Newman's defiance in *Cool Hand Luke*" rather than to any literary heroes.[25]

Newman took over Brando's role as brooding charismatic over the half decade of 1958–63, beginning with a Tennessee Williams role (*The Long, Hot Summer*) and then a similar role in *Cat on a Hot Tin Roof* about a Southern man frustrated by his father's imperious control and the blistering limits of the region's social norms. Newman then absorbed frontier masculinity in *Hud* and as Billy the Kid (in *The Left Handed Gun*), bringing a new roguish sexuality that turned away from John Wayne's sculpted authority or Gary Cooper's decent indestructibility. Newman had Brando's "wounded, bruised quality," as one film critic reflected on his appeal, yet infused it with a certain ironic distance such that "women wanted to console [him] and men could identify with [him]."[26]

As with all the postwar rebel cool figures, Newman played the young white male resistant to social norms and his own privilege. In *The Hustler*, Newman found a new register of anomie and disgust with postwar American triumphalism as he "captured the underside of America's postwar self-satisfaction," according to historian Richard Pells. As Fast Eddie Felson, Newman's performance in *The Hustler* raises these two related questions that harken back to emergent noir: What could a young man do to protest a seemingly empty, materialistic society except to master an impractical skill (like being a pool hustler) and handle it with bravado? How else could he show it wasn't simply laziness that kept him from supporting the status quo?

This is precisely what both African-American cool *and* noir cool brought into postwar society as a mode of silent indictment. By 1968, the Rolling Stones were singing that question in an anthem, "What can a poor boy do? / Except to sing for a rock-and-roll band?" A half century after *The Hustler*, the *London Times* still deemed the essential qualities of "Newman's star persona" to be the charismatic rebellion we call cool: "The irreverence, the obtrusive cool, the sheer gall that made him an idol for a disaffected younger generation, but also embodying its vulnerability."[27]

Newman's alienation in these films squares with Amiri Baraka's original definition of postwar cool for African-Americans: it was "nonparticipation in an absurd society." Much of the association of Newman with cool comes from his performance as a convict in *Cool Hand Luke* (1967), an allegory of society as prison set in a Southern prison camp. Luke is often beaten or made to suffer for his defiance—akin to Elvis in *Jailhouse Rock*—yet he is always beat but never beaten. He gets his nickname from the iconic line of his character when he bluffs out a table full of convicts: "Sometimes nothin' can be a pretty cool hand."

The film illuminates why cool remains a supreme compliment: to be cool suggests the embodiment of dignity without social status, of integrity uncoupled from authority. Newman had walked the definitive noir line between cop and convict the year before in *Harper* (1966), playing Ross McDonald's detective, Lew Harper. Yet it was with *Cool Hand Luke* that he became the "the first star . . . to successfully cross over from the ranks of Hollywood leading men to hero of the counter-culture." Of course, no black actor or non-white figure—not even Sidney Poitier—could then serve as a cool anti-hero, admired for being "authority-averse" for the boomer generation and for "endur[ing] savage beatings in prison simply because he refuses to knuckle under."[28]

Finally, since the 1980s, white jazz musicians have retrospectively reinserted a missing jazz soundtrack to film noir. Bassist Charlie Haden created his Quartet West band in 1986 to celebrate the '50s noir aesthetic of Los Angeles, releasing four albums that have reanimated the postwar noir soundscape. New York jazz session musicians Joe Locke and Bob Sneider have released two CDs in their ongoing Film Noir Project. Classical composer John Adams recently drew on noir's themes and later jazz soundtracks for a three-movement, forty-minute orchestral work about the genre as a shadow urban self, *City Noir: The City and Its Double* (2011). Befitting the Central European heritage of many noir directors, Carlos Franzetti and the City of Prague Philharmonic released an orchestral tribute to the genre—titled *Film Noir*—that included symphonic versions of Herbie Hancock's "Still Time" and Burt Bacharach's "Alfie." Finally, New York jazz drummer Bobby Previte's *Set the Alarm for Monday* (2008) can be usefully heard as a soundtrack for an unproduced noir. Consider these song titles: "Were You Followed?" "Drive South, Along the Canyon," "I'd Advise You Not to Miss Your Train," and "I'm on to Her." Noir has become a sustaining force in American music, film, literature, TV, and in the pop-cultural imagination of masculinity.

Cool Survives

James Dean remains the most enduring cool icon of the postwar era, a freeze-frame of youthful beauty and style. There is a permanent James Dean gallery in the local museum of his hometown, Fairmount, Indiana, while the Grant County website used to claim Dean "represents the cool, bold spirit of youth" absorbed from this staid Midwestern region. In this revisionist history, the website claimed that it was Indianans who "defied convention and *established* the adventurous, self-assured style known as cool that is the hallmark of our community"—against all evidence to the contrary of the history of cool. This rhetoric is easy to mock and yet quite revealing concerning the legacy and trajectory of cool. Invoking a cluster of *cool* keywords—"defiance," "adventure," "self-assured style"— the website sold rebellion as intrinsic to regional identity and doubled down by invoking Dean's roots for context to tourists. A banner across the top proclaimed "Grant County, Indiana—It's All Cool" and the site offered an itinerary called "Fun for Rebels."[29] What happened to cool such that we all began to imagine ourselves as rebels? That is a question for works focused on the period from 1960 to 1980, such as Grace Eliza-beth Hale's *A Nation of Outsiders: How the White Middle Class Fell in Love with Rebellion in Postwar America* (2011).

The end of the postwar cool matrix came about on the cusp of the 1980s due to the revaluation of wealth acquisition along with renewed pride in upper-class affiliation. Ronald Reagan was the political and eco-nomic figurehead of this shift but it permeated nearly all cultural pro-duction. As Michael Douglas preached in the iconic *Wall Street* (1986), "greed is good," and such an attitude manifested in the cultural emblems of the period—from the upper-class pride in the best-selling *Preppie Handbook* (1980) to Vietnam revisionism to the hit song, "It's Hip to Be Square" (1985). A renewal of blind patriotism in "America"—in its original mythic associations of freedom—accompanied the right-wing rise to power and a profound lack of empathy for the less privileged. Everyone still wanted to be cool but *cool*—as a concept—lost its force as the password of an alternative success system.

Here's an evocative comparison. When Elvis sang, "(You're So Square) Baby, I Don't Care" (1957), it was a declaration of difference between a bad boy's wild hip masculinity and a good girl who just likes to go to the movies "and sit there holdin' hands." Yet the bad boy's "heart flips" to just hold her hand. It was a two-minute musical version of *The Wild One* and came courtesy of the prolific Jewish-American song-writing team, Jerry Leiber and Mike Stoller. When Huey Lewis and the News collapsed these terms in "It's Hip to Be Square," the group revealed a society in which "hip" had lost its original meanings of tolerance or creative thinking or social change; hip had been reduced to a signifier of simply what's in vogue. The emblematic sitcom of this shift was *Family Ties*, in which Michael J. Fox played a suited-up market-driven teenager who worships capitalism and entrepreneurial vigor to the embarrass-ment of his ex-hippie parents. When the alt-rocker Mojo Nixon referred to Michael J. Fox as "the anti-Elvis" on his 1987 song, "Elvis Is Every-where," he was calling out an essential difference between a transforma-tive icon of cool and a popular, likable actor.[30]

Yet if "hip" and "hipster" are now pejorative, the word "cool" drifted free of its postwar origins and connotations. "Cool" retains its associa-tion with personal rebellion, anti-authoritarian behavior, and simply *not giving a shit* in terms of artistic risk or even in everyday life. The slang expert Tom Dalzell recently wondered, "What makes 'cool' last for 68 years without fading? What is it about 'hip' that let it morph into hep, hipcat, hipster, hippie (jazz sense), hippie (flower child), hip-hop, and hipster—new hipster?"[31]

Cool has not faded but its meanings have morphed with every generation. Its value remains intact since it is a crucial myth of the American self-concept. Like the image of James Dean, cool continues to exist as a floating signifier of rebellion through youthful daring, stylish self-confidence, sexual charisma, and knowing skepticism. Much of the content in the retro visions of filmmakers such as Jim Jarmusch and Quentin Tarantino are attempts to find the magic rites and symbols back to this mythic American cultural concept.

To consider (or call) someone cool remains the supreme compliment of American and global culture—even as it has been nearly emptied of generational and ideological conflict, of artistic risk and vision, of old transgressions and social change. The recuperation of the deeper meanings of cool will require a reckoning with the past, the reintegration of the many split American selves historically marked by the concept of cool's emergence at the outset of World War II.

Acknowledgments

I have been working on this book in some form for nearly twenty-five years and so I hereby express my gratitude to all my friends and colleagues collectively for a quarter century's worth of conversations about cool. My original plan was to publish this work before the *American Cool* exhibit I co-curated at the National Portrait Gallery in 2014 with Frank Goodyear. It was to be the exhibit's intellectual infrastructure since "cool" as a word and concept remains widely seen as superficial and lacking in history. So it finds the light of day about three years too late—the best-laid plans and all that. And thanks to Frank for being an exemplary collaborator.

The first chapter, "Lester Young and the Birth of Cool," appeared in an excellent anthology edited by Gena Caponi-Tabery, *Signifyin(g), Sanctifyin', and Slam Dunking.* It was my first published academic article, and I will always be grateful to Gena for her encouragement. Much of the second chapter, "Humphrey Bogart and the Birth of Noir Cool from the Great Depression," was first published in different form in 2008 in the UK *Journal of American Studies* under the title, "'Emergent Noir': Film Noir and the Great Depression in *High Sierra* and *This Gun for Hire*." I am grateful to Benjamin Cawthra and the University of Chicago's other reader for their insightful readings of the manuscript and for forcing me to strengthen aspects of the final two chapters with regard to the early 1960s. Thanks as well to Andrew Erish for being my go-to film scholar and for his friendship over the years.

At a key moment, I attended two international conferences on cool: (1) Coolness: Interdisciplinary Perspectives was held in 2010 at Freie Universität in Berlin, organized by Ulla Haselstein and Catrin Gersdorf; (2) Is It 'Cause It's Cool? Affective Encounters with American Culture was held in Salzburg in 2011, organized by Astrid Fellner for that year's Austrian American Studies Conference. The keynote I gave at the latter conference was the first iteration of the "Generational Interlude" here. And in an encounter worthy of film noir, at the Salzburg conference I met and had lunch with Frederick Baker, the director of the documentary *Shadowing the Third Man*. After discussing this project, he persuaded me that *The Third Man* fit my argument perfectly, and so it sits at the intersections of noir and existentialism in chapter 5.

I worked in many excellent archives for this project and wish to recognize these libraries for their assistance: for film noir in Los Angeles, the Warner Brothers collection at the University of Southern California, the Margaret Herrick Library of the Academy of Motion Pictures, and the University of California at Los Angeles's Special Collections (RKO collection, the Raymond Chandler Papers); for jazz, the Ross Russell Papers at the Harry Ransom Center at the University of Texas at Austin and the oral histories and photographs at the Institute of Jazz Studies at Rutgers (Newark); for literature, the Richard Wright Papers at Yale's Beinecke Library, the Walker Percy Archives at the University of North Carolina, Chapel Hill, and Lorraine Hansberry's papers at the Schomburg Center for Research in Black Culture at the New York Public Library. Hansberry's sparkling humanism was one of the surprising revelations of my research: may the nation be worthy of her vision one day.

I want to thank Tulane's School of Liberal Arts for subvention funds that helped license the rights for some of the iconic images in this work. Tulane was also pivotal in my obtaining a summer stipend from the National Endowment for the Humanities' We the People Fund that made possible some pure writing time at a pivotal moment of this book's development.

Finally, to name some essential names. Jeff Cowie has been my intellectual brother for much of this long, cool ride and helpful in more ways than I can count (or remember). And I am a lucky man in that two of my closest friends—my sister Adele Dinerstein and Kenny Fass—are also smart, excellent editors that I impose on regularly. I finished this work with a lot of help from my friends.

Notes

Prelude

1. This narrative is constructed from the following sources: Ross Russell, "Bird and Sartre," Ross Russell Papers, Harry Ransom Center, University of Texas, Austin; "Juliette Gréco, interview by Philippe Carles, "Sartre Asked Miles Why We Weren't Married," trans. Richard Williams, *Guardian*, May 25, 2006, https://www.theguardian.com/music/2006/may/25/jazz; Agnès Poirier, "Juliette Gréco: 'We Were Very Naughty,'" *Guardian*, February 17, 2014, https://www.theguardian.com/music/2014/feb/17/juliette-greco-miles-davis-orson-welles-sartre; Miles Davis with Quincy Troupe, *Miles: The Autobiography* (New York: Simon and Schuster, 1990), 70–71, 125–27, 197, 207, 216; Simone de Beauvoir, *Memoirs of a Dutiful Daughter* (1963; repr. New York: HarperPerennial, 2005); Pierre Michelot and Marcel Romano, liner notes, Miles Davis, *Ascenseur pour l'échafaud* (1958; reissued, Polygram CD, 1990); James Campbell, *Exiled in Paris: Richard Wright, James Baldwin, Samuel Beckett and Others on the Left Bank* (New York: Scribner, 1995), 14–15; Harvey Levenstein, *We'll Always Have Paris: American Tourists in Paris* (Chicago: University of Chicago Press, 2004), 150–52; Ashley Kahn, *The Making of* Kind of Blue (New York: Da Capo, 2001), 64–65; Mark Gardner, liner notes, *Bird in Paris* (Spotlite CD SPJT18); Ian Carr, *Miles Davis: The Definitive Biography* (New York: Thunder's Mouth, 1998), 126–27, 207–8, 217–18; Tyler Stovall, *Paris Noir: African Americans in the City of Light* (New York: Houghton Mifflin, 1996), 179–81; Graham Robb, *Parisians: An Adventure History of Paris* (New York: Norton, 2011), 301–14;

Alyn Shipton, *Groovin' High: The Life of Dizzy Gillespie* (New York: Oxford, 1999), 206–7; Ross Russell, *Bird Lives!* (1976; repr., New York: Da Capo, 1996), 271–73; Mike Hennessey, *Klook: The Story of Kenny Clarke* (Pittsburgh: University of Pittsburgh Press, 1994), 149.

2. Boris Vian, *Round about Midnight: The Jazz Writings of Boris Vian*, ed. Mike Zwerin (London: Quartet, 1988), 78.

3. Gréco, "Sartre Asked Miles."

4. Stovall, *Paris Noir*, 179–81.

5. In effect, the silence—the lack of soundtrack—becomes more effective as it rises and falls in contrast to the improvised passages. This is a hallmark of Davis's jazz phrasing—the balance of silence, sound, and accent.

6. Tom Vallance, "Obituary: Eartha Kitt," *Independent,* December 27, 2008, http://www.independent.co.uk/news/obituaries/eartha-kitt-singer-and-actress-with-a-difficult-reputation-who-was-described-as-the-most-exciting-1212439.html; on Orson Welles and Eartha Kitt, see also Duke Ellington, *Music Is My Mistress* (New York: Da Capo, 1973), 241.

7. Miles Davis with Quincy Troupe, *Miles: The Autobiography* (New York: Simon and Schuster, 1990), 125–27.

8. Audrey Hepburn's son called Gréco one of Hepburn's "prototypes." Sean Hepburn Ferrer, *Audrey Hepburn, An Elegant Spirit: A Son Remembers* (New York: Atria, 2003), 86; Roy Carr, Brian Case, and Fred Dellar, *The Hip: Hipsters, Jazz, and the Beat Generation* (London: Faber and Faber, 1986), 109–11; George Cotkin, *Existential America* (Baltimore, MD: Johns Hopkins University Press, 2003), 104.

9. Eric Nisenson, *'Round about Midnight: A Portrait of Miles Davis* (New York: Da Capo, 1996), 281, on Miles as "the ultimate existentialist artist"; on Miles and existentialism, see also Carr, *Miles Davis*, 502.

10. Will Friedwald, *Jazz Singing* (New York: Da Capo, 1996), 283–84.

Introduction

1. For "playing it cool," see Erving Goffman, *Asylums* (New York: Doubleday/Anchor, 1961), 61–65, and "Cooling the Mark Out: Some Aspects of Adaptation to Failure," *Psychiatry* 15 (November 1952): 451–63.

2. Duke Ellington, *Music Is My Mistress* (New York: Da Capo, 1973), 140.

3. For the abandonment of a European classical ideal for jazz and ethnic idioms among American composers, see Macdonald S. Moore, *Yankee Blues* (Bloomington: University of Indiana Press, 1983).

4. Norman Mailer, Box 1014, Folder 1, Norman Mailer Papers, Harry Ransom Center (HRC), University of Texas–Austin.

5. David Denby, "Out of the West: Clint Eastwood's Shifting Landscape," *New Yorker*, March 8, 2010, http://www.newyorker.com/magazine/2010/03/08/out-of-the-west-6.

6. Andrew Gilbert, "Clint Eastwood: Mise en Swing," *JazzTimes*, September 2007, jazztimes.com/articles/18861-clint-eastwood-mise-en-swing.

7. The cool jazz movement started with Miles Davis and Gil Evans. Most of its major innovators and icons in the mid-1950s were white musicians such as Chet Baker, Gerry Mulligan, and Art Pepper. Gary Giddins and Scott DeVeaux, *Jazz* (New York: W. W. Norton, 2009), 337–76. In 1958, NBC made a half-hour show, *The Subject Is Jazz: Cool*, that can still be found on YouTube.

8. Denby, "Out of the West."

9. Boris Vian's review was titled "The Ears of a Faun," an allusion to Debussy's "Afternoon of a Faun," and an attempt to create equivalence between jazz and classical music (reprinted in *Round about Midnight: The Jazz Writings of Boris Vian*, ed. Mike Zwerin [London: Quartet, 1988], 76–77).

10. Albert Murray, *Stomping the Blues* (New York: Da Capo, 1976), 42. I developed Murray's phrase into a critical term for a broader continuum of African-American culture in my *Swinging the Machine: Modernity, Technology, and African-American Culture between the World Wars* (Amherst: University of Massachusetts Press, 2003), 22–23 and passim.

11. Stephanie Zacharek, "Nothing but a Man: Roemer Directs Abbey Lincoln in Malcolm X's Favorite Movie," *Village Voice*, October 8, 2014, http://www.villagevoice.com/2014-10-08/film/nothing-but-a-man/full/.

12. In the late 1990s, trombonist J. J. Johnson recalled how Lester Young paved the way for finding one's own unique voice in the 1940s. Bob Bernotas, "An Interview with J. J. Johnson," *Online Trombone Journal*, 1999, http://trombone.org/articles/library/jjjohnson-int.asp. "We'd get together and dissect, analyze, discuss, and listen to Lester Young's solos for hours and hours and hours. . . . What struck me about Lester Young then, and still does after all these years, was his maverick approach to tenor sax improvisation. . . . After two or three notes, you'd know, 'That's Lester Young!' It could be no one else, 'cause his playing had a persona that was uniquely Lester Young."

13. When Galatea Dunkel silences Dean Moriarty and descends into melancholy, Sal Paradise exclaims: "He was BEAT—the root, soul, of Beatific." Jack Kerouac, *On the Road* (1957; repr., New York: Penguin, 1991), 195. See also James Campbell, *This Is the Beat Generation* (Berkeley: University of California Press, 2001), 78–81.

14. André Bazin, "The Death of Humphrey Bogart," in *Cahiers du Cinema: The 1950s*, ed. Jim Hillier (Cambridge, MA: Harvard University Press, 1985), 100. Emphasis added.

15. Lee Server, *Robert Mitchum: "Baby, I Don't Care"* (New York: St. Martin's, 2001).

16. Harry Carey Jr., quoted in ibid., 114–15.

17. Allen Ginsberg, *Composed on the Tongue* (Bolinas, CA: Grey Fox Press, 1980), 48–49.

18. Ibid., 80. For Ginsberg, one of the most "important thing[s]" in his poetry was "to get that continuous locomotive rhythm going." A *New Yorker* reporter referred to Young as "pres of cool" in 1954: Lillian Ross, "You Dig It, Sir?" (1954), in *Reading Jazz*, ed. Robert Gottlieb (New York: Vintage, 1999), 700; Billie Holiday,

quoted in Nat Shapiro and Nat Hentoff, *Hear Me Talkin' to Ya* (New York: Dover, 1955), 310. One biographer tells a different version of the origins of these nicknames: first, that Young originally called Holiday's mother "Lady Day" but her daughter stole it; second, that Holiday meant Young and herself were the "president" and "vice-president" of the Vipers Club, since they smoked marijuana most in the Basie orchestra. Douglas Henry Daniels, *Lester Leaps In: The Life and Times of Lester 'Pres' Young* (Boston: Beacon Press, 2002), 216.

19. Zora Neale Hurston first caught the term in the process of linguistic development in the late 1920s in her novel *Mules and Men*. A rich period of new vocabulary developed among young black men during the Great Migration that is well documented in glossaries of African-American slang published in the 1930s and 1940s, including *Cab Calloway's Hepster Dictionary* (see the appendix to Cab Calloway and Bryant Rollins, *Of Minnie the Moocher and Me* [New York: Crowell, 1976], 251–61); *Dan Burley's Original Handbook of Harlem Jive* (New York: D. Burley, 1944); and the glossaries at the end of Mezz Mezzrow's *Really the Blues* (with Bernard Wolfe [1946; repr., New York: Citadel Press, 1990], 371–80); and Zora Neale Hurston's short story, "Now You Cookin' with Gas" (in *The Complete Stories* [New York: HarperPerennial, 2008], 240–41).

20. Jack Kerouac, *Visions of Cody* (New York: Penguin, 1993), 393.

21. B. B. King with David Ritz, *Blues All around Me* (New York: Avon, 1996), 111.

22. Joe Turner, "Cherry Red," on *Boss of the Blues* (1956; reissued, Collectables CD COL-6327, 2002). See also Hot Lips Page, "Ain't No Flies on Me" (1950), a song that begins with a woman simply saying, "He's a cool cat, ain't he?" Hot Lips Page, *Jump for Joy!* (Columbia Legacy CD).

23. It was widely understood that Holiday picked up her musical attack from Young's instrumental phrasing even if neither of them declared it outright. Young modestly suggested that "this was a useful way to put it," that is, his influence on Holiday. Chris Albertson, "My Awkward Q&A with Lester Young: WCAU, Philadelphia, August 26, 1958," *Stomp Off* (blog), February 12, 2011, stomp-off.blogspot .com/2011/02/my-interview-with-lester-young.html.

24. Young and Sinatra, quoted in Will Friedwald, *Sinatra! The Song Is You* (New York: Da Capo, 1997), 405; Young, quoted in Hentoff, "Pres," in *A Lester Young Reader*, ed. Lewis Porter (Washington, DC: Smithsonian Press, 1991), 163.

25. Reinhold Wagnleitner, "Jazz—the Classical Music of Globalization; or: When the Cold War Morphed into the Cool War," in *Is It 'Cause It's Cool? Affective Encounters with American Culture* (Vienna: LIT Verlag, 2013), 51–53.

26. Snyder, quoted in Lewis MacAdams, *Birth of the Cool: Beat, Bebop, and the American Avant-Garde* (New York: Free Press, 2001), 180; the documentary compiled of the Merry Pranksters cross-country bus trip is named for this quest, *Magic Trip: Ken Kesey's Search for a Kool Place* (Magnolia Home Entertainment, 2011, DVD).

27. Ralph Ellison, "The World and the Jug," in *The Collected Essays of Ralph Ellison*, ed. John F. Callahan (New York: Modern Library, 2003), 161.

28. Ellison, quoted in Albert Murray and John F. Callahan, eds., *Trading*

Twelves: The Selected Letters of Ralph Ellison and Albert Murray (New York: Modern Library, 2000), 31.

29. Alan Liu, *The Laws of Cool: Knowledge Work and the Culture of Information* (Chicago: University of Chicago Press, 2004), 383, and see 181–85.

30. Tony Judt, *Postwar: A History of Europe since 1945* (New York: Penguin, 2006), 4–5.

31. Ian Buruma, *Year Zero: A History of 1945* (New York: Penguin, 2013), 7, 22–23, 40–43. Mark Mazower, *Dark Continent: Europe's Twentieth Century* (New York: Vintage, 2000), 307–11.

32. Simone Weil, *The Need for Roots* (New York: G. P. Putnam's Sons, 1952), 101, 146, 168–69; Mazower, *Dark Continent*, 196; Pankaj Mishra, "The Western Model Is Broken," *Guardian*, October 14, 2014. See also Susan Sontag, "Simone Weil," review of *Selected Essays*, by Simone Weil, *New York Review of Books*, February 1, 1963, http://www.nybooks.com/articles/1963/02/01/simone-weil/.

33. Geoffrey Barraclough, *History in a Changing World* (Norman: University of Oklahoma Press, 1956), 221, and see also vii, 203–20 ("The End of European History").

34. Geoffrey Barraclough, *An Introduction to Contemporary History* (New York: Penguin, 1991), 268; Arthur Koestler, *"The Yogi and the Commissar" and Other Essays* (London: Hutchinson, 1945), 202.

35. Judt, *Postwar*, 61, 63, 113.

36. MacAdams, *Birth of the Cool*, 23.

37. Sarah Relyea, *Outsider Citizens: The Remaking of Postwar Identity in Wright, Beauvoir, and Baldwin* (New York: Routledge, 2006), 3, 46–47, 53–56; Beauvoir, quoted in Margaret A. Simons, *Beauvoir and the Second Sex: Feminism, Race, and the Origins of Existentialism* (Lanham, MD: Rowman & Littlefield, 1999), 170.

38. Paul Gilroy, *The Black Atlantic: Modernity and Double Consciousness* (Cambridge, MA: Harvard University Press, 1993), 186.

39. On the phrase "post-Western," see Timothy Garton Ash, "From the Lighthouse," *New York Review of Books*, November 7, 2013, 52. Ash believes Western political frameworks remain a "modernized Enlightenment." My claim here is cultural: any analysis of artistic production in the United States since 1945 must take account of global interpenetration in terms of music, film, and art, such that it is more accurately termed "post-Western."

40. George Cotkin, *Existential America* (Baltimore, MD: Johns Hopkins University Press, 2005), 225–51; Margo Jefferson, "19 Questions," in *What Was the Hipster? A Sociological Investigation*, ed. Mark Greif, Kathleen Ross, and Dayna Tortorici (New York: N+1 Foundation, 2010), 97.

41. Lorraine Hansberry, "Images and Essences: Dialogue with an Uncolored Egg-head," *Urbanite*, May 1961, 10, 11, 36, Box 57, Folder 1, Lorraine Hansberry Papers, Schomburg Center for Research in Black Culture, New York Public Library.

42. James Baldwin, *No Name in the Street* (New York: Vintage, 2007), 85, and *Notes of a Native Son* (Boston: Beacon, 1955), 149.

43. John Gennari, *Blowin' Hot and Cool: Jazz and Its Critics* (Chicago: University of Chicago Press, 2006), 113.

44. Parker, quoted in Carl Woideck, *Charlie Parker: His Music and Life* (Ann Arbor: University of Michigan Press, 1998), 1.

45. On noir and pulp fiction, see William Hare, *Pulp Fiction to Film Noir: The Great Depression and the Development of a Genre* (Jefferson, NC: McFarland, 2012).

46. Camus, quoted in Herbert R. Lottman, *Albert Camus: A Biography* (New York: Gingko Press), 7; Jean-Paul Sartre, *The War Diaries of Jean-Paul Sartre: November 1939–March 1940* (New York: Pantheon, 1984), 88.

47. Camus Folder, Section IV: Folder 7, Walker Percy Papers, Southern Historical Collection, Wilson Library, University of North Carolina-Chapel Hill, n.d. (ca 1972); Albert Camus, *Notebooks, 1951–59* (Chicago: Ivan R. Dee, 2008), 132.

Chapter One

1. Ted Gioia confirmed earlier scholarly speculation on Young's dissemination of the word "cool" through interviews with a dozen swing-era musicians and friends from Young's generation. All of them said he was the only musician who used the term at the time. The younger alto saxophonist Jackie McLean once concurred Young was first to use "that's cool," and by way of emphasis, "Anyone who tells you otherwise is bullshitting." Ted Gioia, *The Birth and Death of the Cool* (Golden, CO: Speck, 2009), 77–78; McLean, quoted in Lewis MacAdams, *The Birth of the Cool: Beat, Bebop, and the American Avant-Garde* (New York: Free Press, 2001), 19. See also Joachim Berendt, *The New Jazz Book* (New York: Lawrence Hill, 1975), 79, Leonard Feather, "Pres Digs Every Kind of Music," in *A Lester Young Reader*, ed. Lewis Porter (Washington, DC: Smithsonian Institution Press, 1991), 149.

2. Ben Sidran, *Black Talk* (1969; repr., New York: Da Capo, 1980), 112.

3. Richard Williams, "The Conception of the Cool," in *The Miles Davis Companion*, ed. Gary Carner (New York: Schirmer, 1996), 93–97; Bill Kirchner, "Miles Davis and the Birth of the Cool: A Question of Influence," in *A Miles Davis Reader*, ed. Bill Kirchner (Washington, DC: Smithsonian Institution Press, 1997), 38–46. *Birth of the Cool* was a reissue of a series of two-sided ten-inch recordings made in 1949–50 in California with an integrated group of musicians.

4. Gunther Schuller, *The Swing Era* (New York: Oxford University Press, 1988), 547; for "genius soloist," see Sidran, *Black Talk*, 93.

5. "Shoe Shine Boy" can be listened to at https://www.youtube.com/watch?v=mHmAIuoIw2g; "Oh! Lady Be Good" at https://www.youtube.com/watch?v=STkDwdpAC7s.

6. Fletcher Henderson's musicians hounded Young from the band in 1934 for having too "thin" a tone for a tenor saxophone. Count Basie thought Young's tone the "weirdest" he had ever heard at first and "wasn't even sure he liked it." Bassist Walter Page heard the speed first: "Who's that fast saxophone?" he asked. Quoted

in Nathan Pearson, *Goin' to Kansas City* (Urbana: University of Illinois Press, 1987), 200–204.

7. Dizzy Gillespie with Al Fraser, *To Be or Not . . . to Bop* (New York: Doubleday, 1979), 212.

8. Young stated openly at an army court-martial hearing that these substances were necessary for a musician to cope with life on the road. Frank Büchmann-Müller, *You Just Fight for Your Life: The Story of Lester Young* (New York: Praeger, 1990), 123–24.

9. The connotations of cool are so varied and innovative in the postwar era that definitions and phrases take up nearly three pages in the definitive study of jazz language in this period. Robert S. Gold, *Jazz Lexicon* (New York: Knopf, 1964), 65–68.

10. Nelson George, *Elevating the Game* (New York: Fireside, 1992), 62; Ross Russell, *Jazz Style in Kansas City and the Southwest* (1971; repr., New York: Da Capo, 1997), 159.

11. Douglas Henry Daniels, "Goodbye Pork Pie Hat: Lester Young as a Spiritual Figure," *Annual Review of Jazz Studies* 4 (1988): 172.

12. Johnny Otis, *Upside Your Head! Rhythm and Blues from Central Avenue* (Middleton, CT: Wesleyan University Press, 1993), 78. African-Americans often honor an important artistic synthesis with the term, "cool." See Donnell Alexander, "Are Black People Cooler Than White People?" *Might*, July–August 1997: 44–53.

13. Green, quoted in Büchmann-Müller, *You Just Fight*, 84. A typical reflection comes from Texas blues pianist Sammy Price. "I don't ever remember having met a person that was as unique. He was just a cute man . . . sweet, high, nice, polite, kind, but mean as hell [when he wanted to be]." Sammy Price, interview by Dan Morganstern, Jazz Oral History Project (hereafter, "JOHP"), Institute of Jazz Studies (IJS), Rutgers University, January 1980, 57–58.

14. Sadik Hakim, "Reflections of an Era: My Experiences with Bird and Prez," unpublished pamphlet, IJS, n.d.

15. Whitney Balliett, *American Musicians: Fifty-Six Portraits in Jazz* (New York: Oxford University Press, 1986), 234–40; Berendt, *New Jazz Book*, 76–83.

16. Quoted in Lewis Porter, *Lester Young* (Boston: Twayne, 1985), 2; Leonard Feather, "Here's Pres!" in *A Lester Young Reader*, ed. Porter, 142.

17. Cornel West, *Keeping Faith* (New York: Routledge, 1994), xii–xiv.

18. John Blassingame and Mary Frances Berry, *Long Memory* (New York: Oxford University Press, 1982), 368. For the influence of swing-era musicians on 1930s African-American culture, see Sidran, *Black Talk*, 78–115; Lewis Erenberg, "News from the Great White World: Duke Ellington, Count Basie and Black Popular Music, 1927–1943," *Prospects* 18 (1993): 483–506; Gunther Schuller, *The Swing Era* (New York: Oxford University Press, 1988), 1–6.

19. W. C. Handy, *Father of the Blues* (1941; New York: Da Capo, 1969), 62 (quote) and 30–54.

20. Mel Watkins, *On the Real Side* (New York: Touchstone, 1994), 80–133; Thomas L. Riis, *Just before Jazz: Black Musical Theater in New York, 1890–1915*

(Washington, DC: Smithsonian, 1989), 4–7; W. T. Lhamon, *Raising Cain: Black-face Performance from Jim Crow to Hip Hop* (Cambridge, MA: Harvard University Press, 1998), passim.

21. Jesse Stone, interview by Chris Goddard, JOHP, IJS, 2:131.

22. Robert Toll, *Blacking Up: The Minstrel Show in Nineteenth-Century America* (New York: Oxford University Press, 1974), 75–79; Eric Lott, *Love and Theft* (New York: Oxford University Press, 1993), 23, 222.

23. Kenneth Burke, *Attitudes towards History* (1937; repr., Boston: Beacon Press, 1961), 20–22; Toll, *Blacking Up*, 274.

24. William Carlos Williams, *In the American Grain* (1925; repr., New York: New Directions, 1956), 208–11; Watkins, *On the Real Side*, 160; Eric Ledell Smith, *Bert Williams: A Biography of the Pioneer Black Comedian* (Jefferson, NC: McFarland & Co., 1992), 81–82, 228; Ann Charters, *Nobody: The Story of Bert Williams* (New York: MacMillan, 1970), 102, 107. On affirmation, see Murray, *Stomping the Blues* (New York: Da Capo, 1976), 21–42; and Ralph Ellison, *Shadow and Act* (1964; repr., New York: Vintage, 1972), 189. On "somebodiness," see James Cone, *The Spirituals and the Blues: An Interpretation* (Maryknoll, NY: Orbis Books, 1972), 16.

25. The construction of whiteness as an American ethnic identity led to the projection of those traits that fell outside the ideal of Republican virtue (e.g., joy, pleasure, appetite, passion, enthusiasm) onto blacks. In the revolutionary era, Englishmen traded in their European identities for as yet unknown American ones, and these tensions played out in minstrelsy: "Far from English civilization, they had to remind themselves constantly what it meant to be civilized—Christian, rational, sexually controlled, and white" (Ronald Takaki, *Iron Cages* [New York: Oxford University Press, 1991], 1–12). See also David Roediger, *The Wages of Whiteness* (London: Verso, 1991), 3–15; Edmund Morgan, *American Slavery, American Freedom* (New York: W. W. Norton, 1975), 328–37.

26. Ralph Ellison, *Going to the Territory* (New York: Vintage, 1986), 163–68, and *Shadow and Act*, 45–59.

27. Gerald Early, *Tuxedo Junction* (New York: Ecco, 1989), 279.

28. Calloway, quoted in Tom Scanlan, *The Joy of Jazz: The Swing Era, 1935–1947* (Golden, CO: Fulcrum Publishing, 1996), 68; see also James Haskins, *The Cotton Club* (New York: Hippocrene Publishers, 1977); and Kathy J. Ogren, *The Jazz Revolution* (New York: Oxford University Press, 1989), 76.

29. Early movies fastened on such stereotypes as "[the tom], the coon, the tragic mulatto, the mammy, and the brutal black buck . . . to entertain by stressing Negro inferiority" (Donald Bogle, *Toms, Coons, Mulattoes, Mammies and Bucks* [New York: Continuum, 1994], 3–4).

30. Panama Francis, interview by Milt Hinton, JOHP, IJS, 4:7–9; Charles S. Johnson, *Patterns of Negro Segregation* (New York: Harper & Brothers, 1943), 244; see also Gillespie with Fraser, *To Be or Not . . . to Bop*, 295–97.

31. Cab Calloway and Bryant Rollins, *Of Minnie the Moocher and Me* (New York: Thomas Y. Crowell Co., 1976), 184.

32. Carl Cons, "A Black Genius in a White Man's World," *Downbeat*, July 1936, 6.

33. Otis, *Upside Your Head!* 77. George Morrison, interview by Gunther Schuller in Schuller's *Early Jazz* (New York: Oxford University Press, 1968), 359–72.

34. Jacqui Malone, *Steppin' on the Blues* (Urbana: University of Illinois Press, 1996), 108.

35. Morroe Berger, Edward Berger, and James Patrick, *Benny Carter: A Life in American Music* (Metuchen, NJ: Scarecrow Press, 1982), 238.

36. Quotes from George T. Simon, *The Big Bands* (New York: Schirmer, 1981), 115–16, 483–84; and Berger, *Carter*, 105–6.

37. Young, quoted in Allan Morrison, "You Got to Be Original, Man," and Pat Harris, "Pres Talks about Himself," both in *A Lester Young Reader*, ed. Porter, 132, 138. See also Büchmann-Müller, *You Just Fight*, 9; John McDonough, liner notes, *The Giants of Jazz: Lester Young* (Alexandria, VA: Time-Life Records, 1980).

38. François Postif, "Interview with Lester Young," in *A Lester Young Reader*, ed. Porter, 181.

39. Lee Young, quoted in Büchmann-Müller, *You Just Fight*, 12; McDonough, *Giants of Jazz*, 708. Many African-American bandleaders were middle-class college graduates who found conventional career paths closed to them. Hsio Wen Shih, "The Spread of Jazz and the Big Bands," in *Jazz*, ed. Nat Hentoff and Albert J. McCarthy (New York: Da Capo, 1959), 177–79.

40. Büchmann-Müller, *You Just Fight*, 8–9 and 18–20.

41. Harris, "Pres Talks about Himself," 138.

42. Luc Delannoy, *Pres: The Story of Lester Young* (Fayetteville: University of Arkansas Press, 1993), 25–37; Büchmann-Müller, *You Just Fight*, 27–40; Porter, *Lester Young*, 6–9; Russell, *Jazz Style*, 151–52.

43. The *Chicago Defender* and the *New York Amsterdam News* both reported Young's new assignment in their April 14, 1934, issues. Citations reprinted in Walker C. Allen, *Hendersonia* (Highland Park, NJ, 1973), 294–95.

44. Mezz Mezzrow with Bernard Wolfe, *Really the Blues* (1946; New York: Citadel Press, 1990), 140–42; Berger, Berger, and Patrick, *Benny Carter*, 105–6.

45. As critic Leonard Feather put it, "Lester . . . augured the slow changeover from hot jazz to cool jazz" ("Pres Digs Every Kind of Music," 144–45).

46. Erenberg, "New from the Great White World," 483–503.

47. Milt Hinton, interview by the author, August 19, 1997.

48. Stanley Dance, *The World of Earl Hines* (New York: Da Capo, 1977), 81; David W. Stowe uses the term "soldiers of music" in *Swing Changes: Big-Band Jazz in New Deal America* (New York: Harvard University Press, 1994), 10–13.

49. Malcolm X with Alex Haley, *The Autobiography of Malcolm X* (New York: Grove, 1966), 35–136; Ellison, *Going to the Territory*, 220; Douglas Henry Daniels, "Schooling Malcolm: Malcolm Little and Black Culture during the Golden Age of Jazz," *Steppingstones* (Winter 1983), 45–60; Nat Hentoff, *Boston Boy* (New York: Knopf, 1986), 119–24.

50. Russell, *Jazz Style*, 152–53; Büchmann-Müller, *You Just Fight*, 33.

51. Balliett, *American Musicians*, 234–35.

52. Ellison, *Shadow and Act*, 236–37.

53. Quoted in Büchmann-Müller, *You Just Fight*, 109.

54. Krin Gabbard, "Signifyin(g) the Phallus: Mo' Better Blues and Representations of the Jazz Trumpet," in *Representing Jazz*, ed. Krin Gabbard (Durham, NC: Duke University Press, 1995), 104–30.

55. Kerouac, *Visions of Cody* (New York: Penguin, 1993), 391–96; for an analysis of Kerouac's hero worship of Young, see W. T. Lhamon, *Deliberate Speed: The Origins of a Cultural Style in the American 1950s* (Washington, DC: Smithsonian Institution Press, 1991), 166–67, 177–78.

56. Harry Edison, quoted in Büchmann-Müller, *You Just Fight*, 115.

57. For the best short discussion of Young's musical style and achievement, see Schuller, *The Swing Era*, 547–62. For a longer technical analysis of Young's solos, see Porter, *Lester Young*, 38–98, and the musicological analyses by Dave Gelly, Louis Gottlieb, Lawrence Gushee, Don Heckman, and Bernard Cash in Porter, ed., *A Lester Young Reader*, 208–76.

58. Earle Warren, quoted in McDonough, *Giants of Jazz*, 13. For a longer analysis of Young's synthesis, see Bennie Green, *The Reluctant Art* (New York: Da Capo, 1962), 91–118.

59. Paramount News, "Jitterbugs Jive at Swingeroo" (1938), newsreel, Ernie Smith Collection 491.230, Smithsonian Institution Archives Center, Washington, DC. See also "All Day Swing Carnival Draws 25,000," *Metronome*, July 1938, 9.

60. Photos dating back to 1937 show Lester Young wearing sunglasses on stage, pre-dating all other jazz musicians. See Büchmann-Müller, 119, and Delannoy, *Pres*, 105–6.

61. Martin Williams, liner notes, *The Smithsonian Collection of Classic Jazz* (Smithsonian / Columbia Special Products P6 11891); see also bassist Gene Ramey's comments in Delannoy, *Pres*, 45.

62. Schuller, *The Swing Era*, 222–62; George T. Simon, *The Big Bands* (New York: Macmillan, 1971), 79–87.

63. Jo Jones, quoted in Stanley Dance, *The World of Count Basie* (New York: Da Capo, 1980), 53–54.

64. Saxophonist Dave Brubeck thought this relationship of individual to community crucial to jazz, "a fusion of African group consciousness with the Renaissance concept of individualism" (Brubeck, "Jazz Perspective," in *Reading Jazz*, ed. David Meltzer [San Francisco: Mercury House, 1993], 206).

65. Eddie Barefield, quoted in McDonough, *Giants of Jazz*, 13.

66. Cited in Frank Driggs, *Black Beauty, White Heat* (New York: Da Capo, 1982), 148; on social aspects of Kansas City, see Russell, *Jazz Style*, 3–24.

67. Jo Jones, quoted in Hentoff, *Boston Boy*, 121; Young, quoted in Pat Harris, "Pres Talks about Himself, Copycats," in *A Lester Young Reader*, ed. Porter, 138–39.

68. John Hammond, "Kansas City a Hotbed for Fine Swing Musicians," *Downbeat*, September 1936, 1, 9. Roy Eldridge, quoted in liner notes, *The Kansas*

City Six with Lester Young: A Complete Session (1944; reissued, Commodore XFL 15352, 1961). On Young's improvisatory prowess in jam sessions, see Count Basie with Albert Murray, *Good Morning Blues* (New York: Random House, 1985), 147–48; and Delannoy, *Pres*, 44–47. For the importance of the jam session in Kansas City, see Nathan W. Pierson Jr., *Goin' to Kansas City* (Urbana: University of Illinois Press, 1987), 107–20; Murray, *Stomping the Blues*, 149–78; Ellison, *Shadow and Act*, 208–11.

69. David W. Stowe, "Jazz in the West: Cultural Frontier and Region during the Swing Era." *Western Historical Quarterly* 23, no. 1 (February 1992): 53–74. During the 1920s and 1930s, the territory bands provided the most dynamic new musical elements of big band swing: a more free-wheeling sense of improvisation, a focus on "head" arrangements and a blues-based hard-swinging drive. On this legacy, see Thomas J. Hennessey, *From Jazz to Swing: African-American Jazz Musicians and Their Music, 1890–1935* (Detroit: Wayne State University Press, 1994), 103–21; Schuller, *The Swing Era*, 770–805; Murray, *Stomping the Blues*, 166–70.

70. Buck Clayton, *Buck Clayton's Jazz World* (London: Macmillan, 1986), 89–90; Büchmann-Müller, *You Just Fight*, 45–48.

71. This famous jam session is described by various sources in Shapiro and Hentoff, *Hear Me Talkin' to Ya* (New York: Dover, 1955), 291–93, and in Büchmann-Müller, *You Just Fight*, 45–48. In a 1939 jam session in New York City, Hawkins felt so confident of victory that he walked off the bandstand after only ten minutes yet Young refused to concede. "Pres walked out right behind him and was playing his horn right behind Hawk as Hawk was going to his car in the street" (Cozy Cole, interview by Bill Kirchner, April 1980, IJS, 22–24).

72. Lee Young with Patricia Willard, "The Young Family Band," in *A Lester Young Reader*, ed. Porter, 20; Billie Holiday with William Dufty, *Lady Sings the Blues* (New York: Doubleday, 1956), 56–57; Mary Lou Williams, quoted in Shapiro and Hentoff, *Hear Me Talkin' to Ya,* 309; Büchmann Müller, *You Just Fight*, 75.

73. The few white musicians who attended Kansas City jam sessions spoke of the communal spirit at the clubs and an easy acceptance of their presence. See, for example, Cliff Leeman, interview by Milt Hinton, IJS, 30–42.

74. A bartender at Monroe's Uptown House in Harlem remembered: "Lester Young and Ben Webster used to tie up in battle like dogs in the road. They'd fight on those saxophones until they were tired out, then they'd put in long-distance calls to their mothers . . . and tell them about it" (quoted in Ellison, *Shadow and Act*, 210).

75. Gordon Wright, "DISCussions," *Metronome*, March 1940, 46. Of a Ziggy Elman recording, he wrote, "[I] wish that Jerry Jerome would be his natural self instead of trying to imitate Lester Young," and of a Harlan Leonard recording: "The Lester Youngish tenor and rhythm section aren't too exciting." John Chilton, *The Song of the Hawk: The Life and Recordings of Coleman Hawkins* (Ann Arbor: University of Michigan Press, 1993), 191; James Lincoln Collier, *Benny Goodman and the Swing Era* (New York: Oxford University Press, 1989), 203, 223.

76. See Dexter Gordon's comments quoted in Russell, *Jazz Style*, 154. Gordon based his stellar performance as Dale Turner in *'Round Midnight* on his memories of Young's last years.

77. Joe Newman, quoted in Ira Gitler, *Swing to Bop* (New York: Oxford University Press, 1986), 39.

78. Arthur Knight, "The Sight of Jazz," in *Representing Jazz*, ed. Gabbard, 11–53; Büchmann-Müller, *You Just Fight*, 113–15; and Kerouac, quoted in Lhamon, *Deliberate Speed*, 166–67.

79. A short discussion of "the middle state" can be found in David Nye, *American Technological Sublime* (Cambridge, MA: MIT Press, 1994), xiii–xiv. As early as 1764, Immanuel Kant described the English as "cool," "steady," "reasonable," and "indifferent" in his essay "On National Characteristics."

80. Robert Farris Thompson, "An Aesthetic of the Cool," *African Arts* 7, no. 1 (Fall 1973): 40–43, 64–67, 89.

81. This discussion of West African cool relies on the following sources: Robert Farris Thompson, "An Aesthetic of the Cool: West African Dance," *African Forum* 2, no. 2 (Fall 1966): 85–102, *Flash of the Spirit* (New York: Vintage, 1984), 9–16, and *African Art in Motion* (Los Angeles: University of California Press, 1974), 1–44; John Miller Chernoff, *African Rhythm and African Sensibility* (Chicago: University of Chicago Press, 1979), 30–115; John Collins, *West African Pop Roots* (Philadelphia: Temple University Press, 1992), 1–15. Collins's work contains a useful discussion of how Africans view hot and cool rhythms.

82. Chernoff, *African Rhythm*, 105–11; see also Ayo Bankole, Judith Bush and Sadek H. Samaan, "The Yoruba Master Drummer," *African Arts* 8, no. 2 (Winter 1975): 48–56, 77–78. Master drummers are the conductors of West African indigenous music: they control the texture of the musical event through the beat, making sure it is deep and steady but always changing.

83. In West African societies, couples do not dance together; a dancer needs his or her whole body to communicate with other dancers and musicians.

84. Toni Morrison, quoted in Paul Gilroy, *The Black Atlantic: Modernity and Double Consciousness* (Cambridge, MA: Harvard University Press, 1993), 78.

85. Mary Lou Williams, interview by John S. Wilson, New York, June 1973, IJS, 119.

86. Jonny King, *What Jazz Is* (New York: Walker & Co., 1997), 24–26.

87. See A. M. Jones, *Studies in African Music* (London: Oxford University Press, 1959), 1–55; John Storm Roberts, *Black Music of Two Worlds* (New York: Praeger, 1972), 1–16.

88. Oscar Peterson, quoted in Büchmann-Müller, *You Just Fight*, 162.

89. Burt Korall, *Drummin' Men* (New York: Schirmer, 1990), 29; see also Norma Miller with Evette Jensen, *Swingin' at the Savoy: The Memoir of a Jazz Dancer* (Philadelphia: Temple University Press), 69.

90. Green, *The Reluctant Art*, 99–108; Young, quoted in Allan Morrison, "You Got to Be Original, Man," in Porter, ed., *A Lester Young Reader*, 132.

91. Johnny Carisi, quoted in Gitler, *Swing to Bop*, 39–40.

92. Young, quoted in Nat Hentoff, "Pres," in *A Lester Young Reader*, ed. Porter, 161–62.

93. Douglas Henry Daniels explored Young's humor, musical approach, philosophy and spirituality from the perspective of West African oral traditions in "Goodbye Pork Pie Hat," 161–77.

94. Marshall Stearns and Jean Stearns, *Jazz Dance* (1968; repr., New York: Da Capo, 1994), 140. Tap-dancing drummers included Jo Jones, Buddy Rich, Cozy Cole, and Louis Bellson. Cozy Cole, interview by Bill Kirchner, IJS, 2:27.

95. Malone, *Steppin' on the Blues*, 91–110. In the Broadway show *Runnin' Wild* (1923), the chorus boys danced the Charleston solely to hand clapping and foot stamping, "the way it had been danced for many years in the South." Stearns and Stearns, *Jazz Dance*, 134.

96. Tom Davin, "Conversation with James P. Johnson," in *Jazz Panorama,* ed. Martin T. Williams (New York: Crowell-Collier, 1962), 56–57.

97. Korall, *Drummin' Men*, 50–51; Mezzrow, *Really the Blues*, 142–47. According to Mezzrow, white drummers from Chicago—Gene Krupa, Davey Tough, Ben Pollack—learned from black drummers that keeping a steady beat was not equivalent to just keeping time. Rather it was about balancing "a sequence of different sounds accented at the right intervals."

98. Willis Lawrence James, *Stars in de Elements: A Study of Negro Folk Music* (1945; repr., Durham, NC: Duke University Press, 1995), 456.

99. Stravinsky, quoted from *Stravkinsky: In Conversation with Robert Craft* (Harmondsworth, England: Penguin, 1962), as reprinted in *Reading Jazz*, ed. Meltzer, 252; William "Sonny" Greer, interview by Stanley Crouch, New York 1977, IJS, 4:15–16; Korall, *Drummin' Men*, 29–30; Basie, quoted in Stanley Dance, *The World of Count Basie* (New York: Da Capo, 1980), 14.

100. Theodore Dennis Brown, "A History and Analysis of Jazz Drumming to 1942," Ph.D. diss., University of Michigan, 1976, 1–42 (on African influences), 102–33 (on the trap set), 424–48 (on Chick Webb); Cosmo Anthony Barbaro, "A Comparative Study of West African Drum Ensemble and the African-American Drum Set," Ph.D. diss., University of Pittsburgh, 1993, 62.

101. LeRoi Jones [Amiri Baraka], *Blues People* (New York: Quill Morrow, 1963), 111–12; Ellison, *Going to the Territory*, 166–67.

102. Manning Marable, *Black American Politics: From the Washington Marches to Jesse Jackson* (London: Verso, 1985), 74–87; Charles S. Johnson, *To Stem This Tide* (Boston: Pilgrim Press, 1943), 109; Nat Brandt, *Harlem at War* (Syracuse, NY: Syracuse University Press, 1996); Russell Gold, "Guilty of Syncopation, Joy, and Animation: The Closing of Harlem's Savoy Ballroom," *Studies in Dance History* 5, no. 1 (Spring 1994): 50–64.

103. Chester Himes, *If He Hollers Let Him Go* (New York: Thunder's Mouth Press, 1986), 121. For the relationship between jazz musicians and the Double-V campaign, see Eric Lott, "Double-V, Double-Time: Bebop's Politics of Style," in *Jazz among the Discourses*, ed. Krin Gabbard (Durham, NC: Duke University Press, 1995), 245–50.

104. Ellison, *Going to the Territory*, 166–67. "Coolness kept our values warm, and racial hostility stoked our fires of inspiration."

105. Young's army experience is discussed in detail in Daniels, *Lester Leaps In*, 250–66; Büchmann-Müller, *You Just Fight*, 117–30; Delannoy, *Pres*, 134–48; McDonough, *Giants of Jazz*, 25–27.

106. Young, quoted in Allan Morrison, "You Got to be Original, Man," in *A Lester Young Reader*, ed. Porter, 135.

107. McDonough, *Giants of Jazz*, 5; Bill Coss, "Lester Young," in *A Lester Young Reader*, ed. Porter, 154.

108. Basie trumpeter Harry Edison said, "The army just took all his spirit" (Büchmann-Müller, *You Just Fight*, 129). Young's close friend Gene Ramey believed he lost some of his technical skill from the beatings he received; see Ramey interview, IJS, 5:37–41. In the late 1940s, European writers expressed disbelief when they first saw Lester Young in concert, shocked this was the same man they heard on recordings. See Delannoy, *Pres*, 140–55, and Ross Russell, *Bird Lives!* (1976; repr., New York: Da Capo, 1996), 327.

109. Lewis Porter, liner notes, *Sarah Vaughan/Lester Young: One Night Stand* (1947; reissued, Blue Note CD, 1997); and Porter, *Lester Young*, 102–3.

110. Bobby Scott, "The House in the Heart," in *A Lester Young Reader*, ed. Porter, 99–118; Büchmann-Müller, *You Just Fight*, 174–77 and 181–84.

111. Porter, *Lester Young*, 27.

112. For an extended analysis, see Joel Dinerstein, "'Uncle Tom Is Dead!' Wright, Himes, and Ellison, Lay a Mask to Rest," *African-American Review* 43, no. 1 (Spring 2009): 83–99.

113. Ellington referred to it as a "social significance show," and the show was originally set to open with Uncle Tom lying on his death bed. Ellington, *Music Is My Mistress* (New York: Da Capo, 1973), 175. Gena Caponi-Tabery, *Jump for Joy: Jazz, Basketball, and Black Culture in 1930s America* (Amherst: University of Massachusetts Press, 2008), 175–86.

114. Ellison, *Shadow and Act*, 56.

115. Ralph Ellison, *Invisible Man* (1952; repr., New York: Vintage International, 1981), 439–44. Invisible Man spots the cool young men at a pivotal moment regarding his faith in social equality, having just witnessed the arrest and subsequent murder of his friend, Tod Clifton.

116. Ellison, *Invisible Man*, 441; George, *Elevating the Game*, 62.

117. Gillespie with Fraser, *To Be or Not . . . to Bop*, 295–96. Struggling for the right to self-definition from both white assumptions and outmoded Southern self-defense strategies, bebop musicians rebelled against show business traditions and the clichés of swing. Neil Leonard, *Jazz: Myth and Religion* (New York: Oxford University Press, 1987), 16–18; Berger, Berger, and Patrick, *Benny Carter*, 18.

118. Sidran, *Black Talk*, 112–13; Ellison, *Shadow and Act*, 226–27; Amiri Baraka, cited in Lott, "Double-V, Double Time," 248.

119. Orrin Keepnews, *The View from Within* (New York: Oxford University

Press, 1988), 39. Bebop musicians completed the job that swing-era musicians had started. Lott, "Double-V, Double-Time," 243–55.

120. Gillespie with Fraser, *To Be or Not . . . to Bop*, 116–17, 185, 241, 502. Young was the tenor saxophonist in Gillespie's first bebop band for a short time (October–December 1943), but his father's death compelled him to travel to California. See also Dempsey Travis, *An Autobiography of Black Jazz* (Chicago: Urban Research Institute, 1983), 341.

121. Russell, *Bird Lives!* 68, 89–95; Parker, quoted in Shapiro and Hentoff, *Hear Me Talkin' to Ya*, 355; Schuller, *The Swing Era*, 794–96.

122. This photo can be found in Ross Russell, *Jazz Style in Kansas City and the Southwest* (Berkeley: University of California Press, 1973), 198–99.

123. Ellison, *Shadow and Act*, 221–32; Sidran, *Black Talk*, 110–12.

124. Amiri Baraka, *Transbluesency: The Selected Poems of Amira Baraka/LeRoi Jones, 1961–1995* (New York: Marsilio, 1995), 171–72.

125. Miles Davis with Quincy Troupe, *Miles: The Autobiography* (New York: Simon and Schuster, 1989), 44–45, 99; Sadik Hakim, quoted in Jack Chambers, *Milestones I: The Music and Times of Miles Davis to 1960* (Toronto: University of Toronto Press, 1983), 16; see also Andre Hodeir, *Jazz: Its Evolution and Essence* (New York: Grove Press, 1956), 116–36, and especially his definition of the "cool sonority" in jazz.

126. Ian Carr, *Miles Davis: A Critical Biography* (Quartet: London, 1982), 26.

127. Max Gordon, "Miles—a Portrait," in *The Miles Davis Companion*, ed. Carner, 93–97; see also Chris Albertson, "The Unmasking of Miles Davis," in *A Miles Davis Reader*, ed. Kirchner, 190–97.

128. Evan Hunter, "Streets of Gold" (excerpt), in *Reading Jazz*, ed. Meltzer, 196–97; Russell, *Bird Lives!* 43; Hentoff, *Boston Boy* (New York: Knopf, 1986), 125–26; Murray, *Stomping the Blues*, 89.

129. This conversation is related in Büchmann-Müller, *You Just Fight*, 210. Bassist Gene Ramey, one of Young's closest friends, recalls Getz and other white musicians "would come around to his [Young's] room every night" at the Alvin Hotel to "sit around and listen to his old records and have him explain to them" how he created certain sounds. Young often begged Ramey not to leave. "'Stay here,' Ramey recalls Young saying. "Maybe we can get these guys to leave." Gene Ramey, interview by Stanley Dance, IJS, 5:39–41; Donald L. Maggin, *Stan Getz: A Life in Jazz* (New York: William Morrow & Co., 1996), 38–43. An excellent analysis of how Young's ideas diffused into jazz in the 1950s can be found in Green, *The Reluctant Art*, 113–18.

130. Büchmann-Müller, *You Just Fight*, 137–39, 201–12; Hentoff, "Pres," 126.

131. Daniels, "Goodbye Pork Pie Hat"; Jo Jones, quoted in Büchmann-Müller, *You Just Fight*, 212; Jo Jones, interview by Milt Hinton, January 1973, IJS, 92.

132. Morroe Berger, "Jazz: Resistance to the Diffusion of a Culture Pattern," in *American Music*, ed. Charles Nanry (New Brunswick, NJ: Transaction, 1972), 6, 11–43.

133. Thad Mumford, "Where Is the Class of '96?" *New York Times*, May 5, 1996, sec. 5, 25.

134. Thad Jones, quoted in Frank Büchmann-Moller, "The Last Years of Lester Young," in *A Lester Young Reader*, ed. Porter, 125; Otis, *Upside Your Head!* 78; Marshall McLuhan, "Media Hot and Cold," in *Understanding Media: The Extensions of Man* (New York: McGraw-Hill, 1965), 31.

135. Ellington, *Music Is My Mistress*, 421; John Szwed, "Foreword," in *I Remember: Eighty Years of Black Entertainment, Big Bands, and the Blues*, by Clyde E. B. Bernhardt (Philadelphia: University of Pennsylvania Press, 1986), ix; Kenneth Burke, *Permanence and Change* (Berkeley: University of California Press, 1954), xxix.

Chapter Two

1. The term was stamped on promotional stills from *The Glass Key* (1942). Margaret Herrick Library of the Academy, Los Angeles, California (MHL).

2. Erin A. Smith, *Hard-Boiled: Working-Class Readers and Pulp Magazines* (Philadelphia: Temple University Press, 2000).

3. "By Request of the Ladies: Humphrey Bogart Turns Lover," pressbook, *Casablanca: 18*. Warner Brothers Archives, University of Southern California (WB/USC); Linda Williams, "Of Kisses and Ellipses," *Critical Inquiry* 32, no. 2 (Winter 2006): 36.

4. David Denby, "Out of the West: Clint Eastwood's Shifting Landscape," *New Yorker*, March 8, 2010. http://www.newyorker.com/magazine/2010/03/08/out-of-the-west-6.

5. Malcolm X with Alex Haley, *The Autobiography of Malcolm X* (New York: Grove, 1966), 99; V. S. Naipaul, *Miguel Street* (1959; repr., New York: Vintage, 2002), 1–5, and *The Middle Passage* (1962; repr., New York: Vintage, 2002), 59. Naipaul's favorite Bogart film was *High Sierra*. Stefan Kanfer, *Tough without a Gun: The Life and Extraordinary Afterlife of Humphrey Bogart* (New York: Knopf, 2011), 239.

6. C. L. R. James, *American Civilization* (London: Blackwell, 1993), 126.

7. André Bazin, "The Death of Humphrey Bogart," in *Cahiers du Cinema, the 1950s*, ed. Jim Hillier (Cambridge, MA: Harvard University Press, 1985), 100; David Desser, "The Wartime Films of John Huston: Film Noir and the Emergence of the Therapeutic," in *Reflections in a Male Eye: John Huston and the American Experience*, ed. Gaylyn Studlar and David Desser (Washington, DC: Smithsonian University Press, 1993), 23; Frank Krutnik, *In a Lonely Street: Film Noir, Genre, Masculinity* (New York: Routledge, 1991), 35–36; Robert Porfirio, "Introduction," in *Film Noir Reader 3: Interviews with Filmmakers of the Classic Noir Period*, ed. Robert Porfirio, Alain Silver, and James Ursini (New York: Limelight, 2002), 2.

8. This is an original periodization of the genre of film noir. Joel Dinerstein, "'Emergent Noir': *Film Noir* and the Great Depression in *High Sierra* (1941) and *This Gun for Hire*," *Journal of American Studies* 42, no. 3 (December 2008): 415–48,

and "The Mask of Cool in Postwar Jazz and Film Noir," in *The Cultural Career of Coolness*, ed. Ulla Haselstein and Catrin Gatsdorf (Lanham, MD: Lexington Books, 2013), 109–26.

9. Stanley Cavell, *The World Viewed* (New York: Viking, 1971), 68.

10. Ibid.; Christopher Breu, *Hard-Boiled Masculinities* (Minneapolis: University of Minnesota Press, 2005), 188, 193n1, 197.

11. John Houseman, quoted in David Thomson, *Rosebud: The Story of Orson Welles* (New York: Knopf, 1996), 73; John Morton Blum, *V Was for Victory* (New York: Harcourt Brace Jovanovich, 1976), 91.

12. John T. Irwin, *Unless the Threat of Death Is behind Them: Hard-Boiled Fiction and Film Noir* (Baltimore, MD: Johns Hopkins University Press, 2008), 217–18.

13. For Thomas Schatz, the genre is a domestic wartime development, that is to say, an inquiry into the "dark side" of human nature as revealed in war. Sheri Biesen extends this analysis by locating the origins of noir's expressionist sensibility—its dark shadows, fervid anxiety, and innovative lighting techniques—in the everyday experience of West Coast power blackouts, paranoia about Japanese attacks, and limited studio budgets. Biesen admits that *Citizen Kane* "anticipated film noir" with its "self-destructive antihero," documentary style, and "bitter, existential *noir* finale," yet does not grapple with the temporal discrepancy. Thomas Schatz, *Boom and Bust: The American Cinema in the 1940s* (New York: Scribner, 1997), 3–5, 138, 204–6, 232–39; Sheri Chinen Biesen, *Blackout: World War II and the Origins of Film Noir* (Baltimore, MD: Johns Hopkins University Press, 2005), 1–6, 34–35, and, on *Citizen Kane*, 59–95.

14. This is an intervention in current academic and historical paradigms of film noir. Feminist film criticism requires a postwar paradigm for its trenchant analysis of the femme fatale, an object of desire so threatening to the controlling male gaze that she must first be demonized and then killed off. In this paradigm of what some scholars recast as "male melodrama," the femme fatale reflects white male anxiety over shifting gender roles in the workplace first during wartime and then in veterans' readjustment to civilian life. Postwar social historians extend this analyze to characterize noir as a genre reflecting anxieties of class identity and the disruption of small-town life, as well as patriarchal resistance to domestication and consumerism. The genre is full of "justified resentments against a corporatist culture of conformity into atomized individualistic self-pity," historian George Lipsitz suggests, as it "aestheticiz[es] alienation" and also satisfies "a craving for revenge." George Lipsitz, *Rainbow at Midnight* (Urbana: University of Illinois Press, 1994), 286; Mike Davis, *City of Quartz: Excavating the Future in Los Angeles* (London: Verso, 1990), 40–41; Krutnik, *In a Lonely Street*, 57–72. See also Joan E. Copjec, *Shades of Noir: A Reader* (London: Verso, 1993), E. Ann Kaplan, ed., *Women in Film Noir* (1978; repr., London: BFI, 1998); and James F. Maxfield, *The Fatal Woman: Sources of Male Anxiety in American Film Noir, 1941–1991* (Madison, NJ: Fairleigh Dickinson University Press, 1996), 10–11.

15. Interview with Billy Wilder, in *Film Noir Reader 3*, ed. Porfirio, Silver, and Ursini, 101. Many scholars link the genre's atomized, isolated, haunted protagonists

to the artistic vision of Central European (often Jewish) immigrant directors in Hollywood (such as Wilder). After escaping Nazism or fascism, these directors allegedly galvanized an intellectual "left culture" in Hollywood. James Naremore rightly presses Orson Welles's political aspirations and John Huston's popular-front ideology to serve his argument. Rather than film noir representing any kind of "a national zeitgeist," Naremore insists that its "atmosphere of death and disillusionment" reflected a small core of artists and, in addition, Hollywood's liberals and Communists—in other words, the very groups facing congressional prosecution first in 1947 and later through McCarthyism and blacklisting. With the end of World War II, and the two entrenched superpowers organized around rival economic systems, the political left in Hollywood "could no longer maintain its Depression-era faith that America would someday evolve into a socialist democracy."

Naremore's paradigm remains dominant: noir's cynicism, claustrophobia, and Marxist critique marry cultural-front politics to imported proto-existentialism. Noir's dark moods and alienated protagonists thus follow from its auteurs, caught between the popular front politics of the Depression and postwar evisceration of their political hopes. Naremore, *More Than Night: Film Noir in its Contexts* (Berkeley: University of California Press, 1998), 104, 123–35; see also Davis, *City of Quartz*, 40–41, and Paula Rabinowitz, *Black and White and Noir: America's Pulp Modernism* (New York: Columbia University Press, 2002).

16. *The Grapes of Wrath* (1940) is as much an emergent noir as a film of social protest while *The Glass Key* was taken from a Dashiell Hammett novel. On Hammett and Huston, see Naremore, *More Than Night*, 63.

17. With regard to the French genre of poetic realism, actor Jean Gabin's characters are always entrapped by family, history, or local loyalties—a more familiar naturalist paradigm—in *Le Jour se Leve*, *La Bête Humaine*, and *Pépé le Moko*. In contrast, noir protagonists act upon an *imagined* agency. Mark Bould, *Film Noir: From Berlin to Sin City* (London: Wallflower, 2005), x, 32 (Lang quote), 36–40.

18. Orson Welles, quoted in Frank Brady, *Citizen Welles* (New York: Scribner, 1989), 81; Richard Slotkin, *Regeneration through Violence* (Middleton, CT: Wesleyan University Press, 1973).

19. Thomson, *Rosebud*, 151–55, 241n35, 398; Michael Walker, "Introduction," in *The Book of Film Noir*, ed. Ian Cameron (New York: Continuum, 1993), 32.

20. Raymond Chandler, *Raymond Chandler Speaking*, ed. Dorothy Gardiner, Katherine Sorley Walker, and Paul Skenazy (1962; repr., Berkeley: University of California Press, 1997), 232.

21. Ibid., 249.

22. Ibid., 232, 249.

23. Nathanael West, "'A Cool Million': A Screen Story," in *Novels and Other Writings* (Library of America, 1997), 745; West's screen treatment here is related only in name to his literary deconstruction of the Alger formula in his novel, *A Cool Million* (1934). Richard Wright, "Alger Revisited; or, My Stars! Did We Read That Stuff?" *PM*, September 16, 1945, 8.

24. James, *American Civilization*, 127.

25. James Naremore, "Introduction," in Raymond Borde and Étienne Chaumeton, *A Panorama of American Film Noir: 1941–1953* (1955; repr., San Francisco: City Lights, 2002), ix; Borde and Chaumeton, *A Panorama of American Film Noir*, 21, 24–25, 33; Krutnik, *In a Lonely Street*, 28; Foster Hirsch, *The Dark Side of the Screen: Film Noir* (1978; repr., New York: Da Capo, 2001), x–xi; Paul Schrader, "Notes on Film Noir," in *Film Noir Reader*, ed. Alain Silver and James Ursini (New York: Limelight, 2000), 52–63.

26. Warren Susman, *Culture as History* (New York: Pantheon, 1973), 196–97; see also Sherwood Anderson, *Puzzled America* (New York: Scribners, 1935), 29, 46, 147.

27. J. P. Telotte, *Voices in the Dark: The Narrative Patterns of Film Noir* (Urbana: University of Illinois Press, 1989), 1–2, 14; Andrew Dickos, *Street with No Name* (Lexington: University Press of Kentucky, 2002), 8.

28. Telotte, *Voices in the Dark*, 14.

29. Thomson, *Rosebud*, 167; interview with Robert Wise in *Film Noir Reader 3*, ed. Porfirio, Silver, and Ursini, 121.

30. Shoshana Felman and Dori Laub, *Testimony: Crises of Witnesses in Literature, Psychoanalysis and History* (Routledge, 1992), 7, 59–62.

31. Angela Martin, "'Gilda Didn't Do Any of Those Things You've Been Losing Sleep Over!' The Central Women of 40s Films Noirs," in *Women in Film Noir*, ed. Kaplan, 209–10, 218–25.

32. James, *American Civilization*, 126; Kanfer, *Tough without a Gun*, ix, 234.

33. Cavell, *The World Viewed*, 75–76. For the studio era, Cavell writes, "An account of the paths of stars across their various films must form part of the internal history of the world of cinema." This is similar to Richard Dyer's theory of stars as cinematic texts in *Stars* (London: BFI, 2008).

34. Humphrey Bogart, telegram to Hal Wallis, May 4, 1940, WB/USC Archives.

35. Rabinowitz, *Black and White and Noir*, 19–20, 106, 110.

36. Smith, *Hard-Boiled*, 42–47.

37. Mat 208, pressbook, *High Sierra*, WB/USC; "Movies to Watch For," *Kansas City Star*, January 26, 1941, 12, clipping file, *High Sierra*, WB/USC Archives.

38. Various posters and mats, pressbook, *High Sierra*, WB/USC Archives.

39. Various posters and mats, pressbook, *High Sierra*, WB/USC Archives.

40. "Second Day Advance" (article), pressbook, *High Sierra*, WB/USC Archives; Bosley Crowther, "The Screen: 'HS' at the Strand, Considers the Tragic and Dramatic Plight of the Last Gangster," January 25, 1941, *New York Times*, n.p., and "'High Sierra' New Tenant at Strand," *New York Journal-American*, January 25, 1941, n.p., clipping file, *High Sierra*, WB/USC Archives.

41. Krutnik, *In a Lonely Place*, 198–201; Alain Silver and James Ursini, *Film Noir* (New York: Taschen, 2004), 112.

42. "Bogart Packs Punch in New Hit" and "Third Day Advance," pressbook, *High Sierra*, WB/USC Archive.

43. Huston won out over two other script doctors in voting to option Burnett's

High Sierra. Internal memoranda, *High Sierra* file, WB/USC Archive. Together, Huston and Bogart teamed up in *The Treasure of Sierra Madre, Key Largo, The African Queen*, and *Beat the Devil*.

44. Dickos, *Street with No Name*, 116.

45. André Bazin, "The Death of Humphrey Bogart," *Cahiers du Cinema*, ed. Hillier, 99.

46. Billy Wilder and Edward Dmytryk, quoted in *Film Noir Reader 3*, ed. Porfirio, Silver, and Ursini, 108–9; see also Biesen, *Blackout*, 97.

47. Edward Dmytryk, Billy Wilder, Robert Wise, and Fritz Lang are quoted in interviews by Robert Porforio in *Film Noir Reader 3*, ed. Porfirio, Silver, and Ursini, 30, 35, 101–2, 122, 133.

48. Nicholas Christopher, *Somewhere in the Night: Film Noir and the American City* (New York: Free Press, 1997), 37–38; Thomson, *Rosebud*, 166, 206.

49. Michael Walker, quoted in Cameron, *Book of Film Noir,* 32; see also Schrader, "Notes on Film Noir," 58–59.

50. Marc Vernet, *"Film Noir* on the Edge of Doom," in *Shades of Noir: A Reader*, ed. Joan Copjec (London: Verso, 1993), 14, 20; William Marling, *The American Roman Noir: Hammett, Cain, and Chandler* (Athens: University of Georgia Press, 1995), ix; Barton Palmer, *Hollywood's Dark Cinema: The American Film Noir* (Boston: Twayne, 1992), 4.

51. Biesen, *Blackout*, 43–45.

52. James H. Cain, quoted in Lloyd Shearer, "Crime Certainly Pays on the Screen," *New York Times Magazine*, August 15, 1945, 77.

53. Naremore analyzes the influence of Graham Greene on the noir genre in *More Than Night*, 72–74.

54. Crowther's review quoted in Beverly Linet, *Ladd: The Life, the Legend, the Legacy of Alan Ladd* (New York: Arbor House, 1979), 71.

55. Lewis Erenberg, *Swingin' the Dream: Big Band Jazz and the Rebirth of American Culture* (Chicago: University of Chicago Press, 1998), 35–64.

56. Borde and Chaumeton, *A Panorama of Film Noir*, 37–38; Marilyn Henry and Ron DeSourdis, *The Films of Alan Ladd* (Secaucus, NJ: Citadel Press, 1981), 15; Veronica Lake with Donald Bain, *Veronica* (London: W. H. Allen, 1969), 85. For a recent retrospective of Ladd and Lake films, one critic called attention to "the stars' icy good looks and temperaments," and how "together, they became a national sensation." "The Tough and the Peek-A-Boo," *American Movie Classics*, August 1995, p. 14, clipping file, *This Gun for Hire*, MHL.

57. "The Tough and the Peek-A-Boo."

58. Laura Mulvey perceives a similar hero vs. heavy split in the postwar Western, as early as *Duel in the Sun* (1946) and culminating in *The Man Who Shot Liberty Valence* (1962). Laura Mulvey, "Afterthoughts on 'Visual Pleasure and Narrative Cinema' inspired by *Duel in the Sun*,'" in *Feminism and Film Theory*, ed. Constance Penley (New York: Routledge, 1988), 69–79.

59. "The Current Cinema: That Odd Miss Lake," *New Yorker*, May 13, 1942, n.p., clipping file, *This Gun for Hire*, MHL.

60. Naremore, *More Than Night*, 73.

61. "Movie of the Week: *This Gun For Hire*—Lake and Ladd Make an Unusual Melodrama," *Life*, June 22, 1942, 49–53; "The Current Cinema: That Odd Miss Lake"; "Alan Ladd, Lake, Cregar Intrigue in 'Gun for Hire,'" *Los Angeles Times*, June 26, 1942, n.p.; Alan Ladd, "The Role I Liked Most . . . ," *Saturday Evening Post*, December 28, 1946, n.p., clipping file, *This Gun for Hire*, MHL.

62. Naremore, *More Than Night*, 74; Henry and DeSourdis, *The Films of Alan Ladd*, 13–14.

63. "T G F H," *Hollywood Reporter*, March 17, 1942, n.p.; "The Current Cinema," *New Yorker*; "T G F H," *Variety*, March 17, 1942, n.p. clipping file, MHL. For Borde and Chaumeton, Ladd's cool-masked masculinity was both revelatory and disturbing. He walked out of every scene "ever silent, ever unfeeling," and within this "expressionlessness" he seemed to inhabit a "great tension reveal[ing] a fearsome, inhuman frigidity" (*A Panorama of Film Noir*, 37–38).

64. Promotional stills, *This Gun for Hire*, MHL; "Alan Ladd Added to Hollywood's List of 'Heavies,'" unidentified clipping, October 30, 1942, MHL; Borde and Chaumeton, *A Panorama of Film Noir*, 37–38.

65. "That Odd Miss Lake," *New Yorker*, clipping file, *This Gun for Hire*, MHL.

66. Scorsese and Jarmusch, quoted in Lee Server, *Robert Mitchum: "Baby, I Don't Care"* (New York: St. Martin's, 2001), 534; Jim Jarmusch, July 1997, statement made upon Mitchum's death to the *Village Voice* (jimjarmusch.tripod.com /profiles.html). See also Jim Trombetta, "Robert Mitchum," in *The Catalog of Cool*, ed. Gene Sculatti (New York: Warner Books, 1982), 128–30; Alex Simon, "Jim Jarmusch: Ghost Story," *Venice Magazine*, March 2000. See also TCM promotional stills for *Out of the Past*, Turner Classic Movies, http://www.tcm.com/tcmdb/title /361/Out-of-the-Past/tcm-archives.html.

67. "Treatment by Geoffrey Homes" (a.k.a. Daniel Mainwaring), *Out of the Past*–Box 1184, RKO-S Archives, UCLA Special Collections; Server, *Robert Mitchum*, 118–19.

68. Ibid.

69. David Thomson, "The Noir to End All Noir," *Independent* (UK), May 5, 1998, 7. This ad appeared in *Life*, November 3, 1947, along with this description of the film: "High-powered romance that begins with a double-cross and ends in double-trouble . . . for a guy without a future and a girl with too much past!" For an overview of the filming of *Out of the Past*, see Server, *Robert Mitchum*, 118–30.

70. Promotional still BMG-22, *Out of the Past*, MHL.

71. Pressbook, *Out of the Past*, and Daniel Mainwaring, original script, *Out of the Past*, Boxes 1183 and 1884, RKO-S Archives, UCLA Special Collections.

72. Charles L. Franke, "Out of the Past," *Motion Picture Daily*, November 17, 1947, n.p.; and Bosley Crowther, "Out of the Past" (review), *New York Times*, November 26, 1947, n.p., clipping file, USC/WB; Robert B. Pippin, *Fatalism in Film Noir: Some Cinematic Philosophy* (Charlottesville: University of Virginia Press, 2012), 12.

73. "Jane Greer, Slick Menace," pressbook, *Out of the Past*, WB/USC.

74. Slavoj Žižek, *Looking Awry* (Cambridge, MA: MIT Press, 1991), 66.

75. Simone de Beauvoir, *The Second Sex* (New York: Knopf, 2010), 206–7.

76. Pippin, *Fatalism in Film Noir*, 12–41; Žižek, *Looking Awry*, 62–66; Fredric Jameson, "The Synoptic Chandler," in *Shades of Noir*, ed. Copjec, 33–57.

77. Server, *Robert Mitchum*, 511.

Chapter Three

1. "Albert Camus—Banquet Speech" (emphasis added), December 10, 1957, Stockholm, http://nobelprize.org/nobel_prizes/literature/laureates/1957/camus-speech.html.

2. In Paris, Camus enjoyed national celebrity such that a young movie critic once jumped up on a bar to declare his envy: "It's Camus—he has everything you need to seduce, to be happy, to be famous, and in addition . . . he dares to have all the virtues!" Herbert R. Lottman, *Albert Camus: A Biography* (New York: Doubleday, 1979), 243, 391, 415, 640; Jean Daniel, quoted in Michael Scammell, *Koestler: The Literary and Political Odyssey of a Twentieth-Century Skeptic* (New York: Random House, 2009), 292.

3. Lottman, *Albert Camus*, 37, 46, 52, 71–72, 290–91, 310, 432–33. Camus called it his "Castilian pride," a result of his family's "silence, their reserve, their natural sober pride."

4. See, e.g., Penny Vlagopoulos, "Voices from Below: Locating the Underground in Post-World War II American Literature," PhD diss., Columbia University, 2008.

5. Jean-Paul Sartre, *The War Diaries, November 1939—March 1940* (New York: Pantheon, 1984), 273–74, 319–20; Annie Cohen-Solal, *Jean-Paul Sartre: A Life* (New York: New Press, 2005), 69, 79.

6. Sartre, *War Diaries*, 52, 95–96; for the code hero, see Philip Young, *Ernest Hemingway* (Minneapolis: University of Minnesota Press, 1965), 11.

7. Italo Calvino, *The Road to San Giovanni* (New York: Vintage, 1994), 50–51; C. L. R. James, *American Civilization* (1950; repr., London: Blackwell, 1993), 147; see also Selwyn Reginald Cudjoe and William E. Cain, eds., *C. L. R. James: His Intellectual Legacies* (Amherst: University of Massachusetts Press, 1993), 25.

8. Albert Camus, *The Rebel: A Study of Man in Revolt* (1951; repr., New York: Vintage, 1991), 15; Sartre, quoted in Steven Earshaw, *Existentialism* (London: Continuum, 2006), 137; Camus, *Notebooks 1951–1959* (Chicago: Ivan R. Dee, 2008), 67, and *Notebooks 1935–1942* (New York: Marlowe & Company, 1963), 71.

9. Sartre, *War Diaries*, 50–52. Sartre felt superior to anyone who did not, like him, "freely seek . . . authenticity."

10. Sartre, *War Diaries*, 75; Albert Camus, *Lyrical and Critical Essays* (New York: Vintage, 1970), 9.

11. Simone de Beauvoir, *A Transatlantic Love Affair: Letters to Nelson Algren* (New York: New Press, 1998), 137, 204, 207, 223, 308–9, 325, 404, 417, 484, 508.

12. Camus, *Lyrical and Critical Essays*, 114–15, and *Notebooks 1951–59*, 230.

13. Sarah Relyea, *Outsider Citizens: The Remaking of Postwar Identity in Wright, Beauvoir, and Baldwin* (New York: Routledge, 2006), 7–8 and 43–44 (quote). Beauvoir credits Wright for the influence on race (and the Other) in *The Second Sex*, 297–98, and in *America Day by Day* (1948; repr., Berkeley: University of California Press, 1999), 34–39, 57–58, 272–76; Sartre discusses Wright in *What Is Literature? And Other Essays* (Cambridge, MA: Harvard University Press, 1988), 71–74.

14. Paul Gilroy, *The Black Atlantic: Modernity and Double Consciousness* (New York: Oxford University Press, 1993) 151, 154.

15. John Dewey, *Art as Experience* (1934; repr., New York: Perigee, 2005), 62, 69; Friedrich Nietzsche, *The Gay Science* (New York: Vintage, 1974), 232.

16. Simone de Beauvoir, *The Ethics of Ambiguity* (1948; repr., New York: Citadel, 1976), 14. On situatedness, see Barbara S. Andrew, "Beauvoir's Place in Philosophical Thought," and Eva Gothlin, "Reading Simone de Beauvoir with Martin Heidegger," both in *The Cambridge Companion to Simone de Beauvoir*, ed. Claudia Card (Cambridge: Cambridge University Press, 2003), 24–44 and 50–56, respectively; on Beauvoir's ethics within situatedness, see Karen Vintges, *Philosophy As Passion: The Thinking of Simone de Beauvoir* (Bloomington: Indiana University Press, 1996), 67–102.

17. Walker Percy, quoted in Lewis A. Lawson and Victor A. Kramer, eds., *Conversations with Walker Percy* (Jackson: University Press of Mississippi, 1985), 275–76, 87.

18. Tony Judt, *Reappraisals: Reflections on the Forgotten Twentieth Century* (New York: Penguin, 2009), 101, 103.

19. Camus, *The Rebel*, 13, 18; Jean-Paul Sartre, *Being and Nothingness: An Essay in Phenomenological Ontology* (New York: Kensington, Citadel, 1956), 18, 21.

20. Camus, *The Rebel*, 13, 104, 250; he adds to this declaration "and we are alone," therefore without ideological or institutional appeal.

21. Ibid., 23; Larry Neal, "Any Day Now: Black Art and Black Liberation," in *Write Me a Few of Your Lines*, ed. Steven C. Tracy (Amherst: University of Massachusetts Press, 1999), 425–28.

22. Camus, *The Rebel*, 15, 23–25; Albert Camus, "*Bahia de Tous Les Saints* by Jorge Amado (The Reading Room)," *Alger Republicain*, April 9, 1939, reprinted in *PMLA* 124, no. 3 (May 2009): 924.

23. Camus, *Lyrical and Critical Essays*, 6–7, 249; for the importance of the sensual life represented by "the sun and the sea," see Avi Sagi, *Albert Camus and the Philosophy of the Absurd* (Amsterdam: Rodopi, 2002), 25, 61, 115, and passim.

24. Camus, *The Rebel*, 25, 194, and passim.

25. Ibid., 55–61.

26. Ibid., 25; Ray Davison, *The Challenge of Dostoevsky* (Devon: University of Exeter Press, 1997), 86–116, 191 (quote); Judt, *Reappraisals*, 95–115.

27. Jean-Paul Sartre, *The Aftermath of War (Situations III)* (London: Seagull, 2008), 198, 240–41.

28. Ibid., 240.

29. Beauvoir, *Ethics of Ambiguity*, 25, 142.

30. Albert Camus, *Camus at Combat: Writing 1944–1947*, ed. Jacqueline Lévi-Valensi (Princeton, NJ: Princeton University Press, 2006), 266; Sartre, "Individualism and Conformity in the United States," in *Aftermath of War*, 87–99 and 107–32; Simone de Beauvoir, *The Mandarins* (1956; repr., New York: W. W. Norton, 1991), 173–75, 323.

31. Beauvoir, *The Mandarins*, 248.

32. Beauvoir, *A Transatlantic Love Affair*, 140.

33. Richard Wright, "Richard Wright," in *The God That Failed*, ed. Richard H. Crossman (1949; repr., Washington, DC: Gateway, 1983), 147.

34. Ronald Aronson, *Camus and Sartre: The Story of a Friendship and the Quarrel That Ended It* (Chicago: University of Chicago Press, 2004); Camus is quoted and *The Rebel* reevaluated in Judt, *Reappraisals*, 96; Camus, *Notebooks: 1951–1959*, 189.

35. Sartre, *The Aftermath of War*, 208–9. Jonathan Judaken has summarized Sartre's impressive contribution to critical race theory: "(1) he was the first to argue that 'race' is a social construct [about Jews]; (2) that 'race' is formed by social struggles and informs processes of inclusion and exclusion, racial subjectification and subjection; (3) he developed the dialectic of the gaze as intrinsic to defining the individual and collective Self and Other; (4) he was an early critic of the shortcomings of the liberal, humanist, Enlightenment tradition for combating racism; (5) he examined how racism was shaped in discourse—considering the semiology of the racialized other and the necessity to deconstruct the stereotypes; (6) he also maintained that discrimination was institutionalized in the strictures and rituals of everyday life; (7) he saw how the system of rules and norms establishing hierarchy and subjugation within the social order could be revealed from the perspective of the racially oppressed; and (8) his vision broadened over time to an appreciation of how race and racism function within the neocolonial global order." Jonathan Judaken, "Sartre on Racism," in *Race after Sartre: Anti-racism, Africana Existentialism, Postcolonialism*, ed. Jonathan Judaken (Albany: State University of New York Press, 2008), 8–9.

36. Camus, quoted in William Hubben, *Dostoevsky, Kierkegaard, Nietzsche and Kafka* (1952; repr., New York: Touchstone, 1997), 34.

37. Camus, *The Rebel*, 301; Vaclav Havel, *The Power of the Powerless* (New York: Routledge, 1985).

38. Chester Himes, *My Life of Absurdity* (New York: Thunder's Mouth Press), 1 (emphasis added).

39. Judt, *Reappraisals*, 9–105, 122, 134; Judt quotes the critic Pierre de Boisdeffre as calling Camus in 1964 "the most noble witness of a rather ignoble age"; Shoshana Felman and Dori Laub, *Testimony: Crises of Witnesses in Literature, Psychoanalysis and History* (Routledge, 1992), 93–119 (on *The Plague*) and 165–203 (on *The Fall*); Jim McWilliams, ed., *Passing the Three Gates: Interviews with Charles Johnson* (Seattle: University of Washington Press, 2003), 193, 251; Danzy Senna refers to Camus three times as a unifying writer in her autobiographical novel, *Cau-*

casia (New York: Riverhead, 1999), 392, 19, 368. Elizabeth Ann Bartlett, *Rebellious Feminism: Camus's Ethic of Rebellion and Feminist Thought* (New York: Palgrave-Macmillan, 2004), xi; Darryl Pinckney, "Forward Passes," *New York Review of Books*, December 17, 2015, 68. See also Charles Mills, *The Racial Contract* (Ithaca, NY: Cornell University Press, 1999).

Philosopher Shannon Sullivan perceives that the intransigence of racism and white supremacy has created an absurd mode in society. Race is akin to "the plague" as it affects the city of Oran in Camus's *The Plague*: it will never go away and always wins, "even if one achieves some minor victories against it[, yet] it's crucial to fight it. . . . The plague spares no one." George Yancy and Shannon Sullivan, "White Anxiety and the Futility of Black Hope," *The Stone* (blog), *New York Times*, December 5, 2014, http://opinionator.blogs.nytimes.com/2014/12/05/white -anxiety-and-the-futility-of-black-hope/.

Charles Mills traces this plague back to the creation of a "racialized world" in early modern European expansionism, since this led to new categories within individuality and equality with separate "categories of personhood and subperson-hood," based on white and non-white, male and female. George Yancy and Charles Mills, "Lost in Rawlsland," *The Stone* (blog), *New York Times*, November 16, 2014, http://opinionator.blogs.nytimes.com/2014/11/16/lost-in-rawlsland.

40. Orlando Patterson, *The Ordeal of Integration* (New York: Basic Civitas, 1998), 108–11.

41. Ibid., 108–11; emphasis mine. Patterson's concept of "creative defiance" is analogous to Kierkegaard's "leap of faith" into the ethical stage of existential freedom.

42. Ibid., 108–9; Lewis R. Gordon, *Existencia Africana: Understanding Africana Existential Thought* (New York: Routledge, 2000), 41–61.

43. Frederick Douglass, *My Bondage and My Freedom* (1855; repr., New York: Barnes & Noble Classics, 2005), 274; Gordon, *Existencia Africana*, 41–61.

44. Richard Wright, *Pagan Spain* (1957; repr., Jackson: University Press of Mississippi, 1995), 21.

45. Richard Wright, "Journal 1945, January 1–Apr. 19," Richard Wright Papers, Yale Collection of American Literature, Beinecke Rare Book and Manuscript Library (hereafter "RW Papers, Beinecke"); Wright, quoted in Margaret A. Simons, *Beauvoir and the Second Sex: Feminism, Race, and the Origins of Existentialism* (Oxford: Rowan & Littlefield, 1999), 178.

46. Wright in Ralph Ellison, *Going to the Territory* (New York: Vintage, 1986), 212; Relyea, *Outsider Citizens*, 87; Wright, "Richard Wright," in *The God That Failed*, ed. Crossman, 130, 147.

47. Wright, "Journal 1945," 9 (emphasis mine), RW Papers, Beinecke.

48. Wright, quoted in Gilroy, *The Black Atlantic*, 159.

49. Wright, "Journal 1945," RW Papers, Beinecke, 10, 17; Wright, quoted in Campbell, *Exiled in Paris*, 10.

50. Richard Wright, "Journal—1947, July 30–September 23: En Route to Europe and In Paris," 10, 55, RW Papers, Beinecke.

51. Simone de Beauvoir, letter to Richard Wright, July 2, 1947, Box 94 ("De Beauvoir"), RW Papers, Beinecke.

52. Wright, "Journal—1947," 53–54; Richard Wright, *The Outsider* (New York: HarperPerennial), 35; Relyea, *Outsider Citizens*, 59–90.

53. "Biographical data for book cover of *The Outsider*," Box 63, Folder 639, RW Papers, Beinecke.

54. Wright, quoted from a 1953 interview in Gilroy, *The Black Atlantic*, 165.

55. Ralph Ellison, letter to Richard Wright, November 3, 1941, "Richard Wright and Ellison—Correspondence," Box 97, RW Papers, Beinecke; Ralph Ellison, "American Negro Writing—a Problem of Communication and Identity," lecture at Bennington College, November 2, 1945, Ralph Ellison Papers, Library of Congress.

56. Ellison, letter to Wright, November 3, 1941.

57. Albert Murray and John F. Callahan, eds., *Trading Twelves: The Selected Letters of Ralph Ellison and Albert Murray* (New York: Modern Library, 2000), 43, 47–48; Albert Murray, *The Omni-Americans* (1970; New York: Da Capo, 1990), 142–70; Maryemma Graham and Amritjit Singh, eds., *Conversations with Ralph Ellison* (Jackson: University Press of Mississippi, 1995), 76, 345.

58. Ellison and Murray, *Trading Twelves*, ed. Murray and Callahan, 24–25, 31, 43, 156, 193–94. Ellison's explication of a blues aesthetic can be found in "An Extravagance of Laughter" in *The Collected Essays of Ralph Ellison*, ed. John F. Callahan (New York: Modern Library, 2003), 617–62; and useful analyses in Timothy Parrish, *Ralph Ellison and the Genius of America* (Amherst: University of Massachusetts Press, 2012), 56–57, 99–103, 117; and in Barbara A. Baker, *Albert Murray and the Aesthetic Imagination of a Nation* (Tuscaloosa: University of Alabama Press, 2010), 132–35.

59. Charles Simic, "No Cure for the Blues," in *The Life of Images: Selected Prose* (New York: Ecco, 2015), 68.

60. Ralph Ellison, "Lectures, Undated," Box 174—Folder 4, ca. 1959, Bard College, Ralph Ellison Collection, Library of Congress; Graham and Singh, eds., *Conversations with Ralph Ellison*, 28.

61. Ralph Ellison, "Hemingway's Romeo and Juliette," typescript, "Lectures, Undated," Ralph Ellison Collection, Library of Congress.

62. Ibid.

63. Jean-Paul Sartre, "American Novelists in French Eyes," *Atlantic Monthly*, August 1946 (emphasis added).

64. Beauvoir, quoted in James R. Mellow, *Hemingway: A Life without Consequences* (New York: Da Capo), 541, and in Beauvoir, *America Day by Day*, 54; Richard Pells, *Modernist America: Art, Music, Movies, and the Globalization of American Culture* (New Haven, CT: Yale University Press, 2012), 261–63; Marling, *American Roman Noir*, 238–39. See also Claire Gorrara, "Cultural Intersections; The American Hard-Boiled Detective Novel and Early French Roman Noir," *Modern Language Review* 98, no. 3 (July 2003): 590–601.

65. Marling, *American Roman Noir,* 93–96 (on Hammett), 148–50 (on Cain), 188–200 (on Chandler).

66. Albert Camus, *The Stranger* (New York: Vintage International, 1989), 3.

67. Matthew Ward, "Translator's Note," in Camus, *The Stranger*, v–vi.

68. David Madden, *Cain's Craft* (Metuchen, NJ: Scarecrow Press, 1985), 79–89.

69. On the absurd in Camus's work, see Sagi, *Albert Camus*, 59–65; Camus, quoted in Lottman, *Albert Camus*, 143; emphasis mine. For Sagi, the key tension in the absurd was between "a rationalist ideal" that is unrealistic and the necessity of "critical rationalism" without conceding to either passion or nihilism.

70. Walker Percy's lecture notes, Camus Folder, Walker Percy Papers, Southern Historical Collection, Wilson Library, University of North Carolina at Chapel Hill.

71. Beauvoir, *America Day by Day*, 55; Camus, *Rebel*, 265.

72. Beauvoir, *America Day by Day*, 31–32, 54–56, 263.

73. John T. Irwin, *Unless the Threat of Death Is behind Them: Hard-Boiled Fiction and Film Noir* (Baltimore, MD: Johns Hopkins University Press, 2008), 13, 19; Joyce Carol Oates, "Man under Sentence of Death," in *Tough Guy Writers of the Thirties*, ed. David Madden (Carbondale: Southern Illinois University Press, 1968), 116–17.

74. See, e.g., Walter Redfern, "Praxis and Parapraxis: Sartre's 'Le Mur,'" in *Jean-Paul Sartre Modern Critical Views*, ed. Harold Bloom (Philadelphia: Chelsea House, 2001), 149–58.

75. Cohen-Solal, *Sartre*, 187, 334.

76. On the progression of Camus's thought through his novels, see Sagi, *Albert Camus*, 155–57; and Walker Percy, untitled lecture notes, Section IV Folder 7, Walker Percy Papers, Southern Historical Collection, Wilson Library, University of North Carolina at Chapel Hill.

77. W. C. Handy, quoted in "Words of the Week," *Jet*, December 31, 1953, 30; LeRoi Jones [Amiri Baraka], *Blues People* (New York: Quill Morrow, 1963), xii.

78. Handy, quoted in "Words of the Week," 30; Mitsutoshi Inaba, *Willie Dixon: Preacher of the Blues* (Lanham, MD: Scarecrow Press, 2011), 9.

79. Ralph Ellison, *Shadow and Act* (1964; repr., New York: Vintage, 1972), 78.

80. Ralph Ellison, *Living with Music* (New York: Modern Library, 2002), 259.

81. Ellison, quoted in Robert O'Meally, "Introduction," in *Living with Music*, xxiii–iv.

82. Ibid.

83. Camus, *Notebooks 1951–1959*, 112.

84. Albert Camus, *The Myth of Sisyphus* (New York: Vintage, 1991); Sagi, *Albert Camus*, 1–2.

85. B. B. King with David Ritz, *Blues All around Me* (New York: Avon, 1996), 83; George Cotkin, "Ralph Ellison, Existentialism and the Blues," *Lettarature d'America* 15, no. 60 (1995): 33–52.

86. King with Ritz, *Blues All around Me*, 130.

87. Big Bill Broonzy with Yannick Bruynoghe, *Big Bill Blues* (London: Cassell and Company, 1955), 44, 56–57, 60–61. On Dylan's deep immersion in the blues during his teenage years, see Toby Thompson, *Positively Main Street: Bob Dylan's*

Minnesota (1971; repr., Minneapolis: University of Minnesota Press, 2008), 65; and Elijah Wald, *Dylan Goes Electric* (New York: Dey Street, 2015), 36, 78–80, 137.

88. Broonzy with Bruynoghe, *Big Bill Blues*, 63.

89. Richard Wright, "So Long, Big Bill Broonzy," liner notes, Mercury Records 7198, Box 5, RW Papers, Beinecke; Broonzy with Bruynoghe, *Big Bill Blues*, 9.

90. Wright, "So Long Bill Broonzy," and "Foreword," in Paul Oliver, *Blues Fell This Morning: Meaning in the Blues* (1960; repr., Cambridge: Cambridge University Press, 1990), xiii–xvii.

91. Muddy Waters, quoted in Jim O'Neal and Amy Van Singel, *The Voice of the Blues* (New York: Routledge, 2002), 183. On blues and African-American culture as they overlapped prewar, wartime, and postwar eras, see Adam Green, *Selling the Race: Culture, Community, and Black Chicago, 1940–1955* (Chicago: University of Chicago Press, 2007), 5–6, 53–55, 70–80.

92. John Milward, *Crossroads: How the Blues Shaped Rock 'n' Roll (and Rock Saved the Blues)* (Boston: Northeastern University Press, 2013), 20, 38–39.

93. Ellison, *Collected Essays of Ralph Ellison*, 128–44.

94. This is one reason why Norman Mailer's "The White Negro" (1957) remains an important document of the post–World War II years for all of its misguided primitivism.

95. To Harold Bloom, Sartre's novels have become dated (except *Nausea*), and he wonders if the works will ever again have an American readership. See Bloom, ed. *Essayists and Prophets* (Philadelphia: Chelsea House, 2005), 202–3.

96. Walker Percy, "Which Way Existentialism?" Walker Percy Papers, University of North Carolina at Chapel Hill.

Chapter Four

1. Ralph J. Gleason, *Celebrating the Duke . . . and Other Heroes* (New York: Da Capo, 1995), 76; see also Gleason, "The Golden Years," in *The Billie Holiday Companion*, ed. Lesley Gourse (New York: Schirmer Books, 1997), 77.

2. Simone de Beauvoir, *The Second Sex* (New York: Knopf, 2010), 17.

3. Ellington, quoted in John Chilton, *Billie's Blues: The Billie Holiday Story, 1933–1959* (New York: Da Capo, 1975), 146; Specs Powell, quoted in Donald Clarke, *Wishing on the Moon* (New York: Da Capo, 2002), 151; Cassandra Wilson, quoted in Farah Jasmine Griffin, *If You Can't Be Free, Be a Mystery: In Search of Billie Holiday* (New York: Free Press, 2001), 14.

4. Milt Gabler, "A Lady Named Billie and I," in *The Billie Holiday Companion*, ed. Gourse, 83–84; Ned Rorem, quoted in Robert O'Meally, *Lady Day: The Many Faces of Lady Day* (New York: Da Capo, 2000), 43; Barney Josephson with Terry Trilling-Josephson, *Café Society: The Wrong Place for the Right People* (Urbana: University of Illinois Press, 2009), 124. Clarinetist Tony Scott once explained the difference of singing a lyric and living it: "A singer like Ella says, 'My man's left me,' and you think the guy went down the street for a loaf of bread or something. But when Lady says, 'My man's gone,' or 'my man's left me,' man, you can see the guy

going down the street. His bags are packed, and he ain't never coming back. I mean like *never*." Scott, quoted in O'Meally, *Lady Day*, 52.

5. Tad Hershorn, *Granz: The Man Who Used Jazz for Justice* (Berkeley: University of California Press, 2012), 89; Marie Bryant, quoted in Donald Clarke, *Wishing on the Moon* (New York: Da Capo, 2002), 202–3; Eric Hobsbawm, *Uncommon People: Resistance, Rebellion and Jazz* (New York: New Press, 1998), 294.

6. Simone Beauvoir, *America Day by Day* (1948; repr., Berkeley: University of California Press, 1999), 44.

7. Interview with Dave Dexter, *Down Beat*, November 1939; see also, Josephson with Trilling-Josephson, *Café Society*, 52, 78.

8. Will Friedwald, "Lady Day . . . Billie Holiday," in *The Billie Holiday Companion*, ed. Grouse, 121.

9. Whitney Balliett, "Billie, Big Bill, and Jelly Roll: Three Graphic Views of the Negro Jazz Musician," *Saturday Review*, July 14, 1956, 32–33.

10. Johann Hari, "The Hunting of Billie Holiday," *Politico Magazine*, January 17, 2015, http://www.politico.com/magazine/story/2015/01/drug-war-the-hunting-of-billie-holiday-114298.

11. Hettie Jones, *How I Became Hettie Jones* (New York: Penguin, 1990), 59, 182; Ira Gitler, quoted in Bret Primack, "Billie Holiday: Assessing Lady Day's Art and Impact," *Jazz Times*, April 1996, 110. http://www.ladyday.net/life/jaztimes.html.

12. Billie Holiday, "Lady Day Has Her Say" (1950), in *Reading Jazz*, ed. Robert Gottlieb (New York: Vintage, 1999), 635–37; Josephson with Trilling-Josephson, *Café Society*, 56; O'Meally, *Lady Day*, 67; Clarke, *Wishing On the Moon*, 230.

13. Margaret A. Simons, *Beauvoir and the Second Sex: Feminism, Race, and the Origins of Existentialism* (Lanham, MD: Rowman & Littlefield, 1999), 167–84; Simone de Beauvoir, *Philosophical Writings*, ed. Margaret A. Simons (Urbana: University of Illinois Press, 2004), 5, 312–13.

14. Josephson with Trilling-Josephson, *Café Society*, 55–57; Griffin, *In Search of Billie Holiday*, 30; O'Meally, *Lady Day*, 97.

15. Angela Y. Davis, *Blues Legacies and Black Feminism: Gertrude "Ma" Rainey, Bessie Smith, and Billie Holiday* (New York: Vintage, 1999), 161–80.

16. Marie Bryant, quoted in Clarke, *Wishing on the Moon*, 202–3.

17. O'Meally, *Lady Day*, 73; Clarke, *Wishing on the Moon*, 307–9.

18. Clarke, *Wishing on the Moon*, 27–50, 290–92; O'Meally, *Lady Day*, 18, 97.

19. Balliett, "Billie, Big Bill, and Jelly Roll," 33. Lester Young, Buck Clayton, and Harry Edison all kept their distance from Holiday after 1943.

20. Albert Murray, *Stomping the Blues* (New York: Da Capo, 1976), 89; Teddy Wilson, quoted in Nat Hentoff, *Jazz Is* (New York: Limelight, 1984), 94–95.

21. Specs Powell, Honi Coles, and Bea Colt, quoted in Clarke, *Wishing on the Moon*, 80–81, 105, 151.

22. Beauvoir, *The Second Sex*, 45.

23. Beauvoir scholars persuasively claim Beauvoir first considered the problem of the Other, influencing both Sartre and Merleau-Ponty.

24. Beauvoir, *The Second Sex*, 643.

25. Annie Dillard, *An American Childhood*, in *Three by Annie Dillard* (New York: Harper Perennial, 1990), 317–21.

26. Beauvoir, *The Second Sex*, 343.

27. Simone de Beauvoir, *A Transatlantic Love Affair: Letters to Nelson Algren* (New York: New Press, 1998), 185 (quote), 177–78. The community of French Africans associated with the journal *Présence Africaine* formally welcomed Armstrong in Paris, along with the African-American expatriate community; Beauvoir, *The Mandarins*, 19, 22, 59, 118, 162, 447, 472, 474.

28. Beauvoir, *A Transatlantic Love Affair*, 84.

29. Beauvoir, *America Day by Day*, 51–52. Mezzrow gave Beauvoir an autographed copy of *Really the Blues* (with Bernard Wolfe [1946; New York: Citadel Press, 1990]), turned her on to marijuana, and explained the prevalence of drugs among musicians.

30. Beauvoir, *America Day by Day*, 265; James Baldwin, "A Question of Identity," in *The Price of the Ticket: Collected Nonfiction, 1948–1985* (New York: St. Martin's, 1985), 92.

31. Davis, *Blues Legacies and Black Feminism*.

32. Darryl Pinckney, "Looking Harlem in the Eye," *NYR Daily* (blog), *New York Review of Books*, February 19, 2015, http://www.nybooks.com/daily/2015/02/19/carl-van-vechten-harlem-photographs/.

33. Davis, *Blues Legacies and Black Feminism*, 8–17.

34. Paul Oliver, *Bessie Smith* (Cranbury, NJ: A. S. Barnes & Co., 1971), 28–29.

35. Ibid., 37–38; Charles Keil, *Urban Blues* (Chicago: University of Chicago Press, 1966); Murray, *Stomping the Blues*.

36. Studs Terkel interviews James Baldwin, 1961, "Studs Terkel Radio Archive Blog," http://studsterkel.wfmt.com/blog/studss-interview-james-baldwin-published/.

37. Chris Albertson, *Bessie* (New York: Stein and Day, 1972), 189, 205, 213. John Hammond scheduled a recording session for Smith with a small unit from the Count Basie orchestra but she died in an auto accident before the session.

38. Betty Carter, quoted in Stanley Crouch, "A Song for Lady Day," *The Root*, July 17, 2009, http://www.theroot.com/articles/culture/2009/07/a_song_for_lady_day/.

39. Bobby Tucker, quoted in Julia Blackburn, *With Billie* (New York: Pantheon Books, 2005), 180.

40. Malcolm X with Alex Haley, *The Autobiography of Malcolm X* (New York: Grove, 1966), 125.

41. Sinatra, quoted in Clarke, *Wishing on the Moon*, 96.

42. Emily Wortis Leider, *Becoming Mae West* (New York: Farrar, Straus and Giroux, 1997), 122–48 and 219–33. See the section "Women and Cool" in my essay, "The Art and Complexity of American Cool," in *American Cool*, ed. Joel Dinerstein and Frank Henry Goodyear III (Munich: Prestel, 2014).

43. Victoria Wilson, *A Life of Barbara Stanwyck*, vol. 1, *Steel-True, 1907–1940* (New York: Simon & Schuster, 2013).

44. James Agee, *Agee on Film: Criticism and Comment at the Movies* (New York: Modern Library, 2000), 340.

45. Quoted in Will Friedwald, *Jazz Singing* (New York: Da Capo, 1996), 283–84.

46. Anita O'Day, *High Times, Hard Times* (New York: Limelight, 1981), 17–18, 22.

Chapter Five

1. "'Round Midnight" was co-written by Thelonious Monk and trumpeter Cootie Williams in 1944.

2. André Bazin, quoted in David Forgacs, *Rome Open City* (London: BFI, 2008), 23.

3. James Jay Carafano, *Waltzing into the Cold War: The Struggle for Occupied Austria* (College Station: Texas A&M University Press, 2002), 4–9 and passim.

4. Frederick Baker, writer and director, *Shadowing the Third Man* (documentary, Criterion Collection); see also James Naremore, *More Than Night: Film Noir in Its Contexts* (Berkeley: University of California Press, 1998), 77–81.

5. Graham Greene, *The Third Man and the Fallen Idol* (New York: Penguin, 1992), 15, 56.

6. Ibid., 14, 60.

7. Rob White, *The Third Man* (London: BFI Film Classics, 2008), 55, 60.

8. Ibid., 56.

9. Ibid., 56, 60.

10. Ibid., 7, 64, 70.

11. Greene, *The Third Man*, 102–3.

12. Ibid., 60–61; White, *The Third Man*, 70.

13. Timothy Snyder, *Bloodlands: Europe between Hitler and Stalin* (New York: Basic, 2012). See also the literary versions of these scenes in Greene, *The Third Man*, 45, 86.

14. Greene, *The Third Man*, 82.

15. The film's climactic scene is a Western-style shoot-out in the sewers where the cops do indeed get the bad guy and Martins himself has to shoot his boyhood friend. For an alternate reading of the moral ambiguity and complexity of the Western as a genre, see Robert B. Pippin, *Hollywood Westerns and American Myth: The Importance of Howard Hawks and John Ford for Political Philosophy* (New Haven, CT: Yale University Press, 2012).

16. *The Quiet American* is a cautionary tale about the U.S. errand in Vietnam and features a naïf named Alden Pyle who, much like Holly Martins, gets his ideas of righteous morality from books. Like Martins, Pyle believes God is always on America's side in its inevitable errand of nation building and the spread of democracy. During the Cold War, the United States took over a warped form of colonialism from European nations, particularly in French Indochina (Vietnam).

17. *The Third Man* is Greene's postwar tribute to a beloved prewar film, *Pépé le Moko* (1937), a work of poetic realism about a French fugitive hiding out in the Algerian casbah that Hollywood remade as *Algiers* (1937), a proto-noir. The film's

use of shadow and key lighting earned an Academy Award for James Wong Howe, one of the acclaimed cinematographers of noir. In the catacombs of the city, le Moko is beloved for his democratic spirit and stylish nonchalance, then hunted down by the police. Harry Lime is heir to Pépé le Moko, living underground on his own guts and guile. Greene acclaimed *le Moko*'s theme of "no freedom anywhere" and credited his existential courage with "the [new] experience of exile common to everyone." The final image is the same: Pépé le Moko clutches the bars of a fence as he watches a French beauty sail back to his beloved Paris; when Harry Lime is shot, he clutches a sewer grate that leads to a street from whose freedom he has seceded. See Greene's review of the film in *The Graham Greene Film Reader: Reviews, Essays, Interviews and Film Stories*, ed. David Parkinson (New York: Applause, 1995), 193–94.

18. Greene, quoted in White, *The Third Man*, 49.

19. In a preface to Anita O'Day's autobiography, Harry Reasoner defined a canary as "the pretty girl in the bouffant dress who spent most of the evening sitting in a chair in front of the big band, snapping her fingers and bouncing a little to the music." Harry Reasoner, "Preface," in Anita O'Day, *High Times, Hard Times* (New York: Limelight, 1981), 11.

20. David Butler, *Jazz Noir: Listening to Music from "Phantom Lady" to "The Last Seduction"* (Westport, CT: Praeger, 2002), 1–2.

21. Robert Mitchum, quoted on *The Dick Cavett Show*, 1971 (Shout Factory DVD, 2006); Catherine L. Benamou, *It's All True: Orson Welles's Pan-American Odyssey* (Berkeley: University of California Press, 2007); Alex Ross, "The Shadow: A Hundred Years of Orson Welles," *New Yorker*, December 7, 2015, http://www .newyorker.com/magazine/2015/12/07/the-shadow; and Ellington, *Music Is My Mistress* (New York: Da Capo, 1973), 240. On Young's love of Westerns, see Ross Russell, "Pres," Ross Russell papers, Box 5, HRC, University of Texas–Austin; Miles Davis with Quincy Troupe, *Miles: The Autobiography* (New York: Simon and Schuster, 1989), 70, 395; Richard Wright, *12 Million Black Voices* (1941; repr., New York: Thunder's Mouth, 2002), 130.

22. Ross Russell, letter to Albert Goldman, Box 7, Folder 7, Ross Russell Papers, HRC, University of Texas–Austin; Ernest Borneman, "Black Mask," *Go* [UK], February–March 1952, 63–66, clipping file, Raymond Chandler Papers, UCLA Special Collections.

23. Comfort lip-synchs the song; Kitty White sings it.

24. Mattie Comfort was married to Los Angeles jazz bassist Joe Comfort, who played with Nat King Cole and sang on several of Frank Sinatra's classic 1950s sessions.

25. Robert Coover, *Noir: A Novel* (New York: Overlook, 2010), 107–9; T. S. Eliot, "The Dry Salvages," in *Four Quartets* (London: Faber, 1941).

26. Raymond Chandler, *The Simple Art of Murder* (New York: Vintage Crime, 1988), 18; Duke Ellington quoted in "Ellington Defends His Music" (1933), in *The Duke Ellington Reader*, ed. Mark Tucker (New York: Oxford University Press,

1995), 81; Max Roach, quoted in Nat Hentoff, "The Constitution of a Jazzman," *Village Voice*, September 5–11, 2007, 22–23.

27. "Interview with Art Blakey," in Art Taylor, *Notes and Tones: Musician-to-Musician Interviews* (New York: Da Capo, 1993), 243.

28. On *Star Trek: The Next Generation*, an episode called "The Big Goodbye" functions as a tribute to the noir detective with Captain Jean-Luc Picard (Patrick Stewart) as PI Dix Hill (season 1, episode 12, airdate January 1, 1988).

29. Norman Mailer, "Dialectic of the American Existentialist," in Box 30–Folder 8, "The White Negro: Handwritten Drafts and Notes," Norman Mailer Papers, Harry Ransom Center, University of Texas–Austin; Norman Mailer, "The White Negro" in *Advertisements for Myself* (1959; repr., Cambridge, MA: Harvard University Press, 1992), 340–41.

30. James Baldwin, "Fifth Avenue, Uptown: A Letter from Harlem," in *Esquire*, July 1960; Richard Wright, "I Choose Exile," Box 6, RW Papers, Beinecke.

31. Chester Himes, *If He Hollers Let Him Go* (New York: Harper & Row, 1945), 15; Mailer, "The White Negro," 340–41.

32. Sartre, "The Republic of Silence," in *The Aftermath of War (Situations III)* (London: Seagull, 2008), 3–4; Jean Guéhenno, *Diary of the Dark Days 1940–1944: Collaboration, Resistance, and Daily Life in Occupied Paris* (New York: Oxford University Press, 2014), 101, 104, 116; Mark Mazower, *Dark Continent: Europe's Twentieth Century* (New York: Vintage, 2000), 192.

33. Liner notes, *Blues in the Mississippi Night* (Rounder CD, 2003). This is a transcript of a conversation between Broonzy, Willie Dixon, and Memphis Slim from March 2, 1947, in New York, as recorded by Alan Lomax.

34. Guéhenno, *Diary*, xxviii, 38; David Ball, "Introduction," in Guéhenno, *Diary*, xi, n2.

35. Ralph Ellison, *Shadow and Act* (1964; repr., New York: Vintage, 1972), 78–79; Sidney Bechet, *Treat It Gentle* (New York: Da Capo, 1960), 211.

36. Big Bill Broonzy, quoted in liner notes, *Blues in the Mississippi Night*; Bob Riesman, *I Feel So Good: The Life and Times of Big Bill Broonzy* (Chicago: University of Chicago, 2011), 131–32.

37. William Irwin Thompson, *The American Replacement of Nature* (New York: Doubleday, 1991), 51.

38. James Campbell, *Exiled in Paris* (New York: Scribner, 1995), 14–15; Sartre, "Jazz in America," in Gottlieb, *Reading Jazz*, ed. Robert Gottlieb (New York: Vintage, 1999), 710–12; Albert Camus, *American Journals* (London: Sphere, 1990), 41.

39. Ellison and Murray, quoted in *Trading Twelves: The Selected Letters of Ralph Ellison and Albert Murray*, ed. Albert Murray and John F. Callahan (New York: Modern Library, 2000), 197–98, 212.

40. "True jazz is an art of individual assertion within and against the group," Ellison observed about big band swing, and Hobsbawm called Count Basie's band, in particular, "a marvelous combination of solo creation and collective exhilaration." Ralph Ellison, *Living with Music: Ralph Ellison's Jazz Writings*, ed. Robert O'Meally

(New York: Random House / Modern Library, 2001), 36; Eric Hobsbawm, *Uncommon People: Resistance, Rebellion and Jazz* (New York: New Press, 1998), 252–53; Joel Dinerstein, *Swinging the Machine: Modernity, Technology, and African-American Culture between World Wars* (Amherst: University of Massachusetts Press, 2003), 22–23, 154–76; West, *Keeping Faith*, xii–xiv.

41. Mailer, "The White Negro," 338.

42. Mailer, "Dialectic of the American Existentialist," NM Papers, HRC, University of Texas–Austin.

43. Mailer, "The White Negro," 338.

44. Albert Camus, *The Fall* (1956; repr., New York: Vintage International, 1991), 45, 118.

45. Archie Shepp, "Foreword," in John Clellon Holmes, *The Horn* (1958; repr., New York: Thunder's Mouth Press, 1987), v.

46. Mailer, "The White Negro," 341.

47. Sartre, *The Aftermath of War*, 259–60.

48. Malcolm X read and reread this essay many times. See Hisham Aidi, "The Music of Malcolm X," *New Yorker*, February 28, 2015, http://www.newyorker.com /culture / culture-desk / the-music-of-malcolm-x.

49. Sartre, *The Aftermath of War*, 259–60, 269.

50. Ben Sidran, *Black Talk* (New York: Da Capo, 1980), xi.

51. James Baldwin, *The Price of the Ticket: Collected Nonfiction, 1948–1985* (New York: St. Martin's, 1985), 89–90; Shepp, "Foreword," in *The Horn*, v.

52. Murray, letter to Ellison, *Trading Twelves*, 65.

53. Baldwin, "Foreword," in *The Price of the Ticket*, xiv.

54. Christopher Small, *Music of the Common Tongue: Survival and Celebration in African American Music* (Middleton, CT: Wesleyan University Press, 1998), 137–62.

55. Questlove, "Does Black Culture Need to Care about What Happens to Hip-Hop?" *Vulture*, May 27, 2014, www.vulture.com /2014/05/questlove-part-6-does -black-culture-need-to-care-about-hip-hop.html.

56. Ross Russell, "Lester and Alienation," Ross Russell Papers, Box 5, Folder 5, HRC, University of Texas–Austin.

57. "Privately Lester thought the lot of white Americans only a . . . thin cut above his own." This is a projection. At times Young had lived a satisfactory domestic life, yet it was in his last dissolute years that white jazz critics viewed him as an existential figure. Douglas Henry Daniels, *Lester Leaps In: The Life and Times of Lester 'Pres' Young* (Boston: Beacon Press, 2002), 243–47, 277–81.

58. Murray, *Stomping the Blues*, 6, 10, 42.

59. Albert Murray, *The Blue Devils of Nada* (New York: Pantheon, 1996), 16, and *The Hero and the Blues* (New York: Vintage, 2012), 107; see also Murray, *Stomping the Blues*, 99, 102, 250–58.

60. François Postif, "Interview with Lester Young," in *A Lester Young Reader*, ed. Lewis Porter (Washington, DC: Smithsonian Press, 1991), 181.

61. Jo Jones, quoted in Nat Hentoff, *Jazz Is* (New York: Limelight, 1984), 19.

62. Gil Evans, quoted in ibid., 196.

63. Murray, *Stomping the Blues*, 162–63.

64. Ellington, *Music Is My Mistress*, 90–92; Blakey, quoted in Taylor, *Notes and Tones*, 248; Denardo Coleman, quoted in Larry Blumenfeld, "Message at Charlie Haden Memorial: 'Hey, Man—We're Family,'" January 16, 2015, *BlouinArtInfo.com*, http://www.blouinartinfo.com/news/story/1072881/message-at-charlie-haden-memorial-hey-man-were-family.

65. Willie Jones, quoted in Büchmann-Müller, *You Just Fight*, 193.

66. Ibid., 193, 212.

67. Dick Pountain and David Robbins, *Cool Rules: Anatomy of an Attitude* (London: Reaktion, 2000), 19.

68. Ernest Hemingway, *A Farewell to Arms* (New York: Scribner, 2012), 161.

69. See, e.g., Paul Fussell, *The Great War and Modern Memory* (New York: Oxford University Press, 1975).

70. Quoted in James M. Salem, *The Late, Great Johnny Ace and the Transition from R&B to Rock 'n' Roll* (Urbana: University of Illinois Press, 2001), 157–58.

A Generational Interlude

1. Lewis MacAdams, *Birth of the Cool: Beat, Bebop, and the American Avant-Garde* (New York: Free Press, 2001), 46.

2. Ibid., 13–14, 46.

3. Gene Sculatti, ed., *The Catalog of Cool* (New York: Warner Books, 1982), 1.

4. Dan Burley, *Dan Burley's Jive*, ed. Thomas Aiello (DeKalb: Northern Illinois University Press, 2009), 72; Zora Neale Hurston, "Story in Harlem Slang," and "Harlem Slanguage," both in *The Complete Stories (P.S.)* (New York: HarperPerennial, 2008) ,134–38, 227–32; William Burroughs, *Junky* (New York: Penguin, 1952), 153–58; *Cab Calloway's Hepster Dictionary*, 6th ed., appears as an appendix in Cab Calloway with Bryant Rollins, *Of Minnie the Moocher and Me* (New York: Thomas Y. Crowell, 1976). A slang glossary can be found in an appendix to Mezz Mezzrow with Bernard Wolfe, *Really the Blues* (1946; repr., New York: Citadel), 371–80. On Mailer as "the philosopher of hip," see Fred Kaplan, *1959: The Year Everything Changed* (London: Wiley, 2010), 15–26.

5. Robert S. Gold, *The Jazz Lexicon* (New York: 1962), 65–67.

6. Joel Dinerstein, "Hip vs. Cool: Delineating Two Key Concepts in American Popular Culture," in *Is It 'Cause It's Cool? Affective Encounters with American Culture*, ed. Astrid M. Fellner, Susanne Hamscha, Klaus Heissenberger, and Jennifer J* Moos (Vienna: LIT Verlag, 2013), 20–45.

7. Thomas Frank, *The Conquest of Cool* (Chicago: University of Chicago Press, 1998). During a symposium titled "American Cool," Thomas Frank suggested his study was more precisely about "the conquest of hip" rather than "cool." Personal conversation with the author, March 18, 2014, "American Cool," Edgar P. Sampson

Symposium of the National Portrait Gallery, Smithsonian Institution, March 18, 2014.

8. Ellington, *Music Is My Mistress*, 79–80.

9. Dizzy Gillespie with Al Fraser, *To Be or Not . . . to Bop* (New York: Da Capo), 296–97.

10. The list of "hip" vs. "square" can be found in *Advertisements for Myself* (1959; repr., Cambridge, MA: Harvard University Press, 1992), 425.

11. Mailer, "The White Negro," in *Advertisements for Myself*, 354.

12. Ibid., 425.

13. Jack Kerouac, *On the Road* (1957; repr., New York: Penguin, 1991); Jonah Raskin, *American Scream: Allen Ginsberg's "Howl" and the Making of the Beat Generation* (Berkeley: University of California Press, 2004), 18; Tennessee Williams, *"Orpheus Descending" with "Battle of Angels": Two Plays* (New York: New Directions, 1958), 27.

14. Robert S. Gold, *Jazz Lexicon* (New York: Knopf, 1964), 65–67 ("cool") and 144–48 ("hip").

15. Ross Russell, *The Sound* (London: Cassell, 1961), 11, 14, 74; Del Close and John Brent, *How to Speak Hip* (1959; reissued by 101 Distribution CD 2009), liner notes by Roy Carr.

16. John Clellon Holmes, *Go* (New York: Scribner, 1952), 209; Burroughs, *Junky*, 143. Burroughs's phrase "not hot with the law" has a double meaning here since the police were known as "the heat" in the postwar era. The opposite of being loyal to "the heat"—and law abiding—was being among "the cool" and open to breaking the law, especially with regard to the use of drugs.

17. Pianist Larry Ham, interview with the author, New Orleans, LA, May 13, 2011; pianist Marc Irwin, interview with the author, Baltimore, MD, November 28, 2011.

18. MacAdams, *Birth of the Cool*, 60.

19. "A Teen-Age Bill of Rights," *New York Times Magazine*, January 7, 1945, SM9; Bob Reisman, *The Life and Times of Big Bill Broonzy* (Chicago: University of Chicago Press, 2011); Uta Poiger, *Jazz, Rock, and Rebels: Cold War Politics and American Culture in a Divided Germany* (Berkeley: University of California Press, 2000), 71–105.

20. Daniel Belgrad, *The Culture of Spontaneity: Improvisation and the Arts in Postwar America* (Chicago: University of Chicago, 1999); and W. T. Lhamon, *Deliberate Speed: The Origins of a Cultural Style in the American 1950s* (Washington, DC: Smithsonian Institution Press, 1991), 179, 184.

21. Louis Menand, "Drive, He Wrote," *New Yorker*, October 17, 2007, http://www.newyorker.com/magazine/2007/10/01/drive-he-wrote.

22. James T. Patterson, *Grand Expectations: The United States, 1945–1974* (New York: Oxford University Press, 1996), 311–42.

23. James Ellroy, commentary, *Crime Wave* DVD (1954; reissued, Warner Brothers, 2007).

24. Bogart, quoted in Stefan Kanfer, *Tough without a Gun: The Life and Extraordinary Afterlife of Humphrey Bogart* (New York: Knopf, 2011), 199–202.

25. Dashiell Hammett, "Introduction" to *The Maltese Falcon* (1930; repr., New York: Modern Library, 1934), ix; Dorothy Parker, "The Maltese Falcon," *New Yorker*, April 25, 1931, 92.

Chapter Six

1. *Jack Kerouac: Selected Letters, 1940–1956,* ed. Ann Charters (New York: Penguin, 1996), 231–32; the letter is dated October 6, 1950.

2. Jack Kerouac, *Some of the Dharma* (New York: Viking, 1997), 270. Here is the full quote: "O [Buddha,] Noble. Your coolness! Your true love, so quiet, remote, beneficent! The truth is the only Gift . . . and the truth is Non-Suffering!"

3. William Burroughs, *Junky* (1953; repr., New York: Penguin, 1977), 143; *Jack Kerouac: Selected Letters*, 231–32.

4. Kerouac, *On the Road* (1957; repr., New York: Penguin, 1991), 12.

5. Ibid., 179–80, 240–41; Kerouac, *Visions of Cody* (New York: Penguin, 1993), 142–44, 157–64, 391–93.

6. Daniel Belgrad, *The Culture of Spontaneity: Improvisation and the Arts in Postwar America* (Chicago: University of Chicago, 1999), 196–221 (on the Beats) and 200–206 (on Kerouac), and passim; W. T. Lhamon, *Deliberate Speed: The Origins of a Cultural Style in the American 1950s* (Washington, DC: Smithsonian Institution Press, 1991), 152–54; Scott DeVeaux, "This Is What I Do," in *Art from Start to Finish: Jazz, Painting, Writing, and Other Improvisations*, ed. Howard S. Becker, Robert R. Faulkner, and Barbara Kirshenblatt-Gimblett (Chicago: University of Chicago, 2006), 118–25.

7. Jack Kerouac and William S. Burroughs, *And the Hippos Were Boiled in Their Tanks* (New York: Grove, 2008). *Hippos* was only published in 2008 after Lucien Carr's death and at his request. He was a professional journalist and never discussed his younger Beat days on the record.

8. Allen Ginsberg, *Composed on the Tongue* (Bolinas, CA: Grey Fox Press, 1980), 83.

9. William Burroughs and Dr. Paul Federn, quoted in Lewis MacAdams, *Birth of the Cool: Beat, Bebop, and the American Avant-Garde* (New York: Free Press, 2001), 113, 126; see also Peter Schjeldahl, "The Outlaw: Williams S. Burroughs," *New Yorker*, February 3, 2014, 72.

10. Gerald Nicosia, "And the Hippos Were Boiled in Their Tanks," *San Francisco Chronicle*, November 9, 2008, M-1.

11. Kerouac and Burroughs, *Hippos*, 172; Kerouac, *On the Road*, 195.

12. "Who wouldn't want to wake out of a nightmare? Seems to say the Eightfold Path." Kerouac, *Some of the Dharma*, 299; Kerouac, *On the Road*, 278. Toward the end of *On the Road*, Kerouac combines the postwar ideal of cool with his own primitivism by perceiving it in the easygoing nonchalance of the old men of Mex-

ico: "the *old men* are so cool and grand and not bothered by anything" (278). See, e.g., Thich Nhat Hanh, *Anger: Wisdom for Cooling the Flames* (New York: Riverhead, 2002), 23–46 and 89–100.

13. Allen Ginsberg, *Howl and Other Poems* (San Francisco: City Lights, 1955), 3.

14. Samuel Charters, "Jack and Jazz," lecture delivered at "On the Road: The Jack Kerouac Conference," July 26, 1982, Naropa Institute, Boulder, CO, https://archive.org/details/On_the_road__The_Jack_Kerouac_conference_82P261; Kerouac, *On the Road*, 12.

15. For example, the documentary of the Prankster bus invokes this notion of the "cool place"—*Magic Trip: Ken Kesey's Search for a Kool Place* (Magnolia Home Entertainment, 2011, DVD).

16. Jack Kerouac, "Are Writers Made or Born?" *Writer's Digest*, January 1962, reprinted in *My Archival Wanderings: Jack Kerouac* (blog), March 12, 2008, http://www.writersdigest.com/editor-blogs/writers-perspective/writers-digest-news/my-archival-wanderings-jack-kerouac; Hettie Jones, *How I Became Hettie Jones* (New York: Penguin, 1990), 59.

17. Kerouac, *On the Road*, 197–98, 209; for Kerouac's cheerleading at the premiere of "Howl," see Jonah Raskin, *American Scream: Allen Ginsberg's "Howl" and the Making of the Beat Generation* (Berkeley: University of California Press, 2004), 15, 18; Ginsberg, *Composed on the Tongue*, 80.

18. Jack Kerouac, "The Essentials of Spontaneous Prose," in *Good Blonde and Others* (New York: Grey Fox, 2001), 69–71; Kerouac, *Selected Letters*, 515–16.

19. Charters, "Jack and Jazz."

20. Kerouac, *On the Road*, 207; my emphasis.

21. "Toni Morrison, the Art of Fiction No. 134: Interviewed by Elissa Schappell, with Additional Material from Claudia Brodsky Lacour," *Paris Review*, no. 128 (Fall 1993), http://www.theparisreview.org/interviews/1888/the-art-of-fiction-no-134-toni-morrison.

22. Norman Mailer, Box 1014, Folder 1, Norman Mailer Papers, HRC.

23. Lawrence Sutin, *All Is Change: The Two-Thousand Year Journey of Buddhism in the West* (New York: Little, Brown, 2006), 304–5.

24. Truman Capote made this quip on the talk show *Open End* on WNTA-TV (NY, later WNET) on January 18, 1959, as reported by Leonard Lyons, Lyons Den, *Daily Defender*, January 27, 1959.

25. Kerouac, *Some of the Dharma*, 173, 182, 184.

26. For cool as a "Negro Zen," see William Jelani Cobb, "The Genius of Cool: The 25 Coolest Brothers of All Time," *Ebony*, August 2008, 68–69.

27. Snyder, quoted in MacAdams, *Birth of the Cool*, 180; Sutin, *All Is Change*, 296. Watts popularized Buddhism but did not invoke either hip or cool despite his role in crossing over Buddhism to the West. Kerouac mocked Watts in *The Dharma Bums* as Arthur Whane, a man ever in search of the next cocktail party where he could dispense cryptic wisdom. Snyder's invocation of the Big Bopper's sly aside from "Chantilly Lace" (1958) would have been understood within Beat circles of the 1950s.

28. Jack Kerouac, *Dharma Bums* (1958; repr., New York: Penguin, 1986), 6.

29. Sutin, *All Is Change*, 248–49, 294.

30. Alan Watts, *"This Is It" and Other Essays on Zen and Spiritual Experience* (New York: Random House / Vintage, 1973).

31. Kerouac, *Some of the Dharma*, 238.

32. D. T. Suzuki, *An Introduction to Zen Buddhism* (New York: Grove, 1964), 71–72. On Suzuki and Buddhist cool (including Watts and Snyder), MacAdams, *Birth of the Cool*, 146–50.

33. Ginsberg, *Howl and Other Poems,* 3; Kerouac, *Dharma Bums*, 244.

34. Kerouac, *Dharma Bums*, 12, 29. This was after "an entire year of celibacy based on my feeling that lust was the direct cause of birth which was the direct cause of suffering and death and I had really[—]no lie[—]come to a point where I regarded lust as offensive and even cruel" (29).

35. Kerouac, *Some of the Dharma*, 325, 417.

36. Ibid., 56, 66, 238.

37. Kerouac, *Dharma Bums*, 202.

38. Kerouac, *Some of the Dharma,* 325, 417.

39. Ibid. 166; Kerouac, *Dharma Bums*, 169.

40. Kerouac, *Dharma Bums,* 169; Kerouac, *Some of the Dharma,* 24, 166.

41. Kerouac, *Some of the Dharma*, 251.

42. Jack Kerouac, *Mexico City Blues* (New York: Grove, 1959), 241–44. Some page numbers for this work are provided within this section.

43. Kerouac's ability to improvise poetically and rhythmically with the musicians is especially impressive on the fourteen-minute track, "Poems from the Unpublished 'Book of Blues.'" Ginsberg thought of Kerouac as a musician (of a kind) in his ability to fit his voice into the jazz grooves on *Blues and Haikus*. Ginsberg, *Composed on the Tongue*, 68.

44. Kerouac, *Some of the Dharma*, 342.

45. Kerouac, *Mexico City Blues*, 115; Red Pine, *The Platform Sutra: The Zen Teaching of Hui-Neng* (New York: Counterpoint, 2006), 140–44. Hui-Neng is the Buddhist monk Kerouac most admired. After copying out nearly two pages of his writings and responding in kind, he writes "HE [is] GREAT" (*Some of the Dharma,* 405–6).

46. Kerouac, *Mexico City Blues*, 116.

47. Ibid., 241.

48. Ibid., 242.

49. Ibid., 243.

50. Ibid.

51. Ibid.

52. Kerouac, *Some of the Dharma*, ix, 417.

53. Kerouac echoes Julio Cortazar's two-pronged perception in *The Pursuer* (1959), his novella about a Charlie Parker surrogate named Johnny Carter. Cortazar suggests that Parker's blank black face was a mask that hid a sophisticated engagement with time, consciousness, and artistry. The novella ends with Johnny

Carter's deathbed words, "O make me a mask!" Julio Cortazar, *The Pursuer*, in *The Jazz Fiction Anthology*, ed. Sascha Feinstein and David Rife (Bloomington: Indiana University Press, 2009), 115–65.

54. Kerouac, *Mexico City Blues*, 244.

55. Ginsberg, quoted in Lawrence Sutin, *All Is Change*, 305 and 310–11. This experience led to the establishment of the Jack Kerouac School of Disembodied Poetics at the Naropa Institute as well as Trungpa's theory of "crazy wisdom." See also Chögyam Trungpa, *Crazy Wisdom* (1991; repr., Boston: Shambhala, 2010).

56. *The Gary Snyder Reader* (Berkeley, CA: Counterpoint, 2000), 99.

57. Ginsberg, *Composed on the Tongue*, 65.

58. Ibid., 65.

59. Kerouac, *Some of the Dharma*, 114, 324.

60. Ibid., 79, 105.

61. Ibid., 95.

62. Ibid., 285.

63. Kerouac, *Some of the Dharma*, 403.

64. Jack Kerouac, *The Scripture of the Golden Eternity* (1960; repr., San Francisco: City Lights, 1994).

65. Kerouac, *Some of the Dharma*, 176, 253, 411.

66. Albert Camus, *Notebooks 1951–1959* (Chicago: Ivan R. Dee, 2008), 189.

67. Red Pine, *The Platform Sutra*, 175, 186. A rare comparative analysis can be found in Sander H. Lee, "Notions of Selflessness in Sartrean Existentialism and Theravadin Buddhism," Paideia Project Online, February 29, 2000, http://www.bu.edu/wcp/Papers/Reli/ReliLee.htm. For an interesting example from cognitive philosophy and neuroscience, see Evan Thompson, *Waking, Dreaming, Being: Self and Consciousness in Neuroscience, Meditation and Philosophy* (New York: Columbia University Press, 2014).

68. Thomas Merton, *Zen and the Birds of Appetite* (New York: New Directions, 1968), 32, 59.

69. Alan Watts, *The Way of Zen* (1957; repr., New York: Vintage, 1985), 88–89; Gary Snyder, *Earth House Hold* (New York: New Directions, 1969), 113–14.

70. Snyder, *Earth House Hold*, 113–14.

71. Albert Camus, *"The Myth of Sisyphus" and Other Essays* (New York: Vintage, 1991), 181.

72. Kerouac, *Some of the Dharma*, 408, 413.

73. Merton, *Zen and the Birds of Appetite*, 90.

74. *The Gary Snyder Reader*, 95; Watts, *The Way of Zen*, 101.

75. Merton, quoted in MacAdams, *Birth of the Cool*, 150; Watts, *The Way of Zen*, 102–3.

76. MacAdams, *Birth of the Cool*, 150.

77. To be glib, Kerouac probably should have avoided alcohol—something he never had under control—and smoked more marijuana. Edie Parker, Kerouac's first wife, claimed Lester Young gave Kerouac his first taste of marijuana. Blues

scholar Samuel Charters heard this from Parker in the early 1980s. Charters, "Jack and Jazz."

78. MacAdams, *Birth of the Cool*, 150.

Chapter Seven

1. Carole K. Fink, *Cold War: An International History* (Boulder, CO: Westview Press, 2014), 123–24; David Halberstam, *The Fifties* (New York: Ballantine, 1994), 473–87.

2. Pete Hamill, *Why Sinatra Matters* (Boston: Little, Brown, 1998), 69 and passim.

3. Arnold Shaw, quoted in Stanislo G. Pugliese, "Introduction," in *Frank Sinatra: History, Politics, and Italian American Culture*, ed. Stanislo G. Pugliese (New York: Palgrave Macmillan, 2004), 3–4; Douglas Brinkley, "Frank Sinatra and the American Century," in *Frank Sinatra*, ed. Pugliese, 20.

4. Barbara Ehrenreich, *Hearts of Men: American Dreams and the Flight from Commitment* (New York: Anchor, 1983), 52–67; Elizabeth Fraterrigo, *Playboy and the Making of the Good Life in Modern America* (New York: Oxford University Press, 2009).

5. On Sinatra as the "O.G.," see John Gennari, "Passing for Italian: Crooners and Gangsters in Crossover Culture," in *Frank Sinatra*, ed. Pugliese, 127–34; on Dean Martin, see Nick Tosches, *Dino: Living High in the Dirty Business of Dreams* (New York: Dell, 1992).

6. Scott Timberg, "The Peak of Sinatra's Power," interview with biographer James Kaplan, November 21, 2015, Salon.com, http://www.salon.com/2015/11 /21/the_peak_of_sinatras_power_every_sinatra_performance_was_acting_his _greatest_performance_was_as_himself/.

7. From a Chandler letter to Bernice Baumgarten dated May 25, 1952, in *Raymond Chandler Speaking*, ed. Dorothy Gardiner, Katherine Sorley Walker, and Paul Skenazy (1962; repr., Berkeley: University of California Press, 1997), 233; Raymond Chandler, *The Long Goodbye* (1953; repr., New York: Vintage Crime, 1992), 378–79. See also Steven Weisenburger, "Order, Error, and the Novels of Raymond Chandler," in *The Detective in American Fiction, Film, and Television*, ed. Jerome H. Delamater and Ruth Prigozy (Westport, CT: Greenwood Press, 1998), 17–18.

8. In Mann's *Railroaded*, e.g., a cop played by Hugh Beaumont (Beaver's father in the TV series *Leave It to Beaver* from the 1950s and 1960s) is caught between the lab's evidence and his affections for a young neighbor. He declares to the suspect's sister, "I'm only interested in facts."

9. Eddy von Mueller, "The Police Procedural in Literature and on Television," in *The Cambridge Companion to American Crime Fiction*, ed. Catherine Ross Nickerson (Cambridge: Cambridge University Press, 2010), 100.

10. George N. Dove, *The Police Procedural* (Bowling Green, OH: Bowling Green University Popular Press, 1982), 1–4.

11. The positive postwar tropes of normalcy and being "average" are explored in

Anna G. Creadick, *Perfectly Average: The Pursuit of Normality in Postwar America* (Amherst: University of Massachusetts Press, 2010).

12. Roger Sabin, "Dragnet," in *Cop Shows: A Critical History of Police Dramas on Television*, ed. Roger Sabin (Jefferson, NC: McFarland, 2015), 15–22; Dove, *Police Procedural*, 1–4 and 38–42, with specific reference to Chandler's novels.

13. Richard Layman, ed., *Discovering "The Maltese Falcon" and Sam Spade* (San Francisco: Avery Books, 2005), 327–35.

14. von Mueller, "The Police Procedural," 100–104.

15. Trailer, *Crime Wave* DVD (Warner Home Video, 2007).

16. Toth, quoted in "Andre de Toth—an Interview," in *Film Noir Reader 3: Interviews with Filmmakers of the Classic Noir Period*, ed. Robert Porfirio, Alain Silver, and James Ursini (New York: Limelight, 2002), 18; James Ellroy, commentary, *Crime Wave* DVD (Warner Home Video, 2007).

17. Bogart's best roles in Postwar II were as a journalist or convict, as in, respectively, *The Harder They Fall* and *The Desperate Hours*.

18. On technology and the network in films of the '40s, see Dana Polan, *Power and Paranoia: History, Narrative, and the American Cinema, 1940–1950* (New York: Columbia University Press, 1986), 161–65, 169.

19. Dana Polan, commentary, *Naked City* (1948; reissued, Criterion DVD, 2007).

20. Eric P. Kaufmann, *The Rise and Fall of Anglo America* (Cambridge, MA: Harvard University Press, 2004), 19–21, 177–86.

21. C. Wright Mills, *The Power Elite* (1956; repr., New York: Oxford University Press, 2000), 171–79, 183–86.

22. Film scholars waver between an end date of 1955 and 1959 for the classic period of film noir.

23. As with Bogart, Edward G. Robinson symbolized urban grit and the ambiguity of modernity. He created the gangster archetype in Hollywood in *Little Caesar* (1931) and added to this figure's existential bravado in noirs such as *Key Largo* (1947) and up to *The Cincinnati Kid* (1961). Yet at the same time he played weak, virtuous men unable to control their desires and in thrall to femme fatales in Fritz Lang's *Scarlet Street* and *The Woman in the Window*.

24. James Kaplan, *Frank: The Voice* (New York: Doubleday, 2010), 509–603; Will Friedwald, *Sinatra! The Song Is You* (New York: Da Capo, 1997), 163–200; Hamill, *Why Sinatra Matters*, 162–64.

25. Hamill, *Why Sinatra Matters*, 170, 175, 176.

26. Ibid., 37–38, and see also, 44, 71.

27. Ibid., 94; Milt Bernhart, quoted in Rob Jacklosky, "Someone to Watch over Him: Images of Class and Gender Vulnerability in Early Sinatra," in *Frank Sinatra*, ed. Pugliese, 94.

28. Rollins, quoted in Eric Nisenson, *Open Sky: Sonny Rollins and His World of Improvisation* (New York: Da Capo, 2000), 24; Duke Ellington recalled Sinatra making "a tour of racially disturbed high schools preaching race tolerance" in *Music Is My Mistress* (New York: Da Capo, 1973), 239; Kaplan, *Frank: The Voice*, 249–51.

29. Sinatra, quoted in Hamill, *Why Sinatra Matters*, 115–16; Friedwald, *Sinatra!* 145, 155–56.

30. Hamill, *Why Sinatra Matters*, 88.

31. Friedwald, *Sinatra!* 154–75; Robert Christgau, "Frank Sinatra 1915–1998," reprinted from *Details*, http://www.robertchristgau.com/xg/music/sinatra-det.php.

32. Friedwald, *Sinatra!* 224; Miles Davis and Quincy Jones, quoted in Hamill, *Why Sinatra Matters*, 172–73.

33. Joel Whitburn, *Joel Whitburn's Top Pop Albums, 1955–2001: Chart Data Compiled from "Billboard"* (Menomonee Falls, WI: Record Research, Inc., 2001), 1165, 1177. See also Friedwald, *Sinatra!* 229–30.

34. Brinkley, "Frank Sinatra," in *Frank Sinatra*, ed. Pugliese, 20.

35. Tosches, *Dino*, 302, 408.

36. Thomas J. Ferraro, "Urbane Villager," in *Frank Sinatra*, ed. Pugliese, 135–46, and 145–46n3 (quote by Herbert Gans).

37. Friedwald, *Sinatra!* 404.

38. Timberg, "The Peak of Sinatra's Power."

39. Gay Talese, "Frank Sinatra Has a Cold," in *The Gay Talese Reader: Portraits and Encounters* (New York: Walker & Company, 2000), 19.

40. Ibid., 19–20.

41. The noir detective resurfaced for this generation in the late 1960s: Paul Newman played *Harper* (1966), featuring the detective Lew Archer, and adapted from Ross Chandler's 1949 detective novel, *The Moving Target*, while James Garner played Philip Marlowe in *Marlowe* (1969).

42. Kerouac, *Some of the Dharma*, 420; Robert Love, "Bob Dylan Does the American Standards His Way," interview with Bob Dylan, *AARP Magazine*, February–March 2015, http://www.aarp.org/entertainment/style-trends/info-2015/bob-dylan-aarp-magazine.html.

Chapter Eight

1. Jack Kerouac, "America's New Trinity of Love: Dean, Brando, Presley" (1957), performed by Richard Lewis on *Kerouac: Kicks, Joy, Darkness* (1996), Rykodisc CD 118566; see also "Old Western Movies" performed by William S. Burroughs on this collection.

2. Peter Guralnick, *Last Train to Memphis: The Rise of Elvis Presley* (Boston: Little, Brown, 1994), 322–23.

3. Elvis should be considered a singer in the African-American vocal tradition: witness his hits on *Billboard*'s rhythm-and-blues charts (a.k.a., the "black" charts) in the mid-1950s. Elvis was fully engaged with various strains of American popular music—country, blues, gospel—and I will not here consider the arguments over his love and theft of black music since it doesn't affect my argument more broadly. In addition, the myth of Presley's racism has fueled an irrelevant discourse. See Peter Guralnick, "How Did Elvis Get Turned into a Racist?" *New York Times*, August 11, 2007, A15.

4. For example, Marlon Brando was in therapy daily for eleven years and close friends urged James Dean to go into therapy. Peter Manso, *Brando* (New York: Hyperion, 1995), 244–46, 281–82; Donald Spoto, *Rebel: The Life and Legend of James Dean* (New York: HarperCollins, 1996), 204–5. Lee Server, *Robert Mitchum: "Baby, I Don't Care"* (New York: St. Martin's, 2001), 117.

5. Leonard Rosenman, quoted in Spoto, *Rebel*, 185–86, 205–6, and also see reflections here by Elia Kazan, Nicholas Ray, and Brando. When Rosenman met Dean's father he called him "[a] monster, a person without any . . . sensitivity," and began to have sympathy for Dean's emotional confusion.

6. Kerouac, *On the Road* (1957; repr., New York: Penguin, 1991), 101, 307.

7. In T-Bone Walker's "Why Not?" (1955)—"why not / let me be your Daddy-O"—the blues singer replaces the father's role with the lover-protector, "Daddy-O." The song can be found on T-Bone Walker, *T-Bone Blues* (Atlantic 1989 CD 8020-2).

8. Dennis Stock, *James Dean Revisited* (San Francisco: Chronicle Books, 1987), 107; Dean, quoted from a letter to Barbara Glenn, in Spoto, *Rebel*, 191.

9. Helen Hall, "Letter from Jack Kerouac to Marlon Brando," *Culture* (blog), *Collectors Weekly*, January 10, 2011, http://www.collectorsweekly.com/articles /letter-from-jack-kerouac-to-marlon-brando/.

10. John Clellon Holmes, "The Philosophy of the Beat Generation" (1958), in *Beat Down to Your Soul: What Was the Beat Generation?* ed. Ann Charters (New York: Penguin, 2001), 228–38; Kingsley Widmer, "The Way Out: Some Life-Style Sources of the Literary Tough Guy and the Proletarian Hero," in *Tough Guy Writers of the Thirties*, ed. Dave Madden (Carbondale: Southern Illinois University Press, 1968), 4 ("hipster cool"), 3–12.

11. Richard Pells, *Modernist America: Art, Music, Movies, and the Globalization of American Culture* (New Haven, CT: Yale University Press, 2012), 274; on European response to Brando's biker image, see Uta Poiger, *Jazz, Rock, and Rebels: Cold War Politics and American Culture in a Divided Germany* (Berkeley: University of California Press, 2000), 1, 71–81 and 171–72, and for Italy, James Gavin, *Deep in a Dream: The Long Night of Chet Baker* (Chicago: Chicago Review Press, 2011), 156–57. Mark Rydell, quoted in the documentary *James Dean: Sense Memories*, a documentary written and directed by Gail Levin that aired May 11, 2005, as part of the *American Masters* television series (season 19, episode 1).

12. Louis Menand, "Drive, He Wrote," *New Yorker,* October 1, 2007, 88, http:// www.newyorker.com/magazine/2007/10/01/drive-he-wrote. For "eroticizing the rebel," see Leerom Medovoi, *Rebels: Youth and the Cold War Origins of Identity* (Durham, NC: Duke University Press, 2005), 169–172, 265–66.

13. Logan, quoted in Truman Capote, "The Duke in His Domain," in *Selected Writings* (New York: Random House, 1963), 409. Capote's profile first appeared in the *New Yorker*, November 17, 1957.

14. Rene Jordan, *Marlon Brando* (New York: Pyramid, 1973), 40–42; Presley, quoted in Guralnick, *Last Train to Memphis*, 452.

15. Patricia Bosworth, *Marlon Brando* (New York: Viking, 2001), 34; on Dean's worship of Brando, see Spoto, *Rebel*, 78–83, 146–47, 204–5, 244–45; Dean, quoted in Joe Hyams, *James Dean: Little Boy Lost* (New York: Warner, 1992), 26, 82–83.

16. Elia Kazan, *A Life* (New York: Knopf, 1988), 428; Tennessee Williams, quoted in David Thomson, "Marlon Brando," *Guardian*, July 2, 2004, http://www.guardian.co.uk/news/2004/jul/03/guardianobituaries.artsobituaries.

17. Jordan, *Marlon Brando*, 40; Hunter, quoted in Bosworth, *Brando*, 53; Maureen Stapleton, quoted in Manso, *Brando*, 511–12; see also David Thomson, "*The Fugitive Kind*: When Lumet Went to Tennessee," April 26, 2010, Criterion Collection, http://www.criterion.com/current/posts/1449-the-fugitive-kind-when-sidney-went-to-tennessee

18. Jordan, *Marlon Brando*, 15, 17, 27. Kazan mentored Brando's use of improvisation in acting. "Improvisation . . . that's the boy's [Kazan's] specialty," Burl Ives said of the director after *East of Eden*. Quoted in William Baer, ed., *Elia Kazan: Interviews* (Jackson: University of Mississippi Press, 2000), 29.

19. Bosworth, *Brando*, 34, 57, 49, 68–70. For the legacy of Brando and his tight T-shirts, see Tim Gunn with Ada Calhoun, *Tim Gunn's Fashion Bible* (New York: Gallery, 2012), 27; "Dean's Jeans," pressbook for *Rebel Without a Cause*, USC/WB, p. 4.

20. Jordan, *Marlon Brando*, 17.

21. Bosworth, *Marlon Brando*, 93.

22. John Patrick Diggins, *The Proud Decades: America in War and Peace* (New York: W. W. Norton, 1989), 197–98.

23. See, e.g., Michael DeAngelis, *Gay Fandom and Crossover Stardom: James Dean, Mel Gibson, and Keanu Reeves* (Durham, NC: Duke University Press, 2001), 45–63 and 157–58, and Eric Braun, *Frightening the Horses: Gay Icons of the Cinema* (London: Reynolds & Hearn Ltd, 2007). In 2009, Dean was number fifteen and Brando number forty-one in "The Top 50 Gay Icons" on the website stoppingthehate.com.

24. Thomson, "Marlon Brando."

25. Kazan, *A Life*, 331; Sidney Gottlieb, ed., *Alfred Hitchcock: Interviews* (Jackson: University Press of Mississippi, 2003), 206. "Actors are cattle," Hitchcock said, as if echoing producers, "[and] all actors should be treated like cattle."

26. Manso, *Brando*, 283.

27. "Brando an Individualist," pressbook, *A Streetcar Named Desire*, WB/USC, p. 25.

28. Bosworth, *Marlon Brando*, 114.

29. Manso, *Brando*, 53.

30. Pells, *Modernist America*, 343–47.

31. Capote, "Duke in His Domain," 433; Manso, *Brando*, 329.

32. Manso, *Brando*, 275–79, 339.

33. Roy Carr, Brian Case, and Fred Dellar, *The Hip: Hipsters, Jazz, and the Beat*

Generation (London: Faber and Faber, 1986), 96; John Clellon Holmes, quoted in David Sterritt, *Mad to Be Saved: The Beats, the '50s and Film* (Carbondale: Southern Illinois University Press, 1998), 80.

34. Camille Paglia, "Brando Flashing," in *Sex, Art, and American Culture: Essays* (New York: Vintage, 1992), 91–95. See also Pells, *Modernist America*; Manso, *Brando*, 329–30.

35. Bogart, quoted in Stefan Kanfer, *Tough without a Gun: The Life and Extraordinary Afterlife of Humphrey Bogart* (New York: Knopf, 2011), 166, 171.

36. Kazan, *A Life*, 145, 428, 517, 525–27.

37. Capote, "Duke in His Domain," 414, 437; Manso, *Brando*, 373.

38. Bosworth, *Marlon Brando*, 10.

39. Capote, "Duke in His Domain," 443.

40. Manso, *Brando*, 269, 273; Capote, "Duke in His Domain," 405–15, 430; Miles Davis with Quincy Troupe, *Miles: The Autobiography* (New York: Simon and Schuster, 1989), 197, 216.

41. Holmes, "The Philosophy of the Beat Generation," in *Beat Down to Your Soul*, ed. Charters, 233.

42. Kazan, *A Life*, 135–36. Kazan famously named names at the House Un-American Activities Committee investigations and made many permanent enemies in the process.

43. Brando and James Baldwin were roommates in 1944, long before either was famous. At the height of his fame, Brando lent his friend $500 in 1952 to sail back from Paris to New York to sell his first novel. Douglas Field, *A Historical Guide to James Baldwin* (New York: Oxford University Press, 2011), 36. Background on the so-called Hollywood Roundtable from 1963 can be found at *Unwritten Record* (blog), September 21, 2012, National Archives, http://blogs.archives.gov/unwritten-record/2012/09/21/hollywood-roundtable/, and the roundtable itself: "Civil Rights 1963—James Baldwin and Marlon Brando," posted on May 29, 2014, https://www.youtube.com/watch?v=ZjZBZxPk4Pc.

44. This video, "Brando and Panthers at Bobby Hutton's Funeral," which originally aired April 12, 1968, can be viewed here: https://diva.sfsu.edu/collections/sfbatv/bundles/188783. Brando talks about his activism on behalf of Native Americans in his autobiography, *Brando: Songs My Mother Taught Me* (New York: Random House, 1994), 380–402.

45. Brando, quoted in Bosworth, *Marlon Brando*, 216.

46. Jordan, *Marlon Brando*, 135–36; Bosworth, *Marlon Brando*, 218.

47. An empirical article intended to explore cool as a "descriptor" meaning "likability or popularity" found that it signified equally as rebellious. James Dean was the main example given among 918 subjects. Ilan Dar-Nimred et al., "Coolness: An Empirical Investigation," *Journal of Individual Differences* 33, no. 3 (2012): 175–85.

48. *Born Cool*, directed by Dennis Pietro (DVD 2005); the poster, which is no longer available, was found at http://www.allposters.com/-sp/James-Dean-4EVR-COOL-License-Plate-Posters_i995196_.htm; for "epitome of cool," see

Jel D. Lewis Jones, *James Dean: The Epitome of Cool* ([Philadelphia]: Xlibris, 2007); and Jaime O'Neill, "The Epitome of Cool," *Los Angeles Times*, September 30, 2010, http://articles.latimes.com/2010/sep/30/opinion/la-oe-oneill-jamesdean-20100930.

49. The working-class dancers of Depression-era swing culture actually constituted the first national youth culture—the ones for whom the "teen-ager" was named—but they went off to war after the Depression and their dance-hall years. Their styles and music remain an unexcavated bottom layer of postwar youth culture, only occasionally explored in films like *Swing Kids*.

50. David Dalton, *The Real James Dean* (2005). This is a documentary written and narrated by Dalton.

51. Dennis Hopper, quoted in ibid.; Dean, quoted in Spoto, *Rebel*, 140; William K. Zinsser's review appeared in the *New York Herald-Tribune* and was quoted in the documentary, *The James Dean Story* (1957); Bosley Crowther, "The Screen: 'East of Eden' Has Debut; Astor Shows Film of Steinbeck Novel," *New York Times*, March 10, 1955, http://www.nytimes.com/movie/review?res=9C0DEFD6143EE53ABC4852DFB566838E649EDE; see also Bosley Crowther, "Rebel without a Cause," *New York Times*, October 27, 1955, 28; "Rebel without a Cause," *Variety*, October 26, 1955, Cinefiles, University of California, Berkeley, Art Museum & Pacific Film Archive, https://cinefiles.bampfa.berkeley.edu/cinefiles/DocDetail?docId=10102.

52. James Dean, letter to Barbara Glenn, in Spoto, *Rebel*, 204.

53. Frank H. Goodyear III, "Shooting Cool: Photography and the Making of an American Persona," in *American Cool*, ed. Joel Dinerstein and Frank H. Goodyear III (New York: Prestel, 2014), 57–58; David Dalton, in the documentary *The Real James Dean*.

54. Kazan, quoted in Spoto, *Rebel*, 198.

55. David Dalton, *James Dean: The Mutant King* (Chicago: Chicago Review Press, 2001), 120–25; Barbara Glenn, quoted in Hyams, *James Dean*, 100, 241.

56. Pells, *Modernist America*, 365.

57. Pressbook, *Rebel Without a Cause*, Warner Brothers Archives, University of Southern California (WB/USC).

58. Stern, quoted in the documentary *James Dean: Sense Memories*.

59. Mat 305, pressbook, *Rebel Without a Cause*, WB/USC; *James Dean: Sense Memories*; Hyams, *James Dean*, 218–20.

60. Mats 301 and 305, pressbook, *Rebel Without a Cause,* WB/USC.

61. John Clellon Holmes, *Passionate Opinions: The Cultural Essays* (Fayetteville: University of Arkansas Press, 1988), 69–70.

62. Elvis Presley in an interview with reporter Lloyd Shearer on August 6, 1956, as, quoted in Guralnick, *Last Train to Memphis*, 323.

63. Quoted in Patrick Higgins, *Before Elvis, There Was Nothing* (New York: Carroll & Graf, 1992).

64. Greil Marcus, *Mystery Train: Images of America in Rock'n'Roll Music* (New York: E. P. Dutton, 1976), 177. Historian David Halberstam counts Elvis as one

of the three most important cultural events of the 1950s (*The Fifties* [New York: Ballantine, 1994], 456–61).

65. Peter Guralnick, *Sam Phillips: The Man Who Invented Rock and Roll* (New York: Little Brown, 2015), 11–12, 18, 32–34, 122–26, 137–38, 142–48, 207, 419; Sam Phillips, quoted in Richard Buskin, "Sam Phillips: Sun Records," *SOS* (*Sound on Sound*), October 2003, https://web.archive.org/web/20150606112655/http://www.soundonsound.com/sos/oct03/articles/samphillips.htm.

66. Guralnick, *Sam Phillips*, 235, 260.

67. Greil Marcus, *Mystery Train*, 180–81. On Leiber and Stoller as "the original cool cats," see Ken Emerson, *Always Magic in the Air: The Bomp and Brilliance of the Brill Building Era* (New York: Viking, 2005), 1–16. As late as 1999, Leiber and Stoller claimed, "We thought we *were* black" in an interview with Nick Spitzer, *American Routes: Songs and Stories from the Road* (Highbridge CD, 2008); Paul Simon, quoted in Dave Marsh, "Echoes of Love: Elvis' Friends Remember," *Rolling Stone*, September 22, 1977, 53; Howlin' Wolf, quoted by Peter Guralnick, liner notes, Elvis Presley, *Reconsider Baby* (RCA LP, 1985); B. B. King with David Ritz, *Blues All around Me* (New York: Avon, 1996), 188–89.

68. Camille Paglia, "Sullen Hero," review of *Brando: A Life in Our Times*, by Richard Schickel, *New York Times*, July 21, 1991, http://www.nytimes.com/1991/07/21/books/sullen-hero.html?pagewanted=all.

69. Captions for promotional stills, *King Creole*, Margaret Herrick Library, Paramount Collection, Los Angeles, CA. The opening duet, "Crawfish," with Jean "Kitty" Bilbrew (a.k.a. Kitty White), can be seen on You Tube (2:08, uploaded by "Swancourt," February 3, 2007, https://www.youtube.com/watch?v=oa7gT2V8WE4).

70. Medovoi, *Rebels*, 169–72, 265–66; see also Virginia Wexman, *Creating the Couple* (Princeton, NJ: Princeton University Press, 1993), 169–70.

71. David R. Shumway, "Watching Elvis: The Male Rock Star as Object of the Gaze," in *The Other Fifties: Interrogating Midcentury American Icons*, ed. Joel Foreman (Urbana: University of Illinois Press, 1997), 124–43.

72. Kazan, *A Life*, 529–30.

73. Quoted in the documentary, *The James Dean Story*.

74. Jordan, *Marlon Brando*, 17–18.

75. Donnell Alexander, *Ghetto Celebrity: Searching for My Father in Me* (New York: Crown, 2003), 14.

76. Bob Dylan, quoted in Higgins, *Before Elvis There Was Nothing*, 42.

77. Springsteen, quoted in Peter Ames Carlin, *Bruce* (New York: Touchstone, 2013), 19–20. Springsteen's contemporary, Tom Petty, recalled his first encounter with Elvis in strikingly similar terms. Petty saw and heard Elvis for the first time during a location shooting for *Follow That Dream* (1962) near his hometown of Ocala, Florida. "Elvis appeared like a vision—he didn't look anything like I'd ever seen. I'm [there] just dumbstruck." Then only ten years old, Petty was spellbound by the hundreds of people in the streets of the small town. "I went home a changed

man," he said (as told in the documentary film about Tom Petty and the Heart-breakers, *Runnin' Down a Dream*, directed by Peter Bogdanovich [DVD 2007]).

78. Dave Hickey, "American Cool," in *Pirates and Farmers* (Santa Monica, CA: Ram, 2013), 97–106.

79. Ibid.

80. Sean Axmaker, "Interview: Stewart Stern, Part 1," *Cinematical* (blog), September 1, 2005, http://blog.moviefone.com/2005/09/01/interview-stewart-stern-part-one/ (site discontinued). See also Sean Axmaker, "Interview: Stewart Stern on 'Rebel Without a Cause,'" *Parallax View* (blog), November 11, 2013, http://parallax-view.org/2013/11/11/interview-stewart-stern-rebel-without-cause/.

81. John Lennon and Paul McCartney, quoted in Mark Lewisohn, *Tune In: The Beatles—All These Years*, vol. 1 (New York: Crown, 2013), 41–42; see also Bob Spitz, *The Beatles: The Biography* (New York: Little, Brown, 2012), 9, 89–90: Paul McCartney sings "That's All Right, Mama" on The Beatles, *Live at the BBC* (Capitol CD, 2013).

82. David Dalton, *Who Is That Man? In Search of the Real Bob Dylan* (New York: Hachette, 2012), 18–20; Elijah Wald, ed., *Dylan Goes Electric!* (New York: William Morrow/Dey Street, 2015), 2, 41.

Chapter Nine

1. George W. Goodman, "Sonny Rollins at Sixty-Eight," *Atlantic Monthly*, July 1999, http://www.theatlantic.com/past/docs/issues/99jul/9907sonnyrollins.htm.

2. Martin Williams, *The Jazz Tradition* (New York: Mentor, 1970), 18, 20, 21, my emphasis. On Hentoff, Williams, and Balliett, see John Gennari, *Blowin' Hot and Cool: Jazz and Its Critics* (Chicago: University of Chicago, 2006), 12, 166–71, and 189–91.

3. Kenny Clarke, quoted in Lewis MacAdams, *Birth of the Cool: Beat, Bebop, and the American Avant-Garde* (New York: Free Press, 2001), 45.

4. James Baldwin, quoted in Joe Goldberg, *Jazz Masters of the '50s* (1965; repr., New York: Da Capo, 1983), 82.

5. See, e.g., the collaboration of Charles Mingus and Langston Hughes, *The Weary Blues* (Polygram CD, 1991) or Kenneth Rexroth, *Poetry and Jazz at the Blackhawk* (Fantasy LP 7008, 1959).

6. Ross Russell Papers, Box 8, Folder 2, "Salvage from the Sound," Harry Ransom Center (HRC), University of Texas–Austin.

7. On Ross Russell's complex relationship with Charlie Parker, see John Gennari's "Race-ing the Bird," in *Blowin' Hot and Cool*, 299–338.

8. Ross Russell, *Bird Lives!* (1976; repr., New York: Da Capo, 1996), 242; Jack Kerouac, *Visions of Cody* (New York: Penguin, 1993), 393.

9. Marshall Stearns, quoted in Lillian Ross, "You Dig It, Sir?" (1954), in *Reading Jazz*, ed. Robert Gottlieb (New York: Vintage, 1999), 686–701.

10. Russell, *Bird Lives!* 5, 10–11.

11. James Gavin, *Deep in a Dream: The Long Night of Chet Baker* (New York: Knopf, 2002), 31–34, 58, 77, 81, 115–16, 188. Pianist Paul Bley explained, about cool as minimalism, "It mean[t] you get done in a sentence what somebody else would take a paragraph for." See also Roy Carr, Brian Case, and Fred Dellar, *The Hip: Hipsters, Jazz, and the Beat Generation* (London: Faber and Faber, 1986), 75–76, 80 (on Art Pepper and Chet Baker). Baker's sound was first "based on the cool Miles Davis," and Pepper recalled, "I wanted to be black because I felt such an affinity to the music."

12. Ross, "You Dig It, Sir?" 700. Musicians who renounced the more affective side of instrumental color, such as Lennie Tristano or Lee Konitz, were dubbed "ultra-cool." Ross set out these categories: "Kenton [was] one of the first of the 'cool' musicians, meaning musicians whose emotions are controlled and ordered, [which included] George Shearing (modified cool) . . . Lennie Tristano (ultra-cool), Lee Konitz (ultra-cool), Jo Jones (swing), Milt Hinton (swing), Lester Young (prez of cool, non-cool, swing, and modern), Gil Melle (ultra-ultra-cool), Gene Krupa (immortal)."

13. Søren Kierkegaard, "Concluding Unscientific Postscript to the 'Philosophical Fragments,'" in *A Kierkegaard Anthology*, ed. Robert Bretall (New York: Modern Library, 1946), 201–5, 209–17.

14. Robert Farris Thompson, *Aesthetic of the Cool: Afro-Atlantic Art and Music* (Pittsburgh: Periscope, 2011), 28–29.

15. Farah Jasmine Griffin and Salim Washington, *Clawing at the Limits of Cool: Miles Davis, John Coltrane, and the Greatest Jazz Collaboration Ever* (New York: Thomas Dunne / St. Martin's, 2008), 254, my italics. See also Amiri Baraka, "Miles Later," in *Digging: The Afro-American Soul of American Classical Music* (Berkeley: University of California Press, 2011), 9–18.

16. On Monk and the Five Spot, see Martin Williams, "A Night at the Five Spot," in *Reading Jazz*, ed. Gottlieb, 679–85; W. T. Lhamon, *Deliberate Speed: The Origins of a Cultural Style in the American 1950s* (Washington, DC: Smithsonian Institution Press, 1991), 103, 129, 236; Robin D. G. Kelley, *Thelonious Monk: The Life and Times of an American Original* (New York: Free Press, 2010), 225–36.

17. Thomas Pynchon, *V.* (New York: Harper Perennial, 1961), 366, my italics.

18. Ibid., 366. In his theory of speed as the cultural style of the 1950s, W. T. Lhamon suggests that Pynchon's "Keep cool, but care" is the obverse of the imperative to integrate the schools with all "deliberate speed." Through Pynchon, Lhamon suggests the function of cool as counterforce—as if to say, as the arts and culture accelerate, we will need to be cool about the necessary social changes. Lhamon, *Deliberate Speed*, 236–39.

19. Mingus, quoted in Goldberg, *Jazz Masters of the '50s*, 134.

20. Mingus, quoted in Nat Hentoff, *Jazz Is* (New York: Limelight, 1984), 158, 160, 162.

21. Ralph Ellison, *Shadow and Act* (1964; repr., New York: Vintage, 1972), 234; James Baldwin, quoted in Walton Muyumba, *The Shadow and the Act* (Chicago: University of Chicago Press, 2009), 39; Toni Morrison, cited in Paul Gilroy, *Black*

Atlantic: Modernity and Double Consciousness (Cambridge, MA: Harvard University Press, 1993), 78. Ironically, "the jazz metaphor" of entrepreneurship—through improvisation and expressive individuality—has become a cliché in management studies since the late 1990s. See, e.g., Chris Arnot, "Business and All That Jazz," *Guardian*, January 2, 2012, https://www.theguardian.com/education/2012/jan/02/jazz-leaders-lessons-for-business.

22. David Steinberg, quoted in the PBS comedy series, *Make 'Em Laugh*, which began airing January 14, 2009 (http://www.pbs.org/wnet/makeemlaugh/about/). Albert Goldman, *Ladies and Gentlemen, Lenny Bruce!* (New York: Penguin, 1992), 347. Goldman wrote of Bruce's improvisatory meditations on his Carnegie Hall concert set: "The performance contained in this album is that of a child of the jazz age. Lenny worshipped the gods of Spontaneity, Candor and Free Association." See also Hampton Hawes with Don Asher, *Raise Up off Me* (1974; repr., New York: Thunder's Mouth Press, 2001), 45.

23. On the appeal of jazz and its clubs for other artists, see MacAdams, *Birth of the Cool*, 20, 47, 82–85, 224. On the Five Spot, see Goldberg, *Jazz Masters of the '50s*, 33–35.

24. Hettie Jones, *How I Became Hettie Jones* (New York: Penguin, 1990), 34–36, 170–72.

25. Robert Kotlowitz, "Monk Talk," *Harper's*, September 1961, 21–23; Kelley, *Thelonious Monk*, 131–36.

26. On Gillespie, see Richard O. Boyer, "Bop," *New Yorker*, July 3, 1948, 28–37; on Miles Davis as an icon of style—one of the nation's best-dressed men—see George Frazier, "The Art of Wearing Clothes," *Esquire*, September 1960 (reprinted at http://www.dandyism.net/the-art-of-wearing-clothes/); Monk appeared on the cover of *Time* in "Jazz: Bebop and Beyond," February 28, 1964.

27. Blakey, quoted in Goldberg, *Jazz Masters of the '50s*, 51.

28. MacAdams, *Birth of the Cool*, 224.

29. On Art Blakey, see Goldberg, *Jazz Masters of the '50s*, 47, 56; on Miles Davis, see John Szwed, *So What: The Life of Miles Davis* (New York: Simon & Schuster, 2004), 179–82; on Monk being bullied by policemen, see Valerie Wilmer, *Jazz People* (New York: Da Capo, 1977), 50.

30. *The Collected Works of Langston Hughes*, vol. 7, *The Early Simple Stories*, ed. Donna Akiba Sullivan Harper (Columbia: University of Missouri Press, 2002), 228; italics in original. Duke Ellington, "The Duke Steps Out" (1931), in *The Duke Ellington Reader*, ed. Mark Tucker (New York: Oxford University Press, 1995), 49.

31. Rollins, quoted in Goodman, "Sonny Rollins at Sixty-Eight"; Sonny Rollins, interview by Kalamu ya Salaam on-stage at Jazzfest, New Orleans, Louisiana, May 7, 2011; Jack Kerouac, *The Subterraneans* (New York: Grove, 1958), 84.

32. Patrick Burke, *Come in and Hear the Truth: Jazz and Race on 52nd Street* (Chicago: University of Chicago Press, 2008); Goldberg, *Jazz Masters of the '50s*, 21; Ingrid Monson, *Freedom Sounds: Civil Rights Call out to Jazz and Africa* (New York: Oxford University Press, 2007), 286; Ishmael Reed, "Sonny Rollins: Three Takes," in *Mixing It Up* (New York: Da Capo, 2008), 63–64.

33. Monson, *Freedom Sounds*, 286.

34. Kenny Clarke said simply, "Bird was a genius. . . . It's rare to get a genius on the scene. . . . Dizzy was different: He's a saint. Dizzy personally taught all the trumpet players . . . and a lot of the drummers, too." Clarke, quoted in Art Taylor, *Notes and Tones: Musician-to-Musician Interviews* (New York: Da Capo, 1993), 193. Sonny Rollins said in 2005, "Of course Charlie Parker was our god." Stated in a video on his website, "Sonny Meets Miles," YouTube video, 10:19, the Sonny Rollins Podcast, episode 4, posted by "Jazz Video Guy," April 22, 2007, https://www.youtube.com/watch?v=3WfRlyUKv8Y.

35. Scott DeVeaux, *The Birth of Bebop: A Social and Musical History* (Berkeley: University of California Press, 1997), 43.

36. Eric Lott, "Double-V, Double-Time: Bebop's Politics of Style," in *The Jazz Cadence of American Culture*, ed. Robert O'Meally (New York: Columbia University Press, 1998), 457–68.

37. Hawes with Asher, *Raise Up off Me*, 76–77. Gillespie said something similar about Parker: "He wasn't strong enough to last long. It's hard out there for a black man in this society. If you let all those pressures get to you and then start to slide all the way along with them, they will do you in." Gillespie, quoted in Hentoff, *Jazz Is*, 67. On Parker's politics and intelligence, see Dizzy Gillespie with Al Fraser, *To Be or Not . . . to Bop* (New York: Doubleday, 1979), 287, 290.

38. Russell, *Bird Lives!* 5, 10–11. Lester Young's porkpie hat, double-breasted suits, shades, and slang were the sartorial extension of his swing-era tenor sound. Parker was more proletarian in his style.

39. Leonard Feather, quoted in DeVeaux, *The Birth of Bebop*, 14. Before bebop, in the swing era, a musician would complain to Duke Ellington about a solo, "Man this thing ain't got no keys on it," until Ellington coached him. After the bebop transformation, Ellington said, "it came to be that young musicians could play anything you set down." Ellington, quoted in Hentoff, *Jazz Is*, 27.

40. Don Byas interview in Taylor, *Notes and Tones*, 54, my italics.

41. Amiri Baraka, *The Autobiography of LeRoi Jones* (New York: Freundlich, 1984), 56–61.

42. Sonny Rollins, quoted in Eric Nisenson, *Open Sky: Sonny Rollins and His World of Improvisation* (New York: Da Capo, 2000), 105.

43. Kelley, *Thelonious Monk*, 106; Gillespie with Fraser, *To Be or Not . . . to Bop*, 148; Francis Davis, "Bebop and Nothingness," in *The Charlie Parker Companion*, ed. Carl Woideck (New York: Schirmer, 1998), 255. "The second world war severely altered the texture and tempo of American life and jazz reflected those changes with greater acuteness by far than the other arts with the arguable exception of painting" (Gary Giddins, *Celebrating Bird* [New York: William Morrow/Beech Tree, 1987], 4); see also Lhamon, *Deliberate Speed*, 103, 129.

44. Kelley, *Thelonious Monk*, 106; Crouch, quoted in Craig Morgan-Teicher, "Sax, Drugs and Jazz: Charlie Parker's 'Lightning-Fast' Rise," review of *Kansas City Lightning: The Rise and Times of Charlie Parker*, by Stanley Crouch, *NPR*, Sep-

tember 27, 2013, http://www.npr.org/2013/09/27/225766018/sax-drugs-and-jazz
-charlie-parkers-lightning-fast-rise?sc=17&f=1032.

45. James Baldwin, "Sonny's Blues," in *Jazz Short Stories: Hot and Cool*, ed.
Marcella Breton (New York: Plume, 1990), 129–30.

46. Ingrid Monson, *Freedom Sounds* (New York: Oxford University Press,
2007), 302.

47. Rollins, interview by Kalamu ya Salaam on-stage at Jazzfest, New Orleans.

48. Gunther Schuller, *Early Jazz: Its Roots and Musical Development* (New
York: Oxford, 1968), 57; on the jazz profession as "the life," see Travis A. Jackson,
"Jazz Performance as Ritual: The Blues Aesthetic and the African Diaspora," in *The
African Diaspora: A Musical Perspective*, ed. Ingrid Monson (Routledge, 2000),
23–82; Ellison, *Shadow and Act*, 209; Blakey, quoted in Carr, Case, and Dellar, *The
Hip*, 85.

49. Quoted in Luc Delannoy, *Pres: The Story of Lester Young* (Fayetteville:
University of Arkansas Press, 1993), 73.

50. John Chilton, *Song of the Hawk: The Life and Recordings of Coleman Hawkins* (Ann Arbor: University of Michigan Press, 1993), 370.

51. Ellington, quoted in Hentoff, *Jazz Is*, 27. "After a man has been in the band
for awhile, I can hear what his capacities are, and I write to that."

52. Ben Ratliff, *Coltrane: The Story of a Sound* (New York: Picador, 2009), x.

53. "Blindfold Test: Charles McPherson," *Downbeat*, December 2009, 98; my
emphasis.

54. Ibid.

55. Betty Carter, quoted in Taylor, *Notes and Tones*, 277–80.

56. Hentoff, "Pres," in *The Lester Young Reader*, ed. Lewis Porter (Washington,
DC: Smithsonian Institution Press, 1991), 158–59, 162 (quote); and Ross Russell,
Jazz Style in Kansas City and the Southwest (1971; repr., New York: Da Capo, 1997),
150, 152–53.

57. Ingrid Monson, *Saying Something: Jazz Improvisation and Interaction* (Chicago: University of Chicago Press, 1997).

58. Young, quoted in Nat Shapiro and Nat Hentoff, *Hear Me Talkin' to Ya* (New
York: Dover, 1955), 310; Gillespie with Fraser, *To Be or Not . . . to Bop*, 148. Drum-
mer Andrew Cyrille recalled being told to stop copying his idol, Philly Joe Jones.
"It's [like] what all the older cats would tell me: 'Don't copy, find something for you
to say.' And they were right." Quoted in Bill Miklowski, "Overdue Ovation: Andrew
Cyrille, Still Searching at 70," *JazzTimes*, November 2009, 27.

59. Clarke, quoted in Mike Hennessey, *Klook: The Story of Kenny Clarke* (Pittsburgh: University of Pittsburgh Press, 1994), 148.

60. Miles Davis with Quincy Troupe, *Miles: The Autobiography* (New York: Simon and Schuster, 1990), 3, 7–8, 399. "The greatest feeling I ever had in life—with
my clothes on," Davis says at the opening of his autobiography, "was when I first
heard Diz and Bird together . . . in 1944" (7).

61. Gillespie, quoted in Hennessey, *Klook*, 30.

62. Thomas Owens, *Bebop* (New York: Oxford, 1995), 168–73.

63. Hampton Hawes with Don Asher, *Raise Up off Me* (1974; repr., New York: Thunder's Mouth Press, 2001), 6; Teddy Wilson and Gil Evans, quoted in Hentoff, *Jazz Is*, 94, 140.

64. Hentoff, *Jazz Is*, 12, 99, 246–48.

65. DeVeaux, *The Birth of Bebop*, 17–18.

66. Jim Hall and Rex Stewart, quoted in Hentoff, *Jazz Is*, 12, 99. Interview with Timothy Brennan, "On His Book *Secular Devotion: Afro-Latin Music and Imperial Jazz*," *Rorotoko*, December 5, 2008, http://rorotoko.com/interview/20081205 _brennan_timothy_secular_devotion_afro-latin_music_imperial_jazz/?page=4; see also Timothy Brennan, *Secular Devotion: Afro-Latin Music and Imperial Jazz* (London: Verso, 2008).

67. Gregory Corso, "For Miles"; Bob Kaufman, "Walking Parker Home"; Edward Hirsch, "Art Pepper"; and Keorapetse Kgostitsile, "Art Blakey and the Jazz Messengers"—all in *Jazz Poems*, ed. Kevin Young (New York: Knopf/Everyman's, 2006), 81–82, 114, 125–27, 185–86.

68. Patricia Spears Jones, "The Blues of This Day (for Miles Davis); and Ted Joans, "Lester Young," in *Jazz Poems*, ed. Young, 106, 117–18. Joans does not use "hipster" as a pejorative term here, but in its original definition, a person "exceptionally aware of or interested in the latest trends and tastes, especially a devotee of modern jazz" (*The American Heritage College Dictionary*, 3rd ed., s.v. "hipster").

69. Ed Sanders, "The Legacy of the Beats," in *Beat Culture and the New America, 1950–1965*, ed. Lisa Phillips (New York: Whitney Museum of American Art; Paris: Flammarian, 1996), 246.

70. Lorenzo Thomas, "'Communicating By Horns': Jazz and Redemption in the Poetry of the Beats and the Black Arts Movement," *African American Review* 26(2) (Summer 1992): 291–98.

71. Monson, *Freedom Sounds*, 28.

72. The poems by Young and Baraka can be found in *Jazz Poems*, ed. Young, 111, 164–65, 168.

73. Goodman, "Sonny Rollins at Sixty-Eight."

74. Sonny Rollins, liner notes, *Freedom Suite* (Riverside LP, 1958). He restates his intentions of this message in Taylor, *Notes and Tones*, 171–72.

75. Rollins, quoted in Reed, *Mixing It Up*, 69.

76. Jackie McLean, quoted in "Sonny Rollins Still Rolling along at 75," *Orange County Register*, April 5, 2006 (updated August 21, 2013), http://www.ocregister .com/articles/rollins-142807-jazz-sonny.html.

77. Rollins, quoted in Nisenson, *Open Sky*, 146–47, and see 148–53; Blakey, Lacy, and Rollins, quoted in Goldberg, *Jazz Masters of the '50s*, 106, 107, 110.

78. Rollins, quoted in Taylor, *Notes and Tones*, 167, 169–70; Timothy Brennan, *Secular Devotion: Afro-Latin Music and Imperial Jazz* (London: Verso, 2008).

79. Rollins, quoted in Taylor, *Note and Tones*, 169; on Rollins's engagement with Eastern religions, see Nisenson, *Open Sky*, 182–85.

80. John Clellon Holmes, *The Horn* (1958; repr., New York: Thunder's Mouth Press, 1987), 5; italics added.

81. Holmes wrote the first two published essays on "The Beat Generation" in the *New York Times*, both published in *Beat Down to Your Soul: What Was the Beat Generation?* ed. Ann Charters (New York: Penguin, 2001), 222–38, and the first Beat novel, *Go* (New York: Scribner, 1952).

82. Holmes, *The Horn*, introduction, n.p. The American Renaissance writers "[first] defined . . . the situation of the artist here." Epigraphs for each "chorus" develop analogies between Poe and Young, Dickinson and Billie Holiday, Thoreau and Parker, Melville and Monk.

83. Ibid.

84. Holmes, quoted from letters in Ann Charters and Samuel Charters, *Brother-Souls: John Clellon Holmes, Jack Kerouac, and the Beat Generation* (Jackson: University Press of Mississippi, 2010), 279–81.

85. Holmes, *The Horn*, 69, 92. This scene is based on an infamous recording session in which producer Ross Russell forced a strung-out Charlie Parker to record under his contractual obligations. This incident was also famously fictionalized in Elliott Grennard, "Sparrow's Last Jump," *Harper's*, May 1947, 419–26.

86. Holmes, *The Horn*, 8 (long quote), 201, 233–34.

87. Holmes, *The Horn*, 11; Ross Russell, "Gin for Breakfast" (unpublished), Box 6, Ross Russell Papers, HRC, and for a more musicological analysis, Russell, *Jazz Style in Kansas City and the Southwest*, 153–54.

88. Holmes, *The Horn*, 59, 73.

89. Ibid., 25, 149. Holmes adapted the idea of the holy fool from Kerouac.

90. Ibid., 242.

91. Ibid., 92; Archie Shepp, introduction to *The Horn*, v.

92. Holmes, *The Horn*, 91; ellipses and italics in original.

93. Miles Davis, "*Playboy* Interview with Alex Haley," in *Miles Davis and American Culture*, ed. Gerald Early (St. Louis: University of Missouri Press, 1999), 198–207; Jones, *How I Became Hettie Jones*, 188–89.

94. See, e.g., Thomas Frank, *The Conquest of Cool* (Chicago: University of Chicago, 1998); Richard Majors and Janet Mancini Bilson, *Cool Pose: The Dilemmas of Black Manhood in America* (New York: Touchstone, 1993); and Marlene Connor, *What Is Cool? Understanding Black Manhood in America* (New York: Crown, 1995).

95. For example, a major exhibit called "Beat Culture and the New America" at New York's Whitney Museum in 1996 featured a few album covers as the representation of jazz's influence on the Beats (or Kerouac in particular). There was no reference to jazz method or practice. In Mona Lisa Saloy's "Black Beats and Black Issues," an essay on jazz from the exhibit catalog, a photo with a caption "Charlie Parker at Birdland 1949," includes no mention of Lester Young (standing next to him) or other musicians. Phillips, ed., *Beat Culture and the New America*, 152–53.

96. I am making a connection to Emerson's "The Poet" here, but for an analysis of Parker as the kind of "liberating god" Emerson calls for in this essay, see

Muyumba, *The Shadow and the Act*, 43–44. For an analysis of the triangulation of pragmatism, experience, and self-invention from Emerson and William James to blues musicians and Elvis, see Tim Parrish, *Walking Blues: The Making of Americans from Emerson to Elvis* (Amherst: University of Massachusetts Press, 1999).

97. On the Orphic mode in African-American literature and culture, see Saadi A. Simawe, *Black Orpheus: Music in African American Fiction from the Harlem Renaissance to Toni Morrison* (New York: Garland, 200), xi–xxi; and A. Yemisi Jimoh, *Spiritual, Blues, and Jazz People in African-American Fiction* (Knoxville: University of Tennessee Press, 2002).

98. Susan McClary, *Conventional Wisdom: The Content of Musical Form* (Berkeley: University of California Press, 2000), xi.

Chapter Ten

1. On the filming of *The Fugitive Kind*, see Peter Manso, *Brando* (New York: Hyperion, 1995), 497–514.

2. Robert Bretall, ed., *A Kierkegaard Anthology* (New York: Modern Library, 1946), 204–17; this section is from Kierkegaard's *Concluding Unscientific Postscript to the'' "Philosophical Fragments."* See also Steven Earshaw, *Existentialism* (London: Continuum, 2006), 31–32, 113–34.

3. On the blues as a model for '60s counterculture, see Dennis McNally, *On Highway 61: Music, Race and the Evolution of Cultural Freedom* (New York: Counterpoint, 2014); and John Milward, *Crossroads: How the Blues Shaped Rock 'n' Roll (and Rock Saved the Blues)* (Boston: Northeastern University Press, 2013).

4. Albert Murray, letter to Ralph Ellison, November 15, 1958, in *Trading Twelves: The Selected Letters of Ralph Ellison and Albert Murray*, ed. Albert Murray and John F. Callahan (New York: Modern Library, 2000), 200.

5. Tennessee Williams, *"Orpheus Descending" with "Battle of Angels": Two Plays* (New York: New Directions 1958), 26–27.

6. "Juke" probably comes from the Wolof *dzug*, to live wickedly; in any case, "juke" seems to derive from West African linguistic origins. Maciej Widawski, *African American Slang: A Linguistic Description* (Cambridge, MA: Harvard University Press, 2015), 56, 79, 87, 95.

7. Williams, *"Orpheus Descending" with "Battle of Angels,"* 26–27.

8. This is taken directly from the play and riffed directly from Sartre: "Nobody ever gets to know no body! We're all of us sentenced to solitary confinement inside our own skins, for life! You understand me, Lady!" Lady demurs and refuses to "agree with something as sad as that sentiment." Williams, *"Orpheus Descending" with "Battle of Angels,"* 47.

9. For an analysis of lynching as a social ritual of the U.S. South, see Orlando Patterson, *Rituals of Blood* (New York: Basic Civitas, 1999), 169–232.

10. Kerouac, *On the Road*, 5–6.

11. Thomas M. Pryor, "A 'Defiant One' Becomes a Star," *New York Times*, Jan-

uary 25, 1959, SM27. William Jelani Cobb, "The Genius of Cool," *Ebony* 63, no. 10 (2008): 68–69; and Shirley Henderson, "What Makes Sidney Cool," in *Ebony* 63, no. 10 (2008): 72.

12. Aram Goudsouzian, *Sidney Poitier: Man, Actor, Icon* (Chapel Hill: University of North Carolina Press, 2004), 103.

13. Harry Belafonte, quoted in Richard W. Nason, "Evaluating the Odds," *New York Times*, March 15, 1959, 415; Goudsouzian, *Sidney Poitier*, 2, 4, 234.

14. Krin Gabbard, "*Paris Blues*: Ellington, Armstrong, and Saying It With Music," in *Uptown Conversation: The New Jazz Studies*, ed. Robert G. O'Meally, Brent Hayes Edwards, and Farah Jasmine Griffin (New York: Columbia University Press, 2004), 301–02.

15. Goudsouzian, *Sidney Poitier*, 3; Harold Flender, *Paris Blues* (New York: Ballantine, 1957), 2.

16. Ruth Feldstein, *How It Feels to Be Free: Black Woman Entertainers and the Civil Rights Movement* (New York: Oxford University Press, 2013), 48–49.

17. Tracey Davis with Nina Bunche Pierce, *Sammy Davis, Jr.: A Journey with My Father* (Philadelphia: Running Press, 2014).

18. Pryor, "'A Defiant One' Becomes a Star."

19. Ibid.

20. Bosley Crowther, "Screen: Stagelike Version of 'A Raisin in the Sun,'" *New York Times*, March 30, 1961, 24.

Chapter Eleven

1. *Raisin* is now even further misunderstood along these lines due to the success of the play *Clybourne Park*, something of a sequel to the play.

2. Lorraine Hansberry with Robert Nemiroff, *To Be Young, Gifted, and Black* (New York: Vintage, 1995). Simone wrote the song during the off-Broadway run of *Young, Gifted and Black* off-Broadway and explained its gestation in an interview at Moorhead College in June, 1969 ("Nina Simone: To Be Young, Gifted and Black," YouTube video, 9:21, posted by the estate of Nina Simone, February 21, 2013, https://www.youtube.com/watch?v=_hdVFiANBTk&feature=share); Ruth Feldstein, *How It Feels to Be Free: Black Woman Entertainers and the Civil Rights Movement* (New York: Oxford University Press, 2013), 107.

3. Frank Rich caught some of Hansberry's prescience in retrospect in 1983. In his review of the twenty-fifth-anniversary revival of *Raisin*, he wrote that the play "encompasses everything from the rise of black nationalism in the United States and Africa to the advent of black militancy to the specific dimensions of the black woman's liberation movement. And she always saw the present and future in the light of the past—clear back to the slavery of the Old South and the new slavery that followed for black workers who migrated to the industrial ghettos of the North." Frank Rich, "'Raisin in Sun,' Anniversary in Chicago," *New York Times*, October 5, 1983.

4. Lorraine Hansberry, *The Collected Last Plays: Les Blancs, The Drinking Gourd, What Use Are Flowers?* ed. Robert Nemiroff (New York: New American Library, 1983), 269–70.

5. Untitled Lecture, Brandeis University, April 27, 1961, Lorraine Hansberry Papers, Box 56 Folder 3.

6. Lorraine Hansberry, "The Negro Writer and His Roots: Toward a New Romanticism," *Black Scholar*, March–April 1981, 2. She delivered this lecture on March 1, 1959, two weeks before the Broadway opening of *A Raisin in the Sun*.

7. Hansberry prepared a fourteen-page typed précis for DuBois, "The Belgian Congo: A Preliminary Report on Its Land, Its History, and Its Peoples." Handwritten across the top, she wrote, "For Dr. DuBois—African History Seminar, Jefferson School, NYC 1953." Lorraine Hansberry Papers, Schomburg Center for Research in Black Culture, New York Public Library (LH Papers, Schomburg). See also Lorraine Hansberry, "A Speech @ Carnegie Hall, 2/23/64," reprinted in "The Legacy of W.E.B. DuBois," *Freedomways* 5 (Winter 1965): 19–20.

8. A similar event did take place at Town Hall three years later when Ossie Davis, Ruby Dee, James Baldwin, Amiri Baraka, and Hansberry debated David Susskind, Charles Silberman, and columnist James Wechsler. Hansberry once explained that African-Americans were not interested in assimilation within white frameworks: "For generations it has been assumed that what Negroes wanted more desperately than anything was simply to be absorbed into 'this house.' . . . Perhaps it seems an affront to some that the most thoughtful elements of the Negro people would like to see this house rebuilt" (quoted in Goudsouzian, *Sidney Poitier*, 177).

9. Hansberry, *To Be Young, Gifted and Black*, 36.

10. Lorraine Hansberry, letter to Edythe Cohen, 1951, Box 2, Folder 14, LH Papers, Schomburg.

11. Hansberry's FBI file is heavily redacted. Box 72, Folders 1 and 2, LH Papers, Schomburg.

12. Lorraine Hansberry, "The Negro in Hollywood Films," *New Foundations*, 1952, 12–14, clipping file, Box 58 (Other Writings), LH Papers, Schomburg.

13. Letter to the Editor of "Sunday Magazine," *New York Times* . . . dated March 4, 1956, Box 63—Professional Correspondence, Folder 25, LH Papers, Schomburg. She also referred—with prescience and patriotism—to DuBois and Douglass as "among the most remarkable products of this American nation."

14. "Notes on Women's Liberation," Box 56 Folder 6, LH Papers, Schomburg.

15. Typescript, "Some Rather Indecisive Thoughts on M. Gide and his 'Corydon'" (1955), Box 56, Folder 18, LH Papers, Schomburg. Here's her rundown of the social hierarchy: "In the United States men oppress women; the working-class . . . joins vigorously in the political persecution of . . . the Communist Party; the whites . . . murder the blacks almost at will in certain regions; a slowly evolving U S still treats its intelligentsia as freaks . . . and all unite against social acceptance of the homosexual."

16. "October 19, 1956," fragment, Box 1 Folder 1, "Autobiographical Notes 1957–1963," LH Papers, Schomburg.

17. The American Society of African Culture was an organization of diasporic intellectuals and artists founded in 1957 with the objective of educating Americans about the cultural contributions of people of African descent. The society sponsored lectures and conferences as well as art exhibits and musical performances, often highlighting issues of black nationalism or pan-Africanism. They began publishing their own American-based journal, *African Forum*, in 1964.

18. Hansberry, "The Negro Writer," 5.

19. Ibid., 7.

20. Ibid.

21. Ibid., 12.

22. Ibid., 11–12.

23. Ibid., 6.

24. Hansberry, letter to Nemiroff, ca. 1956–57, Box 2, LH Papers, Schomburg.

25. Ibid.

26. Lorraine Hansberry, "Simone de Beauvoir and *The Second Sex*: An American Commentary," in *Words of Fire: An Anthology of African-American Feminist Thought*, ed. Beverly Guy-Sheftall (New York: New Press, 1995), 128–42.

27. "Make New Sounds: Studs Terkel Interviews Lorraine Hansberry," *American Theatre*, November 1984, 6. The interview took place on May 12, 1959, but wasn't published until 1984.

28. Hansberry, "Beauvoir and *The Second Sex*," 132, 19–40.

29. Simone de Beauvoir, *The Second Sex* (New York: Knopf, 2010), 44, 46.

30. Hansberry, quoted in Margaret B. Wilkerson, "Introduction," in *The Collected Last Plays*, 7–8.

31. Julius Lester, "Foreword," in Hansberry, *The Collected Last Plays*, 8.

32. "Make New Sounds," 5–8, 41.

33. Hansberry, letter to Nemiroff ca. 1956–57, Box 2—Correspondence, LH Papers, Schomburg.

34. Unpublished MS, n.d., Box 1, "Autobiographical Notes," LH papers, Schomburg.

35. Robert Nemiroff, "Introduction," in *Lorraine Hansberry's "A Raisin in the Sun,"* 30th anniversary ed., rev. (New York: Samuel French, 1989), 6, 148; see also Steven R. Carter, *Hansberry's Drama: Commitment amid Complexity* (Urbana: University of Illinois Press, 1991), 51.

36. Lorraine Hansberry, *"A Raisin in the Sun" and "The Sign in Sidney Brustein's Window"* (New York: New American Library, 1987), 72.

37. Ibid., 72–74.

38. Dick Gregory, quoted in Geneva Gay, "Ethnic Identity Development and Black Expressiveness," in *Expressively Black: The Cultural Basis of Ethnic Identity*, ed. Geneva Gay and Willie L. Baber (New York: Praeger, 1987), 65.

39. Hansberry, *To Be Young, Gifted, and Black*, 30.

40. Hansberry, *"A Raisin in the Sun" and "The Sign in Sidney Brustein's Window"*, 106, and "And Bird Blowin' Back: I Am!" in Box 57, Folder 1, LH papers.

41. LH, Raisin and Sidney, 77–81.

42. Hansberry, quoted in Anne Cheney, *Lorraine Hansberry* (Boston: G. K. Hall & Co., 1984), 60; "Studs Terkel Interviews Lorraine Hansberry," 8, 41.

43. Hansberry, *"A Raisin in the Sun" and "The Sign in Sidney Brustein's Window"*, 135–37.

44. Baldwin, "Sweet Lorraine," in *To Be Young, Gifted, and Black*, xviii; Lester, "Afterword," in Hansberry, *The Collected Last Plays*, 267.

45. Hansberry, "A Raisin in the Sun: Screenplay—Scenes from Earlier Drafts," Box 15, Writings—Play Scripts, LH Papers, Schomburg; see also Carter, *Hansberry's Drama*, 42.

46. Kalamu ya Salaam, "What Use Is Writing? Re-reading Lorraine Hansberry," *Black Collegian*, March–April 1984, 45–46, clipping file, Box 61, LH Papers, Schomburg. See also, Julius Lester, "Afterword," in Hansberry, *The Collected Last Plays*, 262–74; Carter, *Hansberry's Drama*, 25.

47. Bosley Crowther, "Screen: Stagelike Version of 'A Raisin in the Sun,'" *New York Times*, March 30, 1961."

48. Stanley Kauffman, "With Negroes in Suburbia," *New Republic*, March 20, 1961, clipping file, Box 15, Folder 7, LH Papers, Schomburg; Harold Cruse, quoted in Carter, *Hansberry's Drama*, 21.

49. Hansberry, quoted in Carter, *Hansberry's Drama*, 45.

50. Sam Briskin: "There are too many 'jive' expressions, such as 'man,' 'I mean,' 'like,' and . . . as many as possible [should] be deleted" ("Studio Memoranda: Sam Briskin's Notes on Raisin in the Sun," Folder 5, LH Papers, Schomburg; Goudsouzian, *Sidney Poitier*, 184–85).

51. Norman Mailer, "Theatre: The Blacks," *Village Voice*, May 11, 1961, 11, 14, and "Theatre: The Blacks (Contd.)," *Village Voice*, May 18, 1961, 11, 14–15; Lorraine Hansberry, "Genet, Mailer and the New Paternalism," *Village Voice*, June 1, 1961, 11, 14, 15; Norman Mailer, "Mailer to Hansberry," *Village Voice*, June 8, 1961: 11–12. See also, Hansberry, "The New Paternalism," several versions, Box 58, Folder 10, LH Papers, Schomburg.

52. Mailer, "The Blacks (Contd.)," 11, 14 (emphasis added), 15.

53. Ibid.

54. Lorraine Hansberry continued to revise this essay for five years—as many subsequent drafts show—in an attempt to publish a more pointed version in another publication.

55. The term "postmodern minstrel show" has become common. See, e.g., Jenny Sandman, "The Blacks: A Clown Show," *CurtainUp: The Internet Theater Magazine of Reviews, Features, Annotated Listings*, accessed August 4, 2014, http://www.curtainup.com/blacks.html.

56. Mailer, "Theatre: The Blacks," 11, 14.

57. Hansberry, "Genet, Mailer and the New Paternalism," 11.

58. Ibid.

59. Mailer, "Theatre: The Blacks," 14.

60. Hansberry, *"A Raisin in the Sun" and "The Sign in Sidney Brustein's Window,"* 283–84.

61. Hansberry, quoted in Carter, *Hansberry's Drama*, 65.

62. Hansberry with Nemiroff, *To Be Young, Gifted and Black*, 176.

63. Lorraine Hansberry, "The Arrival of Mr. Todog: A Bit of Whimsy, or A Little Camp on a Great Camp," Box 50, Folder 5, LH Papers, Schomburg. Hansberry submitted the story to *Harper's Magazine* in 1965 but it was rejected.

64. Hansberry, *What Use Are Flowers?* in *The Collected Last Plays*, 223–60, and letter to Mme. Chen Jui-Lan, *To Be Young, Gifted and Black*, 223.

65. Lorraine Hansberry, "On Arthur Miller, Marilyn Monroe, and 'Guilt,'" in *Women in Theatre: Compassion and Hope*, ed. Karen Malpede (New York: Drama Books Publishers, 1983), 174; Hansberry, *To Be Young, Gifted and Black*, 11, 227; Carter, *Hansberry's Drama*, 92.

66. Lorraine Hansberry, "Images and Essences: Dialogue with an Uncolored Egg-head," *Urbanite*, May 1961, 10, 11, 36, Box 57—Articles, Folder 1, LH Papers, Schomburg.

67. Ibid., and *To Be Young, Gifted and Black*, 210.

68. Nemiroff tells the story of the play's extended run in *"A Raisin in the Sun" and "The Sign in Sidney Brustein's Window,"* 171–83, 178 (quote from Shelley Winters).

69. Hansberry, letter to Nemiroff, ca. 1956, Box 1, LH Papers, Schomburg. This was a pet peeve of Hansberry's. In her letter about *The Mandarins*, she mocked armchair intellectuals "rearing back in their chairs and saying . . . 'Well—that's the system!'"

70. Hansberry, *"A Raisin in the Sun" and "The Sign in Sidney Brustein's Window,"* 330–31.

71. Ibid., 267; see also Carter, *Hansberry's Drama*, 85.

72. Nemiroff, quoted in *"A Raisin in the Sun" and "The Sign in Sidney Brustein's Window,"* 170.

73. "A Note to Readers: Toussaint," December 1958, "final WNET typescript for WNET," Box 42, LH Papers, Schomburg; emphasis added. *Toussaint* was originally scheduled to be shown on WNET-TV in New York.

74. Hansberry, quoted in Ruth Feldstein, *How It Feels to Be Free*, 94; and in Nina Simone, *I Put a Spell on You: The Autobiography of Nina Simone* (New York: Pantheon, 1991), 86–87.

75. Lorraine Hansberry, *The Movement: Documents of a Struggle for Equality* (New York: Simon & Schuster, 1964), 52.

Epilogue

1. Norman Mailer, "Superman Comes to the Supermarket," in *Mind of an Outlaw: Selected Essays*, ed. Phillip Sipiora (New York: Random House, 2013), 109, 113, 121–28, 131, 143; Michael Sheridan, *Sinatra and the Jack Pack: The Extraordinary Friendship between Frank Sinatra and John F. Kennedy* (New York: Skyhorse, 2016), 171–79.

2. Mailer, "Superman Comes to the Supermarket," 113, 121.

3. Ibid., 113, 121–22, 131.

4. Ibid., 131.

5. Michael Lydon, *Rock Folk: Portraits from the Rock 'n' Roll Pantheon* (New York: Doubleday, 1971), 15.

6. Juliette Gréco, quoted in Roy Carr, Brian Case, and Fred Dellar, *The Hip: Hipsters, Jazz, and the Beat Generation* (London: Faber and Faber, 1986), 110.

7. Elizabeth Wilson, *Adorned in Dreams: Fashion and Modernity* (Berkeley: University of California Press, 1987), 187–88; Marshall McLuhan, *Understanding Media: The Extensions of Man* (New York: McGraw-Hill, 1965), 22–32.

8. McLuhan, *Understanding Media*, v.

9. Tom Wolfe, *The Electric Kool-Aid Acid Test* (1968; repr., New York: Bantam, 1999), 10.

10. For example, Mailer changed his associations for cool to Anglo-American exemplars such as writers and astronauts in the 1960s, in particular in *Of a Fire on the Moon* (Boston: Little, Brown 1970). This work opposes heroism and courage of astronauts to writers and begins with a meditation on Hemingway's suicide. Yet Mailer still referred to himself as a hipster positively, not pejoratively, in 1975. *Conversations with Norman Mailer*, ed. J. Michael Lennon (Jackson: University Press of Mississippi, 1988), 215.

11. William H. Pipes, *Death of an Uncle Tom* (New York: Carlton, 1967), 5–6.

12. Bernard Wolfe, "Uncle Remus and the Malevolent Rabbit," in *Mother Wit from the Laughing Barrel*, ed. Alan Dundes (Englewood Cliffs, NJ: Prentice-Hall, 1973), 538 (quote), 524–40; Simone de Beauvoir, *America Day by Day* (1948; repr., Berkeley: University of California Press, 1999), 208, 242. Both Wolfe and Beauvoir owe their observations, in part, to Mezz Mezzrow's *Really the Blues* (1946; New York: Citadel Press, 1990), the first insider analysis of African-American culture by a white musician, co-written by Wolfe, which also influenced Jack Kerouac and Allen Ginsberg.

13. Stephanie Zacharek, "Nothing but a Man: Roemer Directs Abbey Lincoln in Malcolm X's Favorite Movie," *Village Voice*, October 8, 2014, http://www .villagevoice.com/film/nothing-but-a-man-roemer-directs-abbey-lincoln-in -malcolm-xs-favorite-movie-6442997.

14. Haruki Murakami, "Jazz Messenger," *New York Times*, July 8, 2007, http:// www.nytimes.com/2007/07/08/books/review/Murakami-t.html?_r=0.

15. Ellington theorizes the importance of rhythm in the 1931 article, "The Duke Steps Out," in *The Duke Ellington Reader*, ed. Mark Tucker (New York: Oxford University Press, 1995), 47–48; Murakami, "Jazz Messenger."

16. Charlie Musselwhite, liner notes, *Blues Masters: The Very Best of Lightnin' Hopkins* (Rhino CD, 2000); Dave Alvin quoted in Timothy J. O'Brien and David Ensminger, *Mojo Hand: The Life and Music of Lightnin' Hopkins* (Austin: University of Texas Press, 2013), 124–25. White blues guitarist Mike Bloomfield attended the same concert as Musselwhite in Gary, Indiana, in April 1965, and left similar testimony of Hopkins upstaging the larger band of J. B. Lenoir. Two months later, he introduced Hopkins at the Newport Folk Festival: "I got one favorite [singer who]

to me . . . most typifies the blues . . . the king of the blues, Lightning Sam Hopkins." Quoted in O'Brien and Ensminger, *Mojo Hand*, 156–57 and 167.

17. David Ritz, quoted in liner notes, *Blues Masters: The Very Best of Lightnin' Hopkins*; and see also O'Brien and Ensminger, *Mojo Hand*, 157–58.

18. Richard Wright, *Uncle Tom's Children* (1938; repr., New York: HarperPerennial, 1991), frontispiece; J. C. Furnas, *Goodbye to Uncle Tom* (New York: Sloane and Associates, 1956), 8, 10.

19. Miles Davis, quoted in *"Playboy* Interview with Alex Haley," in *Miles Davis and American Culture*, ed. Gerald Early (St Louis: University of Missouri Press, 1999), 207.

20. "I Just Adored That Man," interview with Quincy Jones, in *Miles Davis and American Culture*, ed. Early, 42; for musicians who spoke of Miles Davis's shell, see John Szwed, *So What: The Life of Miles Davis* (New York: Simon & Schuster, 2004), 332–35, 347–49 (e.g.).

21. Ta-Nehisi Coates, *The Beautiful Struggle* (New York: Spiegel & Grau, 2008), 36. Coates's analysis of the logic of black male urban bravado aligns with Richard Majors's theory of black male "cool pose" in the 1980s, a swagger reflecting the difference in cool from postwar jazz to post–civil rights hip-hop; Ben Ratliff, "Far from Cuba, but Not from His Roots: Listening with Bebo Valdes," *New York Times*, October 13, 2006, http://www.nytimes.com/2006/10/13/arts/music/13vald.html.

22. David Brooks, "Sam Spade at Starbuck's," *New York Times*, April 13, 2012, A31.

23. "Cool Cops," special issue of *TV Guide*, March 2–8, 1996 (the cover for which can be seen at http://coverarchive.tvguidemagazine.com/archive/suboffer /1990s/1996/19960302_c1.jpg.html). Mark Schwed, "Homicide: There's New Life on This Street," in "Cool Cops," special issue of *TV Guide*, March 2–8, 1996 http:// members.tripod.com/waterfront_bar/cool_cops.htm.

24. Uri Klein, "Legendary Actor Paul Newman Dies after Struggle with Cancer," *Haartez*, September 27, 2008, http://www.haaretz.com/jewish/2.209 /legendary-actor-paul-newman-dies-after-struggle-with-cancer-1.254680.

25. I accessed these articles on September 30 and October 1, 2008. Several of them have been taken down from the websites of these newspapers. Steven Winn, "Paul Newman, an Icon of Cool Masculinity," *San Francisco Chronicle*, September 28, 2008, http://www.sfgate.com/news/article/Paul-Newman-an -icon-of-cool-masculinity-3267704.php; Bush, quoted in Maureen Dowd, "Cool Hand Paul," *New York Times*, September 30, 2008, A29; Mark Juddery, "Cinema's Cool Hand," *Australian*, September 28, 2008 (no longer online); "World Mourns 'King of Cool' Paul Newman," Reuters, September 28, 2008, http://www.stuff .co.nz/entertainment/649924/World-mourns-king-of-cool-Paul-Newman; "Schwarzenegger Remembers Newman as 'Ultimate Cool,'" *San Diego Union Tribune*, September 28, 2008 (no longer online).

26. Winn, "Paul Newman, an Icon of Cool Masculinity."

27. Richard Pells, *Modernist America: Art, Music, Movies, and the Globalization of American Culture* (New Haven, CT: Yale University Press, 2012),

271–73; "The Ultimate Mr. Cool—Paul Newman, 1925–2008," *The Times* (London), September 27, 2008, http://www.thetimes.co.uk/tto/opinion/obituaries/article2083111.ece.

28. Bruce Newman, "Paul Newman, Coolest Hand in Hollywood, Dead at 83," *Mercury News*, September 27, 2008, http://www.mercurynews.com/news/ci_10576934.

29. This website has changed its rhetoric and muted the central place of James Dean since my accessing of its homepage on April 1, 2012. It now offers only a photo of his gravestone without calling its visitors to be Indiana-style rebels (http://www.showmegrantcounty.com/grant-county-attractions/james-dean/james-dean-gallery-and-james-dean-museum-exhibits/).

30. Mojo Nixon's "Elvis Is Everywhere" can be found on the album *Bo-Day-Shus!!!* (1987; reissued, Mojo Nixon, 2004) and a performance can be found online (YouTube video, 3:48, posted by William Forsche, January 8, 2012, www.youtube.com/watch?v=mpb4ZAAP6Z4).

31. Linton Weeks, "7 Lost American Slang Words," NPR Arts and Culture, April 23, 2015, http://www.mprnews.org/story/2015/04/23/npr-slang-words.

Index

Page numbers in italics indicate illustrations.